Human Exceptionality

Fourth Edition

Human Exceptionality
Society, School, and Family

MICHAEL L. HARDMAN

University of Utah

CLIFFORD J. DREW

University of Utah

M. WINSTON EGAN

University of Utah

BARBARA WOLF

Indiana University

ALLYN AND BACON

BOSTON / LONDON / TORONTO / SYDNEY / TOKYO / SINGAPORE

Series Editor: Ray Short
Developmental Editor: Alicia Reilly
Production Administrator: Rowena Dores
Editorial Assistant: Christine Shaw
Cover Administrator: Linda K. Dickinson
Composition Buyer: Linda Cox
Manufacturing Buyer: Louise Richardson
Editorial-Production Service: Karen Mason
Text Designer: Karen Mason
Photo Research: Photosynthesis/Gloucester, Mass.
Cover Designer: Paradise Design

Library of Congress Cataloging-in-Publication Data

Human exceptionality: society, school, and family / Michael L. Hardman . . . [et al.].—4th ed.
    p.   cm.
    Includes bibliographical references and index.
    ISBN 0-205-13801-2
1. Handicapped. 2. Exceptional children. 3. Handicapped—Services for. 4. Learning disabilities. I. Hardman, Michael L.
HV 1568.H83 1993
362–dc20   92-26306
                                            CIP

Printed in the United States of America
10 9 8 7 6 5 4 3 2   96 95 94 93

Photo Credits for Chapter Openers and Window Openers

Chapter One: Opener, Stephen Brady/PhotoEdit; p. 2, Harvey Lloyd/The Stock Market
Chapter Two: Opener, Tony Freeman/PhotoEdit; p. 39, David Young-Wolff/PhotoEdit
Chapter Three: Opener, Bob Daemmrich/Stock, Boston; p. 60, David Young-Wolff/PhotoEdit
Chapter Four: Opener, Mario Ruiz/The Picture Group; p. 94, Courtesy of Very Special Arts
Chapter Five: Opener, Kevin Horan/The Picture Group; p. 131, Andy Levin/Photo Researchers, Inc.
Chapter Six: Opener, Spencer Grant/Monkmeyer Press; p. 172, C. Higgins/Photo Researchers, Inc.
Chapter Seven: Mark Lunenberg/The Picture Group; p. 208, L. Druskis/Photo Researchers, Inc.

Chapter Eight: Opener, Myrleen Ferguson/PhotoEdit; p. 230, Freda Leinwand/Monkmeyer Press
Chapter Nine: Opener, Schwartzberg/The Stock Market; p. 260, Barbara Feigles/Stock, Boston
Chapter Ten: Opener, Bob Daemmrich; p. 278, Chester Higgins, Jr./Photo Researchers, Inc.
Chapter Eleven: Opener, Rogers/Monkmeyer Press; p. 312, Ida Weyman/Monkmeyer Press
Chapter Twelve: Opener, Barbara Laing/Black Star; p. 340, Duncan/Courtesy of Dr. Richard Johns
Chapter Thirteen: Opener, Richard Howard/OffShoot Stock; p. 376, John Telford
Chapter Fourteen: Opener, Ellis Herwig/Stock, Boston; p. 412, Laura Dwight/Peter Arnold, Inc.

*This book is dedicated
to people with differences everywhere,
who have risen to the challenge of living
in a society that is sometimes nurturing,
but all too often ambivalent.*

THE NEW YORK TIMES and Allyn and Bacon are sponsoring A CONTEMPORARY VIEW: a program designed to enhance student access to current information of relevance in the classroom.

Through this program, the core subject matter provided in the text is supplemented by a collection of time-sensitive articles from one of the world's most distinguished newspapers, THE NEW YORK TIMES. These articles demonstrate the vital, ongoing connection between what is learned in the classroom and what is happening in the world around us.

To enjoy the wealth of information of THE NEW YORK TIMES daily, a reduced subscription rate is available in deliverable areas. For information, call toll-free: 1-800-631-1222.

Allyn and Bacon and THE NEW YORK TIMES are proud to co-sponsor A CONTEMPORARY VIEW. We hope it will make the reading of both textbooks and newspapers a more dynamic, involving process.

Brief Contents

Contents

Chapter Three

Education through the Life Span   59

Chapter Four

Mental Retardation   93

Chapter Five

Behavior Disorders   131

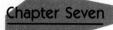

Chapter Six   *Learning Disabilities   171*

Chapter Seven   *Cross-Categorical Perspectives   207*

Chapter Eight

Communication Disorders   229

Chapter Nine

Autism   259

xvi CONTENTS

Features

TODAY'S TECHNOLOGY

Preface

There is a hope, I believe, in seeing the human adventure as a whole and in the shared trust that knowledge about mankind sought in reverence for life, can bring life.

Margaret Mead

As you begin your study of the fourth edition of *Human Exceptionality: Society, School, and Family*, we would like to provide some perspective on those features that continue from our third edition as well as on what is new and different. It is important to remember that this text is about *people*. Namely, it is about people with diverse needs, characteristics, and life-styles. It is about people who, for one reason or another, are called *exceptional*.

What does the word *exceptional* mean to you? For that matter, what do the words *disordered, deviant,* or *handicapped* mean to you? Who or what influenced your knowledge and attitudes about these terms and the people behind them? It is likely that you were influenced most by life experiences and not by formal training. You may have a family member, friend, or acquaintance who is exceptional in some way. Or perhaps you are a person with exceptional characteristics. Then again, you may be approaching the study of human exceptionality with little or no background on the topic. You will find that such study is the study of being human. Perhaps you will come to understand yourself better in the process.

ORGANIZATIONAL FEATURES

In addition to providing you with current and informative content, we are committed to making your first experience in the area of exceptionality interesting, enjoyable, and productive. To accomplish this, we have incorporated some features in the fourth edition of the text that should greatly enhance your desire to learn more and become acquainted with people who are exceptional.

To Begin With . . .

To Begin With . . . boxes, found at the beginnings of chapters, are designed to introduce and stimulate interest on topics. Each offers a variety of fascinating and current quotes, facts, and figures related to the subject covered in the chapter.

Windows

Windows present a series of personal statements that focus directly on individuals with differences. The purpose of the Windows is to share with you some personal insights into the lives of these people. These insights may come from teachers, family members, friends, peers, and professionals, as well as from individuals who are exceptional. Most chapters in this fourth edition open with at least one Window; others are usually included throughout the chapter. Note that these Windows are in no way representative of the range of characteristics associated with a given area of exceptionality. At best, they provide you with a frame of reference for your reading; they let you know that we are talking about real people who deal with life in many of the same ways. We believe that you will find the Windows to be one of the most enriching aspects of your introduction to exceptionality.

In the News

In the News boxes are scattered throughout the book, highlighting current events relating to various exceptionalities. For example, Chapter One (page 16) features an article on breaking down the barriers of discrimination through passage of the Americans with Disabilities Act of 1990. The In the News feature is designed to keep you up to date on issues and people who are making news.

Reflect on This

Every chapter includes at least one section entitled Reflect on This. Each highlights a piece of interesting and relevant information that will add to your learning and enjoyment of the chapter content. These Reflect sections give you a temporary diversion from the chapter narrative, while providing some engaging facts about a variety of subjects, including misconceptions regarding people with Down syndrome, information on preventing a hearing or visual impairment, or what to tell a friend who is contemplating suicide.

Today's Technology

New to the fourth edition is a feature on the expanding use of technology for people who are exceptional. Today's Technology highlights some of the innovations in computers, biomedical engineering, and public communication systems and the impact they have on individuals with differences. These Technology boxes focus on such topics as learning language skills through devices that synthesize speech, electronic readers for people with visual impairments, and word-processing programs with specialized features that assist students with learning disabilities in developing writing skills.

Interacting in Natural Settings

Also new to the fourth edition is Interacting in Natural Settings. This feature is intended to provide the reader with brief tips on ways to communicate, teach, or socialize with people who are exceptional across a variety of settings (home, school, and community) and age spans (early childhood through the high school years). Certainly, there are many possible ways to interact effectively with people who are exceptional. We hope that these tips provide some stimulus for further thinking on how to include these individuals as family members, school peers, friends, and neighbors.

Debate Forum

The text discussion in every chapter is followed by a Debate Forum. The purpose of this element is to broaden your view of the issues concerning people with differences. The Debate Forum in each chapter focuses on an issue about which there is some difference of opinion, such as federal involvement in education, children with AIDS in the public schools, educating students who are disabled with nondisabled peers, and the appropriateness of intervention strategies. For each issue discussed, opposing positions are presented, *Point* and *Counterpoint*. Remember, the purpose of the Debate Forum is not to establish right or wrong answers but to help you better understand the diversity of issues concerning individuals who are exceptional.

IMPROVING YOUR STUDY SKILLS

Each chapter in this text is organized in a systematic fashion. We encourage you to consider these brief suggestions in order to increase your learning effectiveness.

Preview the Chapter

In the margins of each chapter, you will find a series of Focus questions to guide your reading. Survey the Focus questions before reading the chapter; each question highlights important information to be learned. After surveying the Focus questions, examine key chapter headings to further familiarize yourself with chapter organization. Also scan the text for key terms, which are set in boldfaced type. Consult the Glossary at the end of the book for definitions of these terms.

Ask Questions

Using the Focus questions as a guide, ask yourself what you want to learn from the chapter material. After previewing the chapter, write down any additional questions you may have and use them as a supplement to guide your reading. Then organize your thoughts, and schedule time to actively read the chapter.

Read

Again, using the Focus questions as your guide, read the chapter.

Recite

After you have completed reading the chapter, turn back to the Focus questions and respond orally and in writing to each. Develop a written outline of the key points to remember.

Review

Each chapter in this text concludes with a section entitled Review. Each Focus question in the chapter is repeated in this section along with key points to remember from the material presented. Compare your memory of the material and your written outline to the key points addressed in the Review. If you forgot or misunderstood any of the important points, return to the Focus question in the chapter and reread the material. Review key terms cited within the chapter, as well; consult the Glossary as needed to become familiar with the meanings of these terms. Follow this process for each chapter in the book. In addition, consider developing your own short-answer essay tests to further enhance your understanding of the material in each chapter.

A Study Guide is also available to help you master the information included in this fourth edition of *Human Exceptionality*. Each chapter of the Study Guide is organized around effective methods for studying. Students are provided with information on what to preview, questions to ask, keys to effective reading, and how to recite, review, and reflect on the most important concepts in each chapter of the book. The guide includes exercises for mastering key terms, multiple-choice practice tests, fill-in-the-blank study sections, and activities that encourage further exploration into various topics of interest.

The study of human exceptionality is relatively young and unexplored. Those of you seeking careers in fields concerned with people who are exceptional will be part of the exploration. If, after reading this book, you are excited and encouraged to study further in this area, then we have met our primary goal. We would be unrealistic and unfair if we said this book will provide you with everything you ever wanted to know about people who are exceptional. What it does provide, however, is an overview on the lives of these people within their own communities, schools, and families.

LANGUAGE AWARENESS

As mentioned earlier, the study of human exceptionality is relatively new; thus, the parameters that define it are continually evolving. This is true of the language used to describe human exceptionality, as well.

Great care has been taken in this fourth edition of *Human Exceptionality* to discuss people with exceptionalities in a sensitive and positive manner. We have chosen to emphasize that these are indeed *people* first; the fact that they have exceptional characteristics is secondary. For example, rather than refer to *learning-disabled individuals,* we refer to *individuals with learning disabilities.* Likewise, we discuss *students at risk* rather than *at-risk students.* In short, the written style followed in this book is such that the person is always mentioned first; what makes him or her exceptional is mentioned second.

Care has also been taken to use appropriate terminology in describing people with exceptionalities. What is considered appropriate has evolved considerably over the years and will likely continue to do so. For instance, the term *handicapped,* once commonly used, is now considered to be derogatory in most contexts; terms such as *disabled* and *impaired* are preferred. (We address these issues in Chapter One in the discussion on labeling.) Similarly, terms such as *disturbances* (as in *emotional/behavioral disturbances*) have been replaced with less derogatory terms such as *disorders.* Although terms are necessary to describe categories of exceptional individuals, these descriptions need not be stigmatizing.

We encourage readers to review how language is used in this book and adopt these practices in their own communications. Consider that thought and language are interactive. The very words you choose to express your *ideas* about a subject also convey your *attitudes* toward it.

ACKNOWLEDGMENTS

We wish to thank our colleagues from around the country who provided in-depth and constructive feedback on various chapters within this fourth edition of *Human Exceptionality.* We extend our gratitude to the following national reviewers: Robert A. Berner, Slippery Rock University; Phillip Chinn, California State University at Los Angeles; Nancy Dalrymple, Indiana Resource Center for Autism at Indiana University; William E. Davis, University of Maine; Thomas P. DiPaola, Providence College; Deborah Gartland, Towson State University; Joan Herrick, Ferris State University; Bennett Leventhal, University of

Chicago; Isaura Barrera Metz, University of New Mexico; Donald Moorose, Fairmont State College; Susan Moreno, Editor, *The Maap,* Crown Point, Indiana; John J. O'Kane, State University of New York at Brockport; Christopher Pellikan, University of Illinois at Chicago; Cathy Pratt, Indiana University at Bloomington; Ramon Rocha, State University of New York at Geneseo; Raymond Rodriguez, Colorado State University; Stuart E. Schwarz, University of Florida; Kathlene S. Shank, Eastern Illinois University; and Jerry Wellik, St. Cloud State University.

We extend a special thank-you to those adopters from the third edition who took the time to complete a survey that was most helpful in shaping this new edition. Thanks to: Diana Caldwell, Alaska Pacific University; William Callahan, University of Nebraska at Omaha; Bill Casile, Duquesne University; Raymond J. Dalfonso, Kutztown University; Ken Gerlach, Pacific Lutheran University; Elaine Haglund, California State University at Long Beach; Peggy E. Hockersmith, Shippensburg University; Carolann Houser, Delta College; Betty Holdt, Western Oregon State College; Helmi Odems, Pacific Lutheran University; Joan C. Post-Gorden, University of Southern Colorado; and Julie Roncadori, University of Georgia.

We also extend our gratitude to the faculty and students at the University of Utah and Indiana University, who taught us a great deal about writing textbooks. Many of the changes incorporated into this fourth edition are a direct result of critiques from students in our classes.

We are indebted to our Series Editor Ray Short and his editorial assistant Christine Shaw. Ray has now been with us through the highs and lows of the last two editions. (Fortunately, there have been many more ups than downs.) He has spent numerous hours helping us to shape and then reshape the manuscript for this fourth edition. Ray's knowledge of the needs and interests of professors and students in the fields of education and psychology helped us cast this edition into a comprehensive text for the 1990s.

We have also not only appreciated but genuinely enjoyed our work with Developmental Editor Alicia Reilly, whose constant vigilance over quality issues has resulted in a product of which we are all very proud. We again thank Rowena Dores, who was our Production Administrator for the third and fourth editions.

The production team continues to amaze us as they consistently improve the readability, utility, and appearance of this book from edition to edition. To Susan Freese, our thanks for the careful and in-depth editing of the original manuscript and for the meticulous tracking of permissions. We have appreciated the opportunity of working with Karen Mason, who showed considerable patience as we all sought perfection in the final galleys and page proofs.

To Stephanie Gordon, Carolyn Osterman, Lisa Roosendaal, and Ruth Summers, we express our appreciation for the painstaking keyboarding, copying, and mailing of the manuscript. Thank-you for caring so much about the caliber of the finished product.

To those professors who have chosen this book for adoption and to those students who will use it as their first information source on people with differences, we hope our fourth edition of *Human Exceptionality* meets your expectations.

Finally, to our families, thanks for being there as we strived to do our best in preparing yet another edition of this book.

Michael L. Hardman
Clifford J. Drew
M. Winston Egan
Barbara Wolf

Human Exceptionality

Chapter One

A Multidisciplinary View of Exceptionality

TO BEGIN WITH . . .

- No specific behavior is inherently deviant; behavior becomes deviant only when others define it as such (Kammeyer, Ritzer, & Yetman, 1990, p. 184).

- Today, America welcomes in the mainstream of life all people with disabilities. Let the shameful wall of exclusion finally come tumbling down (President George Bush, signing into law the Americans with Disabilities Act, July 26, 1990).

- To: The Access Committee
       Attention: Handicapped Romeo

    There is now a suitable ramp installed at my balcony.

                        Impatiently,
                        Miss Juliet
    (Baird & Workman, 1986)

PETER

IS PETER NORMAL?   Peter is 12 years old and in the seventh grade at McAllister Junior High School. In the basic subjects of reading, writing, and arithmetic, Peter's performance is typical for a boy of his age. Achievement tests indicate that Peter is at approximately the seventh-grade level in all his subject areas. Recently, he took a test that indicated he has an intelligence quotient (IQ) of 106. Peter has 20/20 vision and no measurable hearing loss. He is physically active and healthy, with no serious medical problems. Emotionally, he has developed appropriate family and peer relationships.

*I*NTRODUCTION

If your career goals lie in the field of education, the behavioral and social sciences, medicine, or law, it is important that you view the individual who is exceptional from a broader perspective than that projected by a single profession. Exceptional people live and function in many contexts, not just school. Their differences affect them as they try to adjust to each new environment, but the differences also affect their families and society at large in significant ways.

Although exceptionality is sometimes described as a human problem, we prefer to characterize it as just being human. Exceptionality may present certain obstacles for the individual, but it should not be viewed as always being difficult to deal with or to understand.

In Window 1–1, we meet a child named Peter. Is Peter normal? We can say that Peter meets the basic medical, educational, and social criteria of normalcy. But what is normal, and how do we determine who is and who is not normal?

Normal is a relative term that is defined within the context of any given culture. Every society develops procedures to define what it means. The vast majority of individuals who belong to that society fall within the range of accepted physical and behavioral criteria. There are, however, individuals who exhibit differences that do not meet the cultural expectations of normalcy. These differences may be physical, such as the inability to walk. They can also be overt behaviors, such as a discipline problem or an inability to learn in the same way or at the same rate as siblings or peers.

How does society deal with these human differences? Everyone is in some way different from everyone else. Therefore, the issue is not merely being different; rather, it is the type and extent of the difference. To address these differences, every society creates descriptors to identify people who vary significantly from the norm. This process is called *labeling*.

LABELING PEOPLE WITH DIFFERENCES

FOCUS 1

Why do we label people according to their differences?

Labels are an attempt to describe, identify, and distinguish one person from another. Sociologists use labels to describe people who are socially deviant; educators and psychologists use labels to identify students with learning, physical, and behavioral differences; and physicians use labels to distinguish the sick from the healthy.

Common labels used by professionals to describe physical and behavioral differences include **disorder, disability,** and **handicap.** These terms are not synonymous. *Disorder,*

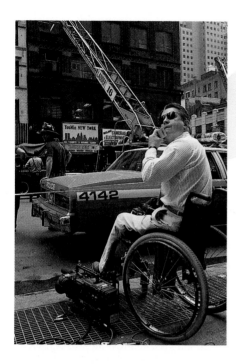

It is important to remember than an exceptional person is not necessarily a handicapped person. (Robert Brenner/PhotoEdit)

the broadest of the three terms, refers to a general malfunction of mental, physical, or psychological processes. It is defined as a disturbance in normal functioning. A *disability* is more specific than a *disorder* and results from a loss of physical functioning (e.g., loss of sight, hearing, or mobility) or difficulty in learning and social adjustment that significantly interferes with normal growth and development. A *handicap* is a limitation imposed on the individual by environmental demands and is related to the individual's ability to adapt or adjust to those demands. For example, a person who is confined to a wheelchair has a physical disability—the inability to walk. He or she is dependent on the wheelchair for mobility. When the physical environment does not accommodate the wheelchair (e.g., in a building without ramps, accessible only by stairs), the disability becomes a handicap.

When applied as an educational label, handicapped has a narrow focus and a negative connotation. The word *handicapped* literally means "cap in hand"; it originates from a time when people with disabilities begged in the streets in order to survive. This term may be used to describe only those individuals who are deficient in or lack ability.

Exceptional is a much more comprehensive term. It may be used to describe any individual whose physical, mental, or behavioral performance deviates substantially from the norm, either higher or lower. A person with exceptional characteristics is not necessarily a person with a handicap. Persons with exceptional characteristics may need additional educational, social, or medical services to compensate for physical and behavioral characteristics that differ substantially from what is considered normal. These differences can be **learning disorders, behavior disorders, speech and language disorders, sensory disorders, physical disorders, health disorders,** or **gifts and talents.**

Labels are only rough approximations of characteristics. Consequently, their effects differ from person to person. Some labels, such as *deaf,* describe permanent qualities; others, such as *overweight,* describe temporary qualities. Some labels are positive, and others are negative.

Labels communicate whether a person meets the expectations of the culture. A society establishes criteria that are easily exceeded by some but cannot be met by others. For example, a society may value creativity, innovation, and imagination. Someone with these attributes will be valued and rewarded with positive labels, such as *bright, intelligent,* or *gifted.* However, anyone whose ideas drastically exceed the limits of conformity may be branded with negative labels, such as *radical, extremist,* or *rebel.* The same label may have different connotations for different groups, depending on each group's viewpoint. For example, a high school student may be labeled a *conformist.* From the school administration's point of view, this is probably a positive characteristic, but to the student's peer group, it may have strong negative connotations.

What are the professional ramifications of using labels to describe people? Reynolds, Wang, and Walberg (1987) contend that the use of labels such as **learning disabled** and **emotionally disturbed** has produced mixed results at best. On the one hand, these labels have been the basis for access to educational services; however, they have also been unreliable. "The boundaries of the categories have shifted so markedly in response to legal, economic, and political forces as to make diagnosis largely meaningless" (Reynolds et al., p. 396). Thus, even though labels have been the basis for developing and providing services to people, they have also been used to promote stereotyping, discrimination, and exclusion. This view is shared by several researchers who indicate that the practice of labeling children in order to provide appropriate services has perpetuated and reinforced both the label and the behaviors implied by it (Graham & Dwyer, 1987; Leitch & Sodhi, 1986; Smith, Osborne, Crim, & Rhu, 1986).

If the use of labels can have negative consequences, why is labeling done so extensively? One reason is that many social services and educational programs for exceptional individuals require the use of labels to distinguish who is eligible for services and who is not. Funding may even be contingent on the numbers and types of individuals who are deemed eligible. To illustrate, Maria is a child with a hearing problem. By federal and state law, she must be assessed and labeled as hearing impaired before specialized educational or social services can be made available to her. A second reason for the use of labels is that they assist professionals in communicating effectively with one another and provide a common ground for evaluating research findings. A third reason is that labeling helps identify the specific needs of a limited number of people. Labeling is a means by which we can determine degrees of need when limited societal resources are available.

Formal versus Informal

Labels may be applied by both formal and informal labelers (Kammeyer et al., 1990). Formal labelers are sanctioned by society. For example, the criminal justice system—including the arresting officer, jury, and court judge—labels the person who commits a crime a criminal. A criminal may be incarcerated in a penal institution and consequently be labeled a convict. Formal labelers have the sanction of their society, as when a court judge pronounces sentence upon a convicted felon on behalf of all who live in the community. Other formal labels include *gifted and talented, mentally ill,* **mentally retarded,** *blind,* and so forth. Additional examples of formal labelers include doctors, educators, and behavioral and social scientists. Formal labels change our perception of the individual and in turn may change the individual's self-concept.

An informal labeler is usually some significant other—such as a family member, friend, teacher, or peer—and the applied label is meaningful only to this person or a restricted group. Informal labels may be expressed in a number of ways. They can be derogatory slang terms, such as *stupid, cripple, fat,* and *crazy.* Some informal labels reflect more favorably on the individual, such as *witty, smart,* and *cool.* Other informal labels, such as *ambitious* and *conformist,* are open to individual interpretation.

Approaches to Labeling

Significant physical and behavioral differences are found infrequently in every society. Most people in any given culture conform to its established standards. Conformity—people doing what they are supposed to do—is the rule for most of us most of the time (Baron & Byrne, 1991). Usually, we look the way we are expected to look, behave the way we are expected to behave, and learn the way we are expected to learn.

In some cases, however, people do not conform. When someone deviates substantially from the norm, a number of approaches can be used to describe the nature and extent of the differences (see Figure 1–1).

The Developmental Approach. The **developmental approach** to labeling is based on deviations from what is considered normal physical, social, or intellectual growth. Human differences are the result of an interaction of biological and environmental factors. To understand these differences, we must first establish what is normal development.

According to the developmental view, normal development can be described statistically. We observe large numbers of individuals and look for those characteristics that occur most frequently at a specific age. For example, the average 3-month-old infant is able to follow a moving object visually. *Average* is a statistical term based on observations of the behavior of 3-month-old infants. An individual child's growth pattern is then compared to the group average. Differences in development (either advanced or delayed) are labeled accordingly.

FOCUS 2
Identify three approaches that can be used to describe the nature and extent of human differences.

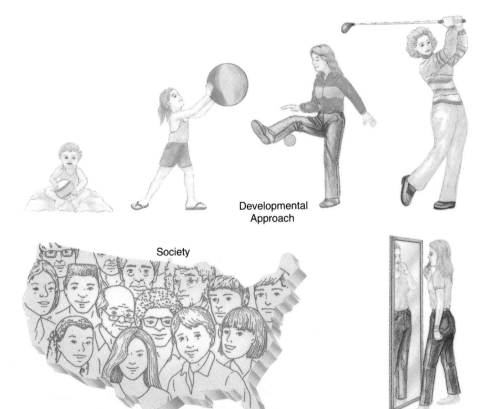

Society

Developmental
Approach

Cultural Approach

Individual Approach

FIGURE 1–1

Approaches to Labeling:
What Is Normal?

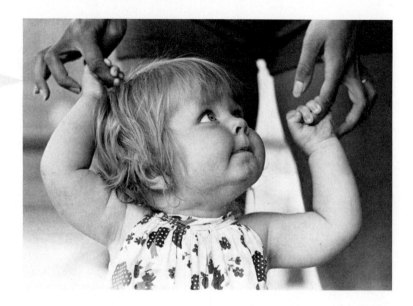

According to the developmental approach to labelling, this child would not be considered normal if her motor capabilities were far behind those of her peers. (Fredrik D. Bodin/ OffShoot Stock)

The Cultural Approach.   The **cultural approach** defines what is normal according to the standards established by a given culture. Whereas a developmental approach considers only the frequency of behaviors to define differences, a cultural approach suggests that differences can also be explained by examining the values inherent within a culture. What constitutes a significant difference changes over time, from culture to culture, and among the various social classes within a culture. As suggested by Kammeyer et al. (1990), "The process of becoming deviant usually begins when people perform acts that are disapproved of by certain members of society" (p. 184). For example, in some cultures, intelligence is described in terms of how well someone scores on a test measuring a broad range of abilities, while in other cultures, intelligence relates much more to how skillful someone is at hunting or fishing.

The idea that human beings are the products of their cultures has received its greatest thrust from anthropology, which emphasizes the diversity and arbitrary nature of cultural rules regarding dress, eating habits, sexual habits, politics, and religion. The human infant is so flexible that it is possible for the child to adjust to nearly any environment.

The Individual Approach.   The **individual approach** asserts that all people engage in a self-labeling process that may not be recognized by others. Self-imposed labels reflect how we perceive ourselves, although those perceptions may not be consistent with how others see us. The opposite may also occur: The culture uses a given label to identify a person, but that label may not be accepted by that person. Such was the case with Thomas Edison. While the schools labeled Edison as a child who was intellectually incapable, he eventually recognized that he was an individualist. He proved himself by identifying his individual abilities and pursuing his own interests.

The Effects of Labeling

Several studies have indicated that reactions to a label differ greatly from one person to another (Aloia & MacMillan, 1983; Bak, Cooper, Dobroth, & Siperstein, 1987; Dotter & Roebuck, 1988; Fiedler & Simpson, 1987; Graham & Dwyer, 1987; Van Bourgondien,

1987). However, researchers have been unable to draw consistent conclusions about how labeling a person influences our view of him or her.

Rosenthal and Jacobsen (1968) examined this issue in a well-known study involving intelligence. A group intelligence test was administered to elementary-age schoolchildren. The teachers were informed that the test was an effective method for determining intellectual potential. They were then provided with a list of about 20 percent of the children who had taken the test and told that these children had the greatest potential for intellectual growth. The list was in fact composed of children who had been randomly selected from the entire elementary school population. The test was administered again later in the schoolyear, and the children who had been identified to the teachers as having had the greatest potential scored significantly higher than the rest of the children in the school. The researchers concluded that teacher expectations contributed to the differences in scores. This effect is known as the **self-fulfilling prophecy,** or "you become what you are labeled."

The research of Rosenthal and Jacobsen (1968) contained many methodological flaws and has not been consistently replicated. In recent years, investigation of that research has stimulated considerable controversy. It has been suggested that the theory is without foundation when viewed in relation to everyday experience (Rosenthal, 1987; Wineburg, 1987). Does it make sense to suggest that a child acts out inappropriately simply because a teacher labels him or her a behavior problem?

The issue of teacher bias as a function of *negative* labels has also been investigated (Aloia & MacMillan, 1983; Foster, Ysseldyke, & Reese, 1975; Smith et al., 1986). Foster et al. (1975) studied the expectations of special education teacher trainees relative to children who were labeled emotionally disturbed. The researchers found that the trainees held negative, stereotyped expectations of these children. Ysseldyke and Foster (1978), in a study of elementary schoolteachers, reported that negative labels (e.g., *emotionally disturbed, learning disabled*) "generated initial negative stereotypes, which were retained in the observance of behaviors inconsistent with the labels" (p. 615). Aloia and MacMillan (1983), in a study of teachers in regular (i.e., not special education) classrooms, found similar results with children labeled as mentally retarded who were being educated in regular class programs. Smith et al. (1986) surveyed special education teachers, school officials, and parents to determine their perceptions of the label *learning disabilities* and found that these individuals attached multiple and sometimes conflicting meanings to the term.

From *Is It Really Only Monday?* by David Sipress. Copyright © 1981 by Fearon Teacher Aids. Simon and Schuster Supplementary Education Group.

Separating the Person and the Label.   Once a label has been affixed to an individual, the two may become inseparable. For example, instead of saying that Becky does not possess age-appropriate intellectual or socialization abilities, we may refer to her as retarded, losing sight of the fact that she is a human being with exceptional characteristics. To treat Becky as a label rather than as a person with special needs is an injustice, not only to Becky but to everyone else, as well.

Environmental Bias.   The environment in which we view someone can clearly influence our perceptions of him or her. For example, it can be said that, if you are in a mental hospital, you must be insane. Rosenhan (1973) investigated this premise by having himself and seven other sane individuals admitted to a number of state mental hospitals across the United States. Once these subjects were in the mental hospitals, they behaved normally. The question was whether the staff would perceive them as people who were healthy instead of patients who were mentally ill. Rosenhan reported that the pseudopatients were never detected by the hospital staff, although several of the real patients recognized the impostors. Throughout their hospital stays, the pseudopatients were incorrectly labeled and treated as schizophrenics. In fact, when a staff nurse observed one experimenter writing, she noted, "Patient engages in writing behavior." Rosenhan's investigation showed that the perception of what is normal can be biased by the environment in which the observations are made.

MEDICAL, SOCIAL, AND EDUCATIONAL SERVICES FOR PEOPLE WITH DIFFERENCES

In order to gain a broader understanding of the nature and extent of human differences, let us briefly examine several disciplines concerned with individuals who are exceptional. These disciplines include medicine, psychology, sociology, and education. Each is unique in its approach to exceptionality, which is reflected in the labels used to describe a person with exceptional characteristics. Figure 1–2 provides the common terminology associated with each field.

Medicine

The **medical model** has two dimensions: normal and pathological. *Normal* is defined as the absence of a biological problem. **Pathological** is defined as alterations in an organism caused by disease. The emphasis is on defining the nature of the disease and its pathological effects on the individual. *Disease* is a state of ill health that interferes with or destroys the integrity of the organism.

The medical model, often referred to as the *disease model,* focuses primarily on biological problems. The model is universal and does not have values that are culturally relative. It is based on the premise that being healthy is better than being sick, regardless of the culture in which one lives.

When diagnosing a problem, a physician carefully follows a definite pattern of procedures that includes questioning the patient and obtaining a history, conducting a physical examination and laboratory studies, and in some cases, performing surgical exploration. The person who has a biological problem is labeled the patient, and the deficits are then described as the patient's disease.

FOCUS 3

How did the work of nineteenth-century physicians and philosophers contribute to our understanding of people with differences?

Contributions of Notable Physicians.   We must go back more than 200 years to find the first documented attempts to personalize treatment programs to the needs of people with differences. During the sixteenth and seventeenth centuries, people who were disturbed mentally or emotionally were viewed as mad persons, fools, and public threats who had to

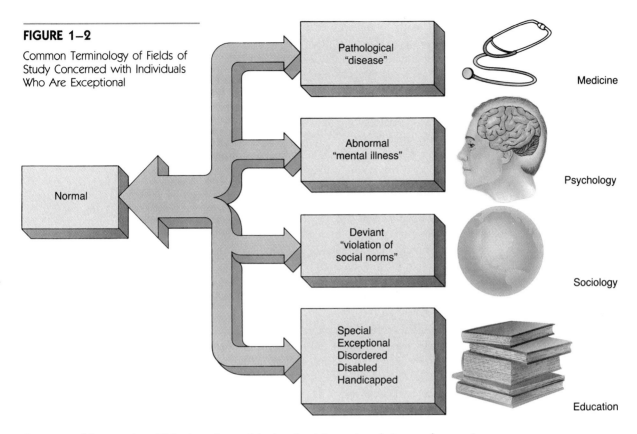

FIGURE 1–2

Common Terminology of Fields of Study Concerned with Individuals Who Are Exceptional

be removed from society. This view changed during the eighteenth and nineteenth centuries, when many physicians contributed to expanding our understanding of human differences. Jean-Marc Itard (1775–1838) epitomizes the orientation of professionals during this period, and his work is reflected in our modern medical, psychological, social, and educational intervention models.

In 1799, as a young physician and authority on diseases of the ear and education of the deaf, Itard worked for the National Institute of Deaf-Mutes in Paris. He believed that the environment, in conjunction with physiological stimulation, could contribute to the learning potential of any human being. Itard was influenced by the earlier work of Philippe Pinel (1742–1826), a French physician concerned with mental illness, and John Locke (1632–1704), an English philosopher. Pinel advocated that people characterized as insane or idiots needed to be treated humanely. However, his teachings emphasized that such individuals were essentially incurable and that any treatment to remedy their disabilities would be fruitless. Locke's philosophy was contrary to that of Pinel. Locke described the mind as a "blank slate" that could be opened to all kinds of new stimuli. The positions of Pinel and Locke represent the classic **nature versus nurture** controversy: What are the roles of heredity and environment in determining a person's capabilities?

Itard tested the theories of Pinel and Locke in his work with Victor, the so-called wild boy of Aveyron. Victor was 12 years old when he was found in the woods by hunters. He had not developed any language, and his behavior was virtually uncontrollable, described as savage or animal-like. Ignoring Pinel's diagnosis that the child was an incurable **idiot,** Itard took responsibility for Victor and put him through a program of sensory stimulation that was intended to cure his condition. After five years, Victor developed some verbal language and became more socialized as he grew accustomed to his new environment.

Itard's work with Victor documented for the first time that learning is possible even for individuals described by most professionals as totally helpless.

Following Itard's groundbreaking work in the early nineteenth century, some European countries began establishing special schools and segregated living facilities for people with disabilities (e.g., the **feebleminded, deaf, blind,** and **insane**). As explained by McCleary, Hardman, and Thomas (1990), expertise and knowledge about people with disabilities was extremely limited during this period. Most programs focused on care and management rather than treatment and education. Although many professionals had demonstrated that positive changes in individual development were possible, they had not been able to cure such conditions as insanity and idiocy.

Medical Services in the 1990s.   Medical services for people with disabilities have evolved considerably. The typical course in the early part of the twentieth century involved treatment primarily in a hospital or institutional setting. The focus today is directly on the individual in family and community settings.

In many cases, the physician is the first professional with whom parents have contact concerning their child's disability. This is particularly true when the child's problem is identifiable immediately after birth or during early childhood. The physician is the family advisor and communicates with parents regarding the medical prognosis and recommendations for treatment. However, too often, physicians assume that they are the family's only counseling resource (Drew, Logan, & Hardman, 1992). Physicians should be aware of additional resources within the community, including other parents, social workers, mental health professionals, and educators.

Medical services are often taken for granted simply because they are readily available to most people. This is not true, however, for many people with disabilities. It is not uncommon for a pediatrician to suggest that parents seek treatment elsewhere for their child with a disability, even when the problem is a common illness such as a cold or a sore throat.

It would be unfair to stereotype medical professionals as unresponsive to the needs of exceptional people. On the contrary, medical technology has prevented many disabilities from occurring and enhanced the quality of life for many people. However, in order for people with disabilities to receive comprehensive medical services in a community setting, several factors must be considered. The physician in community practice (e.g., the general practitioner, pediatrician, etc.) must receive more medical training in the medical, psychological, and educational aspects of disability conditions. This training could include instruction regarding (1) developmental milestones; (2) attitudes toward children with disabilities; (3) disabling conditions; (4) prevention; (5) screening, diagnosis, and assessment; (6) interdisciplinary collaboration; (7) working effectively with parents; (8) long-term medical and social treatment programs; and (9) community resources.

Physicians must also be more willing to treat patients with disabilities for common illnesses when the treatment is irrelevant to the patient's disability. Physicians need not become disability specialists, but they must have enough knowledge to refer patients to appropriate specialists when necessary. For instance, physicians must be aware of and willing to refer patients to other nonmedical community resources, such as social workers, educators, and psychologists. The medical profession must continue to support physician specialists and other allied health personnel who are well equipped to work with people who are disabled. These specialized health professionals include **geneticists** and **genetic counselors, physical therapists** and **occupational therapists,** public health nurses, and nutritional and dietary personnel.

Psychology and Sociology

Psychology and sociology are similar in that both fields are concerned with the study of human behavior. Sociology is the science of social behavior, whereas psychology studies the person as a separate being.

Abnormal Behavior. Modern psychology is the science of human and animal behavior, the study of the overt acts and mental events of an organism that can be observed and evaluated. Broadly viewed, psychology is concerned with every detectable action of an individual. Behavior is the focus of psychology, and when the behavior of an individual does not meet the criteria of normal, it is labeled abnormal.

Psychology, as we know it today, is more than 100 years old. In 1879, Wilhelm Wundt (1832–1920) defined *psychology* as the science of conscious experience. His definition was based on the principle of introspection—looking into oneself to analyze experiences. William James (1842–1910) expanded Wundt's conception of conscious experience in his treatise *The Principles of Psychology* (1890), to include learning, motivation, and emotions. In 1913, John B. Watson (1878–1958) shifted the focus of psychology from conscious experience to observable behavior and mental events.

In 1920, Watson conducted an experiment with an 11-month-old child named Albert. Albert showed no fear of a white rat when initially exposed to the animal. He saw it as a toy and played with it freely. Watson then introduced a loud, terrifying noise directly behind Albert each time the rat was presented. After a period of time, the boy became frightened by the sight of any furry white object, even though the loud noise was no longer present. Albert had learned to fear rats through **conditioning,** the process in which new objects or situations elicit responses that were previously elicited by other stimuli. Watson thus demonstrated that abnormal behavior could be learned through the interaction of the individual with environmental stimuli (Watson & Rayner, 1920).

In spite of Watson's work, most theorists during the first half of the twentieth century considered the medical model to be the most logical and scientific approach to understanding abnormal behavior. The public was more accepting of the view that psychologically disturbed people were sick and not fully responsible for their problems.

The **ecological approach,** which emerged in the latter half of the twentieth century, was supportive of Watson's theories (Cowen, 1973). This approach views abnormal behavior more as a result of an individual's interaction with the environment than as a disease within him or her. The approach theorizes that social and environmental stress, in combination with the individual's inability to cope, lead to psychological disturbances. Bogdan (1986) indicated that there is "symbolic meaning" in what "society honors and what it degrades" (p. 351).

We cannot live in today's society without encountering the dynamics of abnormal behavior. The media are replete with stories of murder, suicide, sexual aberration, burglary, robbery, embezzlement, child abuse, and other incidents that display behavioral disorders. Each case represents a point on the continuum of personal maladjustment that exists in society. Levels of maladjustment range from behaviors that are slightly deviant or eccentric (but still within the confines of normal human experience) to **neurotic disorders** (partial disorganization characterized by combinations of anxieties, compulsions, obsessions, and phobias) to **psychotic disorders** (severe disorganization resulting in loss of contact with reality and characterized by delusions, hallucinations, and illusions).

The study of abnormal behavior is historically based in philosophy and religion in Western culture. Until the Middle Ages, the disturbed or mad person was thought to have "made

FOCUS 4

Distinguish between abnormal behavior and social deviance.

Each culture determines the range of behaviors that will be labelled either normal or deviant. (R. Laura Diez/Leo de Wys Inc.)

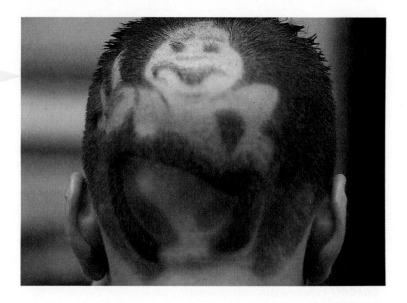

a pact with the devil," and the psychological affliction was a result of divine punishment. A psychological disturbance was thought to be caused by devils, witches, or demons residing within the person. The earliest known treatment for mental disorders, called *trephining,* involved drilling holes in a person's skull to permit evil spirits to leave (Carlson, 1990).

Social Deviance.   Sociology is concerned primarily with modern cultures, group behaviors, societal institutions, and intergroup relationships. It examines an individual in relation to the physical and social environment. When individuals meet the social norms of the group, they are considered normal. When individuals are unable to adapt to social roles or to establish appropriate interpersonal relationships, their behaviors are labeled **deviant.** Unlike medical pathology, social deviance cannot be defined in universal terms. Instead, it is defined within the context of the culture, in any way the culture chooses to define it.

> Even within the same society, different social groups often define deviance differently. Groups of people who share the same norms and values will develop their own rules about what is and what is not deviant behavior. Their views may not be shared by members of the larger society, but the definitions of deviance will apply to group members. (Kammeyer et al., 1990, p. 224)

Four principles serve as guidelines in determining who will be labeled socially deviant.

1. Normal behavior must meet societal, cultural, or group expectations. *Deviance* is defined as a violation of social norms.
2. Social deviance is not necessarily an illness. Failure to conform to societal norms does not imply that the individual has pathological or biological deficits.
3. Each culture determines the range of behaviors that are defined as normal or deviant and then enforces these norms. Those people with the greatest power within the culture can impose their criteria for normalcy on those who are less powerful.
4. Social deviance may be caused by the interaction of several factors, including genetic makeup and individual experiences within the social environment.

THE MOVEMENT FROM SOCIAL ISOLATION TO SOCIAL INCLUSION

Social Isolation

The early twentieth century was marked by contrasts in the treatment of exceptional individuals. On the positive side, the **scientific method** was applied to the measurement of intelligence, as with the Binet-Simon Intelligence Test developed in 1905 (see later in this chapter, "Special Education in U.S. Schools: 1900–1975"). What's more, services that had been denied to exceptional individuals for centuries became more accessible. Special classes in urban public schools were developed for children with learning problems as well as those with visual and hearing impairments. Public sentiment had been aroused, and more federal, state, and local monies were channeled into human services.

By contrast, many misconceptions held during the early twentieth century resulted in people being afraid of individuals with disabilities and a movement to isolate them from society. Many people feared that the mentally and morally defective would defile the human race.

Henry Herbert Goddard, an American psychologist, believed that inferior intelligence was caused solely by hereditary factors. He attempted to convince the scientific and lay communities that feeblemindedness was indeed transmitted from generation to generation (Goddard, 1912). He later hypothesized that there was an irrefutable link between intelligence and social deviance: The less intelligence people have, the less responsible they are for their actions. Therefore, less intelligent people are more likely to exhibit socially deviant or unacceptable behavior. Goddard's definition of social deviates included criminals, alcoholics, the sexually immoral, **epileptics,** the mentally ill, and the feebleminded. Goddard's thesis was widely accepted by American and European psychologists in the 1920s and 1930s, although it is no longer accepted by contemporary professionals in psychology or sociology (Drew et al., 1992).

One outcome of Goddard's theory was a widespread movement toward selective breeding and the overall prevention of deviance. This brought about an extended period of alarm and fear of many people with disabilities, as well as an indictment against them. In the latter half of the twentieth century, we have come to recognize that hereditary factors play a less significant role in the causes of mental and social deviance than was once thought, especially when compared to maternal health and sociocultural factors (Westling, 1986).

The focus of early twentieth-century preventive measures was the passage of state legislation that prohibited mental and social deviates from marrying. Eventually, legislation was expanded to include sterilization of such individuals. Compulsory surgical **sterilization** became widespread, and laws were passed throughout the United States in an effort to reduce the number of deviates. Sterilization laws in some states contained provisions for sterilizing mentally retarded people, individuals with epilepsy, the sexually promiscuous, and criminals. In addition to marriage and sterilization laws, large numbers of individuals were moved from the communities in which they lived to isolated, special-care facilities whose sole purpose was maintenance. These facilities became widely known as **institutions.**

An *institution* is defined as an establishment or facility governed by a collection of fundamental rules. Institutions for people with disabilities have had many different labels: *school, hospital, colony, prison,* and *asylum.* The term *institution* did not originate with the facilities of early twentieth-century America. Asylums were prominent in many parts of Europe in the seventeenth century and were used to segregate, dehumanize, and punish moral defectives.

FOCUS 5

Why has the early twentieth century been described as a period of contrast in meeting the needs of people with differences?

Humanitarian Reforms

Through the work of Philippe Pinel, a French physician, and Benjamin Rush, the father of American psychiatry, an era of humanitarian reform began in the last half of the eighteenth century. Such reform continued into the early nineteenth century, which brought optimism concerning the treatment and eventual cure of people described as deviant. However, hope eventually eroded into despair and fear of deviant people returned because social and mental deviance was not being cured. Because deviance continued to be a major social problem, many professionals were convinced that it was necessary to segregate large numbers of both mental and social deviates.

Institutions became more and more concerned with social control as they grew in size and financial resources became scarce. These facilities had to establish rigid rules and regulations in order to manage large numbers of individuals with a limited financial base. In many cases, rules stripped away individuals' identities and forced them into group regimentation. For example, individuals could not have personal possessions. They were also forced to wear institutional clothing and were given identification tags and numbers. Institutions were characterized by locked living units, barred windows, and high walls enclosing the grounds. Organized treatment programs declined, and the number of "terminal," uncured patients grew. This forced even more expansion and the erection of new buildings, which was a problem, given that public and professional pessimism concerning the value of treatment programs meant diminishing funds for mental health care.

This alarming situation remained unchanged for nearly five decades and declined even further during the Depression years of the 1930s. By the early 1950s, more than 500,000 persons were committed to mental hospitals throughout the United States.

In the early 1950s, the first attempts to reform mental hospitals were initiated by the American Psychiatric Association, which led efforts to inspect and rate the nation's 300 mental hospitals and called attention to the lack of therapeutic intervention and deplorable living conditions. In 1950, parents of children with mental retardation organized and founded the National Association for Retarded Children (now known as the **ARC,** A National Organization on Mental Retardation). The purpose of the ARC is to promote the general welfare of people who are mentally retarded of all ages everywhere: in homes; in communities; in institutions; and in public, private, and religious schools. The parent movement in the United States was paralleled by many others in countries around the world, as families organized to lobby policymakers for more appropriate services (McCleary et al., 1990).

Legal Reforms

Several court cases of the past three decades have been significant in reforming state institutions for people who are mentally retarded and mentally ill. A U.S. district court ruled in the case of *Wyatt v. Stickney* (1972) that the patients at an institution in Alabama who were mentally retarded were being deprived of the right to individual treatment that would give them a realistic opportunity for habilitation. This case was the first major court action on behalf of people with mental retardation residing in public institutions. The court described the institutional facilities as human warehouses, steeped in an atmosphere of psychological and physical deprivation. It further specified that the state must make changes to ensure a therapeutic environment.

During the early 1980s, several court cases expanded on the Wyatt case (*Homeward Bound v. Hissom Memorial Center,* 1988; *Pennhurst State School and Hospital v. Halderman,* 1981; *Youngberg v. Romeo,* 1982). In the case of *Homeward Bound v. Hissom Memorial Center* (1988), a U.S. district court ruled that, because they were institutionalized, persons who were mentally retarded and residing at Hissom State School and Hospital had been denied opportunities for a quality life. The court directed the state of Oklahoma to close the school within a four-year period and to create community alternatives for people with mental retardation.

What constitutes a good institution continues to be a matter of legal and moral debate. Objective criteria have not been agreed on by parents or professionals. We do know that the original rationale for the social segregation model in the early twentieth century is not valid. The institutional accomplishments of the past 80 years can be summed up in a few rather negative statements: Institutions have become isolated asylums, concerned more with social management and regimentation than with education or treatment. In addition, the civil rights of individuals are often ignored.

Lakin and Bruininks (1985) summarized the research on large public and private institutions: "Once virtually the only model of extrafamilial care of [disabled] persons, [these facilities] are both aberrant social settings and have debilitating effects that increase the probability of segregated living" (p. 12). As we move through the 1990s, there is hope that the era of social segregation will be replaced with one of inclusion, resulting in more access and opportunities in community life for people with differences.

Social Inclusion

The integration of people with disabilities into community settings—such as schools, places of employment, and neighborhood homes—is based on a philosophy that recognizes and accepts the range of human differences within a culture. One way to evaluate the success of community services for any individual is to look at whether and how such services make a difference in his or her life. As such, the effectiveness of community services for people with disabilities can be viewed in terms of: Do such services promote personal autonomy? Do opportunities for social interaction and integration exist? Does the individual have a choice of life-style? Do opportunities for economic self-sufficiency exist?

Each of these questions relates to different outcomes, depending on the age of the individual. For the preschool-age child, the world is defined primarily through the family and a small, same-age peer group. As the child grows older, the world expands to include the

FOCUS 6

Identify four primary issues involved in the right-to-treatment cases that have come before the courts in the latter half of the twentieth century.

Children with disabilities are now more likely to be actively involved in mainstream society.
(Richard Hutchings/Info Edit)

Americans with Disabilities Act: Opening Doors

In the past, individuals with disabilities have had to contend with the reality that learning to live independently did not guarantee access to all that society had to offer in terms of services and jobs. Although several states have long had laws that promised otherwise, access to places such as public restrooms and great restaurants and success in mainstream corporate America has often eluded those with disabilities, primarily because of architectural and attitudinal barriers.

The Americans with Disabilities Act (ADA), phase 1 of which began January 26, 1992, has promised to change all that, giving 43 million Americans with disabilities new legal rights, at an estimated cost to businesses of $1 billion to $2 billion. All businesses that serve the public—such as laundromats, retail stores, hospitals, and banks—are required to remove architectural barriers. Included among those changes considered to be "readily achievable" and therefore required are:

♦ Making curb cuts in sidewalks
♦ Repositioning shelves, desks, and telephones
♦ Widening doors
♦ Removing or providing convenient alternatives to turnstiles

Employers are also required to make "reasonable efforts" to hire people with disabilities. Under ADA, employers may not:

♦ Use hiring or firing practices to discriminate against a worker or applicant who has a disability

♦ Ask whether a person has a disability or has had prior medical treatments (employers may ask only about the applicant's ability to perform a particular job)
♦ Use tests or requirements that could screen out an applicant or worker due to his or her disability
♦ Deny access to employment or advancement to someone living with or involved in a relationship with a person who has a disability
♦ Limit job classifications or promotion opportunities

American Telephone and Telegraph (AT&T) and local carriers are required to provide services that enable individuals with hearing and speech impairments to make and receive calls on regular telephones. Mass transit services must also be made accessible to all people with disabilities.

Clearly, individuals with disabilities are a minority group that has been discriminated against regularly in the past. As a result, many such people either cannot get jobs or have stopped looking altogether, making the community of individuals with disabilities one of the poorest in the nation. According to the President's Committee on the Employment of People with Disabilities, two-thirds of these individuals of working age cannot get jobs, even in sound economic times.

Much as the Civil Rights Act of 1964 gave clout to the African-American struggle for equality, the Americans with Disabilities Act has promised to do the same for those with disabilities. The degree to which it will be successful in eliminating the fears and prejudices of the general community remains to be seen.

neighborhood, the school, and eventually a larger heterogeneous group called the community. The questions for professionals then become: How can services be structured to foster full participation as the individual's world expands? What barriers obstruct full participation, and how do we break them down? We will now examine some of the ways in which society supports as well as limits the participation of people with disabilities in community settings.

The Americans with Disabilities Act of 1990

FOCUS 7

What was the purpose of the Americans with Disabilities Act of 1990 (Public Law 101–336)?

On July 26, 1990, President George Bush signed into law the most sweeping civil rights legislation in the United States since the **Civil Rights Act of 1964: the Americans with Disabilities Act (ADA)** (Public Law 101–336). The purpose of ADA was to provide a national mandate to end discrimination against individuals with disabilities in private-sector employment, all public services, and public accommodations, transportation, and telecommunications. The legislation defined a person with a disability as (1) having a physical or mental impairment that substantially limits him or her in some major life activity and (2) having experienced discrimination resulting from this physical or mental impairment. ADA

R E F L E C T O N T H I S

1-1 The Americans with Disabilities Act of 1990: Breaking Down the Barriers

Did you know that, in public and private employment . . . ?

◆ Employers cannot discriminate against an individual with a disability in hiring or promotion if the person is otherwise qualified for the job.
◆ Employers can ask about someone's ability to perform a job but cannot inquire if he or she has a disability or subject him or her to tests that tend to screen out people with disabilities.
◆ Employers need to provide reasonable accommodation to people with disabilities, such as job restructuring and modification of equipment.

Did you know that, in public transportation . . . ?

◆ New public transit buses, bus and train stations, and rail systems must be accessible to individuals with disabilities.
◆ Transit authorities must provide transportation services to individuals with disabilities who cannot use fixed-route bus services.
◆ All Amtrak stations must be accessible to people with disabilities by the year 2010.

Did you know that, in public accommodations . . . ?

◆ Restaurants, hotels, and retail stores may not discriminate against individuals with disabilities.
◆ Physical barriers in existing facilities must be removed, if removal is readily achievable. If not, alterna-

tive methods of providing the services must be offered.
◆ All new construction and alterations of facilities must be accessible.

Did you know that, in government . . . ?

◆ State and local agencies may not discriminate against qualified individuals with disabilities.
◆ All government facilities, services, and communications must be accessible to people with disabilities.

Did you know that, in telecommunications . . . ?

◆ Companies offering telephone service to the general public must offer telephone relay services to individuals who use telecommunication devices for the deaf or similar devices.

charged the federal government with the task of ensuring that these provisions be enforced on behalf of all people with disabilities (West, 1991).

Such legislation, coming almost 30 years after the Civil Rights Act of 1964, was truly needed, for several reasons. First, it was clear that people with disabilities were being discriminated against in employment, access to public and private accommodations (e.g., hotels, theaters, restaurants, grocery stores), and services offered through state and local governments (Harris & Associates, 1987, 1989; National Council on Disability, 1986). Second, the historic Civil Rights Act of 1964 did not even mention people with disabilities. Therefore, these individuals had no federal protection against discrimination except through some

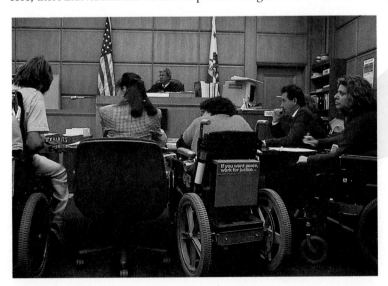

The Americans with Disabilities Act (ADA) will provide the constitutional basis for lawsuits by individuals who feel they have been denied employment or access to services. (Alon Reininger/Woodfin Camp & Associates)

limited provisions in **Section 504 of the Vocational Rehabilitation Act of 1973** (Public Law 93–112). As suggested by Senator Tom Harkin, a leading proponent of ADA in the U.S. Senate:

> Discrimination is sometimes the result of prejudice; sometimes it is the result of patronizing attitudes; and still other times it is the result of thoughtlessness or indifference. Whatever its origin, the results are the same: segregation, exclusion, or denial of equal, effective and meaningful opportunities to participate in programs and opportunities. (Harkin, 1990, p. 1)

Living and Learning in Community Settings.   Legislating against discrimination is one thing; enforcing laws against it is another. The purpose of ADA was to ensure that comprehensive services (e.g., employment, housing, educational programs, public transportation, restaurant access, and religious activities) be available to individuals within or as close as possible to their family and community lives (see Figure 1–3). Individuals should also be able to purchase additional services at will: dental examinations, medical treatment, life insurance, and so forth. Access to these services allows people the opportunity to be included in community life. In order to accomplish integration, two factors should be taken into account: (1) the individual's ability, with appropriate education and training, to adapt to societal expectations; and (2) the willingness of society to adapt to and accommodate individuals with differences.

FOCUS 8

What services must be available to ensure that an individual with a disability is able to live and learn successfully in a community setting?

FIGURE 1–3

Community Services

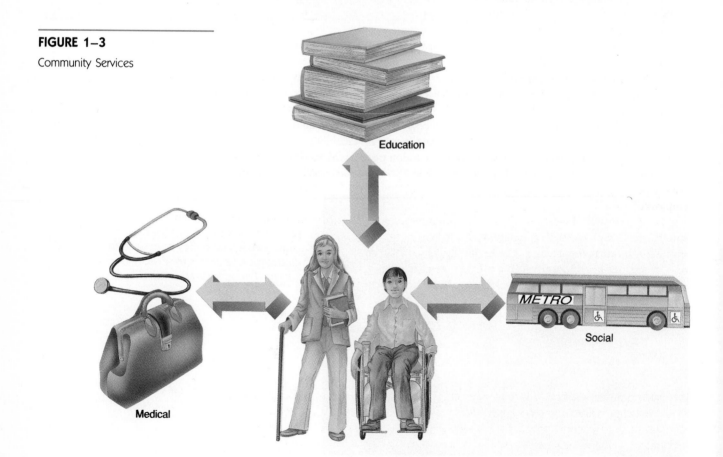

Education

Medical

METRO

Social

Access to adequate housing and **barrier-free facilities** is essential for people with physical disabilities. A barrier-free environment may be created by renovating existing facilities and requiring that new buildings and public transportation incorporate barrier-free designs. People in wheelchairs or on crutches need entrance ramps to and within public buildings; accessibility to public telephones, vending machines, and restrooms; and lifts for public transportation vehicles. Available community living environments could include private homes, specialized boarding homes, supervised apartments, group homes, and foster homes.

Recreation and leisure-time opportunities within the community will vary substantially according to the individual's age and the severity of his or her disability. Thus, the availability of services will also vary from community to community. Many families may not have access to such activities as dance and music lessons, tumbling, swimming, and scouting; yet all of these activities are generally available for other children within the community. Similar problems exist for adolescents and adults with exceptional characteristics. Many cannot adapt to the community because they cannot use their leisure time constructively. Adults may do little with their leisure time beyond watching television.

Recreational programs must be developed to assist individuals in developing worthwhile leisure-time activities and more satisfying life-styles. Therapeutic recreation is a profession concerned specifically with this goal: using recreation to help people adapt their physical, emotional, or social characteristics to take advantage of leisure-time activities more independently in a community setting.

Work is essential to the creation of successful life-styles for adults, including those with disabilities. Yet many individuals with disabilities are unable to gain employment during their adult years. Recent Harris polls found that two-thirds of disabled people between the ages of 16 and 64 were not working but that 66 percent of those not working (and of working age) indicated that they would like to. A comparison of working and nonworking disabled individuals revealed that working individuals were more satisfied with life, had more money, and were less likely to blame their disability for preventing them from reaching their potential (Harris & Associates, 1987, 1989).

A report by the Organization for Economic Cooperation and Development (OECD, 1986) suggested that the worldwide common denominator that makes employment difficult for people with disabilities is "the lack of flexibility of systems which on occasion discourage the search for employment. A further feature of many [countries' policies] is that benefits cease when employment is found, but are not easily obtained again if the individual is unemployed" (p. 18).

For the individual with a disability, the messages are indeed mixed: One government entity urges that people with disabilities strive to be contributing members of society, while another supports their dependence. OECD concluded that the proper role of government may be to stimulate opportunities for people with disabilities in both the private and public sectors. This role would include legislation and policy development, a mandated process for interagency coordination, strategies to change public attitudes, and the dissemination of information regarding effective model programs that enhance community living and participation.

Education

As children progress through formal schooling, their parents, teachers, peers, and others expect that they will learn and behave according to established patterns. Most students move through their educational programs in about the same way, requiring the same level of service and within similar timeframes. Students who do not meet educational expectations of normal growth and development are labeled according to the type and extent of their deviation. They are provided services and resources that are different from those provided for students who are typical.

Access to education is a basic American value, one that reflects the expectation that all individuals have an opportunity to learn and develop to the best of their abilities. From this value emerges some of the most fundamental goals of education. Resnick (1987) described *school* as a place to prepare people for life, as well as an environment in which they can engage in reflection and reasoning. Schools exist to promote literacy, personal autonomy, economic self-sufficiency, personal fulfillment, and citizenship.

Regardless of the purpose of education—be it to reason, reflect, or gain practical knowledge for living and learning—in a democratic society, the expectation is full participation for everyone regardless of race, cultural background, socioeconomic status, physical disability, or mental limitation. Unfortunately, in the United States, it has taken more than two centuries to translate this value into actual practice for students with disabilities.

FOCUS 9

What educational services were available for students with disabilities during most of the twentieth century?

Special Education in U.S. Schools: 1900–1975.   In the United States education of children with exceptionalities began in the early 1900s with the efforts of many dedicated professionals. Those efforts consisted of programs that were usually separate from the public schools, the majority of which were for children who were slow learners or deaf or blind. Students were usually placed in segregated classrooms in a public school building or in separate schools. *Special* education meant *segregated* education. Moreover, if the student's deviation from normal peers was too substantial, he or she would be excluded from public education entirely.

Because the schools needed to have some way of determining who would receive a public education, an assessment device was developed to determine who was intellectually capable of attending school. The result was an individual test of intelligence developed by Alfred Binet and Théodore Simon (1905). It was first used in France to predict how well students would function in school. In 1908, it was translated into English. The **Binet-Simon Scales,** revised and standardized by Lewis Terman at Stanford University, were published in 1916 as the **Stanford–Binet Intelligence Scale.** This test provided a means of identifying children who deviated significantly from the average in intellectual capability, at least in terms of what the test actually measured.

From 1920 to 1960, the availability of public school programs for exceptional children continued to be sporadic and selective. Most states only *allowed* for special education; they did not *require* that it be made available. Services to children with mild emotional disorders (i.e., discipline problems) were initiated in the early 1930s, but mental hospitals continued to be the only alternative for most individuals with severe emotional problems. Special classes for children with physical disabilities were also started in the 1930s, primarily for those with crippling conditions, heart defects, and other health-related problems that interfered with participation in regular education programs. Separate schools became very popular for these children during the late 1950s. Such schools were specially equipped to accommodate the needs of students with physical disabilities; facilities included elevators and ramps and modified doors, toilets, and desks.

During the 1940s, placement of students with disabilities in special versus regular schools emerged as an important policy issue. Polloway (1984) asserted that, during this period, educators were determined to find the most effective placement for students with disabilities as well as to ensure that they had the opportunity for normal social interaction.

By the 1950s, many countries began to expand educational opportunities for students with disabilities in special schools and classes funded through public education. Two separate events had a significant impact on the evolution of education for students with disabilities.

First, in many countries, parents of children with disabilities organized as a constituent group to lobby policymakers for more appropriate social and educational services for their children. Second, professionals from both the behavioral and medical sciences became more interested in services for individuals with disabilities, thus enriching knowledge through research into effective practice.

These events provided the setting for the current period, in which significant departures from past practice have been initiated (McCleary et al., 1990). During the late 1950s, there was an increase in the number of public school classes for students with mild mental retardation and those described as emotionally disturbed. For the most part, these children continued to be educated in an environment that isolated them from nondisabled peers. The validity of segregation continued to be an important issue in the field of education. Several studies in the 1950s and 1960s (e.g., Cassidy & Stanton, 1959; Johnson, 1961; Jordan, 1959; Thurstone, 1959) examined the efficacy of special classes for children with mild mental retardation. Johnson (1962), summarizing this research, suggested that the academic achievement of learners who were retarded was consistent regardless of whether they were placed in special or regular education classes, although the child's social adjustment was not harmed by the special program.

Although numerous criticisms regarding the design of efficacy studies have been made over the years, they did result in a movement toward expanding services beyond special classes in public schools. An example of this outcome was the development of a model whereby a child could remain in the regular class program for the majority if not all of the school day, receiving special education when and where it was needed. This concept became widely known as **mainstreaming**—integrating students with disabilities into general education classes with their nondisabled peers.

The 1960s brought other major changes in the field of special education, as well. The federal government took on an expanded role in the education of children who were exceptional. University teacher preparation programs received federal financial support and initiated programs to train special education teachers throughout the United States. The Bureau of Education for the Handicapped (BEH) in the U.S. Office of Education (presently the Office of Special Education and Rehabilitative Services in the U.S. Department of Education) was created as a clearinghouse for information at the federal level. Demonstration projects were funded nationwide to establish a research base for the education of students with disabilities in the public schools.

The rights of children with disabilities to an appropriate education have been mandated by state and federal legislation. (Bob Daemmrich/Stock, Boston)

FOCUS 10

Identify the principal issues in the right-to-education cases that led to eventual passage of Public Law 94–142 (now referred to as IDEA).

A National Mandate to Educate Students with Disabilities.* The 1970s have often been described as a decade of revolution in the field of special education. Many of the landmark cases addressing the right to education for students with disabilities were brought before the courts during this period. In addition, major pieces of state and federal legislation were enacted to reaffirm the right of individuals with disabilities to a free public education.

What is often overlooked is that the rights of individuals with disabilities came to the public forum as a part of a larger social issue: the civil rights of all minority populations in the United States. The civil rights movement of the 1950s and 1960s awakened the public to the issues of discrimination in employment, housing, access to public facilities (e.g., restaurants and transportation), and public education.

Education was reaffirmed as a right and not a privilege by the U.S. Supreme Court in the landmark case of *Brown v. Topeka, Kansas, Board of Education* in 1954. In its decision, the Court ruled that education must be made available to everyone on an equal basis. A unanimous Supreme Court stated, "In these days, it is doubtful that any child may reasonably be expected to succeed in life if he is denied the opportunity of an education. Such an opportunity, where the state has undertaken to provide it, is a right which must be made available to all on equal terms" (*Brown v. Topeka, Kansas, Board of Education,* 1954).

Although usually heralded for striking down racial segregation, this decision also set a major precedent for the education of students with disabilities in the United States. Unfortunately, it was nearly 20 years before federal courts were confronted with the issue of a free and appropriate education for these students.

In 1971, the Pennsylvania Association for Retarded Citizens filed a class-action suit on behalf of children with mental retardation who were excluded from public education on the basis of intellectual deficiency (*Pennsylvania Association for Retarded Citizens v. Commonwealth of Pennsylvania,* 1971). The suit charged that these children were being denied their right to a free public education. The plaintiffs claimed that children with mental retardation can learn if the educational program is adjusted to meet their individual needs. The issue was whether public school programs should be required to accommodate children who were intellectually different. The court ordered Pennsylvania schools to provide a free public education to all retarded children ages 6 to 21, commensurate with their individual learning needs. In addition, preschool education was to be provided for children who were retarded if the local school district provided it for children who were normal.

Later that year, the case of *Mills v. District of Columbia Board of Education* (1972) expanded the Pennsylvania decision to include all children with disabilities. District of Columbia schools were ordered to provide a free and appropriate education to every school-age child with a disability. The court further ordered that, when regular public school assignment was not appropriate, alternative educational services had to be made available.

Thus, the right of students with disabilities to an education was reaffirmed. The Pennsylvania and Mills cases served as catalysts for several court cases and pieces of legislation in the years that followed. Table 1–1 summarizes precedents that were established between 1954 and 1990.

In 1975, Congress saw the need to bring together the various pieces of state and federal legislation into one comprehensive, national law. **Public Law 94–142** (Part B of the Education of the Handicapped Act [EHA]) and the federal regulations that accompanied the act in 1977 made available a free and appropriate public education to nearly 4 million students with disabilities in the United States. As originally passed, Public Law (PL) 94–142 mandated that all eligible students, regardless of the extent or type of handicap, were to receive at public expense the **special education** services necessary to meet their individual needs.

FOCUS 11

Identify the four major components of the Individuals with Disabilities Education Act of 1990 (Public Law 101–476).

* Because the legislation discussed in this section excluded students who are gifted and talented, the more narrowly defined term *disability* has been used.

■ Table 1–1 Major Court Cases and Federal Legislation Focusing on the Right to Education for Individuals Who Are Disabled (1954–1990)

Court Cases and Federal Legislation	Precedents Established
Brown v. Topeka, Kansas, Board of Education (1954)	Segregation of students by race held unconstitutional. Education is a right that must be available to all on equal terms.
Hobsen v. Hansen (1969)	The doctrine of equal educational opportunity is a part of the law of due process, and denying an equal educational opportunity is a violation of the Constitution. Placement of children in educational tracks based on performance on standardized tests is unconstitutional and discriminates against poor and minority children.
Diana v. California State Board of Education (1970)	Children tested for potential placement in a special education program must be assessed in their native or primary language. Children cannot be placed in special classes on the basis of culturally biased tests.
Pennsylvania Association for Retarded Citizens v. Commonwealth of Pennsylvania (1971)	Pennsylvania schools must provide a free public education to all school-age retarded children.
Mills v. Board of Education of the District of Columbia (1972)	Declared exclusion of individuals with disabilities from free, appropriate public education is a violation of the due-process and equal protection clauses of the Fourteenth Amendment to the Constitution. Public schools in the District of Columbia must provide a free education to all children with disabilities regardless of their functional level or ability to adapt to the present educational system.
Public Law 93–112, Vocational Rehabilitation Act of 1973, Section 504 (1973)	Individuals with disabilities cannot be excluded from participation in, denied benefits of, or subjected to discrimination under any program or activity receiving federal financial assistance.
Public Law 93–380, Educational Amendments Act (1974)	Financial aid was provided to the states for implementation of programs for children who are exceptional, including the gifted and talented. Due-process requirements (procedural safeguards) were established to protect the rights of children with disabilities and their families in special education placement decisions.
Public Law 94–142, Part B of the Education of the Handicapped Act (1975)	A free and appropriate public education must be provided for all children with disabilities in the United States. (Those up to 5 years old may be excluded in some states.)
Public Law 99–457, Education of the Handicapped Act amendments (1986)	A new authority extended free and appropriate education to all children with disabilities ages 3 to 5 and provided a new early intervention program for infants and toddlers.
Public Law 99–372, Handicapped Children's Protection Act (1986)	Reimbursement of attorneys' fees and expenses was given to parents who prevail in administrative proceedings or court actions.
Public Law 101–336, Americans with Disabilities Act (1990)	Civil rights protections were provided for people with disabilities in private-sector employment, all public services, and public accommodations, transportation, and telecommunications.
Public Law 101–476, Individuals with Disabilities Education Act (1990)	The Education of the Handicapped Act amendments were renamed the Individuals with Disabilities Education Act (IDEA). Two new categories of disability were added: autism and traumatic brain injury. IDEA requires that an individualized transition plan be developed no later than age 16 as a component of the IEP process. Rehabilitation and social work services are included as related services.

R E F L E C T   O N   T H I S

| 1-2 | The Individuals with Disabilities Education Act |

In the summer of 1990, Congress made some significant changes in the Education of the Handicapped Act (EHA), including renaming the law the Individuals with Disabilities Education Act (IDEA). These changes went into effect on October 30, 1990, and the law will not be reviewed by Congress again until 1995. The following are some of the changes found in IDEA, Public Law 101–476, the 1990 Amendments to the Education of the Handicapped Act:

Source: Reprinted with permission from *Education of the Handicapped,* Capitol Publications, Inc., P.O. Box 1453, Alexandria, Va. 22313-2053, (703) 683-4100.

Old Law	New Law
THE EDUCATION OF THE HANDICAPPED ACT	**INDIVIDUALS WITH DISABILITIES EDUCATION ACT (IDEA)**
Children eligible for special education services defined as mentally retarded, hard-of-hearing, visually impaired, speech impaired, seriously emotionally disturbed, orthopedically impaired, other health impaired, or learning disabled	Children eligible for special education services include everyone who was eligible under the original law plus students with autism and traumatic brain injury
Special education is defined as specially designed instruction provided in the classroom, in physical education, at home and in hospitals	Definition of special education is expanded to include instruction in all settings, including the workplace and training centers
Defines related services as transportation and other support services, including speech pathology, psychological services, physical and occupational therapy, recreation and medical services needed for a disabled child to benefit from special education	Adds rehabilitation counseling and social work services to related services list
Defines individualized education program (IEP) as a written statement drawn up by the teacher, parent and a school representative that must include: the child's present educational level; annual goals, including short-term instructional objectives; the specific educational services to be provided and the extent to which the child will participate in regular education programs; initiation date and length of services; and evaluation procedures	Requires that the IEP be expanded to include a transition services statement for students by age 16, or younger when appropriate. The IEP team must reconvene when any agency fails to provide transitional services
No language on *attention deficit disorders* (ADD)	Requires the U.S. Department of education to study the issue of providing special education to students with attention deficit disorders

As defined in the law, *special education* meant specially designed instruction provided in the classroom, in physical education, at home, and in the hospital.

The Individuals with Disabilities Education Act of 1990.   In 1990, Congress amended the Education of the Handicapped Act and introduced some significant changes to its original mandate, including PL 94–142 (Part B of EHA). Arguably, the most important of these changes was renaming the law the **Individuals with Disabilities Edu-**

cation Act (IDEA) (PL 101–476).★ IDEA expanded the definition of special education to include instruction in all settings, including the workplace and training centers. As was true with PL 94–142, IDEA also stipulated that students with disabilities had to receive any **related services** necessary to ensure that they benefited from their educational experience. Related services were to include special transportation and other support services, including speech pathology, psychological services, physical and occupational therapy, recreation, rehabilitation counseling, social work, and medical services.

Eligible students were described in IDEA by disability condition and included those with mental retardation, specific learning disabilities, serious emotional disturbances (behavior disorders), speech or language impairments, visual impairments (including blindness), hearing impairments, **orthopedic impairments,** other health impairments, **autism,** and **traumatic brain injury.** Autism and traumatic brain injury were added to the list of conditions that made students eligible under IDEA in the 1990 amendments. Each condition will be defined and described in depth in subsequent chapters of this text.

IDEA provided for:

1. **Nondiscriminatory and multidisciplinary assessment** of educational needs
2. Parental involvement in developing each child's educational program
3. Education in the **least restrictive environment (LRE)**
4. An **individualized education program (IEP)**

Nondiscriminatory and multidisciplinary assessment. IDEA incorporated several provisions related to the use of nondiscriminatory testing procedures in labeling and placement of students for special education services. Those provisions include:

1. The testing of students in their native or primary language, whenever possible
2. The use of evaluation procedures selected and administered to prevent cultural or racial discrimination
3. The use of assessment tools validated for the purpose for which they are being used
4. Assessment by a **multidisciplinary team** utilizing several pieces of information to formulate a placement decision

Students with disabilities were too often placed in special education programs on the basis of inadequate or invalid assessment information. One result of such oversights was a disproportionate number of ethnic minority children and children from low-socioeconomic-level backgrounds being placed in special education programs.

Parent involvement in the educational process. IDEA described the role of parents in the education of their children. Parents were granted rights to:

1. Consent in writing before the child is initially evaluated
2. Consent in writing before the child is initially placed in a special education program
3. Request an independent education evaluation if they feel the school's evaluation is inappropriate
4. Request an evaluation at public expense if a due-process hearing finds that the public agency's evaluation was inappropriate
5. Participate on the committee that considers the evaluation, placement, and programing of the child
6. Inspect and review educational records and challenge information believed to be inaccurate, misleading, or in violation of the privacy or other rights of the child
7. Request a copy of information from the child's educational record

★ Provisions in law that were originally enacted under PL 94–142 will be described in this chapter as components of IDEA.

REFLECT ON THIS

| 1–3 | An Analysis of the Success in Meeting the Needs of Students with Disabilities |

The Robert Wood Johnson Foundation completed a five-year collaborative study of children with special needs in an attempt to document whether the procedural guarantees of PL 94–142 (now referred to as IDEA) were securely in place. The study was conducted in five large metropolitan school districts located throughout the United States. Some of the findings are as follows:

The Positive Side

◆ Parents are generally satisfied with the services their children with disabilities receive. In fact, the researchers believed that parents of special education students were more satisfied with the public schools than were parents of school-children in general.

◆ Schools are committed to the principle of serving children with disabilities in the least restrictive environment. The vast majority of special education students are in the mainstream, attending regular schools and spending at least part of the day in regular classes.

◆ Schools remain the major site of identification for most children with special needs. Physicians do, however, identify between 15 and 25 percent of children with learning disabilities, speech impairments, emotional disorders, and hyperactivity.

◆ Many therapeutic services are now provided in schools. Nearly half of all children in special education receive speech or hearing therapy.

◆ Most children with disabilities have a regular source of health care, although they may not see the same physician at every medical visit.

The Negative Side

◆ Although parents are generally favorable regarding special education services for their child, less than half actually attend their child's IEP meeting.

◆ On average, special education costs nearly twice as much as regular education. The concern is whether special programs for children with disabilities can be maintained against the onslaught of cost-containment pressures facing school districts.

◆ Serious gaps still exist in services. Some children find themselves in a kind of "gray area" with respect to defining their problems and meeting their needs. Specifically, students with disabilities who remain in school until they reach age 21 rarely have access to services that help them make the transition to adult life.

Source: From *Serving Handicapped Children: A Special Report,* 1988 (Princeton, NJ: The Robert Wood Johnson Foundation). Adapted by permission.

---

8. Request a hearing concerning the school's proposal or refusal to initiate or change the identification, evaluation, or placement of the child or the provision of a free, appropriate public education

These safeguards were instituted to protect the student and family from decisions that could adversely affect their lives. In addition, families could be more secure in the knowledge that every reasonable attempt was being made to educate their child appropriately.

Education in the least restrictive environment.   All students have the right to learn in an environment consistent with their academic, social, and physical needs. Such a setting constitutes the least restrictive environment (LRE). IDEA mandated that students with disabilities receive their education with nondisabled peers to the maximum extent appropriate. In order to meet this mandate, federal regulations required schools to develop a continuum of placements, ranging from regular classrooms with support services to homebound and hospital programs. An educational services model is presented in Figure 1–4.

At Level I in this continuum, a student remains in the regular classroom and receives no additional support services. Adaptations necessary for a given student would be handled by the classroom teacher. Consequently, a student's success depends on whether his or her teacher has skills in developing and adapting programs to meet individual needs.

A student placed at Level II also remains in the regular classroom, but **consultative services** are available to both the teacher and student. These services may be provided by a variety of professionals, including special educators, speech and language specialists, behavior specialists, physical education specialists, occupational therapists, physical therapists,

---

WINDOW 1-2

I ENJOY WORKING WITH PARENTS

As a special education teacher for the past five years, I have to say that one of the most satisfying aspects of my career has been working with some of the parents of the children with disabilities in my class. As a parent of a normal 7-year-old, I have to admit that, it seems to me, for the most part, the schools have done little to encourage parent involvement in education. The only time I hear from my child's teacher, outside of the two 10-minute parent conferences held each year, is when there is a problem. I guess you could say that, from where I sit, "no news is good news" from the school. For the children with disabilities in my class, this is simply not true. The parents of students in my class are involved at every phase of their child's program. They work on the

development of goals for their child and participate in activities at home that encourage learning. Sure, it's true that, at first, I resented being told where parents had to be involved and why. The law seemed to be telling me how I should run my classroom. Now, I not only work with my parents because the law says that is what I am supposed to do; I value having parents involved. It is very true that not all of my parents choose to be actively involved. However, for those who do, it has made a big difference in the development of appropriate educational experiences for their child. It has also taught me a lot about how important parent participation is to a good educational program for all children.

Roxanne, A Special Education Teacher in an Elementary School

FIGURE 1–4 Educational Service Options for Students Who Are Exceptional

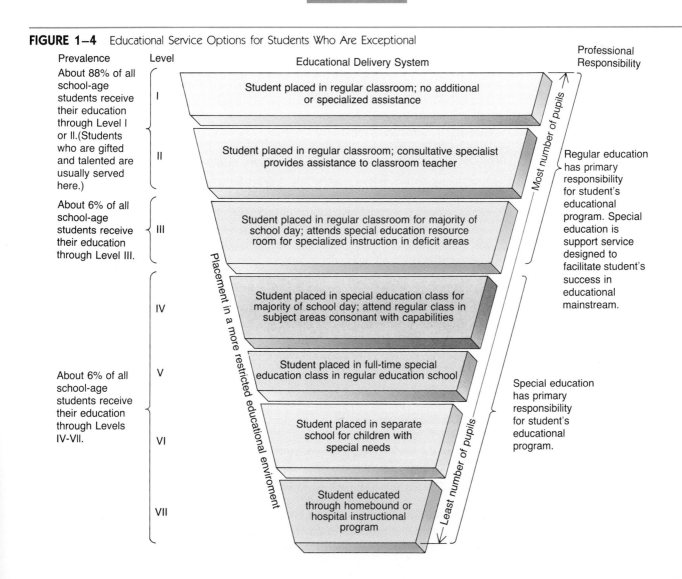

school psychologists, and social workers. Services may range from assisting a teacher in the use of tests or modification of curriculum to direct instruction with students in the classroom setting.

The student placed at Level III continues in the regular classroom for the majority of the school day but also attends a **resource room** for specialized instruction in deficit areas. A resource-room program is under the direction of a qualified special educator. The amount of time a student spends there varies according to his or her needs; it may range from as short as 30 minutes to as long as 3 hours a day. Instruction in a resource room is intended to reinforce or supplement the student's work in the regular classroom. The student receives necessary assistance to ensure his or her keeping pace with regular education peers. About 6 percent of all school-age children are served in a resource-room setting. It is the most widely used public school setting for students with disabilities.

At Levels I, II, and III, the primary responsibility for the student's education lies with the regular classroom teacher. Consultative services, including special education, are intended to support the student's regular class placement. At Levels IV and beyond, the primary responsibility shifts to special education providers.

The student placed at Level IV is in a **special education classroom** for the majority of the school day. At this level, provisions are made for him or her to be integrated with regular education peers whenever possible and consistent with his or her learning capabilities. For students who are moderately to severely disabled, integration is usually recommended for nonacademic subject areas.

Level V placement involves full-time participation in a special education class. Although still in a regular school, the student is not integrated with regular education students for formalized instructional activities. However, some level of social integration may take place during recess periods, lunch assemblies, field trips, and tutoring.

Placement at Level VI involves removing the student from the regular education facility and placing him or her in a classroom in a separate facility specifically for students with disabilities. These facilities include **special day schools,** where the educational program is one aspect of a comprehensive treatment program.

Those students who, because of the severity of their disabilities, are unable to attend any school program must receive services through a homebound or hospital program. Placement at Level VII generally indicates a need for an **itinerant teacher** who visits an incapacitated student on a regular basis to provide tutorial assistance. Some students with chronic conditions, such as certain types of cancer, may be placed at this level indefinitely, whereas others are served while recuperating from short-term illnesses.

The issue of placement in the LRE continues to be a matter of public and private debate. IDEA clearly favored educating students in regular education settings. It mandated that students with disabilities be educated with their nondisabled peers to the maximum extent appropriate.

A recent examination of the placement of students in segregated environments (Danielsen & Bellamy, 1989) suggested that about 6 percent of all students with disabilities receive their education in segregated schools. Approximately 24 percent of all students with disabilities are educated in separate special education classes. These authors also reported that, in spite of the law's strong preference for integrated placements, the use of "separate educational environments has been relatively stable over the 10 years in which the Department of Education has collected national data" (p. 452).

An Individualized Education Program.   IDEA also provided a vehicle for developing an education program based on multidisciplinary assessment and designed to meet the individual needs of exceptional students. That vehicle, the individualized education pro-

Many feel that interaction among individuals with and without disabilities is mutually beneficial. (Bob Daemmrich/Stock, Boston)

gram (IEP), provides an opportunity for parents and professionals to join together in establishing an appropriate educational experience for the student with a disability. The result should be more continuity in the delivery of educational services for students on a daily as well as an annual basis. The IEP also promotes more effective communication between school personnel and the home.

The 1990 amendments to the law (PL 101–476) added a new requirement to the IEP. Beginning no later than age 16 and annually thereafter, the IEP must include a statement of the transition services needed for students as they leave school and enter adulthood. (See Chapter Three for more information on the transition from school to adult life.)

An example of an IEP form is shown in Figure 1–5. All IEPs contain information about the following: (1) the student's present level of performance; (2) annual goals; (3) short-term instructional objectives; (4) related services; (5) percentage of time spent in regular education; (6) beginning and ending dates for special education services; and (7) annual evaluation.

A Mandate for Preschool Children with Disabilities.   In 1986, Congress amended the Education of the Handicapped Act (now IDEA) to include provisions for preschool-age students with disabilities. This important legislation, **Public Law 99–457,** established a new mandate to provide a free and appropriate education for all children with disabilities ages 3 through 5. Thus, all the rights and protections extended to school-age children (ages 5 through 21) were extended to preschoolers.

This law required that all states receiving funds under IDEA assure that 3- to 5-year-old children receive a free, appropriate public education by the 1990–1991 schoolyear. One significant difference, however, between the requirements of IDEA and this new law was that states were not required to report preschool children by disability category (e.g., learning disabilities, mental retardation, deafness, etc.).

Public Law 99-457 was to be administered directly through state and local education agencies. To support states in meeting the requirements of this law, several new initiatives were mandated including, (1) the establishment of demonstration and outreach programs for preschool-age children with disabilities, (2) the authorization of early childhood institutes to generate and disseminate research findings on early childhood education, and (3) the development of projects to demonstrate cost-effective methods of delivering educational services.

FOCUS 12
Identify the major components of the Education of the Handicapped Act Amendments of 1986 (Public Law 99–457).

FIGURE 1–5   A Sample Individualized Education Program (IEP)

	PRIMARY CLASSIFICATION _____
	SECONDARY CLASSIFICATION _____
STUDENT NAME _Diane_____	**TESTS UTILIZED**
DATE OF BIRTH _5-3-81_____ CA _11___	INTELLECTUAL _WISC-R_____
SCHOOL _Elementary School_ GRADE _5___	EDUCATIONAL _Key Math Woodcock Reading_
PRIMARY LANG: HOME _English_ STUDENT _English_	BEHAVIORAL/ADAPTIVE _Burks_____
DATE OF IEP MEETING _April 27, 1992___	SPEECH/LANGUAGE _____
ENTRY DATE TO PROGRAM _April 27, 1992_	OTHER _____
PROJECTED TERMINATION DATE _April 27, 1993_	VISION _Within Normal limits_ HEARING _Within Normal limits_
SERVICES REQUIRED: Specify amount of time in educational and/or related services per day or week	CLASSROOM OBSERVATION DONE _____ _____

RESOURCE _____
RES. SELF-CONT. _____
SELF-CONTAINED _6 Hours daily_____
REG. CLASS _____
RELATED SERV. _group 45 min. 2x weekly_
P.E. PROG. _45 min. daily_____
OTHER _Individual Counseling 1 hour 1x weekly_

STRENGTHS: (INDICATE PRESENT LEVEL OF FUNCTIONING) _____
① _Polite to teachers and peers_____
② _Helpful and cooperative in the classroom_
③ _Good grooming skills_____
④ _Good in sports activities_____

TEAM SIGNATURES	IEP DATE	REVIEW DATE
LEA REP. _____	____	____
PARENT _____	____	____
SP. ED. TCHR. _____	____	____
GUID. SPEC. _____	____	____
COUNSELOR _____	____	____
SP-LANG PATH. _____	____	____
STUDENT _____	____	____
OTHER _____	____	____

LIMITATIONS: (INDICATE PRESENT LEVEL OF FUNCTIONING) _____
① _Limited interaction skills with peers and adults 90%_
② _Excessive tics and grimaces 70%_
③ _Difficulty with on task behaviors 60%_
④ _Difficulty expressing feelings_
⑤ _Below grade level in Math 3.9_
⑥ _Below grade level in Reading 4.3_

JUSTIFICATION FOR PLACEMENT: _Student needs indicated specialized placement and curriculum to deal with behavioral problems_

ANNUAL REVIEW: DATE: _____
COMMENTS/RECOMMENDATIONS _____
_____
_____

Another provision of PL 99–457 was the establishment of a state grant program for infants and toddlers up to 2 years old. Infants and toddlers who were developmentally delayed, as defined by each state, were eligible for services that included a multidisciplinary assessment and an **individualized family service plan (IFSP).** Such a plan is to be developed cooperatively by a multidisciplinary team that includes parents. Although this provision did not mandate that states provide services to all infants and toddlers who were developmentally delayed, it did establish financial incentives for state participation.

(We will discuss the IFSP and other provisions of PL 99–457 in more depth in Chapter Three of this text.)

FOCUS 13

Identify the factors that are most closely associated with students identified as at risk.

Students Who Are At Risk but Not Disabled

While most of this section on education has focused on students who have been identified as disabled, there is a growing number of children in U.S. public schools who do not necessarily meet the definitions of disability but are at considerable risk for academic and

FIGURE 1–5 (continued)

IEP – ANNUAL GOALS AND SHORT TERM OBJECTIVES	PERSONS RESPONSIBLE	OBJECTIVE CRITERIA AND EVALUATION PROCEDURES
#1 ANNUAL GOAL: Diane will improve her interaction skills with peers and adults.	Classroom teachers guidance	Classroom data target behavior
S.T. OBJ. Diane will initiate conversation with peers during an unstructured setting 2x daily.		
S.T. OBJ. When in need of assistance, Diane will raise her hand and verbalize her needs to teachers or peers		
S.T. OBJ. without prompting 80%.		
#2 ANNUAL GOAL: Diane will increase her ability to control hand and facial movements.	Teachers guidance	Data: classroom observation
S.T. OBJ. During academic work, Diane will keep her hands in an appropriate place and use writing		
S.T. OBJ. materials correctly 80%.		
S.T. OBJ. Diane will maintain a relaxed facial expression with teacher prompt 80%.		
#3 ANNUAL GOAL: Diane will improve on task behaviors.	Teachers guidance	Classroom observation and data
S.T. OBJ. Diane will work independently on an assigned		
S.T. OBJ. task with teacher prompt 80% of time.		
S.T. OBJ. Diane will complete academic work on time 90% as specified by teacher.		
#4 ANNUAL GOAL: Diane will improve her ability to express her feelings	Teachers guidance	Data observation
S.T. OBJ. When asked how she feels, Diane will give an		
S.T. OBJ. adequate verbal description of her feelings or moods with teacher prompting 80%		
S.T. OBJ. Given a conflict or problem situation, Diane will state her feelings to teachers and peers 80%.		
#5 ANNUAL GOAL: Diane will improve math skills from a 3.9 grade level.	Teachers	Precision teaching Addison Wesley Math Program
S.T. OBJ. Diane will improve rate and accuracy in oral		
S.T. OBJ. 1 digit division facts to 80 ppm without errors		
S.T. OBJ. Diane will improve her ability to solve word problems involving + − x ÷ $^8/_{10}$.		
#6 ANNUAL GOAL: Improve reading skills from a 4.3 grade level.	Teachers	Precision teaching Barnell + Loft materials
S.T. OBJ. Diane will answer progressively more difficult		
S.T. OBJ. comprehension questions in level D+E specific skills series with 80% accuracy.		
S.T. OBJ. Diane will increase her rate and accuracy of vocabulary words to 80 wpm without errors.		

social failure. Definitions of **students at risk** are very broad and vague. As suggested by Levin (1988), definitions are so vague that "they could easily encompass gifted and talented children, the physically or mentally [disabled], the obese, the shy, and so on" (p. 1).

For the purposes of our discussion, we will address students at risk from the perspective that the individual is not identified as disabled but, due to myriad factors, needs specialized instruction and/or support to succeed in a school setting. At-risk students include but are not limited to the growing number who:

◆ Drop out of school each year (1 million annually)
◆ Live below the poverty line (20 percent to 25 percent)
◆ Use alcohol or drugs or have immediate family members with substance abuse problems (3 million)
◆ Are homeless (100,000)
◆ Have no access to regular and appropriate medical care (10 million)
◆ Are **latchkey kids** with no after-school support (estimated to be 7 million below age 10)
◆ Are abused and/or neglected by family members (more than 2.2 million cases annually)

1-4   At Risk and Disabled: Latchkey Kids with Special Needs

The local newspaper lead sentence read "Special Student Can't Get After-School Care." The reporter had talked with social service workers, a child advocacy organization director, some parents, day care workers, and school personnel. It was a common dilemma. Finding after-school care for any child is difficult, but it is even more demanding and frustrating for a parent who has a child with special needs.

Joey cannot get the after-school care he needs. He is 14 years old and a student at a special school for students with mental disabilities. Joey is mentally developed only to the level of a 6-year-old, and he has a learning disability. He leaves school at 3 P.M. His mother, a single parent, works in a nearby city until 6 P.M. There is another son, a high school junior. "Joey's somebody you can't tell you're going to the store for an hour and go," his mother said. "Even letting Joey out to play can end up in a neighborhood search" (Peterson, 1988).

In the county where Joey lives, there are no government-sponsored day care programs for children with mental disabilities. Private day care operators seldom take anyone older

than 12 years of age, and their staffs are not trained to manage children with special needs. Even when after-school care can be found, it is not usually year round, and it offers no program during the summer or on holidays.

Joey is only one case of an unknown number of latchkey children with special needs whom we have come across in our work with parents, teachers, and school administrators. The number of these children who regularly care for themselves before and after school, on weekends, and during summer vacations and holidays is not known. However, it *is* known that their numbers are growing proportionately to the number of all latchkey children—as many as 7 million below age 10 by some estimates (U.S. Department of Labor, 1982). Speculation is that the numbers of children with disabilities who are at home alone are high. This is difficult to document, however, because their well-being and survival require full-time supervision well into adolescence—long after their non-disabled peers have become self-sufficient (Fink, 1988).

Although many children without disabilities seem to fare well caring for themselves, research findings reveal an array of problems some of these children must face on their own (Robinson, Rowland, & Coleman, 1986).

Workable latchkey arrangements depend upon each child's unique situation, including the following elements:

1. The parents' attitudes.
2. The child's age.
3. The child's maturity level.
4. The degree of self-care preparation.
5. The location of the neighborhood.
6. Community resources.
7. Daily length of time left alone.
8. Type of verification and backup system in parent's absence (Robinson, Rowland, & Coleman, 1989).

The success of latchkey arrangements for children with disabilities is further complicated by the nature and severity of their disabilities.

Parents of children with disabilities who need after-school care are faced with solving their problems in less than satisfying ways. They may elect to make do and not work; they may choose to leave their children home alone and hope for the best; or they may seek help from the community and schools to establish high-quality activity programs for children with special needs.

Source: From "Latckhkey kids with special needs" by B. H. Rowland and B. E. Robinson, *Teaching Exceptional Children, 23*(3), 1991, pp. 34–35. Copyright 1991 by The Council for Exceptional Children. Reprinted with permission.

♦ Live in single-parent families (15.3 million, or 90 percent, live with their mothers)
♦ Become pregnant during the teenage years (1.5 million annually)
♦ Come from different cultural backgrounds and may have limited English-speaking abilities (Davis & McCaul, 1991)

Students at risk are often described as **educationally disadvantaged,** because they enter school with "two strikes" against them. By the time they get to high school, many of these students have not mastered even the basic level of skills necessary to complete school or succeed in adult living. Levin (cited in National School Boards Association, 1989) suggested that, "because of poverty, cultural obstacles, or linguistic differences, these children tend to have low academic achievement and high drop out rates. Such students are heavily concentrated among minority groups, immigrants, non-English speaking families, and economically disadvantaged populations" (p. 6).

Although the schools are the target of discontent, due to their inability to meet the needs of students at risk, it is clear that these individuals are the products of conditions that go far beyond the education system. It will take the cooperation of many agencies—including health, social services, and education—to even begin to understand the extent of the problems, let alone find the solutions. Conservative estimates have suggested that at least 40 percent of the nation's school-age children are at risk of failure due to living in poverty, being of ethnic or minority status, living in a single-parent family, having a poorly educated mother, and having limited English proficiency (Natriello, McDill, & Pallas, 1990).

What can be done to meet the needs of students at risk? Given the complexity of factors associated with failure in the schools, the solutions are obviously not short term. Davis and McCaul (1991) have suggested that, first and foremost, it must be recognized that the problem exists. From there, successful efforts need to be identified, and this knowledge must be incorporated into the system. We know, for example, that early intervention programs benefit children who are both disadvantaged and disabled. We also know that:

◆ Early and frequent prenatal care can significantly reduce the risk of low-birthweight babies.
◆ Quality child-care programs and parenting classes held in schools allow many young teenage women to complete their education.
◆ Appropriate sex education courses are effective in reducing the risks of sexually transmitted diseases (e.g., AIDS) and unwanted pregnancies.
◆ Early health care, including necessary immunizations along with proper nutrition, can prevent the occurrence of serious and even fatal diseases in children.
◆ Intensive instructional programs, conducted in school climates that are safe and conducive to both learning and promoting positive self-esteem, can remarkably enhance the chances of disadvantaged children to become literate, self-assured, and eventually productive adults (Davis & McCaul, 1991, pp. 130–131).

As we move into subsequent chapters on multicultural education, education through the life span, categories of people with disabilities, people who are gifted and talented, as well as the family, the focus will be on effective practices for all students with exceptional characteristics, including those defined as at risk.

Debate Forum

Government Intrusion in the Education of Students with Disabilities

The debate over the federal government's role in the education of children in the United States continues as we move closer to the twenty-first century. The passage of PL 94–142 (now called IDEA) fanned the fires of this debate, once again raising the issue of whether the federal government should have such an extensive role in the education of students with disabilities.

Point   Prior to the passage of PL 94–142, the vast majority of students with disabilities did not receive an appropriate education in U. S. schools, if they received any education at all. This vital legislation created a long overdue entitlement for these students to receive a free and appropriate public education that would greatly enhance their opportunities of being able to contribute to society rather than always being cast in the role of consuming society's resources. PL 94–142 represented an investment in children that results in positive outcomes for everyone. Without this strong federal role, little change would have taken place in many states or local schools. The National Commission on Excellence, in its report *A Nation at Risk,* indicated the need for the federal government to take a primary responsibility in identifying the national interest in education. The continued support and expansion brought by PL 94–142 is clearly within the framework of our national interest.

Counterpoint   Federal intrusion into education violates the intent of the Constitution. Education is the responsibility of the states. The federal government's role should not extend beyond limited support to individual states as they attempt to meet the diverse needs of children throughout the United States. Certainly, this supportive role doesn't extend to the type of intrusion imposed by PL 94–142, including exhaustive procedural requirements such as IEPs, multidisciplinary teams, parental consent, related services, and so on. Without question, this law drains resources needed for other equally deserving students while continuing the unnecessary process of labeling children in order to get them specialized instruction. The federal role in the education of students with disabilities is at best a misguided effort and at worst a fiscal nightmare.

REVIEW ....

FOCUS 1 Why do we label people according to their differences?

◆ Labels are an attempt to describe, identify, and distinguish one person from another.

◆ Many medical, social, and educational services require that an individual be labeled in order to determine who is eligible to receive special services.

◆ Labels help professionals to communicate more effectively with each other and provide a common ground for evaluating research findings.

◆ Labels enable professionals to differentiate more clearly the needs of one group of people from those of another.

FOCUS 2 Identify three approaches that can be used to describe the nature and extent of human differences.

◆ The developmental approach is based upon differences that occur in the course of human development from what is considered normal physical, social, and intellectual growth. Human differences are the result of interaction between biological and environmental factors. Normal growth can be explained by observing large numbers of individuals and looking for characteristics that occur most frequently at any given age.

◆ The cultural approach to describing human differences defines *normal* according to established cultural standards. Human differences can be explained by examining the values of any given society. What is considered to be normal will change over time and from culture to culture.

◆ The individual approach to labeling suggests that labels may be self-imposed. Such labels reflect how we perceive ourselves, although those perceptions may not be consistent with how others see us.

FOCUS 3 How did the work of nineteenth-century physicians and philosophers contribute to our understanding of people with differences?

◆ Early nineteenth-century physicians emphasized that people with disabilities should be treated humanely.

◆ Jean-Marc Itard demonstrated that an individual with a severe disability could learn new skills through physiological stimulation.

FOCUS 4 Distinguish between *abnormal behavior* and *social deviance*.

◆ Behavior is the focus of psychology. When the behavior of an individual does not meet the criteria of normal, it is labeled abnormal.

◆ Sociology is concerned with modern cultures, group behaviors, societal institutions, and intergroup relationships. When people are unable to adapt to social roles or establish interpersonal relationships, their behaviors are labeled deviant.

FOCUS 5 Why has the early twentieth century been described as a period of contrast in meeting the needs of people with differences?

◆ On one hand, social and educational services that had been denied to people with differences for centuries become more accessible.

◆ On the other hand, many misconceptions during the early twentieth century resulted in fear of people with disabilities and a movement to isolate them from society.

FOCUS 6 Identify four primary issues involved in the right-to-treatment cases that have come before the courts in the latter half of the twentieth century.

◆ Individuals residing in institutions were being deprived of the right to individual treatment that would give them a realistic opportunity for habilitation.

◆ Current law establishes a national policy to improve treatment and provides financial incentives for states to do so.

FOCUS 7 What was the purpose of the Americans with Disabilities Act of 1990 (Public Law 101–336)?

◆ ADA provided a national mandate to end discrimination against individuals with disabilities in private-sector employment, all public services, and public accommodations, transportation, and telecommunications.

FOCUS 8 What services must be available to ensure that an individual with a disability is able to live and learn successfully in a community setting?

◆ Comprehensive community services must be available, including access to housing, employment, public transportation, recreation, and religious activities.

◆ The individual should be able to purchase such services as medical and dental care as well as adequate life insurance.

FOCUS 9 What educational services were available for students with disabilities during most of the twentieth century?

◆ Educational programs at the beginning of the twentieth century were provided primarily in separate special schools.

◆ For the first 75 years of this century, the availability of educational programs for special students was sporadic and selective. Special education was allowed in many states but required in only a few.

◆ Research on the efficacy of special classes for students with mild disabilities suggested that there was little or no benefit in removing students from regular education classrooms.

FOCUS 10 Identify the principal issues in the right-to-education cases that led to eventual passage of Public Law 94–142 (now referred to as IDEA).

◆ Education was reaffirmed as a right and not a privilege by the Supreme Court.
◆ In Pennsylvania, the court ordered the schools to provide a free public education to all retarded children ages 6 to 21.
◆ The Mills case extended the right to a free public education to all school-age children with disabilities.

FOCUS 11 Identify the four major components of the Individuals with Disabilities Education Act of 1990 (Public Law 101–476).

◆ The labeling and placement of students with disabilities in educational programs required the use of nondiscriminatory and multidisciplinary assessment.
◆ Parental involvement in the educational process included consent for testing and placement and participation as a team member in the development of an IEP. Procedural safeguards were included (e.g., due process) to protect the child and family from decisions that could adversely affect their lives.
◆ All children were given the right to learn in an environment consistent with their academic, social, and physical needs. The law mandated that children with disabilities receive their education with nondisabled peers to the maximum extent appropriate.
◆ Each child must have an IEP.

FOCUS 12 Identify the major components of the Education of the Handicapped Act Amendments of 1986 (Public Law 99–457).

◆ This law established a federal mandate to provide a free and appropriate public education to preschool-age children from 3 to 5 years of age.
◆ States did not have to report eligible preschool-age children by disability category.
◆ New initiatives were established to support implementation of the law, including demonstration programs, early childhood institutes, and projects on cost-effective methods of service delivery.
◆ A state grant program for infants and toddlers was also established.

FOCUS 13 Identify the factors that are most closely associated with students identified as at risk.

◆ High dropout rates
◆ Living below the poverty line
◆ Serious substance abuse by themselves or immediate family members
◆ Homelessness
◆ No access to adequate health care
◆ No after-school support
◆ Abuse and/or neglect
◆ Single-parent home
◆ Adolescent pregnancy
◆ Different cultural background
◆ Limited English-speaking ability

Chapter Two
Multicultural and Diversity Issues

TO BEGIN WITH . . .

◆ Ethnic minority groups are a rapidly growing proportion of the U.S. population. It is projected that, from 1990 to the year 2000, the Hispanic population will increase by 26.8 percent, the African American by 12.8 percent, and the Caucasian by 5.2 percent (U.S. Bureau of the Census, 1990).

◆ It is estimated that as many as 41 percent of all students in special education are from culturally divergent backgrounds (Bedell, 1989).

◆ By mid-1987, 37 state legislatures had made attempts to pass laws designating English as the official language, known as English-only laws (Pai, 1990).

CHRISTINA

TESTING THE SYSTEM: WHO NEEDS SPECIAL EDUCATION?

CHRISTINA.   Christina, age 8, has great difficulty understanding much of what goes on in the world around her. In school, her classmates and teacher speak a language that she has heard now for a rather long time, but it is not the same one her mother and father speak. When Christina's teacher speaks, the sound seems harsh and unpleasant to her; the words have none of the softness that she hears at home and in the fields when she helps pick berries. At this school, Christina has two teachers and goes to different classrooms at different times of the day. She can't understand why her classmates laugh at her when she goes to the afternoon special teacher. She feels like she must have done something wrong because their laughter isn't a cheerful sound; they are making fun of her, it seems.

Moving is something that Christina is very accustomed to; her family moves two or three times a year. When the berries are all picked, the family gets in the truck and drives a long way, to another farm, where they work on onions. Christina thinks that moving is fun because she and her brothers get to ride in the back of the truck.

RAYMOND.   Raymond is in the eleventh grade, a junior in high school. He is exceptionally tall, listed at 6 feet, 11 inches tall on the basketball programs. He is a little older than most of his classmates because he was held back in the fifth grade when he still couldn't read.

There are many dilemmas in Raymond's life right now, and reading remains a problem. At this point, he is only able to read at about a fourth-grade level, which makes his classes very difficult. For a time, Raymond's mother wanted to get him special help but finally gave in to arguments against it by his coach and his father, as well as Raymond's own fear of being ridiculed by his friends. Raymond's life is not simple right now. He is very confused.

The coach didn't want Raymond to receive special help in school because he thought it would make him ineligible to play basketball. Raymond has an uncanny ability to get the ball in the basket and averaged 39 points per game this year. The coach thinks that Raymond may be heavily recruited by the best universities and could easily move into the professional ranks after a little seasoning. Raymond's father is excited about that and doesn't worry about the school difficulties. The coach has been able to arrange easier classes for Raymond so that his grades will remain satisfactory. This type of arrangement would continue in college. Raymond doesn't want special help for his school work either. For one thing, such behavior is seen as "acting white" by his friends. Besides, all the kids that he knows who get special help are called "tardos" by the others. Raymond just wants to play basketball. He trusts the coach's assurances that the school stuff will be alright. School is mainly a way to play ball and later make money.

*I*NTRODUCTION

The situations presented in Window 2–1 are very different from one another, each testing the educational system in a different way. Is the system serving Raymond appropriately, or is it failing him? If he receives special help, does he become labeled as a student with a disability? If so, what does that mean? In Christina's case, no one in the system is fighting to keep her from being labeled as disabled. Does she receive special education services? Is she considered disabled primarily because of her cultural and language differences? In this chapter, we will examine the very complex issues related to cultural and ethnic diversity and their impact on the education system.

Special interests in the field of education tend to emerge when any particular subgroup's needs are not adequately addressed by the majority. Discontent with what is available emerges if a segment of the student population is left out, discriminated against, or treated unfairly or if the potential of these students is not being appropriately developed. When the mainstream activities of a system are too narrow to accommodate diversity, the system becomes inadequate, and modifications are necessary.

This was the case with respect to the emergence of both **multicultural education** and **special education.** Multicultural education arose from a belief that the needs of certain children—those with cultural backgrounds different from those of the majority—were not being appropriately met. Other societal unrest related to racial discrimination fueled and augmented this belief. Likewise, special education evolved from the failure of general education to meet the needs of certain children. These children were not learning as rapidly or in the same way as their age-mates. With regard to both multicultural and special education, there was also a belief that students within their respective realms of interest were being *mistreated*—in one case, because of their cultural or racial background, and in the other, because of their learning, behavior, or physical problems.

We will examine two basic factors as we introduce multicultural and diversity issues. Initially, we will explore the basic purpose of general education and the conventional approaches used to achieve this purpose. We will then make a comparison with the underlying purposes and approaches of special and multicultural education. Second, we will discuss the linkages between multicultural and special education. With these points as background, we then examine multicultural perspectives and diversity issues in the context of this book's focus: human exceptionality in society, school, and family.

PURPOSES AND APPROACHES TO EDUCATION

Education in the United States is aimed at producing a literate citizenry. To achieve this end, it follows that education in the United States is presumably intended for everyone. All children are supposed to be provided a free and appropriate public education through high school. The manner in which this is usually implemented involves grouping and teaching students by chronological age. Student performance is evaluated based on what society expects children of each age to achieve. Society uses an average of what youngsters of each age learn as its yardstick for this expectation. In other words, American education is aimed

FOCUS 1

Identify three ways in which the purposes and approaches to general American education sometimes differ from those of special education and multicultural education.

In typical U.S. classrooms, students are grouped according to age and taught what society expects them to know. Education is aimed at the masses and performance is judged on an average. (David Young-Wolff/PhotoEdit)

2-1 A Better Understanding of Different Cultures for All

Multicultural education is intended to teach all students about different cultures. Yet a study of history textbooks by the U.S. Commission on Civil Rights in 1980 found different ethnic groups portrayed largely by traditional and unfavorable stereotypes. For example, African Americans were presented in occupational roles that were primarily in service, sports, and entertainment fields. Native Americans were included in historical settings but not in contemporary circumstances. Further, the account of historical events did not reflect the perspective of Native Americans but was solely the viewpoint of the cultural majority, which reflected a biased account of many incidents. Hispanic people, both Mexican Americans and Puerto Ricans, were frequently associated with violence and portrayed as living in segregated, poor neighborhoods.

Textbooks are powerful in the sense that they are a primary means of information for young people who are still developing many attitudes. The attitudes that these individuals form about cultures may be shaped initially by what they learn in school. Although such views can change, early learning often is quite durable. It may be that the attitude of Raymond's coach (whom we met in Window 2–1) toward African Americans was partially shaped from a textbook of the late 1970s. He certainly does not see Raymond as a person who needs attention beyond his training in basketball, which coincides with part of the stereotype noted above. We must ask: What is the probability that Raymond will be recruited by a major university and then make it further to play professional basketball? Only about 1 percent of those who play college basketball go on to perform at the professional level. The coach may well have other motives, but we must seriously question why he is not more concerned with Raymond's academic performance. Raymond will have to read, even if he does play professional basketball.

Stereotypical presentation of different cultures does little to improve the understanding of people from those backgrounds.

at the masses, and performance is judged on an average. The purpose of this system is to bring most students to a similar level of knowledge, at least to a minimum.

Most special education professionals would agree, at least in principle, that the basic purpose of special education in contemporary society is to provide an education that maximizes the development of each student with a disability, given his or her individual potential. The current manner in which this is implemented focuses on individual strengths and limitations. Such an approach is important because the students being served in special education seem unable to function well when instruction is broadly directed at large groups.

Currently, multicultural education is viewed as education that values and promotes **cultural pluralism.** It is not intended to be limited to those of cultural or racial minorities but more appropriately teaches all students about cultural diversity. Gollnick and Chinn (1990) have cited five goals of multicultural education. Namely, it promotes: "(1) the strength and value of cultural diversity, (2) human rights and respect for those who are different from oneself, (3) alternative life choices for people, (4) social justice and equality for all people, and (5) equity in the distribution of power and income among groups" (p. 31). Adding to this description, Rodriguez noted that "multicultural education rejects the view that schools should seek to melt away cultural differences or the view that schools should merely tolerate cultural pluralism" (1982, p. 221).

Comparing Purposes and Approaches

Certain differences emerge as we discuss the fundamental purposes of education, special education, and multicultural education. First, the primary purpose of general education runs counter to both that of special education and that of multicultural education. General education is aimed at serving the masses. Thus, it creates a leveling effect to some extent—bringing everyone to more or less the same level and teaching similar topics in groups, with evaluation based on a norm or average. Special education tends to focus on the individual, presumably promoting growth to each person's maximum potential. Thus, rather than focusing on broad groups and broad topics, special education tends to emphasize individuals and specific skill levels. Evaluation, at least in part, is based on individual growth to a specified mastery level and only partly on **norm-based averages.**

Likewise, the contemporary view of multicultural education is that it promotes recognition and respect for differences and diversity. At a certain level, this means encouraging differences and diversity, which is somewhat at odds with the goal of general education to achieve consistency (i.e., to bring the population to a comparable level of performance in similar areas of knowledge). Further, general education largely reflects a societal self-portrait of the United States as a "melting pot" for peoples of all backgrounds. The **melting pot** perspective, although perhaps outdated, still has great influence on many aspects of society. Contemporary multicultural education, on the other hand, sees the school as a powerful tool for promoting diversity (Hernandez, 1989).

■ **Table 2-1 Myths and Realities about Multicultural Education**

Myth	Reality
Multiethnic education creates divisiveness by emphasizing ethnic differences. We should be emphasizing commonalities among groups.	Commonalities cannot be recognized unless differences are acknowledged. For too long we have ignored ethnic differences; we have treated ethnic differences as bad characteristics and thereby have not recognized commonalities or differences in American society.
Multiethnic education would shatter the melting pot.	A genuine melting pot society—one that molds its ethnic groups into one great society—has never existed in the United States. Actually, this kind of society is an ideal that must be continually nurtured. When U.S. society truly interweaves the best of all its cultures, it will be a melting pot society.
Multiethnic education would not build a harmonious society.	One reason U.S. society is not harmonious is that certain groups have been denied their cultural rights. Multiethnic education would restore those rights by emphasizing cultural equality and respect.
Multiethnic education detracts from the basics in public schools. Students should be taught to read, write, and compute.	Multiethnic education need not detract from the basics of education. Students can be taught basic skills while also learning to respect cultures. A strong argument can be made for multiethnic education as a basic in education.
Multiethnic education is to enhance the self-concepts of ethnic minority students.	A half-true myth. Multiethnic education should enhance the self-concepts of all students because it provides a more balanced view of American society.
Teaching ethnic pride, such as black pride or Chicano pride, would also teach ethnic minority students to dislike white cultures and students.	*Pride* is the wrong word. Teaching ethnic respect, respect for oneself and one's group, would cause the opposite reaction. To engender respect, a student must learn to respect others.

Source: From *Fostering a pluralistic society through multiethnic education* (pp. 44–45) by R. L. Garcia, 1978, Bloomington, IN: Phi Delta Kappa Education Foundation. Reprinted by permission.

The differences in goals and approaches noted among general, special, and multicultural education are not just theoretical. They create a certain amount of difficulty as one faction (multicultural education) attempts to make inroads into the broader domain of another (general education). An adversarial or competitive situation may result due to misunderstanding, which may be diminished with thoughtful examination. Table 2–1 presents a summary of myths and realities about multicultural education.

Prevalence

FOCUS 2

Describe the population status of and trends among culturally diverse groups in the United States. How do they impact the educational system?

Addressing prevalence in the context of a discussion about multiculturalism and diversity raises many different issues. Generally, **prevalence** refers to the number of persons in a given population who exhibit a condition, problem, or particular status (e.g., who have a hearing loss or who have red hair). Thus, in general terms, determining prevalence is a process of counting how often a phenomenon occurs. In this section, we are examining prevalence in a somewhat different sense. Here we discuss the level of occurrence of certain factors that are relevant to the relationship between human exceptionality and multicultural issues.

In Chapter One, we identified several factors that are associated with students being at risk for academic and social failure. Many of these factors are identified as indicators that are associated with educational disadvantage in students, such as poverty, different cultural backgrounds, and limited-English-speaking backgrounds (Davis & McCaul, 1991; Natriello, McDill, & Pallas, 1990). In large part, these factors also emerge in consideration of multicultural and diversity issues. It is important to emphasize that these factors are used as indicators in determining whether students are at risk for difficulties in school; such factors do not necessarily destine a youngster for special education (see also Chapter One).

The distribution of cultural backgrounds in the general U.S. population is considerably different than that found in some programs within the educational system. For example, a very high percentage—perhaps as high as 41 percent—of all special education students are from culturally divergent backgrounds (Bedell, 1989). African-American children appear more frequently than would be expected in classes focusing on serious emotional disturbance and moderate mental retardation. Hispanic Americans also represent a large and rapidly growing group in special education (Fradd, Figueroa, & Correa, 1989). At the other end of the spectrum, programs for the gifted and talented seem to have fewer than expected students who are African American, Hispanic, or Native American (American Indian) (Gollnick & Chinn, 1990). Students from cultural minorities also drop out of school more frequently than their peers from the cultural majority. In 1988, 10.8 percent of the white population between 16 and 24 years of age were dropouts, whereas the figure for African Americans was 12.4 percent and that for Hispanics was 29.7 percent (U.S. Bureau of the Census, 1990). Recent figures indicate that 36 percent of those dropping out of school are African American and 44 percent are Hispanic (Wagner, 1989).

Several populations from culturally or ethnically diverse backgrounds are growing rapidly, due to both birthrates and immigration levels. For example, the number of African Americans, who represented approximately 12.5 percent of the total population in the United States in 1990 (U.S. Bureau of the Census, 1990), is increasing at a rate more than twice that of the Caucasian population. Growth of culturally and ethnically diverse groups will continue to place an increased load on the educational systems as diverse needs for appropriate services are addressed.

Having a diverse student population also means having language differences. Baca and Cervantes (1989) found that approximately 7.9 million children of school age spoke languages other than English in 1980, a growth of nearly 3 million students over 1976 figures.

These authors also estimated that 948,000 of these youngsters were both disabled and linguistically different. Immigration levels since the Vietnam conflict suggest that Southeast Asian people constitute a continually growing population. The general non-English-speaking population had a projected growth of 24 percent from 1976 to 1990 and 43 percent (to 40 million people) by the year 2000 (Baca & Cervantes, 1989). This will continue to place an obvious demand for linguistically appropriate instruction on school systems in the United States. The increasing need for vigilance and caution in assessment is demonstrated, as well.

These figures represent mainly the number of students who are either bilingual or linguistically different. Certainly, many of these students come from backgrounds that permit them to achieve academically in a school system that is based primarily on the English language. However, the National Foundation for the Improvement of Education estimated that approximately 3.5 million children in the United States could benefit from bilingual programs (NFIE, 1982). While this estimate was certainly not as high as the 1980 prevalence figure of 7.9 million, it suggested a considerable need for appropriate bilingual services. With this level of need, which is magnified considerably when we consider other multicultural factors, it is clear why a careful examination of educational purposes must accompany the services provided.

Multicultural and Diversity Linkages to Special Education

The link between multicultural education and special education is not always a comfortable one nor one that was intended. In fact, to a significant degree, much of the relationship between the two areas has been viewed with concern—a problem of both racial discrimination and inappropriate educational programing. Part of the link grew from the way special education operates, serving children who are essentially failing in the general education

The benefits of special education interventions are lost if the child does not understand the language being used. (Tony Freeman/PhotoEdit)

system. Unfortunately, many youngsters placed in special education are from minority backgrounds—again, a number disproportionately large, given the percentage of minority people in the population at large (Bedell, 1989). Such circumstances seem to suggest that special education has been used as a tool of discrimination, a means of separating racial and ethnic minorities from the majority. This is certainly not a desirable situation. We will examine this issue further as we proceed through this chapter.

There are other links between special and multicultural education. Some of the environmental influences mentioned earlier that appear to have an impact in special education also seem operative in multicultural education. In part, these influences are causes of behavioral or academic difficulties in school. Additionally, certain instructional interventions in special and multicultural education may have common elements. They often surface when academic problems require specific or focused instructional approaches. As this chapter proceeds, our discussion will unfold primarily within the context of the four major elements of the Individuals with Disabilities Education Act (IDEA), presented in Chapter One: (1) nondiscriminatory and multidisciplinary assessment; (2) parental involvement in developing each child's educational program; (3) education in the least restrictive environment; and (4) an individualized education program.

NONDISCRIMINATORY AND MULTIDISCIPLINARY ASSESSMENT

Perhaps nowhere is the link between special and multicultural education more obvious than in issues of nondiscriminatory assessment. As noted earlier, a disproportionate number of minority students are found in special education classes. Decisions regarding referral and placement in these classes are based on psychological assessment, often standardized evaluations of intellectual and social functioning. It is questionable as to whether such assessments discriminate or are biased against children from ethnically and culturally different backgrounds. In several cases, this issue was presented to the courts, where determination was made that such evaluations *were* discriminatory to Hispanic students (*Diana v. State Board of Education,* 1970, 1973) and African-American students (*Larry P. v. Riles,* 1972, 1979). Although both of these cases were decided in the state of California, they have had an impact nationwide and greatly influenced the drafting of IDEA.

The case of *Diana v. State Board of Education,* for example, established two precedents that are prominent in IDEA: (1) that children tested for potential placement in special education must be assessed in their native or primary language and (2) that children cannot be placed in special classes on the basis of culturally biased tests. In order to prevent discriminatory evaluation practices, IDEA includes several safeguards against discriminatory assessment. To comply with the law, students must be tested in their native or primary language whenever possible. The evaluation procedures used must be selected and administered to prevent cultural or racial discrimination, and assessment tools must be validated for the purpose for which they are being used. Finally, evaluation should involve a multidisciplinary team using several sources of information to formulate a placement decision. To place these safeguards in a proper context, it is necessary to discuss the assessment process generally and examine how cultural bias can occur.

Assessment is a topic of central importance in all special education and has been throughout its entire history. Assessment is important because, in special education, professionals usually measure discrepancies from a standard and determine whether extra or specialized interventions are necessary. Assessment of academic and behavioral differences represents the basis on which referrals are made and instructional programs are implemented and evaluated.

Assessment Error

Assessment, or more correctly, assessment error, has been a major focal point of controversy and concern involving special and multicultural education. The major difficulty has been one of bias in the measurement instruments employed. **Measurement bias,** in this context, refers to error introduced during testing when results are unfair or inaccurate due to the student's cultural background, reflecting "artifacts of the test" (artificial results) rather than actual mental abilities or skills (Reynolds, 1987). Cultural and ethnic minority groups argue that cultural bias and prejudice are involved in both the construction/development and use of assessment instruments (Roberts & DeBlassie, 1983; Slate, 1983). This has particularly been the case with standardized, norm-referenced instruments, where minority children's performances are often compared with norms developed from other populations. Under these conditions, minority children often appear at a disadvantage because of cultural differences (Wood, Johnson, & Jenkins, 1986).

Bias in psychological assessment has been recognized as a problem for many years (Burt, 1921) and continues to concern experts (Lopez, 1988; Malgady, Rogler, & Constantino, 1987; Miller-Jones, 1989). Some assessment procedures simply do not document the same level of performance by individuals with differing backgrounds, even if they have similar abilities. For many years, this phenomenon was referred to as **test bias,** and considerable effort was expended to develop culture-free or culture-fair instruments (Cattell, 1940; Cattell, Feingold, & Sarason, 1941; Raven, 1938). This effort was rooted in the belief that the test itself was the major element contributing to bias or unfairness. Such a single-minded perspective was fundamentally flawed, although over the years improvements were made. Revision focused on minimizing the most glaring problems by reducing both the amount of culture-specific content in test items and culture-specific language required to perform test tasks (Luftig, 1989). However, even these refinements have limited effectiveness when the use of the test is not appropriate and conceptually sound (Drew, 1973; Kaufman, 1979). More recent attention has focused on minimizing assessment bias in procedures as well as instrumentation (Reynolds & Brown, 1984), with an emphasis on the need for improved professional preparation (Elbert, 1984). Personal impressions are formed, *sometimes based on a single cue,* which trigger biased categorization, even in the face of evidence to the contrary (Skowronski & Carlston, 1989).

Language Differences

A major culprit in assessment difficulties with culturally diverse students over the years has been language differences. Historically, assessment of children who are linguistically different has often been biased, an inaccurate reflection of abilities (Figueroa, 1989). If language differences are not considered during assessment and educational planning, the result may be an inappropriate special education placement for a child who is culturally different (Duran, 1989). As indicated in the prevalence section (see earlier in this chapter), a substantial number of children in the American educational system do not speak English. Children who are linguistically different are found in the school systems of every state in the country, with several states having more than a million each (Baca & Cervantes, 1989).

A particularly difficult situation exists when a student has a language difference (e.g., primarily speaks Japanese) that contributes to learning problems but also has a disabling language deficiency, such as delayed language development. This type of case presents a very perplexing problem for the professional (Langdon, 1989). It is extremely difficult to determine the degree to which each of the problems contributes to deficiency in academic achievement. The question arises whether such a child should be placed in special education

FOCUS 3
Identify two ways in which assessment may contribute to the overrepresentation of students who are culturally different and receive special education.

FOCUS 4
Identify three ways in which language differences may contribute to assessment difficulties with students who are culturally different.

and, if so, whether such placement occurs because he or she is linguistically different culturally or linguistically deficient developmentally.

Assessment of a child in his or her native language was specifically addressed as one of the safeguards in IDEA. While this represents an important positive step toward treating linguistically different students fairly, certain difficulties have emerged as the law has been implemented. The legislation defines *native language* as that used in the home. However, regulations written to implement IDEA defined *native language* as that which is normally used by the youngster in school (Fradd, Figueroa, & Correa, 1989). This latter perspective of native language may present some serious difficulties for a bilingual student who has achieved a conversational fluency in English. Although the child may normally converse in English at school, his or her proficiency may not be adequate to sustain academic work. For this child, testing in English is likely to be biased, even though it would be the native language according to regulations.

Professional Training

Professionals involved in psychoeducational assessment, particularly with ethnic minority children, must be properly trained to obtain accurate data and minimize the formation of impressions that may bias their procedures. Additionally, professionals must be constantly alert to potential bias due to language differences as well as other contributing factors that may mask students' abilities and be reflected in evaluation results. In many cases, information about the child's home life and other environmental matters can provide valuable insight to aid professionals in both assessment administration and interpretation of results. Table 2–2 summarizes guidelines for obtaining information regarding students' cultural and environmental influences. Namely, a series of questions probe vital information that assessment professionals should become aware of in evaluating students of all backgrounds. Uninformed expectations about family constellations and circumstances can lead to inaccurate assessment from a number of perspectives.

Assessment is one of several important tools in education, a particularly important one in both special and multicultural education. For assessment to function properly as part of the education process and not introduce bias, assessment instruments must be correctly constructed and used. Furthermore, the purposes of assessment must be considered from the outset for an instrument or procedure to be correctly designed and used. To determine purpose, several questions should be asked: Are we attempting to bring the bulk of citizenry to a similar point in education or knowledge? In so doing, are we creating a leveling effect, attempting to make all people alike to some degree? Or are we promoting individual growth and development and encouraging cultural diversity and individual differences?

PARENTAL INVOLVEMENT IN THE EDUCATIONAL PROCESS

FOCUS 5

Identify three ways in which differing sociocultural mores may affect the manner in which parents become involved in the educational process.

IDEA specifically provided for parental involvement in the educational process. Parents have the right to a variety of levels of participation. It is important to note, however, that these rights are based on certain assumptions. Perhaps the most fundamental assumption is that parents are proactive and inclined to challenge the school if their child is not being treated properly. However, this assumption has not always been a good one. Many parents are reluctant or afraid to interact with the educational system in any but a passive manner. This is particularly true of parents from some culturally diverse backgrounds.

Accepting a disabling condition is not easy for any parent, and a family's attitude toward exceptionality can have a major influence on how a child's intervention proceeds. People

■ **Table 2–2** Guidelines for Obtaining Information about Cultural and Environmental Influences

After talking with community members about the general cultural characteristics of the community, it is still necessary to discover what experiences each child has had. The following set of questions can be used to find out about the direct cultural and environmental experiences of the child so that appropriate educational programs can be planned.

1. What language(s) do the parents speak to each other?
2. What language(s) do the parents speak to the child?
3. What language(s) do the children use with each other?
4. What language does the referred child prefer to use when playing with friends?
5. Who takes care of the child after school? What language is used?
6. Who lives in the home (parents, grandparents, etc.)?
7. How much time does each parent have to interact with the child?
8. With whom does the child play when at home?
9. What television programs are seen in each language?
10. Are stories read to the child? In what language is the reading material written?
11. What language is used in church services, if attended?
12. What does the child do after school and on weekends?
13. What responsibilities does the child have in the home?
14. How is the child expected to act toward parents, teachers, and other adults?
15. In what cultural activities does the family participate?
16. How do the parents expect adults to act toward the child?
17. Are there any specific prohibitions in the everyday interactions between adults and children, for example, do not look adults in the eye when talking to them, do not pat children on the top of the head, do not ask children questions?
18. How long has the family been in this country?
19. How long has the family been in the local community?
20. How much contact does the family have with the homeland? What kind of contact?

Source: Reprinted with permission from Mattes, L. J., & Omark, D. R. (1984). *Speech and language assessment for the bilingual handicapped*. Boston: College-Hill Press, Appendix A, pp. 111–112.

with differing cultural backgrounds may often have perspectives and beliefs regarding disabling conditions that are different from those held by the cultural majority—the main group that has designed, developed, and perpetuated the existing educational system. For example, Hispanic families often have great difficulty accepting disabilities such as visual impairments (Correa, 1987), and religious beliefs and superstitions tend to have a considerable impact on such acceptance (Smith, 1987). The extended family structures common in African-American and Hispanic cultures are the foundation for differing beliefs regarding the provision of care from a larger community as well as anxieties about adjusting to the

Cultural diversity also applies to attitudes toward disabilities. (Alon Reininger/Contact Press Images)

new or alien cultural influences that may be represented by special education (Fishgrund, Cohen, & Clarkson, 1987; Turner, 1987; Yacobacci-Tam, 1987). Parents of children with disabilities who are poor, who are from a minority background, and who have a primary language other than English face enormous disadvantages interacting with the special education system (Harry, 1992).

In addition to differences in the acceptance of disabling conditions, matters pertaining to delivering service to children of families who are culturally different require certain consideration. For example, the importance of manners and deference to others in traditional Hispanic families needs to be taken into account by educational professionals (Smith, 1987). Likewise, interactions with Asian-American families may be unique due to their reluctance to receive assistance from outside the family (Leung, 1987). Southeast Asian parents may feel great shame that their child has been identified as disabled, which influences not only their acceptance of the situation but also their attitude toward service delivery (Morrow, 1987). And to make matters even more complex, professionals should also keep in mind that the immigration status of some families may influence the manner in which they react to education professionals attempting to provide services for their children (Smith, 1987). Although immigration status is more of a pragmatic consideration than a belief difference, it certainly impacts the delivery of special education in many cases. A family who is residing in the United States illegally or who is somewhat unsure about their residency status will likely avoid the additional interaction with an educational system that may be required to obtain special services for their child.

Public education in the United States predominantly reflects the philosophy of the cultural majority. This is not surprising, since social institutions—in this instance, formal schooling—are typically founded on such mainstream views. However, in a situation where multiple cultures live together, as reflected in the broad diversity of beliefs evident in the United States, social mores in the many subcultures often emphasize different priorities. Table 2–3 illustrates some of the differences in cultural values between the dominant U.S. culture and the Native American culture. Activities that are of the utmost importance to one cultural group may be less crucial to another or even viewed with disdain. For example, although mental retardation is universally recognized by differing cultures, its conceptual-

■ **Table 2–3** Native American versus Dominant Culture Values

Native American	Dominant Culture
Wisdom of age and experience is respected. Elders are revered by their people.	Older people are made to feel incompetent and rejected.
Excellence is related to a contribution to the group—not to personal glory.	Competition and striving to win or to gain status are emphasized.
Cooperation is necessary for group survival.	Competition is necessary for individual status and prestige.
Children participate in adult activities.	Adults participate in children's activities.
Family life includes the extended family.	Family life includes the nuclear family.
Time is present oriented—this year, this week—NOW—a resistance to planning for the future.	Time is planning and saving for the future.
Clocktime is whenever people are ready—when everyone arrives.	Clocktime is exactly that.
Work is when necessary for the common good. Whatever Native American people have, they share. What is mine is ours.	Work is from 9–5 (specified time) and to obtain material possessions and to save for the future. What is mine stays mine.
Good relationships and mutual respect are emphasized.	Success, progress, possession of property, and rugged individualism are valued above mutual respect and maintaining good relationships.
People express their ideas and feelings through their actions.	People express themselves and attempt to impress others through speech.
People conform to nature.	People try to dominate and desecrate nature.
Early childhood and rearing practices are the responsibility of the kin group.	Early childhood and rearing practices are the responsibility of the nuclear family.
Native religion was never imposed or proselytized to other groups.	Religious groups proselytize, coerce, and impose their beliefs on others.
Land gives the Native American his or her identity, religion, and life. It is not to be sold, not owned, but used by all.	Land is for speculation, for prestige, to be owned, sold, or torn up.
Going to school is necessary to gain knowledge. Excelling for fame is looked down upon.	Going to school is necessary to gain knowledge and to compete for grades.
Native Americans have a shorter childhood. The male is held to be a responsible person at the age of 16.	There is an extended childhood. The male is held to be a responsible person at the age of 21.
People are usually judged by what they do.	People are usually judged by their credentials.

Source: From "Teaching the American Indian child in mainstream settings" by F. C. Pepper, in *Mainstreaming and the minority child* (pp. 135–136), ed. R. L. Jones, 1976, Reston, VA: Council for Exceptional Children.

ization, social interpretation, and treatment are culturally specific (Manion & Bersani, 1987). Similarly, certain behaviors that might suggest a learning problem may in fact be a product of the acculturation process or considered normal within a child's cultural background (Collier & Hoover, 1987). Table 2–4 compares some Western and non-Western cultural perspectives.

■ **Table 2–4** Non-Western versus Western Cultural Values

Polynesian Native American	Asian	Western
1. Individual valued as part of family	1. Individual valued as part of family	1. Individual held as supreme value
2. Self-control, humility	2. Self-control, humility	2. Self-expression, pride
3. Submit to family system	3. Submit to family rule	3. Negotiates within family
4. Spiritual harmony	4. Spiritual harmony	4. Spiritual duality
5. Reverence/respect for life	5. Partnership with nature	5. Master nature
6. Cooperation, mutual help	6. Cooperation, mutual help	6. Competition, self-reliance
7. Loyalty, obedience, shared responsibility	7. Obedience, duty, honor	7. Self-pride, honor, duty
8. Do what is necessary, play more	8. Hard work, little play	8. Work hard, then play

Source: From *Exceptional children in focus* (p. 189). J. R. Patton, J. S. Payne, J. M. Kauffman, G. B. Brown, and R. A. Payne, 1987, Columbus, OH: Merrill. Reprinted with permission.

Most professional educators agree that parental involvement in the educational process is beneficial. This is one reason that legislators included such participation as a major element in IDEA. What is not considered in this perspective, however, is that all parents do not view the educational system in the same way. Some parents do not know how to interact with the schools in an effective manner. Others simply do not care what transpires at school, or at least, that is how it appears to teachers who are trying to encourage parental involvement. These teachers may be correct, or they may be misinterpreting behaviors that reflect differing cultural mores. As we have seen, people from divergent cultures view the world from vastly different perspectives.

EDUCATION IN THE LEAST RESTRICTIVE ENVIRONMENT

FOCUS 6

Identify two considerations that represent particular difficulties in serving children who are culturally different in the least restrictive environment.

Education in the least restrictive environment (LRE) involves a wide variety of placement options, as discussed in Chapter One (see Figure 1–4). The guiding principle is that instruction should take place in an environment that is as similar to that of the educational mainstream as possible. IDEA required that students with disabilities be taught in settings with nondisabled peers to the maximum extent appropriate. For the child who is culturally different who is also receiving appropriate special education services, the same is true. However, some unique circumstances arise that require additional attention.

Exceptional children who also have language differences may well require further consideration, since they may also receive assistance from bilingual education staff. In some cases, the language instruction may be incorporated into other teaching that focuses on remediation of a learning problem. In situations where the disability is more severe or the language difference is extreme (perhaps little or no English proficiency), the student may be placed in a separate setting for a portion of the instructional time.

Cultural and language instruction may vary as the child grows older and as a function of the model used in a given school district. Figure 2–1 illustrates how various approaches might be structured into a daily or weekly educational schedule as a student moves through the grades from kindergarten to the twelfth grade. Each approach is somewhat different in the degree of integration it recommends. Part I, the *transition model,* is aimed at moving the student into the instructional mainstream as rapidly as possible while addressing issues of linguistic performance and disability remediation. Parts III-a and III-b involve instruction

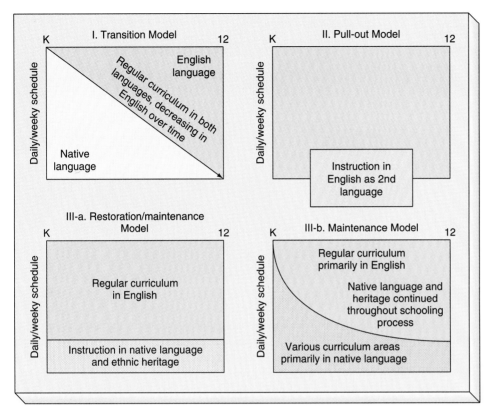

FIGURE 2–1 Models of Bilingual and Bicultural Service Delivery

Source: Reprinted with permission of Merrill, an imprint of Macmillan Publishing Company, from *The bilingual special education interface* (2nd ed.) by L. M. Baca and H. T. Cervantes. Copyright © 1989 by Merrill Publishing Company.

that takes place while the student remains in an integrated setting as much as possible. Part II represents what has long been known as a **pull-out program** and does not reflect integrated instruction. While some students may require placement in such an educational setting, pull-out programs have not been viewed favorably in recent years. Baca and Cervantes (1989) noted that pull-out instructional placements are a particularly sensitive issue in bilingual/bicultural education because they represent segregation. In some cases, placement decisions are based on training limitations of the staff rather than students' needs.

INDIVIDUALIZED EDUCATION PROGRAMS

IDEA required the development of an individualized education program (IEP) for each student with a disability. Most school districts have considerable experience in this process. However, addressing the needs of a child with cultural and/or linguistic differences will present an additional challenge. Depending on the student's background and capabilities, he or she may need remediation for a specific learning disability, catch-up work in academic subjects, and instruction in English as a second language. The IEP must consider cultural factors, such as language differences, as well as learning and behavior problems. A student with a disability and a language difference may receive specialized instruction from different professionals for each facet of his or her education. Rarely will a single professional have the training and background in relevant cultural or linguistic areas as well as the specialized skills

FOCUS 7

Identify two areas that require particular attention when developing an individualized education program (IEP) for a student who is culturally different.

The success of multicultural special education depends more on the teacher than on any single factor. (Paul Conklin/PhotoEdit)

needed to remediate disabilities. Baca and Cervantes noted that, with "the potential for larger numbers of highly specialized personnel to be involved in the provision of services, it becomes extremely critical for school districts to recognize that coordination and sequencing of instruction are a primary concern" (1989, pp. 189–190).

An IEP for a student who is culturally different and also disabled may address many facets of his or her life. If, for example, a child who lives in poverty comes to school, his or her experiences and development will differ from those of peers from more affluent backgrounds. Children from different economic levels will have different instructional needs. The IEP should address these matters if it is to be maximally effective for each particular child.

It is also vital that ethnic or cultural assumptions be discarded to avoid perpetuating stereotypes in a student's educational plan. For example, such stereotypes may involve well-intentioned but misguided efforts at instruction on what are thought to be culturally relevant foods. However, assumptions about what part such foods play in a given student's life may be in error and do more to perpetuate an unfortunate stereotype than to enrich a child's understanding of his or her heritage (Baca & Cervantes, 1989; Hernandez, 1989). IEPs written for children who are culturally different must truly be developed in an individualized fashion. Namely, more factors must often be considered for children with disabilities who come from groups other than the cultural majority.

OTHER MULTICULTURAL CONSIDERATIONS

Other influences come into play as we consider multicultural and diversity issues. In some cases, societal problems contribute to the development of a child's learning problems. In other cases, a variety of factors contribute to the complicated linkages between educating those of different cultures and those of different abilities.

Poverty

Perhaps the most evident example of how social and cultural factors interrelate is found in the conditions pertaining to poverty. A child from an impoverished environment may be

FOCUS 8

Identify two ways in which poverty may contribute to the academic difficulties of children from culturally different backgrounds, often resulting in their referral to special education.

Conditions of poverty may contribute to poor academic performance and special education referrals. (John Sohn, Chromosohn/The Stock Market)

destined for special education before he or she is even born. Gelfand, Jenson, and Drew (1988) cited statistical data and described the prenatal development circumstances in this way: "Only 5 percent of white upper-class infants suffer complications at birth, compared with 15 percent of low-socioeconomic-status (low-SES) whites and *51 percent* of all nonwhites (who have very low incomes as a group)" (p. 64, emphasis in the original). Children who begin their lives facing such problems are more likely to have difficulty later than those who do not. Children who live in poverty may be frail, sick more often, and exhibit more neurological problems that later contribute to academic difficulties (Magrab, Sostek, & Powell, 1984).

As children develop during the important early years, living in an impoverished environment places them further at risk due to factors such as malnutrition, the presence of toxic agents (e.g., lead), and generally insufficient parental care. As with the statistics cited above, these conditions are found more often in the family circumstances of those from cultural and ethnic minorities (Brooks-Gunn & Furstenberg, 1986; Children's Defense Fund, 1990a, 1990b; Field, 1980). Furthermore, poverty is associated with ethnic minority status (Davis & McCaul, 1991; Natriello, McDill, & Pallas, 1990). In 1989, 31.6 percent of the African-American population and 26.8 percent of the Hispanic population in the United States lived below the poverty level, compared to 10.1 percent of the white population (U.S. Bureau of the Census, 1990). The 1990 census data presented an even more disturbing picture when considering children: Twenty percent of children from all races were considered to be living below the poverty level. Analyzed by ethnic origin, over 45 percent of African-American children and over 39 percent of Hispanic children fell below the poverty level while white children represented 15 percent.

The conditions of poverty often contribute to poor academic performance, place children in at-risk situations, and generate special education referrals. Clearly, conditions of poverty are found more often in populations having multicultural education concerns, which contributes to the link between special and multicultural education.

Migrancy

Our opening window about Christina suggested at least two circumstances that might contribute to her experiencing school-related difficulties: a language difference and the fact that

FOCUS 9

Identify two ways in which migrancy among culturally diverse populations may contribute to academic difficulties.

her family moves often at harvest times to obtain employment. But migrancy may or may not be associated with minority status and poverty. In a certain number of cases, neither poverty nor minority status are involved in situations where students move often. Frequent mobility sometimes characterizes families of considerable affluence, such as when a family moves from a summer home to a winter home on a schedule that suits parents rather than school schedules. Children living in these circumstances may also find themselves in and out of school due to extended intercontinental vacations or other trips, which the wealth of their parents permits. Likewise, children of military personnel may change schools frequently and on a schedule that does not coincide with the academic year.

Regardless of the reason for mobility, forces that interrupt the continuity of schooling have an impact on learning, teacher and peer relationships, and general academic progress (Barresi, 1982). The mobility of wealthy people and others subject to frequent reassignment (e.g., military personnel) has an impact, but it is often offset by other circumstances that contribute to a child's general education (e.g., opportunity for travel, help of tutors). Although these children are mobile and migrant, they are not subject to the same risks as children from families who migrate as a way of life. Unlike military personnel, migrant workers are not assured of such matters as employment, housing, or a welcoming sponsor.

In many cases, the circumstances of migrancy are associated with ethnic or cultural differences as well as both economic disadvantage and language differences. Hunter (1982) cited figures indicating that 74.7 percent of the migrant farm workers in Alaska, Oregon, Idaho, and Washington were Hispanic and 20.2 percent were African American. While consistent data are not available for other regions of the country, migrancy is a situation that is widespread, affecting an estimated 15 percent of the American population (Barresi, 1982). Migrant workers are often from Hispanic backgrounds but may also be African American, Asian American, or Native American.

Migrancy generally has a detrimental effect on a child's academic progress. The problems created by poverty and language differences are difficult to address when the child moves three or four times each year (Salend, Michael, & Taylor, 1984). Children from migrant families have limited continuity and considerable inconsistency in educational programing as they move about. They often have limited access to services due to their short-term enrollments or the schools' limited capabilities to deliver services. While it is difficult to determine the singular effects of mobility on children's academic progress, the problem is a significant one.

Other Contributing Factors

FOCUS 10

Identify three conceptual factors that have contributed to heightened attention and concern regarding the placement of children from cultural and ethnic minority groups in special education.

A number of other factors contribute to the link between special and multicultural education. Some of these elicit serious concern regarding the placement of minority children in special education, while others pertain to how such placements might occur.

Special education focuses on *differences*. If a young girl has academic difficulty, perhaps failing reading and math, then she is singled out as being different. She is different in that her math and reading performances are far below those of her peers. Because of this difference, the student may receive special help in reading and math in an attempt to improve her performances. Several questions emerge as we consider this example: (1) How do we determine that the student is doing poorly in reading and math? (2) Is the student a candidate for special education? (3) What is the primary reason the student might be a candidate for special education? and (4) What if the student comes from a culturally different background, such as Christina in Window 2–1?

Certainly, one major point that arises in this case relates to the third question: Is Christina considered disabled due to her academic performance, or is she in this situation because of her culturally different background? This is not an easily answered question. In fact, it may not have a clear answer. Contributing factors may be so intertwined that they cannot be separated in any meaningful manner. Christina may be appropriately considered for special education as long as her performance is *not* preeminently a cultural matter (i.e., just because she is from a background other than that of the majority). Some might argue that it does not matter why Christina is receiving special help as long as she is being served—receiving extra instructional assistance. While this perspective has a certain degree of intuitive appeal, it is not a satisfactory position for professionals involved in multicultural education. If Christina is receiving special education because of her cultural background and not primarily because she is disabled, she is being labeled and placed inappropriately.

Special education often carries with it a certain degree of stigma. When a child receives special education, it is implied that he or she is somehow inferior to those children who do not require such extra or different instruction. Unfortunately, this view remains, despite all efforts by professionals to change it. Peers may ridicule children who are in special education. Furthermore, some parents are more comfortable when their children are among the faceless students in regular education classes. Even parents of children who are gifted and talented are often quick to point out that their children are in some type of accelerated class rather than special education.

This negative perspective of special education is especially harmful to children such as Christina if their placement stems from mislabeling. Multicultural advocates may correctly claim that placing students in special education because of cultural differences is nothing more than another means of discrimination and perhaps oppression by the cultural majority. From this view, it is not difficult to see why multicultural education advocates are concerned, even angry, when culturally different children appear to be overrepresented in special education.

There may be an additional problem if Christina's special education placement is not one that is multiculturally sensitive and appropriate. Special education intervention alone does not often promote cultural pluralism. Furthermore, even the most effective math instruction available will be ineffective if it is provided in English, which the student may not comprehend or speak fluently. Thus, just as the reason Christina is in special education may be in error, so the intervention may be in error as well. As noted in the earlier section in this chapter on IEPs, designing and implementing an appropriate instructional program for Christina will likely be complex and involve a number of different specialists.

Christina's placement in special education may impede her academic progress to the extent that it becomes a self-fulfilling prophecy (see Chapter One). In short, Christina may become what she has been labeled. Christina's poor performance in reading and mathematics may be due to cultural differences, not a learning disability. If the initial assessment is based on her cultural differences and thus inaccurate, Christina may be made a poor reader or math student by the system.

The **self-fulfilling prophecy** concept has been discussed for many years. It was first mentioned directly by Merton (1948) and catapulted into the center of attention by Rosenthal and Jacobson (1968a, 1968b, 1968c), whose work stimulated immediate and ongoing controversy (Rosenthal, 1987; Wineburg, 1987). A great deal remains to be learned about the effects of expectations, specifically, how and the degree to which they affect performance (Merton, 1987). This factor warrants particular attention as we consider multicultural and special education matters (Wineburg, 1987).

INTERVENTIONS

Intervention strategies that consider multicultural issues must be based on the individual needs of the child. Figure 1–5 from Chapter One presented a format for generating an IEP that addressed many different dimensions of the child's abilities. Modifications and additions to the illustrated IEP must include specific cultural considerations that are relevant for that particular child. It may be necessary for assessment to determine language dominance and evaluate language proficiency both in terms of conversational and academic skills. The IEP may also need to address the type of language intervention, which might include enrichment (either in a native tongue or in English), or language development intervention, which may also be in either a native tongue or in English.

These are only examples of the considerations that may need attention, and they primarily relate to language differences. Environmental conditions, such as extreme poverty and developmental deprivation, may dictate that interventions focus on cognitive stimulation that was lacking in the child's early learning. The individual strategies possible are as many and varied as the different factors in a child's background. Effective interventions must be based on the fundamental principles of individualized educational planning.

It is also important to note that most children from culturally different backgrounds do not require special education interventions. While certain factors that we have discussed may place them at risk for such referral, a variety of available instructional elements may meet their needs without special education services. When this is possible, it would be a mistake to label such students disabled.

Debate Forum ·················· English-Only or Bilingual Education? ·······················

Declaring English as the official language has had a certain level of support by lawmakers at several levels during the past few years. Initiatives to promote such legislation have been evident in nearly 75 percent of the states in the United States as recently as 1987. Yet English is not the primary language for many Americans. Students from culturally diverse backgrounds represent a very large portion of the school enrollment across the country. Critics claim that bilingual education places an unacceptable burden on the educational system, compromising its ability to provide specialized educational services to meet students' needs.

Point   Children from different cultures must have certain skills to survive in the world of the cultural majority.

They should be taught in English and taught the knowledge base of the cultural majority for their own good. This knowledge will prepare them for success and more efficiently utilize the limited funds available, since specialized culturally sensitive services will not be required.

Counterpoint   Children from cultures different from that of the majority must have an equal advantage to learn in the most effective manner possible. This may mean teaching them in their native language, at least for some of the time. To do otherwise is a waste of talent, which can ultimately affect the overall progress of our country. To force students who are culturally different to use English is also a means of discrimination by the cultural majority.

REVIEW ···

FOCUS 1   Identify three ways in which the purposes and approaches to general American education sometimes differ from those of special education and multicultural education.

◆ A major purpose of general education is to provide education for everyone and to bring all students to a similar level of performance.

◆ Special education focuses on individual differences and often evaluates performance on an individually set or prescribed performance level.

◆ Multicultural education promotes cultural pluralism and therefore differences.

FOCUS 2   Describe the population status of and trends among culturally diverse groups in the United States. How do they impact the educational system?

◆ Ethnically and culturally diverse groups—such as Hispanic Americans, African Americans, and others—represent substantial portions of the United States population, some individual groups over 12 percent.

◆ Population growth in ethnically and culturally different groups is increasing at a phenomenal rate; in some cases, the rate is twice that of Caucasians. Both immigration and birthrates contribute to this growth.

◆ Increased demands for services will be placed on the educational system as culturally diverse populations gradually acquire appropriate services and as significant growth rates continue.

FOCUS 3 Identify two ways in which assessment may contribute to the overrepresentation of students who are culturally different and receive special education.

◆ Through assessment instruments that are designed and constructed with specific language and content favoring the cultural majority

◆ Through assessment procedures (and perhaps due to personnel) that are negatively biased, either implicitly or explicitly, toward people who are culturally different

FOCUS 4 Identify three ways in which language differences may contribute to assessment difficulties with students who are culturally different.

◆ Non-English-speaking students may be thought to have speech or language disorders and be referred and tested for special education placement.

◆ A child's native language may appear to be English because of conversational fluency at school, but he or she may not be proficient enough to engage in academic work or assessment.

◆ A child's academic or psychological assessment may be an inaccurate portrayal of ability due to his or her language differences.

FOCUS 5 Identify three ways in which differing sociocultural mores may affect the manner in which parents become involved in the educational process.

◆ Parents from some cultural backgrounds may view special assistance from educational institutions with disdain or shame and be reluctant to accept aid from sources outside the family unit.

◆ Parents from certain cultural backgrounds may be reluctant to take an active role interacting with the educational system.

◆ Certain behaviors that may suggest a disabling condition needing special education assistance are viewed as normal in some cultures, and parents may not see them as problematic.

FOCUS 6 Identify two considerations that represent particular difficulties in serving children who are culturally different in the least restrictive environment.

◆ Cultural or language instruction may be superimposed on other teaching that focuses on remediation of a learning prob-

lem, making integration into the educational mainstream more difficult.

◆ Training limitations of school staff, rather than the child's needs, may influence placement decisions.

FOCUS 7 Identify two areas that require particular attention when developing an individualized education program (IEP) for a student who is culturally different.

◆ Coordination of different services and professional personnel becomes critical.

◆ Cultural stereotypes should not be perpetuated by assumptions that are inappropriate for an IEP.

FOCUS 8 Identify two ways in which poverty may contribute to the academic difficulties of children from culturally different backgrounds, often resulting in their referral to special education.

◆ Circumstances resulting in disadvantaged prenatal development and birth complications occur much more frequently among those of low-level socioeconomic status and nonwhite populations.

◆ Environmental circumstances, such as malnutrition and the presence of toxic agents, that place children at risk are found most frequently in impoverished households, and poverty is most frequently evident among ethnic minority populations.

FOCUS 9 Identify two ways in which migrancy among culturally diverse populations may contribute to academic difficulties.

◆ In many cases, migrant families are characterized by economic disadvantages and language differences.

◆ Children in migrant households may move and change educational placements several times a year, contributing to limited continuity and inconsistent educational programing.

FOCUS 10 Identify three conceptual factors that have contributed to heightened attention and concern regarding the placement of children from ethnic and cultural groups in special education.

◆ A stigma is attached to special education.

◆ Special education placement for children from cultural and ethnic minorities may not be educationally effective in meeting their academic problems.

◆ A self-fulfilling prophecy may be operative, resulting in youngsters' becoming what they are labeled.

Chapter Three

Education through the Life Span

TO BEGIN WITH . . .

◆ By the year 2000, all children in the United States will start school ready to learn (Goal 1 from *America 2000,* U.S. Department of Education, 1991).

◆ The number of all preschool children in the United States has increased by more than 3 million since 1980. The number of elementary school children is projected to increase through the year 2000 before declining. The number of secondary school youth, which declined between 1980 and 1990, will increase by the year 2000 (National Association of State Directors, 1991).

◆ Approximately 2 million children in the United States under 6 years of age are considered to be at risk and likely to experience problems in their physical, intellectual or emotional development (Peterson, 1987).

◆ Most school reform initiatives appear to be responses to charges of declining academic achievement rather than efforts to find ways for schools to meet the diverse needs of all students. School reform efforts have not specifically addressed the needs of students with disabilities (National Council on Disability, 1989).

◆ High school special education students take the majority (68 percent) of their courses in regular education. This fact highlights the compelling responsibility of regular education in the transitional outcomes of special education students (U.S. Department of Education, 1991).

ANITA

ANITA.   Anita was elated. She had just learned during an ultrascan that she was going to have twin girls. As the delivery date neared, she thought about how fun it would be to take them on long summer walks in the family's new double-stroller.

Her estimated delivery date passed, but the babies remained in utero. It was not until two weeks later that she found herself in the hospital, bearing down to greet the first of her two twins. The first little girl arrived without a problem. Unfortunately, this was not the case for the second twin.

There was something different about her. It became obvious almost immediately after the birth. Yvonne just didn't seem to have the same body tone as her sister. Within a couple days, she was diagnosed as having cerebral palsy. Her head and the left side of her body were affected most seriously. The pediatrician calmly told the family that Yvonne would undoubtedly have learning and physical problems throughout her life. The doctor referred Anita and her husband to a division of the state health agency responsible for assisting families with children who are disabled.

Further testing was done, and Yvonne was placed in an early intervention program for infants with developmental problems. At the age of 3, Yvonne was enrolled in a preschool program where she would have the opportunity to interact with children of her own age who were both nondisabled and disabled. As neither of Yvonne's parents had any previous direct experience with a child who is disabled, they were uncertain of how to help her. Would this program really help her that much, or should they only be working with her at home? It was hard for them to have this little girl go to school so very early in her young life.

*I*NTRODUCTION

We continue our overview of educational services for students who are exceptional with a focus on issues from birth through the years of transition from school into adult life (see Figure 3–1). Schooling is successful for all students who are exceptional, as it is for everyone, when it provides the skills and experiences necessary to participate in a heterogeneous world. Such participation involves establishing personal autonomy, choosing one's life-style, having opportunities for social interaction, and becoming economically self-sufficient. For infants, toddlers, and preschool-age children, the world is defined primarily through family and a small, same-age peer group. As the child progresses chronologically and developmentally, the world expands to include the neighborhood, the school, and eventually, a larger heterogeneous group called the *community*. For educators, the question is: How can we work with families to structure a child's instructional program to effectively foster full participation, whether it be in the home, the school, or the community setting?

THE EARLY CHILDHOOD YEARS

FOCUS 1

Why is it so important to provide early intervention services as soon as possible to students at risk?

Over the past decade, there has been a growing recognition of the educational, social, and health needs of young children with disabilities. The early experiences of infants and children who are at risk provide the basis for subsequent learning, growth, and development (Casto & White, 1984; Ramey & Baker-Ward, 1982; Ramey & MacPhee, 1985). These first years of life are critical to the overall development of children, including those defined as at risk. Moreover, classic studies in the behavioral sciences from the 1960s and 1970s indicated that early stimulation is critical to the later development of language, intelligence, personality, and a sense of self-worth (Bloom, 1964; Hunt, 1961; Piaget, 1970; White, 1975).

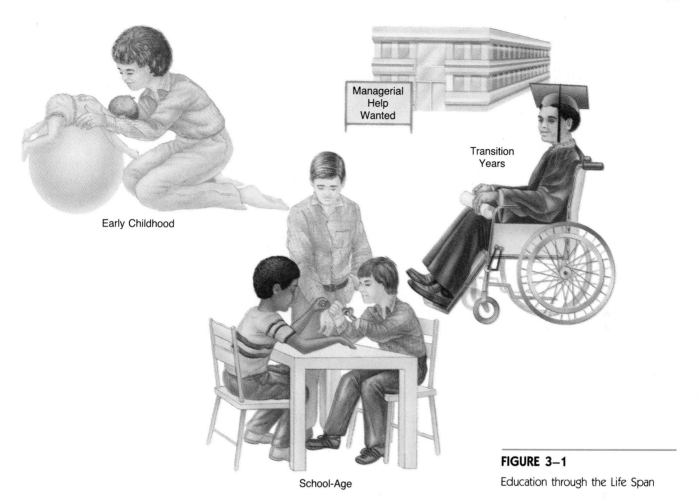

Managerial
Help
Wanted

Transition
Years

Early Childhood

School-Age

FIGURE 3–1

Education through the Life Span

Advocates of early intervention services for children at risk believe that intervention should begin as early as possible in an environment that is free of traditional categorical labels (e.g., *mentally retarded,* emotionally disturbed), particularly if there is any uncertainty about the permanency of the present assessment of the child's condition. Carefully selected interventions have the potential to lessen the long-term impact of the disability and counteract any negative effects of waiting to intervene. The postponement of services may, in fact, undermine a child's overall development as well as his or her acquisition of specific skills.

The efforts of parents and professionals to gain national support to develop and implement services for young children at risk culminated with the passage of Public Law (PL) 99-457, amendments to the Education of the Handicapped Act, passed in 1986 (see Chapter One). PL 99-457 is the most important piece of legislation ever enacted on behalf of infants and preschool-age children with disabilities. With its passage, a new era of services was opened up for young children with disabilities. PL 99-457 required that all states assure a free and appropriate public education to every eligible child with a disability between 3 and 5 years of age. For infants and toddlers (birth to 2 years of age), a program was established to help states develop and implement programs for early intervention services. In this section, we will discuss the comprehensive services necessary to meet the needs of infants, toddlers, and preschool-age children with disabilities.

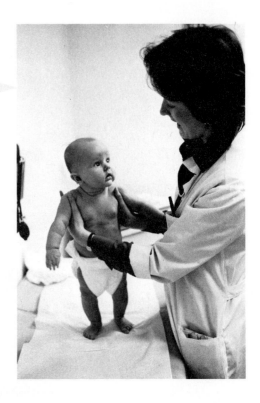

Disabilities should be identified and intervention by special needs professionals should begin as early as possible in an individual's life. (Richard Howard/OffShoot Stock)

Early Intervention Services for Infants and Toddlers

Early intervention is a term often used in myriad ways. For our purposes, *early intervention* is defined as "a comprehensive cluster of services that incorporates goals in education, health care, and social service for young children who are disabled or at-risk for developing developmental disabilities and their families" (Hanson & Lynch, 1989, p. xiii). These services are focused on infants and toddlers from birth to about 3 years of age.

Hanson and Lynch suggested that four factors support the rationale for providing early intervention services to infants and toddlers at risk: (1) the importance of early environmental interactions; (2) the prevention of secondary disabilities/effects; (3) the needs of families of children who are disabled or at risk; and (4) the benefits of early intervention to society (1989, p. 8).

Increasingly, technology has contributed to the number of at-risk infants who survive birth. **Intensive-care specialists** who work with sophisticated medical technologies are able to save the lives of infants who years ago would have died in the first days or weeks of life. This decrease in mortality due to improved technology is a major reason for the increased demand for trained early intervention specialists.

Early intervention and prevention pay substantial dividends to infants and toddlers as well as to their families and society at large. In all likelihood, many infants who, in the past, grew up disabled could have developed normally if appropriate preventative steps had been taken early in their lives. Additionally, in most cases, people with disabilities are far less disabled if effective interventions have been applied from birth.

The intent of intervention programs for infants and toddlers at risk is multifaceted. Goals include diminishing the effects of the disabling condition on the child's growth and development and preventing, as much as possible, the worsening of the at-risk condition.

Timing is critical in the delivery of the interventions. The maxim "the earlier, the better" is very true. Moreover, early intervention may be less costly and more effective than providing services later in the individual's life (Casto & Mastropieri, 1985; Casto & White, 1984; Garber et al., 1991; Reaves & Burns, 1982; Strain, 1984; White, Mastropieri, & Casto, 1984).

According to Peterson (1987), interventions for infants and young children who are at risk or disabled must be "intensive, comprehensive, continuous, and focused upon the individual needs of each child" (p. 74). *Intensity* refers to the frequency and amount of time an infant or child is engaged in intervention activities. If the intensity requirement is to be met, the child should participate in intervention activities that involve two to three hours of contact each day, about four or five times a week.

Comprehensive intervention services are broad in scope. PL 99-457 specified that these services are to include:

♦ Family training, counseling, and home visits
♦ Special instruction
♦ Speech and language instruction
♦ Occupational therapy and physical therapy
♦ Psychological testing and counseling
♦ **Case management** services
♦ Medical services necessary for diagnostic and evaluation purposes only
♦ Early identification, screening, and assessment services
♦ Health services necessary to enable the infant or toddler to benefit from the other early intervention services (Hutinger, 1988, pp. 31–32)

These services are provided to infants and toddlers on the basis of need as established in the individualized family service plan (IFSP) (see Figure 3–2). The IFSP is structured much like the individualized education plan (IEP) but broadens the focus to include not only the individual but all members of the family. The IFSP must contain statements pertaining to:

1. The child's present levels of development (cognitive, speech/language, psychosocial, motor, and self-help)
2. The family's strength and needs related to enhancing the child's development.
3. Major outcomes expected to be achieved for the child and family and the criteria, procedures, and timeframes for determining progress
4. Specific early intervention services necessary to meet the unique needs of the child and the family
5. Projected dates for initiation of services and expected duration
6. The case manager who will be responsible for implementing the plan
7. Procedures for transition from early intervention into a preschool program

Given the breadth of services necessary to meet the individual needs of infants and toddlers, a multidisciplinary intervention team must be in place. It should include professionals with varied experiential backgrounds—such as speech and language, physical therapy, nursing, and education—and also at least one of the child's parents or his or her guardian. The team reviews the IFSP at least annually. Parents are to receive progress updates on the IFSP every six months. Coordination of early intervention services across disciplines and with the family is critical if the goals of the program are to be realized.

The traditional academic-year programing (approximately nine months) common to many public school programs is not in the best interests of infants and toddlers at risk. Continuity is essential. Services must be provided throughout the early years without significant periods of interruption.

FIGURE 3–2 A Sample Individualized Family Service Plan (IFSP)

Background Information

Child's Name:	Mary	
Family's Name:	Smith	
Date of Birth:	12-26-87	Age: 20 mo.
County:		

Family Member's Name: / Relationship to Child:

Family Member's Name:	Relationship to Child:
Susan Smith	mother
Ann Smith	older sister

Family Support Plan Team

Name	Title	Agency	Date
Susan	Parent		
Jane Jones	Case Coordinator	Home-Based Program	8-1-88
John Johnson	Speech Pathologist	Home-Based Program	8-1-88
Linda Williams	Teacher	Home-Based Program	8-1-88
Don Hunter	Psychologist	Home-Based Program	8-1-88
Pat Bennett	Nurse	Public Health Department	8-1-88

Team Review Dates

30 Days:	3 Months:	6 Months:	9 Months:
9-1-89	11-3-90	2-2-90	5-4-90

Source: From *Developing Individualized Family Support Plans* (pp. 168–170) by T. Bennett, B. V. Lingerfelt, and D. E. Nelson, 1990, Cambridge, MA: Brookline Publishing. Copyright 1990 by Brookline Publishing. Reprinted by permission.

Child's Name _____ Mary Smith

Family's Name _____ Smith

CHILD'S FUNCTIONING LEVEL

Domain	CA	Age Level/Range	Domain	CA	Age Level/Range
Social Adapt.	20 mo.	14 mo. (10-16)	Fine motor	20 mo.	10 mo. (7-12)
Gross motor	20 mo.	13 mo. (11-14)	Hearing/Speech	20 mo.	14 mo. (12-16)
Per-social	20 mo.	11 mo. (9-15)	Performance	20 mo.	10 mo. (8-10)

CHILD'S STRENGTHS

She is alert and interacts a lot with people. She engages in smiling behavior. She attends to sounds and voices and uses several words (yes, no). She explores her environment through crawling and shows a lot of initiative.

FAMILY'S STRENGTHS

Commitment to staying together and helping Mary live as normal a life as possible. Communication between mother and children is good. Has wide informal support network with family and friends, has positive outlook on the situation.

RESOURCES AND SUPPORT SERVICES

	Dates	
	Started	Ended
Department of Social Services	8-1-88	3-89
SSI	8-1-88	
Home-based services	8-1-88	
Employment Security Commission	9-18-88	

RESOURCES AND SUPPORT SERVICES

	Dates	
	Started	Ended

| Child's Name | Mary | | Family's Name | Smith | | IFSP # | | FIPP Staff Member | Jane Jones |

Date / #	NEED/PROJECT OUTCOME STATEMENT	SOURCE OF SUPPORT/ RESOURCE	COURSE OF ACTION	FAMILY'S EVALUATION Date	Rating
9-1-89 / 3	Mary will locate food placed in front of her in order to learn to feed herself.	mom, family, friends case coordinator will provide information on feeding strategies	Adults caring for Mary will place her in her high chair with a cracker on the tray at snacks and mealtimes. During weekly home visits, the case coordinator will present information on feeding and answer questions.	9-1-89 9-18-89 9-29-89	2 3 3
9-1-89 / 4	Mary will make sounds when presented with familiar objects, sounds, and smells to increase her communication abilities.	mom, family, friends case coordinator will provide information on teaching strategies	Adults caring for Mary will talk with her about familiar objects, sounds, and smells during everyday activities and reinforce her sounds, encourage Mary to repeat the name of the object, sound, or smell. During weekly home visits, the case coordinator will present information on encouraging vocalizations.	9-1-89 9-29-89 10-13-89 11-3-89	2 3 3 3
9-1-89 / 5	Mary will find toys placed just out of her reach to begin exploring her environment.	mom, family, friends case coordinator will provide information on teaching strategies	Mom will arrange an area at home for Mary with her toys, and adults caring for Mary will encourage her to find toys within this area. During weekly home visits, the case coordinator will present information on encouraging exploration.	9-1-89 9-18-89 9-29-89 11-3-89	2 2 3 7
9-1-89 / 6	Mary will make transitions from sitting to standing in order to eventually walk.	mom, family, friends case coordinator will provide information on teaching strategies	Adults caring for Mary will place cushions on the floor and use a favorite toy to encourage her to climb on the cushions and pull to standing at the couch. During weekly home visits, the case coordinator will present information on motor development.	9-1-89 9-18-89 9-29-89 10-13-89 11-3-89	2 2 2 3 3

Family's Evaluations:
1...Situation changed, no longer a need
2...Situation unchanged, still a need, goal or project
3...Implementation begun, still a need, goal or project

4...Outcome partially attained or accomplished
5...Outcome accomplished or attained, but not to the family's satisfaction
6...Outcome mostly accomplished or attained to the family's satisfaction
7...Outcome completely accomplished or attained to the family's satisfaction

Date	#	NEED/PROJECT OUTCOME STATEMENT	SOURCE OF SUPPORT/ RESOURCE	COURSE OF ACTION	FAMILY'S EVALUATION Date	Rating
9-1-89	1	Susan will obtain employment in order to adequately meet her financial responsibilities for herself and her two children.	case coordinator—support to mom Susan Susan's mother—babysitting Susan's brother—babysitting Employment Security	Susan will fill out the appropriate forms at Employment Security Commission to start the process of finding a job. She will familiarize herself with their process and be aware of what her responsibilities are. Susan will talk with her mother and brother about babysitting while she interviews for	9-1-89 9-18-89 9-29-89 10-13-89 11-3-89	2 3 3 3 7
			Commission—employment possibilities	jobs. Susan will also continue to read the classified ads in the paper and follow through on any job leads she feels might pertain to her. During weekly home visits, the case coordinator will check with Susan about progress in looking for a job.		
9-1-89	2	Susan will find a day-care center in order to provide adequate supervision of her children enabling her to maintain a full-time job.	case coordinator—will act as consultant and resource to mom Chamber of Commerce—list of day-care ctrs. friends—names of day-care centers church members—names of day-care centers	Susan will obtain a list of possible day-care centers from friends, the Chamber of Commerce, church members, Department of Social Services (DSS), and the newspaper. Susan will find out information such as types and ages of children served, cost, hours open, and other general information. At weekly home visits, the case coordinator will share information about what to look	9-1-89 9-18-89 9-29-89 10-13-89 11-3-89	2 3 2 4 7
			Dept. of Soc. Services—names of day-care centers newspapers—names of day-care centers Susan's mother—babysitting Susan's brother—babysitting	for in day-care centers. Susan will narrow her list down to her top three choices and visit these programs personally before coming to a final decision. Susan's mother and brother can babysit while Susan visits day-care centers. Susan's children will then be enrolled in the chosen day-care center.		

Family's Evaluations:
1...Situation changed, no longer a need
2...Situation unchanged, still a need, goal or project
3...Implementation begun, still a need, goal or project

4...Outcome partially attained or accomplished
5...Outcome accomplished or attained, but not to the family's satisfaction
6...Outcome mostly accomplished or attained or attained to the family's satisfaction
7...Outcome completely accomplished or attained to the family's satisfaction

Children with disabilities have the right to the same educational opportunities available to all other children. (Bob Abraham/The Stock Market)

■ **Table 3–1** A Synthesis of "Best Practice" Guidelines for Early Childhood Services

INTEGRATED

Supported placement in generic early childhood service sites.

Systematic contact with [nondisabled] peers.

Planned integration at all levels.

COMPREHENSIVE

Comprehensive assessment, planning, programming, service coordination, and evaluation.

Models theoretically and procedurally well-defined.

Transdisciplinary approach to the delivery of related services.

Direct instruction of generalized responding.

NORMALIZED

Support for parenting role.

Age appropriate skills and instructional strategies.

Concurrent training across skill areas.

Distributed practice across settings.

Establishment of self-initiated responding.

Avoidance of artificial reinforcement and aversive control techniques.

ADAPTABLE

Flexible procedures within noncategorical models.

Support of different family structures.

Emphasis on function rather than form of response.

Programming changes based on individual, formative evaluation.

PEER AND FAMILY REFERENCED

Curriculum that is referenced to individual child, family, peers, and community.

Parents are full partners in educational planning and decision making.

Systematic communication between family and service providers.

Planned enhancement of child's skill development within daily family routine.

OUTCOME BASED

Variety of outcome measures.

Preparation for future integrated settings.

Curricular emphasis on skills with present and future utility.

Transition planning.

Source: From "A Synthesis of 'Best Practice' Guidelines for Early Childhood Services" by A. P. McDonnell and M. L. Hardman, 1988, *Journal of the Division for Early Childhood, 12*(4), 328–341. Copyright by the Division for Early Childhood, the Council for Exceptional Children.

Early Childhood Services for Preschool-Age Children

The right to special education and related services, as mandated in PL 94-142 (now referred to as IDEA), was extended directly to children between the ages of 3 and 5 years by PL 99-457 (amendments to the Education of the Handicapped Act, 1986). Programs for preschool-age children with disabilities have several critical aspects. First, a **child-find** system is set up in each state to attempt to locate young children who are at risk and make referrals to appropriate agencies for preschool services. An IEP is then developed for each eligible child, using a multidisciplinary approach. Specialists from several disciplines—including physical therapy, occupational therapy, speech and language therapy, pediatrics, social work, and special education—participate in the development and implementation of IEPs for these children.

The purpose of preschool programs for young children with disabilities is to assist them in living in and adapting to a variety of environmental settings, including the home, neighborhood, and school. Depending on individual needs, preschool programs may focus on such content areas as language development, social skills, motor proficiency, and preacademic instruction. Westlake and Kaiser (1991) proposed several principles for guiding early childhood services for students with severe disabilities that have direct relevance for all preschool-age children with disabilities. First, young children with disabilities have the right to services that improve the quality of life and maximize developmental potential. In addition, the earlier the services begin, the more effective they will be in improving quality of life. Finally, services that involve families are more effective than those that do not.

In a review of the literature on "best practice" guidelines for early childhood services, McDonnell and Hardman (1988) identified six characteristics of exemplary programs for young children with disabilities. Exemplary programs are (1) integrated, (2) comprehensive, (3) normalized, (4) adaptable, (5) peer and family referenced, and (6) outcome based. Table 3–1 provides a synthesis of these guidelines.

In summary, early childhood programs for children with disabilities focus on teaching skills to improve opportunities and access within family, school, and neighborhood environments. These children are prepared as early as possible for meaningful experiences with

FOCUS 2

Identify the critical components of programs for preschool-age children under Public Law 99-457.

R E F L E C T   O N   T H I S

3–1 A Preschool Classroom That Accommodates Diversity

This classroom is organized around several play areas. You immediately notice that more than one activity is happening at once. In one area, three children are naming animals shown in bright, colorful photographs held up by the teacher. In another area, one child is practicing buttoning with large buttons sewn to canvas fabric. Four children are playing quietly with blocks near a teacher, who calls them from this group one at a time and works with each child for 10 to 15 minutes. At the back of the room, one child is walking on a long, wooden board about 6 feet long and 12 inches wide. A paraprofessional is working with the child on balance as she counts each step on the board and praises the child for her efforts.

If you were to stay for an entire session in this classroom, you would notice that children change activities under teacher direction. The daily schedule paces the children through a sequence of specific learning activities. At several points, the children come together as a group. One such point is for lunch, where careful attention is paid to the task of getting ready to eat, to some of the children's eating skills, and to cleaning up. The music time is for everyone, as is a brief outdoor play period, but most of the time is spent in small groups or one-to-one instruction. If you were to ask the head teacher of this classroom how he decided what the children would do, he would tell you that the decision was different for each child. He would explain that decisions were based on a battery of tests administered to each child to determine individual needs and by the daily recording of each child's progress in each instructional area.

Source: From *Early Intervention for Handicapped and At-Risk Children* by N. L. Peterson, 1987, Denver: Love Publishing. Copyright 1987 by Love Publishing. Adapted by permission.

same-age peers. Additionally, early childhood programs lessen the impact of conditions that may worsen or become more severe without timely and adequate treatment and may prevent children from developing other, secondary disabling conditions. The intended outcomes of these programs will not, however, be accomplished without consistent family participation and professional collaboration.

THE SCHOOL-AGE YEARS

FOCUS 3

What is meant by *adaptive fit* and *adaptive instruction* for students with disabilities?

As we move from preschool into the elementary school years, the emphasis shifts to whether the child who is exceptional can adapt (academically, behaviorally, and physically) to the demands of the regular education environment. The degree to which the child is able to cope with these demands depends on the type and severity of the disability as well as how effectively the school will accommodate his or her needs. A student with a mild disability may be viewed as a discipline problem, a slow learner, or a poorly motivated child. The differences are more pronounced for students with moderate and severe problems and require more extensive educational interventions. Performance deficits of these individuals are evident in several environmental settings, including the home, community, and school.

The degree to which a student is able to cope with requirements of a school setting and the extent to which the school recognizes and accommodates individual diversity is known as **adaptive fit.** The process is dynamic and involves continuous negotiation between the individual and the environment in order to support mutual coexistence.

From the perspective of the student who is exceptional, adaptive fit describes his or her attempt to meet the expectations of various learning environments. Such a student may find that the requirements for success within public education are beyond his or her adaptive capabilities and that the system is not able to accommodate his or her academic, behavioral, physical, sensory, and communicative differences. The result is the development of negative student attitudes toward the educational environment. Imagine yourself in a setting that constantly disapproves of how you act and what you do, a place where activities are difficult and overwhelming, a setting in which your least desirable qualities are emphasized. What would you think about spending more than 1,000 hours a year in such a place?

Over the years, education has responded in several ways to situations where the needs of the student and the demands of the environment do not match. One approach has been to remove the student from the environment and place him or her in a situation that is more conducive to his or her needs. Another approach has been to leave the student in the negative situation and do nothing until there is inevitable failure. Still another approach has been to attempt to create the adaptive fit between the student and the learning environment through instruction. **Adaptive instruction**

W I N D O W   3–2

YVONNE

Yvonne left her preschool program at age 5 to attend her neighborhood elementary school. From kindergarten through sixth grade, she divided her day between a regular education classroom with her friends who were not disabled and a special education class with her friends who were disabled. Her educational program during the elementary years focused on developing basic academic skills, learning to manage her own personal affairs, and promoting socialization activities with her friends. Yvonne's rate of academic learning was significantly slower than that of other children her age, and she required extensive specialized instruction in reading and arithmetic. She also needed assistance in such areas as developing age-appropriate personal hygiene skills, managing her time, socially interacting with her peers, and participating in recreational and leisure-time activities.

modifies the learning environment to accommodate the unique learning characteristics and needs of individual students, and it provides direct or focused intervention to improve each student's capabilities to successfully acquire subject-matter knowledge and higher-order reasoning and problem-solving skills, to work independently and cooperatively with peers, and to meet the overall intellectual and social demands of schooling. (Wang, 1989, p. 183)

Adaptive instruction focuses on assessing each student's individual characteristics and capabilities. A variety of instructional procedures, materials, and alternative learning sequences are utilized in the classroom setting to help students master content at a rate consistent with their abilities and interests. Students are expected to take on increased responsibility for planning and monitoring their learning (Walberg & Wang, 1987; Wang 1989).

For some time, the regular classroom teacher has had to work with students who are disabled without the assistance of any effective support systems. This is no longer the case in many of today's schools. The emergence of collaborative efforts between the classroom teacher and the specialists available in the public schools represents a major breakthrough in the education of individuals who are exceptional.

Educational Partnerships: Sharing the Responsibility

Collaboration may be defined as one or more people working together to attain a common goal. There are several models for partnerships between regular educators, special educators, and other support professionals in the public schools that are intended to enhance each student's educational experience. We will discuss two of these models: the **consulting teacher,** and the **resource-room teacher.** Services provided through each of these collaborative models are intended to support a student in meeting the demands of the regular education environment.

FOCUS 4
Define *collaboration,* and distinguish between the consulting teacher and resource-room teacher.

The Consulting Teacher.   The regular classroom teacher, particularly at the elementary level, is expected to teach nearly every school-related subject area. The elementary classroom teacher is responsible for teaching the basic subjects—reading, writing, and arithmetic—as well as developing students' appreciation for the arts, good citizenship, and physical health. This teacher is trained as a *generalist,* acquiring basic knowledge of every subject

Professionals representing many different disciplines and viewpoints may work together to establish educational programs for students with special needs. (Susan Fish)

area. However, when the regular classroom teacher is confronted with instructional needs that are beyond his or her experience and training, the result is often frustration for the teacher and failure for the student. Given the present structure of public education (large class sizes), it is unrealistic and unnecessary for classroom teachers to become specialists in every school subject.

Many school districts offer support to regular classroom teachers through the services of professionals who have extensive background in specialized areas, such as reading, arithmetic, language, motor development, and behavior and classroom management techniques. Professionals in these areas are usually referred to as *consulting teachers,* although the terms **curriculum specialists, master teachers,** and **itinerant teachers** may also be used.

Effective consultants usually have several important characteristics. They are often professionals with advanced training beyond the basic teacher certification program, and are "knowledgeable about a variety of instructional strategies" (Schulz, Carpenter, & Turnbull, 1991). They are able to build mutually trusting relationships through positive interactions with other professionals. Effective consultants are responsive to others and have a good understanding of the dynamics of social interaction. They view consultation as a learning experience for themselves as well as the professionals and students they serve. Effective consultants are also very concrete and specific in making suggestions to improve students' educational experiences but are capable of looking at issues from broad theoretical perspectives. Finally, effective consultants are good researchers who know how to locate and use resources effectively (Reynolds & Birch, 1988).

The consulting-teacher model includes training and support for regular classroom teachers and an emphasis on modifying the regular education environment to accommodate students who are exceptional, rather than move them to separate settings. In a class of 25 to 30 children, 2 or more students are likely to have learning or behavioral needs that require the classroom teacher to access the services of a consulting teacher.

The Resource Room.   In the resource-room model, the student receives specialized instruction in a classroom that is separate from the regular education setting but still within the same school building. While still receiving the majority of instruction in their regular education classroom, students come to the resource room for short periods during the day to supplement their school curricula. The resource room is not intended to be a study hall, where students do their homework or spend time catching up on other classwork. Instead, the resource room is under the direction of a qualified special education teacher whose role is to provide individualized instruction in academic or behavioral areas that negatively affect each student's chances for success in the regular classroom. The resource-room teacher identifies high-risk skill areas in collaboration with an educational team that includes the student's regular classroom teacher. This team then develops and implements instruction intended to increase proficiency to a level where the student is competitive with classmates.

It can be anticipated that approximately 1 or 2 students in a classroom of 25 to 30 (about 6 percent of the school-age population) will need the additional instructional services offered by the resource-room program. In order to support resource-room programs through federal and state special education funds, many states require that all students who receive direct special education services be labeled. Therefore, in order to adhere to the concept of the least restrictive environment, students who receive instruction through resource-room programs, by definition, have educational needs that require assistance beyond that available in regular classrooms.

The resource-room model has some important features that differ from the traditional self-contained special education classroom. The resource-room model allows students to remain with age-mates for the majority of the school day, eliminating a great deal of the

3-2 Working as a Team Member— What's My Role?

A team is a group of professionals, parents, and/or students who join together to plan and implement an appropriate educational program for a student at risk or with a disability. Team members may be trained in different areas of study, including education, health services, speech and language, school administration, and so on. The idea behind the team approach is that these individual people sit down together and coordinate their efforts to help the student, regardless of where or how they were trained. In order for this to work, each team member must clearly understand his or her role and responsibilities as a member of the team. Let's visit with some team members and have them share their perceived role in relationship to working with a student.

Consultant or Resource-Room Teacher

It's my responsibility to coordinate the student's individualized education program. I work with each member of the team to assist in selecting, administering, and interpreting appropriate assessment information. I maintain ongoing communication with each team member to ensure that we are all working together to help the student. It's my responsibility to compile, organize, and maintain good, accurate records on each student. I propose instructional alternatives for the student and work with others in the implementation of the recommended instruction. To carry this out, I locate or develop the necessary materials to meet each student's specific needs. I work directly with the student's parents to ensure that they are familiar with what is being taught at school and can reinforce school learning experiences at home.

Parents

We work with each team member to ensure that our child is involved in an appropriate educational program. We give information to the team about our child's life outside school and suggest experiences that might be relevant to the home and the community. We also work with our child at home to reinforce what is learned in school. As members of the team, we give our written consent for any evaluations of our child and any changes in our child's educational placement.

School Psychologist

I select, administer, and interpret appropriate psychological, educational, and behavioral assessment instruments. I consult directly with team members regarding the student's overall educational development. It is also my responsibility to directly observe the student's performance in the classroom and assist in the design of appropriate behavioral management programs in the school and at home.

School Administrator

As the school district's representative, I work with the team to ensure that the resources of my district are used appropriately in providing services to the student. I am ultimately responsible for ensuring that the team's decisions are implemented properly.

Regular Classroom Teacher

I work with the team to develop and implement appropriate educational experiences for the student during the time that he or she spends in my classroom. I ensure that the student's experiences outside my classroom are consistent with the instruction he or she receives from me. In carrying out my responsibilities, I keep an accurate and continuous record of the student's progress. I am also responsible for referring any other students in my classroom who are at risk and may need specialized services to the school district for an evaluation of their needs.

These individuals generally constitute the core members of the team, but the team is not limited to this group. Depending on the needs of the student, many other professionals sometimes serve as team members, including speech and language specialists, social workers, school counselors, school nurses, occupational or physical therapists, adaptive physical education teachers, vocational rehabilitation counselors, juvenile court authorities, physicians, and school media coordinators.

stigma associated with segregated special education classrooms. The resource-room model also provides support to the regular classroom teacher, who, despite realizing that these students have potential for success in the regular classroom, finds it extremely difficult to provide appropriate individualized instruction to one or two students.

Collaboration through Schoolwide Assistance and Support. With the movement toward a stronger collaborative relationship among regular educators, special educators, and other school support personnel there has been an increased emphasis on developing schoolwide support or assistance to professionals and students. This essentially means

FOCUS 5
Describe several approaches to achieving a collaborative relationship between regular and special educators.

sharing both a school's human and material resources to meet the individual needs of students who are at risk or disabled. Typically, resources within a school are distributed based on standard staffing patterns: Regular educators work with "their kids," and special educators work with "their kids." Although this procedure may ensure equitable distribution of resources across students who are at risk, it is not sensitive to their varying needs. If a school is to be effective in meeting the needs of all students, flexibility is necessary in order to address individual diversity.

To meet the challenges of individual student diversity, schools have developed support networks that facilitate collaboration across professionals. **Teacher assistance teams (TATs),** sometimes referred to as **schoolwide assistance teams (SWATs),** involve groups of professionals, students, and/or parents working together to "brain storm, problem solve, and exchange ideas, methods, techniques, and activities directed at assisting a teacher and/or student requiring help" (Stainback & Stainback, 1989, p. 73). TATs use strategies designed to assist teachers in making appropriate referrrals of students who may need special education services as well as those at risk in the regular classroom who may not qualify for such services but still need additional support.

There are several perspectives on how to effectively use the variety of professionals required to implement TATs and SWATs. The three common teaming approaches are (1) **multidisciplinary,** (2) **interdisciplinary,** and (3) **transdisciplinary.** These approaches are somewhat different in the way they view the assessment, implementation, and evaluation process.

A *multidisciplinary* approach involves the expertise of several professionals who usually work independently of one another. These professionals conduct independent assessments, write and implement separate program plans, and evaluate progress within the parameters of their own disciplines. This process may be modified by having each of the professionals conduct an independent assessment and write a separate program plan but then forward the data to one person (usually, the educator), who alone would be responsible for implementing and evaluating the entire program.

The *interdisciplinary* approach represents a significant alteration in the process. During the assessment phase, team members still undertake independent assessments, but program development is carried out as a collaborative effort. A group decision is made about what areas are of greatest priority for the student. Based on these priorities, a program is developed and appropriate personnel are assigned to implement it. A student is viewed from several perspectives in order to ascertain the areas of need that must be met in the time available. One problem with the interdisciplinary approach, however, is that, beyond the program development phase, interaction among professionals often ceases, since no single person coordinates their efforts.

The *transdisciplinary* approach is essentially a response to the shortcomings of the other two approaches (see Figure 3–3). In this approach, the critical concept is the introduction of a primary therapist or teacher. This person is designated as the transdisciplinary team leader to avoid compartmentalization and fragmentation of services, thus reducing the number of professionals working in isolation of each other in implementing a student's program. Although the transdisciplinary approach is similar to the interdisciplinary approach in that team members cooperate during both the initial assessment and planning phases, instruction is carried out by one member in collaboration with the others. Each team member supports the primary therapist and other members of the team in meeting individual needs, although no one individual dominates the others (Hart, 1977; Morskink, Thomas, & Correa, 1991).

Regardless of what approach is used in the schools, the team process is the key to an appropriate education program. Interaction among professionals in conjunction with input from parents forms the core to greater understanding and eventual long-term success.

FIGURE 3–3 The Transdisciplinary Approach to Teaming

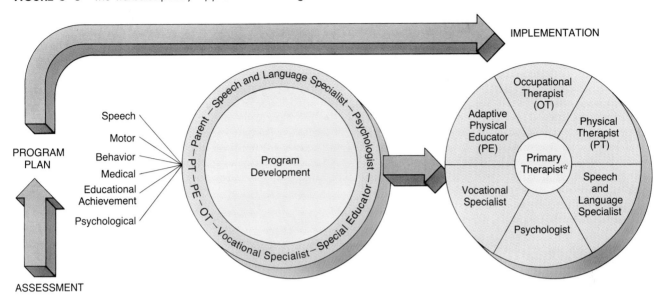

☆ This role may be filled by a special educator.

Role of the Regular Education Classroom Teacher. Today's classroom teachers are confronted with the challenge of educating all students to the point that they will be able to face the complex demands of society. At the same time, classroom teachers are faced with an increased responsibility to meet the needs of those students who require additional instructional support in order to succeed in school. The integration of students who are at risk or have disabilities into regular education schools and/or classrooms need not be met with frustration, anger, or refusal on the part of teachers. These reactions are merely symptomatic of the confusion surrounding the term mainstreaming.

Mainstreaming, in many educational circles, has been synonymous with *dumping,* that is, returning the student with a disability to regular education without any support service to the classroom teacher and at the expense of other students in the class. As we discussed earlier in this chapter, placing students in regular education classrooms without needed support services is not in the best interests of teachers or students.

Regular classroom teachers often have the responsibility for implementing an appropriate educational program for students at risk or with a disability in conjunction with schools' TATs. In order to meet the needs of these students and to function as informed team members, regular classroom teachers should receive expanded training during both their initial university preparation and as a component of their ongoing professional development. It is important for classroom teachers to:

1. Understand how a student's learning, behavior, communication, and physical differences affect his or her ability to acquire academic skills or cope socially in the educational environment
2. Identify students who may be in need of additional educational support
3. Make referrals to the TAT for testing and evaluation of students perceived as being at risk

FOCUS 6
Describe the role of the regular classroom teacher in meeting the needs of students with disabilities.

INTERACTING IN NATURAL SETTINGS ·············· Working with Consultants ················

The following tips are recommended for regular classroom teachers working directly with consultants:

◆ You are in charge of the problem and the class procedures that are under consideration.

◆ Be sure to reach early agreement with the consultant on the nature of the problem and how plans for the solution will be made. An oral or written contract on goals, methods, and responsibilities should be agreed on early in the relationship.

◆ It should be made clear that you are the client and that all communication should go directly to you. The consultant is there to help structure your work, not somebody else's. This relationship does not preclude some direct assessment of children and observations by the consultant, if they are agreed on as part of the contract.

◆ Status problems should be avoided. You and the consultant are coequals.

◆ Avoid interjecting personal problems. The content of the relationship should center on the student and/or the instructional situation.

◆ Try to seek alternative suggestions from the consultant rather than a single or set plan that might not work.

◆ Try to use each consultation as a learning experience to increase effective communication and listening, build trust, and maximize instructional effectiveness.

◆ Each consultation experience should be evaluated objectively, and you should share your conclusions with the consultant.

Source: From *Adaptive Mainstreaming: A Primer for Teachers and Principals* 3d ed. by Maynard Reynolds and Jack W. Birch. Copyright © 1988 by Longman Publishing Group. Reprinted with permission.

4. Work with team members to develop and implement individualized instruction in the regular classroom
5. Initiate and maintain ongoing communication with parents

The role for the regular classroom teacher extends not only to students with mild differences but also to those with more severe disabilities. As is true for all students, an important component of success in the regular education environment for students with severe disabilities is the cooperative relationship among the regular classroom teacher, special education teacher, and school support team. The role of the regular classroom teacher is to work with the team in creating opportunities for inclusion of students with disabilities in natural settings. Inclusion may be achieved by having the regular class serve as a homeroom for the student; by developing opportunities for students with severe disabilities to be with their nondisabled peers as often as possible during the day in such activities as recess, lunch, assemblies, and music classes; and by developing a peer support program (Giangreco & Putnam, 1991; Sailor, Gerry, & Wilson, 1991; Stainback & Stainback, 1989).

WINDOW 3–3

WHAT WILL I DO WITH THESE KIDS?

I remember the first year that I taught third grade and someone mentioned to me that there would undoubtedly be at least one or two students with disabilities in my class. I thought to myself, No kidding? I don't have the training, background, or experience to be dealing with these students. What on earth will I do with these kids?

It didn't take long for me to find out that these two students, labeled *learning disabled* and *behavior disordered,* could and should be in my classroom with their nondisabled peers. Oh, I've needed help, but through the assistance of our school's special education consultant, these kids have progressed right along with the rest of my third-graders. Marie, our special education consultant, has given me some terrific ideas about behavior management, adapting instructional programs, and dealing with my students' questions about children who don't learn in the same way that they do. These students belong in my class, and they deserve the support that will help them stay there. I know that neither they nor I would have it any other way.

Tricia, A Third-Grade Teacher

W I N D O W 3–4

PEER TUTORING
A Growth Experience for Everyone*

Dear Ronaldo:

I would like to thank you for making my first period one of the most enjoyable classes in all of my educational days. You lightened up those days that started out badly and I walked out of that class smiling from ear to ear. So that is the purpose of this note my friend, so that you will know how much you did for my self-esteem. A little help is all it takes from someone special to put a person back on his feet again and that is what you have always done. You are a true friend.

Justin

Peer tutoring at Viewmont High School has developed into more than just a class to take or an empty slot to fill in a student's schedule. At Viewmont students sign up for peer tutoring to learn something about persons with disabilities and leave peer tutoring with a better understanding of themselves, human relationships, differences, abilities, and the worth of each student as an individual. As one former tutor stated, "At first I was a little uncomfortable, but after a relationship is established with the students the learning process begins for both me and the student. This I think is the goal of peer tutoring."

To achieve this goal the teacher must of course go through the process of recruitment, training, and evaluation of peer tutors. But more importantly, the teacher needs to be committed to the idea of peer tutors being a valued and integral part of the overall program. I tell my tutors that they are the life blood of the program. They enjoy more freedom in my class than in most others but I point out that with freedom comes responsibility. I expect and demand the best from them and I always get it.

To ensure that peer tutoring will be a growth experience for both the tutor and the student with a disability the teacher should be committed to the usefulness and success of the program, treat tutors as responsible individuals, establish TRUST between teacher and tutor, have high expectations, be firm but fair, be or-

ganized, have a sense of humor, be a role model for acceptance of individual differences, and LOVE WHAT YOU ARE DOING.

Peer tutoring without question benefits the individual with a disability. As we continue from year to year with the program we discover that perhaps it is the nondisabled student who benefits the most.

Gayle Baker, A High School Teacher of Students with Severe Disabilities

Being a Peer Tutor**

Mike, a first-string tackle on the football team:

Before I started the [peer tutor] program, I thought kids with mental retardation couldn't even learn to do the basic things. Now I realize that they do learn and that the program is worth the time.

Dave, the student body president at his high school:

I know my job is to teach them, but really they teach me just as much if not more. I've learned that everybody can learn and that everybody has something to contribute. I've learned they're more like me than they are different.

Sheila, who has been a peer tutor for two years:

Sometimes it's hard. The improvements that these guys make are small and they have to work hard to make those changes . . . I feel for them. But it puts my own schoolwork into perspective. If they can work that hard, I guess I should be able to.

Sources: * Baker, G. (1990). Peer Tutoring: A Growth Experience for Both Sides. *Utah Special Educator, 2* (2), 1990. Reprinted with permission. ** From *Secondary Programs for Students with Developmental Disabilities* (p. 230) by J. McDonnell, B. Wilcox, and M. L. Hardman, 1991, Boston: Allyn and Bacon. Copyright 1991 by Allyn and Bacon. Reprinted by permission.

Peer Support. One resource to classroom teachers that is readily available within the school but often overlooked is students. Peers can be a powerful support system within the classroom in both academic and behavioral areas. They often have more influence on their classmates' behavior than the teacher does. Peer support programs may range from simply creating opportunities in the class for students with disabilities to socially interact with their nondisabled peers on a regular basis to highly structured programs of **peer-mediated instruction.** Peer-mediated instruction includes "a variety of structured interactions between two or more students, designed or planned by a school staff member . . . to achieve academic and social-emotional goals" (Miller & Peterson, 1987, p. 81). This instruction generally falls into three areas: (1) group–oriented contingency programs; (2) **peer and cross-**

age tutoring; and (3) **cooperative learning.** As described by Zins, Curtis, Graden, and Ponti (1988):

> Cross-age and peer tutoring emphasize individual student learning, while cooperative learning emphasizes the simultaneous learning of students as they strive to achieve group goals or group rewards. Group contingencies provide consequences to group members based on group behavior, but they do not directly promote the goals inherent in cooperative learning, such as group collaboration. (p. 114)

Peers are often very reliable and effective in implementing both academic and behavioral programs with their classmates who are disabled. The effectiveness of peers, however, is dependent on carefully managing the program so that students both with and without disabilities benefit (see Window 3–4). It is important for teachers to carefully select, train, and monitor the performance of students working as peer tutors (McDonnell, Wilcox, & Hardman, 1991).

Special Education Classrooms and Schools

FOCUS 7

Describe special education classrooms and schools for students with disabilities.

It is the view of some professionals and parents that neither the consulting-teacher model nor the resource-room model is appropriate to meet certain students' needs. These students require more intensive and specialized educational services provided in either a self-contained special education classroom or a special school for students with disabilities.

The Self-Contained Special Education Classroom.   The self-contained special education classroom employs the expertise of a qualified special education teacher to work with students who are disabled during most if not all of the school day. This teacher may still create opportunities for students with disabilities to interact with nondisabled peers whenever appropriate, for instance, through academically and nonacademically oriented classes, lunch and playground breaks, school events, peer-tutor programs, and so forth.

The Special School.   Students with disabilities may also be placed in special schools. Proponents of this arrangement have argued that special schools provide services for large numbers of disabled students and therefore provide greater homogeneity in grouping and programing. This type of arrangement has also been supported because it allows teachers to specialize in their subject areas. For example, one individual might decide to teach art, another physical education, and a third math. In small programs, where there are only one or two teachers, these individuals may be required to teach everything from art and home economics to academic subjects. Proponents have also argued that special schools provide for the centralization of supplies, equipment, and special facilities.

Opponents have argued that research on the efficacy of special schools does not support the proponents' rationale. Several authors have contended that, regardless of the severity of their disabling condition, children benefit from placement in a regular education facility, where opportunities for inclusion with nondisabled peers are systematically planned and implemented (Brinker, 1985; McDonnell & Hardman, 1988; Sailor et al., 1989; Sailor et al., 1990; Snell, 1991; Stainback, Stainback, & Forrest, 1989).

Full Inclusion versus Pull-out Programs

FOCUS 8

Identify the arguments for and against the pull-out of students with disabilities from regular education classrooms.

The philosophy behind resource rooms and self-contained special education classrooms has been the predominant instructional approach for students with disabilities over the past two decades. This approach is commonly referred to as **pull-out programs**—removing the student with a disability from the regular classroom to a separate class for at least part of the school day.

A growing group of both regular and special educators has argued that, even though there have been some accomplishments in the pull-out programs, there have also been some negative effects or obstacles to the appropriate education of students with disabilities (Allington & McGill-Franzen, 1989; Gartner & Lipsky, 1987, 1989; Jenkins, Pious, & Jewell, 1990; Lipsky & Gartner, 1991; Stainback & Stainback, 1991; Will, 1986). The proponents of **full inclusion** (sometimes referred to as the **regular education initiative**) have argued that the current system of pulling students out of regular education simply does not work. It fails to serve the individualized needs of each student. Such programs result in a fragmented approach to the delivery of special education programs, with little cooperation between regular and special educators. Students in pull-out programs are stigmatized when segregated from their nondisabled peers.

The proponents of full inclusion have also argued that placement in regular education classrooms with a partnership between regular and special educators results in a learning environment that is diverse and rich, rather than just a series of discrete programing slots and funding pots. A partnership between regular and special education personalizes each student's instructional program and implements it in the least restrictive environment, rather than removing the child to a separate program. Additionally, special educators are more effective in a partnership because they can bring their knowledge and resources to assist regular educators in developing intervention strategies that are directly oriented to student needs in the natural setting of the regular education classroom.

Opponents of full inclusion, as discussed above (Braaten, Kauffman, Braaten, Polsgrove, & Nelson, 1988; Fuchs & Fuchs, 1991; Kauffman, 1991), have argued that regular education has little expertise in assisting students with learning problems and is already overburdened with large class sizes and inadequate support services. Special educators have been specifically trained to develop instructional strategies and use teaching techniques (e.g., behavior management) that are not part of the training of regular education teachers. More specialized academic and social instruction can be provided in a pull-out setting, and such a setting can more effectively prepare the student to return to the regular education classroom. Specialized pull-out settings also allow for centralization of both human and material resources.

A question appropriate to both supporters and detractors of shared responsibility focuses on whether professionals in the education system—including school administrators, regular class teachers, and special educators—are ready to embrace full inclusion in regular classrooms for students with disabilities. Jenkins et al. (1990) have formulated several questions that need to be addressed by schools in assessing their readiness for full inclusion:

1. To what extent do classroom teachers accept responsibilities for
   a. educating all students assigned to them,
   b. making and monitoring major instructional decisions for all students in their class,
   c. providing instruction that follows a normal developmental curriculum in the basic skills area that is designed to bring students to a level of adult competence,
   d. managing instruction for diverse populations, and
   e. seeking, using, and coordinating assistance for students who require more intense service than those provided to their peers;
2. To what extent do principals have sufficient knowledge about instruction and learning to distribute resources across classrooms so that students with special needs can be accommodated and served effectively?

3. To what extent are "specialists" . . . able to collaborate and communicate with classroom teachers and relinquish to them final authority regarding instructional decision making?

4. To what extent are multidisciplinary teams prepared to require hard evidence that students have received high-quality direct instruction from classroom teachers and support staff?

5. Are multidisciplinary teams prepared to decide that students will not develop competency in basic skills during their school career, and recommend that the students be segregated from their regular classroom peers? (pp. 481–482, 489)

FOCUS 9

Identify three curricular approaches that can be used in teaching students with disabilities.

An Instructional Decision-Making Model

Learning is a continual process of adaptation for students with disabilities as they attempt to cope with the demands of school. These students learn to adapt to the limited time constraints placed on them by the educational system. They do not learn as quickly or as efficiently as their classmates and are constantly fighting a battle against failure. They must somehow learn to deal with a system that is often rigid and allows little room for learning or behavior differences. Students with mild disabilities must also be able to adapt to a teaching process that may be oriented toward the majority of students within a regular classroom and not based on individualized assessment of needs or personalized instruction.

In spite of major obstacles, however, students with disabilities can learn to survive in the educational environment as well as develop social and academic skills that can orient them toward striving for success rather than fighting against failure. Success can be achieved only if the professional team remains flexible, adapting to meet the needs of these students.

An educational team plays an important role in creating the adaptive fit between the school environment and student needs. The team makes critical decisions concerning educational goals and objectives, the appropriate curricula, and least restrictive environment

FIGURE 3–4

An Instructional Decision-Making Model

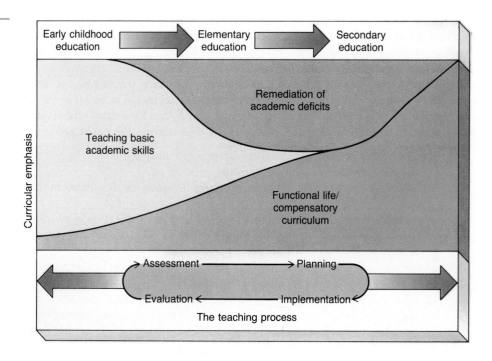

alternatives. The magnitude of these decisions is illustrated in Figure 3–4, which shows a three-dimensional model for instructional decision making. The first dimension of this model represents the curricular approaches that may be used in teaching students who are at risk or have disabilities. The second dimension focuses on the processes involved in teaching, including assessment, planning, implementation, and evaluation of a program. The third dimension is temporal: Only so much instructional time is available from the early childhood through the secondary years. Difficult decisions about what must be taught and when are critical in creating an appropriate educational experience for a child.

Three curricular approaches may be used in teaching students. The primary approach, termed the *learning of basic skills,* stresses that the student must learn a specified set of sequenced skills, each of which is prerequisite to the next. This process, sometimes referred to as the *developmental approach,* can be illustrated by briefly analyzing the foundation approach to teaching reading.

Hansen and Eaton (1978) defined the reading process as "a blend of many separate skills working in harmony. If one skill or cluster of skills is missing, the entire process breaks down and the child is unable to read or comprehend" (p. 41). The teaching of basic reading skills can be divided into three phases: (1) the development of readiness skills (left-to-right sequencing, visual and auditory discrimination skills, and memory skills); (2) the development of word-recognition or decoding skills (breaking the code and correctly identifying the abstract symbols in sequence); and (3) the development of reading comprehension (giving symbols meaning). The **basic-skills approach,** whether in reading or any other content area, lays the groundwork for further development and higher levels of functioning.

However, not all children learn basic skills within the timeframe dictated by the schools. Several alternatives are available to educators to assist students who do not learn in the traditional way or within the specified timeframe. One alternative is to remediate deficiencies in the student's repertoire of skills. According to the **remediation approach,** specific deficiencies are identified by determining what skills the student does or does not have and then locating appropriate materials and instructional approaches to achieve mastery. This approach focuses on helping the learner to adapt to the content and method of instruction that is provided for a majority of students in the learning situation. Skill deficiencies may be the result of either poor teaching or lack of ability on the part of the student. Therefore, it is doubtful that the learner's behavior can be changed by simply repeating that which resulted in failure—asking the student to try harder, in other words. Teaching must be more systematic and precise if deficits are to be remediated.

Another alternative for educators is to teach skills using a **functional life/compensatory approach.** Following this approach, students are taught only those skills that will facilitate their accommodation to the natural setting, whether it be the classroom, family, or neighborhood. As described by Brimer (1990), "The skills necessary for a person to control, modify, and interact with the environment receive the highest priority" (p. 364). Content areas taught within a functional approach might include daily living (e.g., self-care, consumer financing, and community travel), personal-social development (e.g., learning socially responsible behaviors), communication skills, recreational/leisure-time activities, and employment skills.

The functional approach is based on the premise that, if these practical skills are not taught through formal instruction, they will not be learned. Most students do not need to be taught functional skills because they have already learned them through everyday experience. However, the functional approach may be suited to students who cannot learn through basic or remedial approaches to instruction. This does not mean that students being taught using a functional approach are not also learning basic academics, such as reading, arithmetic, and handwriting. Instruction may occur in these areas but not in the same sequence as in the basic-skills approach. For example, a functional reading approach would

In order for mainstreaming programs to succeed, classroom teachers must be adequately trained to meet the learning and behavioral needs of students with disabilities. (Bachman/Stock, Boston)

initially teach words that are used frequently and are necessary for survival within the environment (e.g., *danger, exit, restrooms*). These words are paired directly with an environmental cue. Other examples of goals for functional reading programs might include:

♦ The student will locate information on restaurant menus and place an order.
♦ The student will carry out the directions written on grocery items, games, or specific items that require assembly.
♦ The student will respond appropriately to written information found on employment forms, work time cards, check stubs, grocery store receipts, and so on.

The educational team is confronted with some difficult decisions about how and what to teach. These decisions must take into account such factors as the student's age, previous learning history, performance demands in the natural setting, and available resources. In addition, decisions regarding a student's educational experience must consider time constraints. Instructional time in the classroom is limited, and decisions have to be made concerning how to use available time efficiently. Figure 3–4, the curricular decision-making model, illustrates that the time factor can be separated into three educational dimensions: early childhood, elementary, and secondary. The curricular emphasis is different for each dimension. For the young child (up to age 5), the world is defined primarily through the family and a small, same-age peer group. In the elementary school years, the child's world expands to include the school and neighborhood. During adolescence (i.e., secondary education) and eventually the adult years, the life space increases to a much larger heterogeneous environment called the community.

THE TRANSITION FROM SCHOOL TO ADULT LIFE

FOCUS 10

Cite three reasons why it is important to study the relationship between what is taught in school and the needs individuals have during adulthood.

For many years, the development of appropriate services for people with exceptionalities has focused primarily on school-age children. As we move toward the twenty-first century, one of the most critical issues facing students, parents, and professionals is determination of the relationship between school instruction and individual needs/preferences during adulthood. There are some substantial reasons why this issue is receiving such attention.

WINDOW 3–5

YVONNE AND MARK—CONTRASTING OPPORTUNITIES FOR TRANSITION SERVICES

Yvonne

Yvonne is now 22 and leaving school for adult life. During most of high school, she was in special education classes, receiving extra assistance and tutoring in reading and math. During the last term, she attended a class on finding and keeping jobs. This class was required for graduation, but it didn't make much sense to Yvonne. She had never taken anything like that before, and it didn't seem to be related to her other schoolwork.

Yvonne wants to get a job now that she is out of school, but she hasn't had much success. She doesn't have a driver's license, and her parents don't have much time to take her around to apply for jobs. The businesspeople she has approached work close to her home and know her well. They say they are unable to give her a job, even though several have signs in their windows saying "Help Wanted." Yvonne's parents are not very enthusiastic about her finding employment because they are afraid she might lose some of the benefits she receives from social services. Yvonne is able to go to movies but only with her parents. She is lonesome for her old friends from school.

Mark*

Mark's opportunities as a young adult in his local community were strongly influenced by his secondary school program that focused on preparing him for the transition to community life. From the time he was 16 years old, much of his school program was outside the classroom in experiences focusing on vocational training, recreation, and management of his personal life. His training for employment included three years of sampling various jobs in the local community to match his interests and abilities with the demands of various employment opportunities. These experiences included direct training and support from teachers and school support staff, vocational education personnel, and vocational rehabilitation counselors. At age 19, Mark was hired at a local supermarket as a part of his individualized transition plan where he continued to receive training and support from school personnel until he was 22 years old. In addition to employment training, Mark's program during the secondary school years also concentrated on teaching recreation and personal management opportunities within the community setting. Mark learned to access various community activities, such as parks, theaters, and restaurants. Personal management training focused on many different areas, including hygiene, using a personal schedule, [and] a time management system.

Source: ★ From *Secondary Programs for Students with Developmental Disabilities* (p. 257) by J. McDonnell, B. Wilcox, and M. L. Hardman, 1991, Boston: Allyn and Bacon. Copyright 1991 by Allyn and Bacon. Reprinted by permission.

Research has suggested that many individuals with disabilities are not able to access the services necessary for successful life in the community either during high school or following graduation (Edgar, 1987; Hasazi, Johnson, Hasazi, Gordon, & Hull, 1989; Mithaug, Horiuchi, & Fanning, 1985; Wagner, 1989). A recent Harris poll conducted in the United States found that (1) two-thirds of disabled people between the ages of 16 and 64 were not working; (2) 66 percent of those not working and of working age indicated that they would like to have jobs; and (3) a comparison of working and nonworking individuals with disabilities revealed that those who were working were more satisfied with life, had more money, and were less likely to blame their disability for preventing them from reaching their individual potential (Harris & Associates, 1987).

A recent study in Vermont directly linked employment following school to an effective transition-planning process that included opportunities for students with disabilities to work while still in school. Researchers at the University of Vermont found that students who were employed prior to leaving high school were more likely to be employed as adults and that participation in vocational education was related to eventual employment and higher wages (Hasazi et al., 1989). The U.S. Department of Education's National Longitudinal Transition Study (Wagner, 1989) reported that paid employment during high school had become more common, with 42 percent of students with disabilities being placed in community vocational or employment programs. However, one out of four of these students worked less than 10 hours per week and was paid below minimum wage. Additionally, most students were in service and manual labor positions.

The increasing emphasis on the **transition from school to adult life** has altered many previously held perceptions about people who are exceptional, particularly those we would describe as disabled. Without question, the potential of adults with disabilities has been significantly underestimated. A thorough study of people with disabilities as they move through adult life is one of the most important and challenging areas for professionals to study in the remaining years of this century.

Window 3–5 should raise some questions for you: Why was Yvonne's employment preparation limited to one term with graduation so near? What vocational counseling and transition support services were provided during her last years of school? While Yvonne had little support in making the transition from school to adult life, Mark had opportunities for community training that began early in high school and included individualized transition planning. The transition to adult life for people with disabilities presents some perplexing but interesting issues. Yvonne's situation is not unusual. Fortunately, transition services and adult support systems for people with disabilities, such as Mark, are undergoing considerable change and expansion.

In recent years, professionals and parents have begun to address some of the critical issues facing adolescents with disabilities as they prepare to leave school and face life as adults in their local communities. More than one-quarter of a million students with disabilities exit school each year (U.S. Department of Education, 1991). Since the passage of Public Law 94-142 in 1975 (called IDEA since 1990), schools have made significant strides in preparing youth with disabilities for adult life, but much remains to be done. Many of the current graduates from special education programs, like Yvonne, are neither adequately prepared for employment nor able to access other critical services necessary for success as adults in their local communities (Florian & West, 1991; Hasazi et al., 1989; Hasazi, Gordon, & Roe, 1985). Long waiting lists for vocational and housing services prove frustrating for many of these individuals (McDonnell, Wilcox, & Boles, 1985).

FOCUS 11

Identify three factors involved in the definition of *transition*.

Defining Transition

The transition from school to adult life is a complex and dynamic process that should begin during the early years in high school. The entire process should culminate with the transfer of support for the student from the school to an adult service agency or with the individual moving on to live as an independent adult (Blalock, 1988; Gillet, 1987). Transition procedures involve a series of choices about what experiences students with disabilities should have in their remaining school years to better prepare them for what lies ahead in the adult world. Will (1984) defined *transition* as a "bridge between the security and structure offered by the school and adult life" (pp. 6–7). This "bridge" requires a sound preparation program during high school, support for individuals as they finish school, and opportunities to access services when needed during the adult years.

The requirement that every student with a disability receive transition services was enacted into law through the Individual with Disabilities Education Act (IDEA) of 1990 (PL 101-476). This law defined **transition services** as

> a coordinated set of activities for a student, designed within an outcome-oriented process, which promotes movement from school to post-school activities, including post-secondary education, vocational training, integrated employment (including supported employment), continuing and adult education, adult services, independent living, or community participation. The coordinated set of activities shall be based upon the individual student's needs, taking into account the student's preferences and interests, and shall include instruction, community experiences, the development of employment and other post-school adult living objectives, and, when

appropriate, acquisition of daily living skills and functional vocational evaluation. (PL 101–476, § 602[a][19])

While there is some disagreement about the specific programs that are necessary to bridge the gap between school and adult life, there is consensus about the principal components of a transition system. These components should include:

1. Effective high school programs that reference instruction to community activities and demands
2. An array of adult services that can meet the unique vocational, residential, and leisure needs of youth who are disabled
3. A cooperative system of transition planning that ensures access to needed post-school services (McDonnell, Wilcox, & Hardman, 1991)

Transition is obviously much more than the mere transfer of administrative responsibility for an individual from the school to an adult service agency. It is a process that involves many agencies as well as the family in developing activities and services that are appropriate to the individual.

The Role of the School

Transition begins with a solid foundation on which to build. The school is that foundation. High school programs must provide those activities that lead directly to outcomes facilitating success for the individual during the adult years. For Mark (see Window 3–5), these activities included learning to shop in a neighborhood grocery store and training for a job in the community.

What, then, are the expected outcomes for youth with disabilities as they enter adulthood? First, adults should be able to function as independently as possible in their daily lives; their reliance on others to meet their needs should be minimized. Adults with disabilities

FOCUS 12

Describe five aspects of the school's role in preparing a student with disabilities for adulthood.

Working in the community offers monetary benefits as well as a sense of identity and contribution to others. (MacPherson/Monkmeyer Press)

should also be involved in the economic life of the community. There should be opportunities for both paid and unpaid work. Working in the community is of value to the individual with a disability both for the monetary benefits it offers and for the opportunities for social interaction, personal identity, and contribution to others. Finally, an adult should be able to participate in social and leisure-time activities that are an integral part of community life.

High schools are in the unique position of being able to coordinate activities during the school years that enhance student participation in the community and link students such as Mark with needed services. Schools have many roles in the transition process: assessing individual needs, developing a transition plan for each student, coordinating transition planning with adult service agencies, and participating with parents in the planning process.

Assessing Individual Needs.   The needs of an adult with a disability vary according to his or her functioning level in relationship to the requirements of each environmental setting. People with severe disabling conditions may require significant and long-term support in order to be involved in activities within their communities. Adults with mild disabilities may need only short-term assistance or no support system whatsoever during their adult years. However, Brolin (1982) suggested that even students with mild disabilities must receive more than vocational training experiences while in school.

Schools must broaden their focus on vocational preparation to include career education. Career education systematically coordinates all school, family, and community components. Thus, an individual's potential for economic, social, and personal fulfillment is greatly enhanced. Given the number of individuals with disabilities who may need assistance during the adult years, a transition-planning system must take into account the level of support

FIGURE 3–5 A High School Transition Plan for a Student with a Severe Disability

Student: ___Bob Robins___	Meeting Date: ___10/15/92___	
	Graduation Date: ___6/7/93___	
Participants:		

Parents(s)	Mrs. Robins
School	William Bailey, Special Education Teacher
DSH Casemanager	Susan Love, Developmental Disabilities Agency
DVR Casemanager	N/A

Planning Area: Vocational Services	*Responsible Person*	*Timelines*
Transition Goal		
Bob will initiate work training in Wasatch Work Crew Program	Mr. Bailey	12/15/92
Support Activities		
1. Complete application process	Ms. Robins Ms. Love	11/1/92
2. Obtain city bus pass	Ms. Robins	11/1/92
3. Teach bus route to Wasatch business office	Mr. Bailey	11/14/92
4. Establish planning meeting with Wasatch WCP director	Ms. Love	1/10/93

Source: From "Planning the Transition of Severely Handicapped Youth from School to Adult Services: A Framework for High School Programs" by J. McDonnell and M. L. Hardman, 1985, *Education and Training of the Mentally Retarded, 20*(4), 275–286. Adapted by permission.

necessary for successful participation in a particular community. In order to identify the levels of support that an individual will require, parents and schools must be able to assess the individual during high school across a variety of performance areas (e.g., self-care, work, residential living, recreation, and leisure time). In the area of self-care, for example, assessments should be made for activities such as riding buses, using grocery stores, keeping schedules, crossing streets, and the like.

Developing Transition Plans.   The development of a **transition plan** for each student enhances opportunities for success following school and provides a vehicle for students, parents, and professionals to review options for postschool services (National Council on Disability, 1989). IDEA required that each student's IEP include a statement on the transition services needed beginning no later than age 16 or earlier, if appropriate. This statement should incorporate a description of interagency responsibilities or linkages prior to the student leaving the school setting. McDonnell et al. (1991) suggested that the purpose of the transition plan is to (1) identify the range of services needed by the individual to participate in the community, (2) identify activities that must occur during high school to facilitate the individual's access to an adult service program, and (3) establish timelines and responsibilities for completion of these activities. Figure 3–5 provides an example of a transition plan.

Working with Adult Service Agencies.   A critical component of the transition process is coordination between the schools and **adult service agencies.** Adult service agencies focus on providing the necessary services to assist individuals with disabilities to become more independent, such as vocational rehabilitation services, social services, and mental health services. It is important for these agencies to become involved early in the student's high school program in order to begin targeting the services that will be needed once he or she leaves school. This involvement includes direct participation in the development of the

---

W I N D O W 3–6

THEY DIDN'T PREPARE ME FOR THIS!

They really didn't prepare me for this! The job is incredible, it's satisfying—no, more than that—it's downright fun! But in a lot of ways, the professors didn't prepare me for all that I have to do. When you think about it, though, there's really no way they could do any more than they did. All they could do was train me with the general skills of counseling, analysis of individual needs, program development, provide some examples and practical experience, and tell me to be creative in my approach to helping clients. They did a fantastic job of these things, and actually, I had the very best preparation available. It's just that there is so much to do.

Let me back up a second. I have a job that is called *transition specialist*. I work with young individuals with disabilities who are in the process of leaving high school or have already graduated. I locate resources for employment and housing, arrange for transportation, and sometimes help with personal problems. So at one time or another during the week, I'm working with prospective employers and lining up others, counseling and advising clients, meeting with politicians and community groups arguing for more

services, and arranging for recreation events. I guess I'm a jack-of-all-trades, so to speak. Things are never boring, and each individual's case needs are different. It's really fun to see some of these people having successes that were never thought possible a few years ago. It's also wonderful to see some of the community people respond to what adults with disabilities can accomplish in a work environment.

So what am I complaining about? Really, nothing. I guess I wouldn't change much at all. It's exciting to be a part of these people's lives, and sometimes, I wake up really early in the morning with a new idea for some aspect of the program. When I say they didn't prepare me for this, I'm really referring to the wide variety of things I do and the fact that I enjoy it so much that I don't think about much else. There isn't any way to prepare a person for all of that. Would I recommend to others that they go into the training program and this profession? Only if they want to get "hyped" by their job and do something that helps others at the same time!

Doreen, A Transition Specialist

student's transition plan. Adult service professionals should collaborate with the disabled student, his or her parents, and the school in establishing transition goals and identifying appropriate activities for the student during the final school years. Additionally, adult service professionals must be involved in developing information systems that can effectively track students as they leave school programs and monitor the availability and appropriateness of services provided during adulthood (Wehman, Kregel, & Barcus, 1985).

Involving Parents in the Transition Process.   When a student with a disability leaves school and enters the adult world, many parents receive a considerable shock. First, there is the realization that the services their child was entitled to during the school years are no longer mandated by law. As such, there may be a significant loss in services at a critical time. In addition, many parents know little if anything about adult service systems.

To avoid this problem, during the student's high school years, parents must be educated about critical components of adult service systems, including the characteristics of agencies, criteria for evaluating programs, and potential as well as current service alternatives for their child. McDonnell, Wilcox, and Hardman (1991) suggested two strategies for getting information to parents. First, school districts need to offer ongoing information seminars for parents to acquaint them with the issues involved in their child's transition from school to adult life. Second, every school district should develop and use a transition-planning guide to help parents complete critical planning activities.

As we move toward the twenty-first century, the importance of developing and implementing effective transition services for students with disabilities is clear. Despite significant federal and state investment in educational services for these students, many still remain unemployed, are socially isolated, and depend on the family and community service programs during adulthood. Model transition programs and services have now been developed in most areas in the United States, which demonstrates that students with disabilities can achieve post-school outcomes that will enhance their access and opportunities in nearly every aspect of community life.

Unfortunately, despite the success of model programs, there has not been widespread adoption of these innovations. In response to this concern, the Association for Persons with Severe Handicaps (TASH) has identified several areas of research viewed as critical to the adoption of effective transition services for students with disabilities:

1. The development and validation of strategies to promote inclusion of student values and needs in the transition-planning process
2. Identification of factors that contribute to the implementation of successful transition programs
3. Examination of the effects of recent educational reform efforts in general education on the design of transition programs
4. Longitudinal studies that examine the impact of transition programs on the quality of life achieved by students with disabilities following high school
5. Research examining the reasons behind high unemployment and underemployment of people with disabilities (TASH, 1990)

From early childhood through the high school transition years, the issues in delivering quality educational services to students with disabilities are varied and complex. With the information in this chapter as background, we now move into chapters that focus on each of the areas of exceptionality. The discussion will continue to highlight the nature of educational services while also examining both medical and social services. Definitions for each of the areas of exceptionality are presented, along with overviews of prevalence, characteristics, and causation.

| Debate | Forum | ·················· | Full Inclusion or Pull-out of Students with Disabilities from Regular Education Classrooms? ·················· |

The debate over which educational placement constitutes the least restrictive environment for a student with a disability began long before the passage of Public Law 94–142 (now IDEA) in 1975 and continues into the 1990s. Is any educational placement that "pulls" students out of the natural setting of the regular classroom ever the least restrictive environment?

Point   The purpose of special education is to provide students with disabilities the instruction necessary to meet their unique needs. These students require specially designed academic and social instruction that can often be provided only in a setting outside the regular education classroom. The reality of the general education system is that regular educators have little expertise to assist students with learning problems and are already overburdened with large class sizes and inadequate support services. A special educator is specifically trained to develop instructional strategies and use teaching techniques that are not part of the training of regular education teachers. A specialized classroom setting that provides instruction intended to prepare the student to cope with academic and behavioral challenges and then eventually prepares him or her to return to the regular education classroom is the most effective approach to meeting individualized needs. It is also important to remember that specialized pull-out settings allow for centralization of both human and material resources.

Counterpoint   It is time to face up to the fact that, although special education has been successful in providing access for students with disabilities to a free public education, it has failed to meet their individual needs when it has removed them from natural classroom settings. It is not necessary or effective to separate students from each other on the basis of a label. The time has come to bring the services to the students, not to force students to leave the natural setting of the regular education classroom in order to receive help. Placement in a regular education classroom, forming a partnership between regular and special educators, results in an environment that is diverse and rich, rather than just a series of discrete programming slots and funding pots. A partnership between regular and special education personalizes each student's instructional program and brings the program to the student, rather than forcing the student to go to the program. Additionally, special educators are more effective in a partnership because they can bring their knowledge and resources to assist regular educators in developing intervention strategies that are directly oriented to student need. Finally, this is all accomplished in the natural setting, the regular classroom, where effective learning and behavior are supposed to occur in the first place.

REVIEW ···

FOCUS 1   Why is it so important to provide early intervention services as soon as possible to students at risk?
◆ The first years of life are important to the overall development of all children—normal, at risk, and disabled.
◆ Early stimulation is critical to the later development of language, intelligence, personality, and self-worth.
◆ Early intervention has the potential of preventing and lessening the overall impact of disabilities as well as counteracting the negative effects of delayed intervention.
◆ Early intervention may in the long run be less costly and more effective than providing services later in the individual's life.

FOCUS 2   Identify the critical components of programs for preschool-age children under Public Law 99-457.
◆ A child-find system must be established in each state to attempt to locate young children at risk and make referrals to appropriate agencies for preschool services.
◆ An individualized education program (IEP) must be developed for each eligible child using a multidisciplinary approach.
◆ Specialists from several disciplines and at least one of the parents must participate in the development and implementation of an IEP for each child.

FOCUS 3   What is meant by adaptive fit and adaptive instruction for students with disabilities?
◆ The degree to which an individual is able to cope with the requirements of the school setting is described as *adaptive fit.*
◆ The purpose of adaptive instruction is to modify the learning environment to accommodate the unique learning characteristics and needs of individual students.
◆ Adaptive instruction focuses on assessing each student's individual characteristics and capabilities.

FOCUS 4   Define *collaboration,* and distinguish between the consulting teacher and resource-room teacher.
◆ *Collaboration* may be defined as one or more people working together to attain a common goal.
◆ Consulting teachers work directly with regular classroom teachers on the use of appropriate assessment techniques and intervention strategies.
◆ Students who work with consulting teachers are not removed from the regular classroom program but remain with their nondisabled peers while receiving additional instructional assistance.
◆ Resource-room teachers provide specialized instruction to stu-

dents who are disabled in a classroom that is separate from the regular education classroom.

◆ Under the resource-room program, the student still receives the majority of instruction in the regular education classroom but is removed for short periods to supplement his or her educational experience.

FOCUS 5 Describe several approaches to achieving a collaborative relationship between regular and special educators.

◆ Teacher assistance teams (TATs) involve groups of professionals, students, and/or parents working together to meet the needs of students with disabilities.

◆ The multidisciplinary approach involves the expertise of several professionals who usually work independently of one another in conducting assessments and implementing separate programs.

◆ The interdisciplinary approach represents a significant alteration in the process. During the assessment phase, team members undertake independent assessments, but program development is carried out as a collaborative effort among professionals.

◆ The transdisciplinary approach introduces the idea of a primary therapist or teacher who is designated as team leader to facilitate professionals working with each other in implementing a student's program. The implementation of the instructional program is carried out by one of the members in collaboration with the others. Each team member supports the primary therapist and other members of the team in meeting an individual student's needs.

FOCUS 6 Describe the role of the regular classroom teacher in meeting the needs of students with disabilities.

◆ To understand how a student's learning, behavior, communication, and physical differences affect his or her ability to acquire academic skills and cope socially in the educational environment.

◆ To identify students who may be in need of additional educational support

◆ To make referrals to the team for testing and evaluation of students perceived as being at risk

◆ To work with team members to develop and implement individualized instruction in the regular classroom

◆ To initiate and maintain ongoing communication with parents

◆ To effectively use nondisabled peers as support for students with disabilities

FOCUS 7 Describe special education classrooms and schools for students with disabilities.

◆ The self-contained special education classroom employs the expertise of a qualified special education teacher to work with students who are disabled for all or part of the school day.

◆ The self-contained classroom teacher may still create opportunities for students with disabilities to interact with nondisabled peers whenever appropriate.

◆ Special schools provide services for large numbers of disabled students in a setting away from a regular education school and classroom.

FOCUS 8 Identify the arguments for and against the pull-out of students with disabilities from regular education classrooms.

◆ Arguments against removing students from the regular education classroom include: (a) the current system of pulling students out of regular education simply does not work; (b) pull-out programs result in a fragmented approach to the delivery of special education, with little cooperation between regular and special educators; and (c) students in pull-out programs are stigmatized when segregated from their nondisabled peers.

◆ Arguments for removing students to separate environments include: (a) regular education has little expertise to assist students with learning problems and is already overburdened with large class sizes and inadequate support services; (b) special educators have been specifically trained to develop instructional strategies and use teaching techniques that are not part of the training of regular education teachers; (c) more specialized academic and social instruction can be provided in pull-out settings, and such settings can more effectively prepare students to return to the regular education classroom; and (d) specialized pull-out settings allow for centralization of both human and material resources.

FOCUS 9 Identify three curricular approaches that can be used in teaching students with disabilities.

◆ The basic-skills approach stresses that each student must learn a specified set of sequenced skills, each of which is a prerequisite to the next.

◆ The remediation approach identifies gaps in a student's skill development and then focuses on correcting the problems through the use of appropriate materials and instructional strategies.

◆ The functional life/compensatory approach teaches only those skills that facilitate the student's successful adaptation to the environment.

FOCUS 10 Cite three reasons why it is important to study the relationship between what is taught in school and the needs individuals have during adulthood.

◆ Students with disabilities who leave the public schools are not adequately prepared for life as adults in their local communities.

◆ Adult service systems do not have the resources to meet the needs of students with disabilities following the school years.

◆ The capabilities of adults with disabilities have been underestimated.

FOCUS 11 Identify three factors involved in the definition of *transition*.

◆ Transition is a process that involves a series of choices about school experiences that will help the individual who is disabled attain a successful adult life.

◆ Transition is the bridge between the security of the school and the reality of adult life in the community.

◆ The components of a transition system include an effective high school program, an array of adult services geared to the needs of each individual, and cooperative efforts across agencies for transition planning.

FOCUS 12   Describe five aspects of the school's role in preparing a student with disabilities for adulthood.

◆ High schools must provide activities that facilitate success during the adult years.

◆ The needs of each high school student should be assessed across a variety of performance areas, including self-care, work, residential living, and recreation and leisure time.

◆ Schools must develop a formal transition-planning process that analyzes options during the adult years.

◆ Adult service agencies must become involved in each student's high school program in order to target needed services during the adult years.

◆ Parents must be educated in the critical components of the adult service system.

Chapter Four
Mental Retardation

TO BEGIN WITH . . .

◆ "The fact that a person is born with mental retardation or acquires mental retardation during development is not a justifiable reason, in and of itself, for terminating the life of that person. Mental retardation alone is not a nullification of quality or worth in an individual's life and should not be used as a rationale for the termination of life through direct means nor withholding of nourishment or life sustaining procedures" (Smith, 1988).

◆ "As Americans, . . . we believe in rugged individualism, the sanctity of the family and in taking care of our own. We grow from the experience of living together in the community. We admire those who work and we work hard so that our children can have the best life and education possible. We have sacrificed to maintain our freedom and a life which is nonrestrictive. These values are our heritage which we preserve so that it can be passed down to our children—all of our children. The quality of life made available in the United States as a result of this value base is the best in the world for those who are allowed to share in it. The "American Dream" rests at the foundation of the values we defend. From the evidence presented it is apparent that these values have been denied to that portion of the citizens . . . who carry the label of "mental retardation." Therefore, this Order shall include "Guiding Principles" . . . as follows:

> All persons . . .
> > are capable of growth and development.
> > deserve to be treated with dignity.
> > have value.
> > must be involved in and carry the primary responsibility for the decisions which affect their lives.
> should live in and be a part of the community.
> All children . . .
> > should live with families.
> > have the right to a free and appropriate education"
> > > (Judge Ellison, 1988 — Court Order to close the Hissom State School and Hospital in Oklahoma).

ROGER

ROGER. Roger is 19 years old and lives at home with his parents. During the day, he attends high school and works in a local toy company in a small work crew with five other individuals who are disabled. Roger and his working colleagues are closely supervised by a trained vocational specialist. Roger assembles small toys and is learning how to operate power tools for wood- and metal-cutting tasks. He earns wages but not enough to be financially independent. It is likely that he will always be dependent on either his family or society for some financial assistance. Roger is capable of caring for his own physical needs. He has learned to dress and feed himself and understands the importance of personal grooming and hygiene skills. He can communicate many of his needs and desires verbally but is limited in his social language abilities. Roger has never learned to read, and his leisure hours are spent watching television, listening to the radio, and visiting with friends.

KIM. Kim developed much more slowly than her older brother, which caused some concern for her parents. They also became concerned about Kim's hearing because of her slow speech development, but this was judged to be normal when she was tested last year at the age of 6. The **audiologist** referred the family to a psychologist for further evaluation. Although the audiologist said nothing specific, Kim's responses during the hearing test led her to suspect an overall developmental delay. A psychologist conducted a series of observations and administered a standardized intelligence test along with tests to measure Kim's performance in reading and math. The test scores indicated that Kim's IQ was about 60, which placed her between two and three standard deviations below the average of 100. Her reading and math scores were also behind those expected for a child of her age. Observations by her teacher suggested that Kim was delayed in the area of socialization skill development, as well. Although she is now 7 years old, Kim's functioning in many areas is much like that of a child three or four years younger. She does interact with other children her age in play activities, but if the game is complex or involves more than one or two children, she tends to withdraw. Kim has learned the required self-help skills for her age level, including dressing, feeding, and personal hygiene. Kim is a child with mild mental retardation.

BECKY. Becky is a 6-year-old who has significant delays in intellectual, language, and motor development. These problems have been evident from birth. Her mother experienced a long, unusually difficult labor, and Becky endured severe heartrate dips; at times, her heartrate was undetectable. During delivery, Becky suffered from birth asphyxiation and epileptic seizures. The attending physician described her as flaccid (soft and limp), with abnormal muscle reflexes. Becky has not yet learned to walk, is not toilet trained, and has no means of communication with others in her environment. She lives at home and attends a local elementary school during the day. Her educational program includes work with therapists to develop her gross motor abilities in order to improve her mobility. Speech and language specialists are examining the possibility of teaching her several alternative forms of communication (e.g., a language board or manual communication system) because Becky has not developed any verbal skills. The special education staff is focusing on decreasing Becky's dependence on others by teaching some basic self-care skills such as feeding, toileting, and grooming. The medical and educational prognosis for Becky is unknown. The professional staff does not know what the ultimate long-term impact of their intervention will be, but they do know that, although Becky is a child with severe mental retardation, she is learning.

INTRODUCTION

In this chapter, we focus on people whose intellectual and social capabilities are significantly different from the norm. The growth and development of these individuals depends on the educational and social opportunities made available to them. Kim (see Window 4–1), who has mild retardation, may achieve academically somewhere between the second- and fifth-grade levels if afforded an appropriate educational experience. As she grows older, she may achieve at least partial independence occupationally and socially within the community. Most likely, Kim will need some support from her family or other agencies to assist her in adjusting to adult life in the community.

Roger has completed school and is just beginning life as an adult in his community. Roger is a person with moderate mental retardation. Although he will probably require ongoing support on his job for a lifetime, he is earning wages that contribute to his successful adjustment in the community. Within a few years, he will most likely move away from his family and into a group home or a supervised apartment of his own.

Becky has severe mental retardation. Although the long-term prognosis is unknown, she has many opportunities for learning and development that were not available until recently. Through a positive home environment and specialized educational services, Becky can reach a level of functioning that was once considered impossible.

Kim, Roger, and Becky are people with mental retardation, but they are not necessarily representative of the range of people who are characterized as mentally retarded. A 6-year-old child described as mildly retarded may be no more than one or two years behind in the development of academic and social skills. Many children with mild mental retardation are not identified until they enter school at the age of 5 or 6 because they may not exhibit physical problems that are readily identifiable during the early childhood years. As these children enter school, developmental lags become more apparent in the classroom environment. During early primary grades, it is not uncommon for the intellectual and social difficulties of children with mild mental retardation to be attributed to immaturity. However, within a few years, school personnel generally recognize the need for specialized educational services beyond regular classroom instruction. Unfortunately, for many children with mild retardation, valuable time has already been lost.

Individuals with moderate to severe mental retardation have difficulties that transcend the classroom. Many are impaired in nearly every facet of life. Some have significant multiple disabling conditions, including sensory, physical, and emotional problems. Individuals with moderate retardation are capable of developing skills that allow a degree of independence within their environment. These self-help skills include the abilities to dress and feed themselves, to care for their personal health and grooming needs (e.g., toileting), and to develop safety habits that allow them to move safely wherever they go. These people have some means of communication. Most can develop verbal language skills, but some may be able to learn only manual communication. Their social interaction skills are limited, however, making it difficult for them to relate spontaneously to others.

Contrast the above characteristics with those of individuals who have severe to profound retardation and the diverse nature of these people becomes clear. Individuals who are profoundly retarded depend on others to maintain even their most basic life functions, including feeding, toileting, and dressing. They may not be capable of self-maintenance and often do not develop functional communication skills. The significance of their disabilities may require a lifetime of supervision, whether it be in a special-care facility or at home. In terms of treatment or educational intervention, the only realistic conclusion that can be drawn about this group is that the long-term prognosis for development is unknown.

This does not mean that treatment beyond routine care and maintenance is not beneficial. The extreme nature of these disabilities is the primary reason such individuals were excluded from the public schools for so long. Drew, Logan, and Hardman (1992) have indicated that exclusion was more for the protection of the schools rather than for the educational or social needs of the child with differences. Mori and Masters (1980) concluded that exclusion could be justified "on the basis of lack of resources, lack of facilities, and lack of trained personnel to provide an adequate educational experience for this population" (p. 17). Given the present emphasis on research and alternative intervention approaches for people with mental retardation, the future may hold some answers and bring about a different outlook.

DEFINITIONS AND CLASSIFICATION

Definitions

FOCUS 1

Identify the three components of the definition of *mental retardation*.

People with mental retardation have been studied for centuries, by a variety of professional disciplines. The most widely accepted definition of *mental retardation* is that of the **American Association on Mental Retardation (AAMR),** an organization of professionals from many backgrounds such as medicine, law, and education. The AAMR definition states that "mental retardation refers to significantly subaverage general intellectual functioning resulting in or associated with concurrent impairments in **adaptive behavior,** and manifested during the **developmental period**" (Grossman, 1983, p. 11). The essential features of this definition have also been adopted by the American Psychiatric Association. The AAMR definition has three major components: intelligence, adaptive behavior, and the developmental period.[1]

Intelligence.   Significantly subaverage general intellectual functioning is assessed through the use of a standardized intelligence test. On an intelligence test, a person's score is compared to the statistical average of age-mates who have taken the same test. The statistical average for an intelligence test is generally set at 100. We state this by saying that the person has an intelligence quotient (IQ) of 100. Psychologists use a mathematical procedure to determine the extent to which an individual's score deviates from this average of 100. This measurement is called a **standard deviation.** According to Best and Kahn (1989), standard deviations measure the dispersion of scores in a distribution. A score that deviates more than two standard deviations from the mean of 100 is considered to be significantly different. An individual who scores two standard deviations below the average on an intelligence test is in the range that characterizes mental retardation. Depending on the test, this means that individuals with IQs of approximately 70 to 75 and lower would be considered as having mental retardation. In the case of Kim from Window 4–1, her IQ of 60 placed her in the range of persons with mental retardation, at least on the basis of an intelligence test.

Adaptive Behavior.   Impairments in adaptive behavior are defined by the AAMR as significant limitations in a person's ability to meet standards of maturation, learning, personal independence, and social responsibility that would be expected of another individual of comparable age level and cultural group (Grossman, 1983). Consider Becky from Window 4–1. She has significant impairments in her adaptive behavior skills. She is unable to walk and has a limited repertoire of self-help skills. At 6 years old, she still has no means of communicating with others.

[1] In June 1992, as this book was going to press, the American Association on Mental Retardation adopted a new definition to be field-tested throughout the country over the next several years. A discussion of this definition may be found on pages 439–440.

Participation in normal activities and opportunities for success enable this boy, as he grows up, to share common experiences with other children. (Jose Carrillo/PhotoEdit)

As is true with intelligence, adaptive behavior can be measured by standardized tests. These tests are most often referred to as *adaptive behavior scales,* and generally use structured interviews or direct observations to obtain information. Adaptive behavior scales generally compare an individual to an established norm and measure "the extent to which an individual takes care of personal needs, exhibits social competencies, and refrains from engaging in problem behaviors" (Bruininks & McGrew, 1987). Adaptive behavior may also be assessed through informal appraisal, such as observations by people who are familiar with the individual or through anecdotal records of the individual's adaptive skills.

Developmental Period. In the AAMR definition, the *developmental period* is defined as "the period of time between birth and the eighteenth birthday" (Grossman, 1983, p. 1). The reason for the inclusion of a developmental period within the definition is to clearly distinguish mental retardation from other conditions that may not originate until the adult years, such as head injuries or strokes.

The AAMR definition of mental retardation has evolved through years of effort to define the condition clearly. During the Middle Ages, people with mental retardation were considered fools, demons, and witches. In the sixteenth century, terms such as *sot, simpleton,* and *idiot* were common names for those with mental retardation. Throughout the nineteenth century, many individuals with mental retardation were identified according to their medical condition, such as cretinism, gargoylism, and mongolism. During this period, the most common term to describe people with mental retardation was *feebleminded*. Feeblemindedness was broken down into three levels of retarded behavior: idiot (lowest level of functioning), imbecile, and moron.

Over the years, definitions of mental retardation have emphasized routine care and maintenance rather than treatment and education. However, legislation (including the Individuals with Disabilities Act, IDEA) and litigation (e.g., *Homeward Bound v. Hissom Memorial Center, 1988*) have opened new doors for people with mental retardation and put pressure on professionals to develop and use definitions aimed at assisting individuals in receiving appropriate services and improving their quality of life.

R
E
F
L
E
C
T

O
N

T
H
I
S

4–1   Kennedy Family's Support
of People with Mental
Retardation

In July 1990, the Kennedy family matriarch, Rose Fitzgerald Kennedy, celebrated her one-hundredth birthday and a lifetime of commitment to improving the lives of people with mental retardation. Here are just a few of the Kennedy family's contributions in this century:

♦ In the 1940s, Rose and Joseph Kennedy openly acknowledged that daughter Rosemary is mentally retarded, thus focusing public attention on the needs of people with mental retardation.

♦ In 1946, the Kennedy family established the Joseph P. Kennedy, Jr., Foundation, the only foundation in the world solely devoted to people with mental retardation.

♦ In 1961, President John F. Kennedy established the President's Committee on Mental Retardation to examine critical medical, social, and educational issues affecting people with mental retardation. As both a family member and statesman, the president became a powerful impetus for social reform.

♦ In 1962, the Kennedy foundation established the International Awards in Mental Retardation (sometimes referred to as the Nobel Prize of the field) to recognize individuals and organizations that have had significant impacts on the lives of people with mental retardation.

♦ In 1963, President Kennedy publicly promoted prevention of both mental retardation and mental illness and openly supported legislation intended to reduce the size of U.S. mental institutions. He focused the country's attention on family and community living for all people with mental retardation.

♦ In 1968, Eunice Kennedy Shriver established the Special Olympics to create opportunities for people with mental retardation to participate in sports training and athletic competition.

♦ In July 1991, the Eighth International Summer Special Olympic Games were held in the United States. Over 6,000 athletes with mental retardation participated, representing 100 countries. This was the largest sporting event in the world held that year.

FOCUS 2

Identify the three methods of classifying people with mental retardation.

Classification

The purpose of developing classification systems is to provide a frame of reference for studying, understanding, and treating people labeled mentally retarded. People with mental retardation are often stereotyped as a homogeneous group of individuals, "the retarded," with similar physical characteristics and learning capabilities. Actually, mental retardation is a condition that results in a broad range of functioning levels and characteristics. In order to more clearly understand the diversity of people labeled mentally retarded, several classification systems have been developed. We discuss three methods of classifying individuals with mental retardation: according to the severity of the condition, educability expectations, and medical descriptors.

Severity of the Condition.   The extent to which a person's intellectual capabilities and adaptive behavior deviate from what is considered normal can be described by using such terms as *mild, moderate, severe,* and *profound.* Each of these four terms describes the significance of the intellectual deficit. *Mild* describes the highest level of performance for individuals classified as mentally retarded; *profound* describes the lowest level of performance for this population.

The distinction between each of the severity levels associated with mental retardation is primarily determined through the use of scores on intelligence tests as well as indicators of maladaptive behavior. The AAMR (Grossman, 1983) uses four levels of intellectual functioning to group individuals with mental retardation according to the severity approach: (1) mild, IQ 55 to 70; (2) moderate, IQ 40 to 55; (3) severe, IQ 25 to 40; and (4) profound, IQ 25 or lower (IQ scores based on standard deviations of Wechsler Intelligence Scales). The American Psychiatric Association employs the same four severity classifications and uses basically the same IQ groupings.

A person's adaptive behavior, or the ability to adapt to or cope with environmental demands, can also be broken down into mild through profound severity descriptors. Grossman (1983) drew the distinction between intelligence and adaptive behavior: "Adaptive behavior refers to what people do to take care of themselves and to relate to others in daily living rather than the abstract potential implied by intelligence" (p. 42). As is true with intellectual functioning, adaptive behavior deficits may be described in terms of the degree to which an individual's performance differs from what is expected for his or her chronological age. For example, in the area of independent functioning, average 3-year-olds are expected to feed themselves unassisted with the proper eating utensils, take care of their own personal hygiene, and be fully toilet trained. A child with mild adaptive deficits may be able to use eating utensils but with considerable spilling. This child can dress and take care of personal hygiene but only with help. The child may be partially toilet trained; toileting accidents are common. The level of independence for each of the above skill areas decreases for individuals with moderate, severe, and profound adaptive behavior deficits. A 3-year-old with profound adaptive behavior deficits generally must be fed by another individual, drinks from a cup with help, cannot take care of personal needs, and has no effective speech.

To better understand adaptive behavior, let's return to Window 4–1. Kim is an individual with mild mental retardation. As a 12-year-old, Kim has learned many of the required self-help skills for a child of her age, and although her socialization skills are below those expected, she is able to successfully interact with others in her environment. In contrast, Roger is an individual with moderate mental retardation. At 19, he has developed many skills that allow him to successfully live in his own community with supervision and assistance. It took longer for Roger to learn to dress and feed himself than it did for Kim, but he has learned these skills. His verbal communication skills are somewhat rudimentary; nevertheless, he is capable of communicating basic needs and desires. Becky is a child with severe to profound mental retardation. At age 6, her development is significantly delayed in nearly every area of functioning. However, it is clear that with appropriate intervention, she is learning.

Educability Expectations. In response to the growing number of children with mental retardation entering the public schools, the field of education has developed its own classification system. As the word *expectations* implies, children with mental retardation are classified according to expected achievement in a classroom situation. The specific categories used vary greatly from state to state, depending on the locale and source consulted. Frequently, this type of system specifies a label, an approximate IQ range, and a statement of predicted achievement.

The media have only recently begun to portray individuals with mental retardation as active members of society, capable of having personal relationships with others, as in the popular television series "Life Goes On." (Roman Salicki/Shooting Star)

4–2   Moron, Imbecile, and Idiot

The terms *mild, moderate, severe,* and *profound mental retardation* have been used by professionals as classification descriptors for a relatively short period of time. Perhaps you are more familiar with such terms as *idiot, imbecile,* and *moron,* the forerunners of the current symptom severity descriptors. The use of *idiot* dates back to the late eighteenth century, when John Locke (1632–1704) differentiated between idiocy and insanity by indicating that insane individuals put wrong ideas together and then reason from them but idiots reason scarcely at all.

With the advent of the intelligence test in the beginning of the twentieth century, the terms *idiot* (IQ 0–25), *imbecile* (IQ 25–50), and *moron* (IQ 50–75) were used to identify three levels of retarded functioning. During the decades that followed, these terms became part of our everyday language and took on very derogatory meanings. We have all used such phrases as "You idiot," "What an imbecile," and "He's a moron." It is obvious why professionals and parents have moved away from such labels in developing classification systems for people with mental retardation.

- ◆ *Educable* (IQ 55 to about 70): Second- to fifth-grade achievement in school academic areas. Social adjustment will permit some degree of independence in the community. Partial or total self-support in a paid community job is a strong possibility.
- ◆ *Trainable* (IQ 40 to 55). Learning primarily in the area of self-help skills; some achievement in areas considered academic. Social adjustment is often limited to home and closely surrounding area. Opportunities for paid work include **supported employment** in a community job or **sheltered workshop.**
- ◆ *Custodial* (IQ below 40): Individual may be unable to achieve sufficient skills to care for basic needs; will usually require significant level of care and supervision during lifetime.

Table 4–1 presents a comparison of educability and severity classification approaches according to IQ level.

The educability expectation classification criterion was originally developed to determine for whom the schools would be responsible. As indicated by the terminology, *educable* implied that the child could cope with at least some of the academic demands of the classroom. *Educable* meant the child could learn basic reading, writing, and arithmetic skills. The term *trainable* indicated that the student was *noneducable* and only capable of being trained in noneducational settings. In fact, until the passage of Public Law 94-142 in 1975 (now IDEA), many children who were labeled *trainable* could not get a free public education. Public Law

■ **Table 4–1** Comparison of Educability and Severity Classification Approaches According to IQ Level

	Approach	
IQ Level	Educability Expectation	Severity of Condition
55–70	Educable	Mild
40–55	Trainable	Moderate
25–40	Custodial	Severe
Below 25	Custodial	Profound

94–142 redefined education to include the development of skills (e.g., self-help, motor, communication, etc.) that are not necessarily academic in nature.

The custodial category described children who were only capable of being maintained or cared for in a specialized setting. Inherent within this category was the assumption that learning experiences in a public school would be fruitless. We have learned that such an assumption is entirely false. Many of the children labeled as *custodial* only a few years ago are now receiving appropriate educational experiences that are decreasing their overall dependence on their families and society. The term *custodial* is seldom used in today's public schools. In many states, it has been replaced with the symptom-severity descriptors *severely* and *profoundly retarded*.

Medical Descriptors. Mental retardation may be classified on the basis of the origin of the condition rather than the severity or educational expectations associated with it. A classification system that uses the cause (etiology) of the condition to differentiate retarded individuals is often referred to as a *medical classification system* because it emerged primarily from the field of medicine. The most commonly used medical descriptor system is that proposed by AAMR (Grossman, 1983), which uses the following 10 categories:

1. Infection and intoxication (e.g., syphilis, rubella)
2. Trauma or a physical agent (e.g., injury during birth, prenatal injury)
3. Nutritional or metabolic disorders (e.g., PKU, thyroid dysfunction)
4. Gross postnatal brain disease (e.g., tuberous sclerosis)
5. Diseases and conditions resulting from unknown prenatal influences (e.g., hydrocephalus)
6. **Chromosomal abnormalities** (e.g., **Down syndrome**)
7. Gestational disorders (e.g., prematurity)
8. Psychiatric disorders
9. Environmental influences (e.g., sensory deprivation, social disadvantage)
10. Other conditions (e.g., unknown causes or such known causes as blindness or deafness)

Each of these 10 categories will be discussed more thoroughly in this chapter in the section entitled "Causation."

PREVALENCE

It is generally estimated that from 1 to 3 percent of the total population has mental retardation (Grossman, 1983; Rantakallio & von Wendt, 1986). The U.S. Department of Education (1991) estimated that there are 566,150 students labeled as mentally retarded in U.S. public schools. Approximately 13 percent of all students with disabilities are mentally retarded. Over the past 15 years, there has been a dramatic decrease of more than 300,000 students labeled as mentally retarded in the schools. The reasons for such a decline include changes in definition as well as a tendency for education to use the less stigmatizing label of *learning disabilities* instead of *retardation* (U.S. Department of Education, 1991).

Individuals with mild mental retardation (IQs 55–70) comprise approximately 90 percent of the estimated prevalence. Based on a 3 percent prevalence estimate, approximately 2.5 percent of the general population would be classified as mildly retarded, or about 6 million people in the United States.

Individuals with moderate, severe, and profound retardation constitute a much smaller percentage of the general population. Even if we consider the multitude of conditions, prevalence estimates generally range from no more than 0.1 to 1 percent. Using an estimated

FIGURE 4–1

Prevalence of Mental Retardation (U.S. Department of Education, 1991.)

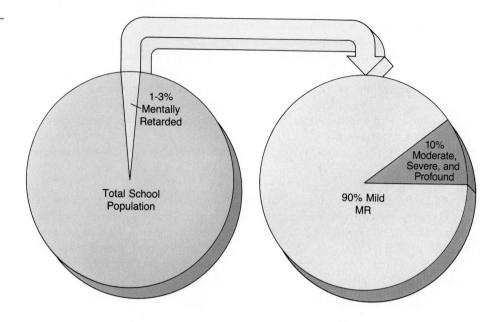

prevalence of 0.5 percent, over 1 million people would fall into the category of moderate to profound mental retardation (see Figure 4–1).

CHARACTERISTICS

Intellectual

The primary characteristic of mental retardation is an intellectual deficiency. There are, however, as many definitions of intelligence as there are people interested in defining the phenomenon. We will refer to *intelligence* as an ability to acquire, remember, and use information

FOCUS 3

Identify four intellectual and adaptive behavior characteristics of individuals with mental retardation.

R E F L E C T O N T H I S

4–3   Did You Know . . .

Did you know that, in the United States . . . ?*

- More than 0.5 million students with mental retardation attend public schools.
- The number of students with mental retardation served in the public schools has declined steadily since 1977. (There are several explanations for this decline, including the preferences of parents and professionals to use labels such as *learning disabled* or *developmentally disabled* rather than *mentally retarded*.)

- Although more than 50,000 special education teachers currently work with students who are mentally retarded, 4,000 more are still needed.
- The number of special education teachers employed to work with students who are mentally retarded is second only to the number of teachers who work with students with learning disabilities.
- The vast majority (69 percent) of students with mental retardation are served in separate special education classes and schools.

  Did you know that, worldwide . . . ?**

- There are more than 300 million

people with mental retardation.
- Mental retardation is more than 7 times as prevalent as blindness or deafness; 10 times as prevalent as physical disabilities; and 12 times as prevalent as cerebral palsy.
- Mental retardation is approximately two to three times as prevalent in the nations of Africa, Asia, and Latin America as in the United States.

Sources:
* Joseph P. Kennedy, Jr., Foundation. (1991). *Facts about mental retardation.* Washington, DC: Author. Adapted with permission.
** From U.S. Department of Education, 1991.

People with Down syndrome are no longer routinely institutionalized. They can live in their own communities and be successfully integrated into regular education settings. (Paul Conklin/ PhotoEdit)

appropriately. People with mental retardation have, by definition, less capability in each of these areas when compared to intellectually normal individuals. People with mental retardation do not learn as effectively or efficiently as their nondisabled peers.

The learning and memory capabilities of people with mental retardation are deficient. Children with mental retardation, as a group, are less able to grasp abstract as opposed to concrete concepts. They benefit from instruction that is meaningful and useful. Children with retardation learn more from contact with real objects, than they do from representations or symbols.

Intelligence is also associated with learning how to learn and the ability to apply what is learned to new experiences. This is known as establishing learning sets. Children and adults with mental retardation develop learning sets at a slower rate than nonretarded peers, and they are deficient in generalizing information to new situations (Agran, Salzberg, & Stowitchek, 1987; Payne, Polloway, Smith, & Payne, 1981).

The greater the severity of intellectual deficit, the greater the deficit in memory. Memory problems in children with mental retardation have been attributed to several factors. Individuals with mental retardation have difficulty in focusing on relevant stimuli in learning situations often attending to the wrong things (Borkowski & Day, 1987; Brooks & McCauley, 1984). Individuals with mental retardation do not appear to develop efficient learning strategies, such as the ability to rehearse a task (i.e., practice a new concept either out loud or to themselves over and over). While most people will rehearse to try and remember, it does not appear that individuals with retardation apply this skill (Borkowski & Cavanaugh, 1979).

Another factor that is often associated with memory deficits in people with mental retardation is the underdevelopment of **metacognitive processes.** As described by Sternberg and Spear (1985), metacognitive processes are "used to plan how to solve a problem, to monitor one's solution strategy as it is being executed, and to evaluate the results of this strategy once it has been implemented" (p. 303). Children with mental retardation appear to be unable to find, monitor, or evaluate the best strategy to use when confronted with a new learning situation. However, research suggests that they can be taught to change their control processes (Borkowski, Peck, & Damberg, 1983; Glidden, 1985).

════════════════════ **W I N D O W 4–2** ════════════════════

HOW HAVE YOU CHANGED IN THE LAST YEAR?

Before I played Becca (on *"Life Goes On,"* the ABC-TV series in which Christopher Burke, who has Down syndrome, plays 19-year-old Corky Thacher, Becca's brother), I would see someone who was disabled and I would be uneasy and look in the other direction. You don't realize that they could be your friend. In fact, you would almost be afraid of being friendly to someone like that, afraid they might *want* to be your regular friend.

When I first knew that there was going to be a boy playing Corky who really had Down syndrome, I was very afraid. I was thinking, "Gosh, I wish they had an actor playing him. This is going to be very hard." But once you've gotten to know someone like Chris, who is such a normal person and so great, everything changes. Now I *feel* like his sister, and I wouldn't have it any other way.

And because of this, I think I've gotten to the point where I would go up and talk to someone else who was "different." I've gotten to understand that you *can* be friends with someone who is like this. The past year has just opened my mind and made me a better person.

Kellie Martin, 14, Los Angeles, California

Source: From "Fresh Voices: Have You Changed in the Last Year?" by L. Minton, 1990, October 14, *Parade Magazine,* p. 24. Copyright 1990 by *Parade Magazine.* Reprinted by permission.

■ **Table 4–2** Adaptive Behavior Skills of People with Mental Retardation

Adaptive Skill	Examples of Skills Needing Possible Training and Support
COPING WITH THE DEMANDS OF SCHOOL	Attending to learning tasks Organizing work tasks Following directions Managing time Asking questions
DEVELOPING INTERPERSONAL RELATIONSHIPS	Learning to work cooperatively with others Responding to social cues in the environment Using socially acceptable language Responding appropriately to teacher directions and cues Enhancing social perception (drawing appropriate conclusions from experiences with others)
DEVELOPING LANGUAGE SKILLS	Understanding directions Communicating needs and wants Expressing ideas Listening attentively Using proper voice modulation and inflection
EMOTIONAL DEVELOPMENT	Seeking out social participation and interaction Decreasing avoidance of work and social experiences (e.g., tardiness, idleness, social withdrawal)
TAKING CARE OF PERSONAL NEEDS	Practicing appropriate personal hygiene Dressing independently Taking care of personal belongings Getting around from one place to another

Adaptive Behavior

The abilities to adapt to the demands of the environment, relate to others, and take care of personal needs are all important aspects of an independent life-style. For people with mental retardation, these social and personal competence skills are often not comparable to those of their nondisabled peers. Table 4–2 presents an overview of the adaptive behavior skills of people with mental retardation. In the school setting, *adaptive behavior* is defined as the ability to apply skills learned in a classroom to daily activities. The child with mental retardation may need to be taught appropriate reasoning, judgment, and social skills that lead to more positive social relationships and personal competence. Some researchers have also suggested that adaptive behavior deficits for people with mental retardation may also be associated with a lower self-image and a greater expectancy for failure in both academic and social situations (Westling, 1986; Zigler & Balla, 1981).

Academic Achievement

Research on the educational achievement of children with mild to moderate mental retardation has suggested that there will be significant deficits in the areas of reading and mathematics. As early as 1940, Kirk indicated that children with IQs between two and three standard deviations below the mean would read anywhere from the first- to fourth-grade level. Westling (1986), in a review of the literature on reading and mental retardation, suggested that "reading is generally considered the weakest area of learning, especially reading comprehension" (p. 127). In general, students with mild retardation are better at decoding words than comprehending their meaning. Most students with retardation read below their own mental-age level. Arithmetic skills are also deficient for these children, although their performance may be closer to what is typical for their mental age. These children may be able to learn basic computations but be unable to apply concepts appropriately (Patton, Beirne-Smith, & Payne, 1990).

A growing body of research (Browder & Snell, 1987) has indicated that children with moderate and severe mental retardation can be taught to read at least enough to develop a protective or survival vocabulary. These children may be limited to recognizing their names and those of significant others in their lives, as well as common survival words, including *help, hurt, danger,* and *stop.*

FOCUS 4
Identify the academic, speech/language, and physical characteristics of children with mental retardation.

Speech and Language Characteristics

One of the most serious and obvious characteristics of individuals with mental retardation is delayed speech and language development. The most common speech problems involve **articulation, voice,** and **stuttering.** Language problems are generally associated with delays in language development rather than the bizarre use of language (Patton et al., 1990). Kaiser, Alpert, and Warren (1987) emphasized that "the overriding goal of language intervention is to increase the individual's functional communication" (p. 248).

The severity of the speech and language problems is positively correlated with the severity of the mental retardation. Miller (1981) indicated that the mental age of the child is the single greatest predictor of language performance. Speech and language difficulties may range from minor speech defects, such as articulation problems, to the complete absence of expressive language. The relationship between language problems and mental retardation was also postulated by Van Riper (1972), who suggested that children may appear to be or even become mentally retarded because they do not learn to speak. Mental retardation may cause speech problems, but speech problems may also directly contribute to the severity of

■ **Table 4–3** Speech and Language Skills for Individuals with Moderate to Profound Mental Retardation

	Severity of Mental Retardation	
Moderate	Severe	Profound
Most individuals are deficient in speech and language skills, but many develop language abilities that allow them some level of communication with others.	Without exception, individuals exhibit significant speech and language delays and deviations (e.g., lack of expressive and receptive language, poor articulation, and little, if any, spontaneous interaction).	Individuals do not exhibit spontaneous communication patterns. Bizarre speech may be evident (e.g., echolalic speech, speech out of context, purposeless speech).

the mental retardation. Table 4–3 describes the range of speech and language skills for individuals with moderate to profound mental retardation.

Physical Characteristics

The physical appearance of most children with mental retardation does not differ from that of children of the same age who are not retarded. However, there is a relationship between the severity of the mental retardation and the extent of physical problems for the individual (Patton et al., 1990; Westling, 1986). For the person with severe mental retardation, there is a significant probability of related physical problems; genetic factors are likely behind both disabilities. The individual with mild retardation, however, may exhibit no physical problems because the retardation may be associated with environmental, not genetic, factors. Table 4–4 describes the range of physical characteristics associated with individuals who have moderate to profound mental retardation.

Research has also suggested that there are higher prevalences of vision and hearing problems among children with retardation (Bensberg & Siegelman, 1976: Fink, 1981), as well as motor difficulties (Drew et al., 1992). The majority of children with severe and profound retardation have multiple disabilities that affect nearly every aspect of intellectual and physical development.

■ **Table 4–4** Physical Characteristics of Individuals with Moderate to Profound Mental Retardation

	Severity of Mental Retardation	
Moderate	Severe	Profound
Gross and fine motor coordination are usually deficient. However, the individual is usually ambulatory and capable of independent mobility. Perceptual-motor skills exist (e.g., body awareness, sense of touch, eye-hand coordination) but are often deficient in comparison to the norm.	As many as 80 percent have significant motor difficulties (i.e., poor or nonambulatory skills). Gross or fine motor skills may be present, but the individual may lack control, resulting in awkward or inept motor movement.	Some gross motor development is evident, but fine motor skills are poor. The individual is usually nonambulatory and not capable of independent mobility within the environment. Perceptual-motor skills are often nonexistent.

The living conditions of children with mental retardation may contribute directly to an increasing incidence of health problems. A significantly higher percentage of children with mental retardation come from low-socioeconomic-level backgrounds in comparison to nondisabled peers. Children, who do not receive proper nutrition, are exposed to inadequate sanitation, and have a greater susceptibility to infections (Drew et al., 1992). Health services for families in these situations may be minimal or nonexistent, depending on whether they are able to access government medical support. As such, children with mental retardation may become ill more often than those who are not retarded. Consequently, children with retardation may miss more school.

CAUSATION

Mental retardation is the result of multiple causes, some known, many unknown. Possible causes of mental retardation include sociocultural differences, infection and intoxication, chromosomal abnormalities, gestation disorders, unknown prenatal influences, traumas or physical agents, metabolic and nutritional factors, and postnatal brain disease.

Sociocultural Influences

For individuals with mild retardation, such as Kim from the opening window, the cause of the problem is not generally apparent. A significant number of individuals with mild retardation come from low-socioeconomic-level families and different cultural backgrounds. Individuals who are environmentally or culturally disadvantaged are often in home situations where there are fewer opportunities for learning, which only further contributes to their problems at school. Additionally, because these high-risk children live in such adverse economic conditions, they generally do not receive proper nutritional care. As stated by Westling (1986), "Poor people have poor nutritional characteristics" (p. 100). MacMillan (1982) further explained that the highest prevalence of mental retardation occurs among

> —people referred to as "culturally deprived," "culturally different," "culturally disadvantaged," or some other term that connotes adverse economic and living conditions. Children of high risk are those who live in slums and, frequently, who are members of certain ethnic minority groups. In these high-risk groups there is poor medical care for mother and child, a high rate of broken families, and little value for education or motivation to achieve. (pp. 86–87)

An important question to be addressed in relationship to individuals who have grown up in adverse sociocultural situations is: How much of the person's ability is related to sociocultural influences as opposed to genetic factors? This issue is referred to as the **nature versus nurture** controversy. Numerous studies over the years have focused on the degree to which both heredity and environment contribute to intelligence. What has been learned from these studies is that, while there is a better understanding of the interactive effects of both heredity and environment, the exact contribution of each to intellectual growth remains unknown.

The term to describe children whose retardation may be attributable to both sociocultural and genetic factors is **cultural-familial.** These individuals are often described as (1) being mildly retarded, (2) having no known biological cause for the condition, (3) having at least one parent or sibling who is also mildly retarded, and (4) growing up in a low-socioeconomic-level home environment.

For the majority of individuals with moderate, severe, and profound mental retardation, problems are evident at birth. The American Association on Mental Retardation has

FOCUS 5
Identify the causes of mental retardation.

grouped the causes of mental retardation into several general categories (Grossman, 1983). In order to gain a greater understanding of the diversity of causes associated with mental retardation, we will briefly review the categories.

Infection and Intoxication

Several types of **maternal infections** may result in difficulties for the unborn child. In some cases, the outcome is spontaneous abortion of the fetus; in others, it may be a severe birth defect. The probability of damage is particularly high if the infection occurs during the first three months of pregnancy. **Congenital rubella** (German measles) is the type of infection that is perhaps most widely known. Rubella is a viral infection that causes a variety of problems, including mental retardation, deafness, blindness, cerebral palsy, cardiac problems, seizures, and a variety of other neurological problems. The widespread administration of a rubella vaccine is one of the major reasons why mental retardation as an outcome of rubella has declined significantly in recent years.

Another infection associated with severe disorders is syphilis. Syphilis transmitted from the mother to the unborn child can result in severe birth defects. With syphilis, bacteria actually cross the placenta and infect the fetus. This results in damage to the tissue of the central nervous system as well as to the circulatory system.

Several prenatal infections may result in other severe disorders. For example, **toxoplasmosis** is an infection carried by raw meat and fecal material. The damage from toxoplasmosis may be significant, resulting in mental retardation and other problems such as blindness and convulsions. Toxoplasmosis is primarily a threat if the mother is exposed during pregnancy, whereas infection prior to conception seems to cause minimal danger to the unborn child.

Intoxication refers to cerebral damage that occurs due to an excessive level of some toxic agent in the mother-fetus system. Excessive maternal use of alcohol or drugs or exposure to certain environmental hazards such as x-rays or insecticides may cause damage to the child. Damage to the fetus that is caused by maternal alcohol consumption is known as **fetal alcohol syndrome.** This condition is characterized by facial abnormalities, heart problems, low birthweight, and mental retardation. It is estimated that more than 50,000 babies are born with alcohol-related problems each year in the United States (National Association, 1991). Similarly, pregnant women who smoke are at greater risk of having a premature baby with complicating developmental problems such as mental retardation (Hetherington & Parke, 1986). The use of drugs during pregnancy has varying effects on the infant, depending on frequency, amount taken, and drug type. According to Peterson (1987), drugs that are known to produce serious fetal damage include LSD, heroin, morphine, and cocaine. Prescription drugs such as **anticonvulsants** and antibiotics have also been associated with infant malformations (Batshaw & Perret, 1986).

Another factor that can seriously affect the unborn baby is an incompatible blood type between the mother and the fetus. The most widely known form of this problem is when the mother's blood is Rh-negative while the fetus has Rh-positive blood. In this situation, the mother's system may become sensitized to the incompatible blood type and produce defensive antibodies that damage the fetus. Medical technology can now prevent this condition through the use of a drug known as *Rhogam*.

Mental retardation may also occur after a baby is born as a result of postnatal infections and toxic excesses. For example, **encephalitis** may damage the central nervous system following certain types of childhood infections (e.g., measles or mumps). Reactions to certain toxic substances—such as lead, carbon monoxide, and drugs—can also cause central nervous system damage.

4–4   Did You Know . . .

Did you know that . . . ?

◆ The United States continues to lag far behind most other industrialized countries regarding maternal and child health care. Ten babies die for every 1,000 live births in the United States. The United States ranks nineteenth in the world for infant mortality and low-birthweight babies.

◆ About 43 percent of the very low-birthweight infants born in the United States who survive have moderate to severe disabilities, including mental retardation.

◆ Approximately 85,000 children between 6 and 15 years of age are in special education programs because of disabling conditions that resulted primarily from being born weighing 2,500 grams or less.

◆ One in five children in the United States has no health insurance.

◆ One out of every four pregnant women in the United States receives no health care during the critical first month of pregnancy (about 20 percent of white mothers and 38 percent of black mothers). Women who do not receive prenatal care have a three to six times greater chance of having a low-birthweight baby.

◆ By the year 2000, one in every five births in the United States and more than one in every three black births will be to a mother who did not receive early prenatal care.

Source: National Association of State Directors of Special Education, 1991.

Chromosomal Abnormalities

Chromosomes are threadlike bodies that carry the genes that play the critical role in determining inherited characteristics. Defects resulting from chromosomal abnormalities are typically dramatic: often severe and accompanied by visually evident abnormalities. Fortunately, genetically caused defects are relatively rare. The vast majority of humans have normal cell structures, and development proceeds without accident. Human body cells normally have 46 chromosomes, arranged in 23 pairs. Aberrations that occur in chromosomal arrangement, either before fertilization or during early cell division, may result in a variety of abnormal characteristics.

One of the most widely recognized types of mental retardation, Down syndrome, results from chromosomal abnormality. Down syndrome is a condition that results in facial

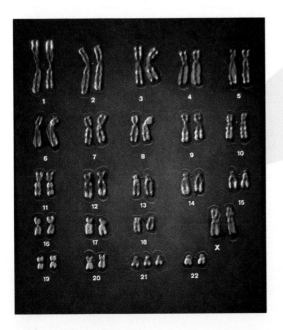

The most common cause of Down syndrome is a chromosomal abnormality known as trisomy 21, in which the twenty-first chromosomal pair carries an extra chromosome. (CNRI/Science Photo Library/Photo Researchers, Inc.)

REFLECT ON THIS

 4–5　　Understanding More about People with Down Syndrome

What Is Down Syndrome?

Down syndrome is a combination of birth defects including mental retardation. Formerly, it was called mongolism because most infants with this birth defect have a somewhat Oriental appearance.

What Does a Child With Down Syndrome Look Like?

The child may have oval-shaped eyes, a tongue that seems big for the mouth and a short neck. The head may be flattened in the back and the ears small and sometimes folded a little at the tops. The nose is also flattened and wide. The child or adult with Down syndrome is often short in stature and has unusual looseness of the joints.

How Serious Is the Mental Retardation?

The degree of mental retardation varies widely, from mild to moderate to severe. Most fall within the moderate range, but all are retarded to some degree. There is no way to predict the mental development of a child with Down syndrome from the physical appearance.

What Can a Child With Down Syndrome Do?

A child with this birth defect can usually do most things that any young child can do, such as walking, talking, dressing and being toilet-trained. However, they do these things later than other children. As with other children, you never can know exactly at what age these developmental milestones will be achieved.

Can a Child With Down Syndrome Go to School?

Yes. There are special programs beginning in the preschool years to help each child develop skills as fully as possible. These programs continue through the school years and there are special work programs designed for adults with Down syndrome. The extent of achievement is determined by the development of the brain and the social environment in which the child lives.

Do Children With Down Syndrome Have Special Health Problems?

Many have heart abnormalities and frequently, surgery can correct these problems. A child with Down syndrome may have many colds, bronchitis and pneumonia. These children, like all others, should receive regular medical care including eye and hearing tests as well as regular immunizations.

Many adults with Down syndrome age faster than their normal age group. Life expectancy among Down syndrome adults is about 50 years of age, but this varies widely.

What Causes Down Syndrome?

A baby is formed when the egg from the mother and the sperm from the father come together. Normally, egg and sperm cells each have 23 chromosomes. Chromosomes are the hereditary information "packets" of every living cell. In the usual case of a child with Down syndrome, either the egg or the sperm cell contributes 24 chromosomes, instead of 23. The result is that the chromosomes present total 47, instead of the normal 46. The extra chromosome causes the mental and physical characteristics of Down syn-

and physical characteristics that are visibly distinctive. Facial features are marked by distinctive epicanthic eyefolds, prominent cheekbones, and a small, somewhat flattened nose. About 5 percent of individuals with mental retardation have Down syndrome (Patton et al., 1990).

Down syndrome has received widespread attention in the literature and has been a favored topic in both medical and special education textbooks for many years. Part of this attention has come because of the apparent ability to identify a cause with some degree of certainty. The cause of such genetic errors has become increasingly associated with the ages of both the mother and the father. MacMillan (1982) reported that, for mothers between the ages of 20 and 30, the chances of having a child with Down syndrome is one in 1,200. The probabilities increase significantly (1 in 20) for mothers older than 45 years of age. Abroms and Bennett (1983) indicated that, in about 25 percent of the cases associated with Trisomy 21, the age of the father (particularly when over 55 years old) is also a factor.

Gestation Disorders

The most typical gestation disorders involve **prematurity** and **low birthweight.** Prematurity refers to infants delivered before 35 weeks from the first day of the last menstrual

drome. This cause of Down syndrome is called trisomy 21, because of the presence of three #21 chromosomes. Certain other accidents involving chromosome #21 in egg, sperm or very early embryo also cause Down syndrome, but account for less than 5 percent of cases.

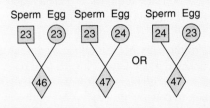

Can a Down Syndrome Baby Be Cured?

There is unfortunately no cure for a child born with this birth defect. Although many claims are made, science has yet to develop the means to prevent the cause of Down syndrome.

Can Down Syndrome Children Marry?

Some young people with Down syndrome have married, but this is unusual. A man with Down syndrome has never fathered a child. A woman with Down syndrome has a 50–50 chance of having a child with the same condition. Many people with Down syndrome require someone to care for them.

Is There Something Wrong With Parents of a Down Syndrome Child?

Usually not. The phenomenon which causes the extra chromosome can happen in any egg or sperm cell. The extra chromosome can come from either parent. In rare cases it occurs in an embryo formed from a normal egg and sperm, or results from a chromosome rearrangement throughout a healthy parent's cells.

Who Has the Greatest Chance of Having a Down Syndrome Child?

Parents who have already had a baby with Down syndrome, a mother or father who has a chromosome rearrangement as mentioned above, a mother who is over 35 years old. The chances of an older woman having a baby with Down syndrome are the same whether it is the mother's first pregnancy or not. Down syndrome is the most common genetic birth defect. It affects all races and economic levels of society equally.

Can Down Syndrome Be Diagnosed Before the Child Is Born?

Yes. If there is reason to be concerned about the possibility, a test called amniocentesis can be done in the fourth month of pregnancy. Any family who has a mentally retarded child or a child with other birth defects can discuss the test with a doctor or other health professional who may refer them to a genetic counseling center. The test cannot guarantee the birth of a normal child, but it can indicate whether Down syndrome is present in the fetus.

What Is the March of Dimes Doing to Prevent and Treat Down Syndrome?

Funding scientific research is the principle means by which March of Dimes is seeking to prevent Down syndrome. Much effort is directed to investigation of the complex structure of chromosomes, and the genes which are contained in all chromosomes, including #21. Other research projects deal with the amelioration of Down syndrome.

Source: March of Dimes Birth Defects Foundation. (1991). *Public health education information sheet: Genetic series.* White Plains, NY: Author. Reprinted with permission.

period. Low birthweight characterizes babies that weigh 2,500 grams (5.5 pounds) or less at birth. Prematurity and low birthweight significantly increase the risk of serious problems at birth, including mental retardation.

Unknown Prenatal Influences

Several conditions associated with unknown prenatal influences can result in extremely severe disorders. One such condition involves malformations of cerebral tissue. The most dramatic of these malformations is known as **anencephaly,** a condition in which the individual has a partial or even complete absence of cerebral tissue. In some cases, portions of the brain appear to develop and then degenerate. The prognosis for individuals with this condition is not very promising; most do not survive beyond a few hours or days.

Hydrocephalus is another condition that results from unknown prenatal influence. In hydrocephalus, an excess of cerebrospinal fluid accumulates in the skull and results in potentially damaging pressure on cerebral tissue. Hydrocephalus may or may not involve an enlarged head, depending on when the production or absorption imbalance occurs. If it is present at birth or shortly thereafter, the seams of the child's skull will not have grown closed and the pressure will result in an enlarged head. Hydrocephaly may result in decreased intellectual functioning. If surgical intervention occurs early, the damage may be slight because the pressure will not have been serious or prolonged. If such intervention does not occur or is not undertaken early, the degree of mental retardation that results may range from moderate to profound.

Traumas or Physical Agents

Traumas or physical accidents may occur either prior to birth (e.g., excessive radiation), during delivery, or after the baby is born. Consider Becky from Window 4–1: The cause of her mental retardation was trauma during delivery. She suffered from birth asphyxiation as well as epileptic seizures.

The continuing supply of oxygen and nutrients to the baby is a critical factor during delivery. One threat to these processes involves the position of the fetus. Normal fetal position places the baby with the head toward the cervix and the face toward the mother's back. Certain other positions may result in fetal damage as delivery proceeds. One of these is known as a breech presentation, in which the buttocks of the fetus, rather than the head, are positioned toward the cervix. The head exits last rather than first and may be subjected to several types of stress that would not occur if the delivery were normal. The head passes through the birth canal under stress, and the pressure of the contractions has a direct impact on the fetal skull rather than on the buttocks, as in a normal position. In a breech presentation, the umbilical cord may not be long enough to remain attached while the head is expelled, or it may become pinched between the baby's body and the pelvic girdle. In either case, the baby's oxygen supply may be reduced for a period of time until the head is expelled and the lungs begin to function. The baby's lack of oxygen may result in damage to the brain. Such a condition is known as **anoxia** (oxygen deprivation).

Other abnormal positions can also result in delivery problems and damage to the fetus. The fetus may lie across the birth canal in what is known as a transverse position. In such cases, the baby may not be able to exit through the birth canal, or if the baby does exit, severe damage may occur. In other cases, labor and delivery proceed so rapidly that the fetal skull does not have time to mold properly or in a sufficiently gentle fashion. Rapid births (generally less than two hours) are known as **precipitous births** and may result in mental retardation as well as other problems.

Metabolism and Nutrition

Metabolic problems are characterized by the body's inability to process (metabolize) certain substances that can then become poisonous and damage tissue in the central nervous system. **Phenylketonuria (PKU)** is one such inherited metabolic disorder. The baby is not able to process phenylalanine, a substance found in many foods, including the milk ingested by infants. The inability to process phenylalanine results in an accumulation of poisonous substances in the body. If it is untreated or not treated promptly (mostly through dietary restrictions), PKU causes varying degrees of mental retardation, ranging from moderate to severe deficits. If treatment is promptly instituted, however, damage may be largely prevented or at least reduced. This is why most states now require mandatory screening for all infants in order to treat the condition as early as possible and prevent lifelong problems.

Milk also presents a problem for infants affected by another metabolic disorder, **galactosemia.** In this case, the child is unable to properly process lactose, which is the primary sugar in milk and is also found in other foods. If galactosemia remains untreated, serious damage results, such as cataracts, heightened susceptibility to infection, and reduced intellectual functioning. Dietary controls must be undertaken, eliminating milk and other foods containing lactose.

Gross Postnatal Brain Disease

Several disorders are associated with gross postnatal brain disease. **Neurofibromatosis** is an inherited disorder that results in multiple tumors in the skin, peripheral nerve tissue, and other areas such as the brain. Mental retardation does not occur in all cases, although it may be evident in about 10 percent (Robinson & Robinson, 1976). The severity of mental retardation and other problems resulting from neurofibromatosis seems to relate to the location of the tumors (e.g., in the cerebral tissue) and their size and growth. Severe disorders due to gross postnatal brain disease occur with a variety of other conditions, including **tuberous sclerosis,** which also involves tumors in the central nervous system tissue and degeneration of cerebral white matter.

Although we have presented a number of possible causal factors associated with mental retardation, it is important to remember that the cause is unknown and undeterminable in many cases. Additionally, many conditions associated with mental retardation are due to the interaction of both hereditary and environmental factors. While we are unable to always identify the causes of mental retardation, measures can be taken to prevent its occurrence.

PREVENTION

Preventing mental retardation is a laudable goal and has for many years been the focus of professionals in the field of medicine. Over the years, prevention has taken many forms, including the sterilization of people with mental retardation. More recently, preventive measures have focused on immunization against disease, maternal nutritional habits during pregnancy, appropriate prenatal care, and screening for genetic disorders prior to and at birth.

FOCUS 6
Identify four measures that may prevent mental retardation.

Children who live in poverty are at terrible risk for mental retardation and other disabilities.
(Mike Jackson/The Picture Group)

Immunization can protect family members from contracting serious illness and in addition guard against the mother becoming ill during pregnancy. Diseases such as rubella, which may result in severe mental retardation, heart disease, or blindness, can be controlled through routine immunization programs.

Improper nutritional habits during pregnancy may also contribute to fetal problems. Moreover, poor nutritional habits are part of a much larger social problem: the lack of appropriate prenatal care during pregnancy. In 1983, the President's Commission for the Study of Ethical Problems in Medicine and Biomedical and Behavior Research indicated that delays in prenatal care can have "significant health consequences, as many conditions that are amenable to timely medical treatment can develop serious complications if neglected" (p. 111). The commission documented several case studies of pregnant women who were unable to obtain prenatal care in their local communities. These women were already in labor when they entered the hospital and were considered to be at high risk for complications at delivery (President's Commission, 1983).

A medical history can alert the attending physician to any potential dangers for the mother or the unborn infant that may result from family genetics, prior trauma, or illness. The physician will be able to monitor the health of the fetus, including heartrate, physical size, and position in the uterus. At the time of birth, several factors relevant to the infant's health can be assessed. A procedure known as **Apgar scoring** evaluates the infant on heartrate, respiratory condition, muscle tone, reflex irritability, and color. This screening procedure alerts the medical staff to infants who may warrant closer monitoring and more indepth assessments. Other screening procedures conducted in the medical laboratory within the first few days of life can detect anomalies that, if not treated, will eventually lead to mental retardation, psychological disorders, physical disabilities, or even death.

Other methods of prevention are more involved with issues of morality and ethics. These include genetic screening and counseling and therapeutic abortion. *Genetic screening* is defined as "a search in a population for persons possessing certain genotypes that (1) are already associated with disease or predisposed to disease, (2) may lead to disease in their descendants, or (3) produce other variations not known to be associated with disease" (National Academy of Sciences, 1975, p. 9). Genetic screening may be conducted at various times in the family-planning process or during pregnancy. When screening is conducted prior to conception, the purpose is to determine whether the parents are predisposed to

Modern technologies such as ultrasound allow for prenatal detection of abnormalities, which may signal the presence of mental retardation. (Keith/Custom Medical Stock Photo)

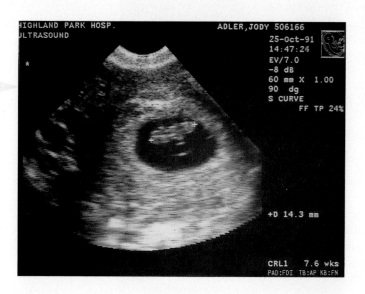

genetic anomalies that could be inherited by their offspring. If screening takes place after conception, the purpose is to determine if the fetus has any genetic abnormalities. This can be accomplished through one of several medical procedures, including **amniocentesis, fetoscopy,** and **ultrasound.**

Once genetic screening has been completed, it is the responsibility of a counselor to inform parents of the results. Parents are then made fully aware of potential outcomes and options. While the genetic counselor does not make decisions *for* the parents regarding family planning, he or she prepares the parents to exercise their rights.

The primary outcome of genetic counseling can be viewed in terms of informing the parents concerning decisions they have to make about whether to (1) have children based on the probability of a genetic anomaly occurring or (2) abort a pregnancy if prenatal assessment indicates that the developing fetus has a genetic anomaly. The decision of whether to abort involves a moral controversy that society has been attempting to deal with for years. For example, if it is detected that a fetus has Down syndrome, what intervention options are available? Certainly, one option involves continuing the pregnancy and making mental, physical, and financial preparations for the additional care that may be required for the child. The other option is to terminate the pregnancy through what is often termed **therapeutic abortion.** This is abortion, nonetheless, and presents ethical dilemmas for many people.

The time immediately following birth, known as the *neonatal period,* may present some of the most difficult ethical dilemmas for parents and professionals. During the neonatal period, the issue is usually whether to withhold medical treatment from a defective newborn. This raises a number of ethical and moral questions: Who makes these decisions? Under what circumstances are such decisions made? What criteria are used to determine whether treatment is to be withheld?

EDUCATIONAL ASSESSMENT

Just as a physician assesses an individual with mental retardation to determine the extent of medical intervention, so do professionals from several disciplines assess the individual's need for special education services. This group of professionals join with the child's parents to assess needs and plan for intervention. They are often referred to as the multidisciplinary team. The professionals on this team usually include the school psychologist, the classroom teacher, and a school administrator. Depending on the needs of the child, other professionals may be involved as well, including a social worker, speech or language specialist, occupational or physical therapist, adaptive physical education teacher, school counselor, and school nurse.

The multidisciplinary team has two critical functions with regard to assessment of a child. First, they must determine whether the child in question meets the criteria of mental retardation before placing him or her in a special education program. Second, it is the responsibility of the team to assess the educational needs of the child so that an appropriate educational program can be developed and implemented.

An intelligence test and a measure of adaptive behavior must be completed to determine whether the child meets criteria. The most commonly used scales for measuring intelligence in school-age children are the Wechsler Intelligence Scales and the Stanford-Binet Intelligence Scale.

Adaptive behavior may be measured by both formal and informal appraisals. Informal appraisals include direct observations as well as asking people who are in regular contact with the child (such as parents and classroom teachers) about his or her ability to cope with the demands of the environment. Formal appraisals include the use of standardized adaptive behavior scales such as the Vineland Social Maturity Scale, the Scales of Independent Behavior, and the AAMR Adaptive Behavior Scale.

Once it has been determined that the child meets the criteria for mental retardation, the team sets in place specific assessment procedures that will determine the nature of an appropriate educational experience for this particular child. The team members contribute information from their areas of expertise to build a broad base for determining the child's needs. The psychologist and the classroom teacher select, administer, and interpret appropriate psychological, educational, and behavioral assessment instruments. In addition, they observe the child's performance in an educational setting and consult with parents and other team members regarding the child's overall development. Parents provide the team with information regarding the child's performance outside of the school setting. They must provide written consent for testing the child in order to change his or her educational placement. Physical therapists, occupational therapists, and adaptive physical education specialists assess the motor development of the child. The speech or language specialist assesses the child's communication abilities. The social worker may collect pertinent information from the home setting as well as other background data relevant to the child's needs. The school nurse assists in the interpretation of information regarding the child's health (e.g., hearing and vision screenings, conferring with physicians, and monitoring medications).

Although each team member has specific responsibilities in assessing the educational needs of the child, it is important that the members work together as a unit. Each member of the team has the responsibility to maintain ongoing communication with other members, actively participate in problem-solving situations, and follow through with assigned tasks.

EDUCATIONAL INTERVENTIONS

Education is a relatively new concept as it relates to students with mental retardation, particularly those with severe disabilities. Historically, many of these students were defined as noneducable by the public schools because they did not fit the programs offered by general education. Such programs were built on a foundation of academic learning that emphasized

---

TODAY'S TECHNOLOGY

Children with Down Syndrome Learn Language through Synthesized Speech

Children with Down syndrome often have significant delays in language development. They may not even be able to speak single words until they are 2 years old and may not be able to string words together until at least 3 or 4 years of age. Even as these children get older and are able to master more language skills, they often apply their vocabulary or new language structure in an inconsistent fashion. Speech is expressed in such a complex and rapid auditory stream that the child with Down syndrome often finds it extremely difficult to comprehend meaning.

Laura Meyers, a specialist in speech and language disabilities, found a way to slow down speech through the use of a computer and assist students with Down syndrome to become more proficient at language acquisition. Two software programs, *Exploratory Play* and *Representational Play*,★ are designed to help children express and receive speech through

computer instruction. Using a computer keyboard, a child may ask for, label, or describe a toy or action by touching a picture on the keyboard. The picture then appears on the screen, and a speech synthesizer says the descriptive word written below it. Using the speech output, the child can then create and describe imaginary play scenes and carry on meaningful conversations with others.

Since synthesized speech can occur at a rate much slower than that of human speech, the child is able to hear more efficiently what is being said. Additionally, through the synthesized speech output the child can generate as many repetitions of exactly the same signal as needed to learn the sound pattern of words, sentences, and phrases.

Source: From *Computer-Enhanced Language Interventions* by L. Meyers, n.d., Calabasas, CA, PEAL Software. Copyright PEAL Software. Adapted by permission.

★ Both available from PEAL Software.

reading, writing, and arithmetic. Thus, students with mental retardation could not meet the academic standards set by the schools and as such were excluded. Schools were not expected to adapt to the needs of students with retardation; rather, the students were expected to adapt to the schools.

Due to both state and federal mandates (e.g., IDEA), the schools that excluded these children for so long face a new challenge: to provide an appropriate education for all children with mental retardation. Based on a new set of values, education has been redefined. No longer do the schools dictate a general curriculum emphasizing only academic learning. Instead, education is defined as advancing an individual to the next highest level of functioning, regardless of how developmentally delayed he or she may be. For those who are severely and profoundly retarded, the differences are substantial and require the provision of services far beyond the scope of a single profession. Although educators have traditionally been autonomous in their classrooms, this practice cannot continue if the needs of students with severe and profound retardation are to be met. When working in harmony, the fields of medicine, the social services, and education form a network of professionals that provide the best means available to educate individuals with mental retardation. To gain a more in-depth perspective on intervention strategies, we will analyze both childhood and adolescent programs for these students.

Early Childhood Education

Education and training for people with mental retardation—particularly individuals such as Becky, who is severely mentally retarded (see Window 4–1)—may be a lifelong process. For people who are severely retarded, interventions should begin at birth and continue to the adult years. The importance of early intervention cannot be overstated. Gentry and Olson (1985) reported that significant advances have been made in the area of early intervention, including (1) improved assessment, curricular, and instructional technologies; (2) increasing numbers of children receiving services; and (3) appreciation of the need to individualize services for families as well as children. McDonnell and Hardman (1988), in a review of the literature in early intervention, suggested that "best-practice" indicators include programs that are integrated with students who are not disabled, as well as comprehensive, normalized, adaptable, peer and family referenced, and outcome based.

Early intervention techniques, such as **infant stimulation** programs, focus on the acquisition of sensorimotor functions and intellectual development. This involves learning simple reflex activity and equilibrium reactions. Subsequent intervention then expands into all areas of human growth and development. Intervention based on normal patterns of growth is often referred to as the *developmental milestones approach* (Bailey & Wolery, 1989) because it seeks to develop, remedy, or adapt learner skills based on the child's variation from what is considered normal. This progression of skills continues as the child ages chronologically. His or her rate of progress will depend on the severity of the condition. Some children who are profoundly retarded may never exceed a developmental age of 6 months. Others with moderate retardation may develop to a level that will enable them to have fulfilled lives as adults, with varying levels of societal support and supervision.

The preschool-age child with mild retardation may exhibit subtle developmental discrepancies in comparison to age-mates, but parents may not identify these discrepancies as significant enough to seek intervention. Even if parents are concerned and seek help for their child prior to school age, they are often confronted with professionals who are apathetic toward early childhood education. Some professionals believe that early childhood services may actually create rather than remedy problems, since the child may not be mature enough to cope with the pressures of structured learning in an educational environment. This maturation philosophy has been ingrained in educators and parents. Simply stated, it means to

FOCUS 7

Why is the need for early intervention services for children with mental retardation so critical?

wait for the child to reach a point of maturation where he or she is ready to learn certain skills. Unfortunately, this philosophy has kept many children out of the public schools for years while waiting for them to mature.

The antithesis of the maturation philosophy is the prevention of further learning and behavior problems through intervention. **Project Head Start,** initially funded as a federal preschool program for disadvantaged students, is a prevention program that attempts to identify and instruct high-risk children prior to their entering public school. Although Head Start did not generate the results that were initially anticipated (the virtual elimination of school-adjustment problems for the disadvantaged student), it did represent a beginning. The rationale for early education is widely accepted in the field of special education and was part of the mandate of IDEA (see Chapters One and Three).

Education for Elementary School-Age Children

FOCUS 8
Identify five skill areas for elementary-age children with mental retardation.

Educational programing for elementary school-age children with mental retardation is concerned with decreasing dependence on others while concurrently teaching adaptation to the environment. Therefore, the educational curriculum must concentrate on those skills that facilitate the child's interaction with others and emphasize independence in the community. Programs for children with mental retardation generally include skill areas such as motor development, self-care, social skills, communication, and functional academics.

Motor Skills.   The acquisition of motor skills is a fundamental component of the developmental process and a prerequisite to successful learning in other content areas, including self-care and social skills. Moon and Bunker (1987) suggested that

> both fine and gross motor skills are involved in the accomplishment of almost all activities within every domain. . . . A general rule of thumb should be to train fine and gross motor skills within the context of functional activities. . . . Walking can be instructed during community activities such as learning to use the neighborhood grocery store or traveling independently to school or work. (p. 232)

Gross motor development involves general mobility, including the interaction of the body with the environment. Gross motor skills are developed in a sequence ranging from movements that make balance possible to higher-order locomotor patterns. Locomotor patterns are intended to move the person freely through the environment. Gross motor movements include head and neck control, rolling, body righting, sitting, creeping, crawling, standing, walking, running, jumping, and skipping.

Fine motor development requires more precision and steadiness than the skills developed in the gross motor area. Fine motor skills include reaching, grasping, and manipulation of objects. The development of fine motor skills is initially dependent on the ability of the child to "visually fix" on an object and "visually track" a moving target (Mori & Masters, 1980). Coordination of the eye and hand is an integral factor in many skill areas as well as in fine motor development. Eye-hand coordination is the basis of social- and leisure-time activities and is essential to the development of the object-control skills required in employment.

Self-Care Skills.   The development of self-care skills is another important content area related to independence. Self-care skills include eating, dressing, and personal hygiene tasks. Eating skills range from finger feeding, drinking from a cup, and proper table behaviors such as the use of utensils and napkins to serving food and etiquette. Dressing skills include buttoning, zipping, buckling, lacing, and tying. Personal hygiene skills also range on a

Computer-assisted communication enables individuals who are nonverbal to express themselves and answer questions. (Spencer Grant/Stock, Boston)

continuum from rather basic developmental skills to high-level skills relevant to adult behavior. Basic skills include toileting, face and hand washing, bathing, tooth brushing, hair combing, and shampooing. Skills associated with adolescent and adult years include skin care, shaving, hair setting, use of deodorants and cosmetics, and menstrual hygiene.

Social Skills.   Social skills training is closely aligned with the self-care area in that it relates many of the self-care concepts to the development of good interpersonal relationships. Social skills training emphasize the importance of physical appearance, proper manners, appropriate use of leisure time, and sexual behavior. The area of social skills may also focus on the development of personality characteristics conducive to successful integration into society.

Communication Skills.   The ability to communicate with others is also essential to growth and development. Without communication, there can be no interaction. Communication systems for children with mental retardation take three general forms: (1) verbal language; (2) **manual communication,** such as sign language and language boards; and (3) a combination of the verbal and manual approaches. The approach used depends on the child's capability. If he or she is able to develop the requisite skills for spoken language, everyday interactive skills will be greatly enhanced. Manual communication must be considered when a child is unable to develop verbal skills as an effective means of communication. What is important is that the individual develop some form of communication.

Functional Academic Skills.   A functional academic curriculum is intended to expand the child's knowledge in daily living, recreation, and employment areas. When teaching functional academic skills, the classroom teacher uses instructional materials that are realistic and part of the child's environment. Browder and Snell (1987), reviewing the literature related to learning functional reading skills, reported that students with mental retardation, including those with moderate to severe difficulties, can learn to read sight words and acquire reading comprehension or decoding skills (p. 437). A functional reading program contains words that are frequently encountered in the environment, such as labels or signs in public places; words that warn of possible risks; and symbols such as the skull and crossbones on poisonous substances. A functional math program involves such activities as learning to use a checkbook, shop in a grocery store, or operate a vending machine.

INTERACTING IN NATURAL SETTINGS ············ People with Mental Retardation ············

EARLY CHILDHOOD YEARS

Tips for the Family

◆ Promote family learning about the diversity of all people in the context of understanding the child with intellectual differences.

◆ Create opportunities for friendships to develop between your child and children without disabilities, both in family and neighborhood settings.

◆ Help facilitate your child's opportunities and access to neighborhood preschools by actively participating in the education planning process. Become familiar with the individualized family service plan (IFSP) and how it can serve as a planning tool to support the inclusion of your child in preschool programs that involve students without disabilities.

Tips for the Regular Preschool Teacher

◆ Focus on the child's individual abilities first. Whatever labels have been placed on the child (e.g., mentally retarded) will have little to do with instructional needs.

◆ When teaching the child, focus on presenting each component of a task clearly while reducing outside stimuli that may distract learning.

◆ Begin with simple tasks and move to more complex ones as the child masters skills.

◆ Verbally label stimuli, such as objects or people, as often as possible to provide the child with both auditory and visual input.

◆ Provide a lot of practice in initial learning phases using short but frequent sessions to ensure that the child has mastered the skill before moving on to more complex tasks.

◆ Create success experiences by rewarding correct responses to tasks as well as appropriate behavior with peers who are not disabled.

◆ It is important for the young child with mental retardation to be able to transfer learning from school to the home and neighborhood. Facilitate such transfer by providing information that is meaningful to the child and where the initial and transfer task are similar.

Tips for Preschool Personnel

◆ Support the inclusion of young children with mental retardation in classrooms and programs.

◆ Support teachers, staff, and volunteers as they attempt to create success experiences for the child in the preschool setting.

◆ Integrate families into the preschool programs as well as children. Offer parents as many opportunities as possible to be part of the program (e.g., advisory boards, volunteer experiences).

Tips for Neighbors and Friends

◆ Look for opportunities for young neighborhood children who are not disabled to interact during play times with the child who is mentally retarded.

◆ Provide a supportive community environment for the family of a young child who is mentally retarded. Encourage the family, including the child, to participate in neighborhood activities (e.g., outings, barbecues, outdoor yard and street cleanups, crime watches, etc.).

◆ Try to understand how the young child with mental retardation is similar to other children in the neighborhood rather than different. Focus on those similarities in your interactions with other neighbors and children in your community.

ELEMENTARY YEARS

Tips for the Family

◆ Actively participate in the development of your son or daughter's individualized education program (IEP). Through active participation, fight for the goals that you would like to see on the IEP that will focus on your child developing social interaction and communication skills in natural settings (e.g., the regular education classroom).

◆ To help facilitate your son or daughter's inclusion in the neighborhood elementary school, help educators and administrators understand the importance of inclusion with peers who are not disabled (e.g., riding on the same school bus, going to recess and lunch at the same time, participating in schoolwide assemblies, etc.).

◆ Participate in as many school functions for parents (e.g., PTA, parent advisory groups, volunteering, etc.) as is reasonable to connect your family to the mainstream of the regular education school.

◆ Create opportunities for your child to make friends with same-age children who are not disabled, both within the family and neighborhood.

Tips for the Regular Classroom Teacher

◆ View children with mental retardation as *children,* first and foremost. Focus on their similarities with other children rather than their differences.

◆ Recognize children with mental retardation for their own accomplishments within the classroom rather than comparing them to those of peers without disabilities.

◆ Employ cooperative learning strategies wherever possible to promote effective learning by all students. Try to use peers without disabilities as support for students with mental retardation. This may include establishing peer-buddy programs or peer and cross-age tutoring.

- Consider all members of the classroom when you organize the physical environment. Find ways to meet the individual needs of each child (e.g., establishing aisles that will accommodate a wheelchair, organizing desks to facilitate tutoring on assigned tasks, locating furniture to support individual hearing or vision differences).

Tips for School Personnel

- Integrate school resources as well as children. Wherever possible, help regular classroom teachers access the human and material resources necessary to meet the needs of students with mental retardation. Instructional materials and programs should be made available to whomever needs them, not just those identified as being in special education.
- Assist regular and special education teachers to develop nondisabled peer-partner and support networks for students with mental retardation.
- Promote the heterogeneous grouping of students. Try to avoid clustering large numbers of students with mental retardation in a single regular classroom. Integrate no more than one or two in each elementary education classroom.
- Maintain the same schedules for students with mental retardation as for all other students in the building. Recess, lunch, school assemblies, and bus arrival and departure schedules should be identical for all students, with and without disabilities.
- Create opportunities for all school personnel to collaborate in the development and implementation of instructional programs for individual children.

Tips for Neighbors and Friends

- Support families who are seeking to have their child with mental retardation educated in their local school with children who are not disabled. This will help children with mental retardation have more opportunities for interacting with children who are not disabled both in school and in the local community.

SECONDARY/TRANSITION YEARS

Tips for the Family

- Create opportunities for your son or daughter to participate in activities that are of interest to him or her beyond the school day with their same-age peers who are not disabled, including high school clubs, sports, or just hanging out in the local mall.
- Promote opportunities for students from your son's or daughter's high school to visit your home. Help arrange get-togethers or parties involving students from the neighborhood and/or school.

- Become actively involved in the development of the individualized education and transition program.
- Become aware of what life will be like for your child in the local community after he or she leaves high school. What is the high school's view on what it should be doing to assist your son or daughter in the transition from school to adult life? What are the characteristics of adult service programs available? Explore postschool services in the local community.

Tips for the Regular Classroom Teacher

- Collaborate with special education teachers and other specialists to adapt subject matter in your classroom (e.g., science, math, or physical education) to the individual needs of students with mental retardation.
- Let students without disabilities know that the student with mental retardation belongs in their classroom. The goals and activities of this student may be different from those of other students, but with support, the student with mental retardation will benefit from working with you and the other students in the class.
- Support the student with mental retardation in becoming involved in extracurricular high school activities. If you are the faculty sponsor of a club or organization, explore whether this student is interested and how he or she could get involved.

Tips for School Personnel

- Advocate for parents of high-school-age students with mental retardation to participate in the activities of the school (e.g., committees and PTA).
- Help facilitate parental involvement in the IEP process during the high school years by valuing parental input that focuses on a desire for including their child in the mainstream of the school. Parents will be more active when school personnel have regular and positive contact with the family.
- Provide human and material support to high school special education or vocational teachers seeking to develop **community-based instruction** programs that focus on students learning and applying skills in actual community settings (e.g., grocery stores, malls, theaters, parks, worksites).

Tips for Neighbors, Friends, and Potential Employers

- Seek ways to become part of the community support network for the individual with mental retardation. Be alert to ways that this individual can become and remain actively involved in community employment, neighborhood recreational activities, local church functions, and the like.
- As potential employers in the community, seek information on employment of people with mental retardation. Find out about programs (e.g., supported employment) that focus on establishing work for people with mental retardation while meeting your needs as an employer.

FOCUS 9

Identify four educational goals for adolescents with mental retardation.

Education and Employment Training for Adolescents

The goals of an educational program for adolescents with mental retardation are to (1) increase personal independence, (2) enhance opportunities for participation in the local community, (3) prepare for employment, and (4) facilitate a successful transition to the adult years.

Independence refers to the development and application of skills that lead to greater self-sufficiency in daily personal life, including personal hygiene, self-care, and appropriate leisure-time activities. Participation in the community includes access to those programs, facilities, and services people who are not disabled often take for granted: grocery stores, shopping malls, restaurants, theaters, parks, and the like. Adolescents with mental retardation should have opportunities for contact with nondisabled peers other than caregivers, access to community events, sustained social relationships, and involvement in choices that affect their lives. Work is a critical measure of any person's success during adulthood, providing the primary opportunity for social interaction, a basis for personal identity and status, and a chance to contribute to the community. These needs are basic to adults who are mentally retarded, just as they are to their nondisabled peers.

Employment training for adolescents with mental retardation was historically fraught with problems because professionals and the general public held a pessimistic attitude about its effectiveness. Today, that negative philosophy has largely been replaced by a commitment to the development of relevant employment-training programs, particularly in competitive employment settings (Brickey, Campbell, & Browning, 1985; McDonnell, Wilcox, & Hardman, 1991; Wehman & Hill, 1985).

Employment training during the high school years is moving away from the isolation and "getting-ready" orientation of a sheltered workshop to activities accomplished in community employment. Goals and objectives are developed according to the demands of the community work setting and in conjunction with the functioning level of the individual. The focus is on assisting the individual to learn and apply skills in a job setting while still receiving the necessary support to succeed. Providing ongoing assistance to the individual while on the job is the basis of an approach known as *supported employment*. Supported employment is defined as work in an integrated setting for individuals with severe disabilities (including those with mental retardation) who are expected to need continuous support services and for whom competitive employment has traditionally not been possible.

Research indicates that individuals with mental retardation, including those with moderate and severe differences, can work in community employment if provided adequate training and support (Hasazi, Johnson, Hasazi, Gordon, & Hull, 1989; McDonnell et al., 1991). Effectively preparing adolescents for community work settings will require a comprehensive employment-training program during the high school years. Adherence to the following guidelines will help enable the student to access and succeed in a community job following school:

1. The student should receive employment training in community settings prior to graduation from high school.

2. Employment training should focus on work opportunities present in the local area where the individual currently lives.

3. The focus of the employment training should be on specific job training as the student approaches graduation.

4. Collaboration between the school and adult service agencies must be part of the employment-training program (Hasazi et al., 1989; McDonnell et al., 1991).

Educational Placement Considerations

The educational placement of students with mental retardation has been a critical concern for school personnel and parents for many years. Prior to the late 1960s, special education for students with mental retardation meant segregated education. Since then, much of the focus on educational placement has been concerned with including, or mainstreaming, these students with their nondisabled age-mates. *Full inclusion* may be defined as the placement of students with mental retardation in regular education classrooms with nondisabled peers, consistent with an established educational plan for each individual (see also Chapter Three). Some students with mental retardation may be only partially included for a small part of the school day and attend only those regular education classes that their individualized education program (IEP) teams consider consistent with their needs and functioning levels (e.g., physical education, industrial arts, home economics). Other students with mental retardation may attend regular education classes for the majority of the school day. For them, special education consists mostly of support services to facilitate their opportunities and success in the regular education classroom.

Segregated educational facilities (often referred to as *special schools*) have been a placement option for students with mental retardation for several years. Proponents of special schools argue that they provide for (1) greater homogeneity in grouping and programing; (2) teacher specialization in such areas as art, language, physical education, and music; and (3) centralization of teaching materials—all of which will result in a more efficient use of available resources. In addition, some parents of students with severe mental retardation believe that their children will be happier in a segregated environment that "protects" them.

However, research on the efficacy of segregated educational environments does not support these contentions (McDonnell & Hardman, 1989). On the contrary, investigations over the past 10 years have strongly indicated that students with mental retardation, regardless of the severity of the condition, benefit from placement in regular education environments where opportunities for interaction with students who are not disabled are systematically planned and implemented (Brimer, 1990; Halvorsen & Sailor, 1990; McDonnell et al., 1991; Meyer, Peck, & Brown, 1991). As stated by Halvorsen and Sailor, "The overwhelming majority of research studies conducted over the past ten years provides clear support for integrated, less restrictive environments" (1990, p. 152). Inclusion for students with mental retardation includes a variety of opportunities, both within the regular education classroom and throughout the school. Besides interaction in a classroom setting, ongoing inclusion may be found in the halls, on the playground, in the cafeteria, and at school assemblies.

Stainback and Stainback (1990) also reported that regular education teachers who have the opportunity for interaction with children who are severely retarded are not fearful of or intimidated by their presence in the school building. Segregated schools generally offer little, if any, opportunity for interaction with normal peers and deprive the child of valuable learning and socialization experiences. McDonnell and Hardman (1989) argued that segregated facilities cannot be financially or ideologically justified. Public school administrators must now plan to include children with retardation in existing regular education schools and classes.

OTHER INTERVENTION STRATEGIES

Medicine

In order to meet the diverse needs of people with mental retardation, several professionals must be involved in intervention. Most individuals with moderate to profound mental

FOCUS 10
Why is the inclusion of students who are mentally retarded with their nondisabled peers important to an appropriate educational experience?

FOCUS 11
Identify the roles of medicine and social services in meeting the diverse needs of people with mental retardation.

retardation exhibit problems that are evident at birth. Consequently, a physician is usually the first professional to come in contact with these children. In a survey of physicians in Texas, more than 85 percent indicated they were the initial informants to parents regarding their child's disabling condition (McDonald, Carson, Palmer, & Slay, 1982). The physician's primary roles are as diagnostician, counselor, and caregiver. As a diagnostician, the physician analyzes the nature and cause of the child's condition and then, based on the medical information available, counsels the family concerning the medical prognosis. The physician's role as a family counselor has been challenged by some professionals in the behavioral sciences and by parents because such counseling often exceeds the medical domain. This concern reflects the opinion that medical personnel should counsel families only on medical matters and recommend other resources—such as educators, psychologists, social workers, clergy, or parent groups—when dealing with issues other than the child's medical needs.

Social Services

The appropriate social services for someone with mental retardation extend into many aspects of his or her life: the primary family, the extended family, the neighborhood, the educational environment, and the community at large. Thus, appropriate social services may be classified into five general categories: (1) community support services; (2) family support services; (3) supported living arrangements; (4) employment services; and (5) leisure-time services. Figure 4–2 illustrates some of the services included within each of these general categories.

The availability of social services provides individuals with mental retardation a greater opportunity to achieve what is commonly referred to as **normalization.** The principle of normalization emphasizes the need to make available to the individual "the patterns and

FIGURE 4–2

Classification of Social Services

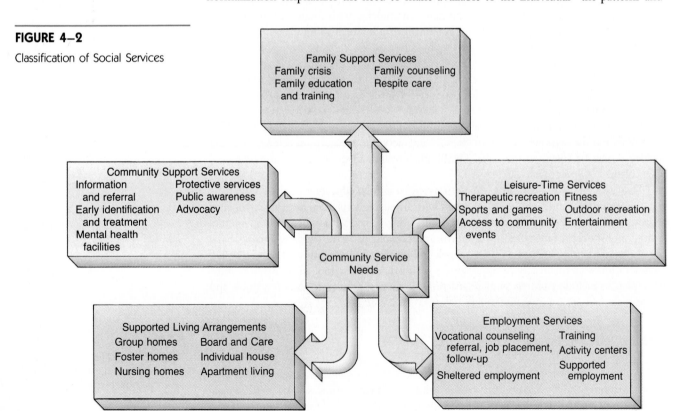

Society has yet to accommodate the needs of elderly individuals with retardation, an issue that will demand attention in the near future. (Boston Globe)

conditions of every day life which are as close to the norms and patterns of mainstream society" (Nirje, 1970, p. 181). Normalization goes far beyond the mere physical integration of the individual into a community. In addition, it promotes the availability of needed support services, such as training and supervision, without which the individual with mental retardation may not be prepared to cope with the demands of community life.

WINDOW 4–3

"FROM WHERE SHE WAS THEN TO WHERE SHE IS NOW IS PHENOMENAL."

When she started into the educational system she was extremely spastic, she made no meaningful movements. She was tube-fed, she was deepsuctioned. . . . She gave no indication of being aware of her environment. Her expression, her demeanor, everything was the same no matter what she was doing. She actually seemed even semicomatose, . . . a perfect candidate to overprotect.

Also a perfect candidate to set artificial barriers for—mental barriers that we set for these kids: "She doesn't even know where she is; how can we improve her quality of life when she doesn't show any indication that she knows where she is?" When we place these artificial barriers there we make them self-fulfilling prophecies. They said, "Let her die" after her accident; "She'll be a vegetable; she'll never know the difference; why ruin three lives for the benefit of one who's never going to do anything anyway?" Then they said to put her in a state hospital. . . . When we brought her home from the hospital the back of her head was touching her buttocks; that's how she was neurologically postured. . . . Our barriers were identified for us: "She won't go any further so what are you worrying about? Get on with your lives and forget about it."

But early on we learned that we don't decide what she'll accomplish or what she won't accomplish. We have to provide *her*

with every opportunity to show *us* what she can accomplish. . . . If they're not on an integrated school site, you're taking away those opportunities to break down those barriers. . . .

Now, she moves, she's totally flexible, she gets herself sitting up; she's starting to pull herself in a kind of crawl; she can stand up; she sits in a wheelchair. She gets herself moving around in a wheelchair; she feeds herself with a spoon, she says a few words, she smiles when she's happy, she's aware, she has a personality. I mean, we've gone so far *beyond* the *optimum* quality of life that was identified for her to us that you can't even talk about it.

Integrated opportunities have been a major part of that ongoing growth. When they're educated in their own communities they are a part of their community—when they're educated outside of that community, they become invisible members of the community.

—Excerpts from a talk by Don Vesey, parent

Source: Reprinted by permission of the publisher from Gaylord-Ross, Robert, *Issues & Research in Special Education,* Volume 1. (New York: Teachers College Press, © 1990 by Teachers College, Columbia University. All rights reserved), pp. 110–111, "Excerpts from a talk with Don Vesey, parent."

4–6   Circles of Friends in Schools

Toronto, Ontario—Marsha Forest came away from her Joshua Committee experiences as if she had put on a better pair of glasses. Her position as a well-ensconced professor of special education at York University suddenly seemed less important to her. She spent long hours on the road helping school boards, principals, and teachers to see how everybody can experience richness when someone with a severe disability is placed in a regular classroom and the so-called regular students are encouraged to form a circle of friends around that person.

Forest always believed in getting teachers down to meticulous detail when it came to educating persons with disabilities. Now, however, she saw that some of the most valuable educational steps can come naturally from regular classmates, if the right conditions exist in the classroom. She saw how peer-group concerns can become a fountainhead of power.

She also knew that parents and teachers fear peer-group pressure. After all, when kids get together these days, they can give themselves quite an education—one that often shapes lives more powerfully than adults can shape them. But peer-group education doesn't always lead to belligerence and destruction and drugs. It can lead to caring and nurturing and helping others do healthy things they had never done before.

This twist, however, generated fears in some teachers when it dawned on them that a circle of friends might foster better growth and development in a student than they were capable of teaching.

And so Marsha moved into regular schools and worked hard at:

- helping boards and principals understand the circles of friends process
- finding a teacher and class willing to include a person with a severe disability
- helping the regular teacher handle any initial fears about the venture
- letting the teacher and class call the shots as much as possible
- providing strong support persons—integration facilitators—who would assist only when they really were needed
- then finding a handful of kids willing to work at being friends with their classmate with the disability

"The first placement in a school is the toughest," she said. "After that, it's usually easy to include others."

Forest sees the building of a circle of friends as a person-by-person process, not an all-encompassing program. And so she focuses on students with disabilities one at a time, setting up a framework that enables a circle to surround that person.

Because no two settings are alike, she watches as the circle, the regular teacher, and the rest of the students develop and coordinate their own routines for helping. Then, never predicting an outcome, she waits. And when new learning takes place in the person with the disability, Forest moves in and makes all the students, the teacher, the principal—even the board members—feel simply great.

According to her, the average school can handle up to twelve of these arrangements. After that, the efficiency of the process may diminish.

She doubts that circles of friends will work in every school. "If a school is all screwed up," she said, "and if it has lost its zest and commitment for really helping kids learn—forget it. On the other hand, I'm sure that circles of friends can help make a good school—especially the kids—better. Then coming to school takes on fresh values and meaning. Some enjoy coming to school as they never did before."

According to Forest. . . .

"Circles of friends are not an alternative to learning. They are a precondition.

"They move us beyond integration—into community.

"I hate labels. I just see people who challenge the school system.

"Wait for schools to be ready for people with challenging behaviors, and you can wait until hell freezes over.

"The term *gifted* is an insult. All people have gifts. Sometimes those with challenging behaviors have the greatest gifts.

"You can't learn to like kids with disabilities by watching puppets. Puppets don't smell or drool. They aren't real. Kids learn to accept people with differences by really living with them."

Source: From *Circles of Friends.* Copyright © 1988 Robert and Martha Perske. Reprinted by permission of Abingdon Press.

Society Faces the "Graying" of People with Mental Retardation

On the day Michael was born, doctors prepared Andrew and Anna Lutz for their son's death.

"They said it was unlikely he would see his twenty-first birthday. Just like that. They said it like we had to accept it as gospel truth," said Anna Lutz, recalling her conversations with doctors on the steamy June morning when her son was diagnosed with Down syndrome.

"We were just heartsick, I mean, just really torn up," she said. "But we told ourselves we would make those 21 years, however brief, as joyous and filled with love and compassion as possible."

Michael recently celebrated his forty-eighth birthday, far outliving the dire predictions of his doctors. He has spent all of his years with his parents: planting tomatoes with his mother in their tiny garden, attending church services with his parents each Sunday, following his beloved Red Sox with his father either on television or at Fenway Park.

Yet with each birthday, Michael's parents are filled with dread and uncertainty, fearing the day when they will no longer be able to care for their only son.

"I'm 76, and my wife is closing in on 75. Mikey, he's closing in on 50. Pretty soon, he's going to be an old man, and then what?" Andrew Lutz asked. "Everyone prepared us for the idea of Mikey dying young, but nobody ever prepared us for Mikey growing old. He's been with us his whole life, but what happens when we die? Who's going to take care of our son when he's an old man and we're gone?"

"We Could Never Do That"

The Lutzes never considered putting Michael in a state institution. Even during the most difficult periods, the Lutzes were determined to keep their son at home.

"It would have been like giving Mikey away. 'Here, you have him. He's too much trouble for us.' We could never do that," Anna Lutz said. "I can't say there hasn't been difficulty, but what child doesn't give his parents some difficulty?"

"I can accept the fact that soon, we won't be able to care for Mikey any more," Mrs. Lutz continued. "It won't be easy on us or on Mikey, but we're trying to get ready for that day. It's just that, when that day comes, I want to know that there is somewhere for Mikey to go."

Despite their condition, elderly people with mental retardation want and deserve the same things as the general elderly population: the opportunity to maintain their health, be productive, socialize, and express their concerns about aging. All people share the same need to grow old with dignity.

Source: From "Society faces the graying of those with mental retardation," by Renee Graham, *The Boston Globe*, September 30, 1991.

Debate / Forum · · · · · · · · · · · · · · ·

Social Inclusion or Social Separation of Students with Mental Retardation? · · · · · · · · · · · · · · ·

The principle of normalization and the least restrictive environment clause in IDEA state that individuals with mental retardation should have available to them conditions and opportunities in everyday life that are as close as possible to those available to individuals who are not disabled. The following are two different viewpoints on the applications of these principles to students with mental retardation in an educational setting. One point of view is from the vantage of professionals working in a special school (separate educational facility for students with disabilities); the counterpoint is from the position of social inclusion for students in a regular education building or classroom.

Point *Special School Programs as the Least Restrictive Environment:*[*] Often times it is a special school program which can provide the least restrictive environment for a student with a disability. It is here where a greater variety of opportunities in which the student can attain full participation is offered. These settings provide the necessary adaptive instruction in a non-competitive environment which leads to the mastery of skills and growth of self-esteem that cannot be duplicated in many of our neighborhood schools. Special school programs can concentrate on adaptive and functional instruction and therapy, leisure activities, social skills, community participation, and vocational preparation.

For many students, special school programs are the least restrictive environment because of the appropriate delivery of services and the 'philosophical' commitment to students with more severe disabilities. . . . Although mainstreaming may provide the most appropriate environment for the majority of students with disabilities, let's not assume that this is the least restrictive environment for all students at all times. There will always be a need for special school programs as long as there are students with unique, special needs.

Counterpoint *The Movement to Social Inclusion:*[**] For the preschool-age child, the world is defined primarily through family and a small same-age peer group. As the child progresses chronologically the world expands to the neighborhood, the school, and eventually to a larger heterogeneous group we call the community. As educators we must then ask how do we structure a student's educational program to effectively foster full participation as the life space of the individual is expanded? What are the barriers to full participation, and how do we work to break them down?

One critical barrier is the separation or segregation of students with severe disabilities from the people with whom they will participate in the heterogenous world, whether it be at school, where they live, at work, or play. Such segregation promotes dependence and isolation, and limits opportunities for students to learn skills that enhance independent living and social participation. . . . Students with severe disabilities are to be educated to the maximum extent appropriate with their nondisabled peers, which includes attending a regular school and class unless extenuating individual circumstances preclude this as an appropriate placement decision.

Recent research on social, educational, and financial outcomes are also supportive of the social inclusion of students with severe disabilities. Appropriately implemented integration efforts include planned sustained interactions between students with severe disabilities and their nondisabled peers. In fact, such interactions yield improved attitudes and interaction patterns, while exposing the student to socially appropriate role models.

Sources:
* From "Special School Programs as the Least Restrictive Environment" by J. Curtis and M. Riding, 1989, *The Special Educator, 9*(5), p. 6. Copyright © 1989 by the Utah Special Education Consortium, Utah State Office of Education. Reprinted with permission.
** From "Educational Services for Students with Severe Disabilities: The Movement toward Social Integration" by M. L. Hardman, 1988, *The Special Educator, 9*(1), pp. 9–10. Copyright © 1988 by the Utah Special Education Consortium, Utah State Office of Education. Reprinted with permission.

REVIEW

FOCUS 1 Identify the three components of the definition of *mental retardation.*

◆ *Significantly subaverage generally intellectual functioning* is defined as two standard deviations below the mean on an individual test of intelligence.

◆ *Adaptive behavior deficits* are defined as significant limitations in a person's ability to meet standards of maturation, learning, personal independence, and social responsibility.

◆ *Developmental period* is defined as birth to 18 years of age.

FOCUS 2 Identify the three methods of classifying people with mental retardation.

◆ Severity of the condition may be described in terms of mild, moderate, severe, and profound mental retardation.

◆ Educability expectations are designated for groups of children who are educable, trainable, and custodial.

◆ Medical descriptors classify mental retardation on the basis of the origin of the condition (e.g., infection, intoxication, trauma, chromosomal abnormality).

FOCUS 3 Identify four intellectual and adaptive behavior characteristics of individuals with mental retardation.

◆ Intellectual characteristics include learning and memory deficiencies, difficulties in establishing learning sets, and inefficient rehearsal strategies.

◆ Adaptive behavior characterisics may include difficulties coping with the demands of school, developing interpersonal relationships, developing language skills, and taking care of personal needs.

FOCUS 4 Identify the academic, speech/language, and physical characteristics of children with mental retardation.

◆ Students with mental retardation exhibit significant deficits in the areas of reading and mathematics.

◆ School-age students with mild mental retardation have poor reading mechanics and comprehension when compared to their same-age peers.

◆ The most common speech problems involve articulation, voice, and stuttering.

◆ Language problems are generally associated with delays in language development rather than the bizarre use of language.

◆ Physical problems generally are not evident for individuals with mild mental retardation because the retardation is usually not associated with genetic factors.

◆ The more severe the mental retardation, the greater the probability of genetic causation and thus compounding physiological problems.

FOCUS 5 Identify the causes of mental retardations.

◆ The cause of mental retardation is generally not known for the individual who is mildly retarded.

◆ Causes associated with moderate to profound mental retardation include infection and intoxication, chromosomal abnormalities, gestation disorders, unknown prenatal influences, traumas or physical agents, metabolic or nutrition problems, and gross postnatal brain disease.

FOCUS 6   Identify four measures that may prevent mental retardation.
◆ Immunizations against disease
◆ Appropriate nutrition for the mother during pregnancy
◆ Appropriate prenatal care
◆ Screening for genetic disorders at birth

FOCUS 7   Why is the need for early intervention services for children with mental retardation so critical?
◆ Early intervention services are needed to provide a stimulating environment for the child to enhance growth and development.
◆ Early intervention programs focus on the development of communication skills, social interaction, and readiness for formal instruction.

FOCUS 8   Identify five skill areas for elementary-age children with mental retardation.
◆ Motor development skills
◆ Self-care skills
◆ Social skills
◆ Communication skills
◆ Functional academic skills

FOCUS 9   Identify four educational goals for adolescents with mental retardation.
◆ To increase the individual's personal independence
◆ To enhance opportunities for participation in the local community
◆ To prepare for employment
◆ To facilitate a successful transition to the adult years

FOCUS 10   Why is the inclusion of students with mental retardation with their nondisabled peers important to an appropriate educational experience?
◆ Regardless of the severity of their condition, students with mental retardation benefit from placement in regular education environments where opportunities for inclusion with nondisabled peers are systematically planned and implemented.

FOCUS 11   Identify the roles of medicine and social services in meeting the diverse needs of people with mental retardation.
◆ The physician's roles include diagnostician, counselor, and caregiver.
◆ Appropriate social services include community support services, family support services, alternative living arrangements, employment services, and leisure-time services.

Chapter Five
Behavior Disorders

TO BEGIN WITH . . .

◆ One Day in the Lives of American Children, 1987: 1,293 teenagers will give birth; 6 teens will commit suicide; 1,849 children will be abused; 3,288 children will choose to run away from home; 1,629 children will be incarcerated in adult jails; 2,989 children will see their parents divorce (Children's Defense Fund, 1989).

◆ The dropout rate for students with behavior disorders is well over 40 percent. Fewer than half are placed in integrated settings. As these students exit secondary school, about one-third are neither working nor engaged in any employment-related training (Peacock Hill Working Group, 1990).

◆ "Many children are growing up healthy, resilient, and skilled, but too many are not. Violence, and poverty, poor health, teen parenthood and school failure dim the future of children. And when their future is dimmed, the lives of all Americans are diminished" (Center for the Study of Social Policy, 1991, p. 2).

◆ There are massive numbers of students having school problems who are screaming at educators with their behaviors. They are telling educators that school is irrelevant, boring, dull, not meeting their needs, and driving them crazy. These students drop out, form gangs, and get in trouble, and yet, society continues to blame the victims rather than looking deeply at itself and the school system for creative answers and alternatives (Forest & Pearpoint, 1990, p. 188).

BRETT

BRETT. Brett's overall appearance and demeanor were something to behold. I have worked with several hundred very difficult boys, but Brett in many ways represented the most difficult of the difficult. It was as if he had become a belligerent vagrant at the early age of 12. His clothing was dirty, or should I say filthy. His countenance, clothing, and conduct said, "Stay away from me, or you'll be very, very sorry!"

I thought I was prepared for almost anything after teaching disturbed children for 10 years, but Brett drew off all the patience and skill that was in me during the first two months in my class. His refusal and outright opposition to almost any request made of him was incredibly frustrating to me and his houseparents. Moreover, he was exceptionally skilled in what I refer to as "teacher torture" techniques. These included various forms of pencil tapping, quiet but distinguishable junglelike vocalizations, and careful applications of mucus applied to reading and math assignments. His other school assignments were rarely submitted without some grotesque or sexually explicit drawing. Assignments replete with numerous erasures and erasure-induced holes and purposeful errors were commonplace.

Brett's feelings of disdain for himself, other students, and his situation were expressed in numerous ways. Spitting was a constant threat to anyone who sat near him or chose to interact with him, particularly when he was upset. He was a time bomb of sorts. The treatment staff, including myself, could rarely predict what it was that set him off, nor could we reliably predict when he would explode. The unpredictability of his behavior kept us continually on our toes. He excelled in irritation and outright intimidation of adults and fellow students. Teasing, bullying, harassing, bothering, and fighting were his specialties. He continually hassled the younger, more demure students in the class. His manipulative skills and capacity to talk one out of an assignment or talk one into a preferred activity of his choosing were well-developed behaviors. Even in fairly informal settings that were recreational in nature and devoid of demands of adults and other authority figures, Brett seemed to be unhappy and unfulfilled.

CHERIE. Cherie was an attractive, bright sixth-grader. Her work was always completed punctually and accurately. She was, in fact, unusually conscientious, conforming, and eager to please. She seemed to enjoy school a great deal and liked being a part of all our classroom activities. The school year came to an end, and delightful Cherie left my classroom to enjoy the summer.

The next school year was an altogether different story. She began her junior high school year with her peers and with much anticipation. Seven teachers per day, lockers and locker partners, and a host of other new school variables were only a few of the features of junior high school life that captured her attention. She did well during the first week of school. Then suddenly, without any real warning signs, Cherie complained about not feeling very well and asked if she could stay home. Her actual request to stay home was preceded by episodes of nausea and vomiting. She also said that she felt dizzy and faint during the afternoon of the previous day. Her mother was prompt in responding to her symptoms of illness and allowed her to stay home that day. This was the beginning of a consistent pattern of refusal to go to school.

The precipitating events appeared to be two low scores that Cherie had received the previous day in two of her classes, history and advanced math. She was also perplexed with the challenges that were an integral part of her P.E. class. Undressing, dressing, and showering with so many peers present was highly stressful for her. She felt as if everyone was watching her. School became socially and psychologically aversive.

Many attempts were made to persuade Cherie to attend school following these events, but they were unsuccessful. Her anxiety actually bordered on what many would describe as sheer panic at times. Sometimes, she would have chest pains; other times, she would feel very dizzy. She fought attempts by her parents to forcibly take her to school. She often locked herself in her room, or she just took off if she felt her parents were going to force her to go to school. Just thinking about school was anxiety provoking for her.

JAN. Jan, our daughter, was very close to completing her junior year in high school. With the exception of the last six months, her behavior had been normal. She didn't have a lot of friends, as she was fairly shy and enjoyed doing things by herself. She didn't like or dislike school.

Occasionally, she would participate in extracurricular school activities if her friends went out of their way to invite her. Her interests, concerns, loves, and fears were like those of any teenager. But after Christmas break, her behavior began to change, not in an abrupt fashion but very slowly. One of the first signs was the deterioration of her relationship with her friends. They stopped calling her, and she had no interest in talking to them.

One morning during this post-Christmas period, after I awakened her for school and began making breakfast, Jan entered the room still attired in her pajamas and told me that she did not need to go to school that day. When I asked her why, she told me that a voice had told her not to go. These voices began to impact her life in many ways. Gradually, I watched as my once competent daughter became another person, and I was powerless to do anything about it. Her face was at times immobile. The normal emotional intensity that was so much a part of her earlier junior high and high school days had practically vanished.

Her thoughts, as expressed in conversations with family members and others, were often disconnected. She rapidly shifted from one topic to another completely unrelated topic of discussion without realizing that she was not making sense.

Another behavior that really concerned us during this time was Jan's loss of self-initiated, goal-directed activity. Her behavior became very random, both in school and at home. At times, she appeared to know what she was doing, and at other times, she seemed to be totally unaware of her behavior and its impact on others.

With the presence of these and other behaviors, we knew that something was definitely wrong with Jan. We consulted with our family physician, and he referred us to Dr. Holmes, a psychiatrist in our area. After a number of preliminary visits, we were told that Jan has schizophrenia.

INTRODUCTION

Individuals with **behavior disorders**—such as Brett, Cherie, and Jan in Window 5–1— experience great difficulties in relating appropriately to peers, siblings, parents, and teachers. They also have difficulty responding to academic and social tasks that are essential parts of their schooling. In some cases, they may exhibit too much behavior. For example, Brett's placement in a specialized treatment facility was a function of his excessive aggressive or oppositional behaviors. In other cases, individuals with behavior or emotional problems may not have learned the coping behaviors necessary for successful participation in school settings, as demonstrated by Cherie. She, for a variety of reasons, was unable to respond to the demands of her new junior high school environment. Jan, as described by her mother, gradually lost her capacity to engage in meaningful relationships and goal-directed behaviors. Her inability to communicate and relate effectively to her family members, teachers, and peers had a profound impact on her achievement educationally, socially, and occupationally.

STUDYING BEHAVIOR DISORDERS

Many factors influence the ways in which we view the behaviors of others. Our perceptions of others and their behaviors are significantly influenced by our personal beliefs, standards, and values about what constitutes normal behavior. If we were to observe Jan hearing voices in our classroom, we would probably become very concerned about her behavior. Also, imagine how her peers might react to her hearing voices in a classroom. Our range of tolerance for various behaviors varies greatly. Brett's aggressive and oppositional behaviors were not tolerated at school, nor were they well liked by his brothers and sisters or his

FOCUS 1

Identify five factors that influence the ways in which we view others' behaviors.

mother, who was often manipulated by his aggressive behaviors. Now he receives education in a more restrictive setting. When he learns to control his behaviors and act more appropriately, he can return to the normal school environment.

What may be viewed as normal by some of us may be viewed by others as abnormal. Brett's toughness and willingness to continually oppose authority was viewed as normal by his father. Others, including his teachers, viewed this behavior as totally inappropriate and abnormal.

The context in which behaviors occur dramatically influences our views of their appropriateness or inappropriateness. For example, if Jan were to hear voices in a church setting or as a part of a religious service, fellow worshippers might view her as being very spiritual. Similarly, Brett's toughness may be highly valued by a little league football coach who observes his zealousness in pursuing and attacking his fellow teammates during practice.

Sometimes it is the intensity or sheer frequency with which a given behavior or cluster of behaviors occurs that leads us to suspect the presence of behavior or emotional problems. Jan's parents observed a gradual change in her behavior. Initially, they were uncertain about the significance of her symptoms. However, with the passage of time and the increase in frequency of certain behaviors (conversation devoid of meaning, hallucinations, and withdrawal from social activities), her parents realized that she needed psychiatric help.

VARIABLES IN BEHAVIOR DISORDERS

FOCUS 2

Identify five variables that influence the types of behaviors that are exhibited or suppressed by individuals with behavior disorders.

Many variables influence the types of behaviors that are exhibited or suppressed by individuals with behavior disorders. These include the parents' and teachers' management styles; the school or home environment; the social and cultural values of the family; the social and economic climate of the community; the responses of peers and siblings; and the academic, intellectual, and social-emotional characteristics of the individuals with the disorders.

The vignettes of Brett, Cherie, and Jan (Window 5–1) help us to partially understand the severity of various behavior disorders. Jan and her family will have to deal with the challenges of schizophrenia throughout her lifetime. Brett's aggressive and oppositional behaviors were extremely difficult to treat, but the staff were successful in helping him learn other, more functional ways of successfully dealing with problems than by acting aggressively. Cherie's refusal to go to school was a major challenge for her parents and therapist, but she eventually returned to her junior high, completed her high school preparation, and went on to graduate from college as a certified teacher. Some behavior disorders are very severe and require the services of many trained individuals working together cooperatively. Other disorders may be treated in a relatively short time, with fewer personnel and at less expense.

TERMINOLOGY: EXTERNALIZING AND INTERNALIZING DISORDERS

FOCUS 3

What differentiates externalizing disorders from internalizing disorders?

At this juncture, it is important to note that a number of terms have been used to describe individuals with emotional, social, and behavioral problems. These terms include **behavior disorders, social maladjustment, emotional disturbance,** and others. Childhood, adolescent, and adult behavior problems can frequently be grouped into two broad but overlapping categories: externalizing and internalizing disorders. The latter category refers to behaviors that seem to be directed more at the self than at others. Depressions and phobias are examples of behaviors that we would include in the internalizing category. Some clinicians would describe individuals with these conditions as being emotionally disturbed.

The behavior of children who exhibit externalizing disorders is often directed more at others than at themselves. (Hermine Dreyfuss/Monkmeyer Press)

Children who exhibit externalizing disorders may be described as engaging in behaviors that are directed more at others than at themselves. Furthermore, these behaviors may have greater observable impact on parents, siblings, and teachers. The juvenile offender who chronically engages in crimes involving property damage or injury to others might be identified as being socially maladjusted. The distinction between the two categories is not clear cut. For example, adolescents who are severely depressed certainly have an impact on their families and others. However, the primary locus of the distress for these youths is internal or emotional.

Throughout this chapter, we use the term *behavior disorders* to describe persons with both external and internal problems. Our use of the term reflects our interest in observable behaviors. Our observations and those of others help to determine whether a child is depressed, aggressive, suicidal, anxious, delinquent, hyperactive, socially withdrawn, or extremely shy. So as we proceed, please keep in mind that behavior disorders as we perceive them may be internal (emotional) and/or external (social) in nature. Our knowledge of their presence is a function of our ability to carefully observe and measure them.

DEFINITIONS AND CLASSIFICATIONS

Definitions

A variety of definitions have been created to describe children with behavior disorders. The current definition, used in conjunction with the rules and regulations governing the implementation of the Individuals with Disabilities Education Act (IDEA), is as follows:

"Seriously emotionally disturbed" is defined as . . . :

(i) The term means a condition exhibiting one or more of the following characteristics over a long period of time and to a marked degree, which adversely affects educational performance:
   (A) An inability to learn which cannot be explained by intellectual, sensory or health factors;

FOCUS 4

Identify six essential features of definitions describing serious emotional disturbances or behavior disorders.

(B) An inability to build or maintain satisfactory relationships with peers and teachers;

(C) Inappropriate types of behavior or feelings under normal circumstances;

(D) A general pervasive mood of unhappiness or depression; or

(E) A tendency to develop physical symptoms or fears associated with personal or school problems.

(ii) The term includes children who are schizophrenic [or autistic]. The term does not include children who are socially maladjusted, unless it is determined that they are seriously disturbed. (U.S. Department of Health, Education and Welfare, 1977, p. 42478)

This description of severe emotional disturbance or behavior disorders was derived from an earlier definition created by Bower (1959). Bower's definition has been severely criticized because of its lack of clarity, incompleteness, and exclusion of individuals described as socially maladjusted (Cline, 1990; Council for Children with Behavior Disorders, 1987, 1989, 1990; Forness & Knitzer, 1990). Additionally, in order for students to be served under this definition, assessment personnel must demonstrate that the disorder is adversely affecting students' school performance. In many cases, students with serious behavior disorders—such as eating disorders, depression, suicidal tendencies, and social withdrawal—do not receive appropriate care and treatment merely because their academic achievement in school appears to be normal or above average. In some cases, these students are gifted (see Chapter Thirteen).

Recently, committees and coalitions from a variety of professional health and educational organizations have proposed a new definition and terminology for *serious emotional disturbance* for federal legislation in the United States (Council for Exceptional Children, 1991; Forness & Knitzer, 1990):

Emotional or Behavior Disorders (EBD) refers to a condition in which behavioral or emotional responses of an individual in school are so different from his/her generally accepted, age-appropriate, ethnic, or cultural norms that they adversely affect educational performance in such areas as self-care, social relationships, personal adjustment, academic progress, classroom behavior, or work adjustment.

EBD is more than a transient, expected response to stressors in the child's or youth's environment and would persist even with individualized interventions, such as feedback to the individual, consultation with parents or families, and/or modification of the educational environment.

The eligibility decision must be based on multiple sources of data about the individual's behavioral or emotional functioning. EBD must be exhibited in at least two different settings, at least one of which must be school related.

EBD can co-exist with other handicapping conditions as defined elsewhere in this law [IDEA].

This category may include children or youth with schizophrenia, affective disorders, or with other sustained disturbances of conduct, attention, or adjustment. (Council for Exceptional Children, 1991, p. 10)

Features of this newly proposed definition represent significant advantages over the present federal definition, including (1) the inclusion of impairments of adaptive behavior as evidenced in emotional, social, or behavioral differences; (2) the use of normative standards of assessment from multiple sources, including consideration of cultural and/or ethnic factors; (3) the examination of prereferral interventions and other efforts to assist children prior to formally classifying them as disabled; and (4) the potential inclusion of individuals previously labeled socially maladjusted.

The press to include children considered to be socially maladjusted in the federal definition of serious emotional disturbance continues to be a sharply debated issue (Clarizio, 1987; Kelly, 1988; Nelson, Rutherford, Center, & Walker, 1991; Slenkovitch, 1983). Proponents for the inclusion of the socially maladjusted have argued that professional practice as well as current research run counter to the exclusionary clause found in the present definition (Center, 1989a, 1989b; Kauffman, 1989; Nelson et al., 1991; Wolf, Braukmann, & Ramp, 1987).

Many professionals believe that greater numbers of young children with behavior disorders will receive preventative treatment if the more inclusive definition is adopted, thereby lessening the need for more intensive and expensive services later in children's lives. Additionally, many clinicians believe that adoption of this definition will lead to greater numbers of children with special needs being served.

Classifications

Classification systems serve several purposes for human services professionals. First, they provide a means for describing various types of behavior problems in children. Second, they provide a common set of terms for communicating with others. For example, children who are identified as having Down syndrome, a type of mental retardation, share some rather distinct characteristics (see Chapter Four). Physicians and other health care specialists use these characteristics and other information as a basis for diagnosing and treating these children.

Unfortunately, there is no consistent use of a standardized set of criteria for determining the nature and severity of behavior disorders (Forness, 1988; Kavale, Forness, & Alper, 1986; Swartz, Mosley, & Koenig-Jerz, 1987). If valid eligibility and classification systems did exist, they would provide educational or psychiatric clinicians with extremely valuable information about the nature of various conditions, effective treatments, and associated complications.

The area of behavior disorders is broad and includes many different types of problems. Thus, it is not surprising that many approaches have been used to classify them. Some classification systems describe individuals according to statistically derived categories. Patterns of behavior that are strongly related to each other are identified through sophisticated statistical techniques. Other classification systems are clinically oriented. They are derived from the experiences of physicians and other social scientists who work directly with children and adults with behavior disorders. Still other classification systems help us understand behavior disorders in terms of their relative severity.

Statistically Derived Classification Systems. For a number of years, researchers have collected information about children with behavior disorders. Data collected from parent and teacher questionnaires, interviews, and behavior rating scales have been analyzed using a variety of advanced statistical techniques. Certain clusters or patterns of related behaviors have emerged from these studies. For example, Peterson (1987) found that the behavior problems exhibited by elementary school children could be accounted for by two dimensions: withdrawal and aggression. Similarly, several researchers have intensively studied child psychiatric patients to develop a valid classification system (Achenbach, 1966; Achenbach & Edelbrock, 1981). Statistical analysis of data generated from these studies revealed two broad clusters of behaviors: externalizing symptoms and internalizing symptoms. Externalizing clusters of behaviors included stealing, lying, disobedience, and fighting. Internalizing clusters of behaviors included physical complaints (e.g., stomachaches), phobias, fearfulness, social withdrawal, and worrying.

FOCUS 5

Identify three reasons why classification systems are important to professionals who diagnose, treat, and educate individuals with behavior disorders.

The behavior of Hannibal in the movie *The Silence of the Lambs* bore some similarities to that defined as conduct disordered. (AP/Wide World Photos)

Other researchers (Quay, 1975, 1979; Von Isser, Quay, & Love, 1980), using similar methodologies, have reliably identified four distinct categories of behavior disorders in children:

1. Conduct disorders involve such characteristics as overt aggression, both verbal and physical; disruptiveness; negativism; irresponsibility; and defiance of authority—all of which are at variance with the behavioral expectations of the school and other social institutions.
2. Anxiety-withdrawal stands in considerable contrast to conduct disorders, involving, as it does, overanxiety, social withdrawal, seclusiveness, shyness, sensitivity, and other behaviors implying a retreat from the environment rather than a hostile response to it.
3. Immaturity characteristically involves preoccupation, short attention span, passivity, daydreaming, sluggishness, and other behavior not in accord with developmental expectations.
4. **Socialized aggression** typically involves gang activities, cooperative stealing, truancy, and other manifestations of participation in a delinquent subculture (Von Isser et al., 1980, pp. 272–273).

Behaviors related to each of these categories may be very severe to very mild in nature. In thinking about these categories, recall for a moment the vignettes of Brett, Cherie, and Jan (see Window 5–1). How would they be classified according to these categories? Did Brett have a conduct disorder? Was Cherie's refusal to go to school and her other related behaviors an anxiety-withdrawal disorder? And what about Jan's behavior? Does she qualify for placement in any of these categories?

R E F L E C T   O N   T H I S

5–1   Internal Suffering: Shyness

We have talked about external versus internal disorders. One of the conditions associated with internal disorders is extreme shyness. What does it feel like to be extremely shy? How does shyness affect an individual? Shirley Radl shares with us what it is like to feel shy, even as a mother.

Having personally suffered from shyness in varying degrees nearly all of my life, I know full well how it got started—skinny, homely little girl, skinnier and homelier teenager—and know all too well that neither the shyness researchers nor those I've interviewed exaggerated how really awful and crazy it feels. I have known what it is to, no matter what the circumstance, feel self-conscious of my every gesture, have trouble swallowing and talking, see my hands tremble for no apparent reason, feel as if I were freezing to death while perspiring profusely, be confused about issues I am thoroughly familiar with, and imagine all sorts of terrible things that might happen to me—the least of which being that I would lose my job for being a public disgrace.

I have experienced dizzy spells and twitching when in the company of absolutely nonthreatening men, women, and children. I've known what it is to avoid going to the grocery store because I couldn't face the checker, to become excessively nervous while chatting with the man who delivers the milk, or to be unable to tolerate the watchful gaze of my children's friends while making popcorn for them. I have known what it is like to have the feeling that I was stumbling naked through life with the whole thing being broadcast internationally. . . . (Radl, 1976, as cited by Zimbardo, 1978, p. 24)

Clinically Derived Classification Systems.   Several clinically derived classification systems have been developed; however, the major system used by medical and psychological personnel is the American Psychiatric Association's (1987) *Diagnostic and Statistical Manual of Mental Disorders* (3rd ed., rev.) (DSM-III-R). It was developed and tested for its usefulness by groups and committees of psychiatric, psychological, and health care professionals. Participants in each of these groups included persons who served or worked closely with children, youth, and adults with behavior disorders. The categories and subcategories of the DSM-III (American Psychiatric Association, 1980) were developed after years of investigation and field testing. The DSM-III was preceded by earlier publications of the DSM-I in 1952 and DSM-II in 1968.

The current manual, DSM-III-R (American Psychiatric Association, 1987), identifies nine major groups of disorders that may be exhibited by infants, children, or adolescents. They include (1) developmental disorders, (2) **disruptive behavior disorders,** (3) **anxiety disorders** of childhood or adolescence, (4) **eating disorders,** (5) **gender identity disorders,** (6) **tic disorders,** (7) **elimination disorders,** (8) **speech disorders** and other disorders of infancy, childhood, or adolescence.

Some of the DSM-III-R categorical groups for infants, children, and adolescents overlap with other exceptionalities. For example, children who exhibit developmental disorders may also be identified as retarded, autistic, and learning disabled. We now explore some of the more prevalent disorders that have been identified in the DSM-III-R.

◆ *Developmental disorders.* Developmental disorders are characterized by severe delays in the acquisition of cognitive, language, motor, and social skills. The disorders may be evidenced as a general delay, as in autism or mental retardation, or as a failure to demonstrate normal growth in specific areas of skill acquisition, as in receptive and expressive language disorders. (Many of these disorders or conditions are discussed in greater detail in subsequent chapters.)

◆ *Disruptive behavior disorders.* Classifications identified as disruptive behavior disorders correspond to some of the clusters of behavior identified earlier in the statistically derived classification system. The first condition is attention–deficit hyperactivity disorder (ADHD). It is closely related to the immaturity category of the statistically derived classification system. Children with this disorder have difficulty attending to and completing tasks, responding carefully and reflectively to academic and social tasks, and controlling or restricting their level of physical activity. In fact, often their activity appears to be very random or purposeless in nature. (ADHD will be discussed in greater depth in Chapter Six.)

The second condition found within the disruptive behavior disorders category is conduct disorders. Does Brett, the young boy described in Window 5–1, meet the prerequisites for this condition, as defined by the DSM-III-R (see Table 5–1)? Actually, we probably have not provided sufficient information about Brett for you

---

■ Table 5–1 Diagnostic Criteria for Conduct Disorder

A. A disturbance of conduct lasting at least six months, during which at least three of the following have been present:
   (1) Has stolen without confrontation of a victim on more than one occasion (including forgery)
   (2) Has run away from home overnight at least twice while living in parental or parental-surrogate home (or once without returning)
   (3) Often lies (other than to avoid physical or sexual abuse)
   (4) Has deliberately engaged in fire-setting
   (5) Is often truant from school (for older person, absent from work)
   (6) Has broken into someone else's house, building, or car
   (7) Has deliberately destroyed other's property (other than by fire-setting)
   (8) Has been physically cruel to animals
   (9) Has forced someone into sexual activity with him or her
   (10) Has used a weapon in more than one fight
   (11) Often initiates physical fights
   (12) Has stolen with confrontation of a victim (e.g., mugging, purse-snatching, extortion, armed robbery)
   (13) Has been physically cruel to people

   Note: The above items are listed in descending order of discriminating power based on data from a national field trial of the DSM-III-R criteria for Disruptive Behavior Disorders.

B. If 18 or older, does not meet criteria for Antisocial Personality Disorder.

Criteria for Severity of Conduct Disorder:

Mild: Few if any conduct problems in excess of those required to make the diagnosis, and conduct problems cause only minor harm to others.

Moderate: Number of conduct problems and effect on others intermediate between "mild" and "severe."

Severe: Many conduct problems in excess of those required to make the diagnosis, or conduct problems cause considerable harm to others, e.g., serious physical injury to victims, extensive vandalism or theft, prolonged absence from home.

Source: American Psychiatric Association: *Diagnostic and Statistical Manual of Mental Disorders, Third Edition, Revised.* Washington, DC, American Psychiatric Association, 1987.

to make an informed choice about his classification; however, if you had access to all the information in Brett's file, the choice would be very clear. He would be identified as conduct disordered.

◆ *Anxiety disorders.* The anxiety disorders of childhood or adolescence category is very similar to the anxiety-withdrawal category of the statistically derived classification system. Children with anxiety disorders have problems dealing with anxiety-provoking situations. They also may have problems separating themselves from parents or other attachment figures (e.g., close friends, teachers, coaches, etc.). Unrealistic worries about future events, overconcern about achievement, excessive need for reassurance, and somatic complaints are characteristic of young people who have anxiety disorders. Cherie, the junior high student, suffered from an anxiety disorder.

◆ *Eating disorders.* The fourth category, eating disorders, provides information about anorexia nervosa and bulimia. These conditions are evidenced by gross disturbances in eating behavior. In the case of anorexia nervosa, the most distinguishing feature is bodyweight that is 15 percent below that which is expected. Bulimia is characterized by repeated episodes of binging, followed by self-induced vomiting or other extreme measures to prevent weight gain.

◆ *Gender identity disorders.* Gender identity disorders were not a part of the previous DSM classification system for infants, children, and youth. At the heart of these disorders is an incongruence between the youth's perception of his or her biologically assigned sex and his or her gender identity.

◆ *Tic disorders.* Tic disorders involve stereotyped movements or vocalizations that are involuntary, rapid, and recurrent over time. Tics may take the form of eye blinking, facial gestures, sniffing, snorting, repeating certain words or phrases, and grunting. Stress often exacerbates the nature and frequency of tics.

◆ *Elimination disorders.* Elimination disorders deal with soiling and wetting behaviors in older children. Children who continue to have consistent problems with bowel and bladder control past their fourth or fifth birthdays may be diagnosed as having an elimination disorder, particularly if the condition is not a function of any physical disorder.

◆ *Speech and other disorders.* The remaining categories in the DSM-III-R refer to speech and other disorders that are not easily placed in other categorical areas. We briefly review two conditions identified in these categories. Elective mutism is a persistent refusal to talk in typical social and school environments. This disorder is really quite rare, occurring less than 1 percent of the time in psychiatric referrals. Identity disorders are characterized by severe stress and uncertainty about one's goals, values, social relationships, sexual orientation, and religious preference. This condition generally surfaces in late adolescence or young adulthood, when individuals are moving away from their families and forming relationships with others.

Classification According to Severity of Behaviors. Various researchers have attempted to differentiate mild to moderate behavior disorders from severe problems. As you might expect, the behavioral characteristics of individuals with severe disorders are identified more easily than those associated with mild disorders. Stainback and Stainback (1980) contrasted the characteristics of individuals with mild and severe disturbances. As illustrated in Table 5–2, children with severe disorders differ significantly from those with mild disorders in a variety of intellectual, social, academic, and behavioral domains.

Persons who exhibit severe behavior disorders are often described as psychotic, crazy, or insane. **Psychosis** is a general term. The DSM-III-R uses such terms as *pervasive developmental disorders, schizophrenia,* and others to refer to infants, children, youth, and adults

■ **Table 5–2** Characteristics of Children Who Exhibit Maladaptive Behavior

Definition	Mildly Disturbed	Severely Disturbed	Comment
INTELLECTUAL OR COGNITIVE ABILITY: as measured by a standardized intelligence test.	Average IQ score in low-normal or dull-normal range.	Average IQ in mentally retarded range.	Actual range for both groups is from retarded to gifted.
ACHIEVEMENT: as measured by achievement test scores predominantly in reading and arithmetic.	Generally achieve at a lower level than their IQ level would imply. Children classified as conduct disordered or delinquents further behind than other categories.	Markedly deficient in academic areas. Generally function at basic levels in language, toileting, eating, rudimentary reading, and math.	Both levels range the spectrum, but most are generally below average. Any seriously disturbed high achievers are usually erratic in responding.
UNDERSELECTIVITY: difficulty focusing on relevant stimuli and screening out irrelevant stimuli. **OVERSELECTIVITY:** attention to limited aspects of a task, lacks ability to zero out.	Difficulty focusing on task at hand. Tend to be underselective.	Tend to be overselective. Often exhibit "gaze aversion," will not make or maintain eye contact.	Both levels as a group have attending problems; however, research indicates that the type of attending problem may be different depending on the seriousness of the emotional disturbance.
HYPERACTIVITY: inability to modulate motor behavior in accordance with the demands of a situation. **IMPULSIVITY:** quick, almost instantaneous response to stimulation.	Frequently exhibit hyperactivity and impulsivity.	Frequently exhibit hyperactivity and impulsivity.	Reflectivity, the tendency to look, think, and consider alternatives, is the reverse of impulsivity.

who are psychotic or very seriously disturbed. The following statements reflect the views of teachers of children with severe behavior disorders about these students:

1. A residential center is the best placement for most of these children.
2. These children are often classified as autistic or schizophrenic.
3. These children usually show no social interest in relating to others.
4. These children are most often multihandicapped.
5. The problems of this group of children are more likely to be genetically or organically based. (Olson, Algozzine, & Schmid, 1980, p. 100)

Work completed by Newcomer (1980) also helps us understand other important features of severe behavior disorders (see Table 5–3). One of these parameters is an insight index, which relates to the child's awareness or understanding of his or her behavior prob-

■ **Table 5–2** (continued)

Definition	Mildly Disturbed	Severely Disturbed	Comment
WITHDRAWAL: includes withdrawal from human contact and/or general overall withdrawal of interest in the environment.	May consistently refrain from initiating conversation, refrain from play with others, or exhibit lack of concern or interest in the environment—shy, immature, wall-flower, but not oblivious to surroundings.	May lack contact with reality and subsequently develop own world—often called autistic, schizophrenic, psychotic.	Depression is sometimes associated with withdrawal.
PHYSICAL AGGRESSION: destructive actions against self and other people and things. **VERBAL AGGRESSION:** includes yelling, cursing, abusive language, threats, and self-destructive statements.	May be obnoxious, negative, oppositional, and/or generally nasty. Generally *not* violent, brutal, destructive, assaultive, or physically damaging to others and self.	May frequently, consistently over a long period of time, display aggressive behaviors of a serious nature.	"Normal" children also display aggressive behaviors, but usually less onerous and at a lower rate.
HELPLESSNESS: does not appear to be interested in trying to do anything, does not set goals for self, often does not respond to assigned tasks.	May exhibit lack of joy and interest in life, fail to perform tasks previously exhibited, unwillingness to try, tends to give up quickly.	May be highly dependent, pessimistic, and suicidal; may be unable to perform basic life skills.	Teacher's task is to provide appropriate training that is based on the level the child is actually functioning.

Source: Reprinted by permission of the authors and the publisher from Susan Stainback and William Stainback, *Educating Children with Severe Maladaptive Behaviors* (New York: Grune & Stratton, 1980), Table 1–2, pp. 26–27.

lems. Is the child aware of the behavioral deviance, and does he or she understand the reasons for the behavior and its impact on self, family, and others? Another parameter of similar importance is the conscious-control dimension, which relates to whether the child makes an attempt to control the behavior problem and the degree to which such attempts are successful. These parameters and others are particularly helpful to professionals and parents who are responsible for referring a student for further evaluation.

Prevalence

Estimates of the prevalence of behavior disorders vary greatly from one source to the next, ranging from 0.05 to 15.0 percent. The U.S. Office of Education estimated that 2 percent of the children in the country have behavior disorders. However, Bower (1982) indicated

■ **Table 5–3** Criteria for Determining Degree of Disturbance

Criteria	Degree of Disturbance		
	Mild	Moderate	Severe
Precipitating events	Highly stressful	Moderately stressful	Not stressful
Destructiveness	Not destructive	Occasionally destructive	Usually destructive
Maturational appropriateness	Behavior typical for age	Some behavior typical for age	Behavior too young or too old
Personal functioning	Cares for own needs	Usually cares for own needs	Unable to care for own needs
Social functioning	Usually able to relate to others	Usually unable to relate to others	Not able to relate to others
Reality index	Usually sees events as they are	Occasionally sees events as they are	Little contact with reality
Insight index	Aware of behavior	Usually aware of behavior	Usually not aware of behavior
Conscious control	Usually can control behavior	Occasionally can control behavior	Little control over behavior
Social responsiveness	Usually acts appropriately	Occasionally acts appropriately	Rarely acts appropriately

Source: From Phyllis L. Newcomer, *Understanding and Teaching Emotionally Disturbed Children.* Copyright © 1980 by Allyn and Bacon. Reprinted with permission.

that "approximately 10% of children in school have moderate to severe emotional problems" (p. 60). Approximately 2 to 4 out of every 10,000 children exhibit some form of severe behavior disorder.

Kauffman (1985) suggested that 6 to 10 percent of the school-age population need specialized services because of behavior disorders. Other specialists have suggested that as many as 33 percent of school-age children experience behavior problems during any given year

TODAY'S TECHNOLOGY

Expert Systems/Artificial Intelligence

Researchers are testing the effectiveness of computers in aiding assessment teams to classify students as behavior disordered, learning disabled, or mentally retarded. Multidisciplinary team members enter assessment data that they have collected and respond to other questions that experts have programed the computer to ask. The so-called artificial intelligence (AI) that the experts have created examines and processes the data that have been provided and then makes a reasoned judgment. Additionally, AI systems are also programed to provide information about interventions that should be applied and the likelihood of their success in treating various learning and behavior problems (Hofmeister & Ferrara, 1986).

You might ask yourself: Are these expert systems superior to human judgment? This is a difficult question to answer. AI systems represent the best judgment of skilled assessment and intervention specialists. They are much like the expert systems used in medicine that assist physicians in making careful diagnoses and identifying potential treatments.

Imagine having an expert system in your own home for identifying potentially serious behavioral problems in your children as well as ways of dealing with them! You would enter the problem, its duration in time, its average frequency per day, and other salient information, and the computer would provide you with some effective strategies for addressing the problems.

(Cullinan & Epstein, 1986). Of this number, about one-third need the assistance provided by personnel outside the typical classroom. Another third need special education and related services.

During the 1989–1990 school year in the United States, less than 1 percent of children 6 to 17 years of age were identified and served as behavior disordered. This prevalence figure is significantly smaller than that of students served elsewhere in developed and undeveloped countries around the world (Juul, 1986). From 1989 to 1990, the number of students with behavior disorders served in special education in the United States increased from 8 to 9 percent of all students classified as disabled (U.S. Department of Education, 1991).

The fact remains, however, that a significant number of students with behavior disorders do not receive special education (Kauffman, 1987; Knitzer, Steinberg, & Fleisch, 1990). Some researchers have suggested that the number of students who receive special education is less than one-third of those who actually need this assistance (Brandenburg, Friedman, & Silver, 1990). This is truly unfortunate. The low number of students served is in part due to the lack of standardized criteria and diverse definitions used by various states (Kavale et al., 1986).

CHARACTERISTICS

Intelligence

Researchers from a variety of disciplines have studied the intellectual capacity of individuals with behavior disorders. In an early national study of children with behavior disorders enrolled in public school programs, the majority of these students exhibited above-average intelligence (Morse, Cutler, & Fink, 1964). However, other research conducted more recently has revealed a different picture.

Rubin and Balow (1978) studied three groups of children. The first group was composed of students who had been referred and identified as disturbed by medical or psychological personnel but not by their teachers. Their average IQs on two separate intelligence tests were 109 and 107. The second group of students, who were consistently referred and identified by teachers, had IQs of 96 and 92 on the same measures. The last group, who were sporadically identified as having difficulties by teachers, had average IQs of 102 on both tests of intelligence. Bower (1982) compared the IQs of children who were disturbed to those of children who were not disturbed. He found that children who were disturbed had average IQs of 92, whereas their nondisturbed peers had average IQs of 103.

Studies dealing with children who have been identified as psychotic reveal still another picture of intellectual functioning. Researchers have found that the majority of these children have IQs in the retarded range of functioning (Kauffman, 1985; Freeman & Ritvo, 1984). Of course, some of these children do have average or above-average IQs, but they are in the minority.

The preponderance of evidence leads to the conclusion that children who are disturbed tend to have average to lower-than-average IQs compared to their normal peers (Coleman, 1986). Additionally, children with severe behavior disorders tend to have IQs that fall within the retarded range of functioning. These inferences closely parallel the conclusions reached by Kauffman (1985).

What impact does intelligence have on the educational and social-adaptive performance of children with behavior disorders? Is the intellectual capacity of a child who is disturbed a good predictor of other types of achievement and social behavior? The answer is yes. Kauffman (1985) asserted that "the IQs of disturbed children appear to be the best single

FOCUS 6
Identify five general characteristics (intellectual, adaptive, and achievement) of children with behavior disorders.

predictor of academic and future social achievement" (p. 143). The below-average IQs of many of these children contribute significantly to the challenges that they experience in mastering academic and social tasks in school and other environments.

Adaptive Behavior

Individuals with behavior disorders exhibit a variety of problems in adapting to their homes, schools, and community environments. Furthermore, they have difficulties in relating socially and responsibly to persons such as peers, parents, teachers, and other authority figures.

Listening, asking for teacher assistance, bringing materials to class, following directions, completing assignments, and ignoring distractions are some of the school-related adaptive behaviors that do not come naturally to children with behavior disorders. Moreover, such behaviors may not have been successfully taught to these children. Socially, they may have difficulty introducing themselves, beginning and ending conversations, sharing, playing typical age-appropriate games, and apologizing. They may be unable to deal appropriately with situations that produce strong feelings, such as anger and frustration. Recall Cherie's difficulty in dealing with fears and frustrations, which profoundly influenced her desire to stay out of school (see Window 5–1).

Social problem solving, accepting consequences of misbehavior, negotiating, expressing affection, and reacting appropriately to failure are not generally part of the behavior repertoire of a child with behavior disorders. Because these children have deficits in these adaptive-social behaviors, they frequently experience difficulties in meeting the demands of the classroom and other environments in which they must participate. Brett, the aggressive boy described in Window 5–1, experienced many difficulties in accepting the consequences of behavior, dealing with strong feelings, and expressing affection. Cherie's refusal to go to school was directly related to her deficits in coping with her first week of junior high school. Jan's problems surfaced much later in her school career. It was a deterioration of her adaptive skills that caused significant problems in completing her schooling and maintaining her relationships with friends and others.

Earlier in the classification section, we talked about statistically derived categories of behaviors that were common to children and adolescents with behavior disorders. You may recall the categories: conduct disorder, anxiety-withdrawal, immaturity, and socialized aggression. Children with conduct disorders engage in verbal and physical aggression; are disruptive, negative, and irresponsible; and defy authority. Children who are characterized as being anxious and withdrawn exhibit behaviors such as anxiety, social withdrawal, seclusiveness, and shyness. Children who exhibit behaviors associated with immaturity have difficulty attending to tasks, particularly academic ones, tend to daydream, and respond to learning tasks in a very lethargic fashion. Gang activities, drug abuse, cooperative stealing, truancy, and other delinquent acts characterize youth who are identified as socialized aggressives. They relate well with each other but engage in antisocial acts that are offensive to the communities in which they take place.

It is easy to see how the behaviors associated with these categories are maladaptive and interfere with school and family success. Moreover, we can see how gang activities and cooperative stealing on the part of youth would antagonize and agitate community members who are affected by these behaviors.

Children with severe behavior disorders exhibit social and adaptive patterns of behaviors that closely parallel children who are moderately to severely retarded. They may need extensive assistance in developing self-help skills (e.g., toileting, grooming, dressing, and caring for themselves), language competency, and social skills that permit them to interact adequately with others in their home environments and elsewhere.

Academic Achievement

A variety of studies have been conducted to assess the academic characteristics of children with behavior disorders. Tamkin (1960) evaluated the achievement of children who had recently been institutionalized for behavior disorders. He found that 41 percent were academically advanced in comparison to their actual grade level, 27 percent were performing at grade level, and 32 percent were performing below grade level. Reading achievement for the group as a whole was significantly higher than math performance. In a more recent study, Coutinho (1986) found a significant relationship between early reading achievement problems and eventual classification as behavior disordered as well as continued subaverage performance in reading at the secondary level.

Other researchers have collected data that provide a different perspective of the academic characteristics of children with behavior disorders. Stone and Rowley (1964) evaluated children referred for psychiatric services on the basis of chronological age. Of the 116 children tested, 20 percent were academically above average for their grade level, 21 percent were at grade level, and 59 percent were below grade level. Graubard (1964) investigated the achievement of institutionalized children in conjunction with their mental age (their intellectual capacity as measured in years and months on an IQ test). In reading and math, these children were found to be severely disabled in relation to their mental ages.

Large-scale studies (Bower, 1981) of children, both disturbed and normal, revealed that those who are disturbed are significantly behind their peers in reading and math achievement. As a rule, the academic achievement of children with behavior disorders is not on a par with their expected achievement as indicated by mental age. In fact, many of these students could be identified as learning disabled if the selection were based primarily on discrepancy scores (the difference between one's ability as represented by IQ scores and one's actual academic performance as represented by achievement test scores) (O'Donnell, 1980; Scruggs & Mastropieri, 1986). This is particularly true for children who have mild to moderate disorders.

The picture is quite different, however, for children who are identified as schizophrenic or psychotic. Very few of them compare favorably to their peers in achievement. Youngsters who are severely disturbed are also generally retarded, and as such, their performance in areas such as math and reading is significantly substandard compared to that of normal children (Coleman, 1986; Kauffman, 1985).

CAUSATION

Theoretical Perspectives

Throughout history, philosophers, physicians, theologians, and others have attempted to explain why people behave as they do. Historically, people who were mentally disturbed were described as being possessed by evil spirits. It was presumed that the presence of evil spirits within these individuals made them behave the way they did. The treatment of choice at that time was religious in nature. Later, Sigmund Freud (1856–1939) and others promoted the notion that behavior could be explained in terms of subconscious phenomena or early traumatic experiences. More recently, some theorists have attributed disordered behaviors to inappropriate learning and complex interactions that take place between individuals and their environments. From a biological perspective, others have suggested that aberrant behaviors are caused by certain biochemical substances, brain abnormalities or injuries, and chromosomal irregularities.

With such a wealth of etiological explanations, it is easy to see why practitioners might choose different approaches to treating and preventing the various disorders. However, the

FOCUS 7
What can we accurately say about the causes of behavior disorders?

■ **Table 5–4** Causal Factors Associated with Behavior Disorders

Theoretical Framework	Causal Factors
BIOLOGICAL	Genetic inheritance Biochemical abnormalities Neurological abnormalities Injury to the central nervous system
PSYCHOANALYTICAL	Psychological processes Functioning of the mind: id, ego, and superego Inherited predispositions (instinctual processes) Traumatic early childhood experiences
BEHAVIORAL	Environmental events: 1. Failed to learn adaptive behaviors 2. Learned maladaptive behaviors 3. Developed maladaptive behaviors as a result of stressful environmental circumstances
PHENOMENOLOGICAL	Faulty learning about self Misuse of defense mechanisms Feelings, thoughts, and events emanating from self
SOCIOLOGICAL/ECOLOGICAL	Role assignment (labeling) Cultural transmission Social disorganization Distorted communication Differential association Negative interactions and transactions with others

variety of theoretical frameworks and perspectives provides clinicians with a number of choices for explaining the presence of certain behaviors. Table 5–4 provides an overview of etiologies and causal factors associated with various theoretical frameworks.

The Biological Approach.   The biological framework explains behavior disorders as a function of inherited or abnormal biological conditions within the body or injury to the central nervous system. Behavior problems presumably surface as a result of some physiological, biochemical, genetic abnormality or disease.

The Psychoanalytical Approach.   Subconscious processes, predispositions or instincts, and early traumatic experiences explain the presence of behavior disorders from a psychoanalytic perspective. The internal processes are unobservable events that occur in the mind among the well-known psychic constructs of the id (the drives component), ego (the reality component), and superego (the conscience component). As we gain insight into psychic conflicts by means of psychotherapy, we may be able to eliminate or to solve the problem behaviors. The return to normalcy may also be aided by a caring therapist or teacher. For children, this process theoretically occurs through play therapy, in which inner conflicts are revealed and subsequently resolved through family therapy and therapeutic play experiences with understanding adults.

The Behavioral Approach.   The behavioral approach focuses on aspects of the environment that produce, reward, diminish, or punish certain behaviors. Through treatment, adults and children are given opportunities to learn new adaptive behaviors by identifying realistic goals and receiving **reinforcement** for attaining these goals. Gradually, aberrant behaviors are eliminated or replaced by more appropriate ones.

The Phenomenological Approach.   From a phenomenological point of view, abnormal behaviors arise from feelings, thoughts, and past events tied to a person's self-perception or self-concept. Faulty perceptions or feelings are thought to cause individuals to behave in ways that are counterproductive to self-fulfillment. Therapy using this approach is centered on helping people develop satisfactory perceptions and behaviors that are in agreement with self-selected values.

The Sociological-Ecological Approach.   The sociological-ecological model is by far the most encompassing explanation of behavior disorders. Aberrant behaviors are presumed to be caused by a variety of interactions and transactions with other people (Patterson & Bank, 1986; Ramsey & Walker, 1988). For some, the deviant behaviors are taught as a part of one's culture. For others, the behaviors are a function of labeling. Individuals labeled as juvenile delinquents, according to this perspective, gradually adopt the patterns of behavior that are associated with the assigned label. In addition, others who are aware of the label begin to treat the labeled individuals as if they were truly delinquent. Such treatment theoretically promotes the delinquent behavior.

Another source of aberrant behavior associated with this model is differential association. This source of deviance is closely related to the cultural-transmission explanation of deviance: People exhibit behavior problems in an attempt to conform to the wishes and expectations of a group with which they wish to join or maintain affiliation. Finally, the sociological-ecological perspective views the presence of aberrant behavior as a function of a variety of interactions and transactions that are derived from a broad array of environmental settings.

Each of these models contributes different explanations for the causes of behavior disorders. Unfortunately, we are rarely able to isolate the exact cause of a child's behavior disorders, but we do have an understanding of many conditions and factors that contribute to disordered behavior. We concur with Wicks-Nelson and Israel (1984), who wrote: "With few if any exceptions, behavior can be explained only by multiple influences and their continuous interaction. A vast array of variables—biological structure and function, inheritance, cognition, social/emotional status, family, social class—can usually be expected to come into play" (p. xvii).

Family and home environments play a critical role in the emergence of behavior disorders. Poverty, malnutrition, increased homelessness, family discord, divorce, childrearing practices, and child abuse have an impact on the behaviors we observe in children (Gelfand, Jenson, & Drew, 1988). Young mothers who are malnourished during pregnancy are likely to give birth to low-birthweight babies. Babies weighing less than 4 pounds are at risk for developing a variety of disabling conditions (e.g., attention-deficit disorders, epilepsy, and other neurological disorders). Young mothers in impoverished environments are often single and inexperienced in child care. Others are experienced in child care but frequently burdened with the survival tasks of providing food, clothing, and housing for themselves and their children. Little time may be available for stimulating and interacting with their infants. Moreover, these mothers may have little energy at the end of the day to play and talk with their children. Lacking appropriate stimulation, these children suffer intellectually, cognitively, socially, and emotionally (Peterson, 1987).

Family discord and divorce also play a role in the development of behavior disorde in some children. The impact of divorce on children is influenced by a variety of facto (e.g., age of the child, financial status of the family, gender of the child, amount of acrimor between the partners, etc.). Therefore, it is difficult to predict with great precision who w be severely affected by divorce. As a rule, boys appear to be more negatively influenced I divorce than are girls (Emery, Hetherington, & DiLalla, 1984). Girls who are affected oft exhibit behaviors associated with anxiety and withdrawal. Boys, in contrast, exhibit a gressive and hyperactive behaviors (Guidubaldi, Perry, & Cleminshaw, 1984).

Child-management and discipline procedures also play important roles in the deve opment of behavior disorders. Parents who are extremely permissive, overly restrictiv and/or aggressive often produce children who are conduct disordered (Kazdin, 1985). Hor environments that are devoid of consistent rules and consequences for child behavior, th lack parental supervision, that reinforce aggressive behavior, and that have parents wl model aggression and use aggressive child-management practices produce children who a very much at risk for developing disruptive behavior disorders. Also, marital discord, fami separation, and divorce are found more frequently in families of children and youths ider tified as having conduct disorders.

Child abuse, too, plays a major role in the development of aggression and other prol lematic behaviors in children and youth. Rogeness, Amrung, Macedo, Harris, & Fish (1986) found that serious abuse during later childhood and adolescence was often followe by destructive, noncompliant, and aggressive behaviors in the child. MacFarlane (197 referred to **sexual abuse** as the "psychological time bomb." The bomb's impact is a functic of several factors: the age at which the child or youth was abused; the degree of violen involved; the relationship of the abuser to the child or youth; the duration of the abuse; tl response of parents and professionals to the abuse; and the degree of guilt or discomfo expressed by the affected child or youth. Most reported victims of sexual abuse are gir between the ages of 11 and 14. Very little research has been devoted to sexual abuse of mal or its impact (Browne & Finkelhor, 1986).

ASSESSMENT

Screening and Referral

The first step in the assessment process is screening. The major purpose of screening is identify infants, childen, and youth who are most in need of treatment. Screening is al based on the belief that early identification leads to early treatment, which may lessen tl overall impact of the behavior disorders on the individual and family. However, very fe school systems or social agencies engage in any kind of grand-scale screening for behavic disorders. First, such a task is generally very expensive and time consuming. Most scho systems and state social service agencies do not have sufficient financial or human resourc to conduct systematic screening programs for behavior disorders. Furthermore, it is possib that many more children would be identified than could be adequately handled by a scho system or social agency. However, research conducted in one statewide screening progra did not confirm this outcome (Smith, 1985).

In most school environments, children are considered for screening only after concerne or perplexed teachers have initiated referrals for them. For example, an experienced ki dergarten teacher became very concerned about a boy named John. He was continuall involved in a variety of behaviors atypical for his age—taking off his clothes, crying fc prolonged periods, and physically attacking children—all for no obvious reason. These behaviors and others prompted John's kindergarten teacher to take some action, not onl with his parents but also with the principal.

Child abuse and neglect play a major role in the development of problematic behavior. (Grant LeDuc/Monkmeyer Press)

The actual submission of a referral for a student is generally preceded by a number of parent-teacher conferences. The conferences help the teacher and parents determine what action ought to be taken. For example, the student's problems may be a symptom of family problems such as an extended parental illness, marital difficulties, or severe financial challenges. If the parents and teacher continue to be perplexed by a child's behavior, a referral may be initiated. Referrals are generally processed by principals, who review them, consult with parents, and then pass them on to a psychologist or assessment team leader.

Once a referral has been appropriately processed and parental or guardian permission for testing and evaluation has been obtained, assessment team members proceed with the tasks of carefully observing and assessing a child's strengths and weaknesses. Their task is to determine whether the child has a behavior disorder and whether he or she qualifies for special education services. Furthermore, the team is responsible for identifying treatment strategies that may be helpful to the parents and teacher.

Factors in Assessment

The severity of behaviors such as those exhibited by the kindergartner John may be examined from several perspectives. First, it is necessary to determine whether any discrepancy exists between his chronological age and the behaviors he consistently displays. This is important in determining John's status in relationship to various norms. In addition to determining whether John's behaviors are age appropriate, assessment team members must analyze the frequency of problem behaviors. They must assess how often his peculiar behaviors occur and under what circumstances. They must also determine if his inappropriate behaviors are related to specific activities or individuals and whether his problems continue even after someone intervenes.

Assessment team members have the responsibility of evaluating the influence of his behaviors on classmates, teachers, and the family unit. Additionally, team members have an obligation to assess the teacher's contribution to the present problems (Slate & Saudargas, 1986). John's interactions with individuals in his school setting and his responses to his home environment significantly influence the recommendations that team members make regarding his classification, placement, and eventual treatment.

FOCUS 8
Identify four factors that need to be carefully assessed in determining whether a child has a behavior disorder.

5–2   Case Study: Peter

Introduction

Peter was referred for individualized care by the local elementary school basic staffing team. His first-grade teacher reported that he was often aggressive, unable to sit still, and that he refused to do anything she asked. In addition, she complained that his hygiene was very poor and that he often came to school tired. At the time of the referral, his parents refused to participate on the school planning team and were openly hostile toward school staff. While Peter was a child with above average intellectual abilities, he was failing in his academic subjects, was disliked by his peers, and spent approximately 70 percent of his school day in "time-out" situations. Peter's teacher felt that his needs could no longer be met within a regular mainstream setting. The initial assessments in school indicated that Peter was a child with significant undercontrolled behaviors occurring approximately every five minutes. Some of his more disruptive and dangerous behaviors included running around the classroom, jumping on the desks, hitting, spitting at the other children and the teacher, bolting out of the school, running into the street, and refusing to work and comply with instructions.

Peter's parents were unable to cope with equally problematic behaviors at home. If they placed any limits on his behavior he would destroy things. They reported that he constantly fought with his younger brother, wet the bed every night, hit and kicked his parents, and required constant supervision because he was like a revved up engine and would get into everything. Their approach to child management was quite punitive and involved yelling, spanking, and locking Peter in his room. An assessment of the home environment revealed a highly punitive and restrictive home situation. Peter's mother and father felt inadequate as parents and rarely interacted with their children. They lacked an understanding of developmental norms and expectations for children, expressed only hostile feelings toward their children, and demanded 100 percent compliance at all times. Their marital relationship was explosive and during one episode the children were physically hurt and had to be placed in foster care for a short period of time. The child protection agency and school personnel felt that there was considerable potential for further abuse. (p. 53)

Source: Excerpted from Burchard, J. D., Clarke, R. T.: The role of individualized care in a service delivery system for children and adolescents with severely maladjusted behavior. *Journal of Mental Health Administration* 1990; 17(1):48–60. Reprinted with permission.

Techniques Used in Assessment

A variety of techniques are used to identify children with behavior disorders. These techniques closely parallel the theoretical framework or philosophical perspective of the evaluator. Usually, an actual diagnosis of the behavioral problems is preceded by a set of screening procedures. Screening is done using behavior checklists or a variety of sociometric devices (e.g., peer ratings) and teacher rating scales.

Parents and teachers are generally asked to respond to a variety of rating-scale items that are descriptive of behaviors that are significantly related to various classifications of behavior disorders. The number of items marked as well as the rating given each item contribute to the behavior profiles that are generated from the ratings. (See Table 5–5, which is drawn from the Child Behavior Checklist for Ages 4–16 [Achenbach, 1988].) In making their assessments, parents and professionals are asked to consider the child's behavior during the past six months.

Behavioral analysis techniques are also used to make comparisons between children suspected of exhibiting serious behavioral problems. One such technique is direct observation. Using this method, a well-trained observer can count and record a variety of behaviors that may be of concern to a teacher or parent while at the same time monitoring these behaviors in a number of other students. Comparisons drawn from these types of observations can be very helpful in accurately assessing the behavior pattern of a student in contrast to his or her peers.

Once the screening process has been concluded, specialists and/or consultants—including psychologists, special educators, social workers, and psychiatrists—complete

■ **Table 5–5** Representative Items from the
Child Behavior Checklist for Ages 4–18

0 = Not True (as far as you know)
1 = Somewhat or Sometimes True
2 = Very True or Often True

0 1 2	1.	Acts too young for his/her age
0 1 2	5.	Behaves like the opposite sex
0 1 2	10.	Can't sit still, restless, hyperactive
0 1 2	15.	Cruel to animals
0 1 2	20.	Destroys his/her own things
0 1 2	25.	Doesn't get along with other children
0 1 2	30.	Fears going to school
0 1 2	35.	Feels worthless or inferior
0 1 2	40.	Hears sounds and voices that aren't there (describe):

_____

_____

0 1 2	45.	Nervous, high strung, or tense
0 1 2	50.	Too fearful or anxious

Source: From *Manual for the Child Behavior Checklist/4–18 and 1991 Profile*, by T. M. Achenbach. Burlington: Department of Psychiatry, University of Vermont. Copyright by T. M. Achenbach. Reproduced by permission.

in-depth assessments of the child's academic and social-emotional strengths and weaknesses in various environmental settings, such as the classroom, home, and playground. The assessment team may analyze classroom and playground interactions with peers and teachers using ecological and behavioral analysis techniques (observations with frequency counts of various types of behaviors or interactions); administer various tests to evaluate personality, achievement, and intellectual factors; and interview the parents and the child. Additionally, they may observe the child at home and apply an array of other assessment procedures.

Unfortunately, many assessment devices, particularly projective and personality inventories, do not provide information that reliably differentiates individuals who have disorders from those who do not (Gelfand et al., 1988). Likewise, information gained from these devices cannot be readily translated into specific programing for individuals with behavior disorders. Of greatest promise at this point are behavioral analysis techniques, which provide a concrete means for evaluating problem behaviors, selecting appropriate individualized education program (IEP) goals, and assessing intervention effects. Unfortunately, the agreement between diagnostic or assessment data and students' IEP goals and associated interventions is poor (Fiedler & Knight, 1986).

FOCUS 9

Identify six major treatment approaches generally used in treating children and adolescents with behavior disorders.

INTERVENTIONS

Approaches to Treatment

Interventions for children and adolescents with behavior disorders include a variety of approaches (Center, 1986). Major approaches to treatment include insight-oriented therapy, play therapy, group psychotherapy, behavior therapy, marital and family therapy, and drug

■ **Table 5–6** Summary of Intervention Approaches

General Goals	Intervention Approaches					
	Insight-Oriented Therapy	Play Therapy	Group Psychotherapy	Behavior Therapy	Marital and Family Therapy	Drug Therapy
Relieve symptoms	■					■
Treat causes of behavior	■		■		■	
Develop therapeutic relationship	■	■	■		■	
Play out emotional problems		■				
Develop positive peer relationships		■	■	■		
Teach language skills				■		
Teach self-help skills				■		
Teach academic skills				■		
Reduce and/or eliminate behaviors				■		
Teach adaptive behavior				■		
Teach social skills		■		■		
Develop problem-solving skills		■	■		■	
Understand unconscious causes of behavior	■		■			
Control disordered or unusual behavior				■		■
Control aggression				■		■
Control behavior				■		■

therapy (see Table 5–6). Unfortunately, many of these therapies are not available to students with behavior disorders (Peacock Hill Working Group, 1990). As a rule, school systems and mental health agencies have not been successful in developing effective collaborative models for serving students with severe behavior disorders (Knitzer, 1982). However, there are some exceptions. Project Wraparound (Burchard, Clarke, & Hamilton, 1988) and the Alaska Youth Initiative (Dowrick, 1988) represent unique and comprehensive programs in which schools and mental health agencies have worked effectively together to provide quality education and related services to students with behavior disorders.

Insight-Oriented Therapy. Insight-oriented therapy includes psychoanalytic, nondirective, and client-centered therapy. These approaches assume that children who feel rage, rejection, and guilt can be helped by an understanding and caring therapist. The therapist endeavors to establish a relationship with the child by creating an atmosphere that is conducive to sharing and expressing feelings. The goal of therapy is to help the child develop insight or self-understanding, which provides the basis for the relief of symptoms and the development of new, more adaptive behaviors.

5–3	Case Study: Peter

Interagency Care and Intensive Family-Based Services

Following initial contacts with Peter's family, an interdisciplinary team was formed consisting of the parents and appropriate representatives from mental health, social services, and education. The interdisciplinary team met as needed for three reasons: (1) to plan and coordinate the various services that were provided to the family and child; (2) to provide multiagency ownership with respect to funding services as well as to discuss the utilization of private third-party payments; and (3) to ensure that all efforts were made to provide the least restrictive care prior to any placement of the child into more costly and/or restrictive educational or residential programs. Peter's parents participated in the interagency team to aid in the identification of services.

Due to the necessity to intervene immediately to prevent the child from being placed in a more restrictive environment, the comprehensive ecological assessment was performed as intervention was being applied. As the evaluation process was progressing, services and plans were revised to meet the individual needs of the family, child, and school. For example, an immediate family concern was the parents' lack of appropriate discipline and child management strategies. A family intervention specialist entered the home within seven hours of the referral and initiated interventions designed to assist the parents in developing alternative approaches. As the parents progressed through the training, the ongoing individualized assessment revealed that the parents did not know how to play with their children and felt insecure about interacting with them. Interventions were then applied to educate them about child play and coach them through play situations. At all stages of the assessment process, emphasis was placed on the parents realistically identifying needs and assisting in the development of services to meet those needs. While the needs identified by the parents did not always coincide with the priorities of the clinician, involving the parents in this manner insured more commitment from them to participate and empowered them to be effective advocates for themselves and their children. During a two-year period, the family experienced intensive home-based services, significant respite care, a variety of interventions designed to meet the individual needs of the child such as dry-bed training and conflict resolution training, individual counseling to address alcohol and physical abuse issues, and two summer education programs to assist the children in skill building around safety, social skills, and cooperative play. (pp. 53–54)

Source: Excerpted from Burchard, J. D., Clarke, R. T.: The role of individualized care in a service delivery system for children and adolescents with severely maladjusted behavior. *Journal of Mental Health Administration* 1990; 17(1):48–60. Reprinted with permission.

Play Therapy. Play therapy for young children serves several purposes. It is designed help them become aware of their own unconscious thoughts and the behaviors that anate from these thoughts. For children who have been emotionally abused or neglected, other purpose is to provide them with an opportunity to interact with a caring, sensitive ult. The vehicle for communication between the therapist and children is free play and her related small-group activities. Through play therapy, children may reveal information out themselves that they cannot talk about, such as sexual abuse, sibling rivalry, and maging discipline practices. Play therapy can be a valuable source of information for erapists.

Group Psychotherapy. Group psychotherapy and other group-oriented treatment proaches are occasionally used with children; however, they are used more frequently th adolescents and young adults. **Activity group therapy** for children is operated much e a club. For example, a mix of aggressive and withdrawn boys meet together weekly club (therapy) meetings. The therapist's role in the group setting is primarily one of deling appropriate, healthy behaviors, helping aggressive children become more cooptive and promoting and developing outgoing behaviors in children who are shy and thdrawn. Group-treatment approaches for older youth are varied and often quite similar the procedures used with adults. The major difference lies in the concerns and issues that the focus of therapy sessions. Vorrath's Positive Peer Culture has been used with a variety

When Gangs Meet Individuals with Disabilities

Salvador used to run with the East Side Longos, but now he's in "the CDC gang." The 16-year-old convicted car thief is one of 35 Los Angeles juvenile felons who, as part of probation, work with children with disabilities.

Today, Salvador is "dancing" with Maria, a teenage girl who uses a wheelchair, gliding her around the school gymnasium to the beat of a tambourine. Maria can't speak, but she shows her gratitude by smiling and spelling out "I Love You" on a message board.

Salvador basks in the affection. "I like working with the children," he says, "and it's a lot better than what I was doing."

The idea is simple: rehabilitation through good deeds. Rather than return to their old schools and haunts, the probationers attend classes at the Southeast Community Day Center (CDC) in Bellflower. For two hours each day, they help train, exercise, and feed 225 children with disabilities.

"Instead of being so-called gangsters, this shows that they are recyclable, valuable people," says Cedric Anderson, a CDC teacher.

The program isn't perfect—after 18 months, 22 of the 105 students have been expelled. But the CDC gang recently saw its first member graduate from high school, and many students have earned better grades.

A "Hard Sell"

Turning gang members into social workers was a "hard sell." At first, parents and administrators balked at mixing car thieves and attempted murderers with children, says Sharon Roberts, the county special education planning director who conceived the program. But the logic proved irresistible. Children with disabilities can often be reached more easily by people their own age, but peer-age volunteers are hard to find. CDC was a rich and ready source. For their part, probation officials wanted to teach the exoffenders responsibility and self-esteem.

"They all say they never had anything," says Roberts. "But they learn that they have it so much better than a kid who can't move and can't talk. And it's better than returning from jail straight to the streets."

"Now I really feel like I can do something," says Alfred, a 17-year-old former gang member.

The county agrees. "We're dispelling the myth that these kids are terrible people and anything they do would turn out badly," says Ted Price, director of Los Angeles County's juvenile court community school program. Next year, the county plans to expand to at least two other locations, giving those who need help more of a chance to help each other.

Source: From "When Gangs Meet the Handicapped," *Newsweek*, May 7, 1990.

of youth-related problems, including disruptive classroom behaviors, delinquency, and substance abuse (Sandler, Arnold, Gable, & Strain, 1987; Vorrath & Brendtro, 1985). This treatment approach capitalizes on the power inherent in peer approval and peer-selected rules, contingencies, and solutions. It requires the skill of an experienced therapist, group leader, or teacher.

Behavior Therapy.   Behavioral interventions for children and youth focus on developing or improving various self-help, social, language, and academic behaviors. Increasing the rates of desirable behavior is achieved in a variety of ways. Teachers and special education personnel make extensive use of the principles of behavior modification in this approach. Rewards, **token reinforcement systems,** contingency contracting, and other motivational systems are used to encourage children to engage in normal, adaptive behaviors (Bauer & Shea, 1988).

Another focus of behavioral interventions is the reduction or elimination of maladaptive behaviors. Reductions in certain behaviors may be achieved through a variety of means. For instance, a young boy's fighting behavior may be reduced by rewarding his cooperative and problem-solving behaviors and punishing his fighting behaviors. For engaging in fighting, he may lose accumulated tokens (response cost) or be placed in a time-out area where he cannot earn tokens or participate in the ongoing, reinforcing activities of the classroom.

A variety of researchers and clinicians have experimented with a relatively new behavioral modification approach known as **cognitive-behavioral training** (Ager & Cole, 1991;

Etscheidt, 1991). This approach emphasizes teaching *internal verbal strategies* as a means of encouraging and maintaining important social or academic behaviors (Meichenbaum, 1977). For example, a child might be taught the following strategic sequence, which combines thinking with behaving:

Step 1 *Motor cue/Impulse delay:* Stop and think before you act, cue yourself.
Step 2 *Problem definition:* Say how you feel and exactly what the problem is.
Step 3 *Generation of alternatives:* Think of as many solutions as you can.
Step 4 *Consideration of consequences:* Think ahead to what might happen next.
Step 5 *Implementation:* When you have a really good solution, try it! (Etscheidt, 1991, p. 111)

Results generated from studies in which this approach has been used with children and youth have been quite promising (Ager & Cole, 1991; Harris & Pressley, 1991).

Marital and Family Therapy.   Marital therapy and family therapy are designed to help married individuals and their families enjoy greater success in dealing with problems and relating more effectively with one another. Several types of family therapy have been developed. Some therapists are psychodynamically oriented; that is, they are interested in helping family members understand the unconscious dynamics and other factors that may be influencing their interactions. Family therapists who adhere to the systems orientation direct their efforts at helping family members understand the roles and functions they play in the family system. They may determine that a child's disturbance serves some specific family function and is thereby supported by the other family members. Structural family therapy emphasizes the assessment of family functioning. The ways in which family members solve problems and interact with each other are assessed. Coalitions within the family are isolated, and the views that family members have of themselves and others are evaluated. Therapists using this approach become actively involved with families by assigning homework between sessions and giving participants other family-related tasks to complete.

Depression is now recognized as a serious and frequent problem among youth. (Kevin Horan/ The Picture Group)

INTERACTING IN NATURAL SETTINGS ············· People with Behavior Disorders ·············

EARLY CHILDHOOD YEARS

Tips for the Family

♦ Become involved with parent training and other community mental health services.

♦ Work closely with family support personnel (e.g., social workers, nurses, and parent group volunteers) in developing effective child-management strategies.

♦ Use the same intervention effective strategies at home that are used in the preschool setting.

♦ Establish family routines, schedules, and incentive systems that reward positive behaviors.

♦ Join advocacy or parent support groups.

Tips for the Preschool Teacher

♦ Work closely with the support personnel in your preschool (e.g., director, psychologist, social worker, parent trainers, special educators, etc.) to identify effective and realistic strategies.

♦ Establish clear schedules, class routines, rules, and positive consequences for all children in your classroom.

♦ Create a learning and social environment that is nurturing and supportive for everyone.

♦ Teach specific social behaviors (e.g., following directions, greeting other children, sharing toys, using words to express anger, etc.) to all children.

♦ Do not be reluctant to ask for help from support personnel. Remember, collaboration is the key.

Tips for Preschool Personnel

♦ Use older, socially competent children to assist with readiness skills and social skills training.

♦ Help others (e.g., teaching assistants, aides, volunteers, etc.) know what to do in managing children with behavior disorders.

♦ Make every effort to involve the children in all schoolwide activities and special performances.

♦ Orient and teach the other preschool children about disabling conditions and how they should respond and relate to their peers with behavior problems.

♦ Collaborate with parents in using the same management systems in your preschool classroom that are used in the home and other specialized settings.

Tips for Neighbors and Friends

♦ Become familiar with the things you should do as a neighbor or friend in responding to the positive and negative behaviors of a child with behavior disorders.

♦ Be patient with parents who are attempting to deal with their child's temper tantrum or other equally challenging behaviors at the grocery store or other like environments.

♦ Offer parents some time away from their preschooler by watching him or her for a couple of hours.

♦ Involve the child in your family activities.

♦ Help parents become aware of advocacy or parent support groups.

♦ Encourage parents to involve their child in neighborhood and community events (e.g., parades, holiday celebrations, and birthday parties).

ELEMENTARY YEARS

Tips for the Family

♦ Use the effective management techniques that are being used in your child's classroom in your home environment.

♦ Help your other children (who are not disturbed) to develop an understanding of behavior disorders.

♦ Establish rules, routines, and consequences that fit your child's developmental age and interests.

♦ Take advantage of parent training and support groups that are available in your community.

♦ Obtain counseling when appropriate for yourself, your other children, and your spouse from a community mental health agency or other public or private source.

♦ Help your other children and their friends understand the things they can do to assist you in rearing your child with behavior disorders.

Tips for the Regular Classroom Teacher

♦ Provide a structured classroom environment (e.g., clearly stated rules, helpful positive and negative consequences, well-conceived classroom schedules, and carefully taught classroom routines).

♦ Teach social skills (e.g., dealing with teasing, accepting criticism, etc.) to all of the children with the aid of members of the teacher assistance team.

♦ Teach self-management skills (e.g., goal selection, self-monitoring, self-reinforcement, etc.) to all children with the aid of members of the teacher assistance team.

♦ Use cooperative learning strategies to promote the learning of all children and to develop positive relationships among students.

♦ Do not be reluctant to ask for help from members of your teacher assistance team or the child's parents.

Tips for School Personnel

♦ Use same-age or cross-age peers to provide tutoring, coaching, and other kinds of assistance in developing the academic and social skills of children with behavior disorders.

◆ Develop a schoolwide management program that reinforces individual and group accomplishments.

◆ Work closely with the teacher assistance team to create a school environment that is positive and caring.

◆ Use collaborative problem-solving techniques in dealing with difficult or persistent behavior problems.

◆ Help all children in the school develop an understanding of how they should respond to students with behavior problems.

Tips for Neighbors and Friends

◆ Involve the child with behavior problems in appropriate after-school activities (e.g., clubs, specialized tutoring, recreational events, etc.)

◆ Invite the child to spend time with your family in appropriate recreational events (e.g., swimming, hiking, etc.).

◆ Teach other children (without behavior problems) how to ignore or support certain behaviors that may occur.

◆ Catch the child being good rather than looking for "bad" behaviors.

◆ As a youth leader, coach, or recreation specialist, get to know each child with behavior disorders well so that you can respond with confidence in directing his or her activities.

SECONDARY/TRANSITION YEARS

Tips for the Family

◆ Continue your efforts to focus on the positive behaviors of your child with behavior disorders.

◆ Assist your child in selecting appropriate post-secondary training, education, and/or employment.

◆ Give yourself a regular break from the tedium of being a parent, and enjoy a recreational activity that is totally enjoyable for you.

◆ Ask for help from community mental health services, your priest or pastor, or a close friend when you are feeling overwhelmed or stressed.

◆ Consult regularly with treatment personnel to monitor progress and to obtain ideas for maintaining the behavioral gains made by your child.

◆ Continue your involvement in advocacy and parent support groups.

Tips for the Regular Classroom Teacher

◆ Create positive relationships within your classroom with co-operative learning teams and group-oriented assignments.

◆ Use all students in creating standards for conduct as well as consequences for positive and negative behaviors.

◆ Focus your efforts on developing a positive relationship with the student with behavior disorders by greeting him or her regularly to your class, informally talking with him or her at appropriate times, attending to improvements in his or her performance, and becoming aware of his or her interests.

◆ Work closely with the members of the teacher assistance team to be aware of teacher behaviors that may adversely or positively affect the student's performance.

◆ Realize that changes in behavior often occur very gradually, with periods of regression and sometimes tumult.

Tips for School Personnel

◆ Create a school climate that is positive and supportive.

◆ Provide students with an understanding of their roles and responsibilities in responding to peers who are disabled.

◆ Use peers in providing social skills training, job coaching, and academic tutoring, and the like.

◆ Use members of the teacher assistance team to help you deal with crisis situations and to provide other supportive therapies and interventions.

◆ Be sure schoolwide procedures are in place for dealing quickly and efficiently with particularly difficult behaviors.

Tips for Neighbors, Friends, and Potential Employers

◆ If you have some expertise in a content area (e.g., math, English, history, etc.), offer to provide regular assistance with homework or other related school assignments for students with behavior disorders.

◆ Provide opportunities for students with behavior disorders to be employed in your business.

◆ Give parents an occasional reprieve by inviting the youth to join your family for a cook-out, video night, or other family-oriented activities.

◆ Encourage other children (who are not disordered) to volunteer as peer partners, job coaches, and social skills trainers.

◆ Do not allow others in your presence to tease, harass, or ridicule a youth with behavior disorders.

Drug Therapy. Drug therapy for children is frequently used to treat a variety of conditions and related behaviors (Epstein & Olinger, 1987; Forness & Kavale, 1988). Children who are hyperactive, inattentive, and impulsive are often treated with stimulant drugs. Children with severe behavior disorders may be treated with medications to control disorganized or highly erratic behavior (Gadow, 1986). In other cases, medications may be prescribed for children who have chronic problems with bed-wetting or involuntary urination. Older teenagers or young adults may be prescribed drugs that are ordinarily taken by adults for depression and other psychiatric conditions.

A number of service delivery systems are used to make these and other treatments available to children, youth, and their families. The type of service delivery and the emphasis of the approach taken depends on the age of the student, the severity of the disorder, the type of disorder, and the theoretical orientation of the providers. Moreover, the effectiveness of past interventions and input from the family must be considered. For example, a preschooler who is out of control will need an altogether different treatment than an adolescent who is severely depressed.

Early Childhood Interventions

Service delivery systems for young disturbed children are many and varied. However, four systems are generally used to provide children who are disturbed with necessary services: the home-based system; the home-based system followed by involvement with a specialized center; the home- and center-based system; and the center-based system. Personnel in these service delivery systems may use a variety of intervention approaches to assist children and families with whom they work (see Table 5–7).

The home-based program approach provides disturbed children with specialized services through a home teacher. The teacher trains parents to use behavior modification and other therapeutic procedures. Parents then employ these techniques to assist their children in learning and mastering new, developmentally appropriate skills. Home-based behavioral interventions seem to produce better results for young children with conduct disorders than do other service delivery systems (Scruggs, Mastropieri, Cook, & Escobar, 1986).

Referrals for home-based service programs come from physicians, local guidance clinics, public school personnel, and county health nurses. Home teachers assist parents in selecting appropriate goals for their children, which are based on actual performance data of the child as observed firsthand by the parents and home teacher. Using these data, the home teacher and parents develop a program that is consistent with the child's needs. The program consists of training related to self-help, language, socialization, and motor skills. On a weekly basis, the family is visited by the home teacher, and the child is observed relative to weekly goals that have been established. The parent is also observed to be sure that he or she is encouraging the behaviors associated with the weekly goal. The home teacher discusses any problems that may be occurring in the training process and also provides demonstrations

■ **Table 5–7** Childhood Service Delivery Systems and Intervention Approaches

Early Childhood Service Delivery Systems	Intervention Approaches					
	Insight-Oriented Therapy	Play Therapy	Group Psychotherapy	Behavior Therapy	Marital and Family Therapy	Drug Therapy
Home-based program				■		■
Home-based program followed by specialized center	■	■		■	■	■
Home- and center-based system	■	■	■	■	■	■
Center-based program	■	■	■	■	■	■

and instructions that are relevant to the goals that the parents and child are presently pursuing.

A home-based program may be followed by a specialized center program. The intent of these programs is to provide a carefully conceived, sequential program in which objectives for the home and center programs are interrelated. In general, children served in this manner receive home-based instruction from birth to approximately 3 years of age. When a child is about 2½ to 3½ years old, he or she is moved into a center-based program that builds on the skills developed in the home program.

Center-based programs for young children with severe emotional problems provide treatments based on a variety of perspectives and orientations. For example, a center may emphasize both behavioral and psychodynamic principles. Teachers and therapists in such a center would attempt to determine all of the dynamics that may play a role in the child's present behaviors. Feelings, thoughts, past negative and positive experiences, relationships with parents and siblings, and family values would all be considered in the treatment process and daily education of a young child. Various forms of play therapy may be used to encourage children to play out their conflicts and to develop trusting relationships with adults. Teacher-child relationships are very important to teachers and other persons who work directly with children in these centers.

Teachers and therapists are also free to use the techniques associated with behavior therapy. Rewards for positive behavior, use of task analysis (breaking down behaviors into their most elementary parts for teaching), behavior shaping (gradually helping a child develop a behavior that has not yet been exhibited or mastered), and other behavioral techniques may be used.

Interventions for Elementary-Age Children

Elementary-age children with behavior disorders are likely to exhibit below-average performance in reading and math as well as other areas within the typical school curriculum. In addition to their academic problems, they may have difficulties relating to others, observing class rules, and handling emotional situations.

Academic problems may be addressed through specialized instruction and materials provided by a consulting teacher. How and when the special materials are used depends on the staffing patterns and resources available in the school. Young children with behavior disorders may be tutored by older, academically capable students. Some children are assisted by aides or regular class teachers, with follow-up provided by consultants or special education resource-room teachers.

Behavioral difficulties may be addressed in a variety of ways. Sometimes, misbehavior is a function of a lack of satisfactory rules, routines, and structures within the regular classroom. If this is the case, a consulting teacher may assist the regular class teacher in developing a classroom-management system that not only benefits the child who is disturbed but other children in the classroom, as well.

Small training groups may be formed by a teacher to assist a youngster in developing social and problem-solving skills (Amish, Gesten, Smith, Clark, & Stark, 1988; Knapczyk, 1988). Structured Learning (McGinnis, Goldstein, Sprafkin, & Gershaw, 1984) is a program that uses (1) **modeling,** (2) **role-playing,** (3) **performance feedback,** and (4) **transfer of training.** Prior to the initiation of training, a careful assessment is completed to determine the skills that need to be taught through the structured learning sequences. The first phase of training consists of modeling activities in which students are given an opportunity to carefully observe various types of prosocial behaviors. For example, a trained peer may model some healthy and effective ways to respond to teasing. Observational learning or

5-4   Case Study: Peter

Intensive School-Based Services

Due to pervasive, cross-setting difficulties, a school-based planning team was established consisting of the classroom teacher, a case worker from social services, a special educator, the parent, a school-based integration specialist, and the school nurse. This team met for one hour each week to coordinate a variety of school programs aimed at helping Peter adjust and improve academic skills and to track his progress in school. Again, all services used were child-centered and designed to meet Peter's needs in the various school environments.

The integration specialist assigned to Peter's planning team provided a variety of services including teacher training in behavior management, behavioral analysis of Peter's behaviors in school, technical assistance to the planning team in designing, implementing and monitoring treatment services within the school; and direct counseling to Peter. The direct counseling Peter received revolved around structured programs to help him gain control of his impulses and manage his own behavior. These programs were supplemented by the school counselor and the classroom teacher through training in social skills and cooperative play behaviors carried out with the entire class. In-school counseling service was provided an average of four times a week.

In addition to individual and group counseling, Peter engaged in a behavior token program with the whole class focusing on improving time on task and work achievement. More structured restitution and time-out procedures were implemented for aggressive behaviors. Over time it was felt that Peter would benefit from more structured positive interactions with other children and the teacher. In order to achieve this, the classroom teacher engaged in scheduled reinforcement of Peter. He was instructed to use a soft voice, work on his assigned task cooperatively, and wait his turn. This reinforcement occurred every five minutes and was decreased by the end of the year to once every half hour. (pp. 54–55)

Source: Excerpted from Burchard, J. D., Clarke, R. T.: The role of individualized care in a service delivery system for children and adolescents with severely maladjusted behavior. *Journal of Mental Health Administration* 1990; 17(1):48–60. Reprinted with permission.

modeling activities are followed by role-playing in which students rehearse and practice the behaviors that have been modeled. Students are then given performance feedback directly related to the success with which they have adequately performed the targeted social behavior. After children have demonstrated a solid level of performance in the small-group setting, they are given many opportunities to try their newly learned skills in regular classrooms, during recess periods, and at home.

Research regarding the effectiveness of programs like Structured Learning is beginning to emerge. These interventions have been effective in teaching specific social skills to students with behavior disorders in well-controlled environments, but the transfer of these skills over time to the home, neighborhood, and employment settings is difficult to achieve (Sasso, Melloy, & Kavale, 1990; Schloss, Schloss, Wood, & Kiehl, 1986; Simpson, 1987).

Children with Moderate to Severe Behavior Disorders. Children who exhibit moderate to severe behavior disorders are primarily served in special classes, which may be housed in a number of types of facilities. In some school systems, special classes are found within the elementary schools. In fact, there may be a small cluster of two to three classes in selected buildings. Other special classes may be found within hospital units, special schools, residential programs, and specialized treatment facilities.

Special classes for children with moderate to severe disorders are characterized by a number of significant features (Morgan & Jenson, 1988). The first is a high degree of structure; that is, rules are clear and consistently enforced. The second feature is teacher monitoring of student performance; students are frequently provided with feedback and reinforcement based on their academic and social behaviors. Furthermore, expectations for student behavior are well known by all class participants.

REFLECT ON THIS

5–5   Case Study: Peter

Summary

To date, Peter and his family have received a host of intensive home and school-based treatment services. They have participated in 2½ years of service planning and have been, at one point or another, involved in the mental health, social service, educational and recreational systems of care. The approach of all these services emphasized individual care and incorporated program tracking of services and adjustment. While Peter and his family continue to access services, their needs are less intense than they were two years ago. His parents are better able to manage his behavior and spend more time interacting with him in positive activities. In addition, both parents are full participants on the school planning team. At present, Peter requires little one-to-one attention, although an intervention is still being provided to foster additional social skills. A major component of Peter's plan at this point in time involves tracking progress and assessing long-term changes. Peter's parents understand that additional services will be provided if they are necessary. (p. 55)

Source: Excerpted from Burchard, J. D., Clarke, R. T.: The role of individualized care in a service delivery system for children and adolescents with severely maladjusted behavior. *Journal of Mental Health Administration* 1990; 17(1):48–60. Reprinted with permission.

In addition to behaviorally oriented interventions, students may also receive individual counseling or group and family therapy. Many children with behavior disorders may be on some form of medication, as well. In these cases, teachers are encouraged to carefully monitor the effectiveness (or ineffectiveness) of the medications that have been prescribed. Signs of negative side effects are immediately reported to parents or guardians.

One of the most comprehensive and successful programs developed for disturbed elementary children was Project Re-Ed (Hobbs, 1965; Weinstein, 1969), which had an ecological focus. Interventions were directed not only at the children but also at their families, schools, and communities. The program was a residential one: Children attended school at

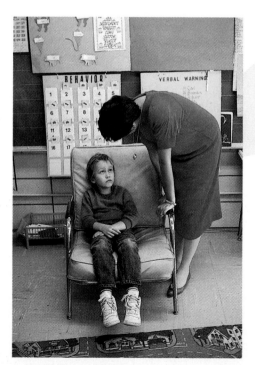

Children with moderate to severe behavior disorders are often served in special, self-contained classrooms. (Bob Daemmrich/Stock, Boston)

a residential site and went home on weekends. Through teacher-counselors, enrolled children received relevant educational and therapeutic support in special class environments. At the same time, the parents of these children and regular school personnel were kept informed of the children's progress by liaison teachers. These liaison teachers were also responsible, in conjunction with other personnel, for helping families and school personnel ready themselves for the reentry of the children into regular classrooms. A variety of treatment approaches were used in helping these children and their families develop the behaviors necessary for successful individual and family living; however, the distinguishing characteristic of this program was its ecological focus. Not only were the children treated, but the major social and education environments of the children were also treated and prepared for their return.

Programs for children who are seriously disturbed and may be described as schizophrenic or exhibiting pervasive developmental disorders are similar in nature to those previously discussed. However, they may involve a variety of other specialized medical, speech or language, and social services personnel. For young children who are autistic, the continued thrust of their training is language development (see Chapter Nine). For children with pervasive developmental delays, the thrust may be training in the self-help skills of toileting, feeding, dressing, bathing, and grooming.

Interventions for Adolescents

Adolescents with behavior disorders represent a significant challenge for educators, mental health specialists, and their families. As a group, they exhibit a variety of problems. For example, the dropout rate for youth with behavior disorders is over 40 percent (U.S. Department of Education, 1991). Of this number, about one-third are neither working nor involved in any postsecondary training (Neel, Meadows, Levine, & Edgar, 1988). Some researchers have suggested that as many as 40 percent of these youth will likely have criminal records within several years of their leaving school (Jay & Padilla, 1987).

Youth who are chronically delinquent and have been found guilty of a number of felony offenses (e.g., physical assault, armed robbery, etc.) present some challenging problems for treatment personnel. Researchers have indicated that as many as 28 percent of the incarcerated youth in the United States are disabled. However, less than 25 percent actually receive the specialized services guaranteed them by law (Rutherford, Nelson, & Wolford, 1985).

Service delivery systems for adolescents with behavior disorders closely parallel those for elementary-age students. The major differences lie in the types of intervention strategies that are applied, the roles educational specialists fulfill, and the types of problems that become the focus of interventions. Additionally, programs for youth with behavior disorders vary according to the severity and nature of the individuals' social and academic problems. We will highlight two programs that have been developed for youth with behavior disorders.

One program that has been developed for youth who are severely aggressive and otherwise very difficult to manage is the aggression replacement training (ART) program (Goldstein & Glick, 1987). This program emphasizes (1) social skills training, (2) anger control instruction, and (3) moral education. Youth involved in this multielement program learn how to respond to anger appropriately, avoid fights, deal with group pressure, and express affection, as well as other pertinent social skills. Additionally, they learn to engage in *self-talk,* a self-instructional strategy that helps them control their verbally or physically aggressive behaviors. What follows is one brief example of self-talk in which the individual talks himself through a situation that, in the past, may have caused him to behave very aggressively: "My muscles are starting to feel tight. Time to relax and slow things down.

REFLECT ON THIS

| 5–6 | Students As Solutions |

Jane's Story

Jane, a 12-year-old student, started doing strange things at school. The principal, teacher, and resource person agreed to call in the "behavior specialists" to design a "compliance training" program.

For a short while Jane stopped being a nuisance and life went on until she suddenly attacked a schoolmate in the schoolyard, knocked the girl to the ground touching her breasts and genital area. She had to be physically pulled away. The "attack" frightened the other child involved but did not seriously injure her.

The principal immediately phoned both sets of parents and to his surprise, the mother of the student who was "attacked" did not become hysterical; she realized her daughter was not hurt. Jane's entire family was called in for a serious talk with the principal.

Two months later these responses were gathered from her classroom peers:

Our S.W.A.T. (Students Who Are Together) team has a weekly meeting with Mrs. Gill (the resource teacher). Jane comes to every meeting. At the first meeting we told Jane we wanted to help and be her friends. We told her that no matter what she did, we'd be there for her.

We apologized for not being around enough before. Sarah invited her to a party and Sue went to visit her at home. Danny, Rose, and Linda call her a lot. Jane's happy now because she's got the S.W.A.T. team and because she has friends. We're making new friends, too. Jane's whole attitude has changed and she hasn't hit or attacked anyone since we talked to her. (p. 191)

Jane has changed since her first meeting with the S.W.A.T. team. These past couple of weeks she's really opened up. She now feels that she belongs, and she knows we are her friends. She hasn't been acting up or annoying us like she used to. Instead she has been cheery and always talks to us.

She was just recently invited to her first party with boys. She really enjoyed it. I think that Jane has really changed. She used to be so quiet and always kept to herself. Now she is more outgoing and talkative. Like any teenager, Jane needs friends and a social life. (p. 192)

Melanie McDermott

Before S.W.A.T. I found Jane moody, babyish, she swore, she spat, and once in awhile she would pee in her pants. When S.W.A.T. started helping, Jane was overjoyed. Jane would always say that she didn't care about anyone or school. About four days after saying how she didn't care about school she got

suspended because she touched a kid in a private spot.

Because of S.W.A.T. she is really changing now. I called her at home and she talked to me for 10 minutes on the phone. Jane is trying to act like us. She's becoming like us! (p. 192)

Krystyne Banakiewiczm

A Poem About Jane
Jane came three years ago
No one did she really know
We tried to teach her wrong from right
Tried to make her days sunny and bright
Still she walked around so sad
And we knew that we had
To make her feel like one of us
And over her we'd all fuss
Now Jane has many good friends
And I hope "our" friendship never ends.

Tammi Washnuk

Source: From "Supports for Addressing Severe Maladaptive Behavior" by M. Forest and J. Pearpoint, 1990, *Support Networks for Inclusive Schooling: Interdependent Integrated Education*, W. Stainback and S. Stainback (Eds.), Baltimore: Paul H. Brookes Publishing Company. Copyright 1990 by Paul H. Brookes Publishing Company. Reprinted with permission. Jack Pearpoint and Marsha Forest are the Directors and Founders of the Centre for Integrated Education and Community and Inclusion Press. For information, write 24 Thome Crescent, Toronto, Ontario, Canada M6H 255, 416-658-5363.

Getting upset won't help. It's just not worth it to get so angry. I'll let him make a fool of himself. I have a right to be annoyed, but let's keep the lid on" (Goldstein & Glick, 1987, p. 73).

The third component of the ART program, moral development, gives youth experiences that are directed at improving their reasoning and problem-solving skills as well as other related behaviors. Groups are formed and directed by trained leaders who carefully expose youth to moral dilemmas and conflicts. Through these dilemma discussions and related activities, youth develop new ways of thinking and reasoning about moral conflicts and learn how it feels to be someone who has been injured, abused, stolen from, or otherwise hurt. Moreover, youth learn how to behave in new, socially appropriate ways when confronted with moral dilemmas.

Another program that is beginning to attract the attention of professionals is individualized care (IC) (Burchard & Clark, 1990). The case study of Peter (see Reflect on This 5–3 through 5–7) is an excellent example of individualized care. IC, as a formalized concept, began with the Alaska Youth Initiative (VanDenBerg, 1989). It is based on several basic principles. The first of these principles, unconditional care, is best characterized by a statement made by Dowrick:

> Yes, we will take care of these children [youth], no matter what they do. If they try to kill themselves, try to kill each other, if they are sexually promiscuous, destroy things, set fires to buildings, assault one another, or generally drive people up the wall, we will take care of them nonetheless. One person will take that responsibility. . . . We won't pass the child [youth] around anymore. We will take care of this child [youth]. (1988, p. 60)

The second principle of IC is least restrictive care. Youth are served within their families and neighborhood schools. They are not moved to other more restrictive environments unless they pose a significant threat to themselves or others. Moreover, they are not placed in other more restrictive environments unless all other less restrictive services have proven to be ineffective.

The third principle is child and family-centered care. Services are precisely designed to meet the needs of the youth and his or her family. For example, a person who already has a special relationship with the youth may be one of the primary caregivers. This may be a neighbor, a fisherman (in an Alaskan village), a carpenter, an artist, or a friend of the family—anyone who is capable of helping the youth, given his or her unique needs at the time.

The fourth and fifth principles of IC are flexible care and flexible funding. Flexible care is essentially the provision of services when and where they are needed with sufficient intensity to address the severity of the youth's or family's needs. Flexible funding is simply the capacity to use funds in a timely manner to address specific needs. For example, a family in crisis might benefit significantly from the skills of a family intervention specialist who actually lives with them during this time.

The last principle upon which IC is based is interagency care. An intervention plan is created, maintained, and altered from time to time by an interdisciplinary team. This team consists of the youth, his or her parents or guardian, and the service providers from mental health, social service, health, vocational, and educational agencies. A major component of interagency care is the proactive client tracking system (PCTS), which provides all team members with weekly assessment of the youth's progress. It also promotes involvement of parties concerned as well as prevention of potential crises.

Overview of Effective Programs

In summary, highly effective programs for children and adolescents with behavior disorders are characterized by a number of features:

1. Interventions that are supported by observational data
2. Assessment and monitoring that are continuous
3. Frequent opportunities for students to practice and use their newly learned skills
4. Treatments and strategies that are carefully targeted at specific problems identified by a multidisciplinary team and parents

FOCUS 10

Identify seven characteristics of highly effective programs for children and adolescents with behavior disorders.

5. Multiple coordinated treatments that are directed at children and youth as well as their families
6. Provisions for assuring that the skills and behaviors learned in treatment settings will be transferred to school, family, and neighborhood environments
7. The commitment to sustained intervention for children and youth who require long-term support and care (Peacock Hill Working Group, 1990)

Debate / Forum ·········· Drugs: Is There Adequate Support for Their Continued Use with Great Numbers of Children? ··········

There is considerable disagreement regarding the practice of prescribing stimulant drugs for children who are disturbed and children who have been identified as inattentive, hyperactive, impulsive, or difficult to manage. Consider for a moment the following:

1. Stimulant drugs do improve school children's short-term academic performance in some language areas and arithmetic skills.
2. IQ scores, grades, and basic learning abilities are not improved with stimulant medication.
3. Researchers report that stimulant medication enhances children's classroom performance and makes them less impulsive, easier to control, and more attentive.
4. Parent-child and teacher-child interactions appear to improve after the child has received stimulant medication.
5. Reduced aggression, more goal-directed activity, enhanced short-term memory, reduced impulsiveness, and improved performance on rote learning and fine motor tasks seem to be the major positive outcomes of stimulant medication for children.
6. Long-term academic achievement does not appear to be significantly affected by stimulant medication.
7. Drug therapy may be a poor substitute for effective teaching and parenting or nothing more than a form of control that makes children more manageable for adults.
8. Research regarding the effectiveness of stimulant medication compared to behaviorally oriented treatment strategies has produced mixed results.
9. Behavioral procedures seem to produce more positive results. Targeted behaviors are increased or reduced. Changes in the child's environment are brought about through the use of behavioral procedures. The child may attribute the changes in behavior to his or her actions rather than to medication.
10. Stimulant medication may temporarily suppress normal growth and weight gains in children, but rapid recuperation occurs during drug "holidays."

11. Several studies suggest that small but significant decreases in height and weight occur with certain individuals with chronic treatment.
12. State-dependent learning may be one of the outcomes of consistent use of medication in that the child is only able to learn and demonstrate learning when he or she is medicated.
13. Medication appears to decrease activity in structured classroom settings and significantly increases activity during physical recreation periods.
14. There is no reliable method for predicting who will respond or benefit from medication.
15. Follow-up studies show that youngsters who have used medication extensively over a long period of time to control their behavior may develop problems associated with substance abuse.

Point The administration of stimulant drugs improves children's functioning in a variety of school-related behaviors. Drugs enhance general classroom performance as observed by teachers, improve children's on-task behaviors, reduce aggression, increase goal-directed activity, and reduce behaviors associated with impulsiveness. They should be prescribed for children who need help in these areas.

Counterpoint The administration of stimulant drugs does not improve children's basic learning abilities or academic achievement over time. It appears that other interventions are equally effective in changing children's behaviors, and these other procedures do not appear to produce any negative side effects. Furthermore, researchers are uncertain as to the long-term effects of continual use of stimulant drugs by children. The regular use of stimulant drugs to change children's behaviors should be stopped.

REVIEW

FOCUS 1   Identify five factors that influence the ways in which we view others' behaviors.

- Our personal beliefs, standards, and values
- Our tolerance for certain behaviors, which varies with our standards, values, and levels of emotional fitness at the time the behaviors are exhibited
- Perceptions of normality, which are frequently in the "eye of the beholder" rather than some objective standard of normality as established by consensus or research
- The context in which a behavior takes place
- The frequency with which the behavior occurs or its intensity

FOCUS 2   Identify five variables that influence the types of behaviors that are exhibited or suppressed by individuals with behavior disorders.

- The parents' and/or teachers' management styles
- The school or home environment
- The social and the cultural values of the family
- The social and economic climate of the community
- The responses of peers and siblings
- The academic, intellectual, and social-emotional characteristics of the individuals with behavior disorders

FOCUS 3   What differentiates externalizing disorders from internalizing disorders?

- Externalizing disorders involve behaviors that are directed at others (e.g., fighting, assaulting, stealing, vandalizing, etc.).
- Internalizing disorders involve behaviors that are directed inwardly or at oneself more than at others (e.g., fears, phobias, depressions, etc.).

FOCUS 4   Identify six essential features of definitions describing serious emotional disturbances or behavior disorders.

- The behaviors in question must be exhibited to a marked extent.
- Learning problems that are not attributable to intellectual, sensory, or health deficits are common.
- Satisfactory relationships with parents, teachers, siblings, and others are few.
- Behaviors exhibited occur in many settings and under normal circumstances are inappropriate.
- A pervasive mood of unhappiness or depression is frequently displayed by children with behavior disorders.
- Physical symptoms or fears associated with the demands of school are common in some children.

FOCUS 5   Identify three reasons why classification systems are important to professionals who diagnose, treat, and educate individuals with behavior disorders.

- They provide a common language for communicating about various types and subtypes of behavior disorders.
- They provide a means of describing and identifying various behavior disorders.

- They sometimes provide a basis for treating a disorder and making predictions about treatment outcomes.

FOCUS 6   Identify five general characteristics (intellectual, adaptive, and achievement) of children with behavior disorders.

- Children who are disturbed tend to have average to lower-than-average IQs compared to their normal peers.
- Children with severe behavior disorders tend to have IQs that fall within the retarded range of functioning.
- Children who are disturbed have great difficulty relating socially and responsibly to peers, parents, teachers, and other authority figures.
- Students who are disturbed perform less well than their ability would predict, as measured by intellectual instruments.
- Students who are seriously disturbed, particularly those with IQs in the retarded range, are substantially substandard in their academic achievement.

FOCUS 7   What can we accurately say about the causes of behavior disorders?

- Behavior disorders are caused by sets of continuously interacting biological, genetic, cognitive, social, emotional, and cultural variables.

FOCUS 8   Identify four factors that need to be carefully assessed in determining whether a child has a behavior disorder.

- The discrepancy between the child's behavior and expected performance, given his or her age, culture, temperament, and intellectual endowment
- The frequency, intensity, and location of the various problematic behaviors
- The relationship of the behaviors to various events and people
- The influence of family and cultural factors

FOCUS 9   Identify six major treatment approaches generally used in treating children and adolescents with behavior disorders.

- Major approaches to treating behavior disorders include insight-oriented therapy, play therapy, group psychotherapy, behavior therapy, marital and family therapy, and drug therapy.
- The therapies are used in conjunction with various types of service delivery systems, including home-based and center-based programs, school-based programs (consulting teacher, resource rooms, self-contained programs, specialized schools), residential programs, hospitals (outpatient and inpatient programs), and one-to-one or family therapy provided by private practitioners.

FOCUS 10   Identify seven characteristics of highly effective programs for children and adolescents with behavior disorders.

- Interventions are based on data that affirm their effectiveness.

- Assessment and monitoring procedures are used continuously to document students' progress or lack thereof.
- Many opportunities are provided for students to practice the skills and behaviors learned.
- Treatments and interventions are carefully selected and matched to problems identified by parents and members of the interdisciplinary team.
- A variety of carefully coordinated treatments are applied si-multaneously to children or youths and their families.
- Precise steps are taken to ensure that the skills and behaviors learned are transferred to home, school, and community settings.
- Sustained and coordinated interventions are provided over time for individuals who may require long-term support and treatment.

Chapter Six
Learning Disabilities

TO BEGIN WITH . . .

◆ Children with learning disabilities comprised 49 percent of the children ages 6 to 21 during the 1988–89 schoolyear. In number, nearly 2 million students have been identified as having learning disabilities (National Association of State Directors of Special Education, 1991).

◆ A college student, in an interview with the author, describing her younger sister who has a learning disability: "It just gets me! The same child who forgets her own telephone number remembers word for word almost any commercial you see on TV. You want the Pepsi jingle? Just ask Sara."

◆ It has been estimated that, in the early 1990s, over 1 million children will receive stimulant medication (Associated Press News Service, 1989).

◆ "More than 90 percent of the prescriptions for psychotropic drugs given children are written by pediatricians, and they are not that knowledge-able about the range of psychotropic drugs for kids" (Youngstrom, 1991).

DEBORAH

DEBORAH. I am LD—I learn differently. Rather than read a textbook like you're doing, I follow along as I listen to a recording of the text. When a recording of the text is unavailable, I rely on a reader. Rather than take notes, I photocopy another student's notes or tape the lecture or sometimes both. Rather than write the complete answer to an essay question, I write a rough outline, and from that I present my answer to the instructor (or record my answer on a cassette tape) so the instructor can assess my knowledge of the subject.

Educators say that background knowledge is extremely important to facilitate learning. To help develop my background knowledge (as well as for my enjoyment), I have a home library somewhat different from that of many people. It consists of illustrated books, books on many subjects that are primarily photographs, children's books (these really helped to begin building background knowledge), and educational books and tapes that go with them. I also have novels and short stories on tapes read by professional artists (these can be purchased at many bookstores). Another important source of both information and enjoyment are videotapes of movies made from books, documentaries, lectures, and classic and more recent movies. I have a specially designed radio that broadcasts the local newspaper, current magazine articles, books or chapters from books, and old-time radio shows. In addition to these, I receive a weekly world newspaper with larger print, less cluttered format, and less difficult reading level than papers available at the newsstand. The last item that I will mention here (I could go on much longer) is a consumer news digest that is extremely important. It covers a wide variety of topics, but the articles are short (*really* short) and therefore easy for me to read. This is a great source of consumer awareness and protection. I use it constantly for background information, and it helps a great deal in social conversation as well.

Learning differently is not without difficulty but I choose to focus on my strengths. It is my strengths that I need to spend time developing. It is by developing and using my strengths that I can compensate for my deficits. It is through utilizing my strengths that I'm successful. By focusing on my strengths and allowing myself to be different, to be creative, to accept that there are many alternatives by which I can get from A to B allows me to accept who I am—helps me to be my own best friend. I am a human being—I am *not* a learning disability, I am *not* an Attention Deficit Disorder, I am *not* a *label!* I am a person who learns differently, a person who approaches learning and living differently. If you let me I will share with you from my world, sensitivity, adventure, and discovery. You may even find new personal options, more creative approaches, and a new way of looking at people and life.

Deborah, A graduate student

Introduction

Since she wrote the material in Window 6–1, Deborah has finished her master's degree in special education and has entered the world of work. She is now a successful business-woman, working in private practice with individuals who have learning disabilities. Compared with other disabling conditions, **learning disabilities** are a recently identified and defined area of exceptionality. They have often been viewed as mild because most individuals with learning disabilities have normal or near normal intelligence but experience problems in academic areas such as reading and mathematics. However, recent thinking suggests that the term *learning disabilities* is a generic label representing a very heterogeneous group of disabilities, ranging from mild to severe. In many cases, people with learning disabilities have been described as having "poor **neurological** wiring" and other such maladies that are somewhat mystical in terms of explaining their problems. They have normal intelligence but experience academic difficulties and perhaps social ones, as well. They represent a substantial challenge to both school and family settings. They present a highly variable and complex set of characteristics and needs.

DEFINITIONS AND CLASSIFICATIONS

Learning disabilities have generated more controversy, confusion, and polarization among contemporary professionals than any other exceptionality. Educational services for students with learning disabilities were virtually nonexistent prior to the 1960s. In the past, many children now identified as having specific learning disabilities would have been labeled **remedial readers,** remedial learners, emotionally handicapped, or even mentally retarded—if they received any special or additional instructional support at all. Today, learning disabilities command the largest single program for exceptional children in the United States. Although relatively new, its growth rate has been unparalleled by any other area in special education (U.S. Department of Education, 1991).

Definitions

Definitions of learning disabilities reflect great variation. This may be because of the field's unique evolution, highly accelerated growth pattern, and strong interdisciplinary nature. Several disciplines (e.g., medicine, psychology, speech-language, and education) have contributed to the confusion associated with inconsistent terminology. For example, education coined the phrase *specific learning disabilities;* psychology uses such terms as **perceptual disorders** and **hyperkinetic behavior;** speech and language employ the terms **aphasia** and **dyslexia;** and medicine uses the labels *brain damage, minimal brain dysfunction, brain injury,* and *impairment. Brain injury, minimal brain dysfunction,* and *learning disabilities* are among the most commonly used terms, although all appear in various segments of the literature.

A child with a brain injury is described as having an organic impairment resulting in perceptual problems, thinking disorders, and emotional instability. A child with minimal brain dysfunction manifests similar problems, but there is often evidence of language, memory, motor, and impulse-control difficulties. Individuals with minimal brain dysfunction are often characterized as average or above average in intelligence, distinguishing the disorder from mental retardation.

Early Definition History.   Kirk (1963) introduced the phrase *specific learning disabilities,* and his original concept remains largely intact today. The concept is presently defined by delays, deviations, and performance discrepancies in basic academic subjects (e.g., arithmetic, reading, spelling, and writing), as well as speech and language problems. Additionally, these disabilities cannot be attributed to mental retardation, sensory deficits, or emotional disturbance. It has become common practice in education to describe individuals with learning disabilities on the basis of *what they are not.* For example, although they have a number of problems, they are not mentally retarded, emotionally disturbed, or deaf. *Learning disabilities* is a general educational term—an umbrella label—that includes a variety of different conditions and behavioral and performance deficits (Gelfand, Jenson, & Drew, 1988).

IDEA Definition.   One widely used definition of learning disabilities was presented by the National Advisory Committee on Handicapped Children (1968) of the U.S. Office of Education. This definition was similar to Kirk's early concept and initially incorporated into Public Law (PL) 91-320, the Learning Disabilities Act of 1969. This definition was also used in the Individuals with Disabilities Education Act (IDEA) of 1990 (PL 101-476), as follows:

> "Specific learning disability" means a disorder in one or more of the basic psychological processes involved in understanding or in using language, spoken or written, which may manifest itself in an imperfect ability to listen, think, speak, read, write, spell, or to do mathematical calculations. The term includes such conditions as

FOCUS 1

Identify four reasons why definitions of learning disabilities have varied.

perceptual handicaps, brain injury, minimal brain dysfunction, dyslexia, and developmental aphasia. The term does not include children who have learning problems which are primarily the result of visual, hearing, or motor handicaps, of mental retardation, of emotional disturbance, or of environmental, cultural, or economic disadvantage. (Section 5[b][4])

Joint Committee Definition. Many think the IDEA definition was exclusionary (a definition of conditions that are *not* learning disabilities rather than a substantive explanation of what learning disabilities *are*) and ambiguous because of a lack of measurement specification. An earlier definition presented by the National Joint Committee for Learning Disabilities (1988) had certain important elements that are not stated in IDEA. This definition states:

> *Learning disabilities* is a general term that refers to a heterogeneous group of disorders manifested by significant difficulties in the acquisition and use of listening, speaking, writing, reasoning, or mathematical abilities. These disorders are intrinsic to the individual, presumed to be due to central nervous system dysfunction, and may occur across the life span. Problems in self-regulatory behaviors, social perception, and social interaction may exist with learning disabilities but do not by themselves constitute a learning disability. Although learning disabilities may occur concomitantly with other handicapping conditions (for example, sensory impairment, mental retardation, serious emotional disturbance) or with extrinsic influences (such as cultural differences, insufficient or inappropriate instruction), they are not the result of those conditions or influences. (1988, p. 1)

This definition is important to the present discussion for several reasons. First, it describes *learning disabilities* as a generic term that refers to a heterogeneous group of disorders. Second, a person with learning disabilities must manifest *significant* difficulties. The use of the word *significant* is an obvious attempt to remove the connotation of a mild problem. Finally, this definition highlights learning disabilities as lifelong problems and places them in a context of other disabilities as well as cultural differences. These matters are important refinements of earlier definitional efforts (Hammill, 1990).

Other Issues in Definition. The wide variety of terminology and definitions in learning disabilities has emerged partly because of the different theoretical views of the problem. For example, **perceptual-motor** theories emphasize an interaction between various channels of perception and motor activity. Perceptual-motor theories of learning disabilities focus on normal sequential development of motor patterns and compare it with the motor development of children with learning disabilities. Children with learning disabilities are seen as having perceptual-motor abilities that are unreliable and unstable, which presents problems when they encounter activities involving time and spatial orientation. In contrast, *language disability theories* concentrate on the child's reception or production of language. Because language is so important in learning, these theories emphasize the relationship between learning disabilities and language deficiencies.

On the basis of only these two theories, it is clear we are examining very different viewpoints. Learning disabilities is a field with many theoretical perspectives regarding the nature of problems as well as causation and treatment.

Recent literature has taken a different view of learning disabilities. Instead of focusing on differing terminology, some researchers have suggested that many different, specific disorders have been grouped under one term. "*Learning disabilities* is a general educational term. . . . The term can be used only as a generalized referent in that it encompasses a variety

People with learning disabilities have widely divergent behaviors and skills. (Mary Kate Denny/PhotoEdit)

of specific types of problems" (Gelfand, et al., 1988, p. 224). Benton and Pearl (1978) also supported this notion, suggesting that even specific *types* of learning disabilities, specifically dyslexia, represent a collection of different disorders.

In one sense, this thinking is not surprising. It has long been acknowledged that people with learning disabilities are a very heterogeneous group. However, professionals have continued to characterize people with learning disabilities as though they were uniform. Such characterizations typically reflect the theoretical or disciplinary perspective of the professional rather than an objective behavioral description of the individual being evaluated. Thus, there has been a tendency to characterize the *disorder* rather than the individual with problems. Such characterizations will inevitably be in error in a population representing a wide variety of disorders.

The problems with defining learning disabilities are evident in research on this topic. The wide range of characteristics associated with children who have learning disabilities and myriad methodological problems (e.g., poor **research design** and measurement error) have caused difficulties in conducting research on learning disabilities (Swanson, 1988). Generalizing research results is questionable, and replication of studies is very difficult. Consequently, efforts to standardize and clarify definitions are important, both for research and intervention purposes.

In past years, educational literature virtually ignored the notion of severity in definitions and concepts of learning disabilities. This has recently changed (Weller, Strawser, & Buchanan, 1985; Wilson, 1985). Additionally, the issue of where measured intelligence fits in defining learning disabilities has emerged as a serious controversy (Wong, 1989). Some researchers have argued that intelligence quotient (IQ) is irrelevant to the definition of learning disabilities whereas others see it as important (e.g., Siegel, 1989; Torgesen, 1989). Such difference of opinion is not unusual in the field of learning disabilities. Learning disabilities have probably been defined in more different ways than any other type of disability. In fact, Hammill (1990) discussed 11 different definitions still being used for this family of disorders.

In our examination of learning disabilities, we describe behavioral characteristics from different theoretical viewpoints. This is a field with an insufficient research base to allow us to select *one* perspective to explain learning disabilities. It is important to provide examples of how a person might be classified as having a learning disability using different perspectives. Hammill (1990) suggested that definitional consensus in the field of learning disabilities is near, despite the historical controversies. The definitional characteristics that have received the most agreement include (1) academic problems with considerable attention to **intraindividual** underachievement, (2) central nervous system dysfunction, (3) potential for learning disabilities at all ages, (4) language problems with listening and speaking, and (5) potential for multiple handicaps (other disorders may coexist with learning disabilities). Additionally, several researchers have defined learning disabilities to include (1) some disruption of psychological processes and/or (2) conceptual problems (e.g., with thinking and reasoning). However, there is considerably less consensus on these latter two characteristics (Hammill, 1990).

Learning Disabilities and ADD

One condition often associated with learning disabilities that is not defined in IDEA is **attention–deficit disorder (ADD).** Nonetheless, the essential features of ADD have long been recognized in many children with learning disabilities. Attention–deficit disorders, as currently conceived, actually include two subcategories, **attention–deficit hyperactivity disorder (ADHD)** and **undifferentiated attention–deficit disorder (UADD)** (APA, 1987). The primary characteristic of both conditions is a child's inability to concentrate for a long period of time. ADD is defined as a disorder in children who have difficulties maintaining an attention span because of their limited ability to concentrate and who exhibit impulsive actions (Lahey, Schaughency, Hynd, Carlson, & Nieves, 1987). The two subcategories—ADHD and UADD—as defined in the *Diagnostic and Statistical Manual of Mental Disorders* (3rd ed., rev.) (DSM-III-R), were developed to distinguish between children who exhibited hyperactive behavior and those who did not (APA, 1987).

Individuals with either of the ADD diagnoses will have attention-span problems, being generally unable to focus on a specific task for a sustained period. They will also evidence impulsiveness and often commit actions with no apparent forethought of what is involved or what the consequences might be. For children who are diagnosed as ADHD, the characteristic of excessive motor activity (especially in inappropriate situations) will be evident. These youngsters are thus seen as being hyperactive, a characteristic long identified with some children who have learning disabilities. Those children who are not hyperactive but exhibit attention or concentration difficulties should be diagnosed as UADD.

While ADD has often been associated with learning disabilities, there is not a complete correspondence in characteristics between the two. As we continue to describe the attributes of learning disabilities in this chapter, it will be evident that concerns with attention problems, impulsiveness, and hyperactivity have emerged periodically in depictions of learning disabilities. However, other characteristics are also evident in many children with learning disabilities. Specific academic deficits are probably the most frequently mentioned difficulty in children with learning disabilities. Additionally, perception difficulties and discrimination problems, among others, are often associated with learning disabilities. The distinctions between learning disabilities and ADD categories are not at all clear, in part because the definitions have historically overlapped and been applied to groups of people that are very heterogeneous.

There is great disagreement about the causes of ADD. Both biological and environmental influences have been implicated. Speculation has included genetic inheritance, neurological injury during birth complications, vitamin deficiencies, and food additives, to name only a few. Most authorities agree that there are likely multiple causes for what is most certainly a family of different specific disorders (Gelfand et al., 1988). Prevalence estimates for ADD suggest that about 3 percent of all children may have the disorder (APA, 1987; Parker, 1990). Research indicates that males with ADD outnumber females in ratios varying from 2:1 to 10:1 (McGee, Williams, & Silva, 1987; Parker, 1990).

6–1   How to Legislatively Define ADD?

Currently, children with ADD cannot receive special services funded by IDEA unless they have another condition that is defined in the law. There are several views regarding how ADD should be included in legislation so that children with this disorder may receive appropriate services. Arguments pro and con cover several topics, including *whether* and *how* this should be handled.

There is some question regarding whether the law should be amended regarding ADD at all. Central to this issue is the question of whether children with ADD need special services that can only be met by making them eligible through legislation. The arguments for and against leaving the law as it is include the following:

OPTION 1. Do not amend the law. Leave matters as they are.

Pro   A person is not disabled if his or her condition has no significant effect on his or her ability to learn in a regular setting. To determine if a condition has a significant effect on a child's ability to learn, the usual standard is a measured discrepancy between ability and achievement. Research has determined that 10 percent of children with ADD have a significant enough discrepancy between ability and achievement to be considered as having learn-

ing disabilities. Therefore, the vast majority of these children have a condition that has no significant effect on their ability to learn and thus cannot be considered disabled. Those with serious aptitude/achievement problems can already qualify under learning disabilities. ADD is not an inherent condition that so adversely affects children's ability to learn that they need special education and related services.

Con   Children with ADD do need access to the special services provided for under the law because they have an inherent condition that interferes with their ability to learn. Children with ADD have academic problems because it takes them longer to learn in most instances. They do not stick with tasks long enough to finish them, have difficulty organizing and completing work correctly, and have other problems that require intervention involving an individualized education program.

OPTION 2. Interpret the term *minimal brain dysfunction* under the definition of *specific learning disability* to include ADD.

Pro   To interpret *minimal brain dysfunction* as including ADD would be the least complicated legislative remedy to specifically recognize that Congress intends children with ADD to be served. This would not change the statute itself, thus avoiding definitional issues that would be raised if the law were amended. If adopted, the language could be included in the *Code of*

Federal Regulations as a "comment" in the appropriate place.

Con   Arguments against this option state that interpreting minimal brain dysfunction as including ADD would be inaccurate. ADD is recognized as a separate entity. Although ADD was once understood as falling under the rubric of minimal brain dysfunction, that is not consistent with current understanding.

OPTION 3. Include ADD in the statutory definition of *other health impairments*.

Pro   Including ADD in the definition of other health impairments would leave no question that Congress intends that children with ADD be eligible for special services. If Congress wants such children served, then the syndrome should be specifically listed in the law.

Con   It is not wise to add ADD to the definition of other health impairments under the law because there is still confusion and controversy over the exact definition and nature of the syndrome. It is inappropriate to include ADD in the definition of other health impairments since that category has traditionally been reserved for conditions that can be identified objectively, such as heart conditions and diabetes.

Source: Aleman, 1990.

Children with ADD do not qualify for special education or related services under IDEA unless they also have another disability condition that is defined in the law (Aleman, 1990). In IDEA, ADD was viewed as a *characteristic* of a specific learning disability but not as a disability by itself. However, the use of ADD terminology has begun to grow during the 1980s. This expanded use, plus the DSM-III-R (APA, 1987) labels noted above, have prompted consideration of including ADD in federal legislation. Exactly how and where ADD might be defined in IDEA remains under debate. Reflect on This 6–1 summarizes some of the positions for and against such legislative change.

FOCUS 2

Identify two ways in which people with learning disabilities can be classified.

Classification

Individuals who are labeled *learning disabled* represent a complex constellation of behaviors and conditions. However, people with learning disabilities have seldom been formally classified into differing severity categories. As noted earlier, learning disabilities have generally been seen as mild disorders, despite the fact that clinicians have observed a range of symptoms, from mild to severe, for years. Instead of a severity scheme, individuals with learning disabilities have been described relative to the classification parameters discussed earlier.

Federal rules and regulations related to IDEA address the issue of severity to some extent, however. According to these rules and regulations, any criterion for classifying a child as having learning disabilities must be based on an already existing *severe* discrepancy between capacity and achievement. The determination for placement was related to:

1. Whether a child achieves commensurate with his or her age and ability when provided with appropriate educational experiences
2. Whether the child has a *severe* discrepancy between achievement and intellectual ability in one or more of seven areas relating to communication skills and mathematical abilities

The child's learning disability must be determined on an individual basis, and the severe discrepancy between achievement and intellectual ability must be in one or more of the following areas: (1) oral expression; (2) listening comprehension; (3) written expression; (4) basic reading skill; (5) reading comprehension; (6) mathematical calculation; and/or (7) mathematical reasoning.

The intended meaning of the term *severe discrepancy* is open to debate among professionals. This concept coincides with severity as a classification parameter, although it is not specified in terms of measurement. What is an acceptable discrepancy between a child's achievement and expected grade level—25 percent? 35 percent? 50 percent? The idea of discrepancy has appeared in the literature for many years, but there has never been general agreement regarding degree.

As indicated in Reflect on This 6–1, it is possible that ADD may be placed in legislation as one interpretation of minimal brain dysfunction under the definition of specific learning disability. The legislative process is far from complete at this writing. However, if this does occur, ADD and its two subcategories may also be included as classifications of learning disabilities. The various pro and con arguments presented in Reflect on This 6–1 indicate clearly that the legislative placement of ADD remains uncertain.

A review of the literature on definitions and classifications of learning disabilities, either historical or current, presents a confusing and conflicting array of ideas. We cannot identify any precise set of concepts with which all researchers totally agree. This causes a number of difficulties with respect to both research and treatment. However, the people who display characteristics of learning disabilities present some of the most interesting challenges in behavioral science today.

FOCUS 3

Identify two estimate ranges for the prevalence of learning disabilities.

PREVALENCE

Determining prevalence (the total number of existing cases) is always difficult because actually counting on a large scale is time consuming and expensive. Problems of determining accurate figures are magnified by the differing definitions, theoretical views, and assessment procedures employed. Wallace and McLoughlin (1988) cited estimates that range from 1 to 28 percent. Briefing papers presented in hearings before the National Council on the Handicapped on June 8, 1989, indicated that 5 to 10 percent is a reasonable estimate of the persons affected by learning disabilities (Stanford Research Institute, 1989) (see Figure 6–1). These figures are remarkably similar to the earlier levels noted.

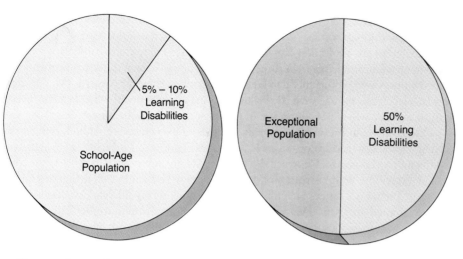

FIGURE 6–1

The Prevalence of Learning
Disabilities

(Stanford Research Institute, 1989)

Since study was begun, the prevalence of learning disabilities has been high in comparison to that of other exceptionalities, a fact that has been controversial for many years. It has been difficult to focus on one prevalence figure that is agreed on by all involved in the field. The 1991 Report to Congress indicated that over 4 million children with disabilities were being served in U.S. schools during the 1989–1990 schoolyear. Of that number, over

R
E
F
L
E
C
T

O
N

T
H
I
S

| 6–2 | Prevalence Distribution by Disability Condition |

Despite the difficulties involved with defining and classifying learning disabilities, this term describes one of the largest groups served in special education. Since use of the term emerged in 1963, the number of people served has grown more rapidly for this group than for any other disability group, while a number of other categories have shown a decrease during the same period. Use of the *learning disabilities* label for service still continues to grow, as illustrated in the adjacent table. The growth and high level of service for students with learning disabilities has come under some criticism. With definitional problems and uncertain research evidence, does it make much sense to have this group of exceptional individuals represent such a high proportion of those served? Do people with learning disabilities really represent such a high proportion of individuals with disabilities in general? Or has this label become a catchall for those in special education?

Net Change between 1988–1989 and 1989–1990 in Number and Percentage of Children Ages 6 through 21 Served under IDEA (by disability condition)

Disability Condition	Net Changes	
	Number	Percentage
Learning disabilities	66,585	+3.4
Speech impairments	7,588	+0.8
Mental retardation	−14,451	−2.8
Emotional disturbances	3,337	+1.0
Hearing impairments	−7	0.0
Multidisabled	2,448	+3.8
Orthopedic impairments	401	+1.0
Other health impairments	2,619	+5.6
Visual impairments	256	+1.5
Deaf-blind	24	+3.0
All conditions	**68,800**	**+1.7**

Source: U.S. Department of Education, 1991.

2 million were classified as having learning disabilities, which represents 50 percent of the population with disabilities being served (U.S. Department of Education, 1991).

Needless to say, professionals and others with vested interests in a particular group view this as somewhat problematic. In some cases, their apprehension is due to competition for limited funds between different disabilities. In other cases, there are concerns that the *learning disabilities* label is being overused to avoid the stigma associated with other labels or because of misdiagnosis, which may not result in the most appropriate treatment.

Discrepancies in prevalence occur in all fields of exceptionality, although the area of learning disabilities seems more variable than most. Part of this diversity can be attributed to different procedures used between the agencies, states, and researchers who do the counting and estimating. Another source of discrepancy may be found when definitions differ or are vague. Prevalence figures are unlikely to be the same when different definitions of what is being counted are used. This situation is not at all uncommon in the field of learning disabilities, where various definitions are evident, the definitions are often ambiguous, and therefore different characteristics may be used by those conducting prevalence studies.

FOCUS 4

Identify seven characteristics attributed to those with learning disabilities, and explain why it is difficult to characterize this group.

CHARACTERISTICS

Although many professionals have characterized specific learning disabilities as mild disorders, little attempt has been made to empirically validate this premise (Gelfand et al., 1988). Identification of subgroups and severity levels in this heterogeneous population have been largely ignored in the past. However, some attempts have been made during the last decade to attend to these issues (Deloach, Earl, Brown, Poplin, & Warner, 1981; Hooper & Willis, 1989; Swanson, Cochran, & Ewers, 1990).

For example, Weller et al. (1985) used model-consolidating criteria from several sources as a means of identifying severity level. This model used functional/adaptive ability criteria to differentiate students with mild disorders from those with more severe problems. It focused on a variety of skill areas, including the effect of the problem on other abilities (such as social skills) and the need to alter the person's future life.

Deloach et al. (1981) suggested that the differences between populations who are mildly and severely disabled may be determined through the perceptions of teachers in the field. Results of this study indicated that teachers view students with learning disabilities as a heterogeneous group functioning at differing levels of severity. These levels range from nonlearning disabled to severe disabilities. Approximately 20 percent of the students in classes for learning disabilities are functioning at a level that warrants classification as having severe learning disabilities. The authors reported that the most significant factors in distinguishing mild from severe problems are the needs of students with severe learning disabilities for individualized instruction, a necessity for alternative curricular approaches for students with severe disabilities, and a significant discrepancy between a student's scores on intelligence scales and grade level as measured by achievement tests.

Teachers in the study by Deloach et al. (1981) indicated that approximately 30 percent of the students in their classrooms had learning problems that they did *not* attribute to learning disabilities. This finding is consistent with the belief that many students currently being served as having learning disabilities may have been inappropriately referred. Larsen (1978) commented on this phenomenon:

> It is . . . likely that the large number of students who are referred for mild to moderate underachievement are simply unmotivated, poorly taught, come from home environments where scholastic success is not highly valued, or are dull-normal in intelligence. For all intents and purposes, these students should not automatically be considered as learning-disabled, since there is little evidence that placement in special education will improve their academic functioning. (p. 7)

Intelligence

When comparing populations with mild behavior disorders and learning disabilities, intelligence is considered a common attribute. By definition, both categories include people thought to be average or near average in intelligence. Differences between mild behavior disorders and specific learning disabilities have focused primarily on social adjustment differences and learner characteristics. However, individuals with learning disabilities may also exhibit secondary behavioral disorders, and students with mild behavior disorders may also have learning difficulties similar to those exhibited by individuals with learning disabilities (Wallace & McLoughlin, 1988).

Student classroom performance also suggests that behavior problems are not specific to any one intellectual functioning level. It is well known that individuals with intellectual deficits and learning disabilities also exhibit a considerable amount of maladaptive social and interpersonal behavior (deHaas, 1986; Margalit, 1989; Reid, 1988). Problems in social adjustment must be viewed as a shared characteristic.

Variability between areas of functioning (e.g., measured intelligence and performance) and between performance areas has long been viewed as characteristic of people with learning disabilities. General descriptions of learning disabilities have often emphasized great intraindividual differences between skill areas (Gelfand et al., 1988). For example, a youngster may have a disability (very low performance) in reading but not in arithmetic. Frequently, this variability in aptitude patterns has been used as a distinguishing characteristic between populations with learning disabilities and those with mental retardation. Typically, individuals thought to be retarded are expected to exhibit a rather flat or consistent profile of abilities (somewhat even, low performance levels in all areas), as contrasted to the pronounced intraindividual variability associated with learning disabilities. As with other attributes, however, intraindividual variability is not limited to students with learning disabilities. Intraindividual variability is definitely evident in students with mental retardation and behavior disorders.

Hyperactivity

Hyperactivity is a behavioral characteristic commonly associated with children labeled as having learning disabilities. Hyperactivity, also termed hyperkinetic behavior, is typically thought of as a general excess of activity. Professionals working in the area of learning disabilities, particularly teachers, often mention hyperactivity first in describing their students. Such children are frequently depicted as fidgeting a great deal and being unable to sit still for even a short time. Most descriptions involve the characterization of an overly active child.

Certain points need to be considered as we discuss hyperactivity in children with learning disabilities. First, not all children with learning disabilities are hyperactive nor vice versa. Rosenthal and Allen (1978) highlighted these facts when they sought to differentiate learning disabilities, hyperkinesis, and minimal brain dysfunction. They noted, "There is probably such a degree of overlap between these categories that perhaps half of the subjects in a learning disability study might also be labeled either minimally brain dysfunctional or hyperkinetic" (p. 693). This should not be interpreted to mean that *half* of those with learning disabilities are hyperactive. More correctly, this statement emphasizes the confusion regarding learning disabilities and how they relate to or are distinguishable from hyperkinesis.

A second point to consider involves the view that hyperkinesis is characterized as a *general* excess of activity. This idea may be more a function of stereotyped expectations than descriptions based on accurate observations. Some research has suggested that it may be more helpful to consider the *appropriateness* of a child's activity *in particular settings;* it may be incorrect to view hyperkinesis as a general excess of activity. Evidence does indicate that

Most people with learning disabilities are thought to be of average intelligence. (Lew Merrim/Monkmeyer Press)

children who are hyperactive have a higher level of activity than their normal peers in structured settings (which may be descriptive of certain classroom circumstances). However, in relatively unstructured settings (e.g., play periods), no differences seem to result between children who are and are not hyperactive (Baxley & LeBlanc, 1976; Whalen & Henker, 1976).

Learning Characteristics

Learning disabilities have also been associated with perceptual abnormalities. Such problems have been conspicuous in the historical development of the field of learning disabilities. Interest in this perspective has declined over the years, although some researchers have continued to view perception difficulties prominently with respect to behavior and causation of learning disabilities.

Perception.   Perception difficulties in people with learning disabilities represent a constellation of behavioral abnormalities, rather than a single characteristic. Descriptions of these problems have included the visual, auditory, and **haptic** sensory systems. Visual perception difficulty has been closely associated with learning disabilities. It is important to remember that the definitions of learning disabilities exclude impaired vision in the traditional sense. Visual perception problems in persons with learning disabilities refers to something distinctly different. This type of abnormality is evident when a child sees a visual stimulus as unrelated parts rather than as an integrated pattern. In such cases, the child may not be able to identify a letter in the alphabet because he or she perceives only unrelated lines rather than the letter as a meaningful whole. Clearly, such perception causes severe performance problems in school.

Visual perception problems may also emerge in **figure-ground discrimination,** the process of distinguishing an object from its background. Most of us have little difficulty with figure-ground discrimination. However, certain children labeled as having learning disabilities are unable to accomplish such a task. They may have difficulty focusing on a word or sentence on the page of a textbook, which of course results in school difficulties. This example also presents an illustration of the theoretical problems in learning disabilities. A given behavior may be interpreted quite differently, depending on the research, theory, or disciplinary perspective being employed. The example above *may* be a figure-ground discrimination disorder, but it may also represent an attention-deficit or memory problem. These have also been associated with the difficulties of children with learning disabilities. Thus, the same abnormal behavior can be accounted for by several theories.

Discrimination.   Other discrimination problems have also appeared in descriptions of people with learning disabilities. Difficulties in **visual discrimination** have often been associated with learning disabilities. Individuals with such problems may be unable to distinguish one visual stimulus from another (e.g., between words such as *sit* and *sat* or letters such as *V* and *W*). This may result in the reversal of such letters as *b* and *d*, which has often been noted in children with learning disabilities. This type of error is common among young children and often causes great concern for parents. However, most youngsters develop normally and show few reversal or rotation errors on visual images by about 7 or 8 years of age. The child who "continues to have difficulty and who makes frequent errors on easily discriminable letters" should be viewed as being a potential problem and perhaps given extra help (Hallahan, Kauffman, & Lloyd, 1985, p. 33).

Auditory perception problems have also been associated with learning disabilities. Some children have been characterized as unable to distinguish between the sounds of different words or syllables, or even to identify certain environmental sounds (e.g., a ringing telephone) and differentiate them from others. Such problems have been termed **auditory discrimination** deficits. People with learning disabilities have also been described as having difficulties in **auditory blending, auditory memory,** and **auditory association.** Those with blending problems may not be able to blend word parts into an integrated whole as they pronounce it. Auditory memory difficulties may result in an inability to recall information presented verbally. Auditory association deficiencies may cause the person to be unable to associate ideas or information presented verbally. Difficulties in these areas naturally create school performance problems for a child (Nix & Shapiro, 1986).

Haptic perception (touch, body movement, and position sensation) problems have also been associated with learning disabilities. Such difficulties are thought to be relatively uncommon but may be important in some areas of school performance. For example, handwriting requires haptic perception because tactile information about the grasp of a pen or pencil must be transmitted to the brain. In addition, **kinesthetic** information is transmitted

Visual and perceptual difficulties have been closely associated with learning disabilities. (Will & Deni McIntyre/Photo Researchers, Inc.)

FIGURE 6-2

Writing Samples of a College Freshman with a Learning Disability

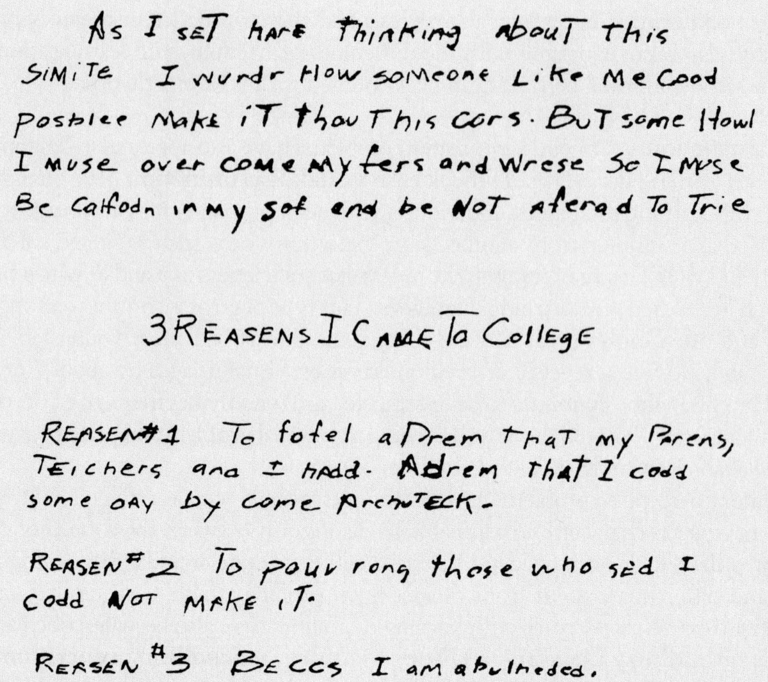

As I set hare thinking abouT This simiTe I wurdr How someone Like Me Cood posbiee Make iT thou This cors. BuT some Howl I muse over come My fers and wrese So I muse Be Calfodn in my sof end be NoT aferad To Trie

3 REASENS I CAME To CollegE

REASEN #1 To fofel a Drem thaT my Prens, Teichers ana I hAdd. A Drem that I codd some oAy by come ArchiTECK.

REASEN #2 To pour rong those who sed I codd NoT MAKE iT.

REASEN #3 BECCS I am abulheded.

The text of these samples reads as follows:

As I sit here thinking about this semester, I wonder how someone like me could possibly make it through this course. But somehow I must overcome my fears and worries. So I must be confident in myself and not be afraid to try.

Three Reasons I Came To College

Reason #1.   To fulfill a dream that my parents, teachers, and I had — a dream that I could some day become an architect.
Reason #2.   To prove wrong those who said I could not make it.
Reason #3.   Because I am bullheaded.

regarding hand and arm movements as one writes. Children with learning disabilities have often been described by teachers as having poor handwriting, with difficulties in spacing letters and staying on the lines of the paper. However, such problems could also be due to visual perception abnormalities. Precisely attributing some behaviors to a single factor is difficult. Figure 6–2 presents an example of writing by a college freshman with learning disabilities. There are two samples in this figure, written on two consecutive days, each in a *40-minute period*. The note provides a translation of what was written.

Not all individuals labeled as having learning disabilities exhibit behaviors that suggest perceptual problems. Widely varying patterns of deficiencies are evident. We should also mention the relative lack of empirical evidence regarding perceptual problems in those labeled as having learning disabilities. In many cases, the notion of perceptual dysfunction is represented more by clinical impressions than by rigorous research. However, such clinical lore is widespread enough that it should be discussed in the learning disabilities area.

Cognition/Information Processing

Many other characteristics have been attributed to those with learning disabilities, some of which are in the area of **cognition** or **information processing** (Reid, 1988). Information processing has long been used in psychology as a model for studying cognition. This approach essentially relates the way a person acquires, retains, and manipulates information. Each of these areas has periodically emerged as problematic for individuals with learning disabilities. For example, teachers have long complained about poor memory in such children. In many cases, the students seem to learn material one day but cannot recall it the next. Research on the memory skills of these children has been relatively scanty, although such study is central to understanding how information is acquired, stored, selected, and recalled. Certain evidence has suggested that children with learning disabilities do not perform as well as normal children on some memory tasks (Agrawal & Kaushal, 1987; August, 1987; Swanson, 1988), whereas other results have shown no differences (Griffith, Ripich, & Dastoli, 1986; Swanson, 1979, 1988). Research in this area needs increased effort to confirm, refute, or clarify clinical impressions.

Research has also suggested that such children have *different* rather than deficient cognitive abilities (Hall, 1980). This type of finding has led to the development of specific, highly focused instruction for individuals with learning disabilities to replace a generic curriculum that assumes their cognitive skills are *generally* poor (Finch & Spirito, 1980; McKinney & Haskins, 1980).

Attention problems have also been associated with learning disabilities. Such problems have often been clinically characterized as a **short attention span.** Parents and teachers often note that their children with learning disabilities cannot sustain attention for more than a very short time. Some evidence has supported observations of a short attention span in these children (Aman & Turbott, 1986), but other research has indicated that children with learning disabilities have difficulty in certain types of attention problems and attending selectively (Cotungo, 1987; Draeger, Prior, & Sanson, 1986; Richards, Samuels, Turnure, & Ysseldyke, 1990; Zentall & Kruczek, 1988). **Selective attention** problems cause difficulty in focusing on centrally important tasks or information rather than peripheral or less relevant stimuli. Such problems might emerge when children with learning disabilities are asked to compute simple math problems that are on the chalkboard (which also means they must copy from the board). They may focus their attention on the copying task rather than the math problems. This example presents a situation where the teacher can easily modify the task (e.g., by using worksheets rather than copying from the board) as a means of facilitating completion of the important lesson.

Academic Achievement

One of the primary areas that resulted in the development of learning disabilities as an identified exceptionality is academic achievement. Individuals with learning disabilities, while generally of normal or above average intelligence, seem to have many academic problems.

Reading.   Students with learning disabilities often have reading problems. In fact, the category learning disabilities grew out of what was once known as *remedial reading*. Some estimates have suggested that over 85 percent of all students with learning disabilities also have reading disabilities (Kaluger & Kolson, 1978). The specific reading problems that these students have are as varied as the many elements involved in the reading process.

Word knowledge and word recognition are important parts of reading that cause difficulty for people with learning disabilities. When we encounter a word that we know, it needs only to be recalled from our mental dictionary to determine the meaning (Samuels

Research has suggested that children with learning disabilities perform below average at tasks involving memory. (Bill Bachmann/Leo de Wys, Inc.)

& Kamil, 1984). Other words, however, are not a part of our mental dictionary, and so we must sound the letters out and pronounce them based on our knowledge of typical rules regarding spelling patterns and pronunciation. Skill in this latter process is particularly important, since there are too many words to memorize, especially when we are constantly encountering and learning new material.

This dimension of word knowledge presents particular problems for students with learning disabilities. To recognize novel words, students must know the rules, be able to generalize letter patterns, and draw analogies with considerable flexibility to attain word recognition. Good readers usually accomplish this rather easily, fairly quickly, and almost automatically. Students with reading disabilities experience great difficulty with this process, and when they can do it, they do so only slowly and laboriously. They can, however, be taught through specific training in the process (Anderson, Hiebert, Scott, & Wilkinson, 1985; Englert & Palincsar, 1988).

Another important element in reading is the use of context to determine meaning. Good readers tend to be very adept at inferring the general meaning of an unknown word from the contextual information surrounding it. Poor readers have difficulty using context to aid in word recognition and reading (Patberg, Dewitz, & Samuels, 1981; Sorrel, 1990). However, specific instruction on using context improves the reading performance of students with learning disabilities (Wong & Sawatsky, 1984).

WINDOW 6–2

MAKING SENSE OF HISTORY

Alice found herself very frustrated with school at this point. She was in the fourth grade, and her grades were very bad. She had worked very hard, but many of the things that were required just didn't seem to make sense.

History was a perfect example. Alice had looked forward to learning more about history; it seemed so fun and interesting when Grandfather told his stories. Alice thought it would have been fun to have lived back then, when all the kids got to ride

horses. But history in school was not fun, and it didn't make any sense at all. Alice had been reading last night, supposedly about a girl who was her age who was moving West with a wagon train. As she looked at the book, Alice read strange things. One passage said, "Mary pelieveb that things would get detter. What they hab left Missouri they hab enough foob dut now there was darely enough for one meal a bay. Surely the wagon-master woulb finb a wet to solve the brodlem." Alice knew that she would fail the test, and she cried quietly in her room as she dressed for school.

Good and poor readers are also different in the degree to which they have and use background knowledge (Sorrel, 1990). Failure to use background information is likewise a problem for students with learning disabilities (Wong, 1980). Similarly, students with learning disabilities do not seem to perceive or use the organization of important ideas in text material, often focusing on details and factors that are less relevant (Bos & Filip, 1984; Englert & Thomas, 1987).

Reading is a complex process, involving many skills that are also found, in one form or another, in other areas (e.g., the ability to focus on the important rather than irrelevant aspects of a task). Thus, some of the difficulties experienced by people with learning disabilities emerge in more than one facet of behavior, as we will see in discussing other academic characteristics. Depending on the severity of the problem, specific instruction may improve performance, although there may not be significant generalization beyond the limited focus of the training. In some cases, if the disability is quite severe (as in dyslexia), a person must be taught to compensate for the difficulty through alternative means of accessing information and even then use reading sparingly.

Writing and Spelling.   Children labeled as having learning disabilities also often have markedly different writing performance than their nondisabled peers, which affects their academic achievement. These difficulties include areas such as handwriting (slow writing, spacing problems, poor formation of letters), poor spelling skills, and immature composition (Bailet, 1990; Hallahan, et al., 1985). Several such problems were illustrated in Figure 6–2, presented earlier.

Some children are poor at handwriting because they have not mastered the basic developmental skills required for the process. Earlier, we discussed theories regarding haptic perception problems in children with learning disabilities. Such deficits contribute to the very fundamental processes of grasping a pen or pencil and moving it in a fashion that results in legible writing on the page. In some cases, fine motor development seems delayed in children with learning disabilities, which can contribute to the inability to physically use handwriting materials well. Handwriting also involves an understanding of spatial concepts such as up, down, top, and bottom. These are abilities that frequently are less well developed in youngsters with learning disabilities than in their nondisabled age-mates. The physical acts involved in using writing tools (e.g., pencil or pen) as well as problems in spatial relationships can contribute to difficulty in forming letters and spacing letters, words, and lines. Some children with rather mild handwriting problems may be exhibiting a slowness in development, which will improve as they grow older, receive instruction, and practice. However, there are also more severe examples (e.g., the young adult whose writing sample appeared in Figure 6–2) where age and practice have not resulted in skill mastery.

Some researchers view the handwriting abilities of students with learning disabilities as being closely related to their reading ability (Seidenberg, 1989). For example, research does not clearly indicate that children with learning disabilities write more poorly than their normally achieving peers who are reading on a similar level (Grinnell, 1988; Tansley & Panckhurst, 1981). Letter reversals and, in severe cases, **mirror writing** have often been used as illustrations of poor handwriting. However, it is also questionable whether children with learning disabilities commit these types of errors more often than their nondisabled peers at the same reading level (Nelson, 1980).

The logic connecting handwriting and reading abilities has certain intuitive appeal. Most children write to some degree on their own prior to receiving instruction in school. In general, children who write spontaneously also seem to read spontaneously and tend to have considerable practice at both before they enter school. Their homes (thereby implicating their parents) tend to have writing materials readily available for experimentation and practice. Likewise, writing is an activity they often observe their parents doing and may be one that the parents and child do together. Further research concerning the relationship between reading and handwriting is definitely in order. Instruction in writing for children with learning disabilities has historically been somewhat isolated from the act of reading, focusing instead primarily on the technical skills (Grinnell, 1988).

Poor spelling is often a problem among students with learning disabilities (also evident in Figure 6–2). These children frequently omit letters or add unnecessary ones. Their spelling also shows evidence of letter-order confusion and reflects developmentally immature mispronunciation (Polloway & Smith, 1982). Interestingly, relatively little research has been conducted on these spelling difficulties, and teaching has been based primarily on opinion (Grinnell, 1988). Recent studies have suggested that spelling skills of students with learning disabilities seem to follow developmental patterns similar to those of their nondisabled peers but are delayed (Gerber, 1985, 1986). Characteristics such as visual and auditory memory problems, deficiencies in auditory discrimination, and phonic generalizations have also been implicated in the spelling difficulties with learning disabilities (Polloway & Smith, 1982). Further research on spelling is needed to more clearly understand this area.

Mathematics.   Arithmetic is another academic achievement area where individuals with learning disabilities have considerable difficulty (Ackerman, Anhalt, & Dykman, 1986). They often have problems with counting, writing numbers, and mastering other simple math concepts.

Counting objects is perhaps the most fundamental mathematics skill and provides a foundation for the development of the more advanced yet basic skills of addition and subtraction. Counting is also an area where students with learning disabilities encounter problems. Some of these youngsters omit numbers when counting sequences aloud (e.g., "1, 2, 3, 5, 7, 9"), whereas others can count correctly but do not understand what the numbers mean with respect to relative value. Students with arithmetic learning disabilities also have additional counting difficulties when they are asked to proceed beyond 9, where more than one digit is used. This is a somewhat more advanced skill than single-digit counting and involves knowledge about place value.

Place value involves even more of a conceptual skill than the simple counting of objects and is fundamental to the arithmetic functions of adding and subtracting. Many students with learning disabilities in math have problems understanding place values and particular difficulty with the idea that the same digit (e.g., 6) represents different magnitudes when placed in various number positions (e.g., 16, 61, 632). Place-value concepts are central to addition and subtraction since they are important to the processes of carrying and borrowing. Grinnell (1988) stated that the four problems students with learning disabilities encounter include "(1) understanding the grouping process, (2) understanding that each position to the left represents another multiple of ten, (3) understanding the placement of one digit per position, and (4) understanding the relationship between the order of the digits and the value of the numeral" (p. 349).

Basic arithmetic difficulties, such as those mentioned, place major problems in the paths of students with learning disabilities. Mastery of beginning quantitative concepts is vital to learning further, more abstract, and complex mathematics. Youth with learning disabilities are increasingly seeking to complete high school and attend colleges or universities. For these young adults, it is essential to achieve a certain level of mathematics mastery, including work in algebra and geometry during their years in secondary education. These topics have traditionally received minimal or no attention in curriculum design because of an emphasis on computation (Fair, 1988). Further research on mathematics difficulties and effective instruction for students encountering such problems is more important as the goals and achievements of such young people change.

Community-Based Learning Programs

Contemporary concepts of what makes an appropriate learning environment are expanding to include more than just traditional classrooms—a change that could be very attractive to young learners, especially those with learning disabilities. The traditional format has called for students to learn academic concepts in the classroom with the hope that they can be used in practical settings in the real world. Advocates of community-based learning programs argue that sometimes *practical experience* can lead to *conceptual understanding,* rather than vice versa.

Community-based learning programs are, of course, commonly used to teach vocational skills. However, they are being used more and more to teach academic skills, as well. For example, one program brings students to a grocery store to learn arithmetic. Among other things, students practice addition and subtraction and consider weights and measures as they browse through the store aisles; they also learn about making change when they go to "pay" at the cash register.

At a time when society is seriously questioning whether public education teaches students basic skills, methods such as these are receiving positive attention. What's more, many educators have found that students can learn more effectively if given the opportunity to apply reading, writing, and arithmetic skills to real-life problems as opposed to learning them in isolation—in the classroom rather than the community.

Schools, libraries, and museums must become flexible, adaptable environments that provide a variety of information and learning experiences. It is possible to implement such programs in the community without providing increased technology. What is required is a creative perspective of the world around students and how it can be used to teach everything from basic skills to lofty ideas. The goal is to develop positive student attitudes toward learning, motivating them by offering educational situations that are intriguing and within reach.

Innovative learning environments may be used to stimulate interest in specific subject areas. For example, U.S. students' indifference to science has been well documented in recent years; innovative programs that provide hands-on, practical experience may help create interest. Similar approaches to teaching mathematics would perhaps improve the performance of U.S. students, who clearly lag behind those from other developed countries. Such performance deficits hold clear ramifications for the future competitive ability and technological growth of the United States. Thus, improving student interest and achievement must be an important educational goal.

Community-based learning programs offer advantages to all students, not only those with learning disabilities. The key to success is to inspire a lust for learning.

Achievement Discrepancy. Students with learning disabilities frequently find the fundamental and basic areas of academic achievement problematic, as indicated above. These students tend to score below their age-mates in achievement, but they also perform below what would be expected based on their measured potential. This has led to the discrepancy notion, which basically involves a discrepancy between academic achievement and what one would expect given the student's assessed ability and age. Attempts to quantify the academic achievement/potential discrepancy in learning disabilities have appeared in the literature for some time (Bennett & Clarizio, 1988; Meyen, 1989; Parrill, 1987). However, the field remains without an agreed on formula. School-age youngsters may be two to four or more years behind their peers in academic achievement. Frequently, a student falls progressively behind as he or she continues in the educational system. This often results in students dropping out of high school (Gartner & Lipsky, 1989; Stanford Research Institute, 1989) or graduating even though they are not proficient in basic reading, writing, or math skills.

Comments

We have described several behavioral characteristics that have been attributed to individuals labeled as having learning disabilities. It is increasingly evident that learning disabilities represent a very heterogeneous set of problems and that many different specific problems are

R E F L E C T   O N   T H I S

6–3   Characteristics, Definitions, and Labels

We have discussed the characteristics and behavior of students with learning disabilities primarily from an academic standpoint. Definitions and even the label used for these students tend to focus on this perspective. Yet children and adolescents with learning disabilities often encounter emotional and interpersonal difficulties that are quite serious. Because of their learning problems, they frequently experience low self-esteem and negative emotional

consequences that present significant problems. They may not be able to interact effectively with others because their perception of social cues is distorted or because they have not learned to discriminate or interpret the subtleties of normal interpersonal associations.

In some cases, the social dimensions of life present greater problems to students with learning disabilities than their specific academic deficits. How would you address this issue with regard to defining and labeling learning disabilities? Remember that *learning disabilities* is already considered a gen-

eral term, with many specific dimensions, and that some view the label as less functional than specific terminology that more precisely describes the problem. Should the definition and label be broadened to incorporate social and emotional problems? Should these problems be viewed as secondary and outcomes of academic difficulties, which would support leaving the definition and label as they currently are? Should the social and emotional aspects receive subcategory labeling, as is the case with ADHD and ADD, in which the presence or absence of hyperactive behavior is distinguished?

involved under this general label. It is important to repeat that *learning disabilities* is a generalized educational term representing many different disorders. In many cases, solid empirical evidence for certain characteristics of those with learning disabilities is scanty or even absent. A substantial amount of what is known about people with learning disabilities can be considered simply clinical lore. This is also evident as we discuss the causes of learning disabilities.

FOCUS 5

Identify four causes thought to be involved in learning disabilities.

CAUSATION

The behaviors of individuals with learning disabilities have been explained in a number of ways, and a number of causes have been suggested. In some segments of the special education profession, determining causation (and classification) in learning disabilities has been viewed from a rather pessimistic standpoint. For example, as Lynn, Gluckin, and Kripke (1979) noted, "In fact, the causes of learning disabilities are unknown. If we knew what caused a learning disability, we would call it by another name" (p. 139). These authors further stated that "no *honest* classification of learning disabilities can be based on causes, because the causes are unknown" (p. 158, emphasis ours).

This view, however, is not held by all professional groups working in learning disabilities. Interest and research on the causes of learning disabilities have been substantial over the years. In learning disabilities, as in many other areas, determining precise causation is difficult. This does not detract from the importance of such efforts; it merely limits the information available at any given time.

Neurological Causation

Over the years, learning disabilities have often been viewed as caused by structural neurological damage or, if not structural, some type of neurological activation abnormality. A number of professionals within the field have supported this contention (Gaddes, 1985; Reid, 1988; Rourke, 1987). Neurological involvement has even been specified as an identification criterion in some studies of learning disabilities (Kavale & Nye, 1981).

A variety of factors may result in neurological damage such as that associated with learning disabilities. Part of what was discussed in relation to mental retardation (Chapter

Four) is relevant here, as well. To repeat, damage may be inflicted on the neurological system at birth in several ways (e.g., abnormal fetal positioning during delivery, or anoxia, a lack of oxygen). Infections may also result in neurological damage and learning disabilities. Specific injury or infection has also long been implicated as a causal factor in brain damage and learning disabilities (Houck, 1984). However, neurological damage as a cause must be largely inferred, since direct evidence is usually not available (Miller, 1990).

Maturational Delay

Somewhat related to neurological causation is that of maturational delay. Some theories have suggested that a maturational delay of the neurological system results in the difficulties experienced by some individuals with learning disabilities. In many ways, the behavior and performance of children with learning disabilities resembles that of much younger individuals (Reid, 1988). They often exhibit delays in skills maturation, such as slower development of language skills, and problems in the visual-motor area and several academic areas, as noted above. Maturational delay is most likely not a causative factor in all types of learning disabilities, but it has received considerable support as one of many.

Genetic Causation

Genetic causation has also been implicated in learning disabilities. Genetic abnormalities, which are inherited, are thought to cause or contribute to one or more of the problems categorized as learning disabilities. This is always a concern for parents with regard to all types of learning and behavior disorders. Some evidence has suggested genetic influences. Most likely, we are examining many different specific problems with multiple causes. Over the years, some research has obtained results suggesting an inheritance linkage (Bonnet, 1989; Healy & Aram, 1986; Smith, 1989), including studies of both **identical** and **fraternal twins** (Hermann, 1959). These findings must be viewed cautiously because of the well-known problems in separating the influences of heredity and environment (Gelfand et al., 1988), but evidence lends a certain degree of support to the inherited causation of some learning disabilities (Houck, 1984).

Environmental Causation

Environmental influences are often mentioned as a possible cause of learning disabilities. Such factors as diet inadequacies, food additives, radiation stress, fluorescent lighting, unshielded television tubes, smoking, drinking, drug consumption, and inappropriate school instruction are now only beginning to be investigated (e.g., Miller, 1990). In some cases, these influences appear to be primarily prenatal concerns, whereas in others, the problems seem limited to the postnatal environment or both. Research on environmental causes remains inconclusive, but it is the focus of continuing study.

Comments

Learning disabilities have many different causes, and in some cases, a given type of learning disability may have multiple causes. We cannot always determine the origins of these problems, although considerable research has been conducted over the years with this aim. In many cases, it is more practical to direct attention to assessment issues in order to determine who can be helped with specialized instruction and what the nature of that instruction should be.

FOCUS 6
Identify four questions that are addressed by screening assessment for learning disabilities.

ASSESSMENT

Assessment for learning disabilities has several purposes. The ultimate goal is appropriate screening, identification, and placement of individuals who require services beyond those needed by most people. This may mean additional help academically, socially, or in various combinations, including nearly all aspects of life and nearly all human service disciplines. Decisions of such a varied nature require differing types of information from a variety of assessment procedures (Achenbach, 1986; Gordon, 1986). We examine here the assessment for learning disabilities in terms of purpose and domain of assessment and focus on the areas of intelligence, adaptive behavior, and academic achievement.

Preliminary Concepts

As we begin discussing the assessment of individuals with learning disabilities, certain preliminary concepts need to be mentioned. These concepts play an important role with respect to both the purpose and method of assessment. An individual's status in performance, skills, and ability may be evaluated in a number of ways. Assessment may involve either formal or informal means. The notions of *formal* and *informal* have grown to mean *standardized* versus *teacher-made* tests or techniques. Standardized instruments are those that are published and distributed widely on a commercial basis, such as intelligence tests and achievement tests. Teacher-made (or those devised by any professional) generally refer to techniques or instruments that are not commercially available. These may be constructed for specific assessment purposes and are often quite formal in the sense that great care is taken in the evaluation process. Both formal and informal assessment techniques are effective ways of evaluating students with learning disabilities and other students, as well. Both are used for various evaluation purposes and in a number of performance or behavior areas.

Two other background concepts are also important, norm- and criterion-referenced assessment. **Norm-referenced assessment** compares an individual's skills or performance with that of others, such as age-mates, usually on the basis of national average scores. Thus, a student's counting performance might be compared with that of his or her classmates, others in the school district of the same age, or state or national average scores. In contrast, **criterion-referenced assessment** does not compare an individual's skills with some norm. Instead, his or her performance is compared with a desired level (criterion) that is a goal. The goal may involve counting to 100 with no errors by the end of the schoolyear or some other criterion, depending on the purpose. One particular application of criterion-referenced assessment that has received a great deal of attention recently is **curriculum-based assessment.** This approach directly uses the objectives in a student's curriculum as the criteria against which progress is evaluated (Blankenship, 1988; Fuchs & Fuchs, 1988; Perkins, 1989). Curriculum-based assessment emphasizes the relationship between evaluation and instructional objectives, which enhances the utility of assessment for instructional decisions and planning.

Both norm- and criterion-referenced assessment are useful for students with learning disabilities. The two types tend to be used for different purposes, however. Norm-referenced assessment tends to be used more often for administrative purposes, such as compiling census data on how many students are achieving at the state or national average. Criterion-referenced assessment is helpful for specific instructional purposes and ongoing interventions planning.

It is very important to note that we are using these two terms as *concepts,* with no implied reference to specific instruments or procedures. Depending on how a technique, instrument, or procedure is employed, it may be used in a norm-referenced or criterion-referenced manner. Some areas of assessment, such as intelligence, are more typically evaluated using norm-referenced procedures. However, even a standardized intelligence test can be scored and used in a criterion-referenced fashion (although then it would become no more than a source of test items, and a student's performance could not be viewed exactly as the test developer intended). Assessment should always be undertaken with careful attention to the purpose and use of evaluation (Fuchs & Fuchs, 1986; Gronlund & Linn, 1990).

Screening

Screening and identification have always been important in assessment. For these purposes, assessment occurs *prior* to any labeling or treatment. Usually, however, clinicians or others (often parents) who come into contact with the child suspect a problem exists. This may occur at a rather young age for some individuals and involve assessment to compare the child with others of a similar age. Screening has the purpose of "throwing up a red flag," suggesting that more investigation is needed for one or more of several reasons.

The questions to ask at this point of the assessment process are:

1. Is there a reason to more fully investigate the abilities of the child?
2. Is there a reason to suspect that the child is disabled in any way?
3. If the child appears disabled, what are the relevant characteristics and how should we move to intervention?
4. How should we plan for the future of the individual?

Answers to all of the above screening questions might well involve classification, placement for services, psychological or educational treatment, and evaluation of progress for the person. It is important to emphasize that assessment is not a simple, isolated event that results in a diagnosis and is then complete. It is complex, involving many different steps. Assessment includes diagnosis, but it must be an ongoing process that provides the basis for a progression of decisions throughout the time an individual is receiving services (Drew, Logan, & Hardman, 1992; Houck, 1984). Approaches to assessment, for our purposes, come back to the three foci of intelligence, adaptive behavior, and academic achievement.

Intelligence.   Individuals with learning disabilities have long been described as having average or near-average intelligence while experiencing problems in school more often characteristic of students having lower intelligence. In many cases, the measured intelligence may not be accurate because of specific visual, auditory, or other limitations that might make assessment inaccurate. However, intelligence assessment remains an important matter for individuals with learning disabilities (Torgesen, 1989) and is typically evaluated with a standardized instrument such as an IQ test.

Adaptive Behavior.   People with learning disabilities have frequently been described as exhibiting behaviors that are not appropriate or adaptive in their environment. This has primarily appeared in clinical reports and has not historically been a routine part of the assessment to the degree it has in other areas of exceptionality such as mental retardation. However, some work has been undertaken to address adaptive behavior assessment for individuals with learning disabilities. Such efforts have been based on the assumption that an ability/academic discrepancy alone is insufficient to fully assess and describe learning disabilities. Adaptive behavior has contributed to concepts of subtypes and severity levels in learning disabilities (Weller et al., 1985; Weller & Strawser, 1987).

Academic Achievement.   Academic achievement has always been a major problem for students with learning disabilities. Achievement assessment is used to determine if there is a discrepancy between a student's ability and his or her academic achievement. Assessment of academic achievement is also of central importance to help evaluate the student's level of functioning in one or more areas. Instruments have been developed and used in an attempt to diagnose specific academic problems. For example, a number of reading tests are used to determine the nature of reading problems, including the Woodcock Reading Mastery Tests, the Diagnostic Reading Scales, and the Stanford Diagnostic Reading Test. Likewise, mathematics assessment has received attention, resulting in instruments such as the Key Math Diagnostic Arithmetic Test and the Stanford Diagnostic Mathematics Test (Gronlund & Linn, 1990).

Academic assessment for students with learning disabilities is very important. For the most part, assessment techniques are the same as those used in other areas of exceptionality. This is because deficits in academic achievement are a common problem among students with disabilities. However, specific skill-deficit diagnosis is more prominent in learning disabilities and has prompted focused skill-oriented academic achievement assessment in other disability areas, as well.

INTERVENTIONS

FOCUS 7

Identify three types of intervention or treatment employed with people diagnosed as having learning disabilities.

Intervention strategies for individuals with learning disabilities have changed as professionals have come to view learning disabilities as a constellation of specific problems rather than a generic category. Much of the current literature has addressed the area in terms of specific disabilities, such as perceptual, cognitive, attention and hyperactivity, social and emotional, spoken language, reading, writing, and mathematics (Dudley-Marling & Searle, 1988; Reid, 1988). A consequence of this current view is intervention aimed at specific problems, rather than general treatment of a problem that includes many discrete disabilities.

Interventions used for adolescents or adults with learning disabilities may be different than those used for children. In some cases, changes in treatment are due to different intervention goals emerging as individuals grow older (e.g., the acquisition of basic counting skills versus math instruction in preparation for college). Educational interventions require a broad range of procedures and placements, depending on the particular problems presented in each case (Wiederholt, 1989). Various professions are also involved in interventions for persons with learning disabilities. Although the different professionals often function as a team, each makes a unique contribution to the overall treatment program.

Early Childhood Interventions

There are several approaches to treatment and education of young children with learning disabilities. Many such children are first diagnosed as having learning disabilities when they enter school and begin to encounter academic difficulties. In these circumstances, it is often the educator and related school personnel that are involved in interventions. Other children with learning disabilities are first evaluated and treated by medical professionals.

Medical Interventions. Physicians often diagnose childhood abnormal or delayed development in the areas of language and behavior as well as motor functions. Pediatricians often participate in diagnosing physical disabilities that may significantly affect learning and behavior, and interpret medical findings to the family and other professionals. Physicians may be involved with a child having learning disabilities early because of the nature of the problem, such as serious developmental delay or hyperactivity. Often, however, a medical professional sees the young child first because he or she has not entered school yet, and the family physician is the primary advisor for parents. When other professional expertise is

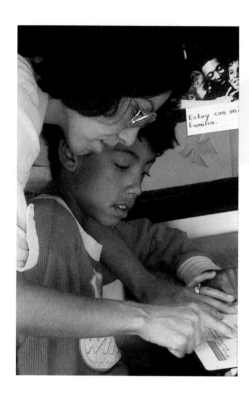

Individualized instruction has proven effective for individuals with many types of learning disabilities. (Tony O'Brien/The Picture Group)

needed, the physician may refer the family to other specialists and then function as a team member in meeting a child's needs (Johnston, 1987).

One example of therapeutic intervention is in the area of hyperactivity. On the surface, hyperactivity may lead one to believe that such children are overly aroused, that is, suffering from greater than normal physiological arousal. Such notions led many researchers to recommend environments with few distracting stimuli, known as low-stimulus or stimulus-free settings. However, one treatment often employed with hyperactive children has called into question the overarousal theory. The medication most often used to control hyperactivity is from the amphetamine family and is known as Ritalin. Although amphetamines increase activity in most people, they decrease activity in children who are hyperactive.

Other theories regarding hyperactivity may make sense of the paradoxical reactions to amphetamines. Some researchers have suggested that individuals who are hyperactive may be plagued by abnormally *low* physiological arousal; they are not functioning at an *optimal* arousal level, rather than being generally overly aroused (Zentall & Kruczek, 1988). It has been hypothesized that the apparent high level of motor activity in individuals who are hyperkinetic may be the result of the person trying to increase stimulation, much as a person who yawns is trying to stay alert. Such a notion would explain the higher level of activity in certain circumstances, plus the apparent quieting effect of amphetamines. Hyperactive children may receive adequate stimulation on the playground but not in a structured instructional setting. If amphetamines actually increase arousal in hyperactive individuals, as they do with most people, then these children might not require an extraordinary level of activity to maintain an adequate level of stimulation.

More research is crucial in this area because much remains unknown about medication and learning disabilities. For example, exactly which drug will be effective is seldom known until after treatment has begun. Adding to the disconcerting confusion is a problem with dosage level. Pelham (1983) stated:

INTERACTING IN NATURAL SETTINGS ·················· People with Learning Disabilities *

EARLY CHILDHOOD YEARS *

Tips for the Family
- Play verbal direction games, like finding certain words or sounds, interspersing those that are difficult with those that are easy for the child with learning disabilities.
- Give the child practice in identifying different sounds (e.g., the doorbell and phone).
- Reinforce the child for paying attention.
- Promote family learning about learning disabilities, their child's specific strengths and limitations, and their respect for their child as a person.

Tips for the Preschool Teacher
- Limit verbal instructions to simple sentences, presented briefly, one at a time.
- Watch content carefully, paying attention to the developmental level of the material.
- Provide multiple examples to make the points clear and have meaning.
- Provide more practice than usual, particularly on new material or skills.

Tips for Preschool Personnel
- Promote a school environment and attitude that respects children of all abilities.
- Promote the development of instructional programs focusing on preacademic skills, which may be unnecessary for all children but very important for young students with learning disabilities.
- Be alert for students that seem to be of average or higher intelligence but, for reasons that may not be evident, are not performing up to ability.

Tips for Neighbors and Friends
- Community activities should be arranged to cover a broad range of maturational levels so that children with learning disabilities are not shut out or experience unnecessary failure at this early age.

ELEMENTARY YEARS

Tips for the Family
- Become involved in the school through parent-teacher organizations and conferences.
- Volunteer as a tutor.
- Learn more about learning disabilities as you begin to understand that your child is affected, perhaps through reading material or enrolling in a short course.

Tips for the Regular Classroom Teacher
- Continue to keep verbal instructions simple and brief. Have the student with learning disabilities repeat directions back to assure understanding.
- Use mnemonics in instruction to aid memory.
- Intensify instruction by repeating the main points several times to aid memory.
- Provide additional time to learn material, including repeating or reteaching.

* Very young children with learning disabilities have typically not been identified, although they may exhibit what appears to be maturational slowness.

One of the problems with previous studies of drug effects on learning is the dosages of psychostimulants that have been administered in the great majority of studies (and in *all* long-term studies) have been considerably higher than the doses shown to maximize cognitive improvement. . . . Teacher ratings show greatest improvement with high doses of medication, with the result that the children in these studies have received mean doses of stimulants that improve *social behavior* but are 50% to 400% higher, than the dose . . . recommended as the maximum to improve *cognitive abilities*. (pp. 15–16)

Some professionals have seriously questioned the use of medication in light of the available evidence on its effectiveness (Pelham, 1986; Rosenberg, 1987). There has also been concern about side effects of the medication as well as possible abuse (Levy, 1989; Weiss & Hechtman, 1986). The physical side effects of using stimulant medication include insomnia, irritability, decreased appetite, and headaches. These side effects seem to be relatively minor

Tips for School Personnel

◆ Encourage individual athletic activities (e.g., swimming) rather than competitive team sports.
◆ Involve the child in appropriate school activities (e.g., chorus or music) where interests are apparent.
◆ Develop programs of peer tutoring, where older students may assist with children who are having difficulty.

Tips for Neighbors and Friends

◆ Learn about advocacy or other groups that can help you learn about and interact with the child with learning disabilities.
◆ Maintain a relationship with the child's parents, talking with them if and when they feel comfortable doing so.
◆ As a friend, encourage parents to seek special assistance from agencies that might provide services such as talking books.
◆ If you are interested as a friend, volunteer to assist the child's parents in whatever form they may need or even volunteer to work with the child as a tutor.

SECONDARY/TRANSITION YEARS

Tips for the Family

◆ Provide extra support for your child in the family setting, encouraging good school performance despite academic problems that may be occurring.
◆ Encourage your child to talk about and think about future plans as he or she progresses into and through the transition from school to young adult life.
◆ Try to be understanding of the academic and social difficulties the student may encounter. Encourage impulse control if impulsiveness may be causing some of the problems.
◆ Do not shy away from the difficult task of encouraging the student to associate with peers who are success oriented rather than those who may be involved in inappropriate behavior.

Tips for the Regular Classroom Teacher

◆ Specifically teach self-recording strategies such as asking: Was I paying attention?
◆ Relate new material to knowledge the student with learning disabilities already has, drawing specific implications from familiar information.
◆ Teach the use of external memory enhancers (e.g., lists and note-taking).
◆ Encourage the use of other devices to improve class performance (e.g., tape recorders).

Tips for School Personnel

◆ Promote involvement in social activities and clubs that will enhance interpersonal interaction.
◆ Where students with learning disabilities have such interests and abilities, encourage participation in athletics or other extracurricular activities.
◆ Where interests and abilities are present, involve students in support roles to extracurricular activities (e.g., as team equipment manager).
◆ Promote the development of functional academic programs for students with learning disabilities that are combined with transitional planning and programs.

Tips for Neighbors and Friends

◆ Encourage students to seek assistance from agencies that may provide services (e.g., special newspapers, talking books, and special radio stations).
◆ Promote involvement in community activities (e.g., scouting).
◆ Encourage a positive understanding of learning disabilities by other neighbors, friends, or community agencies (e.g., enforcement officials) who may encounter these students at this stage of life.

and mostly temporary, although they vary greatly among individuals. Current thinking indicates that the successful treatment of hyperactivity requires multiple interventions, often differing greatly among individuals, and may be a lifelong undertaking (Whalen, 1987).

Academic Interventions. Academic interventions include a variety of programs, such as perceptual, cognitive, attention, spoken language, reading, writing, and mathematics treatment (Choate & Rakes, 1989; Enright, 1989; Rakes & Choate, 1989). Even within these areas, an array of instructional procedures have aimed at pinpointing specific problems. For example, as part of cognitive training, attention has focused on such instructional areas as problem solving, problem-attack strategy training, and social competence (Hamlett, Pellegrini, & Conners, 1987; la Greca, 1987; Osman, 1987). Learning disabilities involve a very heterogeneous population, as our discussions thus far has indicated. Likewise, cognitive interventions also vary; they are tailored to address specific problems and often include combinations of approaches (Whalan & Henker, 1986).

Multiple intervention approaches and programs have been developed for the specific subtypes of learning disabilities noted above, and it is not surprising that controversies have emerged in some. For example, two general approaches to intervention for perceptual disabilities are process-training programs and the behavioral approach. Each has a number of specific procedures that have variously been called *programs, techniques,* or other labels. In all cases, with children, the main purpose is to build skills that seem to be deficient so the students have a more promising potential in later school programs.

One example of building a foundation of skills for later learning is in the area of mathematics. Earlier, we noted that children with arithmetic learning difficulties may have problems with basic counting and place values. For these students, counting may be most effectively taught with manipulative objects. Repetitive experience counting buttons, marbles, or any such objects helps the student to practice counting as well as learn the basic concepts of magnitude associated with numbers. Counting more than 9 objects can help children begin to grasp rudimentary place-value concepts. In these cases, each 10 objects counted are placed separately in a group, with those remaining being counted and grouped separately. For students with learning disabilities, these activities must be quite structured.

The illustration above involves counting, as a beginning math concept, using commonly available objects. However, there are also commercially available programs involving instruction in basic math concepts. Cuisenaire Rods are a set of 291 color-coded rods for manipulative learning experiences. These rods differ in length, with the color and size systematically associated with numbers. They may be used to teach basic arithmetic processes, either with individual students or groups.

Basic computational skills (addition, subtraction, multiplication, and division) may also be taught using the Computational Arithmetic Program (Smith & Lovitt, 1982). This program was developed on the basis of the authors' research on students with learning disabilities. It also may be used with either individuals or groups. The manual includes methods for pupil placement, student performance charting and analysis, and procedures for evaluating progress.

The programs mentioned above are selected from several available that can be used effectively for students with arithmetic learning disabilities. Others include DISTAR Arithmetic (Engelmann & Carnine, 1972), KeyMath Teach and Practice (Connolly, 1985), and Corrective Mathematics Program (Engelmann & Carnine, 1982). (The Corrective Mathematics Program is mentioned here although it is designed for use with students in the third grade through adulthood.)

Rapid advances in computer technology have also found their way into teaching math skills to students with learning disabilities. Kirk and Chalfant (1984) suggested that microcomputers are particularly appealing for teaching math to these students because the fundamental structure of the content can be sequenced and programed to present systematic instruction. Computers also have an advantage in that they provide a great deal of drill and practice on an individualized basis, something that is often difficult for teaching staff to accomplish with several children present, each adding to instructional responsibilities in different ways. Kirk and Chalfant (1984) pointed out that "the computer capability to present forms, objects, number problems, and word problems and to reinforce the student visually in a highly prescriptive, systematic fashion may replace many of the instructional methods used today" (p. 253).

These points are well taken and do provide an effective means of instruction for some students with learning disabilities. One limitation, however, that cannot be addressed through the use of microcomputers is the manipulation of objects for students who find this helpful. Long-term research is needed regarding the effectiveness of computer instruction to determine its most useful application for these children.

TODAY'S TECHNOLOGY

The FredWriter

Writing has long been recognized as an academic area that presents considerable difficulty for children with learning disabilities. Advances in educational applications of technology, especially the development of new computer software, have potential for assisting children with problems such as writing. An example of such software is FredWriter, a word-processing program that has a special writing feature that is particularly useful for children with learning disabilities. This feature, known as *prompted writing,* provides cues or hints to the user regarding what to do. Teachers can use FredWriter and prepare a prompted script to help a student with learning disabilities work through a piece of written composition. Because the prompts can be individualized for each student, this software provides a very powerful tool for personalizing instruction through technology. FredWriter is a program that is in the public domain, which means it is available without charge to educators needing this type of instructional tool. It is currently available for the Apple family of computers.

Reading has been recognized for many years as a serious problem for students with learning disabilities, as indicated earlier. Consequently, this area of instruction has received a great deal of attention, and many different procedures have been used. Each has had some success with certain children but not with all, emphasizing the current belief that many different disabilities are involved even in students experiencing problems in the same area. Instructionally oriented research on specific types of problems, such as the inability to use context to determine meaning, has resulted in significant improvements for students with learning disabilities (e.g., Wong & Sawatsky, 1984). Information based on research like this is being incorporated into instructional programs more than ever before. Combined with the realization that we face many specific disabilities requiring focused instruction—that is, one approach does not fit all students—the instructional picture for students with learning disabilities appears promising.

Developmental reading instruction programs are often successful for students with learning disabilities (Lerner, 1985) and typically use the approach of introducing controlled sight vocabulary with an analytic phonics emphasis. Perhaps the most widely used developmental approaches involve basal readers such as the Holt Basic Reading; Ginn 720 Series; Scott, Foresman Reading; and Macmillan Series E. Basal readers are most useful for group instruction (often designed for three levels), are well sequenced developmentally, and most have sufficient detail for use by relatively inexperienced teachers. They tend to be oriented toward group instruction and therefore may present some limitations for students with learning disabilities who need heavy doses of specific individual attention.

Individualized reading instruction is often required for a student with serious reading disabilities. Such individualization may be accomplished with many different materials (e.g., trade books), which are typically selected for reading levels and topics of high interest to the students. The basis for individualization falls on the shoulders of the teacher, who needs to have considerable knowledge of reading skills and procedures for specific, individually tailored instruction. Effective individualized instruction also requires a high level of progress evaluation, ongoing monitoring, and detailed record keeping. Individualized reading instruction seldom comes in a package (even when a publisher claims it), although most materials can be used in an individualized manner. The teacher's training, skills, and knowledge of effective individualized teaching must be applied in a flexible manner based on student needs.

Specific skill–oriented reading instruction may also be found in several diagnostic-prescriptive programs commercially available, such as the Fountain Valley Reading Support System available from Zweig and Associates and the Ransom Program from Addison-Wesley. There are also diagnostic-prescriptive reading programs that use computer-assisted instruction, such as the Harcourt Brace CAI Remedial Reading Program and the Stanford University CAI Project. Diagnostic-prescriptive reading programs provide for individualization in that the students work at their own pace. However, because they are packaged, commercially available materials, the skills that can be taught are only those that lend themselves to the format used. This reduces, to a degree, the level of individualization, but these programs do not require the high level of teacher knowledge and skill described above for the totally individualized reading instruction. Diagnostic-prescriptive programs generally provide ongoing assessment and feedback, and developmental skills are usually well sequenced.

Many approaches and programs are available for reading instruction beyond those mentioned above, each with strengths and limitations for students with learning disabilities. Other developmentally based approaches include synthetic phonics basals, linguistic phonemic programs, and language experience approaches. In addition, some procedures use multisensory techniques such as Fernald's method, developed initially in 1943 and recently revised by Idol (1988). Selection of an appropriate method and proper application of instructional technique is most effective when a student's particular disability and needs are addressed.

Computer software for use in reading instruction presents some potential assistance for students with learning disabilities and will likely be more commonly seen in the future. For these students, computer-presented reading instruction offers some particular advantages. Individual instruction can be provided to a student, and the computer provides for never-ending drill and practice. Programs can also provide feedback combined with corrective instruction. As more experience is gained in writing computer programs, reading instruction software will improve (currently, word recognition programs seem to be of a higher quality than comprehension software) and become more widely available (Lindsey, 1987).

As children progress into the upper-elementary grades, they may also need to be taught some compensatory skills or methods to circumvent deficit areas that have not been remedied. These interventions may involve tutoring by an outside agency or individual specializing in the problem, or they may mean placement in a resource room or even a self-contained class for students with learning disabilities. Each approach reflects the severity of the difficulty, area of deficiency, and, unfortunately, the resources and attitudes of those involved (e.g., families and school districts).

Behavioral Interventions.   Distinctions between behavioral and instructional interventions are not always sharp and definitive. Both involve learning skills and changing behavior. Behavioral treatments, however, generally use the most basic principles of learning, the pointed use of stimuli or stimulus conditions and manipulation of the consequences of behavior, such as reinforcement. Behavioral interventions such as the structured presentation of stimuli (e.g., letters or words) and reinforcement for correct responses (e.g., specific praise) are used in many instructional interventions, including several mentioned earlier. In this section, we briefly discuss some behavioral treatments that are used outside of traditional academic areas.

With certain children, treatment may include social skills that are causing difficulty. Some students with learning disabilities who experience repeated academic failure become frustrated and depressed despite trying so hard. They may not understand why their classmates who are not disabled seem to do little more than they do yet achieve more success.

These students may show extreme withdrawal or express frustration and anxiety by acting out or becoming aggressive. When this type of behavior emerges, it may be difficult to distinguish these students with learning difficulties from those with behavior disorders as a primary disability. In fact, at this point, there is an overlap between these student groups with regard to many behaviors. Social and behavioral difficulties of students with learning disabilities are receiving increasing attention in the literature (e.g., Deshler & Schumaker, 1983).

One type of intervention often used to change undesirable behavior is the **behavioral contract.** Using this approach, a teacher or behavioral therapist establishes a contract with the child that provides him or her with reinforcement if appropriate behavior is exhibited. Such contracts may be either written or verbal, usually focus on some specific behavior (e.g., remaining in his or her seat for a given period of time), and rewards the child with something that he or she really likes and therefore considers reinforcing (e.g., going to the library or using the class computer). It is important that the pupil understand clearly what is expected and that the event or consequence be appealing to *that child* so that it really does reinforce the appropriate behavior. Behavioral contracts have considerable appeal because they give students a certain amount of responsibility for their own behavior (Brown, 1986). They can also be used effectively outside of school settings, including by parents at home. Contracts also have applications in various forms at widely different ages.

Another behavioral intervention involves what is known as a **token–reinforcement system.** Token-reinforcement systems arrange conditions in a manner where the students can earn tokens for appropriate behavior, which can then be exchanged for something that is of value to them (something rewarding, as noted above). Token systems resemble the work-for-pay lives that most adults have, and so that approximation of life can also teach the child skills that are generalizable later. Token systems require considerable time and effort to plan and implement (Morris, 1985), but they can be used effectively to improve behavior.

Behavioral interventions are based on the fundamental principles of learning and largely developed from the early work of experimental psychologists such as Skinner (1953; 1957; 1971). These principles have been widely applied in many settings for students with learning disabilities as well as other exceptionalities. One of their significant strengths is that, given knowledge of the basic theory, behavioral interventions can be modified to suit a wide variety of needs and circumstances.

One factor that must be considered for all interventions is the age of the person being treated. In this section, we have discussed interventions that may be used during childhood. Obviously, childhood covers a broad age span. The exact elements (content or specific approach) of an appropriate intervention for a child of 6 are not likely to be useful for one who is 12 years old. Age-appropriate modifications are essential to the effectiveness of any treatment and most often must be made by the professional involved in the intervention.

Interventions in Adolescence

Medical Interventions. Intervention for adolescents with learning disabilities is somewhat different than that with children. If adolescents are receiving medication to control hyperactivity or other problems, it is likely that they have been taking it for a number of years, since many physician assessments and prescriptions are made during childhood. There are, however, a number of cases in which youth and adults with learning disabilities have struggled through the earlier years and have not received medication until after childhood. In many cases, the medication to assist with behavior and attentional problems is again one in the amphetamine family (Coons, Klorman, & Borgstedt, 1987). Adolescents with learning

FOCUS 8

How are the interventions used for adolescents with learning disabilities different from those employed with children?

disabilities may have social-behavior deficits somewhat similar to those exhibited by juvenile delinquents (Fleener, 1987; Perlmutter, 1987).

Instructional Interventions. Instructional/academic interventions are also different with adolescents than with younger individuals. Research suggests that the instructional system fails adolescents with learning disabilities. Forty-seven percent drop out of school by the age of 16 (Gartner & Lipsky, 1989) and do not receive diplomas. If the goal of secondary education is to prepare individuals for postschool lives and careers, there is serious doubt that this goal is being accomplished for youth with learning disabilities. Not only do these young people still need to achieve at least minimal survival-skills academically (for some, preparation for college), but they are also often deficient socially, without comfortable interpersonal relationships. Clearly, a comprehensive model, with a variety of components, needs to be developed to address a broad spectrum of needs for adolescents with learning disabilities.

Deshler, Schumaker, and Lenz (1984) discussed such a model and suggested seven components that specifically emphasize (1) motivation, (2) detailed, specific instruction targeting academic and cognitive skills, (3) generalization of mastered skills to other content areas and settings, (4) content to be mastered, (5) communication enabling a coordinated service to the student from various professionals, (6) transition from secondary school to postschool life, and (7) evaluation to obtain intervention feedback (p. 109). Such a comprehensive model program, however, rests primarily in the literature as a recommendation; it remains to be developed or implemented on a widespread basis. To this list, we would add instruction and experiences in socially related areas that are relevant to young people just entering adulthood—information seldom taught but essential to a successful and happy adult life.

One of the continual difficulties that faces teachers of adolescents with learning disabilities is *time*. A limited amount of time is available for instruction for youth, progress is often slow, and determining what to focus on is difficult (Deshler, Schumaker, Lenz, & Ellis, 1984). These adolescents and their teachers face a difficult task. In some areas, the students may not have progressed beyond the fifth grade academically (Warner, Schumaker, Alley, & Deshler, 1980), and they may have only a rudimentary grasp of some academic topics. Yet they are reaching an age where life after secondary school must be addressed. This may mean college plans, which is happening with increasing frequency, vocational goals, and preparations for social and interpersonal life beyond childhood. Thus, at a time when they need to be building and expanding on a firm foundation of knowledge, rather, many adolescents with learning disabilities are operating on a beginning to intermediate level.

Circumstances of deficient academic skills combined with limited instructional time have lead researchers to seek alternatives and supplements for traditional teaching of academic content to students with learning disabilities. One approach that has received considerable attention in recent years has emphasized instruction in strategies for efficient learning where the student is taught *how* to learn and solve problems. The learning-strategies approach is one where the individual is taught in a manner that essentially promotes self-instruction (Ellis & Lenz, 1987). Learning-strategies programs may involve rather complex academic content, such as writing, and are often employed in the regular classroom, as illustrated in Reflect on This 6–4.

Secondary school instruction for youth with learning disabilities may also involve compensatory skills to circumvent those not acquired earlier. These compensations are often focused on specific deficits, such as writing, listening, and social behaviors. For example, tape recorders may be used in class to offset difficulties in taking notes during lectures, which would compensate for a listening (auditory input) problem.

R
E
F
L
E
C
T

O
N

T
H
I
S

6–4   Write, P.L.E.A.S.E.: A Learning
Strategy for Students
Who Have Learning Disabilities

Using a bologna sandwich to teach writing skills may seem a bit strange, but it serves a definite purpose. It camouflages the academic overtones of a video-assisted learning-strategies program that has been successfully employed with typical students, low-efficiency learners who do not qualify for special education, and students with learning disabilities. Write P.L.E.A.S.E. provides students with an easily remembered strategy for planning and executing their written compositions using the mnemonic cues of the title, as follows:

Pick—Students pick the topic, audience, and appropriate textual format in view of the topic and audience.

List—Students list information about the topic to be used in generating sentences.

Evaluate—Students evaluate their list and other elements of their writing as they proceed.

Activate—Students activate their paragraph with a topic sentence.

Supply—Students supply supporting sentences, moving from their topic sentence and drawing on their list of ideas.

End—Students end with a concluding sentence and evaluate.

Combining mnemonics and the sandwich visual metaphor have given students a means of remembering important elements of writing paragraphs. This is a uniquely presented learning strategy that is effective in the regular classroom.

———

Source: Welch & Jensen, 1991.

For some individuals, residual or accompanying personal problems related to their disabilities require counseling or other mental health assistance. Adolescents with learning disabilities tend to have low social status among nearly all the people around them, including peers, teachers, and even parents (Dudley-Marling & Edmiaston, 1985). Certain youth with learning disabilities may also become involved in criminal activities at this time in their lives (Fleener, 1987; Perlmutter, 1987). Despite this fact, which is mentioned periodically in the literature, the empirical link between learning disabilities and juvenile delinquency is inconclusive (Wallander, 1988). Evidence has suggested that arrests of and jail terms for individuals with learning disabilities do not occur at substantially higher rates than for nondisabled peers (McLoughlin, Clark, Mauck, & Petrosko, 1987; White, Deshler, Schumaker, Warner, Alley, & Clark, 1983).

Transitional Interventions. In many cases, adolescents as well as adults with learning disabilities have accomplished adaptation by themselves over the years. However, the difficulties that youth with learning disabilities experience do not disappear, and specialized services are often needed through adolescence, perhaps into adulthood (Kramer, 1986; McCue, Shelly, & Goldstein, 1986). Unfortunately, transition services remain rather sparse for this population on a widespread basis, but they are beginning to receive increased emphasis as interest in adolescence becomes greater. Both research and personnel preparation efforts are now being undertaken on a level that would not have been predicted a few years ago.

Transition programs for adolescents with learning disabilities must basically consider similar life goals as would be relevant for adolescents who are not disabled. Some students view their postsecondary schoolyears as involving employment that does not require further education in a college setting. A portion of these pupils continue their schooling in vocational and trade schools (Stanford Research Institute, 1989). Growing numbers of young people with learning disabilities have definite college or university plans. There is little question that they will encounter difficulties (Vogel, 1982). However, with as much academic mastery as possible, compensatory skills where needed, and perseverance, college education is certainly possible.

College-bound students with learning disabilities find that many of their specific deficit areas are basic survival skills in higher education. Matters such as taking notes during lectures, absorbing lecture information auditorially, written language skills, reading, and study habits are all assumed in normal college classrooms. Transition programs preparing students with learning disabilities must elevate their abilities in these areas as much as possible and show the students how to compensate, as well. Tape recorders may circumvent difficulties in lectures because the student need not receive all the information from notes or auditorially, at least not quickly, *during* the lecture. Taped lectures can be played and replayed many times to help the student understand the information. Students with reading disabilities often obtain the help of readers, who tape textbooks for their use in much the same manner as others tape lectures.

Perhaps the most helpful survival skill that can be taught to youth with learning disabilities is actually more than a specific skill—it is a way of thinking about survival. Recall Deborah, the graduate student in Window 6–1. Deborah describes an amazing array of techniques that she uses to acquire knowledge while circumventing her specific deficit areas. No list of detailed suggestions like those in the last paragraph can cover all possible situations when a college student with learning disabilities will need special assistance. Transition programs preparing these students for college will be most effective if, in addition to suggestions, they can teach a survival attitude or way of thinking about how to compensate for severe deficit areas.

As part of survival skills, students with learning disabilities should also be taught how to establish an interpersonal network of helpers and advocates. In many cases, a faculty member advocate is more successful than the student in asking a colleague to allow for special testing arrangements or other consideration (at least for the first time). Faculty in higher education are bombarded with student complaints and requests, most of which are not based on extreme needs. They are, therefore, wary of students' requests for considerations like extra time. Additionally, many faculty in higher education are uninformed about learning disabilities and thus to receive the initial overtures from a faculty colleague carries more credibility.

Students with learning disabilities can lead productive even distinguished adult lives. Some research has shown that, even after they complete a college education, adults with learning disabilities have limited career choices (Gottfredson, Finucci, & Childs, 1984). A more complete research base is needed in this area. However, we do know that learning disabilities are reported to have plagued notable people like Thomas Edison (scientist and inventor), Woodrow Wilson (President of the United States), Albert Einstein (scientist), and Nelson Rockefeller (Governor of New York and Vice President of the United States). We also know that Deborah graduated with her master's degree and that the young man whose writing we saw in Figure 6–2 did become a successful architect. Such achievements are not accomplished without considerable work, but the outlook for students with learning disabilities can be very promising.

Debate Forum

.... **Is Medication an Appropriately Used Treatment for Children with Learning Disabilities?** ....

There has been growing concern about the use of medication, particularly psychostimulants, to treat students with learning disabilities. For some children, there is no question about the utility of medication for treating problems associated with learning disabilities. Some professionals, however, have seriously questioned the administration of medication as currently practiced.

Point   Several points must be raised regarding the administration of medication to children with learning disabilities. The use of medication for treating learning disabilities and ADHD is very widespread and probably overprescribed. Some estimates place the number of children receiving psychostimulant treatment near 1 million. In the context of such wide usage, a basic concern is raised about how little we actually know regarding dosage and effectiveness. Doses showing improvement in social behavior may range from 50 percent to 400 percent above that recommended as a maximum to improve cognitive abilities. It is unsettling that we know so little about a treatment that is so widely employed.

Counterpoint   For some children with learning disabilities and ADHD, using medication is the only approach that will bring their hyperactivity under control and thereby allow effective instruction to occur. Without such treatment, stu-

dents will be unable to attend to their academic work and will be so disruptive in classroom situations that other students will not be effectively taught. Side effects such as insomnia, irritability, decreased appetite, and others are relatively minor and temporary for the most part. Research has suggested that a substantial proportion of those children receiving medication show an improvement in behavior according to their teacher's judgment.

REVIEW

FOCUS 1   Identify four reasons why definitions of learning disabilities have varied.

◆ *Learning disabilities* is a broad, generic term that involves many different specific types of problems.

◆ The study of learning disabilities has been undertaken by a variety of different disciplines.

◆ The field of learning disabilities per se has existed for only a relatively short period of time and is therefore relatively immature with respect to conceptual development and terminology.

◆ The field of learning disabilities has grown at a very rapid pace.

FOCUS 2   Identify two ways in which people with learning disabilities can be classified.

◆ Whether a child achieves commensurate with his or her age and ability when provided with appropriate educational experiences

◆ Historically, as a mild disorder but with increasing attention to varying severity

FOCUS 3   Identify two estimate ranges for the prevalence of learning disabilities.

◆ From 1 to 28 percent, depending on the source.

◆ From 5 to 10 percent is a reasonable current estimate.

FOCUS 4   Identify seven characteristics attributed to those with learning disabilities, and explain why it is difficult to characterize this group.

◆ Typically, average or near-average intelligence

◆ Uneven skill levels in various areas

◆ Hyperactivity

◆ Perceptual problems

◆ Visual and auditory discrimination problems

◆ Cognition deficits, such as memory

◆ Attention problems

◆ In other words, the group of individuals included under the umbrella term *learning disabilities* is so varied that it defies simple characterization with a single concept or term

FOCUS 5   Identify four causes thought to be involved in learning disabilities.

◆ Neurological damage or malfunction

◆ Maturational delay of the neurological system

◆ Genetic abnormality

◆ Environmental factors

FOCUS 6   Identify four questions that are addressed by screening assessment in learning disabilities.

◆ Is there reason to investigate the abilities of the child more fully?

◆ Is there reason to suspect that the child is disabled in any way?

◆ If the child appears disabled, what are the characteristics and how should we move to intervention?

◆ How should we plan for the future of the individual?

FOCUS 7   Identify three types of intervention or treatment employed with people diagnosed as having learning disabilities.

◆ Medical interventions, in some circumstances involving medication to control hyperactivity

◆ Academic interventions in a wide variety of areas that are specifically aimed at building particular skill areas

◆ Behavioral interventions aimed at improving social skills or remediating problems in this area; behavioral procedures may also be a part of academic instruction

FOCUS 8   How are the interventions used for adolescents with learning disabilities different from those employed with children?

◆ Interventions with children focus primarily on building the most basic skills

◆ Interventions during adolescence may include skill building but also involve assistance in compensatory skills that permit circumvention of deficit areas

◆ Interventions during adolescence should include instruction and assistance in transition skills that will prepare students for adulthood, employment, and further education, based on their own goals

Chapter Seven
Cross-Categorical Perspectives

TO BEGIN WITH . . .

◆ "The labeling system that serves as the entry point for any child receiving special education focuses precisely on identification of *reasons why children can't learn, reasons that are enduring within the child and relatively unchangeable.* Indeed special educators who assume that we've done very well with our categorizing system and need not change it in order to meet present and future needs run the risk of being . . . excluded from the very real and exciting school reform efforts currently underway in this country" (Lilly, 1992, p. 90).

◆ "The classification of children into specific categories, such as learning disabilities, mental retardation, or emotional disturbance, may not be justified. There does not appear to be a relationship between these categories and the instructional needs of each individual student. An example of this is the classification of learning disabilities, described by some professionals as ill-defined and poorly conceptualized. Yet the term is used to describe a vast number of children who are unsuccessful in school" (Goldman & Gardner, 1989).

◆ "Dissatisfaction with current special education labels and diagnostic procedures is quite understandable and appropriate. Calls for improvement in classification and identification systems certainly are warranted and timely—calls for eliminating all classification and identification are premature" (Adelman, 1992, p. 99).

MARILYN

MARILYN. Marilyn is 9 years old and in her second month of fourth grade at Willowbrook Elementary School. Her classroom teacher describes her as a slow learner and a poorly motivated student. Marilyn in unable to cope with the behavioral and academic requirements of the classroom without assistance beyond that required by the other students. She has a reading vocabulary that is beginning-third-grade level and consistently struggles with reading-comprehension activities. In math, she is still attempting to master basic subtraction facts but is proficient in number identification and single-digit addition.

Marilyn has communicated to her parents and teacher the frustrations she encounters at school. She sees school as a negative aspect of her life. Her teacher confirms this negative attitude and reports that Marilyn has difficulty completing assigned tasks and is often reprimanded for daydreaming or visiting with classmates at inappropriate times.

Marilyn was recently referred to the school psychologist for an analysis of her educational skills. A standardized test battery indicated that Marilyn is functioning below the average on an individual test of intelligence (IQ 83); achievement test scores range from the end-of-second-grade level in reading to second grade, first month, in math; and language expression and reception are below the average for students in her classroom.

JARED. Jared is a very disruptive student who has been referred numerous times to a variety of public school and community agencies. From the time he was in second grade until he reached fifth grade, he was in constant trouble, not only with his parents but also with his teachers and neighbors. A review of his school history shows that he has been described as obnoxious, a "holy terror," and downright sneaky. In terms of his academic performance, he has not done well either. He is considerably below the level of his classmates in all subjects except art and physical education. In creative activities, particularly artwork, he does extremely well.

Jared's most obvious problem is his behavior. He is extremely noncompliant. He does things when he feels like doing them, regardless of setting or rules. He has had few if any close friends. He has regularly been involved in fights and teasing. His regular classroom teachers have used all available resources and personnel to assist Jared and his family in dealing with their problem, but these efforts have been to no avail. His misbehavior has not been limited solely to school environments. Children in his neighborhood avoid him, and his family has a difficult time relating to him.

During the middle of Jared's elementary school years, his mother and father were divorced. Jared's father maintained custody of the children (two younger sisters and Jared). Within a year, Jared's father remarried. His new mother made sincere attempts to become Jared's friend, but that friendship never materialized to any significant degree. Over time, Jared and his stepmother became bitter enemies. With the demise of his family relationships and lack of any substantive success in school, his already dismal school record became worse. He was eventually referred at the beginning of the fifth grade for placement in a self-contained class for students with behavior disorders. The placement was finalized during the seventh week of school. Jared now regularly attends this class.

KEVIN. Kevin is 14 years old and attends school at Eastmount Junior High. He does not speak, walk, hear, or see. Throughout the day, his classroom support team works diligently to meet Kevin's most basic needs, including eating and toileting. In spite of his profound and multiple disabling conditions, Kevin has learned to express himself through a communication board, is able to maneuver through his environment in a wheelchair, and is learning to feed himself independently. Kevin lives at home with his family. He participates in all family activities, including shopping at the local mall, eating at a fast-food restaurant, relaxing on the lawn in the neighborhood park, and playing miniature golf at the community recreation center.

INTRODUCTION

Marilyn is a student with a **mild learning and behavior disability** (see Window 7–1). She has remained in the regular classroom environment, with no additional educational services, since she was 6 years old. While Marilyn's academic and behavioral performance in the classroom deviates enough to require some additional instruction beyond that given to her classmates, it is anticipated that, once these services are available, she can remain in the regular classroom. The problems of children with mild learning and behavior disabilities are most evident in school; they have less difficulty adjusting to life outside the classroom setting. Consequently, as these individuals move into adulthood, the learning- and behavior-disabled classification is usually no longer applicable if adequate special services have been provided during the school years.

Jared is a student with a **moderate learning and behavior disability.** His behavior problems occur not only in a school setting but also at home and within his neighborhood. He and his family need additional help beyond educational services, including ongoing counseling provided by the local mental health agency. With considerable effort on the part of teachers, support services, and family, Jared may be back in the regular class in the next school year.

Kevin is an individual with **severe and profound/multiple disabilities.** In one way or another, he will be dependent on others throughout his life. Marilyn, Jared, and Kevin are certainly not representative of all individuals with learning and behavior disabilities, but they are representative of the range of problems experienced by this population.

The previous three chapters discussed learning and behavior disabilities using the traditional **categorical descriptors** of mental retardation, behavior disorders, and learning disabilities. In this chapter, we view individuals with learning and behavior disabilities from the perspective of **cross-categorical definitions** and intervention strategies. Our purpose is to familiarize you with an alternative approach to traditional categorical labels.

CATEGORICAL AND CROSS-CATEGORICAL APPROACHES

Presently, the most common way to classify students for special education services is the traditional categorical approach, in which students are divided into discrete groups based on individual characteristics. Ten separate categories of students with disabilities are recognized in the Individuals with Disabilities Education Act (IDEA). Of these 10 categories, students classified as learning disabled, emotionally disturbed (behavior disorders), and mentally retarded constitute more than 70 percent of all students eligible for special education services in the United States (U.S. Department of Education, 1991).

Proponents for maintaining separate categories in the areas of learning disabilities, behavior disorders, and mental retardation argue that student characteristics are unique to each of the three categories. For example, students with behavior disorders have different characteristics and instructional needs than those with learning disabilities or mental retardation. According to the categorical approach, grouping all these students under one single label will not be functional in terms of meeting their educational needs (Braaten, Kauffman, Braaten, Polsgrove, & Nelson, 1988; Bryan, Bay, Lopez-Reyna, & Donahue, 1991).

While some professionals support the traditional categorical approach, others argue that such classification prohibits clearly defining or adequately differentiating the needs of these students in a classroom setting (Gottlieb, Alter, & Gottlieb, 1991; Jenkins, Pious, & Peterson, 1988; Lilly, 1992; Reynolds, 1991; Reynolds & Birch, 1988; Wang, 1989). Jenkins et al. (1988)

FOCUS 1

Why is the cross-categorical approach considered an alternative way of defining and classifying individuals with learning and behavior disabilities?

concluded, "We can see no justification for separating students by categorical labels" (p. 157). Reynolds (1991) indicated that the traditional approach to categorization results in unnecessary separation of students and "represents a large and expensive error" (p. 31).

Categorical and cross-categorical approaches represent alternative ways of defining and classifying individuals with learning and behavior disabilities. While both approaches are useful in certain instances, neither alone can adequately serve the broad range of people with learning and behavior disabilities. The use of categorical and cross-categorical approaches in defining and classifying learning and behavior disabilities is an issue that has gained considerable attention in the field of education in recent years (Adelman, 1992; Gartner & Lipsky, 1987, 1989; Kauffman & Pullen, 1989; Lilly, 1992; Lipsky & Gartner, 1991; Marston, 1987; Reynolds, 1991; Reynolds, Wang, & Walberg, 1987).

While more and more professionals have attempted to break away from the traditional categories, their efforts have met with limited success. Some so-called new approaches have represented little more than semantic exercises using different terms but maintaining the traditional categorical framework. Other approaches have been dramatically different but accomplished little except to fuel a debate between advocates of cross-categorical and categorical classification systems. Serious examination is needed of the bases or parameters employed for classification as well as the circumstances under which they may be functional.

Our discussion in this chapter will focus on learning and behavior disabilities using a cross-categorical approach that is based on the severity of the student's condition. The learning and behavioral characteristics of the individual are broken down into mild, moderate, and severe and profound/multiple conditions. A mild learning and behavior disability represents the highest level of performance; a severe and profound/multiple condition represents the lowest level of performance.

MILD LEARNING AND BEHAVIOR DISABILITIES

Every educator has been confronted with students who exhibit mild learning and behavior problems. As is true of Marilyn in the opening window, the significance of such problems depends on a number of factors. First, what is the discrepancy between how the student performs on school-related tasks and what is expected? For Marilyn, her reading performance is about a year behind that of her classmates. In math, she is about two years behind peers. Her classroom teacher also describes her as a poorly motivated student. From the school's standpoint, the problem is often viewed in terms of its effect on the student's academic achievement and social adjustment, as well as any negative effect on the student's classmates, which may be evident (or anticipated).

FOCUS 2

Identify the four components of the definition of mild learning and behavior disabilities.

Definition

The framework for our discussion of mild learning and behavior disabilities is the following definition:

> Individuals with mild learning and behavior disabilities exhibit academic and/or social-interpersonal performance deficits that range from one to two standard deviations below average on **norm** and **criterion-referenced assessments.** These deficits generally become evident in a school-related setting. The cause of the performance deficits is generally unknown. A student with a mild disability remains in the regular classroom setting for the majority, if not all, of the school day. Additional support services beyond those typically offered in a regular education setting should be made available as necessary.

7–1 Everything You Ever Wanted to Know about a Standard Deviation

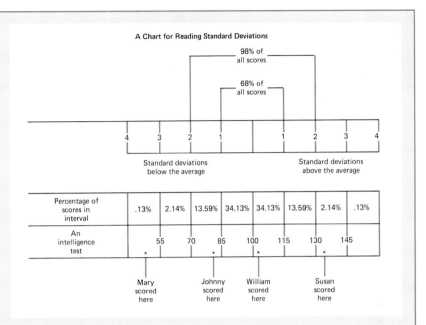

A Chart for Reading Standard Deviations

Standard deviation is a *measure* of the amount that an individual score differs from the average. Put another way, standard deviation gives us a way to measure the difference between the average score of a group of people and how well a given individual performed in comparison to that average.

Let's take, for example, an intelligence test. Questions are put together by a group of researchers that, for the sake of our discussion, measure the construct known as *intelligence*. Once the questions have been developed, this test is administered to a group of people to see how well they do on each of the questions. When all the scores are added up and divided by the number of people who have taken the exam, the average score turns out to be 100. This certainly doesn't mean that everyone scored 100; it is merely a mathematical way of establishing what is average.

When we look at individual scores on the intelligence test, we find that some people actually do score 100, whereas others score either higher or lower. Johnny, for example, has a score of 83. So just what does the score of 83 mean in comparison to the scores of the rest of the people who have taken this test?

We can now use a mathematical procedure to determine the extent to which Johnny's score differs from the average score of 100. This measurement is called a **standard deviation** from the average. Again, for the sake

of discussion, we find that, on this intelligence test, each standard deviation is about 15 points. Now, looking at the chart for reading standard deviations, we can see that, because Johnny scored 83, he is more than one standard deviation *below* the average score on the test. Mary, on the other hand, scored 50. Looking at the chart, we see that she is more than three standard deviations below the average. William scored 104 on the test, so he is less than one standard deviation *above* the average. Susan scored 134, so she is more than two standard deviations above the average.

We now know how many standard deviations each of these individuals is away from the average, but the information is still not very meaningful. Let's convert these standard deviations into percentages. The mathematical procedure used to determine a standard

deviation also reveals the *percentage* of people taking the test who score at each of the standard deviation levels. The chart reveals that Johnny's score of 83 means that he performed better than only 16 percent of all the people who took the test. In other words, 84 percent of the people taking the test had better scores than Johnny. Mary's score of 50 is better than the scores of less than 1 percent of everyone taking the test. William's score is close to the average, so he did better than 50 percent of those taking the test. Susan's score of 134 is better than about 98 percent of all the scores.

The standard deviation is simply a means of measuring percentages. Whether a test is a measure of intelligence, academic achievement, behavior, weight, height, age, or some other characteristic, the idea is the same.

This definition emphasizes the breadth of the population with learning and behavior disabilities and allows for considerable flexibility in identifying and providing educational support services. This cross-categorical definition stresses that the primary reason for identifying this population is to enhance the opportunity for success in the regular education classroom.

FIGURE 7–1

Components of the Definition of
Mild Learning and Behavior
Disabilities

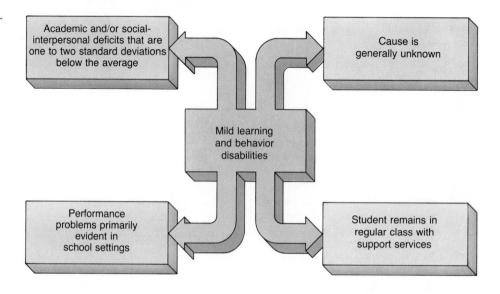

In order to deal with the variety of characteristics exhibited by these students, the definition purposely does not limit the areas for assessment. Depending on the problem that has resulted in a referral, assessment may include several measures, such as adaptive behavior, **academic achievement,** and **cognitive functioning.** This provides the professional with the flexibility of using whatever assessment tools are necessary to determine the extent of the academic or behavioral deficits and to make recommendations for educational intervention.

The definition is meant to emphasize *present* functional deficits that may well be corrected or improved through educational intervention. In the cross-categorical approach, educators must focus directly on functional descriptions of the specific problem behavior, rather than on a label that may have no specific relevance for instruction.

There are four major components in the definition of mild learning and behavior disabilities: (1) academic and/or social-interpersonal deficits are one to two standard deviations below average on normative and criterion-referenced assessments; (2) problems are primarily evident in school settings; (3) the cause of the problems is generally unknown; and (4) the student remains in the regular class and receives support services (see Figure 7–1).

The phrase *academic and/or social-interpersonal performance deficits* is necessary because such deficits are generally shared attributes of these students. It is not uncommon to find a student with a mild disability who is lower in academic ability than his nondisabled classmates and who exhibits social adjustment problems. The definition allows for the independent occurrence of an academic deficit or behavior problem, but it also suggests that, if both disabilities occur in parallel fashion, they should be included within the single definition. For example, Marilyn is unable to cope with either the academic or behavioral requirements of the classroom. We can assume that an individual functioning at this level is generally able to adapt to the social environment outside the classroom setting. Problems that do emerge are not likely to be serious enough to cause a referral on behavior alone.

The phrase *one to two standard deviations below average* specifies severity level. For example, Marilyn's IQ is 83, which is between one and two standard deviations below the mean of 100. This qualification of IQ level differs somewhat from certain trends in more traditional categories. For example, in 1973, the American Association on Mental Retardation (AAMR) moved to two standard deviations as the upper limit on IQ in defining mental retardation and essentially declassified all individuals functioning between that level and the average.

The cross-categorical approach permits individuals with mild disabilities to receive specialized services in *regular education classrooms,* but it avoids using the label *retardation,* which has such a negative connotation. Even though the AAMR has ceased viewing mental retardation as unchangeable, the general connotation of the label is one of permanence and social stigma. The cross-categorical definition emphasizes a person's functional performance, which may well be changed by specific intervention techniques.

It is our contention that the term *mild learning and behavior disabilities* is broad enough that it is unlikely to become a diagnostic term, but it can be used in a number of ways that are functional for intervention purposes. Use of this term would prompt educators to focus more directly on a functional description of the behavior than has historically been the case (labels have become diagnostic entities). For example, Marilyn is a fourth-grade student with a reading vocabulary that is beginning-third-grade level. The deficit in reading vocabulary is a functional description of Marilyn's problem that indicates the discrepancy between actual performance and what is expected for a child of her age. The categorical label placed on Marilyn might be *learning disabled,* which provides no specific information regarding her specific academic problems.

An individual's performance may be described statistically by comparing him or her with others of the same chronological age (**interindividual** differences), or the person may be described in terms of an analysis of his or her individual strengths and weaknesses (**intraindividual** differences).

An interindividual assessment is often referred to as a *norm-referenced* or *standardized* measure of student abilities because the individual is compared to a larger group for which a mean or average score has been determined. Intraindividual assessment, often referred to as *criterion-referenced* measurement, does not compare the student to other students but analyzes the individual's strengths and weaknesses. As with interindividual assessment, a mean or

Even though many learning disabilities are associated with social adjustment problems, these problems alone are not always serious enough to prompt special education referrals. (Mimi Forsyth/Monkmeyer Press)

average is determined. However, the average is calculated on several of the *individual's* performance areas (e.g., giving letter sounds, recognizing common word parts, or sound blending). Then each area of performance is compared to the individual's average, in addition to an assessment of differences between performance areas. Depending on the nature of the problem, it may be necessary to view the student on an interindividual basis, an intraindividual basis, or both. Consideration of average performance (i.e., means) does not restrict this definition by requiring the use of standardized tests in which means have been established through norms. Individual norms can be determined using behavior checklists and **precision teaching** techniques on both inter- and intraindividual bases. The basic premise of this part of the definition is that a functional analysis of the individual's performance areas will be made.

The phrase *on norm- or criterion-referenced assessments* is necessarily broad because of the variety of individual characteristics to be assessed. Depending on the problem that resulted in a referral, the assessment may occur in areas such as adaptive behavior, academic achievement, and intellectual functioning. This provides the flexibility to use norm-referenced (interindividual) instruments, criterion-referenced (intraindividual) assessments, observations, and interviews as well as systems of assessment that combine several types of measures.

In large part, the performance deficits of students with mild disabilities *become evident in school-related settings where the cause of the problem is generally unknown.* Problems may well occur in other settings, such as the home, but the most pronounced difficulties clearly relate to the structured environment of formal schooling. Certain characterizations, such as the "**six-hour retardate,**" have been made based on observations that certain youngsters appear retarded only during the six hours a day they are in school. These children, often from low-socioeconomic-level backgrounds, are labeled as retarded in the school setting, but the label does not follow them to their home and community lives. The retardation label also disappears once the student leaves school and forms an adult life. Given that the occurrence of mild learning and behavior disabilities is associated primarily with the student's educational experience, the estimated prevalence of the condition is based on services provided during the school years.

FOCUS 3

Identify the estimated prevalence and causes of mild learning and behavior disabilities.

Prevalence

Whether a student is labeled *disabled* (as defined by IDEA) depends on the level of educational intervention that is required. This decision is best handled by a multidisciplinary team responsible for determining the most appropriate educational program and environment for the student. Depending on federal and state funding patterns, this team must generally work within the parameters of the 12 percent prevalence figure established under IDEA for services to students with disabilities.

Approximately 13 percent of all school-age children will perform between one and two standard deviations below the mean, and thus be considered as having mild learning and behavior disabilities according to the definition presented in this chapter. Obviously, not all students with mild learning and behavior disabilities qualify for special education services or are eligible to be labeled under IDEA. Given the 12 percent ceiling, we estimate that about 6 percent of the school-age population qualify for IDEA funds under the description *mild learning and behavior disabilities.* An additional 7 percent need educational support services and are considered to have mild learning and behavior disabilities but do not qualify for federal money targeted for students with disabilities. These students, often described as *at risk for school failure,* are caught in the middle: They are ineligible to receive special education services but still need help that is not available in the regular education setting. (See Chapter One for a more indepth description of students at risk.)

Causation

The causes of mild learning and behavior disabilities are largely unknown. Because so many factors can interact and contribute to learning and behavior differences, it may not be possible to determine cause. We do know that individuals with mild learning and behavior disabilities are not usually characterized by physical or sensory deficits. Rather, these individuals' problems are primarily educationally related. In fact, individuals with mild learning and behavior disabilities are not easily identified as such once they are outside the educational environment. It may not be until a child enters school, often at the age of 5, that a disability is actually recognized.

Numerous causal factors have been associated with mild learning and behavior disorders, for example, diverse cultural backgrounds, socioeconomic differences, and poor teaching. Students whose cultural backgrounds are different from the dominant core culture and whose socioeconomic status is on the low end of the continuum, are more likely to be identified and labeled as at risk or disabled (Davis & McCaul, 1991).

Effective teaching practices are critical to the success of students with mild learning and behavior disabilities (Larrivee, 1986). Poor teaching may also be a primary reason for many of the school-related problems exhibited by these students. There is a need to examine more closely the way teachers are educated in university preparation programs and how effectively they apply what they have been taught (Marston, 1987). Do teachers utilize the appropriate procedures, methods, and materials necessary to ensure the maximum growth and development of their students?

Several other factors associated with mild learning and behavior disabilities include high absenteeism during the early school years and differing value systems within the home concerning the importance of school. Poor motivation and inadequate memory and retention skills have also been linked to school-related problems. The list goes on, but the issue of determining specific causality remains unresolved.

Characteristics

Individuals with mild learning and behavior disabilities share a variety of characteristics that cut across the more traditional categorical definitions. Although many special educators have attempted to preserve categorical purity, some professionals indicate that, when the child's actual performance in the classroom is examined, there is considerable overlap, particularly at the mild severity level (Gartner & Lipsky, 1987, 1989; Gottlieb et al., 1991; Jenkins et al., 1988; Reynolds, 1991; Wang, 1989).

Educators have begun to focus on the relationship among learning environment, material content, and individual learner and teacher styles rather than the differences between categorical labels. This new focus has directed attention to specific instructional approaches and away from labels. Historically, educational programing has been based more on definitional expectations according to categorical labels than the individual students' actual performance. This educational phenomenon is illustrated in Table 7–1, a comparison of expectations according to traditional categorical definitions with the actual performance of students within given categories.

There is real danger in adhering strictly to a categorical approach at the mild severity level because such an approach implies that each category is homogeneous. An examination of individuals with mild learning and behavior disabilities reveals that this is not the case. The categories of students with learning disabilities, mental retardation, and behavior disorders are generic classifications that include individuals with a variety of academic, cognitive, and adaptive behavior differences. As Laycock (1980) pointed out, "It is misleading to use the labels as though all children within the category exhibit common attributes. . . .

FOCUS 4

Identify the discrepancies between definitions of mental retardation, behavior disorders, and learning disabilities and the actual performance of children in each category.

■ **Table 7–1** Intelligence, Achievement, and Adaptive Behavior Characteristics Associated with Traditional Categories of Exceptional Students

Characteristic	Students with		
	Learning Disabilities	Behavior Disorders	Mental Retardation
INTELLIGENCE			
Definition	Student must exhibit average or above-average performance on intelligence tests.	Student must exhibit average or above-average performance on intelligence tests.	Student must exhibit significantly subaverage performance on intelligence tests; student must score at least two standard deviations below average to be considered retarded (IQ 70 or below); student who falls between one and two standard deviations below average is not considered retarded.
Actual performance	Students at all intelligence levels can experience learning disabilities.	Students at all intelligence levels can experience behavior problems.	Student performs below average on intelligence tests; student who performs below average but does not have IQ of 70 or below cannot receive special education services.

In addition to variance within categories, there is also overlap between categories. Human beings cannot be pigeon-holed as neatly as definitions would lead us to believe" (p. 53).

Students with mild learning and behavior disabilities are often defined and categorized primarily by exclusion—by what they are *not*. For example, the child with a learning disability is usually defined as one who is *not* intellectually inferior, even though children of varying intellectual functioning levels may exhibit specific learning disabilities. Additionally, students with learning disabilities do not demonstrate distinct and reliable differences from other low achievers in the educational system (Gottlieb et al., 1991; Ysseldyke, Algozzine, Shinn, & McGue, 1982).

When comparing students labeled as behavior disordered with those labeled as learning disabled, intelligence is considered a common attribute. By definition, these two categories involve individuals who have normal intelligence. The differences between behavior disorders and learning disabilities have been explained more in terms of social adjustment dif-

■ **Table 7–1** Continued

Characteristic	Students with		
	Learning Disabilities	Behavior Disorders	Mental Retardation
ACHIEVEMENT			
Definition	Discrepancy between intelligence and achievement is integral to definition; student performs at least one to two years below grade level.	Low achievement is not usually integral to definition.	Criteria associated with achievement are not generally integral to definition; however, if student performs below average on IQ test, it is expected that achievement will be below average, as well.
Actual performance	Student performs below grade level.	Student's low achievement may be secondary effect; behavior problems interfere with academic performance.	Student performs significantly below average on achievement tests.
ADAPTIVE BEHAVIOR			
Definition	Deficits are generally not included in definition.	Deficits in socialization and classroom adaptation skills are integral to definition.	Adaptive behavior is integral to definition.
Actual performance	Student deficits may be secondary effect of learning problems.	Student deficits are apparent in classroom setting.	Student exhibits poor performance relative to socialization and personal independence.

ferences and learner characteristics. However, students with learning disabilities may also exhibit secondary behavioral disorders. In addition, students with behavior disorders may have learning difficulties comparable to those exhibited by individuals defined as learning disabled.

The performance of students in the classroom also suggests that behavior problems are not specific to any one intellectual level. Students with mental retardation may behave in a manner that would be considered socially and interpersonally maladaptive (Drew, Logan, & Hardman, 1992). Problems in social adjustment must therefore be viewed as a characteristic that is shared to a considerable degree by students with learning disabilities, behavior disorders, and mental retardation.

One factor that has long been viewed as characteristic of students with learning disabilities is variability between areas of functioning. General descriptions of learning disabilities have often emphasized great intraindividual differences between skill areas. For example,

Marilyn (see Window 7–1) is a fourth-grader reading at about a third-grade level with some difficulties in comprehension. However, her skills in math are at least a full grade below her reading level and two grades below what is expected for her age. Frequently, this variability in aptitude patterns has been used to distinguish between students with learning disabilities and those with mental retardation. Typically, students thought to have retardation are expected to exhibit a rather flat or consistent profile of abilities as contrasted with the pronounced intraindividual variability associated with learning disabilities. For example, it is expected that a child with mental retardation would achieve at about the same level across all academic areas: reading, writing, and arithmetic. As with other attributes, however, intraindividual variability does not seem to be the sole domain of students with learning disabilities. Intraindividual variability often occurs in students with mental retardation and behavior disorders.

Our discussion has emphasized the considerable similarities of behavioral attributes within traditional categories. This does not negate the fact that differences exist among the traditional categories, especially in terms of overall ability, rate of learning, and attention to task. It does, however, stress that categorical labels may not be useful in developing educational programs for students with mild learning and behavior disabilities. As summarized by Reynolds and Birch (1988):

> In view of the major problems of reliability in the classification of children, it can be fairly concluded that for the present, instruction for exceptional children ought to proceed mainly on the basis of highly individualized evaluations of both children and their situations, disregarding such classification criteria as educational mentally retarded, learning disabled, and emotionally disturbed. (p. 56)

Our effort to conceptualize mild disabilities in a cross-categorical fashion requires that the traditional categories be viewed within an "umbrella" model of symptom severity (i.e., all under one classification of severity). It also requires accommodation for both the shared and discrepant behavioral characteristics of students with mild learning and behavior disabilities.

MODERATE LEARNING AND BEHAVIOR DISABILITIES

Definition

FOCUS 5

Identify the four components of the definition of moderate learning and behavior disabilities.

The definition of moderate learning and behavior disabilities is as follows:

> An individual with moderate learning or behavior disabilities exhibits intellectual, academic, and/or social interpersonal performance deficits that range between two and three standard deviations below average on norm- and criterion-referenced assessments. These performance deficits are not limited to the school setting but are typically evident in the broad spectrum of environmental settings. The causes of the problems may be identified in some cases but typically cannot be precisely determined. Individuals with functional disorders at this level require substantially altered patterns of service and treatment and may need modified environmental accommodations.

This definition presents a cross-categorical framework that is consistent with our approach to mild learning and behavior differences. The four major components of the definition of moderate learning and behavior disabilities are (1) intellectual, academic, and/or social-interpersonal deficits that range from two to three standard deviations below average; (2) performance problems beyond the school setting; (3) identifiable causes in some cases;

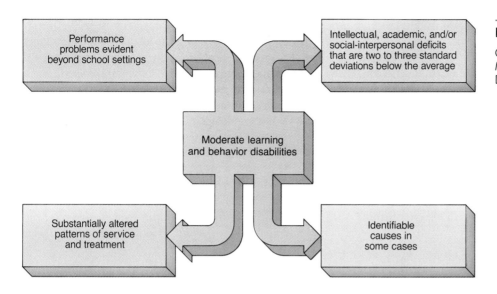

FIGURE 7–2

Components of the Definition of Moderate Learning and Behavior Disabilities

and (4) the necessity for substantially altered patterns of service and treatment (see Figure 7–2).

The phrase *intellectual, academic, and/or social-interpersonal performance deficits* focuses on problems that require a more intense level of service than that provided to students with mild disabilities. The term *intellectual* has been added to the definition because at the moderate severity level, when an intellectual deficit is involved, it is far more evident and pronounced than at the mild severity level. (Some individuals with mild learning and behavior disabilities may exhibit learning or achievement difficulties that suggest intellectual deficits, but the deviations in measured intelligence are not sufficient to be considered a primary problem.)

The term *academic and social-interpersonal performance* was also used in the definition of mild disabilities. In defining *moderate* disabilities, such performance will be different in terms

Children from the low-level end of the socio-economic group are more likely to be identified as having learning and behavior disorders. (C. Vergara/Photo Researchers, Inc.)

of severity and the environment in which a problem may be apparent. Namely, the difficulties that characterize moderate disabilities are evident in a broader range of environments than in the case of mild disabilities. Performance problems may be exhibited in more than one area of functioning. Individuals with moderate disabilities exhibit multiple performance deficits that are more frequent and serious than at the mild severity level. However, the primary disabling condition is more easily identified than with a mild disability. Additionally, causes for some of the conditions may be identifiable at this level of severity.

FOCUS 6

Identify the estimated prevalence and causes of moderate learning and behavior disabilities.

Prevalence

Approximately 2 percent of all school-age individuals exhibit moderate learning and behavior disabilities. This prevalence figure is based on our definition of moderate disorders, which indicates that the performance deficits for these individuals range between two and three standard deviations below interindividual or intraindividual means on any given assessment.

FOCUS 7

Why are many children with moderate learning and behavior disabilities not identified as such until they reach school age?

Causation

The causes of moderate learning and behavior disabilities include the same factors associated with mental retardation, behavior disorders, and learning disabilities. Causal factors may range from socioeconomic differences, poor motivation or achievement orientation, and inadequate memory and retention to identifiable neurological dysfunction, genetic or metabolic error, drug or alcohol abuse, poor maternal nutrition, and infectious disease. The specific cause of the disability is often unknown or unidentifiable.

Characteristics

The primary distinguishing characteristics associated with the traditional categories of mental retardation, behavior disorders, and learning disabilities become more distinct at the moderate level of severity. It is true that many people with moderate learning disabilities also manifest behavior problems and vice versa, but in many cases of moderate disabilities, we can assess which is the primary difficulty and which is the secondary one. This is not as

Children with moderate disorders may go undetected until they enter school, and at which time their developmental lags become more apparent. (Brent Jones)

easily accomplished with those who are described as having a mild learning and behavior disability.

Many children with moderate learning and behavior disabilities are not identified until they enter school at the age of 5 or 6. This is because these children may not exhibit severe physical anomalies that are readily identifiable during the early childhood years. Nevertheless, the preschool child with a moderate disability exhibits one- or two-year delays, particularly in the development of socialization skills and academic readiness. As the child enters school, these developmental lags become more apparent in the classroom environment. During the first one or two years in school, the child's intellectual, academic, and/or social differences may be attributed to immaturity. However, school professionals will eventually realize the need for specialized interventions beyond the regular class. Unfortunately, valuable instruction time may be lost by not intervening when the problem is first suspected. (For a more indepth discussion of the characteristics of these individuals according to the traditional categorical areas of mental retardation, behavior disorders, and learning disabilities, see the "Characteristics" sections of Chapters Four, Five, and Six.)

SEVERE AND PROFOUND/MULTIPLE DISABILITIES

Individuals with severe and profound/multiple disabilities may be impaired in nearly every facet of life. Some of these people have severe intellectual, learning, and behavior disorders; others are physically disabled or sensory impaired. Most have significant, multiple problems. Recall that Kevin, from the opening window, cannot speak, walk, hear, or see.

The needs of these people cannot be met by one profession. The nature of their disabilities extends equally into the fields of medicine, psychology, and social services. Since these individuals present such diverse characteristics and require the attention of several professions, it is not surprising that numerous definitions and intervention strategies have been employed to describe and treat them.

In addition to mental retardation, people with severe and profound disorders may also exhibit problems such as poor muscle tone, epilepsy, and vision and hearing disorders. (Will & Deni McIntyre/Photo Researchers, Inc.)

Definition

Our cross-categorical definition of severe and profound/multiple disabilities is as follows:

Individuals with severe and profound/multiple disabilities exhibit physical, sensory, intellectual, and/or social-interpersonal performance deficits that range beyond three standard deviations below average on norm- and criterion-referenced assessments. These deficits are not limited to any given setting but are evident in all environmental settings and often involve deficits in several areas of performance. Causes are more likely to be identifiable at this level of functioning, but exact causes may be unknown in a number of cases. Individuals with functional disabilities at this level will require substantially altered patterns of service and treatment and will require modified environmental accommodations.

The four major components of this definition are (1) physical, sensory, intellectual, and/or social-interpersonal deficits more than three standard deviations below average; (2) deficits evident in all environmental settings and across several areas of performance; (3) identifiable causes in some cases; and (4) substantially altered patterns of service and treatment (see Figure 7–3).

In comparison to previous definitions of mild and moderate disabilities, the severity of the disabling condition has increased, moving to *beyond three standard deviations below average on the measures being recorded.* The definition continues to focus on the *disability* and carefully avoids labeling it a *handicap.* The reason for this is that the two terms are not synonymous. For example, a person may have a severe visual disability (i.e., blindness) but not be handicapped because of accommodations in the environment, special mobility training, and special instructional technology. Kevin has multiple disabilities, including the inability to communicate verbally (see Window 7–1). However, through the technology of a communication board, he is able to express himself to others. Thus, in certain circumstances, a disability may be severe, but its impact on the individual may be less pronounced.

The term *multiple* is used to describe this category of disabilities because the vast majority of persons with severe and profound disabilities exhibit a number of problems, including a

FIGURE 7–3

Components of the Definition of Severe and Profound/Multiple Disabilities.

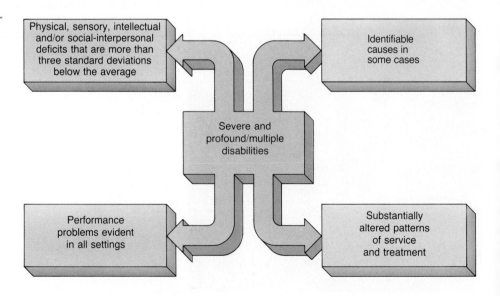

R
E
F
L
E
C
T

O
N

T
H
I
S

7–2

Definitions Tell Us Very
Little about People
with Severe Disabilities

If you have a severe disability, the very first thing that others would most likely be told about you would be a summary of your "deficits." Chances are, whatever you were, there would be a file containing a lengthy description of your intellectual shortcomings, your physical impairments, and your behavior problems. Even the most rudimentary personal information included on a driver's license—your eye color, hair color, height, and weight—remain a mystery throughout hundreds of pages of written records.

Nowhere would someone learn that you had a lovely smile, a strong sense of identity, and a family that cared about you. Instead, we might read about your "inappropriate affect," your "non-compliance," and the "overprotectiveness" of your "difficult" parents. And although you might like to think of yourself as an active teenager interested in the "top 40" hits and the latest fashion in dress, hairstyle, and make-up, you may find yourself listening to nursery rhymes, dressed in a shapeless sweatsuit, your hair cropped short and straight, and with no access to even acne medication much less makeup. Why? Because an assumption has been made that your *disability* tells all there is to know about

you, and from the moment you were diagnosed (or even *dually* diagnosed), you ceased being regarded as a person and became a "subject," a "client," or—worse yet—a "case." Your personality, your identity, and your lifestyle have become minor and even hidden details in a clinical history that tells the world about your weaknesses, faults, and deficits.

Source: From "Definition of the People TASH Serves" by L. H. Meyer, C. A. Peck, and L. Brown, 1991, *Critical Issues in the Lives of People with Disabilities* (p. 17), L. H. Meyer, C. A. Peck, and L. Brown (Eds.), Paul H. Brookes Publishing Company, PO Box 10624, Baltimore, MD, 21285-0624. Reprinted with permission.

combination of any one or more of the several categories of disability. However, mental retardation is a primary symptom in the greatest number of cases. Persons with profound retardation invariably suffer from significant physical and psychological disabilities in addition to subaverage intellectual functioning. For instance, they have a higher incidence of congenital heart disease, **epilepsy,** respiratory problems, diabetes, and metabolic disorders. They also exhibit poor muscle tone and are often plagued with such conditions as **spasticity, athetosis,** and **hypotonia.** Individuals with severe and profound mental retardation may also have sensory impairments, including vision and hearing problems.

Students who do not have disabilities can provide valuable assistance to their peers who do. (Palmer, Kane/The Stock Market)

The relationship between severe retardation and emotional disturbance is not understood as clearly as that between retardation and physical disabilities. In fact, there is a great deal of confusion concerning the overlapping characteristics of these supposedly different populations. The characteristics of individuals with serious emotional disturbances appear to be closely related to those of individuals with severe and profound retardation, but by definition, individuals with emotional disturbances are not truly retarded.

There are also multiple disabilities in which mental retardation is not a primary symptom. One such disability is deafness-blindness. The concomitant vision and hearing difficulties exhibited by people who are **deaf-blind** result in severe communication deficits as well as developmental and educational difficulties.

Many terms are used to describe individuals with severe and profound/multiple disabilities: *severely handicapped, profoundly handicapped,* and *severely multiply handicapped.* Note, however, that few cross-categorical definitions distinguish between severe and profound conditions. There is little consensus on the distinction between the definitions of severe and profound disabilities. These conditions are often treated as a single category within the education system.

Prevalence

FOCUS 9

Identify the estimated prevalence and causes of severe and profound/multiple disabilities.

Individuals with severe and profound/multiple disabilities constitute a very small percentage of the general population. Even if we consider the multitude of conditions, prevalence estimates generally range from no more than 0.1 to 1.0 percent. Approximately 4 out of every 1,000 persons are severely and profoundly disabled where the primary symptom is mental retardation.

Causation

Multiple problems result from multiple causes. For the vast majority of the individuals with severe and profound/multiple disabilities, the problems are evident at birth. Birth defects may be the result of genetic or metabolic disorders, including chromosomal abnormalities, phenylketonuria, or **Rh incompatibility.** Poor maternal health during pregnancy may also cause birth defects. The use of drugs, tobacco, and alcohol, poor maternal nutrition; infectious diseases (e.g., rubella); radiation exposure; venereal disease; and advanced maternal age are all factors. Severe and profound disabilities can also result from incidents or conditions that occur late in life, such as poisoning, accidents, malnutrition, physical and emotional neglect, and disease.

Characteristics

FOCUS 10

Describe people with severe and profound/multiple disabilities in terms of the adaptive fit between them and the environment as well as the nature of their instructional needs.

Individuals with severe and profound/multiple disabilities may exhibit any combination of physical, psychological, intellectual, or sensory differences. However, instead of focusing specifically on the differences, as do most definitions, it is also possible to characterize these individuals in terms of the adaptive fit between them and the environment. Following this approach, we identify the support needed for them to successfully participate in community settings. The Association for Persons with Severe Handicaps (TASH) characterizes these individuals as requiring

> extensive ongoing support in more than one major life activity in order to participate in integrated community settings and to enjoy a quality of life that is available to citizens with fewer or no disabilities. Support may be required for life activities such

as mobility, communication, self-care, and learning as necessary for independent living, employment, and self-sufficiency. (Meyer, Peck, & Brown, 1991, p. 19)

Individuals with severe and profound/multiple disabilities may also be characterized according to their instructional needs. Snell (1987, 1991) suggested that professionals concentrate more on the instructional needs and placement of these individuals in integrated settings and less on general, often stereotyped population characteristics. For Kevin, from Window 7–1, this would mean focusing on educational outcomes that will decrease his dependence on others in his environment and create opportunities to enhance his inclusion at home, at school, and in the community. Instruction would be developed with these outcomes in mind, rather than on the basis of a set of general characteristics associated with the label *severely disabled*. As proposed by Snell, "Such appropriate methods for these difficult-to-teach students include those that reduce errors, and facilitate generalization of skills learned under one set of conditions to other conditions. Further, teachers need to collect accurate student performance data so that progress can be monitored" (1987, p. 3).

The multitude of characteristics exhibited by people with severe and profound disabilities is mirrored by the numerous definitions associated with these conditions. A close analysis of these definitions reveals a consistent focus on people whose life needs cannot be met without substantial assistance from society. With this support, however, individuals with severe disabilities have a much greater probability of escaping the stereotype that depicts them solely as consumers of societal resources and becoming contributing members of families and communities. (For a more extensive discussion of individuals with severe mental retardation, see Chapter Four.)

Debate Forum

The merits of categorical versus cross-categorical programs for students with learning and behavior differences have been a topic of discussion for several years. In Chapters Four, Five, Six, and Seven of this text, you had the opportunity to review such material as definitions, characteristics, and intervention strategies from both categorical (mental retardation, behavior disorders, learning disabilities) and cross-categorical perspectives. The following discussion focuses on some of the issues in the debate on the merits of each approach.

Point   The traditional categories of mental retardation, behavior disorders, and learning disabilities are essentially nonfunctional in an instructional situation. Their use is not necessary because the criteria on which they are based do not adequately differentiate the needs students who are exceptional may have in the classroom setting.

Counterpoint   It is the cross-categorical approach to instruction that is nonfunctional. This approach forces the teacher to deal with children who have a wide variety of educational and behavioral problems. How can individualized programs be implemented when the teacher has to work every day with such a wide range of individual problems and needs?

Categorical versus Cross-Categorical Programs

Point   The cross-categorical approach stresses that the reason children are identified and labeled is to ensure that they receive adequate and appropriate services based on individual need. On the other hand, the categorical approach often forces children into neat and tidy boxes that describe individuals according to sets of characteristics associated with given labels. This may be a self-fulfilling prophecy: "Johnny cannot be expected to read because Johnny is mentally retarded." Using the cross-categorical approach, the professional assesses the individual to determine the range of academic and behavioral needs and to make recommendations for educational intervention. On the other hand, the primary purpose of assessment under the categorical approach is to make sure the child fits into one of the boxes (categories) known as mentally retarded, behavior disordered, or learning disabled.

Counterpoint   Your assumption that the cross-categorical approach results in more clearly defined groups of individuals and consequently adequate programing based on individual needs is certainly questionable. Look at the effect of the cross-categorical approach on research studies concerned with educational programing for these children. Researchers must have clearly defined groups of subjects in order to determine the efficacy of instructional approaches for this population. The cross-categorical approach makes research very difficult to conduct because the groups from which subjects are selected are very broad and not well defined.

What other issues need to be discussed as we assess the merits of categorical and cross-categorical approaches to working with students who have learning and behavior disabilities?

REVIEW

FOCUS 1   Why is the cross-categorical approach considered an alternative way of defining and classifying individuals with learning and behavior disabilities?

◆ The cross-categorical approach does not use the traditional labels mentally retarded, behavior disordered, and learning disabled in defining or classifying students with learning and behavior disabilities.

◆ Some professionals have suggested that the use of traditional categories prohibits clearly defining or adequately differentiating the needs of each student.

◆ According to the cross-categorical approach, students with learning and behavior disorders are characterized according to the severity of the problem: mild; moderate; or severe and profound/multiple disabilities.

FOCUS 2   Identify the four components of the definition of mild learning and behavior disabilities.

◆ An individual with mild learning or behavior disabilities exhibits academic and/or social-interpersonal performance deficits that range from one to two standard deviations below average on norm- and criterion-referenced assessments.

◆ Deficits become evident in school-related settings.

◆ Cause is generally unknown.

◆ Student remains in the regular classroom for the majority if not all of the school day.

FOCUS 3   Identify the estimated prevalence and causes of mild learning and behavior disabilities.

◆ Approximately 13 percent of all school-age children perform between one and two standard deviations below average.

◆ Only 6 percent of school-age children functioning between one and two standard deviations below average receive special education services.

◆ The causes associated with mild learning and behavior disabilities are largely unknown.

◆ Factors such as diverse cultural backgrounds, socioeconomic status, poor teaching, and high absenteeism in school have been associated with mild learning and behavior differences.

FOCUS 4   Identify the discrepancies between definitions of mental retardation, behavior disorders, and learning disabilities and the actual performance of children in each category.

◆ Behavioral difficulties may be evident in children with mental retardation and learning disabilities as well as those with behavior disorders.

◆ Learning disabilities are found in people of all ranges of intelligence.

◆ Low academic achievement is evident in children with behavior disorders as well as in those with learning disabilities and mental retardation.

FOCUS 5   Identify the four components of the definition of moderate learning and behavior disabilities.

◆ An individual with moderate learning or behavior disabilities exhibits intellectual, academic, and/or social-interpersonal deficits that are two to three standard deviations below average.

◆ Problems are evident in a broad spectrum of environmental settings.

◆ Causes are identifiable in some cases.

◆ Individuals with moderate learning and behavior disabilities require substantially altered patterns of service and treatment in comparison to nondisabled peers.

FOCUS 6   Identify the estimated prevalence and causes of moderate learning and behavior disabilities.

◆ Approximately 2 percent of all school-age children exhibit moderate learning and behavior disabilities.

◆ Possible causes associated with moderate learning and behavior disabilities include socioeconomic differences, poor motivation or achievement orientation, inadequate memory and retention, genetic or metabolic errors, and poor maternal nutrition.

FOCUS 7   Why are many children with moderate learning and behavior disabilities not identified as such until they reach school age?

◆ Children with moderate learning and behavior disabilities are generally not identified prior to school age because they do not exhibit physical or learning problems that are readily recognizable during the early childhood years.

FOCUS 8   Identify the four components of the definition of severe and profound/multiple disabilities.

◆ Individuals with severe and profound/multiple disabilities have physical, sensory, intellectual, and/or social-interpersonal deficits that range beyond three standard deviations below average.

◆ These deficits are evident in all environmental settings.

◆ Causes are identifiable in some cases.

◆ Individuals with severe and profound/multiple disabilities require significantly altered environments with regard to care, treatment, and accommodation.

FOCUS 9 Identify the estimated prevalence and causes of severe and profound/multiple disabilities.

◆ Prevalence estimates generally range from 0.1 to 1 percent of the general population.

◆ Problems are generally evident at birth.

◆ Birth defects may be the result of genetic or metabolic problems.

◆ Factors associated with poisoning, accidents, malnutrition, physical and emotional neglect, and disease are also known causes.

FOCUS 10 Describe people with severe and profound/multiple disabilities in terms of the adaptive fit between them and the environment as well as the nature of their instructional needs.

◆ People with severe disabilities may require ongoing support in many life activities in order to fully participate in integrated community settings.

◆ Professionals need to concentrate more on each individual's instructional needs and placement in integrated settings and less on stereotypical population characteristics.

Chapter Eight

Communication Disorders

TO BEGIN WITH . . .

◆ Nearly one-fourth of the children (6–21 years old) with disabilities who were served under federal law during 1989–1990 had speech or language impairments (U.S. Department of Education, 1991).

◆ Babies who are deaf and whose parents are also deaf appear to babble with their hands just as infants who hear babble through speech (Reuter News Agency, 1991).

◆ Welcome to Wendy's! Using the Fast Food Passport, a customer with limited language or speech that is difficult to understand can flip to cards that have pictures of food items and simply point to what he or she wants (Crestwood Company, 1987–1988).

MILLIE

MILLIE.   Millie was 52 years old when the accident happened. She was a successful real estate broker and developer, owning her own agency in Lubbock and working on commercial projects in Brownsville. That basically covered the state of Texas, from north to south, and involved a lot of opportunity, responsibility, and travel. Millie was driving home late one evening when she fell asleep at the wheel. A Texas state trooper found her car lodged against a rock at the bottom of a gulley. Millie had pulled herself out of the wreck and made it about 50 yards up the rock-strewn bank. She was diagnosed in the rehabilitation unit of the hospital as having *aphasia.*

One year after the accident, Millie still has great difficulty speaking, and she communicates mostly through notes. She seems to understand most of what is said to her, although at times, she shakes her head, indicating that she does not comprehend what the speaker is trying to say. She can no longer personally show property to potential investors and can only make suggestions by writing notes to her associate broker, who has worked in her agency for several years. Her rehabilitation program is focusing on relearning language and adjusting to the vocational limitations that might well exist for the rest of her life.

DOUG.   The first years of Doug's life were basically normal. He was an active and intelligent child. His father and mother were both well educated—his father, a chemistry professor; his mother, a nurse. Doug exhibited all the normal behaviors of a young child. There was no evidence of serious abnormality in his initial speech development, but at the age of 4 his parents began to observe an unusual lack of fluency in his speech. Doug's father was the first to label the problem as stuttering, and he began to work with Doug to correct it. Doug's mother was concerned about attempting to solve the problem in this manner. She was inclined to seek professional assistance, but was not successful in convincing Doug and his father to agree.

The results of the corrective program provided by his father were not great. We now find Doug at age 13. In his diary, Doug recounts part of a day in his life:

> The best time of day is before I get out of bed because I don't have to talk. The only problem during this time is that I dread the rest of the day. I have to see my Mom and Dad at breakfast and say something—which will always end up in me stuttering; Dad trying to correct or help me; and Mom trying to anticipate what I am struggling to say. Since I have to go to breakfast, I try to wait until Dad has left for the office so that the number of people I have to deal with is reduced. This morning, I was successful in avoiding Dad, but Mom was still there—trying to please and asking what I wanted for breakfast. God, I wish that she would just put something in front of me. Even if it wasn't great, it would be better than having to talk and stutter. I asked for a hot roll this morning. I really wanted cereal, but I knew that I would block on that, plus Mom would have asked why I didn't want something hot.

FOCUS 1
Identify four ways in which speech, language, and communication are interrelated.

*I*NTRODUCTION

We communicate with others many times a day: to order food in a restaurant; thank a friend for doing us a favor; ask a question in class; call for help in an emergency; or give directions to someone who is lost. **Communication** is one of the most complicated and vital processes people undertake, yet we seldom think much about it unless there is a problem. **Speech** and **language** are two components of communication. They are highly interrelated, and problems in either can significantly affect a person's daily life. Because of their complexity, determining the cause of a problem is often perplexing.

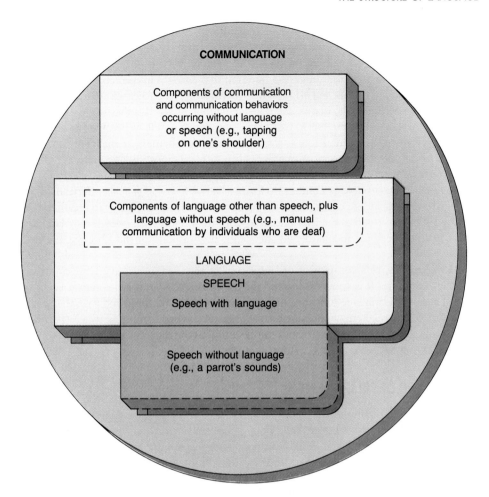

FIGURE 8–1

A Conceptual Model of
Communication, Language,
and Speech

Communication is the interchange of ideas, opinions, or facts between senders and receivers. It requires that a sender (an individual or group) compose and transmit a message and that a receiver decipher and understand the message (Bernstein, 1985). In this manner, the sender and receiver are partners in the communication process. Communication is an extremely important tool that we use to interact with our environment. Part of this tool involves the use of speech and language.

Although related, *speech* and *language* are not synonymous. *Speech* is one means of expressing language but not the only means; it is merely the audible representation. *Language* represents the message that is contained in speech. It is possible to have language without speech, such as sign language by people who are deaf, and speech without languages, such as birds that are trained to talk.

Communication is the broadest concept. Language is a part of communication. Speech is often thought of as a part of language, although language may exist without speech. Figure 8–1 illustrates the interrelationship of speech, language, and communication.

THE STRUCTURE OF LANGUAGE

Language—whether English, Russian, or Arabic—is generally viewed as including several major components: phonology, syntax, morphology, semantics, and pragmatics. **Phonology** represents the system of speech sounds that an individual utters, that is, rules regarding how sounds can be used and combined. For example, the word *cat* has three phonemes. **Syntax** involves the rules governing sentence structure, the way sequences of words are combined into phrases and sentences (Cole & Cole, 1989). For example, the sentence *Will you help Linda?* suggests a question that changes in meaning when the order of words is changed to *You will help Linda.* **Morphology** is concerned with the form and internal structure of words, that is, the transformations of words in terms of such areas as tense and number—like present to past tense, singular to plural. When we add an *s* to *cat,* we have produced the plural form, *cats,* with two morphemes, or meaning units—the concept of cat and the concept of plural. Such transformations involve prefixes, suffixes, and inflections.

Syntax and morphology combine to form what we know as *grammar.* **Semantics** represents the understanding of language, the component most concerned with meaning (Cole & Cole, 1989). It involves the meaning of a word to an individual, which may be unique in each of our personal mental dictionaries (e.g., the meaning of the adjective *nice* in the phrase *nice house*).

Pragmatics, as a component of language, has received increased attention in recent language literature. It is concerned with "the use of language in social contexts, including rules that govern language functions (the reason for communicating) and rules that govern the choice of codes (alternate message forms) to be used when communicating" (Bernstein, 1985, p. 4). An example of pragmatics can be found in the different ways a professor talks when lecturing to a class versus chatting at a party.

LANGUAGE DEVELOPMENT

The development of language is a complex process, one that is fascinating to observe first-hand, as parents of infants know well. Young children normally progress through several stages in developing language, from a preverbal stage to the use of words together in sentences. At first, a baby's verbal communication is limited primarily to crying, which is usually associated with discomfort (e.g., from hunger, pain, or being soiled or wet). Before long (around 2 months), babies begin to coo as well as cry, verbally expressing reactions to pleasure as well as discomfort. They begin to babble at about 3 to 6 months of age, which involves making some consonant and vowel sounds. At this point, babies often make sounds repeatedly when they are alone, seemingly experimenting with their sound making and not necessarily trying to communicate with anyone. They may also babble when their parents or others are with them, playing or otherwise handling them.

A baby's first word is always a momentous event, and parents often attach words to sounds that stretch the imagination of more objective observers and likely have no meaning to the child. What usually happens is that the baby begins to string together sounds that resemble words. To the delight of the parents, these sounds frequently include such utterances as "Da-Da" and "Ma-Ma" which, of course, are echoed, repeated, and reinforced greatly by Father and Mother. As the baby begins to actually listen to the speech of adults, exchanges or "conversations" seem to occur, where the youngster responds by saying "Da-Da" when a parent says that sound. While this type of interchange sounds like a conversation, the child's vocal productions may only be understood by those close to him or her (e.g., parents or siblings); people other than immediate family members may not be able to interpret meaning at all. The baby also begins to use different tones and vocal intensity, which makes the vocalization vaguely resemble adult speech. The interactions between babies and their parents can do much to enhance their developing language at this time. Parents often provide a great deal of reinforcement for word approximations, such as praise in excited tones of voice or hugs. They also provide stimulus sounds and words for the baby to mimic, which gives the youngster considerable directed practice.

The timing of a baby's actual production of his or her first words is obviously open to interpretation, but it usually happens between 9 and 14 months. Often, these words continue to involve echoing (repeating what has been heard) or mimic responses based on verbalizations by those around him or her. Initially, the words may have little or no meaning, although they soon become attached to people or objects in the child's immediate environment, such as Daddy, Mommy, or milk. It is not long before these words begin to have more perceptible intent, as the child uses them for requests and an apparent means of pleasing parents or siblings. Strings of two and three words that resemble sentences typically begin between 18 and 24 months. At this stage, there is little question about meaning because the child can rather clearly indicate that he or she wants something. The child uses reasonably accurate syntax, usually with a word order involving subject-verb-object.

By 3 to 4 years of age, most children whose language is developing normally are able to use all basic syntactical structures. By the time they are 5 years old, they have progressed to using six-word sentences, on the average. A child that is developing language normally articulates nearly all speech sounds correctly and in context somewhere between 4 and 8 years of age.

As we have outlined the process of normal language development, variable age-ranges have been identified for each milestone. Some have been rather broad approximations. Several factors contribute to this variation. For one thing, children exhibit considerable variability in their rates of development, even those that are considered normal. Some of these differences are due to general health and vitality, others are due to inheritance, and others relate to environmental influences, such as the amount of interaction with parents and siblings (Bialystok, 1986; Roberts, Rabinowitch, & Bryant, 1989). Note also that age-ranges become more variable with stages of more advanced development (e.g., 3 to 6 months for babbling; 18 to 24 months for two- and three-word strings). This is partially because there is more variation regarding when advanced developmental events occur than for earlier stages. It is also true, however, that these advanced developments are more complex, some involving subtleties that are not as singularly obvious as, say, the first "Da-Da." Therefore, observation of when they first occur is perhaps less accurate. Table 8–1 summarizes general milestones of normal language and prelanguage development.

The variability noted in normal language development will also be seen as we discuss abnormal language and speaking ability. In some cases, the same factors that influence variability in normal language performance are also considered to be disorders if they are extreme. In others, we will find that definitions differ in the literature and characteristics vary between people, which we have encountered with other disorders.

■ **Table 8–1** Normal Language and Prelanguage Development

Age	Behavior
Birth	Crying and making other physiological sounds
1 to 2 months	Cooing as well as crying
3 to 6 months	Babbling as well as cooing
9 to 14 months	Speaking first words as well as babbling
18 to 24 months	Speaking first sentences as well as words
3 to 4 years	Using all basic syntactical structures
4 to 8 years	Articulating correctly all speech sounds in context

Source: Reprinted with permission of Merrill, an imprint of Macmillan Publishing Company, from *Mental Retardation: A Life Cycle Approach,* Fifth Edition by Clifford J. Drew, Donald R. Logan, Michael L. Hardman. Copyright © 1992 by Macmillan Publishing Company.

SPEECH DISORDERS

Definitions of **speech disorders** vary greatly, some being quite detailed in terms of characteristics and others more general. A synthesis of definitions has been developed by Gelfand, Jenson, and Drew (1988):

> Defective speech or a speech disorder (which are terms often used interchangeably) refers to speech behavior which is sufficiently deviant from normal or accepted speaking patterns that it attracts attention, interferes with communication, and adversely affects communication for either the speaker or the listener. (p. 203)

This definition is broad in that it refers to a wide range of specific speech disorders. Each of these disorders is designated by separate definitions that describe the condition. We highlight these descriptions and definitions in the following sections.

Speech is extremely important in contemporary society. Speaking ability can influence a person's success or failure in both the personal–social and professional arenas. Most people are about average in terms of their speaking ability. They may envy those who are unusually articulate and pity those who have a difficult time with speech. What is it like to have a serious deficit in speaking ability? Certainly, it is different for each individual, depending on the circumstances in which he or she operates and the severity of the deficit. We caught a glimpse of what it may be like in the case of Doug, presented in Window 8–1.

Although we only saw a glimpse of Doug's day, it is obvious that his abnormal speech seriously affects his life. Doug carries some strong emotional reactions to his stuttering. Stuttering also significantly alters his behavior, as when he tries to wait until his father has left before coming to breakfast. It is easy to imagine the impact that stuttering must have on Doug in such settings as the classroom or in social encounters with his peers. Speech is so central to functioning in society that such disorders often have a significant impact on affected individuals. As children, they may be ridiculed by peers, begin to feel inadequate in general, and suffer serious emotional distress.

There are many different speech disorders and considerable diversity in terms of theoretical perspectives regarding causes and treatment. Volumes much longer than this book have focused solely on the topic. We discuss here several speech disorders that represent major communication disorders.

Fluency Disorders

Normal speech is characterized by a reasonably smooth flow of words and sentences. It has a rhythm and timing that is, for the most part, steady, regular, and rapid. There is always a certain degree of variation, both between people and situations. Most of us also have times when we pause to think about what we are saying, either because we have made a mistake or want to mentally edit what we are about to say. However, these interruptions are relatively infrequent and usually do not constitute an ongoing disturbance of the speech flow. In general, our speech can be considered fluent with respect to speed and continuity.

For some people, fluency of speech is a significant problem; they have a **fluency disorder.** The speech of a person with a fluency disorder is characterized by repeated interruptions, hesitations, or repetitions that seriously interrupt the flow of communication. Some people with a fluency disorder speak with what is known as cluttered speech, or **cluttering.** This type of fluency disorder is characterized by speech that is overly rapid (to the extreme), disorganized, and occasionally filled with unnecessary words—unrelated insertions that seem random. People with cluttered speech seem to be either unaware or indifferent to the problem. The most well-known type of fluency disorder, where those affected are painfully aware of the problem, is **stuttering.**

Parents can greatly influence their children's early speech patterns but should not become overly concerned about doing so. (Richard Hutchings/Info Edit)

Stuttering. Stuttering occurs when the flow of speech is abnormally interrupted by repetitions, blocking, or prolongations of sounds, syllables, words, or phrases (Van Riper & Emerick, 1990). Stuttering may be the most studied of all speech disorders, and it has fascinated researchers for decades.

Stuttering is probably the most widely recognized type of speech problem. This recognition and interest is somewhat paradoxical, since stuttering occurs rather infrequently and has one of the lowest prevalence rates compared to other speech disorders (Van Riper & Emerick, 1990). For example, articulation disorders (e.g., omitting, adding, or distorting certain sounds) occur in the United States much more often than do stuttering problems.

The common view of stuttering partly comes from the nature of behavior involved in the problem. Stuttering is typically defined as a disturbance in the rhythm and fluency of speech. It may involve certain sounds, syllables, words, or phrases, and the problem elements may differ among individuals. (Doug's diary described some of his specific problems as he thought about asking for breakfast.) Such interruptions in the flow of speech are very evident to both the speaker and listener. They are perhaps more disruptive to the communication act than any other type of speech disorder. Furthermore, listeners often become quite uncomfortable and may try to assist the stuttering speaker, providing missing or incomplete words. The speaker's discomfort may be magnified by physical movements, gestures, or facial distortions that often accompany stuttering. All this may make the experience very vivid for and easily remembered by the listener, which accounts for part of the prominence of stuttering in the larger picture of speech disorders.

Parents often become unnecessarily concerned about stuttering as their children learn to talk. Most children exhibit some fluency problems as they develop speech. These fluency problems involve disruptions in the rhythm and flow of speech and include some or all of the behaviors mentioned above (e.g., blocking, repetition, and prolonging of sounds, syllables, words, or phrases). Generally, such speech patterns represent normal fluency problems during early speech development, which diminish and cease as maturation progresses. However, these normal fluency problems have also historically played an important role in some theories regarding the causes of stuttering.

Causation of Stuttering. The search for a cause of stuttering has led behavioral scientists in many directions. One difficulty with these efforts has been that researchers have

FOCUS 2
Identify three factors thought to cause stuttering.

often sought a single cause for the disorder. Current thinking has suggested that stuttering may have a variety of causes (Prosek et al., 1987; Rastatter & Dell, 1987), and the search for a single cause has been largely discarded. Theories regarding causes of stuttering seem to take three basic perspectives: (1) theories related to emotional problems, that is, stuttering as a symptom of some emotional disturbance; (2) theories that view stuttering as the result of a person's biological makeup or some neurological problem; and (3) theories that view stuttering as a learned behavior.

Many professionals have become less interested in both the emotional and biological causation theories of stuttering. The emotional-problem theory tends to be held predominantly by psychiatrists and certain counseling psychologists. Van Riper and Emerick (1990) suggested that this may be because the stuttering clients they see in their clinical practice tend to have deep-seated emotional problems. Research in this area is scarce, and the topic is difficult to study due to measurement error in assessing deep emotional problems and trying to establish a causal relationship based on such measurement.

A few studies have been published on the biological-cause theory over the past 15 years. Some research has indicated that the brains of people who stutter may be organized differently from those of their fluent counterparts (Healey & Howe, 1987), but the nature of such differences remains unclear and a matter for speculation. Certain results have suggested that individuals who stutter versus those with fluent speech use different sections of the brain to process material (Pindzola, 1987; Webster, 1988). Some evidence has seemed to indicate that people who stutter may have brain-hemisphere-dominance problems to a greater degree than those who are fluent; that is, the hemispheres of the brain may compete in information processing (Rastatter & Dell, 1987; Rastatter & Loren, 1988). Other research has suggested that neurological problems may disrupt the person's precise timing ability, which is important to speech production (Peters & Hulstijin. 1987). Thus, as we view evidence on biological causes, some interest continues, but the results are mixed.

One persistent theory over the years regarding the causation of stuttering has related to learning. This line of reasoning has viewed stuttering essentially as a learned behavior that comes from the normal nonfluency evident in early speech development. Most young children exhibit nonfluent speech as they develop communication skills. From a learning causation point of view, a typical child may become a stuttering child if considerable attention is focused on normal disfluencies at that stage of development. This may have occurred in Doug's case, as his father focused on his speech and even labeled him as "a stutterer" (see Window 8–1). The disfluency of early stuttering may be further magnified by negative feelings about the self as well as anxiety (Klinger, 1987; Kraaimaat, Janssen & Brutten, 1988). Current thinking and treatment follow this logic, although the theory has been prominent for many years.

There has been some interest in the influence of heredity on stuttering (Cassar, 1988). This issue has been approached from several perspectives, one of which is that stuttering may be gender related. The logic of this theory has a certain appeal on the surface, since males who stutter outnumber females by about four to one. Thus, it is possible that, under certain circumstances, the genetic material that determines gender may also carry material that contributes to stuttering. However, this hypothesis is difficult to test and remains only speculation. Heredity has also been of interest because of the high incidence of stuttering within certain families as well as with twins (Van Riper & Emerick, 1990). Once again, however, we are faced with the difficulty of separating hereditary and environmental influences, a problem that has long been evident in child development and behavioral disorders research (Ausubel, Sullivan, & Ives, 1980; Gelfand et al., 1988).

In sum, the cause of stuttering has been an elusive and perplexing matter for professionals working in speech pathology. Researchers and clinicians continue their search for a cause, with the hope of identifying more effective treatment and prevention measures. The work of Murdoch, Killin, and McCaul (1989) is an example of such effort. These investigators studied subjects ranging in age from 23 to 54. Their findings suggested that stuttering may be a function of speech coordination with respiration. One might view this as a physical dysfunction, but it could also be seen as a result of learning or a combination of the two.

Interventions.   Over the years, many different treatment approaches have been used with people who stutter, but the results have been mixed. Techniques such as play therapy, creative dramatics, parental counseling, and group counseling with parents have been useful in working with children who stutter. Even hypnosis has been used to treat some cases of stuttering, but its success has been limited (Cassar, 1988). Speech rhythm has also been the focus of some therapy for stuttering. In some cases, this approach has included the use of a metronome to establish a rhythm for speaking (Van Riper & Emerick, 1990). Relaxation therapy and biofeedback have also been used, since tenseness has typically been observed in people who stutter (Hasbrouck et al., 1987). In all the techniques noted, outcomes are mixed, with some cases resulting in success and others being disappointing. It has been common for those who stutter to repeat treatments using several approaches. The inability of any one treatment or cluster of treatments to consistently help people who stutter to learn to speak fluently demonstrates the ongoing need for research in this area.

Thus, a complete understanding of stuttering remains elusive. However, treatment approaches have increasingly focused on direct behavioral therapy that attempts to teach individuals who stutter to use fluent speech patterns. In some cases, children are taught to monitor and manage their stuttering (e.g., by speaking more slowly or rhythmically) and to reward themselves for increasing periods of fluency. Some behaviorally oriented therapies include providing knowledge regarding physical factors (e.g., regulating breathing) and direct instruction about correct speaking behaviors. Such research combines several dimensions to create the overall therapy, such as an interview regarding the inconvenience of stuttering, behavior modification training, and follow-up. Because stuttering is a complex problem, effective interventions are likely to be equally complex, perhaps combining different elements from several therapies.

Fluency disorders interfere significantly with spoken communication because they interrupt the flow of ideas. For people who stutter, the stream of communication is broken by severe rhythm irregularities. For people with cluttered speech, the flow of ideas is interrupted by extraneous words and disorganization. However, other people with speech disorders are not dysfluent; rather, they are delayed in their speaking ability.

Delayed Speech

Definition.   **Delayed speech** refers to a deficit in communication ability in which a person speaks like someone who is much younger. From a developmental point of view, this type of difficulty involves a delayed beginning of speech and language. Very young children are generally able to communicate, at least to some degree, before verbal behaviors are learned. They use gestures, facial expressions, other physical movements, and vocalizations that would not be considered speech, such as grunts or squeals (Tiegerman, 1985). This early behavior development illustrates the interrelationships between communication, language, and speech.

Although it is difficult to distinguish among the three functions at this stage, we are concerned here only with speech delay. Delayed speech is considered a failure of speech to develop at the expected age and is often associated with other maturation delays, such as crawling or sitting up alone later than most children (Bishop & Edmundson, 1987). Delayed

FOCUS 3
Identify two ways in which learning theory and home environment relate to delayed speech.

Communication via gestures is very important to young children, especially if they have delayed speech. (Robert Brenner/PhotoEdit)

speech may also be related to hearing impairment, mental retardation, emotional disturbance, and brain injury. Delayed speech may occur for many reasons and take various forms, and treatment differs accordingly.

Children with delayed speech often have few or no verbalizations that can be interpreted as conventional speech. Some communicate solely through physical gestures. Others may use a combination of gestures and vocal sounds that are not even close approximations of words. Still others may speak but in a very limited manner, perhaps using single words (typically nouns without auxiliary words, e.g., *ball* instead of *my ball*) or primitive sentences that are short or incomplete (e.g., *get ball* rather than *would you get the ball*). Such communication behavior is normal for infants and very young children, but here we are referring to children who are well beyond the age at which they should be speaking in at least a partially fluent fashion.

The differences between stuttering and delayed speech are obvious. However, the distinctions between delayed speech and **articulation disorders** are not as clear. In fact, children with delayed speech usually make many articulation errors in their speaking patterns. However, their major problems lie in grammatical and vocabulary deficits, which are more matters of developmental delay (Van Riper & Emerick, 1990).

The current prevalence of delayed speech is very unclear, and government estimates did not even provide data regarding provision of services for delayed speech during 1989–1990 (U.S. Department of Education, 1991). There has been confusion in the past regarding distinctions between *incidence* and *prevalence*. The two terms have been used interchangeably when, in fact, **incidence** refers to the number of *new* cases identified during a particular period of time (often one schoolyear), whereas **prevalence** includes all of the cases existing at a given point in time—the newly diagnosed plus those previously identified. Such problems, plus definition differences between studies, have led many to place little faith in existing prevalence figures (Van Riper & Emerick, 1990).

Causation.   As discussed earlier, cases of delayed speech may take a variety of forms, so it is not surprising that the causes of these problems also vary greatly. Several types of environmental deprivation contribute to delayed speech. For example, partial or complete hearing loss may cause an individual to experience serious delay (or absence) of speech development. If the auditory stimulus and modeling are deficient, learning to speak will be extremely difficult.

For those with normal hearing, the environment may be a factor in delayed speech. Some children live in homes where there is little opportunity to learn speech, such as in families where there is minimal conversation or chance for the child to speak. Other problems may contribute to delayed speech, such as cerebral palsy and emotional disturbances. Even less severe emotional problems may result in delayed speech, such as negativism, which can be viewed as an emotional problem stemming from interpersonal difficulties between parents and child.

Negativism involves a conflict between parents' expectations and a child's ability to perform, which often occurs in some form as children develop speech. A great deal of pressure is placed on children during the period when they are normally developing their speaking skills: to go to bed when told, to control urination and defecation properly, and to learn appropriate eating skills, among other things. The demands are great, and they may exceed a child's performance ability. Children may react in many ways when more is demanded than they are able to produce. Refusal is one way in which they may respond. They may simply not talk, seeming to withdraw from family interactions, remaining silent. In normal development, children occasionally refuse to follow the directions of adults. One very effective area of refusal is speaking; the parents' reprisal options are few and may be ineffective. As a parent, it is relatively simple to punish refusal misbehaviors when they involve such acts as refusing to go to bed or not cleaning one's room. However, it is a different matter when parents encounter the refusal to talk. It is not easy to force a child to talk through conventional punishment techniques. Delayed speech may occur in extreme cases where negativism related to talking is prolonged.

Viewing the problem from another angle, children may be punished *for* talking in other situations. Parents may be irritated by a child's attempt to communicate. A child may speak too loudly or at inappropriate times, such as when adults are reading, watching television, resting, or talking with other adults (even more rules to learn at such a tender age).

From these descriptions, we can see that some children might have delayed speech as a result of environmentally controlled learning due to refusal or rebellion. Not speaking may be rewarded in some instances, and in others, it may be a way of expressing refusal that is unlikely to result in punishment. Thus, in some cases, children may *not learn to speak,* and in others, they may *learn not to speak.* Imagine the effect on a baby who is yelled at for practicing his or her babbling (perhaps loudly) while Mother is on the telephone. Frightened, the child begins to cry, which further angers Mother, who screams, "Shut up!" Of course the baby does not understand, and this episode escalates and becomes even more frightening to the child. Such situations may be alternated with more calm periods, when the mother hugs the baby and talks in soothing tones. A baby in this type of environment is likely to become very confused about the reaction to vocal output; sometimes it is punished, and other times it is rewarded. If such circumstances exist at the time a child normally develops speech and persist for a substantial length of time, seriously delayed speech may result.

As mentioned earlier, delayed speech may emerge from experience deprivation, in which the environment either limits or hinders the opportunity to learn speech. Basic principles of learning suggest that, when one is first learning a skill, the stimulus and reward circumstances are important. A skill that is just beginning to develop is fragile. Stimuli and reinforcement must be reasonably consistent, appropriate, and properly timed. If such conditions do not exist, the skill development may be retarded or even negated. A child who is left alone for many hours each day, perhaps with only a single light bulb and four walls as stimuli, will not be rewarded for cooing, babbling, or approximating the first word. Over a long period of time, this baby will fall behind his or her peers who are being hugged for each sound and hearing adults talk as models. This does not mean that the home environment must be an orchestrated language development program. Most households involve adequate circumstances to permit and promote speech learning.

INTERACTING IN NATURAL SETTINGS ·············· People with ·············· Communication Disorders

EARLY CHILDHOOD YEARS

Tips for the Family

◆ Model speech and language to your infant by talking to him or her in normal tones from a very early age, even though he or she may not yet be intentionally communicating directly with you.

◆ Respond to babbling and other noises the young child makes with conversation, reinforcing early verbal output.

◆ Do not overreact if your child is not developing speech at the same rate as someone else's infant; there is great variation between children.

◆ If you are concerned about your child's speech development, have his or her hearing tested to determine if that source of stimulation is normal.

◆ Observe other areas of development to assure yourself that your child is progressing within the broad boundaries of normal variation.

◆ If you are seeking day-care or a preschool program, search carefully for one that will provide a rich, systematic communication environment.

Tips for the Preschool Teacher

◆ Encourage parental involvement in all dimensions of the program, including systematic speech and language stimulation at home.

◆ Use all situations and events as opportunities to teach speech and language, perhaps focusing initially on concrete objects and later moving to the more abstract, depending on the individual child's functioning level.

◆ Ask "wh" questions, such as *what, who, when,* and so on, giving the child many opportunities to practice speaking as well as thinking.

◆ Practice with the child the use of prepositions *in, on, out,* and so on.

◆ Use all occasions possible to increase the child's vocabulary.

Tips for Preschool Personnel

◆ Preschool and day-care staff all communicate with the young child and can be involved in either direct or indirect communication instruction.

Tips for Neighbors and Friends

◆ Interact with young children with communication disorders as you would with any others, speaking to them and directly modeling appropriate communication.

◆ Intervene if you encounter other children ridiculing the speech and language of these youngsters, attempting to encourage sensitivity to individual differences among your own and other neighborhood children.

ELEMENTARY YEARS

Tips for the Family

◆ Stay involved in your child's educational program through active participation with the school.

Learning to speak is no different from learning other skills. In some homes, conversation is abnormally infrequent, and parents may rarely speak to either each other or to the children. In such cases, a child may have infrequent speech modeling and little reinforcement for speaking, so delayed speech may result. It is also possible that verbal interchanges between parents reflect a strained relationship or emotional problems. The environment in such situations may be unpleasant, tense, and troubled, involving threats, arguments, and shouting. A child learning to speak in this type of setting may learn that speech is associated with unpleasant feelings or even punishment. Seriously delayed speech may result from these environmental circumstances as well. When such contingencies are combined with infrequent interchanges, the learning—whether not to speak or not learning to speak—may be particularly potent.

The environment just described represents an unpleasant set of circumstances, one in which learning speech may be impaired. There may be concern about the amount of love and caring in such a situation and the role that emotional health plays in learning to speak. But delayed speech may also occur in families where there is great love and caring, at least with respect to observable behavior. In some environments, a child may have little need to learn speech. Most parents are concerned about satisfying their child's needs or desires.

◆ Work in collaboration with the child's teacher on speaking practice, blending it naturally into family and individual activities.

◆ Communicate naturally with the child; avoiding "talk down" and thereby modeling the use of more simple language.

Tips for the Regular Classroom Teacher

◆ Continue promoting parental involvement in their child's intervention program in whatever manner they can participate.

◆ Encourage the child with communication disorders to talk about events and things in his or her environment, describing experiences in as much detail as possible.

◆ Use all situations possible to provide practice for the child's development of speech and language skills.

◆ Continue to promote the enhancement of vocabulary for the child in a broad array of topic areas.

Tips for School Personnel

◆ Promote an environment where all who are available and in contact with the child are involved in communication instruction, if not directly then indirectly through interaction and modeling.

◆ Begin encouraging student involvement in a wide array of activities that can also be used to promote speech and language development.

Tips for Neighbors and Friends

◆ Interact with children with communication disorders normally, not focusing on the speaking difficulties that may be evident.

◆ As a neighbor or friend, provide support for the child's parents, who may be struggling with difficult feelings about their child's communication skills.

SECONDARY/TRANSITION YEARS

Tips for the Family

◆ Children who still exhibit communication problems at this level are likely to perform on a lower level, suggesting that communication may focus on functional matters such as grooming, feeding, and so on.

◆ For some children, communication may involve limited verbalization, and consideration should be given to other means of interacting.

◆ To the degree possible, continue to interact with your child as much and as normally as possible.

Tips for the Regular Classroom Teacher

◆ Communication instruction should be embedded in the context of functional areas (e.g., social interactions, request for assistance, choice-making).

◆ Augmented communication devices or procedures may be added to the student's curriculum.

Tips for School Personnel

◆ Encourage the development of school activities that will encourage use of a broad variety of skill levels in speaking (i.e., not just the debate club).

◆ Promote the development of school activities that permit participation through alternative communication modes other than speaking.

Tips for Neighbors and Friends

◆ To the degree that you are comfortable, interact with children with communication disorders using alternative communication approaches (e.g., signs, gesturing, pantomiming).

Carrying this desire to the extreme, a "superparent" may anticipate the child's wants (e.g., toys, water, or food) and provide them even before the child makes a verbal request. Such children may only gesture and their parents immediately respond, thereby rewarding gestures and not promoting the development of speech skills. Learning to speak is much more complex and demanding than making simple movements or facial grimaces. If gesturing is rewarded, speaking is less likely to be learned properly.

If delayed speech is a complex phenomenon, causation is equally complicated—as complicated as the speech development process itself. If you are a new parent or anticipating parenthood, you should know that the vast majority of children learn to speak normally. Certainly, parents should not become so self-conscious that they see a problem before one exists.

Interventions. Treatment approaches for delayed speech are as varied as causes. Whatever the cause, an effective treatment is one that teaches the child appropriate speaking proficiency for his or her age group. In some cases, matters other than just defective learning, such as hearing impairments, must be considered in the treatment procedures. Such cases

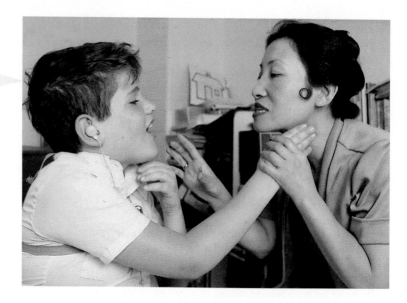

Effective treatment for children with delayed speech involves teaching appropriate speaking proficiency for their age group. (Barbara Kirk/The Stock Market)

may involve surgery and prosthetic appliances like hearing aids, as well as specially designed instructional techniques aimed at teaching speech.

If delayed speech is caused primarily by defective learning, treatment may focus on the basic principles of learned behavior. In a general sense, the stimulus and reinforcement patterns that contributed to delayed speech must be changed. These circumstances must be rearranged so that appropriate speaking behaviors can be learned. This process sounds simple, but the identification and control of such contingencies may be complex. There has been some success over the years with specific teaching interventions using direct instruction as well as other procedures aimed at increasing spontaneous speech (Cole & Dale, 1986; Raver, 1987). Such instruction places a heavy emphasis on the reinforcement of speaking, attempting to modify the child's behavior toward more normal speech. Other interventions involve collaborative efforts between speech clinicians, teachers, and parents (Hornby & Jensen-Proctor, 1984), focusing on modifying not only the child's speech but also the family environment that contributed to the problem. Because each case has different elements that cause the delay, therapies must be individually tailored to fit the situation. Further research on treatment is needed to evaluate the relative effectiveness of different procedures.

Articulation Disorders

FOCUS 4

Identify two reasons why some professionals are reluctant to treat functional articulation disorders in young schoolchildren.

Definition.   Articulation disorders represent the largest category of all speech problems. For most of those affected, the label **functional articulation disorders** is used. This term refers to articulation problems that are not due to structural physiological defects, such as **cleft palate** or neurological problems, but are likely a result of environmental or psychological influences.

An articulation disorder is an abnormality in the speech-sound production process resulting in inaccurate or otherwise inappropriate execution of speaking. Typical problems include omissions, substitutions, additions, and distortions of certain sounds. Omissions most often involve dropping consonants from the ends of words (e.g., *los* for *lost*), although omissions may occur in any position in a word. Substitutions frequently include saying *w* for *r* (e.g., *wight* for *right*), *w* for *l* (e.g., *fowo* for *follow*), and *th* for *s* (e.g., *thtop* for *stop*, *thoup* for *soup*). Articulation errors may also involve transitional lisps, where a *th* sound

==================== **W I N D O W 8–2** ====================

My name is Timothy. I am almost 7½ years old. Mondays after school, I go to the university where I meet with a lady who helps me talk betto. It was my teacha's idea because she said I couldn't say "l" and "r" good. I kinda like it [coming here] but I think I talk okay. I can say "l" good now all the time and "r" when I reeeally think about it. I have lots of friends, fow, no—five. I don't talk to them about coming hea, guess I'm just not in the mood. Hey, you witing this down, is that "mood"? You know the caw got hit by a semi this mowning and the doow handle came off. I'm a little dizzy 'cause we wecked.

Timothy, Age 7½

precedes or follows an *s* (e.g., *sthoup* or *yeths* for *soup* or *yes*). Window 8–2 presents an illustration of a young boy, 7½ years old, who has an articulation problem. Articulation difficulties come in many forms and combinations.

Articulation disorders are a prevalent type of speech disorder. Research indicates that the majority of speech problems seen by speech clinicians involve articulation disorders (Edwards, Cape, & Brown, 1989). Van Riper and Emerick (1990) estimated that articulation problems represent about 80 percent of the speech disorders encountered by such professionals. Although most of these difficulties are functional articulation disorders, not disorders caused by conspicuous physiological defects, a certain number of articulation disorders do not fit into the functional type and may be attributed to physiological abnormalities.

There is some controversy about the treatment of articulation disorders, due in part to the large number that are functional in nature. A predictable developmental progression occurs in a substantial number of functional articulation disorders. In such cases, articulation problems diminish and may even cease to exist as the child matures. For instance, the *r, s,* or *th* problems disappear for many children after the age of 5.

This phenomenon makes many school administrators reluctant to treat functional articulation disorders in younger students, basically because of limited school resources. In other words, if a significant proportion of articulation disorders are likely to correct themselves as the child continues to develop, why expend precious resources to treat them early on? The logic is obvious and has a certain amount of appeal, but it can be applied only with caution. In general, improvement of articulation performance continues until a child is about 9 or 10 years of age. If articulation problems persist beyond this age, they are unlikely to improve unless intense intervention occurs. Furthermore, the longer such difficulties are allowed to continue, the more difficult treatment will become, and the less likely it will be successful (Cruz & Ayala, 1987).

Thus, the decision whether to treat articulation problems in young children is not an easy one. One solution is to combine articulation training with other instruction for all very young children. This may serve as an interim measure for those who have continuing problems, facilitate the growth of articulation for others, and not overly tax school resources. It does, however, require some training for teachers of young children.

Causation. What causes articulation disorders? As with many other speech problems, there are many causes. Some disorders are caused by physical malformations, such as mouth, jaw, or teeth structures that are abnormal. In other cases, articulation disorders are the result of nerve injury or brain damage. Functional articulation disorders are often seen as caused by defective learning of the speaking act in one form or another (Mecham & Willbrand, 1985). However, such categories of causation are not as distinct in practice as may be suggested by textbook discussion. There is definitely a blurring between even such broad types as functional and structural. Function and structure, although often related, are not perfectly correlated, as illustrated by the fact that some people with physical malformations that should result in articulation problems do not have problems, and vice versa.

Despite this qualifying note, we examine causation of articulation performance deficits in two general categories: those due to physical oral malformations and those that are clearly functional because there is no physical deformity. These distinctions remain useful for instructional purposes, since it is the unusual individual who overcomes a physical abnormality and articulates satisfactorily. Even with general types of causes, a variety of specific circumstances may result in articulation difficulties.

We examine physical abnormalities of the oral cavity, noting, however, that other types of physical defects can affect articulation performances, such as an abnormal or absent **larynx.** Speech formulation involves many different physical structures that must be interfaced with learned muscle/tissue movements, auditory feedback, and a multitude of other factors. Although these coordinated functions are almost never perfect, they occur for most people in an unbelievably successful manner. Malformed oral structures alter the manner in which coordinated movements must take place. With certain deformities, normal or accurate production of sounds is extremely difficult, if not impossible.

One oral malformation that most people recognize is the cleft palate, often referred to by speech pathologists as *clefts of the lip* or *palate* or both. The cleft palate is a gap in the soft palate and roof of the mouth, sometimes extending through the upper lip. The roof of the mouth serves an important function in accurate sound production. There is a reduced division of the nasal and mouth cavities with a cleft palate, which influences the movement of air so important to articulation performance. Clefts are **congenital** defects that occur in about 1 of every 700 births and may take any of several forms. Figure 8–2 shows a normal palate in part (A) and unilateral and bilateral cleft palates in (B) and (C), respectively. In cases of cleft palates, it is easy to see how articulation performance would be impaired. These problems are caused by developmental difficulties **in utero** and are often later corrected by surgery.

Dental structure also plays a significant role in articulation performance. Because the tongue and lips work together with the teeth in an intricate manner to form many sounds,

FIGURE 8–2

Normal and Cleft
Palate Configurations

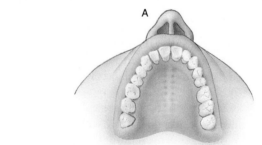

Normal palate configuration

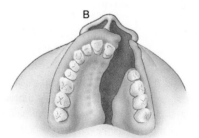

Unilateral cleft palate

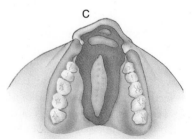

Bilateral cleft palate

dental abnormalities may result in serious articulation disorders. Some dental malformations are side effects of cleft palates, as portrayed in (B) and (C) of Figure 8–2. But other dental deformities not associated with clefts also cause articulation difficulties.

The natural meshing of the teeth in the upper and lower jaws is important to speech production. The general term used to refer to the closure and fitting together of dental structures is **occlusion,** or *dental occlusion*. When the fit is abnormal, the condition is known as **malocclusion.** Occlusion involves several factors, including the biting height of the teeth when the jaws are closed, the alignment of teeth in the upper and lower jaws, the nature of curves in upper and lower jaws, and the positioning of individual teeth.

A normal adult occlusion is portrayed in part (A) of Figure 8–3. The teeth of the upper jaw normally extend slightly beyond those of the lower jaw, and the bite overlap of those on the bottom is about one-third for the front teeth (incisors) when closed.

Although abnormalities take many forms, we discuss only two here. When the overbite of the top teeth is unusually large, the normal difference between the lower and upper dental structure is exaggerated. Such conditions may be due to the positioning of the upper and lower jaws. Part (B) of Figure 8–3 illustrates a malocclusion of the type where there is a misalignment of the jaw structures. In other cases, nearly the opposite situation occurs. This is illustrated in part (C) of Figure 8–3 and is once again a jaw misalignment. Both exaggerated overbites and underbites may also be the result of abnormal teeth positioning or angles as well as jaw misalignment. All of these may result in articulation difficulties.

Functional articulation disorders are generally thought to be caused by faulty learning. In many cases, the sources of defective speech learning are difficult to identify (Mecham & Willbrand, 1985; Van Riper & Emerick, 1990). Like other articulation problems, those of a functional nature have many specific causes (Cruz & Ayala, 1987). For example, interactions between children with articulation disorders and their mothers tend to be quite different than those of children without such problems, resembling interchanges more typical of younger children (Gardner, 1989). In some cases, the existing stimulus and reinforcement contingencies may not be appropriate for developing accurate articulation. It is not uncommon for unthinking adults to view the normal inaccuracies of speech in young children as

FIGURE 8–3

Normal and Abnormal Dental Occlusions

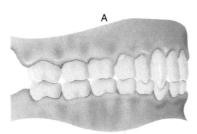

A

Normal dental occlusion

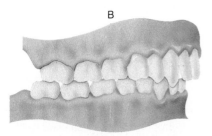

B

Overbite malocclusion

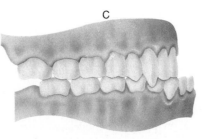

C

Underbite malocclusion

cute or amusing. Consequently such "baby talk" may be reinforced in a powerful manner, as when asking the young child to say a particular word in the presence of grandparents or other guests. This can be very rewarding for the young child, who is then on center stage and may be reinforced by laughter and physical affection like hugs and kisses. Such potent rewards can result in misarticulations that linger long beyond the time when normal maturation would diminish or eliminate them. Related defective learning may come from modeling. Parent (or other adult) modeling can result in articulation disorders when they imitate the baby talk of young children. If parents, grandparents, or friends realized the potential results of such behavior, they would probably alter the nature of verbal interchanges with young children. Modeling is generally a potent tool in shaping learned behavior, although the influence of baby talk between parents and children has been questioned (Harlan & Tschiderer, 1987).

In certain cases, parental reinforcement for accurate articulation may simply be unsystematic. Parents are busy in their daily routines, and encouraging their children to speak properly may not be high among their conscious ordering of priorities. However, such encouragement is important, particularly if misarticulation begins to emerge as a problem.

Interventions.   Treatment of articulation disorders takes many forms. Clearly, the treatment for disorders due to physical abnormalities is different from that for disorders that are functional. However, in many cases, treatment may include a combination of procedures.

In recent years, considerable progress has been made in the surgical repair of cleft palates. Such techniques may involve several different procedures because of the dramatic nature of the structural defect. Some procedures include Teflon implants in the hard portion of the palate, as well as stretching and stitching together the fleshy tissue. As suggested by Figure 8–2, surgery is often necessary for the upper lip and nose structures, and corrective dental work may be undertaken, as well. It may also be necessary to train or retrain articulation in the individual, depending on his or her age at the time of surgery. A child's continued development may result in later problems; for example, the physical growth of the jaw or mouth may create difficulties for someone who underwent surgery at a very young age. Although early correction has resulted in successful healing and speech for a very high percentage of treated cases, the permanence of such results is questionable in light of later growth spurts.

Treatment for cleft-palate cases has also involved the use of **prosthetic** appliances, for example, a device that basically serves as the upper palate or at least covers the fissures. Such an appliance may be attached to the teeth to hold it in position and can be visualized in terms of the palate portion of artificial dentures.

Dental malformations other than those associated with clefts are also often treated by means of procedures aimed at correcting the physical defect. Surgery may be undertaken to alter jaw structure and alignment. In some cases, orthodontic treatment may involve the repositioning of teeth through extractions and pressure applied using braces. Prosthetic appliances, such as full or partial artificial dentures, may also be used. As in other types of problems, the articulation patient who has orthodontic treatment often requires speech therapy to learn proper speech performance.

Treatment of people who have functional articulation disorders typically focuses on relearning the speaking act. Specific causation of defective learning is difficult to identify precisely, but the basic assumption in such cases is that an inappropriate configuration of stimulus and reinforcement was present in the environment during speech development (e.g., inappropriate modeling by parents). Treatment attempts to correct that configuration so that accurate articulation can be learned. Several behavior modification procedures have been employed successfully in treating functional articulation disorders (Mowrer & Conley, 1987). In all cases, treatment techniques are complex to implement because interventions must teach proper articulation plus the generalization of that learning to a variety of word configurations and diverse environments beyond the treatment setting (Koegel, Koegel, VanVoy, & Ingham, 1988; Weaver-Spurlock & Brasseur, 1988).

Voice Disorders

Definition.   **Voice disorders** involve unusual or abnormal acoustical qualities in the sounds made when a person speaks. All voices differ significantly in pitch, loudness, and other qualities from others of the same gender, cultural group, and age. All people have varying acoustical qualities in their voices. However, voice disorders involve characteristics that are habitually and sufficiently different such that they are noticeable and may divert a listener's attention from the content of a message.

Voice disorders have received relatively little attention compared to other speech problems, due to several factors. First, the determination of voice normalcy involves a great deal of subjective judgment. Moreover, what is normal varies considerably according to the circumstances (e.g., football games, barroom conversation, or seminar discussion) and geographical location (e.g., the West, a rural area, New England, the Deep South), as well as family environments, personality, and physical structure of the speech mechanism. Another factor contributing to the lack of attention to voice disorders is related to the acceptable ranges of normal voice. Most individuals' voices fall within acceptable tolerance ranges.

Voice disorders have received relatively little investigation from professionals in speech pathology. As a result, children with voice disorders are often not referred for help, and their problems are quite persistent when not treated (Powell, Filter, & Williams, 1989).

Children with voice disorders often speak with an unusual nasality, hoarseness, or breathiness. Nasality either involves too little resonance from the nasal passages (**hyponasality** or **denasality**), which sounds like the child has a continual cold or stuffy nose, or too much sound coming through the nose (**hypernasality**), which causes a twang in the speech. People with voice disorders of hoarseness have a constant husky sound to their speech, as though they had strained their voices by yelling. Breathiness is a voice disorder characterized

An individual's speaking ability can greatly influence how successful he or she will be in both personal and professional life. (Kevin Horan/The Picture Group)

by very low volume, somewhat like a whisper; it sounds like the person is not sending enough air through the vocal cords. Other voice disorders include overly loud or soft speaking and pitch abnormalities (e.g., monotone speech).

The nature of voice disorders varies greatly. Our description provides considerable latitude, but it also outlines the general parameters of voice disorders often discussed in the literature: pitch, loudness, and quality. An individual with a voice disorder may exhibit deviation in one or a combination of these factors, significantly interfering with communication. Interference occurs when the abnormal voice results in listener attention being focused on the sound rather than the message being conveyed.

Causation.   An appropriate voice pitch is one that is efficient and suited to the situation and the speech content as well as the speaker's **laryngeal** structure. Correct voice pitch permits inflection without voice breaks or excessive strain. Appropriate pitch varies as emotion and meaning change and should not attract attention. The acoustic characteristics of voice quality include such factors as degree of nasality, breathy speech, and hoarse-sounding speech. As with the other parameters of voice, loudness is a subjective determination. The normal voice is not habitually characterized by excessive loudness or unusual softness. Loudness depends a great deal on circumstances surrounding the communication.

Pitch disorders may take several forms. The voice may have an abnormally high or low pitch, it may be characterized by pitch breaks or a restricted pitch range, or it may be monotonal or monopitched. Many individuals experience pitch breaks as they progress through adolescence. Although these are more commonly associated with young males, they also occur in females. Such pitch breaks are a normal part of development, but if they persist much beyond adolescence, they may signal laryngeal difficulties. Abnormally high- or low-pitched voices may be due to a variety of problems. They may be learned through imitation, as when a young boy attempts to sound like his older brother or father. They may also be learned from certain circumstances, such as when an individual placed in a position of authority believes a lower voice pitch is necessary to suggest the image of power. Organic conditions, such as a hormone imbalance, may also result in abnormally high- or low-pitched voices.

Voice disorders involving loudness may likewise have varied causes. Excessively loud or soft voices may be learned either through imitation or through perceptions of the environment, much like those mentioned for pitch disorders. An example of this is mimicking the soft speaking of a female movie star. Other cases of abnormal vocal intensity occur because an individual has not learned to monitor loudness. Beyond learning difficulties, however, some intensity voice disorders occur because of organic problems. For example, abnormally low vocal intensity may result from such problems as paralysis of vocal cords, laryngeal trauma (e.g., larynx surgery for cancer, damage through accident or disease), and pulmonary diseases (e.g., **asthma** or **emphysema**). Excessively loud speech may occur as a result of such organic problems as hearing impairments and brain damage.

Voice disorders that relate to the quality of speech include such production deviances as those of abnormal nasality as well as the hoarse and breathy speech noted earlier. Abnormal nasality may take the form of a voice that sounds overly nasal (hypernasality) or a voice with reduced acoustic sound (denasality or hyponasality) that dulls the resonance of consonants. Hypernasality occurs essentially because the rear opening of the nose does not close adequately. Such conditions can be due to improper tissue movement in the speech mechanism, or they may result from such organic defects as an imperfectly repaired cleft palate. Excessive hypernasality may also be acquired through learning, as in the case of country music or speech that represents an extreme form of the hillbilly dialect. Denasality is a type of voice quality that is experienced with a severe head cold or hay fever. The sounds produced are congested and/or dulled, with reduced acoustic resonance. In some cases, however, denasality is the result of learning or abnormal physical structures rather than these more common problems.

Interventions. Approaches to voice disorder treatment depend on causation. In some cases, when abnormal tissue and/or dental structures result in unusual voice production, surgical intervention may be necessary. In other situations, treatment may involve direct instruction to help the affected individual's learning or relearning of acceptable voice production. Such interventions often include counseling regarding the effects of unusual voice sounds on others and behavior modification procedures aimed at retraining the person's speaking. These efforts are more difficult if the behavior has been longstanding and is well ingrained as a learned habit. We have discussed interventions such as these previously under other speech disorders.

Voice disorders are not frequently the focus of referral and treatment in the United States, although they receive considerable attention in the United Kingdom (Elias, Raven, Butcher, & Littlejohns, 1989; Powell et al., 1989). Some researchers have argued strongly, however, that voice disorders should be treated more aggressively (Kahane & Mayo, 1989). Interested readers may wish to consult other volumes focusing solely on speech problems for further information on interventions with voice disorders (Emerick & Haynes, 1986; Mecham & Willbrand, 1985).

Prevalence

We have already encountered the difficulties involved in estimating the prevalence of other disorders, due to differences in definitions and data-collection procedures. The field of speech disorders is very vulnerable to these problems, and thus, prevalence estimates vary considerably.

The most typical prevalence figures cited for speech disorders indicate that between 7 and 10 percent of the population is affected (Emerick & Haynes, 1986). These figures do not deviate greatly from other estimates over the years, although some data have suggested substantial differences between geographic locales (e.g., significantly higher percentages in some areas of California than in parts of the Midwest). These figures present difficulties when we consider the overall 12 percent ceiling for services to *all* students who are disabled, as specified in the Individuals with Disabilities Education Act (IDEA). Obviously, individuals with speech disorders of a mild nature cannot be eligible for federally funded services. In the *Thirteenth Annual Report to Congress* on the implementation of IDEA, approximately 23 percent of those who received special services during 1989–1990 were classified as having speech or language impairments (U.S. Department of Education, 1991).

The frequency with which speech problems occur diminishes in the population as age increases. Speech disorders are identified in about 12 to 15 percent of the children in kindergarten through grade four. For children in grades five through eight, the figure declines to about 4 to 5 percent. The 5 percent rate remains somewhat constant after grade eight unless treatment intervenes. Thus, age and development serve to diminish speech disorders considerably, more so with certain types of problems (e.g., articulation difficulties) than with others.

LANGUAGE DISORDERS

Language has assumed many forms throughout history. Early Native Americans communicated through systems of clucking sounds made with the tongue and teeth. Such sounds were also used in combination with hand signs and spoken language that often differed greatly between tribes. (These language systems have been described in historical documents. An excellent portrayal of such language differences is found in *Sacajawea* by A. L. Waldo, 1984.)

Current definitions of language reflect the breadth necessary to encompass diverse communication systems. For example, Lucas (1980) noted that language reflects "a system of symbols agreed upon by two or more people and governed by the linguistic properties inherent in phonology, syntax, morphology, and semantics" (p. 242). Bernstein (1985) defined language as "the system of rules governing sounds, words, meaning, and use. . . . These rules underlie both linguistic comprehension (the understanding of language) and linguistic production (the formulation of language)" (p. 6).

The variety of speech disorders discussed earlier all involved problems related to verbal production, that is, vocal expression. Language disorders pertain to serious difficulties in the ability to understand or express *ideas* in the communication system being used. The distinction between speech and language disorders is like the difference between the *sound* of a word and the *meaning* of a word. As we examine language disorders, we discuss difficulties in meaning, both expressing it and receiving it.

Definition

FOCUS 5

Identify two ways in which language delay and language disorders are different.

Language disorders occur when there is a serious disruption of the language development process. Such malfunctions may occur in one or more of the components of language. Because language is one of the most complex sets of behaviors exhibited by humans, language disorders are complex and present some perplexing assessment problems (Allen & Bliss, 1987; Groshong, 1987; Wnuk, 1987). Language involves memory, learning, message reception and processing, and expressive skills. An individual with a language disorder may have deficits in any of these areas, and it may be difficult to identify precisely the nature of the problem. In addition, language problems may arise in the form of language delays or language disorders.

The term **language delay** is used to describe when the normal *rate* of developmental progress is interrupted but the systematic *sequence* of development remains essentially intact (i.e., the development follows a normal pattern or course of growth but is substantially slower than in most children of the same age). The term *language disorder* is different in that it refers to circumstances when language acquisition is not systematic and/or sequential. "A language disordered child is not progressing systematically and sequentially in any aspect of rule-governed and purposive linguistic behavior" (Lucas, 1980, pp. 52, 54). We will use the term *language disorder* in a general sense to discuss several types of behaviors. Where evidence suggests that delay may be a major contributor, we discuss it as such.

Classification

A wide range of terminology is used to describe the processes involved in language as well as disorders in those processes. In many cases, language disorders are classified according to their causes, which may be known or only suspected. In other cases, specific labels tend to be employed, such as **aphasia.** There is some uncertainty in the literature regarding classification of language disorders, although one common approach is to view them in terms of *receptive* and *expressive* problems (Ewing-Cobbs, 1987; Kerbeshian, Gascon, & Burd, 1988). We examine both of these categories as well as aphasia, a problem that may occur in both children and adults.

Receptive Language Disorders.   Difficulties in comprehending what others say result in **receptive language disorders.** In many cases, receptive language problems in children are noticed when they do not follow an adult's instructions. These children may seem inattentive or as though they do not listen to directions (Cole & Cole, 1989). Individuals with receptive language disorders have great difficulty understanding other people's messages and may process only part (or none) of what is being said to them. They have a substantial problem in language *processing,* which is basically half of language (the other part being language *production*). Language processing is essentially listening to and interpreting spoken language (Wiig & Semel, 1984).

Our discussion of some of the behavior noted earlier corresponds to the discussion in Chapter Six on learning disabilities. Namely, it is not uncommon for receptive language problems to appear in students with learning disabilities. Such language deficits contribute significantly to these students' academic performance problems as well as difficulties in social interactions (Smith, 1991).

Expressive Language Disorders.   **Expressive language disorders** are exhibited when individuals have difficulty in language production or formulating and using spoken language (Wiig & Semel, 1984). Those who have expressive language disorders may have limited vocabularies and rely on the same array of words regardless of the situation (Cole & Cole, 1989). Expressive language disorders may appear as immature speech and often result in personal interaction difficulties. People with expressive language disorders also rely on hand signals and facial expressions to communicate.

Aphasia.   Definitions of aphasia have varied over time but still employ strikingly consistent themes. For example, Wood (1971) noted that aphasia was the "partial or complete loss of the ability to speak or to comprehend the spoken word due to injury, disease, or maldevelopment of the brain" (p. 11). Wiig and Semel (1984) viewed aphasia as involving those who have acquired a language disorder because of brain damage resulting in impairment of language comprehension, formulation, and use. Thus, definitions of aphasia commonly link the disorder to brain injury, either through mechanical accidents, as we saw in the case of Millie (Window 8–1) or other damage, such as that caused by a stroke (Henderson, 1990). Over the years, many different types of aphasia and/or conditions associated with aphasia have been identified and labeled, such as agnosia, paraphrasia, and dysprosody. Aphasic language disturbances have also been classified in terms of receptive and expressive problems.

WINDOW 8-3

MILLIE'S PROGRESS: INTERVIEW WITH THERAPIST

Remember Millie from the beginning of this chapter, the Texas real estate broker who developed aphasia following an automobile accident? As the car struck a large boulder, Millie's head was thrown forward against the steering wheel, which caused injury to the front part of her brain. Millie's recovery and relearning of speech are characteristic of such an injury. Although she can understand others reasonably well, she has great difficulty articulating her responses. The following interaction with her therapist illustrates the nature of Millie's language at this point:

Therapist: Good Morning, Millie. How are you today?

Millie: (responding very slowly, with labored speech): I fine.

Therapist: I think today we should finish the magazine article that we started last time.

Millie: Yes. I no book (indicating that she forgot to bring the magazine).

Therapist: That's alright. I have an extra copy right here. We can use it instead of yours.

Millie: Millie betto, I till foget.

Therapist: Yes, you are getting much better. You still forget some things, but everyone does, so don't worry.

Aphasia may be present both in childhood and during the adult years. The term *developmental aphasia* has been widely used with affected children, despite the long-standing association of such problems with neurological damage. Aphasic children often begin to use words at age 2 or later and phrases at age 4. The link between aphasia and neurological abnormalities in children has been of continuing interest to researchers; some evidence has suggested a connection between the two (Cooper & Flowers, 1987). Despite theories and assumptions, in many cases of aphasia in children, objective evidence identifying neurological dysfunction has been difficult to acquire.

Adult aphasia has been defined in as many ways as childhood aphasia. Adult aphasia typically can be linked to accidents or injuries that are more likely to occur during this part of the life span, such as gunshot wounds, motorcycle or auto accidents, and strokes. Current research has suggested that varying symptoms result from damage to different parts of the brain. Those with injury to the front part of the brain often can comprehend better than they can speak; they also have considerable difficulty finding words, have poor articulation with labored and slow speech, omit small words such as *of* and *the,* and generally have reduced verbal production. Individuals with aphasia resulting from injury to the posterior (back part) of the brain seem to have more fluent speech but it lacks content. Speech may also be characterized by use of an unnecessarily large number of words to express an idea or use of unusual or meaningless terms. The speech of these individuals appears to reflect impaired comprehension.

Causation

FOCUS 6

Identify three factors thought to cause language disorders.

Identifying the precise causes of different language disorders can be difficult (Kerbeshian et al., 1988). The answers are not clear regarding what contributes to normal language acquisition, exactly how those contributions occur, and how malfunctions influence language disorders. We do know that certain sensory and other physiological systems must be intact and developing normally for language processes to develop normally. For example, if hearing is seriously impaired, a language deficit may result. Likewise, serious brain damage might deter normal language functioning. Learning must also progress in a systematic and sequential fashion for language to develop appropriately. For example, children must first attend to the communication around them before they can mimic it or attach meaning to it. Language learning is like other learning: It must be stimulated and reinforced in order to be acquired and mastered.

In our discussion of other communication disorders, we have encountered many of the physiological problems that may also cause language difficulties. Neurological damage that may affect language functioning can occur prenatally, during birth, or anytime throughout life. For example, oxygen deprivation before or during birth or an accident later in life can all cause language problems. Serious emotional disorders may be accompanied by language disturbances if an individual's perception of the world is substantially distorted.

Learning opportunities may be seriously deficient or otherwise disrupted and result in language disorders. As with speech, children may not learn language if the environment is not conducive to such learning. Modeling in the home may be so infrequent that a child cannot learn language in a normal fashion. This might be the case in a family where no speaking occurs because the parents are deaf, even when the children have normal hearing. Such circumstances are rare, but when they occur, a language delay is likely. The parents cannot model language for their children, nor can they respond to and reinforce such behavior.

It should be emphasized, however, that learning outcomes are variable. In situations that seem normal, we may find a child with serious language difficulty. In circumstances

=================== **W I N D O W 8–4** ===================

WE DIDN'T KNOW THEY WERE DIFFERENT

My name is Cy, and I am one of the four brothers mentioned. Both of my parents were deaf from a very early age; they never learned to speak. When you ask me how we learned speech, I can't really answer, knowing what I now know about how those very early years are so important in this area. When we were really young, we didn't even know they were deaf or different (except for Dad's active sense of humor). Naturally, we didn't talk; we just signed. We lived way out in the country and were pretty isolated—all four of us just played together and didn't have other playmates. Grandma and Grandpa lived close by, and I spent a lot of time with them. That is when I began to know something was different. We probably began learning to talk there.

When we were about ready to start school, we moved into town. My first memory related to school is sitting in a sandbox,

I guess on the playground. We had some troubles in school, but they were fairly minor as I recall. I could't talk or pronounce words very well. I was tested on an IQ test in the third grade and had an IQ of 67. Both Mom and Dad worked, and so we were all sort of out on our own with friends, which probably helped language, but now I wonder why those kids didn't stay away from us because we were a bit different. Probably the saving grace is that all four of us seem to have pretty well-developed social intelligence or skills. We did get in some fights with kids, and people sometimes called us the "dumby's kids." I would guess that all four of us pretty much caught up with our peers by the eighth grade. One thing is for certain: I would not trade those parents for any other in the world: Whatever they did, they certainly did right.

Cy, Ph.D.

that seem dismal, we may find a child whose language facility is normal. Gelfand et al. (1988) cited an example involving four brothers with normal hearing who were born to and raised by parents who were both deaf and had no spoken language facility. The boys seemed to develop language quite normally, although they could not explain that development. They have distinguished themselves in various manners, ranging from earning Ph.D.s and M.D.s (one holds both degrees) to becoming a millionaire through patented inventions.

This example represents a rare set of circumstances, but it is a good illustration of how variable and poorly understood language learning is. The assumption has long been that language-deprived environments place children at risk for exhibiting language delays or disorders. For example, it has been thought that language acquisition may be delayed when parents use baby talk in communicating with their young children. Such a view is based on the fundamental principles of learning theory that children learn what is modeled and taught.

There is little question that this perspective is sound with most skill acquisition. Many clinical reports of language problems uphold such a notion, and research has also supported certain relationships between parental verbalizations and child language development (Fitzgerald & Karnes, 1987; Gardner, 1989; Richard, 1986). From another view, however, Cromer (1981) reviewed research on language acquisition and concluded that "most studies of baby talk fail to explain the acquisition of [language] structure" (p. 70). The effects of parent modeling on child language development may not be clear and simple.

An assumption of brain damage is usually associated with aphasia during adulthood. The causes of such brain damage are diverse. Various physical traumas may result in aphasia, such as automobile and industrial accidents or shooting incidents. This type of circumstance was illustrated in Window 8–1 about Millie. Other factors (e.g., strokes, tumors, and diseases) that affect brain tissue may have the same result. In most cases, aphasic trauma seems to be associated with damage to the left hemisphere of the brain.

The distinction between speech problems and language problems is blurred because they overlap as much as the two functions of speech and language overlap. Thus, receptive and expressive language disorders are as intertwined as speech and language. When an individual does not express language well, is it because he or she has a receptive problem or an expressive problem? The two cannot be cleanly separated. Thus, causation also cannot be clearly divided into categories.

Interventions

FOCUS 7

Describe two ways in which treatment approaches for language disorders generally differ for children and adults.

Language disorder treatment must take into account the nature of the problem and the manner in which an individual is affected. Intervention is an individualized undertaking, just as with other types of disorders. Some causes are more easily identified than others and may or may not be remedied by mechanical or medical intervention. Other types of treatment basically involve instruction or language training.

Several steps are involved in effective language training, including (1) identification, (2) assessment, (3) development of instructional objectives, (4) development of language intervention program, (5) implementation of the intervention program, (6) reassessment of the child, and (7) reteaching, if necessary (Cole & Cole, 1989). These steps are very similar to the general stages involved in special education interventions for other disorders. Thus, the customary approach to language disorder intervention follows the basic steps for treatment, as outlined in IDEA. Specific programs of intervention obviously include details not evident at this level.

Language-training programs are tailored to an individual's strengths and limitations. In fact, current terminology labels these individualized language plans (ILPs), similar in concept to the individualized educational plans (IEPs) mandated by IDEA. These intervention plans include long-range goals (annual), a set of more short-range and specific behavioral objectives, a statement of the resources to be used in achieving the objectives, a description of evaluation methods, program beginning and ending dates, and an evaluation of the individual's generalization of skills. For young children, such interventions often focus on beginning language stimulation. Treatment is intended to mirror the conditions under which children normally learn language, but the conditions may be intensified and taught more systematically (Chapman & Terrell, 1988). In many cases, parents are trained and involved in the intervention.

Intervention for some individuals involves using means of communicating other than oral language. In some cases, the person may be incapable of speaking because of a severe physical or cognitive disability. For him or her, a nonspeech means of communicating needs to be designed and implemented. Known as **assistive, alternative,** or **augmentative communication,** these strategies may involve a wide variety of approaches, some employing the capability of new technological developments. Today's Technology 8–1 describes an augmentative communication device known as DynaVox, which illustrates such an approach.

Many approaches have been used to remediate aphasia, but consistent and verifiable results have been slow to emerge. As with other disorders, remediation typically involves the development of an individual's profile of strengths, limitations, age, and developmental level (Ylvisaker, 1986). From this profile, an individualized treatment plan can be designed. Several questions or points immediately surface, including what to teach or remediate first and whether teaching should focus on an individual's strong or weak areas. These questions have been raised from time to time with respect to many disorders. Nearly all clinicians have their own opinions or some personal formula for balancing the extremes. Teaching exclusively to a child's weak areas may result in more failure experiences than are either necessary or helpful to his or her overall progress. This may occur because, being taught solely in the weakest areas, the child receives so little success and reinforcement that he or she becomes discouraged about the whole process. Good clinical judgment needs to be exercised in balancing remediation attention to the aphasic child's strengths and weaknesses.

Augmentative Communication Aid

DynaVox is a voice-output communication aid that is activated by a touch screen, such as that shown here. This technology is particularly exciting because the communication options can be designed and created by the therapist to meet the particular needs of an individual client. The touch screen changes, depending on the communication underway. For example, if the person selects *food* in a main display, the screen changes instantly to present a variety of choices related to food, DynaVox provides for voice output, with choices of 10 different voices (male, female, child) and even has the ability to customize a unique voice for the individual, should that be desirable. Selections can be made in a number of fashions, such as touching with a finger or touchstick or using a joystick, such as that used with electronic games. This battery-operated device (rechargeable with up to 14 hours of operation on a charge) represents one type of technology application being used for augmentative communication.

Remediation for adults with aphasia begins from a perspective different than that for children in that it involves relearning or reacquiring language function. Views regarding treatment have varied over the years. Early approaches included the expectation that adult aphasics would exhibit spontaneous recovery if left alone. This approach has largely been replaced by the view that patients are more likely to progress when direct therapeutic instruction is available.

Therapy for adults with aphasia has some predictable similarities to treatment for children. Areas of strength and limitation must receive attention when an individualized remediation program is being planned. However, development of a profile of strengths and deficits may involve some areas different from those of children because of age differences. For example, social, linguistic, and vocational readjustments represent three broad areas that

A Language Tutorial Program

Computer technology has made inroads in many areas of human disability in the past few years and will become increasingly important in the future. Language disability intervention is one example of an area in which advances in both hardware and software have had an impact, with substantial potential for future development. First Words is a language tutorial progam that may have a number of applications for teaching those who are developing or reacquiring language functions. This program uses graphic presentations on a screen that are combined with synthesized speech to teach and test a student's acquisition of high-frequency nouns. The student is presented with two pictures of an object and asked to decide which one represents the word being taught. Students can select an answer via a computer keyboard, or a special selection switch, or by touching the object on the screen. First Words is a relatively inexpensive program, costing about $200. The voice synthesizer and the touch screen options must be added to the basic package but may be essential elements to effective intervention, depending on the student's capability. First Words is currently available for the Apple family of computers.

need attention for most adults with aphasia. Although children need attention beyond just language therapy, some aspects of adult treatment are not relevant (e.g., vocational readjustment), and the notion of readjustment differs substantially from initial skill acquisition.

An individualized treatment program for adult aphasics also involves evaluation, profile development, and teaching in specific behavioral areas within each of the broad domains. Such training should begin as soon as possible, depending on the patient's condition. Some spontaneous recovery often occurs during the first six months after an incident resulting in aphasia. However, waiting beyond two months to begin treatment may not only be unnecessary but also seriously delay recovery to whatever degree may be possible.

Debate   Forum   ·············· To Treat or Not to Treat? ·············

Articulation problems represent about 80 percent of all speech disorders encountered by speech clinicians, making this type of difficulty the most prevalent of all communication disorders. It is also well-known that young children normally make a number of articulation errors during the process of maturation as they are learning to talk. A substantial portion do not conquer all the rules of language and produce all the speech sounds correctly until they are 8 or 9 years old, yet they eventually develop normal speech and articulate properly. In lay terminology, they seem to "grow out of" early articulation problems. Because of this maturation outcome and the prevalence of articulation problems, serious questions are asked regarding treatment in the early years.

Point   Some school administrators are reluctant to treat young children who display articulation errors. The resources of school districts are in very short supply, and budgets are

extremely tight. If a substantial proportion of young children's articulation problems will correct themselves through maturation, then shouldn't the precious resources of school districts be directed to other more pressing problems? Articulation problems should not be treated unless they persist beyond the age of 10 or 11.

Counterpoint   While it is true that articulation improves with maturation, it is a mistake to delay interventions. The longer such problems are allowed to persist, the more difficult treatment will be. Even the issue of financial savings is a false one. If all articulation difficulties are allowed to continue, those children who do not outgrow such problems will be more difficult to treat later, requiring more intense and expensive intervention than if treated early. Early intervention for articulation problems is vitally important.

REVIEW ··········

FOCUS 1   Identify four ways in which speech, language, and communication are interrelated.
◆ Both speech and language are part but not all of communication.
◆ Some components of communication involve language but not speech.
◆ Some speech does not involve language.
◆ In humans, the development of communication, language, and speech overlap to some degree.

FOCUS 2   Identify three factors thought to cause stuttering.
◆ Emotional problems, neurological problems, and learned behavior can contribute to stuttering.
◆ Some research has suggested that people who stutter have a different brain organization from those who do not.

◆ People who stutter may learn their speech patterns as an outgrowth of the normal nonfluency evident when speech development first occurs.

FOCUS 3   Identify two ways in which learning theory and home environment relate to delayed speech.
◆ The home environment may provide little opportunity to learn speech.
◆ The home environment may interfere with speech development when speaking is punished.

FOCUS 4   Identify two reasons why some professionals are reluctant to treat functional articulation disorders in young schoolchildren.
◆ Many articulation problems evident in young children are developmental in nature, and speech may improve with age.

◆ Articulation problems are quite frequent among young children, and treatment resources are limited.

FOCUS 5   Identify two ways in which language delay and language disorder are different.

◆ In language delay, the *sequence* of development is intact but the *rate* is interrupted.
◆ In language disorder, the *sequence* of development is interrupted.

FOCUS 6   Identify three factors thought to cause language disorders.

◆ Defective or deficient sensory systems

◆ Neurological damage occurring through physical trauma or accident
◆ Deficient or disrupted learning opportunities during language development

FOCUS 7   Describe two ways in which treatment approaches for language disorders generally differ for children and for adults.

◆ Treatment for children generally addresses initial acquisition or learning of language.
◆ Treatment for adults involves relearning or reacquiring language function.

Chapter Nine

Autism

TO BEGIN WITH . . .

◆ "His way of walking on the balls of his feet was akin to prancing. . . . Both boys relied heavily on peripheral vision. Even when spoken to, I felt like they listened to me 'sideways'" (Biklen, 1990, p. 291).

◆ "He would spend hours spinning various objects or watching records spin on his parents' phonograph. When his mother took him to nursery school each day, . . . he spent his entire time there spinning objects (Bemporad, 1979, p. 188).

◆ "When he talked, and he rarely did, he sounded very mechanical, echoing back what other people had said but seldom expressing an original thought. Words were only meaningless collections of sounds to him" (Pingree, 1983, p. 57).

KIM

RAIN MAN. The character of Raymond Babbitt, played by Dustin Hoffman in *Rain Man*, was labeled an autistic **savant** in the film. Raymond exhibited a number of unusual behaviors that are characteristic of people with autism. His interaction with other people was somewhat strange, and much of the time, he appeared to function in a world of his own, apart from that experienced by those around him. If someone changed Raymond's environment, which had been arranged meticulously according to his unique sense of order, he became very upset and acted as though the world was coming apart.

These and other significant, sometimes subtle behaviors portrayed by Hoffman made his character appear to have autism. However, perhaps the most spectacular situations in the movie were those in which Raymond's extraordinary skills emerged—knowing phone numbers of people he had never met, knowing the number of toothpicks in a box, or "counting cards" in Las Vegas with computerlike accuracy. These skills represented the savant dimension of his label and, to many people, may seem rather unbelievable. Although the occurrence is very rare, savant skills do exist in some people with autism, as exemplified by Kim, one of the two young men who inspired the story of *Rain Man*.

Forty-year-old Kim is a behavioral contradiction, with performances ranging from extraordinary to quite poor. At one end of the continuum, Kim has encyclopedic knowledge and abilities in at least seven areas (mathematics, history, music, literature, calendar calculation, geography, and map memorization). Tell him your birthday, and he will tell you on which day of the week it occurred and also the day of the week on which you will turn 65. At the other extreme, Kim has significantly below average reasoning skills and motor ability. Conversations with Kim often involve seemingly random changes in direction and thought. Kim is definitely not typical of people with autism, although some of his behaviors have definite autistic qualities. Only about 15 percent of individuals with autism exhibit extraordinarily high performance in given skill areas.

INTRODUCTION

The Individuals with Disabilities Education Act of 1990 (IDEA) added autism as a category of disability to the existing law. Although newly recognized in federal legislation, autism first began to appear in the research literature in the first half of the twentieth century (Kanner, 1943). The word *autism* was taken from the Greek *autos,* meaning "self," to indicate the extreme sense of isolation and detachment from the world around them that characterizes these individuals who are autistic.

Symptoms of autism primarily appear very early. Most cases emerge before the age of 2½; few are diagnosed after the age of 5. Autism is one of the most disruptive of childhood disabilities, resulting in varying degrees of deficiencies in language, interpersonal skills, emotional or affective behavior, and intellectual functioning. It is a disability that impairs the normal development of many areas of functioning.

Autism has received increased attention during the past several years by both researchers and the media. An example of this public visibility is found in the 1988 movie *Rain Man*, which starred Dustin Hoffman as an adult with autism. Although many people first learned about autism through this film, the portrayal was not one of typical autism, as indicated in Window 9–1.

FOCUS 1
Identify four areas of functional challenge often found in children with autism.

The Academy Award-winning film *Rain Man* inspired broader awareness of the complexities of autism. (MGM/Shooting Star)

DEFINITION

Proposed federal regulations for IDEA provided the following definition of autism:

> *Autism* means a developmental disability significantly affecting verbal and nonverbal communication and social interaction, generally evident before age three, that adversely affects educational performance. Characteristics of autism include—irregularities and impairments in communication, engagement in repetitive activities and stereotyped movements, resistance to environmental change or change in daily routines, and unusual responses to sensory experiences. (Department of Education, 1991, p. 41271)

This definition specifically refers to developmental evidence appearing before 3 years of age, since it is commonly accepted that symptoms of autism emerge during the early years. However, it is not the intent of the definition to preclude a diagnosis of autism if a child shows evidence of the condition *after* age 3. It should also be noted that the proposed federal regulations specifically state that a diagnosis of autism should not be made in children with characteristics of serious emotional disturbance, since they are addressed elsewhere in the law (Department of Education, 1991, p. 41266).

Although definitional statements are helpful to some degree, most professionals are reluctant to make sweeping generalizations regarding people with autism. It is important to remember that not all people with autism are alike. It is more accurate to speak of *characteristics* than to *characterize*. The diagnostic criteria employed for autism add to the descriptive picture of these individuals. Table 9–1 provides a summary of the diagnostic criteria outlined for autism by the American Psychiatric Association (APA, 1987).

PREVALENCE

Autism is a relatively rare condition. The American Psychiatric Association has estimated that the prevalence is about 4 to 5 cases per 10,000 (APA, 1987). This rate of occurrence has been supported by some researchers (e.g., Ritvo et al., 1989), although other results have shown considerably higher figures of 10 to 14 per 10,000 (Bryson, Clark, & Smith, 1988; Cialdella & Mamelle, 1989).

FOCUS 2

What are the two general ranges of prevalence estimated for autism?

■ **Table 9–1** Diagnostic Criteria for Autism

At least eight of the following sixteen items are present, these to include at least two items from A, one from B, and one from C.

Note: Consider a criterion to be met *only* if the behavior is abnormal for the person's developmental level.

A. Qualitative impairment in reciprocal social interaction as manifested by the following:

(The examples within parentheses are arranged so that those first mentioned are more likely to apply to younger or more handicapped, and the later ones, to older or less handicapped, persons with this disorder.)

___ (1) marked lack of awareness of the existence or feelings of others (e.g., treats a person as if he or she were a piece of furniture; does not notice another person's distress; apparently has no concept of the need of others for privacy)

___ (2) no or abnormal seeking of comfort at times of distress (e.g., does not come for comfort even when ill, hurt, or tired; seeks comfort in a stereotyped way, e.g., says "cheese, cheese, cheese" whenever hurt)

___ (3) no or impaired imitation (e.g., does not wave bye-bye; does not copy mother's domestic activities; mechanical imitation of others' actions out of context)

___ (4) no or abnormal social play (e.g., does not actively participate in simple games; prefers solitary play activities; involves other children in play only as "mechanical aids")

___ (5) gross impairment in ability to make peer friendships (e.g., no interest in making peer friendships; despite interest in making friends, demonstrates lack of understanding of conventions of social interaction, for example, reads phone book to uninterested peer)

B. Qualitative impairment in verbal and nonverbal communication, and in imaginative activity, as manifested by the following:

(The numbered items are arranged so that those first listed are more likely to apply to younger or more handicapped, and the later ones, to older or less handicapped, persons with this disorder.)

___ (1) no mode of communication, such as communicative babbling, facial expression, gesture, mime, or spoken language.

___ (2) markedly abnormal nonverbal communication, as in the use of eye-to-eye gaze, facial expression, body posture, or gestures to initiate or modulate social interaction (e.g., does not anticipate being held, stiffens when held, does not

Such variation in prevalence is likely due to differences in definition and diagnostic criteria employed and may diminish as greater consensus about what constitutes autism is achieved over time. Gender differences are evident in autism, with males outnumbering females substantially. Estimates of these prevalence differences range from 2.5 to 1 to 4 to 1 (Bryson et al., 1988; Dunlap, Koegel, & O'Neill, 1985).

■ **Table 9–1** Continued

      look at the person or smile when making a social approach, does not greet
      parents or visitors, has a fixed stare in social situations)

__ (3) absence of imaginative activity, such as playacting of adult roles, fantasy
      characters, or animals; lack of interest in stories about imaginary events

__ (4) marked abnormalities in the production of speech, including volume, pitch,
      stress, rate, rhythm, and intonation (e.g., monotonous tone, questionlike
      melody, or high pitch)

__ (5) marked abnormalities in the form or content of speech, including stereotyped
      and repetitive use of speech (e.g., immediate echolalia or mechanical repetition
      of television commercial); use of "you" when "I" is meant (e.g., using "You
      want cookie?" to mean "I want a cookie"); idiosyncratic use of words or
      phrases (e.g., "Go on green riding" to mean "I want to go on the swing"); or
      frequent irrelevant remarks (e.g., starts talking about train schedules during a
      conversation about sports)

__ (6) marked impairment in the ability to initiate or sustain a conversation with
      others, despite adequate speech (e.g., indulging in lengthy monologues on one
      subject regardless of interjections from others)

C. Markedly restricted repertoire of activities and interests, as manifested by the
   following:

__ (1) stereotyped body movements, e.g., hand-flicking or -twisting, spinning,
      head-banging, complex whole-body movements

__ (2) persistent preoccupation with parts of objects (e.g., sniffing or smelling
      objects, repetitive feeling of texture of materials, spinning wheels of toy cars)
      or attachment to unusual objects (e.g., insists on carrying around a piece of
      string)

__ (3) marked distress over changes in trivial aspects of environment, e.g., when a
      vase is moved from usual position

__ (4) unreasonable insistence on following routines in precise detail, e.g., insisting
      that exactly the same route always be followed when shopping

__ (5) markedly restricted range of interests and a preoccupation with one narrow
      interest, e.g., interested only in lining up objects, in amassing facts about
      meteorology, or in pretending to be a fantasy character

D. Onset during infancy or childhood.

Specify if childhood onset (after 36 months of age).

Source: American Psychiatric Association: *Diagnostic and Statistical Manual of Mental Disorders, Third Edition, Revised*, Washington, DC, American Psychiatric Association, 1987.

CHARACTERISTICS

Children with autism exhibit a number of rather unusual behaviors and characteristics, some of which are evident very early in life. For example, significant impairment in interpersonal interaction may be observed by parents of infants with autism. These babies may be notably

FOCUS 3
Identify six characteristics of children with autism.

Children with autism often seem to avoid eye contact with others. (Craig Hammell/The Stock Market)

unresponsive to physical contact or affection. Parents often report that their infants become rigid when they are picked up and are "not cuddly." They may also avoid eye contact, averting their gaze rather than looking directly at another person. Such behavior may continue in older children, as evident in Biklen's description of 11- and 12-year-olds quoted in the "To Begin With" section of this chapter. In many cases, there is heavy reliance on using peripheral vision rather than making direct, face-to-face visual contact.

Children with autism are frequently described as exhibiting social impairments, being socially unresponsive, and having extreme difficulty relating to other people (Ricks, 1989; Szatmari, Bartolucci, & Bremner, 1989). Often, it seems that they prefer interacting with inanimate objects, forming attachments to objects rather than people. Children with autism appear to be insensitive to the feelings of others and in many cases treat other people as objects, even physically pushing or pulling others around to suit their needs (Sue, Sue, & Sue, 1990). Clearly, children with autism interact with their environment in ways that are not typical. It is as if they have difficulty making sense of the world around them.

Impaired or Delayed Language

Children with autism routinely exhibit an impaired or delayed facility with language. Approximately half do not develop speech, and those who do often engage in strange language and speaking behavior, such as **echolalia** (repeating back only what has been said to them) (Loveland, McEvoy, & Tunali, 1990; Szatmari et al., 1989). In many cases, children with autism who speak reproduce parts of conversations that they have heard but do so in a very mechanical fashion, with no sign that they attach meaning to what was said. This echolalic behavior is sometimes misinterpreted as an indicator of high intellectual abilities. Typically, children with autism who develop language have a limited speaking repertoire and fail to use pronouns in speech directed at other people (Oshima-Takane & Benaroya, 1989;

Schreibman, 1988). It appears that these children make little use of semantics in sentence structure (Paul, Fischer, & Cohen, 1988). Additionally, the tonal quality of their speech is often unusual or flat, and in some cases, their speech appears to serve the purpose of self-stimulation rather than communication.

Self-Stimulation

Self-stimulation is a behavior frequently associated with autism, although, like many other characteristics, self-stimulation is not always present (Akyurek & Kalverboer, 1986; Durand & Carr, 1987). Children with autism often engage in physical forms of self-stimulation, such as flicking their hands in front of their faces repeatedly. They also tend to manipulate objects in a repetitive fashion, suggesting self-stimulation. Behavior such as spinning objects, rocking, or hand-flapping may continue for hours. Some behaviors that seem to start as self-stimulation may worsen or take different forms and create potential injury to the child, such as face-slapping, biting, and head-banging. Behavior that becomes self-injurious is more often found in low-functioning children and can understandably cause concern and stress for parents and others around them (Konstantareas & Homatidis, 1989).

Resistance to Change in Routine

Children with autism are frequently characterized as having an intense resistance to change (Schreibman, 1988). Familiar routines—for example, at bedtime—are obsessively important to them, and any deviation from the set pattern may upset them greatly. Youngsters who are affected in this manner may insist on a particular furniture arrangement or one type of food for a given meal (e.g., specific cereal for breakfast); they may even wash themselves in a particular pattern. Often, items must be arranged in a given fashion for things to seem proper for the child with autism.

These obsessive, ritualistic behaviors create numerous problems, as one might expect, particularly if there is an effort to integrate the child into daily life activities. For example, most people pay little attention to the *exact* route that they take when they drive to the grocery store or the *precise* pattern of moving through the store once they arrive. However, for parents attempting to take their child with autism along, minor deviations may cause serious crisis situations (Dunlap, Koegel, & O'Neill, 1985).

Intelligence

Most children with autism exhibit low intellectual functioning, with about 75 percent having measured IQs below 70 (Sue et al., 1990). These children have particular difficulty with verbal and reasoning skills in intelligence testing situations. Intellectual ability varies among children having autism, with high-functioning individuals testing at a normal or near-normal level. While these youngsters may have rather substantial vocabularies, they do not always know the appropriate use of terms that they can spell and define.

Approximately 10 to 15 percent of those with autism exhibit what are known as *splinter skills,* areas of ability in which performance levels are unexpectedly high compared to those of other domains of functioning. For instance, a student with autism may perform unusually well at memory tasks or drawing but have serious deficiencies in language skills and abstract thinking. For parents of such students, these splinter skills create enormous confusion. Although most parents realize early on that their child with autism is exceptional, they also hope that he or she is healthy. These hopes may be fueled by the child's demonstration of unusual skills. In some cases, the parents may believe that whatever is wrong is their fault, as portrayed in Window 9–2.

WINDOW 9–2

REFLECTIONS OF A PARENT

Steven was 2½ years old when our daughter, Katherine, was born. This was the time when I seriously began to search for help. I knew something was wrong shortly after Steve's birth. But when I tried to describe the problem, no one seemed to understand what I was saying. In spite of chronic ear infections, Steve looked very healthy. He was slow in developing language, but that could easily be attributed to his ear trouble. Since he was our first baby, I thought that maybe we just weren't very good parents.

When he was 2½, we enrolled Steven in a diagnostic nursery school. He did not seem to understand us when we spoke. I wondered if he was retarded or had some other developmental problem. The nursery school gave us their opinion when he was 4. They said Steve seemed to have normal intelligence, but he perseverated, was behind socially, and did not seem to process verbs. The school said he had some signs of autism and some signs of a learning disability.

When Steve was 4½, he did some amazing things. He began to talk, read, write, and play the piano. I was taking beginning adult piano lessons at the time, and Steve could play everything I did. In fact, he could play any song he heard and even added chords with his left hand. Relatives and friends began to tell us that he was a genius and that that accounted for his odd behavior. I really wanted to believe this genius theory.

I enrolled Steven in a public kindergarten at age 5. This teacher had another theory about Steve's strange behavior. She believed that we were not firm enough with him. She also sent the social worker to our home to see what we were doing with him.

I often wondered if we were just very poor parents. I certainly had enough people tell us so! Whenever I went to anyone for help, I was likely to begin crying. Then the doctor or whoever would start to watch my behavior closely. I could just see each of them forming a theory in his or her mind: The child is okay, but the mother is a mess. I wondered if I was a very cold mother. Maybe I was subtly rejecting my son. Then again, maybe it was his father. My mother always said he didn't spend enough time with Steve.

I didn't understand when the psychiatrist told me Steve had a **pervasive developmental disorder.** I began to get the picture when the other terms were used. I had heard of autism before. Something was terribly wrong, but it had a physical basis. It was not my fault at all. This was a relief but also a tremendous blow. It has really helped to have a name for the problem. We used to wonder if Steve was lying awake nights, dreaming up new ways to get our attention. We lived from crisis to crisis. We would just handle one problem, only to have a new one develop in its place. Steve still does unusual things, but it doesn't send us into a panic anymore.

Sheri, Steve's Mother

A great deal remains unknown about autism. For example, do the savant characteristics portrayed in *Rain Man* represent extremes of splinter skills? Future research from both biological and behavioral sciences must unravel these puzzles.

The behavior patterns often found in children with autism cause a variety of difficulties. Restricted behavioral repertoires, communication limitations, stereotyped self-stimulation, resistance to changes in routine, and unusual responses to their environment pose problems and limit integration options for some individuals with autism. They may have the ability to perform and the skills necessary to participate in community jobs or living arrangements. However, the presence of a challenging behavior may lead to placement of an individual with autism in a more restricted setting. Continued research on behavior management, social interactions, and program development is essential for these individuals to achieve maximum integration into the community.

Learning Characteristics

The learning characteristics of children with autism are often different than those of their normally developing peers and present a number of challenges from an educational standpoint. Some of the behavioral characteristics described earlier are relevant here. For example, students who resist change may perseverate on a specific item to be learned and encounter difficulties shifting attention to the next topic or problem in an instructional sequence. Because of their problems understanding social cues and relating to people, students with autism may experience difficulty interacting with teachers and other students in a school setting (Mesibov & Stephens, 1990; Volkmar et al., 1987).

The abilities of children with autism often develop unevenly, both within and among skill areas. These children also may not generalize skills that they have learned to other settings or topics. They are often impulsive and inconsistent in their responses, which is a matter that teachers may have to address. Children with autism frequently have difficulty with abstract ideas and may focus on one or more select stimuli while failing to understand the general concept (Rincover & Ducharme, 1987; Sue et al., 1990).

Children with autism may also possess certain qualities that can be viewed as educational strengths or at least be focused on for instructional purposes. For example, although generalizations about these youngsters are difficult to make, individuals with autism are sometimes noted as enjoying routine, which is consistent with their desire to maintain sameness. If a child shows this tendency, teachers may employ it in situations where practice or drill is warranted to learn a skill. Some individuals seem to have relatively strong long-term memory skills, particularly for factual information like names, numbers, and dates. For these students, once they have learned a piece of information, they will not forget it. Their long-term memory skills may equal those of their normally developing peers.

Generalizations regarding children with autism are difficult to make. Despite the fact that there are many stereotypes about these individuals, they are highly variable. Learning characteristics, both limitations and strengths, must be individually assessed and considered in educational programing.

CAUSATION

Historically, two broad theories about the causes of autism have existed, biological and **psychodynamic.** From a psychodynamic perspective, family interactions have been implicated as causal factors in autism. Theorists subscribing to this view have speculated that the child withdraws from rejection and erects defenses against psychological pain. In so doing, he or she retreats to an inner world and essentially does not interact with the outside environment that involves people. Psychodynamic theories have largely fallen out of favor since the 1970s because research has not supported this position.

Much of the current research on causation in autism has explored biological factors, particularly genetics (Prior, 1989). For example, a condition involving damage to the chromosome structure, known as **fragile X syndrome,** emerged in the late 1960s as a potential cause of autism. Researchers found that this condition appeared in a certain percentage of males with autism (e.g., Coleman & Gillberg, 1985). However, other investigators have suggested that fragile X is not a major cause of autism (Fisch, 1989; Ho & Kalousek, 1989).

Information to date has not established a solid research base for genetic causation in autism—certainly not one that allows us to understand it. One problem in developing a body of genetic information arises from the relative infrequency with which autism appears in the population at large. Because the disability is somewhat rare, there are few families to study from a genetic standpoint. Although some research on twins has also suggested a genetic link, weaknesses in investigation methods make the validity of the information questionable (Folstein & Rutter, 1988).

Damage to or impairment of the central nervous system has received attention recently as a cause of autism along with other investigations of neurological problems, such as brain cell differences and neurological chemical imbalances (Dawson, Finley, Phillips, & Lewy, 1989; Du Verglas, Banks, & Guyer, 1988). Major developments in technology have made it possible to conduct research that previously could only be accomplished through autopsy, if at all. For example, in some people with autism, it appears that a portion of the brain is underdeveloped (Courchesne, Yeung-Courchesne, Press, Hesselink, & Jernigan (1988)). This underdeveloped area, known as the **vermis,** is located in the cerebellum and may be related to the cognitive malfunctions found in autism. Further research is needed to confirm

FOCUS 4

Identify the two broad theoretical views regarding the causes of autism that have been considered historically.

this finding in more people with autism. Additionally, investigation regarding the reasons for such developmental abnormality will be essential if we are to address the possibility of prevention.

Neurological damage such as that noted earlier may be caused by a number of problems during prenatal development as well as early infancy. Maternal infections and other problems during pregnancy have great potential of damaging the developing fetus and have been associated with autism as well as other disabilities involving the central nervous system. In particular, viral infections such as rubella have been implicated, although a great deal of research is still needed to explore this area (Gillberg, 1986). Problems during the birth process—such as unusual hemorrhaging, difficult deliveries, and anoxia—are also known causes of neurological injuries in babies. Children with autism seem to have more frequent histories of delivery problems than do children without disabilities, although no single type of trauma has been consistently identified (Gelfand et al., 1988). Toxic agents such as lead have also been implicated in some cases of autism (Accardo, 1988).

The cause of autism remains an unsolved puzzle, although there is constant research interest in the condition. Accumulated evidence has strongly suggested that biological factors are responsible, although it is clear that some biological malfunctions may be related to environmental influences (Prior, 1989; Rothenberger, 1990). Many current researchers have viewed autism as a behavioral syndrome with multiple biological causes (Folstein & Rutter, 1988; Gillberg, 1990a, 1990b; Volkmar et al., 1988). To date, researchers have not identified any single specific factor that causes autism. It appears to be an assortment of symptoms rather than a specific disease, which is why it is often called a *syndrome*. As with many areas of disability, an understanding of causation is important as we attempt to improve treatment. Research continues to unravel the sources of this perplexing disability.

INTERVENTIONS

FOCUS 5

Identify four major approaches to the treatment of autism.

Along with the constant interest in identifying causation in autism, there has also been continual attention to discovering effective treatment. A number of different approaches have been used in the treatment of autism, some based on the theory of causation and others focusing on specific observable behaviors.

Educational Interventions

Education for children with autism requires a full range of instructional options, ranging from specialized individual programs to integrated placement with support services. Observation of unusual maladaptive behaviors has led to the creation of stereotypes about youngsters with autism; this has contributed to imposing rather restrictive treatment placement in the past (Dunlap et al., 1985). However, current literature has emphasized integration for educational purposes to the maximum degree possible (e.g., Wheeler, Rimstidt, Gray, & DePalma, 1991). The specific educational placement will depend on the student's age and functioning level. Under IDEA, students with autism are entitled to a free and appropriate education in the least restrictive environment.

An individualized educational plan (IEP) is required for children with autism, as they are for students with other disabilities, including statements of short- and long-term goals. For most students with autism, it is vital that the IEP have a central component of functional communication and social skills. It is also important to focus on using individual strengths to teach skills required to function as independently as possible (Dalrymple, 1989). Skills and knowledge that are functional will vary among individuals. For some, what is functional will mean heavy use of augmentative communication, social, and self-help skills (Porco, 1989a). For others, functional instruction will focus on what many consider to be traditional academic subjects as well as some that are not always in regular education curricula, like sex education (Dalrymple, Gray, & Ruble, 1991; Porco, 1989b).

One educational matter that is mentioned regarding students with autism perhaps more than students with other disabilities is the need for creative and innovative teachers with positive attitudes (Moreno & Donnellan, 1991; Pingree, 1984). As indicated in the earlier section on learning characteristics, these children present some unique and challenging qualities for instruction. In some cases, seemingly insignificant actions by teachers may create difficulties for students who are autistic. These difficulties can easily be avoided if teachers are informed. For example, many high-functioning individuals with autism who have language skills interpret speech literally. Consequently, it is important to avoid using slang, idiom, and sarcasm. Such phrases might be translated literally by the individual with autism and teach something other than what is desired.

Parental collaboration in preparing children with autism for school can be of great assistance. This preparation can include such matters as instilling a positive attitude in the child, helping him or her with scheduling, and teaching him or her how to find the way around in school (e.g., perhaps drawing a map of where to go based on the daily schedule). It may also be helpful to identify and show the child a "safe" place and a "safe" person in case he or she becomes confused or encounters a particularly upsetting event (Moreno & Donnellan, 1991).

Psychological and Medical Interventions

Therapy based on the psychodynamic theory of causation historically focused on repairing emotional damage and resolving inner conflict. This approach aimed at rectifying the presumably faulty relationship between the child with autism and his or her parents, which involved rejection and resulted in withdrawal by the child. This treatment model has been criticized because of a relative absence of solid empirical evidence supporting its effectiveness. The internal psychological nature of problems, as seen by this approach, makes it very difficult to evaluate effectiveness.

Medical treatment in several forms has also been used for children with autism. Certain early medical therapies (e.g., electroconvulsive shock and psychosurgery) have been discarded because they appeared to have questionable results and harmful side effects (Gelfand et al., 1988). Likewise, certain medications used in the past (e.g., D-lysergic acid, more commonly known as LSD), had doubtful therapeutic value and were considered very controversial. Other medications used for people with autism have often included antipsychotic drugs, which seem to help reduce some of the unusual speech patterns and self-injurious behaviors, particularly with older patients. Decreasing self-injury and social withdrawal has also been evident in some research on responses to other drugs (Lienemann & Walker, 1989; Walters, Barrett, Feinstein, & Mercurio, 1990). However, other research on drug therapy has shown only small or no improvement in the condition (Ekman, Miranda-Linne, Gillberg, Garle, & Wetterburg, 1989; Oades, Stern, Walker, & Clark, 1990; Sherman, Factor, Swinson, & Darjes, 1989).

Generally speaking, medication has shown some promising but mixed results in the treatment of autism. There appears to be potential for improvement, but such treatment should be used thoughtfully in conjunction with a comprehensive treatment plan (Stewart, Myers, Burket, & Lyles, 1990).

INTERACTING IN NATURAL SETTINGS ·················· People with Autism ··················

EARLY CHILDHOOD YEARS

Tips for the Family

- Seek out and read information regarding autism and become knowledgeable about the disability in all areas possible. Be an active partner in the treatment of your child, take parent training classes (e.g., behavior management workshops).
- When working with the child with autism, concentrate on one behavior at a time as the target for change; emphasize work on the *positive*, increasing appropriate behavior rather than solely focusing on inappropriate behavior.
- Involve all family members in learning about your child's disability and working with him or her when appropriate.
- Protect your own health by obtaining respite care when needed to get rest or to get a break. You may need to devise a family schedule that allows adequate time for ongoing sleep/respite. Plan ahead for respite; otherwise, when you need it most, you will be too exhausted to effectively find it.
- Help prepare your child for school by instilling a positive attitude about it, helping him or her with the idea of a school schedule, and how to find a "safe" place and "safe" person at school.

Tips for the Preschool Teacher

- Depending on the child's level of functioning, you may have to use physical cues or clear visual modeling to persuade him or her to do something; children with autism may not respond to social cues.
- Pair physical cues with verbal cues in order to begin teaching verbal compliance.
- Limit instruction to one thing at a time; focus on what is concrete rather than abstract.
- Avoid verbal overload by using short, directive sentences.

Tips for Preschool Personnel

- Encourage the development of programs where older children model good behavior and interact intensely with children with autism.
- Promote ongoing relationships between the preschool and medical personnel who can provide advice and assistance for children with autism.
- Promote the initiation of parent-school relationships to assist both parents and preschool personnel in working together to meet the child's needs and offer mutual support.
- Promote the appropriate involvement of nonteaching staff through workshops that provide information and awareness. Consistent interaction and expectations are important.

Neighbors and Friends

- Be supportive of the parents and siblings of a child with autism. They may be under a high level of stress and need moral support.
- Be positive with the parents. They may receive information that places blame on them, which should not be magnified by their friends.
- Offer parents a respite to the degree that you're comfortable; you may only give them a short time away to go to the store, but the break will be very helpful to them.

ELEMENTARY YEARS

Tips for the Family

- Be active in community efforts for children with autism; join local or national parent groups.
- Use your knowledge and resources to identify a good program for your child; participate in this program in whatever arrangement might be available to parents.
- Consistently follow through with the basic principles of your child's treatment program at home. This may mean taking more workshops or training on various topics.
- Continue family involvement; be sensitive to the feelings of siblings who may be feeling left out or embarrassed by the child with autism.
- It may be necessary to take safety precautions in the home (e.g., installing locks on all doors).

Tips for the Regular Classroom Teacher

- Help with organizational strategies, assisting the student with autism with matters that are difficult for him or her (e.g., remembering how to use an eraser). Keep instruction as unrestrictive as possible, perhaps a prompting note or picture somewhere.
- Avoid abstract ideas unless they are necessary in instruction. Be as concrete as possible.
- Communicate with specific directions or questions, not vague or open-ended statements.
- If the child becomes upset, he or she may need to change activities or go to a place in the room that is "safe" for a period of time.
- If the child is not learning a particular task, it may need to be broken down into smaller steps or presented through more than one medium (e.g., visual and verbal).
- Begin preparing the child with autism for a more variable environment by programing and teaching adaption to changes in routine. Involve him or her in planning for the changes, mapping out what they might be.

Tips for School Personnel

◆ Promote an all-school environment where children model appropriate behavior and receive reinforcement for it.

◆ Develop peer-assistance programs, where older students can help tutor and model appropriate behavior for children with autism.

◆ Encourage the development of strong, ongoing, school-parent relationships and support groups working together to meet the child's needs. Consistent expectations are important.

◆ Do not depend on the child with autism to take messages home to parents for anything unless you are trying this out as a skill for him or her to learn; communication is a major problem, and even a note may be lost.

Tips for Neighbors and Friends

◆ If you interact with the child with autism, be positive and praise him or her for appropriate behavior.

◆ To the degree possible, ignore trivial disruptions or misbehaviors; focus on positive behaviors.

◆ Don't take misbehaviors personally; the child is not trying to make your life difficult or manipulate you.

◆ Avoid using nicknames or cute names such as "buddy" or "pal."

◆ Avoid sarcasm and idiom, such as "beating around the bush." These children may not understand and interpret what you say literally.

SECONDARY/TRANSITION YEARS

Tips for the Family

◆ Be alert to developmental and behavioral changes as the child grows older, watching for changing effects of any medication that may occur.

◆ Continue as an active partner in your child's educational and treatment program, planning for the transition to adulthood.

◆ Acquaint yourself with the adult services that will be available when your child leaves school. If he or she is high functioning, consider or plan for adult living out of the family home.

◆ Seek legal advice regarding plans for your child's future when you are no longer able to care for him or her. Plan for financial arrangements and other needs that are appropriate, such as naming an advocate. Backup plans should be made; do not always count on the youngster's siblings. Consider guardianship by other persons or agencies.

Tips for the Regular Classroom Teacher

◆ Gradually increase the level of abstraction in teaching, remaining aware of the individual limitations the child with autism has.

◆ Continue preparing the student for an increasingly variable environment through instruction and example.

◆ Focus increasingly on matters of vital importance to the student as he or she matures (e.g., social awareness and interpersonal issues between the sexes).

◆ Teach the student with an eye toward postschool community participation, including such matters as navigating the community physically, activities, and employment. Teach the student about interacting with police in the community, since they require responses different than those appropriate for other strangers.

Tips for School Personnel

◆ To the degree possible for children with autism, promote involvement in social activities and clubs that enhance interpersonal interaction.

◆ Encourage the development of functional academic programs for students with autism that are combined with transition planning and programs.

◆ Promote a continuing working relationship with school staff and other agency personnel that might be involved in the student's overall treatment program (e.g., health care providers, social service agencies, and others).

◆ Work with other agencies that may encounter the child in the community (e.g., law enforcement). Provide workshops if possible to inform officers regarding behavioral characteristics of people with autism that might be misinterpreted.

Tips for Neighbors and Friends

◆ Encourage a positive understanding of people with autism by other neighbors and friends who may be in contact with the child and able to provide environmentally appropriate interaction.

◆ Promote the positive understanding of people with autism by community agencies that may encounter these individuals at this stage of life (e.g., law enforcement officials, fire department personnel).

◆ Support the parents as they consider the issues of adulthood for their child. Topics such as guardianship and community living may be difficult for parents to discuss.

Behavioral Management

Behavioral interventions for children with autism are undertaken without concern for an underlying causation of the disability. The focus of this approach is on enhancing appropriate behaviors and decreasing inappropriate or unadaptive behaviors (Dunlap et al., 1985). Behavior management for individuals with autism requires a statement of precise operational

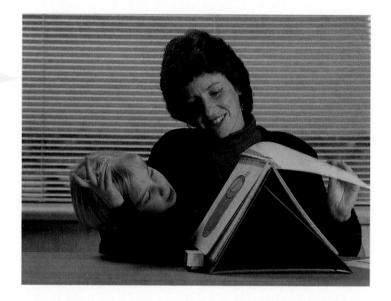

In some cases, behavior management of individuals with autism requires one-on-one instruction. (Kevin Beebe Photography/Custom Medical Stock Photo)

definition, observation, and recording of data on behaviors viewed as appropriate and inappropriate. Accurate and reliable data collection is a cornerstone of behavioral intervention, a process that is being greatly enhanced by new applications of technology, as indicated in the Today's Technology box.

Interventions may initially target such conduct as self-stimulation, tantrum episodes, or self-inflicted injury in children with autism (Ramm, 1990). These problem behaviors have been substantially reduced or eliminated in many cases using behavioral therapy (Sue et al., 1990). Behavioral treatment has also been used effectively with children with autism in remediating deficiencies in fundamental social skills and language development (Groden & Cautela, 1988; Lord, 1988; Paul et al., 1988). Because of the individualized nature of behavioral intervention, treatment is typically undertaken on a one-to-one basis and may be very expensive and time consuming, especially during the early phases. Consequently,

---

TODAY'S TECHNOLOGY

Treatment from the Supermarket

Most of us are familiar with the bar-code scanners used at checkout stands in many stores. The clerk passes the code symbol over a scanner, the price is instantly entered into the cash register, and a record of the sale is made for inventory control. This same technology is now being applied to coding and recording data on behavioral observations.

Known as the *Videx TimeWand*, this device simplifies reliable data collection for behavioral interventions with a variety of conditions, such as autism. Appropriate and inappropriate behaviors are defined very specifically and then given a code, which is translated into a bar-code symbol much like we see at the market. These bar codes are then placed on an observation sheet to be used by the observer. The observer also carries a small, portable bar-code reader with a wand that is passed over the relevant code symbol

when that particular behavior is observed. Data on behavioral occurrences are recorded as well as clock-time stamping that indicates when the behavior occurred. These data are stored electronically (the unit will hold up to 16,000 characters of information) and transferred to a portable computer at the end of an observation session for analysis and graphing.

Use of the *TimeWand* reduces the strain on therapists who were previously required to physically write down behavioral codes while attempting to continue observation. Use of this technology thereby improves the accuracy of data collection and also expedites data processing and translation into treatment action. Information regarding this automated data-collection method is available from Walter Nelson and Gordon Defalco at the Fircrest School in Seattle, Washington, or Richard Saunders at the Parson Research Center, University of Kansas, Parsons, Kansas.

methods of optimizing efficiency are crucial. One approach to accomplishing this that has shown promising results has involved parents in behavioral treatment (Marcus & Mesibov, 1987; Prizant & Wetherby, 1988). Research has also demonstrated that certain students with autism can be effectively taught to employ self-directed behavior management, which further enhances efficiency (Koegel & Koegel, 1990). Although this work has been limited to reducing stereotypic behavior, further research may show promise for applications in other areas, particularly with high-functioning individuals.

It should be noted that behavioral therapy does not make claims of curing autism. The procedures involved are very specific in focusing on limited behavioral areas that need attention. This approach seems effective for many children with autism, prompting decreases in problem behaviors and potential improvement of survival skills. Such gains constitute a significant step toward normalization for both the children and their families (Lovaas, 1987).

Biklen (1990) reported a treatment being used for people with autism in Australia that specifically focuses on their communication problems. Known as **facilitative communication,** this procedure was developed by Rosemary Crossley and her associates in Melbourne and carries an assumption that it is better to "overestimate than underestimate a person's ability" (Biklen, 1990, p. 306). Clients who have received this treatment have included those who have been labeled as having severe autism. Treatment emphasizes the use of typing as a means of communicating, with the therapist providing physical support by touching the student's arm or shoulder and interpersonal support through positive attitudes and interactions. Facilitative communication as a treatment for autism has been controversial (Crossley & McDonald, 1980), as have many other therapies used with this disability. Autism is clearly a complex condition.

IMPACT ON THE FAMILY

The impact of having a child with autism in the family is significant for the other members. Living with such an individual is exhausting and presents a wide variety of challenges. The child may only sleep a few hours a night and spend extensive periods during waking hours engaged in self-abusive or disruptive behavior. One parent described a state of constant chaos generated by her son, who continually disassembled mechanical devices. "When he could find a hidden screwdriver, he would unleash it on heating vents, door hinges, and electrical outlets. One day he slipped outside with a repairman's screwdriver and had the taillights and rear view mirror removed from the repairman's truck before the startled man could begin fixing the dishwasher" (Pingree, 1984, p. 331). Not only is this disruptive to family routine, but it is physically and emotionally draining (Beavers, 1982; Park, 1982; Schopler & Mesibov, 1984). Additionally, the child with autism may demonstrate little affection toward or interest in family members, which means that their efforts will not seem appreciated let alone be rewarded (Bebko, 1987).

Siblings of children with autism may experience a number of problems, particularly during the early years. They may have difficulty understanding the distress their parents have regarding their brother or sister and the level of attention afforded this child (McHale, Sloan, & Simeonsson, 1986). Siblings may also have difficulty accepting the emotional detachment of the youngster, who might seem not to care for them at all. Like the siblings of children with other disabilities, brothers and sisters of a child with autism may be embarrassed and reluctant to bring friends home. However, if they can become informed and move beyond the social embarrassment, siblings can be a significant resource in assisting parents (Harris, 1986).

The arrival of a child with autism will present a significant challenge to parents and other family members. Parents usually have to turn to multiple sources for assistance and

Extraordinary Talents of Individuals with Autism

One of the many mysteries surrounding the phenomenon of autism are the extraordinary talents and abilities demonstrated by some individuals. The Academy Award–winning film *Rain Man*, about a man with autism who also had astonishing memory skills, increased mainstream awareness of people with autism and of those with special abilities in particular.

In the past, such individuals were referred to as *idiot savants*. *Idiot* is an antiquated term for someone with mental retardation, and *savant* means "knower" in French. Some professionals now prefer the term *savant syndrome* to describe a condition in which persons with serious mental limitations demonstrate spectacular "islands of brilliance in a sea of mental disability."

Given the scope of talents in the human repertoire, these "islands" are confined to a narrow range of abilities: a flair for music or visual arts, mathematical aptitude, mechanical wizardry, or mnemonic skills such as calendar calculation (being able to report instantly on what day of the week a particular date will fall in a given year, past or future). The trait that binds these unique abilities is superior memory skills that are idiosyncratic, emotionless, and enigmatic. Indeed, savants often seem to accomplish feats of brilliance as if by rote. No emotion shades their performance.

How are savants able to do what they do? While no conclusive findings exist, theories abound. For example, one theory has suggested that the sensory deprivation and social isolation experienced by many individuals with autism causes them to be bored and thus adopt trivial preoccupations. Another theory has suggested that autism is associated with deficits in the left hemisphere of the brain, which governs the use of language and other logical, conceptual, and abstract skills. Savants' skills are usually associated with right-brain functions—spatial perception, visualization, mechanical dexterity, and movement—suggesting that the right hemisphere is dominant.

Clearly, much remains unknown about both autism and the savant syndrome. Certainly, little is understood about how they exist in the same person. Increased understanding will hopefully benefit those who struggle with autism.

information. Groups such as the Autism Society of America can provide a great deal of help and support from a perspective that is not available elsewhere. Parents may find that they have to become aggressive and vocal in their search for services from various agencies (Donnellan & Mirenda, 1984). They will also have to be conscious of their own health and vitality, since their ability to cope will be significantly affected if they allow personal well-being to diminish. This will require respite time and care from a number of sources, both the family as a whole and outside agencies (Moreno & Donellan, 1991). Perhaps the most difficult issue is the realization that there are no clear-cut answers to many of the questions they have.

Debate   Forum   ·················· Self-Stimulation as a Reinforcer? ·····················

It is difficult to find reinforcers for some children with autism. In many cases, these individuals do not respond to the same types of rewards that others do. Social rewards may not provide reinforcement or have any effect at all on these youngsters. Research has also shown that, in some cases, tangible reinforcers may produce desired results, but they often seem to lose their power for individuals with autism. Given these circumstances, some researchers have suggested that self-stimulation, which appears to be a powerful and durable reinforcer, should be used to assist in teaching appropriate behavior. Self-stimulation is very different for each child and may involve manipulation of such items as coins, keys, and twigs.

Point   Since reinforcers are often difficult to identify for children with autism, it is important to use whatever is available and practical in teaching these youngsters. Self-stimulation has been recognized as providing strong reinforcement for those who engage in it. Although self-stimulation is typically viewed as an inappropriate behavior, it may be very useful in teaching the beginning phases of more adaptive behavior and other skill acquisition. For some children with autism, it may be the most efficient reinforcer available, so why not use it, at least initially?

Counterpoint   Using inappropriate behavior as a reinforcer carries with it certain serious problems and in fact may be unethical. The use of self-stimulation as a reinforcer may cause an increase in this behavior, making it an even more pronounced part of the child's inappropriate demeanor. Should this occur, it may make self-stimulation more difficult to eliminate later.

REVIEW

FOCUS 1   Identify four areas of functional challenge often found in children with autism.

◆ Language
◆ Interpersonal skills
◆ Emotional or affective behaviors
◆ Intellectual functioning

FOCUS 2   What are the two general ranges of prevalence estimated for autism?

◆ Approximately 4 to 5 cases per 10,000
◆ From 10 to 14 cases per 10,000

FOCUS 3   Identify six characteristics of children with autism.

◆ As infants, they are often unresponsive to physical contact or affection from their parents and later have extreme difficulty relating to other people.
◆ Most have impaired or delayed language skills, with about half not developing speech at all.
◆ Those who have speech often engage in echolalia and other inappropriate behavior.
◆ They frequently engage in self-stimulatory behavior.

◆ Changes in their routine are met with intense resistance.
◆ Most have a reduced level of intellectual functioning.

FOCUS 4   Identify the two broad theoretical views regarding the causes of autism that have been considered historically.

◆ The psychoanalytic view places a great deal of emphasis on the interaction between the family and the child.
◆ The biological view has included neurological damage and genetics.

FOCUS 5   Identify four major approaches to the treatment of autism.

◆ Psychoanalytic-based therapy focuses on repairing the emotional damage presumed to have resulted from faulty family relationships.
◆ Medically based treatment often involves the use of medication.
◆ Behavioral interventions focus on enhancing specific appropriate behaviors or on reducing inappropriate behaviors.
◆ Educational interventions employ the full range of educational placements.

Chapter Ten

Hearing Impairments

TO BEGIN WITH . . .

◆ "The ear is an amazingly flexible organ, but it simply was not designed to withstand the strain of modern living. . . . The most endangered kids are those who wander around with cassette players blaring music into their skulls for hours. These personal stereos can funnel blasts of 110 decibels or more into the ear. 'If you can hear the music from a Walkman someone next to you is wearing, they are damaging their ears,' declares Dr. Jerome Goldstein of the American Academy of Otolaryngology. After years of such assaults, notes audiologist Dean Gartecki, head of the hearing-impairment program at Northwestern University, 'we've got 21-year-olds walking around with hearing-loss patterns of people 40 years their senior'" (Toufexis, 1991, p. 50).

◆ "In 1985, the Salem Shopping Mall in Dayton, Ohio, announced the availability of a Santa who could use sign language. More than 250 . . . children [with hearing impairments] visited Mr. Claus. One problem occurred: Santa's bushy beard got in the way for children who also used lip reading to communicate" ("A Very Special Santa," 1985)!

◆ "Closed-caption television programs including 'The Cosby Show,' 'Sesame Street,' news programs, and sports activities are now being used to teach reading to . . . students [both with and without hearing impairments]" (National Captioning Institute, n.d.).

ROSA

ROSA. Rosa is the oldest of three children. She was born with normal hearing, but at the age of 8, she developed **spinal meningitis.** The disease resulted in a severe hearing loss in both ears. Rosa's parents worked diligently with her to retain the precious speech that had been acquired prior to the loss of hearing. Their work was reinforced through her educational experiences. Rosa spent the remainder of her elementary school years in a special class for children with hearing impairments, and as an adolescent, she went on to her neighborhood high school, where she graduated with honors. She continued her education at the university level, receiving an undergraduate degree in philosophy and then completing law school. Rosa is now a successful real estate lawyer and is very active in civic and charitable endeavors. Her leisure time is spent oil painting, reading history books, and relaxing at the local golf course.

*I*NTRODUCTION

Although Rosa is unable to hear a single word, her life is one of independence and fulfillment (see Window 10–1). In Rosa's case, as well as those of many people with hearing disorders, the obstacles presented by the loss of hearing are not insurmountable.

In a world that is often controlled by sound, the ability to hear and speak is a critical link in the development of human communication. Children who can hear learn to talk by listening to those around them. Our everyday communication systems would make little sense without sound. Telephones, loudspeakers, car horns, musical instruments, alarm clocks, fire alarms, radios, stereos, and intercoms would be useless in a world without sound. Our sense of hearing is an important factor in the way we learn to perceive our world and in the way the world perceives us.

How difficult is it, then, for the person who cannot hear to adjust to a hearing world? Most people with hearing impairments, such as Rosa, can and do adjust successfully to life within their local communities. Unfortunately, others feel shunned by their own families and neighbors. Feeling like outsiders, they may deal with their stigma in a number of ways. Some may try to adjust as much as possible to the demands of the hearing world. Others may live a life of isolation, avoiding those who can hear. Still others may become part of organized groups whose members share the common bond of hearing impairment.

THE HEARING PROCESS

FOCUS 1

Describe how sound is transmitted through the human ear.

Audition is defined as the act or sense of hearing. The auditory process involves the transmission of sound through the vibration of an object to a receiver. The process originates with a vibrator—such as a string, reed, membrane, or column of air—that causes displacement of air particles. In order for a vibration to become sound, there must be a medium to carry it. Air is the most common carrier, but vibrations can also be carried by metal, water, and other substances. The displacement of air particles by the vibrator produces a pattern of circular waves that move away from the source.

This movement is referred to as a *sound wave* and can be illustrated by imagining the ripples resulting from a pebble dropped in a pool of water. Sound waves are patterns of pressure that alternately push together and pull apart in a spherical expansion. Sound waves are carried through a medium (e.g., air) to a receiver. The human ear is one of the most sensitive receivers there is; it is capable of being activated by incredibly small amounts of pressure. Perkins and Kent (1986) suggested that, "considering its puny size, the ear is a

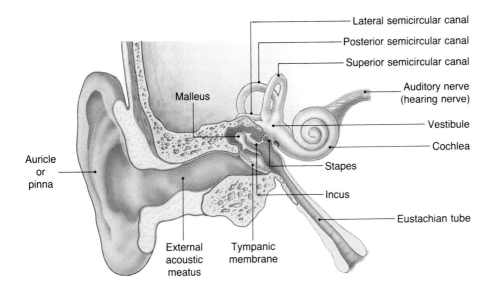

Lateral semicircular canal
Posterior semicircular canal
Superior semicircular canal
Auditory nerve (hearing nerve)
Vestibule
Cochlea
Stapes
Incus
Eustachian tube
Malleus
Auricle or pinna
External acoustic meatus
Tympanic membrane

FIGURE 10–1

The Structure of the Human Ear

prodigious instrument. With equipment that could almost be packaged in a sugar cube, we can distinguish all the sounds of speech, along with nearly a half a million other sounds" (p. 245).

The ear is the mechanism through which sound is collected, processed, and transmitted to a specific area in the brain that decodes the sensations into meaningful language. The anatomy of the hearing mechanism is discussed in terms of the external, middle, and inner ears. These structures are illustrated in Figure 10–1.

The External Ear

The external ear consists of a cartilage structure on the side of the head called the *auricle,* or *pinna,* and an external ear canal referred to as the *meatus.* The auricle is the only outwardly visible part of the ear and is attached to the skull by three ligaments. The purpose of the auricle is to collect sound waves and funnel them into the meatus. The meatus secretes a wax called *cerumen,* which protects the inner structures of the ear by trapping foreign materials and lubricating the canal and eardrum. The *eardrum,* or *tympanic membrane,* is located at the inner end of the canal between the external and middle ear. The concave membrane is positioned in such a manner that, when struck by sound waves, it can vibrate freely.

The Middle Ear

The inner surface of the eardrum is located in the air-filled cavity of the middle ear. This surface consists of three small bones that form the **ossicular chain.** These bones are the *malleus, incus,* and *stapes,* often referred to as the hammer, anvil, and stirrup because of similarities to these common objects. The three bones transmit the vibrations from the external ear through the cavity of the middle ear to the inner ear.

The **eustachian tube** is a structure that extends from the throat to the middle-ear cavity. Its purpose is to equalize the air pressure on the eardrum with that of the outside. This is accomplished by controlling the flow of air into the middle-ear cavity. Although air conduction is the primary avenue through which sound reaches the inner ear, it is possible for conduction to occur through the bones of the skull. Bone conduction appears comparable to air conduction in that the patterns of displacement produced in the inner ear are similar.

The Inner Ear

The inner ear consists of a multitude of intricate passageways. The **cochlea** lies horizontally in front of the *vestibule* (a central cavity where sound enters directly from the middle ear), where it can be activated by movement in the ossicular chain. The cochlea is filled with fluid similar in composition to cerebral spinal fluid. Within the cochlea is **Corti's organ,** a structure of highly specialized cells that translate vibrations into nerve impulses that are sent directly to the brain.

The other major structure within the inner ear is the **vestibular mechanism,** containing the semicircular canals that control balance. The semicircular canals have enlarged portions at one end and are filled with fluid that responds to head movement. The vestibular mechanism integrates sensory input passing to the brain and assists the body in maintaining equilibrium. Motion and gravity are detected through this mechanism, allowing the individual to differentiate between sensory input associated with body movement and that from the external environment. Whenever the basic functions of the vestibular mechanism or any of the structures in the external, middle, and inner ear are interrupted, hearing loss may occur.

DEFINITIONS AND CLASSIFICATION

Definitions

A hearing impairment may be defined according to the degree of hearing loss. This is accomplished by assessing a person's sensitivity to loudness (sound intensity) and pitch (sound frequency). The unit used to measure sound intensity is the *decibel* (db), and the range of human hearing is approximately 0 to 130 db. Sounds louder than 130 db are extremely painful to the ear. Table 10–1 illustrates various common environmental sounds and their measurable decibel levels.

The frequency of sound is determined by measuring the number of cycles that vibrating molecules complete per second. The unit used to measure cycles per second is the **hertz**

■ **Table 10–1** Estimated Decibel (db) Levels of Common Environmental Sounds

Decibel Level (sound intensity)	Source of Sound
140 db	Jet aircraft (80 feet from tail at takeoff)
130 db	Jackhammer
120 db	Loud thunder
110 db	Rock concert/Personal cassette player
100 db	Chain saw
90 db	Street traffic
80 db	Telephone ring
70 db	Door slam
60 db	Washing machine
50 db	Conversational speech (40–60 db)
40 db	Electric typewriter
30 db	Pencil writing
20 db	Watch ticking
10 db	Whisper
0 db	Lowest threshold of hearing for the human ear

(Hz). The higher the frequency, the higher the hertz. The human ear can hear sounds ranging from 20 to approximately 15,000 Hz. The pitch of speech sounds is 300 to 4,000 Hz, whereas the pitches made by a piano keyboard range from 27.5 to 4,186 Hz. Although it is possible for the human ear to hear sounds at the 15,000 Hz level, the vast majority of sounds in our environment range from 300 to 4,000 Hz.

Deaf and Hard of Hearing.   The term *hearing impairment* is generally used to describe the entire range of hearing loss, from mild through profound conditions (Greenberg & Kusche, 1989). Two terms, **deaf** and **hard of hearing** (or *partially hearing*), are commonly used to distinguish between severities of hearing impairments.

Deaf is an often overused and misunderstood term commonly applied to describe a wide variety of hearing impairments; however, the term should be used in a more precise fashion. *Deaf* describes specifically those individuals whose hearing impairment is in the extreme range of loss—90 db or greater. Even with the use of hearing aids or other forms of amplification, the individual's primary means for developing language and communication is through the visual channel (Quigley & Paul, 1989). *Deafness,* as defined by the Individuals with Disabilities Education Act (IDEA), means "a hearing impairment which is so severe that the child is impaired in processing linguistic information through hearing, with or without amplification, which adversely affects educational performance." A person who is deaf is unable to recognize sound or the meanings of sound pressure waves. However, the degree of loss, as measured on an audiometer, should not be the sole criterion for defining deafness. Ross and Calvert (1984) suggested that the definition of deafness must be "a functional description, based on a person's ability to comprehend spoken language auditorily" (p. 129).

For persons defined as *hard of hearing,* audition is deficient but remains somewhat functional. "A person who is hard-of-hearing is one who, generally with the use of a hearing aid, has residual hearing sufficient to enable successful processing of linguistic information through audition" (Brill, MacNeil, & Newman, 1986, p. 67).

The distinction between deaf and hard of hearing, based on the functional use of residual hearing, is not as clear as many traditional definitions imply. New breakthroughs in the development of hearing aids as well as improved diagnostic procedures have made it possible for many children labeled as deaf to use their hearing functionally under limited circumstances.

In addition to measuring a person's sensitivity to loudness and pitch, two other factors are involved in defining a hearing impairment: the age of onset and the anatomical site of the loss.

Age of Onset.   A hearing impairment may be present at birth (congenital) or acquired at any time during life. The distinction between congenital and acquired impairments is an important one. The age of onset will be a critical variable in determining the type and extent of interventions necessary to minimize the effect of the individual's disability (Greenberg & Kusché, 1989; McAnally, Rose, & Quigley, 1987). This is particularly true in relation to speech and language development. As was the case for Rosa in Window 10–1, her parents and teachers worked diligently to maintain the speech and language skills she had acquired prior to her hearing loss. The maintenance of these skills had a crucial effect upon Rosa's subsequent pattern of intellectual development, communication, academic achievement, and social adaptation. In contrast, a person who is born with a hearing impairment has significantly more problems, particularly in the areas of communication and social adaptation (Quigley & Paul, 1989).

FOCUS 2
Distinguish between the terms *deaf* and *hard of hearing*.

FOCUS 3
Why is it important to consider age of onset and anatomical site when defining a hearing impairment?

It is important for people to have regular hearing examinations, as hearing impairments may be aquired at any time during life.
(Bob Daemmrich/Stock, Boston)

Rosa's experiences clearly reflect the need to distinguish between pre- and postlingual disorders. McAnally et al. (1987) identified **prelingual disorders** as those occurring prior to the age of 2, or about the time of speech development. **Postlingual disorders** occur at any age following speech development. Quigley and Paul stressed that "children incurring a profound hearing impairment prior to two or three years of age have been found to perform significantly inferior to those deafened after this age on certain language tasks" (1989, p. 4).

Anatomical Site of the Loss.   The two primary types of hearing loss based on anatomical location are *peripheral* and *central* auditory problems. There are three types of peripheral hearing loss: **conductive, sensorineural,** and **mixed.** Conductive hearing losses result from poor conduction of sound along the passages leading to the sense organ (inner ear). The loss may result from a blockage in the external canal, as well as from an obstruction interfering with the movement of the eardrum or ossicle. The overall effect is a reduction or loss of loudness. A conductive loss can be offset by amplification (hearing aids) and medical intervention. Surgery has proven to be effective in reducing or even restoring a conductive loss.

Sensorineural hearing losses are a result of an abnormal sense organ and a damaged auditory nerve. A sensorineural loss may distort sound, affecting the clarity of human speech. At present, sensorineural losses cannot be treated adequately through medical intervention. A sensorineural loss is generally more severe than a conductive loss, and it is permanent. Losses of greater than 70 db are usually sensorineural and involve severe damage to the inner ear. One common way to determine whether a loss is conductive or sensorineural is to administer an air and bone conduction test. An individual with a conductive loss would be unable to hear a vibrating tuning fork held close to the ear because air passages to the inner ear are blocked. However, if the same fork were applied to the skull, the person with a conductive loss may be able to hear it as well as someone with normal hearing. An individual with a sensorineural loss would not be able to hear the vibrating fork regardless of its placement. However, this test is not always accurate and must therefore be used with caution in distinguishing between conductive and sensorineural losses.

Mixed hearing loss, a combination of conductive and sensorineural problems, may also be assessed through the use of an air and bone conduction test. In the case of a mixed loss, abnormalities are evident in both tests.

Although most hearing losses are peripheral, such as conductive and sensorineural problems, some impairments occur where there is no measurable peripheral loss. This type of loss is referred to as a *central auditory disorder* and occurs when there is a dysfunction in the cerebral cortex. The cerebral cortex is the outer layer of gray matter of the brain. It governs thought, reasoning, memory, sensation, and voluntary movement. Consequently, a central auditory problem is not a loss in the ability to hear sound but a disorder of symbolic processes, including auditory perception, discrimination, comprehension of sound, and language development (expressive and receptive).

Classification

Hearing impairments, like other disabilities, may be classified according to the severity of the condition. Table 10–2 illustrates a symptom severity classification system and presents information relative to a child's ability to understand speech patterns at the various severity levels. In addition, it highlights implications for educational placement.

Classification systems based solely on a person's degree of hearing loss should be used with a great deal of caution when determining appropriate intervention strategies. These systems do not reflect the individual's capabilities, background, or experience; they merely suggest parameters for measuring a physical defect in auditory function. As a child, Rosa was diagnosed as having a severe hearing loss in both ears (see Window 10–1). Yet throughout her life, she successfully adjusted to both school and community experiences. She went on to college and now has a successful career as a lawyer. Consequently, many factors beyond the severity of the hearing loss must be assessed when determining the potential of individuals with hearing losses. In addition to severity of loss, such factors as general intelligence, emotional stability, scope and quality of early education and training, and the family environment must also be considered.

PREVALENCE

It has been extremely difficult to determine the prevalence of hearing impairments. Estimates of hearing loss in the United States go as high as 28 million people, or 11 percent of the total population (Toufexis, 1991). LaPlante (1991) has estimated that there are 813,000 people with hearing impairments who need specialized services in the United States.

It has been difficult to determine accurately the prevalence of hearing impairments due to (1) inconsistent definitional criteria and (2) methodological problems in the surveys. Different criteria have been used to define and classify hearing impairments. For instance, the differentiation between unilateral (one ear) and bilateral (two ears) losses may not have been taken into consideration. Finally, there are questions related to the age of the individuals, since most surveys focus exclusively on school-age children.

The most accurate data source may well be the U.S. Department of Education in its *Thirteenth Annual Report to Congress* (1991). This report indicated there are 57,555 students who are hard of hearing or deaf between the ages of 6 and 21 who are receiving specialized services in U.S. schools. These students account for approximately 1.4 percent of the over 4 million students labeled as disabled. It is important to note that these figures only represent students who receive special services. A number of students with hearing losses who would benefit from additional services are not being served. About 20 percent of the students with

FOCUS 4

What are the estimated prevalence and causes of hearing impairments?

■ **Table 10-2** Classification of Hearing Impairments

Average Hearing Loss in Best Ear as Measured in Decibels (db) (ISO*) at 500–2,000 Hertz (Hz)	Severity Level	Effect on Ability to Understand Speech	Typical Classroom Setting and General Lanugage Characteristics of Students with Hearing Impairments
0–25 db	Insignificant	No significant difficulty with faint or normal speech	Individual is likely to be fully integrated into regular education setting; support services, if any, would be minimal.
25–40 db	Mild (hard of hearing)	Frequent difficulty with faint sounds; some difficulty with normal speech (conversations, groups)	Individual is likely to be integrated into regular education setting with support services available to develop/maintain speech and language; hearing aid is recommended.
40–60 db	Moderate (hard of hearing)	Frequent difficulty with normal speech (conversations, groups); some difficulty with loud speech	Individual is likely to be placed in special class for students who are deaf during significant part of the day but can be integrated for at least some portion of the day; individual exhibits language delays, articulation problems, and omission of consonants.
60–80 db	Severe (range includes hard of hearing and deaf)	Frequent difficulty with even loud speech; may have difficulty understanding even shouted or amplified speech	Individual is likely to be placed in special class with little or no integration into regular education setting; even with amplification, person is unable to process ordinary conversational sound; individual will likely have severe speech and language disabilities.
80 db or more	Profound (deaf)	Usually cannot understand even amplified speech	Individual is likely to be placed in special class or school for people who are deaf; individual will have severe speech and language disability or may have no oral speech.

*International Standards Organization

hearing impairments are being served in regular classrooms full time, 24 percent in regular classes with resource-room support, 35 percent in separate special education classes, 10 percent in separate public or private day schools for students with hearing impairments, and 11 percent in public or private residential living facilities.

CAUSATION

A number of conditions may result in a hearing impairment. These conditions are generally classified as congenital (existing at birth) or acquired factors. The American-Speech-Language-Hearing Association has listed several conditions that place an individual in the high-risk category for hearing loss:

1. Family history of childhood hearing impairment
2. Congenital or perinatal infection
3. Anatomic malformations involving the head and neck
4. Birth weight of less than 1,500 grams
5. **Bacterial meningitis**
6. Severe **asphyxia** at birth

Our discussion focuses on some of these factors while highlighting causal factors related to anatomical site of loss (external, middle, or inner ear).

Congenital Factors

Heredity.   Although more than 60 types of hearing impairments have been related to hereditary factors, the cause of 25 percent of all hearing loss remains unknown (Morgan, 1987). Morgan reported that about one-third to one-half of all profound sensorineural losses result from genetic inheritance. Trybus (1985) sampled 55,000 school-age students with hearing losses and found that approximately 11 percent of all cases were associated with hereditary factors.

One of the most common diseases that affects the sense of hearing is *otosclerosis*. The cause of this disease is unknown, but it is generally believed to be hereditary and is manifested most often in early adulthood. Otosclerosis is characterized by destruction of the capsular bone in the middle ear and the growth of weblike bone that attaches to the stapes. As a result, the stapes is restricted and unable to function properly. Hearing impairments occur in about 15 percent of all cases of otosclerosis, and the incidence is twice as high for females as for males. Victims of otosclerosis suffer from high-pitched throbbing or ringing sounds known as **tinnitus,** a condition associated with disease of the inner ear.

Prenatal Disease.   Several conditions, although not inherited, can result in a congenital sensorineural loss. The major cause of nongenetic congenital deafness is infection, of which rubella, **cytomegalic inclusion** disease, and **toxoplasmosis** are the most common.

The rubella epidemic of 1963–1965 dramatically increased the incidence of deafness in the United States. Abroms (1977) indicated that, during the 1960s, approximately 10 percent of all congenital deafness was associated with women contracting rubella during pregnancy. Morgan (1987) reported that, for about 40 percent of the individuals who are deaf, the cause is rubella. About 50 percent of all children with rubella acquire a severe hearing loss. Most hearing impairments caused by rubella are sensorineural, although a small percentage may be mixed. In addition to hearing impairments, children who have had rubella sometimes acquire heart disease (50 percent), **cataracts** or **glaucoma** (40 percent), and mental retardation (40 percent) (Abroms, 1977). Since the advent of rubella vaccine, the elimination of this disease has become a nationwide campaign, and the incidence of rubella has dramatically decreased. "The hope for prevention of congenital rubella lies in immunization of susceptible populations with the currently available vaccines" (Morgan, 1987, p. 29).

Cytomegalic inclusion disease is a condition in newborns due to infection by cytomegalovirus (CMV). It is characterized by jaundice, microcephaly, hemolytic anemia, mental retardation, hepatosplenomegaly (enlargement of liver and spleen), and hearing impairments. There are some significant barriers to prevention of this virus. Experimental vaccines are available but, due to limited research, have not been approved by the government for general use (Morgan, 1987).

Congenital toxoplasmosis infection is characterized by jaundice and anemia, but frequently, the disease also results in central nervous system disorders (e.g., seizures, hydrocephalus, microcephaly). Approximately 15 percent of the infants born with this disease are deaf.

Other factors associated with congenital sensorineural hearing impairments include maternal Rh-factor incompatibility and the use of **otoxic drugs.** Maternal Rh-factor incompatibility does not generally affect a firstborn child, but as antibodies are produced during subsequent pregnancies, multiple problems can result, including deafness. Fortunately, deafness as a result of Rh-factor problems is no longer common. With the advent of an **anti-Rh gamma globulin (RhoGAM)** in 1968, the incidence of Rh-factor incompatibility has significantly decreased. If injected into the mother within the first 72 hours after the birth of the first child, she does not produce antibodies that harm future unborn infants.

Ototoxic drugs are so labeled because of their harmful effects on the sense of hearing. If these drugs are taken during pregnancy, the result may be a serious hearing loss in the infant. Although rare, congenital sensorineural impairments can also be caused by congenital syphilis, maternal chicken pox, anoxia, and birth trauma.

A condition known as **atresia** is a major cause of congenital conductive impairments. Congenital aural atresia results when the external auditory canal is either malformed or completely absent at birth. A congenital malformation may lead to a blockage of the ear canal due to an accumulation of cerumen. This wax hardens and blocks incoming sound waves from being transmitted to the middle ear.

Acquired Factors

Postnatal Disease.   One of the most common causes of hearing impairments in the postnatal period is infection, although it has shown the most significant decrease in this century (Martin, 1986; Meadow, 1980). Postnatal infections—such as measles, mumps, influenza, typhoid fever, and scarlet fever—are all associated with hearing loss. Remember that Rosa acquired a condition known as spinal meningitis at the age of 8 (see Window 10–1). Meningitis is an inflammation of the membranes that cover the brain and spinal cord and is a cause of severe hearing impairments in school-age children. Loss of hearing, sight, paralysis, and brain damage are all complications of this disease. However, there has been a recent decrease in the incidence of meningitis due to the development of antibiotics and chemotherapy.

Another common problem that may result from postnatal infection is known as **otitis media,** an inflammation of the middle ear. This condition is the result of severe colds and spreads from the eustachian tube to the middle ear. Otitis media has been found to be highly correlated with hearing problems (Martin, 1986).

Environmental Factors.   Environmental factors—including extreme changes in air pressure caused by explosions, physical abuse of the cranial area, foreign objects, and loud music—are also factors that contribute to postnatal hearing impairments. Loud noise is rapidly becoming one of the major causes of hearing problems. All of us are subjected to hazardous noise, such as jet engines and loud music, more often than ever before. With the increasing use of headphones, such as those on portable cassette players, many people (particularly adolescents) are subjected to damaging noise levels. Occupational noise (e.g., from jack-hammers, tractors, and sirens) is now the leading cause of sensorineural hearing loss.

10–1   Now Hear This—
If You Can

Diane Russ of Evanston, Ill., never stays in the kitchen when the dishwasher is running. She wouldn't think of using power tools without wearing earplugs. And on weekends she keeps her windows closed. "Some mornings you can't walk outside because so many people are using their power mowers," she laments. "It's very noisy out there." Who would dispute it? From the roar of airplanes to the wail of sirens, the blast of stereos to the blare of movie sound tracks, noise is a constant part of American life. But few go to the lengths Russ does to avoid it. Noise is annoying and frustrating—and accepted. That tolerant attitude needs to change—and fast.

Increasingly, the racket that surrounds us is being recognized not only as an environmental nuisance but also as a severe health hazard. About 28 million Americans, or 11%, suffer serious hearing loss, and more than a third of the cases result from too much exposure to loud noise. . . .

Much of the clamor is unavoidable because it fills work sites or public places. As many as 10 million Americans are exposed daily to on-the-job noise that could gradually cause some degree of permanent hearing loss. Sixty million Americans endure other noise, including a cacophony of city traffic, that is louder than the Federal Government deems safe, and 15 million live close to busy airports or beneath heavily traveled air routes. In some neighborhoods of northern New Jersey, more than 1,000 flights thunder overhead each day. . . .

Efforts are also beginning to be made to attack unavoidable noise pollution. John Wayne International Airport in Orange County, Calif., boasts the toughest runway noise standards in the country. Observers can stand on the field and carry on conversations in normal tones, even as jets take off and land. Los Angeles International Airport has pledged to be equally quiet by the end of the decade.

Some communities are starting to enforce antinoise ordinances more vigorously. New York City, arguably the noisiest urban center in the country, issued 1,000 citations last year, up from 700 in 1988, primarily targeting air-conditioning equipment, discos, street construction machinery and horn blowing. In Southern California, police in National City and Redondo Beach have been empowered to confiscate big speakers installed in autos to make them what are known as "boom cars." Says Officer Michael Harlan of National City: "If we hear a boom car 50 feet or more away on a public street, we can cite the driver. . . ."

The ultimate hope, says Dr. Patrick Brookhouser of Boys Town National Research Hospital in Omaha, is that people will realize "when you lose hearing you lose, to some degree, one of our most vital attributes, the ability to interact with our environment." In other words, Americans should be making the most noise about noise itself.

——————

Source: From "Now Hear This—If You Can" by A. Toufexis, 5 August 1991, *Time*, pp. 50–51. Copyright 1991 The Time Inc. Magazine Company. Reprinted by permission.

Other factors associated with acquired hearing impairments include the degenerative process in the ear as a result of aging, cerebral hemorrhages, allergies, and intercranial tumors.

CHARACTERISTICS

In this section we examine some of the general characteristics of people with hearing impairments, including intelligence, speech and language skills, educational achievement, and social development. We emphasize that the effect of a hearing impairment on the learning or social adjustment of the individual is extremely varied. The influence may be far reaching, as in the case of prelingual sensorineural deafness, or quite minimal, as in the case of a mild postlingual conductive impairment. Fortunately, increased emphasis has recently been placed on prevention, early detection, and intervention, which has resulted in a much improved prognosis for individuals with hearing impairments.

Intelligence

Over the past 20 years, reviews of the research on the intellectual characteristics of children with hearing impairments have suggested that the distribution of IQ scores for these individuals is similar to that of hearing children, although the mean score is slightly lower

Children with hearing impairments have been shown to have the same intellectual capabilities as their hearing peers, even though difficulties with speech and language might make it appear otherwise. (Jim Erickson/The Stock Market)

FOCUS 5

Describe the basic intelligence, speech and language skills, educational achievement, and social development associated with people who are hearing impaired.

(Greenberg & Kusche, 1989; Meadow, 1980; Vernon, 1969; Vernon & Brown, 1964). However, on the performance subtests of IQ batteries, "deaf children as a group obtain scores that fall within the average range for nonverbal intelligence" (Greenberg & Kusche, 1989, p. 98).

A study conducted by Schlesinger and Meadow (1976) revealed that children without hearing impairments scored higher than children who were deaf on three major tests of intellectual development. One striking find, however, was that the pattern of performance was consistent across the two populations. Children who are deaf, although attaining concepts at a later stage than normal, appear to learn them in approximately the same sequence as children with normal hearing.

Findings made over the past two decades have suggested that intellectual development for people with hearing impairments is more a function of language development than cognitive ability. Their difficulties in performance appear to be closely associated with speaking, reading, and writing the English language.

Speech and Language Skills

Speech and language skills are the areas of development most severely affected for those with hearing impairments. Numerous papers have been published within the last 50 years on just the speech skills of children who are deaf (Levitt, 1989). These publications have clearly suggested that the effects of a hearing impairment on language development vary considerably. For people with mild and moderate hearing losses, the effect on speech and language may be minimal. Even for individuals born with moderate losses, effective communication skills are possible because the voiced sounds of conversational speech remain audible. Although individuals with moderate losses cannot hear unvoiced sounds and distant speech, language delays can be prevented if the hearing loss is diagnosed and treated early (Ling & Milne, 1981). The majority of people with hearing impairments are able to use speech as the primary mode for language acquisition.

For the person who is congenitally deaf, most loud speech is inaudible, even with the use of the most sophisticated hearing aids. These people are unable to receive information through speech unless they have learned to lipread. Sounds produced by the person who is deaf are extremely difficult to understand (low in intelligibility) (McAnally et al., 1987).

Children who are deaf exhibit significant articulation, voice quality, and tone discrimination problems (Levitt, 1989). Researchers have found that, even as early as 8 months of age, babies who are deaf appear to babble less than their hearing peers (Stoel-Gammon & Otomo, 1986).

Persons who are congenitally deaf have a great deal of difficulty adequately communicating with the hearing world. In order to have any chance of overcoming this severe disability, they must have access to early and extensive training in language production and comprehension. A hearing impairment is a serious barrier to verbal learning. "The sense of hearing plays a crucial role not only in the understanding of speech, but also in providing the cues needed for the acquisition of speech and language in the normal, developing child" (Levitt, 1989, p. 23).

Educational Achievement

The educational achievement of students with hearing impairments may be significantly delayed in comparison to that of their hearing peers. Students who are hearing impaired have considerable difficulty succeeding in a system that depends primarily on the spoken word and written language to transmit knowledge. Low achievement is characteristic of students who are deaf (Greenberg & Kusche, 1989; Meadow, 1980); they average 3 to 4 years below their age-appropriate grade levels (Mandell & Fiscus, 1981). However, even students with mild to moderate losses achieve below expectations based on their performance on tests of cognitive ability (Greenberg & Kusche, 1989).

Reading is the academic area most negatively affected for students with hearing impairments. Any hearing loss, whether mild or profound, appears to have very detrimental effects on reading performance (Cole, 1987; Greenberg & Kusche, 1989). Students who are deaf obtain their highest achievement scores in reading during the first three years of school, but by third grade, reading performance is surpassed by both arithmetic and spelling performance (Meadow, 1980). By the time students who are deaf reach adolescence, their reading performance is equivalent to that of about a fifth-grade child with normal hearing (Conrad, 1979).

To counteract the difficulty with conventional reading materials, specialized instructional programs have been developed especially for students with hearing impairments. One such program is the *Reading Milestone* series (Quigley and King, 1984), which uses content that focuses on the interests and experiences of children with hearing impairments while incorporating linguistic controls: the careful pacing of new vocabulary, the clear identification of syntactic structures, and the movement from simple to complex in introducing new concepts (e.g., idioms, inferences, etc.). In less than a decade, *Reading Milestones* has become the most widely used reading program for students who are deaf (LaSasso, 1985).

Spelling performance is also below average for students with hearing impairments but less so than reading performance. Quigley and Kretschmer (1982) reported that students who are deaf leave school with about a seventh-grade spelling ability. Interestingly, these students make far less phonetic spelling errors than their hearing counterparts (Hanson, Shankweiler, & Fischer, 1983).

The written language of students who are deaf is simple and limited in comparison to that of their hearing counterparts (Quigley & Paul, 1989). The sentences written by students with hearing impairments are generally short and rudimentary, resembling sentences written by less mature students without hearing impairments.

Very little research is available on the teaching of mathematics to students with hearing impairments (Lang, 1989). What is available suggests that arithmetic computation skills are deficient for students with hearing impairments in comparison to their hearing peers. Karchmer (1985) reported that the average adolescent who is deaf leaves school with about a seventh-grade mathematical ability. Researchers have found that these students are not very proficient in number conservation, questioning skills, and word-problem solving (Quigley & Paul, 1989).

Allen (1986) examined the overall academic achievement of students who are deaf to see if there was any improvement in scores over a nine-year period. He evaluated student scores from achievement tests taken in 1974 and then did the same evaluation on a different set of students in 1983. He reported that achievement scores for students with hearing impairments were lower than those of their hearing peers in both 1974 and 1983. However, a comparison of 1974 and 1983 data indicated that the scores of students with hearing impairments had improved over the nine-year period and that the gap between student groups was closing. This is an encouraging trend that may reflect advances in instructional techniques for these students.

Social Development

A hearing impairment modifies the individual's capacity to receive and process auditory stimuli. People with hearing impairments receive a reduced amount of auditory information; the information received is also distorted, compared to the input received by those with normal hearing. Consequently, the perceptions of auditory information by people with hearing impairments are different from the norm. Sanders (1980) stated:

> The problem is not simply one involving a reduction of sensitivity to sound; it concerns the whole process of structuring an awareness and understanding of things, events, people, and even self. The hearing impaired child must develop his perceptions using an auditory system which distorts or even eliminates information that the normal developing child uses to build his understanding of the world. (p. 219)

Reviews of the literature on social and psychological development in children who are deaf have suggested that these individuals are less socially mature than hearing children (Greenberg & Kusche, 1989; Meadow, 1980). Delayed language acquisition may lead to more limited opportunities for social interaction (Cole, 1987). Children who are deaf may have more adjustment problems than their hearing counterparts. In spite of these findings, Meadow suggested "that it would be a mistake to conclude that there is a single 'deaf personality type.' *There is much diversity among deaf people, and it is related to education, communication, and experience*" (1990, pp. 96–97; emphasis added).

Social maladjustment patterns are also positively correlated with the severity of the loss and the type of impairment. The more severe the loss, the greater the potential for social isolation. However, it is important to note that most individuals with severe hearing losses, such as Rosa from Window 10–1, are socially well adjusted.

ASSESSMENT AND INTERVENTION

Medical Interventions

Medicine plays a major role in the prevention, early detection, and remediation of hearing impairments. Several specialists are integrally involved in the medical assessment and intervention process. These include the genetics specialist, the **otologist,** the pediatrician, the family practitioner, the neurosurgeon, and the **audiologist.**

The Genetics Specialist.   Prevention of hearing impairments is a primary concern of the genetics specialist. A significant number of hearing impairments are inherited or occur during prenatal, perinatal, and postnatal development. Consequently, the genetics specialist

FOCUS 6

Why is the early detection of hearing loss so important?

10-2   Athletes and Poets: The World Heard Them

Most likely the football huddle was invented at Gallaudet in the 1890s so opposing teams could not see what plays were being worked out. And baseball owes some umpires' calls to the deaf: Raising the right arm to signify a strike was created for William Ellsworth "Dummy" Hoy, a deaf outfielder for Cincinnati and Washington. In one game in 1889, he threw out three runners at home plate, a record that still stands. At least fourteen other pro baseball players have been deaf, as well as pro boxers and wrestlers.

Erastus "Deaf" (pronounced deef) Smith was a Texas soldier, scout, and spy under Sam Houston. He led his men to victory in a famous battle, and a Texas county is named after him.

The French poets Pierre de Ronsard and Joachim duBellay became deaf as young men. And Beethoven, Goya, and Thomas Alva Edison all became profoundly deaf in later life. Helen Keller, of course, was an advocate for the rights of all disabled people.

These days there are deaf doctors, accountants, lawyers, and artists. Actress Marlee Matlin won the Oscar as Best Actress for 1986. In 1976, Kitty O'Neil, a deaf Hollywood stunt woman, set a land speed record for women in a rocket-powered racer. She also set a record in 1970 for the fastest woman on water skis. David Michalowski performed through the 1980s as a world-class figure skater—skating to music by memorizing beats.

Source: From "I Know How to Ask for What I Want" by L. A. Walker, 23 April 1989, *Parade*, pp. 4–6. Reprinted with permission from *Parade*, copyright © 1989.

plays an important role in preventing disabilities through family counseling and prenatal screening.

The Pediatrician and Family Practitioner.   Early detection of a hearing problem can prevent or at least minimize the impact of the disability on the overall development of an individual. Generally, it is the responsibility of the pediatrician or family practitioner to be aware of a problem and to refer the family to an appropriate hearing specialist. In order to meet these responsibilities, the physician must be familiar with family history. It is also

The success of actress Marlee Matlin in mainstream movies and television has been inspirational to people with hearing impairments. (Marianne Barcellona/Shooting Star)

10–3   Testing for a Hearing Loss

Figure A is an example of an audiogram before a hearing test. It shows several things: The numbers along the bottom show the frequency of the tone to be tested. The frequency may be indicated by hertz (Hz), which is another way of describing how many vibrations happen each second. The numbers along the side are shown in decibels (db). As the numbers go from zero to ten to twenty to thirty, the intensity (strength) increases.

When an audiologist tests hearing using the air-conduction test, he or she marks the audiogram with *X* for the left ear and *O* for the right ear.

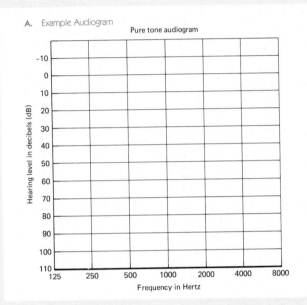

A. Example Audiogram

Pure tone audiogram

Don

Figure B shows Don's audiogram. The line connecting the *X*s shows the hearing level in Don's left ear. The line connecting the *O*s shows the hearing level in his right ear. Don's hearing level is normal. This means he can hear very soft speech sounds with no difficulty. The dark part on Don's audiogram (0–25 db) shows the area that is "within normal limits." Even if a person has a loss in this area, he or she can still follow a normal conversation. People who are talking to each other usually speak at a volume of 55 db. This helps you to see why a slight loss can be within normal limits.

Bill

Bill had his hearing tested also. The audiologist first used the air-conduction test and marked Bill's audiogram. Then the audiologist used another test—a bone-conduction test—to find out where the problem might be. In this test, the sound goes past the middle ear. The test tells if the inner ear is working properly. For the bone conduction test, the audiologist uses a small device called a *vibrator,* which makes the same kind of tones as the earphones. He places the vibrator be-

important for the physician to conduct a thorough physical examination of the child. The physician must be alert to any symptoms (e.g., delayed language development) that indicate potential sensory loss.

The Otologist.   The otologist is the medical specialist who is most concerned with the hearing organ and its diseases. *Otology* is a component of the larger specialty of diseases of the ear, nose, and throat. The otologist, like the pediatrician, screens for potential hearing problems, but the process is much more specialized and exhaustive. The otologist also conducts an extensive physical examination of the ear to identify syndromes that are associated with conductive or sensorineural loss. This information, in conjunction with family history, provides data regarding appropriate medical treatment.

Treatment may involve medical therapy or surgical intervention. Common therapeutic procedures include monitoring aural hygiene (e.g., keeping the external ear free from wax); blowing out the ear (e.g., a process to remove mucus blocking the eustachian tube); and the use of antibiotics to treat infections. Surgical techniques may involve the cosmetic and functional restructuring of congenital malformations such as a deformed external ear or a

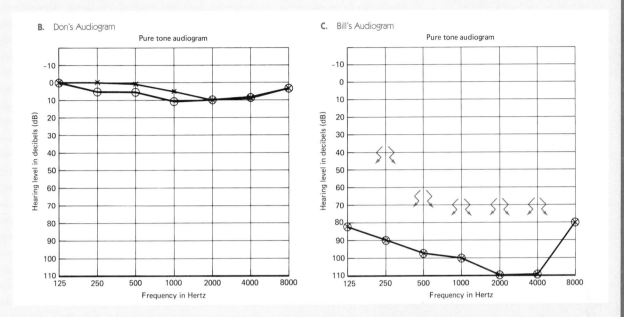

B. Don's Audiogram

Pure tone audiogram

C. Bill's Audiogram

Pure tone audiogram

hind the ear or on the forehead. The individual must respond when he hears a sound from the vibrator. The audiologist marks this response on the audiogram. He may use < for the left ear, and > for the right ear. An arrow (→) added to either symbol means that the person cannot hear the sound from the vibrator. The bone-conduction test tells if the inner ear is working properly.

Figure C is Bill's audiogram. It shows the results of both tests. We can see that Bill did not respond at all to the bone-conduction test. His hearing problem results from trouble in the inner ear or along the auditory nerve. This type of loss is a sensorineural loss.

Bill's audiogram shows that he is profoundly deaf. For Bill, this means that he cannot hear or understand speech. With a hearing aid, he can hear

some speech sounds, but he may not be able to understand them. Bill became deaf when he was two years old, as a result of spinal meningitis.

———
Source: Adapted from *You and Your Deafness* by permission of Gallaudet College Press, 800 Florida Ave. N.E., Washington, DC 20002. Copyright 1982 by Gallaudet College.

closed external canal (atresia). **Fenestration** is the surgical creation of a new opening in the labyrinth of the ear to restore hearing. A **stapedectomy** is a surgical process conducted under a microscope whereby a fixed stapes is replaced with a prosthetic device capable of vibrating, thus permitting the transmission of sound waves. A **myringoplasty** is the surgical reconstruction of a perforated tympanic membrane (eardrum).

A **cochlear implant** is a surgical procedure that has proven to be highly successful. The purpose of the implant is to restore hearing through electronic stimulation of the auditory nerve. The implant consists of a receiver coil, electrodes (internal), a microphone, **transducer,** and transmitter (external). Cochlear implants are becoming more widely used with both adults and children. However, cochlear implants may be inappropriate for some children who are unable to benefit from conventional amplification. Additionally, caution should be exercised because of the risk of possible damage to an ear that has some residual hearing and the risk of infection from the implant.

The Audiologist.   The degree of hearing loss, measured in decibel and hertz units, is ascertained by using a process known as *audiometric evaluation*. The audiometric evaluation

Early testing for hearing impairments is essential so problems can be identified and so children can benefit from early intervention programs. (N. Benn/Stock, Boston)

is conducted by an audiologist, who presents the listener with tones that are relatively free of external noise (pure-tone audiometry) or spoken words, in which speech perception is measured (speech audiometry). An electronic device (**audiometer**) is used to detect a person's response to sound stimuli. A record (**audiogram**) is obtained from the audiometer that graphs the individual's threshold for hearing at various sound frequencies.

Whereas the otologist presents a biological perspective on hearing impairments, the audiologist emphasizes the sociological and educational impact of hearing loss. Hodgson (1987) suggested:

FOCUS 7

Distinguish between an *otologist* and an *audiologist*.

> The first purpose of an audiologist in dealing with children is to identify an auditory disorder. If a hearing loss is found, its nature and magnitude must be determined. The audiologist must ask whether the disorder, as measured, is sufficient to explain observed behavior. The social, educational, and vocational implications of the disorder must be explored. (p. 185)

Although audiologists are not specifically trained in the field of medicine, these professionals interact constantly with otologists to provide a comprehensive assessment of hearing. The audiologist is trained in the measurement of hearing. Patrick (1987) addressed the goals of audiometry: "(1) to identify those individuals who have sufficient hearing loss to compromise communication and/or learning in the typical classroom; (2) to find and send for medical management those students who have middle ear pathologies; and (3) to perform these tasks in the most cost-effective and efficient manner" (p. 402).

Another important function served by audiologists and otologists is to provide assistance regarding the selection and use of hearing aids. At one time or another, most people with hearing impairments will wear hearing aids. Hearing aids make sounds louder, but they do not correct hearing. Hearing aids have been used for centuries. Early acoustic aids included cupping one's hand behind the ear as well as the ear trumpet. Modern **electro-**

Hearing aid technology has been much improved since these early 1800 versions were created. (North Wind Picture Archives)

acoustic aids do not depend on the loudness of the human voice to amplify sound but utilize batteries to increase volume. Electroacoustic aids come in two main types: body aids (strapped to the body) and behind-the-ear aids. These aids may be fitted monaurally (on one ear) or binaurally (on both ears).

Although the quality of commercially available aids has improved dramatically in recent years, they do have distinct limitations. For example, hearing-aid use has been found to be positively related to speech use but appears to have little effect on reading ability (Mertens, 1990). The criteria for effectiveness must be measured against wearability, the individual's communication skill, and educational achievement (Garwood, 1987).

The stimulation of residual hearing through a hearing aid enables most people with hearing impairments to function as hard of hearing. However, as Ross and Calvert (1984) pointed out, use of a hearing aid must be implemented as early as possible, before sensory deprivation takes its toll on the child. It is the audiologist's responsibility to weigh all the factors involved (e.g., convenience, size, weight) in the selection and use of an aid for the individual. The individual should then be directed to a reputable hearing-aid dealer.

Social Interventions

The social consequences of being hearing impaired are highly correlated with the severity of the impairment. For the individual who is deaf, social integration may be extremely difficult because societal views of deafness have reinforced social isolation. The belief that a person who is deaf is incompetent has been predominant from the time of the early Hebrews and Romans, who deprived these people of their civil rights, to twentieth-century America, where, in some areas, it is still difficult for adults who are deaf to obtain drivers' licenses or adequate insurance coverage or to be gainfully employed. Moores (1987) indicated that people who are deaf remained significantly underemployed in the 1980s. Individuals with the greatest difficulty are those born with congenital deafness. The inability to hear and understand speech has often isolated these people from their hearing peers. For example, people who are deaf tend to marry other people who are deaf (Woodward, 1982).

FOCUS 8

Identify factors that may impede the social integration of people who are deaf into the hearing world.

10–4 Regular Classroom Placement for Students Who Are Deaf: Isolation or Inclusion?

SITUATION 1: A Case of Isolation*

It's a Monday in May, near the end of the school year. The classroom door is open, and the hearing students are pouring in, greeting their friends and talking excitedly about their weekend experiences. The deaf student slips in silently, sits down alone and buries his head in a book as he waits for class to begin. He cannot hear the buzz of activity and conversation around him. He was not a part of the weekend activities. No one speaks to him. He looks up as a girl he likes comes up the row to her seat and drops her books down on the desk. He ventures to speak softly to her, not noticing that she is already talking and joking with a guy across the room. The deaf student finally captures her glance and asks his question, but the girl doesn't understand what he says. (His speech is slightly impaired, and the room is noisy.) After two more repetitions of "How was your weekend?" he is rewarded with a perfunctory "Oh, fine!" before she turns around and gets wrapped up in a detailed, secret exchange with her best girlfriend, who sits right behind her. They giggle and talk, glancing up once in a while to catch the eye of the boy across the room. The deaf student rearranges the papers on his desk.

Finally, the teacher begins to lecture, and the lively conversational exchanges become subdued. The hearing students settle into pseudo-attentive postures, reverting to subtle, subversive communications with those around them. The deaf student, in his front row, corner seat, turns his eyes on the interpreter. He keeps his focus there, working to grasp visually what the other students are effortlessly half-listening to. The teacher questions a student in the back of the room. Her hearing friends whisper help. Their encouragement boosts her confidence and she boldly answers the teacher. Satisfied, the teacher moves on to question someone else. The first student joins those whispering to the boy who's now on the spot. He picks up the quiet cues and impresses the instructor with his evident mastery of the subject. A peer support system of companionable cooperation helps keep everyone afloat. However, only those with sensitive hearing and social support can tap into this interwoven network of surreptitious assistance. When a pointed question is directed to the deaf student, he is on his own. No student schemes bring him into the "we" of class camaraderie. Instead, when he speaks, the students suddenly stop talking and stare. But he is oblivious to the awkward silence in the room. He is verbally stumbling, searching for an answer that will pacify the teacher, and yet not be too specific. He strains to minimize the risk of opening himself up for embarrassment of saying something that has already been said, or something that misses the mark entirely. While he is still speaking, the bell rings and the other students pack up and start moving out the back door. The deaf student, his eyes on the teacher, doesn't notice the interpreter's signal that the bell has already sounded. The teacher smiles uncomfortably and cuts him off to give last-minute instructions as the students pour out the door.

In the next class, the first five minutes are set aside for the class to practice sign language. The deaf student has been hoping that the sign lessons would provide at least a spare stock of signs that students could use with him. The presenter demonstrates how to form the signs. A few students follow along, hesitantly imitating these gestures which seem so strange to them. But most of the students just take advantage of a little more time to pass notes, whisper together, and strengthen established friendships. Although they have had almost a year of exposure to signing, the deaf student is still waiting for the day when someone, sometime, will approach him for a few words of simple conversation.

Suddenly, a rapid series of pulsing bells blast into the classroom. Glad for an excuse to get out of class, the students quickly join the mass of people streaming out of all the doorways for the fire drill. The various classes mingle together and the mass of students swarms onto a nearby field. Students find their friends and cluster to chat while they wait for the end of the drill. In the middle of the milling crowd, in a sea of communication, the deaf student thirsts for a drop of conversation. He tries talking with a few people, but when they speak, he cannot understand their words. Impatiently, they turn away, leaving the deaf student to stand alone in awkward silence. When the drill ends, he hurries back to the room, relieved. The other students return reluctantly to their seats.

As class starts, the teacher returns papers she has corrected. The deaf student hopes he won't be singled out again as "different." At the first of the year, he had been one of two students who received the same poor grade on a test. The teacher had suggested to the hearing student that he work harder; then he had asked the deaf student if he wanted to move to a less demanding class. It seemed that people suspected that he might be "dumb" as well as deaf. Perhaps it was the same assumption that led another teacher to react with amazement when the deaf student earned an "A" grade on the first exam in his class. Thankfully, today his paper is returned without incident, and the rest of the period passes uneventfully.

During the afternoon, there is a rally in the gym. The deaf student arrives early, choosing a seat on one of the lower bleachers, where he will be close enough to see the speakers and the interpreter. Students stream in through doors on both sides of the building. It isn't long before the bleachers are jam-packed with talking, laughing, cheering students. The building is fairly bursting with spirited shouting, dynamic energy, and animated conversations. But no one talks with the deaf student. Set apart by silence, he cannot enter the world of words around him. Only an observer, behind a quiet barrier, he is alone in the crowd.

SITUATION 2: A Vision of Inclusion**

It is a crisp autumn morning, the kind that some people breathe in deeply as they look forward to the challenges of the day. School has begun an hour ago. Mrs. Jones' algebra class is examining some equations. Puzzled by Mrs. Jones' explanation, Samantha raises her hand and questions her teacher about an equation. While Samantha signs her question, Mrs. Jones watches Samantha (pleased that she understands much of what Samantha is signing) and listens to Samantha's interpreter. Several of Samantha's classmates watch her signing, nodding in agreement that the explanation was not clear. Later, as the students work some math problems, Samantha and a hearing friend exchange suggestions through signs. As Samantha and her classmates leave for their next class, Mrs. Jones call out to the class and signs to Samantha, "Have a nice day."

Samantha and two of her hearing friends hurry to their next class. On the way, they animatedly sign to each other about the upcoming school dance. Samantha's planning to go with one of her deaf friends from the mainstream program, Jason. As they reach their next class, they meet Mike and Ernestine, two other deaf students in the mainstream program. Samantha and her two friends greet Mike and Ernestine and they enter the class together. During the civics class the students and teachers have a lively ex-

change about the responsibility of citizens when faced with a law they feel is immoral. (Occasionally the teacher reminds the students not to interrupt one another or talk so fast so that all of the students, deaf and hearing, can catch what is being said.) Samantha, Mike, and Ernestine join in through sign language, and several of the hearing students sign as they speak. An interpreter speaks and signs as needed.

After civics, Samantha and Ernestine head to an English class and Mike to a physical education class. The English class is taught by Mr. Roberts, a deaf education teacher in the mainstream program. Being deaf, Mr. Roberts signs gracefully and eloquently. The class is alive as they discuss poetry by hearing and deaf poets. Tony, Margaret, and Lee, three hearing students, are in the class with Samantha and her deaf classmates. They will attend for two weeks as the class discusses and dramatizes poetry. Mr. Roberts uses his voice to help them understand, though they sign quite well. At the end of the two weeks, the class will dramatize and sign several poems for other deaf and hearing students.

At lunch, Samantha, Alice (another deaf youth), and several hearing students gossip about the day's events and their plans for later that day. Alice and Jean, a hearing student, plan to stay after school to finish an assignment in their business course. Both hope to work for a local bank as file clerks when they graduate from high school. Samantha and some of her deaf friends are going to study together for a "big" test in history. After lunch, the students head to their classes for the remainder of the afternoon.

Across town, at the elementary mainstream program, Ms. Moore, the interpreter, is teaching a class of second graders to sign. By leaving recess early, Jimmy, a deaf sixth grader, helps the interpreter instruct the hearing chil-

dren. After helping, Jimmy goes to his reading class with other deaf youth. Mrs. Cary, the deaf education teacher, often uses stories involving deaf characters or deaf people for the reading lessons (as well as other, diverse characters and people — so too do the teachers in the mainstream). After reading, Jimmy and his deaf and hearing classmates in art listen and watch as a local deaf artist demonstrates her sculpting. The artist encourages the students to try their hands at it, and she answers their questions. As several classmates question the artist, Jimmy signs to David, a hearing friend. Their teacher signs to Jimmy and Dave to stop, which they sheepishly do. After class, the guest artist remarks to the art teacher that she did not realize that so many of his students were deaf. He tells her that about one-fourth of the students are deaf, but many of the hearing students sign. As school ends, Jimmy and Dave are picked up by Dave's mother. As they get into the car, Dave's mother greets her son and Jimmy in voice and sign.

After Jimmy, Dave, and the other students leave, Mr. Johnson, the principal, several deaf education and mainstream teachers, a few parents of deaf and hearing students, and a representative from the local chapter of the state association of the deaf discuss how deaf citizens can be more involved in the school. While they all agree that good progress has been made — witness the local deaf artist who guest taught today — they are determined to have deaf adults routinely involved in the education of the deaf and hearing youth.

Sources: *From "Alone in the Crowd" by C. Wixtrom, 1988, *The Deaf American*, 38(12), pp 14–15. **From P. C. Higgins, *The Challenges of Educating Together Deaf and Hearing Youth: Making Mainstreaming Work*, 1990. Courtesy of Charles C Thomas, Publisher, Springfield, Illinois.

A segment of individuals who are deaf is actively involved in organizations and communities specifically intended to meet their needs. The National Association for the Deaf (NAD) was organized in 1880. The philosophy of the NAD is as follows: "All deaf persons have the right to life, liberty, and the pursuit of happiness and . . . this right must be evidenced in ways that meet the satisfaction of the deaf persons themselves rather than that of their teachers and parents, who do not live with the condition" (Schreiber, 1979, p. 565). NAD serves individuals who are deaf in many capacities. Among its many contributions, NAD publishes books on deafness, sponsors cultural activities, and lobbies around the United States for legislation promoting the rights of persons who are deaf.

Another prominent organization is the Alexander Graham Bell Association for the Deaf, which advocates the integration of persons with hearing impairments into the social mainstream. The major thrust of this approach is the improvement of proficiency in speech communications. The Alexander Graham Bell Association is also a clearinghouse for information for people who are deaf and their advocates. The association publishes widely in the areas of parent counseling, teaching methodology, speech reading, and auditory training. In addition, it sponsors national and regional conferences that focus on a variety of issues pertinent to the social adjustment of people who are deaf.

Because of the unique communication problems of persons with hearing impairments, many are unable to benefit from mental health services in their communities. Mental health professionals may be unaware of the communication barriers that prevent people with hearing impairments from obtaining services. Such professionals must be trained to address the unique needs of these people. Mental health professionals should work with parents as early as possible to assist young children in adjusting to their sensory limitation. As children with hearing impairments become older, counselors must be available to help them explore feelings regarding impairment and to cope with the reactions of parents, family, and peers.

FOCUS 9

Why are educational services for students who are hearing impaired described as being in the process of change?

Educational Interventions

In the United States, educational programs for children who are hearing impaired emerged in the early nineteenth century. The residential school for the deaf was the primary model for educational service delivery; it was a live-in facility where students were segregated from the family environment. In the latter half of the nineteenth century, day schools were established, in which students lived with their families while receiving an education in a special school for students identified as deaf (Van Cleve & Crouch, 1989). As the century drew to a close, some public schools established special classes within regular schools for children with hearing impairments.

The residential school continued to be a model for educational services well into the twentieth century. However, with the introduction of electrical amplification, advances in medical treatment, and improved educational technology, more options became available within public school systems. Today, educational programs for students who are hearing impaired range from the residential school to regular class placement with support services.

The delivery of educational services to students with hearing impairments is in the process of change. Since 1986, with the advent of early childhood amendments in Public Law 99-457, an expanding emphasis has been placed on early intervention. As Newton (1987) emphasized, "Early identification is essential, for without it no further intervention will occur. Children with hearing impairments should be identified as close to birth as possible, but at least by one year of age" (p. 323). There is little disagreement that the education of the child with a hearing impairment must begin at the time of the diagnosis.

Educational goals for students with hearing impairments are comparable to those for their hearing peers. The student with a hearing impairment brings many of the same

Rock Music and Hearing Loss

Rock and Roll may never die, but it may become a little difficult to hear for those of us who've ever cranked up the volume louder than a jackhammer in search of that ultimate music "rush": the bass line stirring our very souls, making us feel "forever young." And who hasn't felt the energy of a rock concert, with music blared by amplifiers bigger than most station wagons? If you ever thought that your poor old dad, screaming from the top of the steps to "turn that awful noise down," was hopelessly out of touch, it may be time to eat a little crow.

Many of the loud noises that assault our ears on a daily basis—including one of the worst of modern-day offenders, stereo headsets—seem to cause permanent and sometimes painful hearing problems. During a recent press conference following a concert tour, Pete Townshend of the legendary rock band The Who, who is famous for finishing each concert by smashing his guitar to pieces in an amplifier-blowing crescendo, revealed that he suffers from permanent hearing loss and painful tinnitus (ringing in the ears).

Some loss of hearing is normal with age, particularly among people in industrialized countries. In the 1950s, audiologist Samuel Rosen tested an African tribe tucked away in quiet isolation on the Sudaness-Ethiopian border. He found that men well into their seventies could routinely hear faint murmurs across a distance the length of a football field. In comparison, few people living in noisier parts of the world will be so lucky. By age 65, one in three Americans suffers hearing loss serious enough to interfere with communication. Many other Americans experience serious loss well before that age.

The volume of a live rock and roll concert commonly reaches 120 decibels—louder than a jackhammer. A stereo headset routinely pumps about 115 decibels of noise into vulnerable ears. (If the person standing next to you can hear the music coming out of your headset, it's loud enough to be damaging your ears.) Some customized car stereos can reach sound levels of over 130 decibels, which is roughly as loud as a jet at takeoff.

It seems that the sensory damage done by exposure to these megadecibels is first manifested in the loss of ability to hear soft and high-pitched sounds: a whisper, the chirp of a bird, the soft murmur of people at a nearby table, the laughter of children, the tinkle of piano keys. If the preservation of such sounds is important to you, experts suggest that you seek protection. At about $2 a pair, old-fashioned earplugs are well worth the price.

Source: Peter Jaret, "Turn Down the Racket," *Reader's Digest,* November, 1991

strengths and weaknesses to the classroom as the hearing student. Adjustment to learning experiences is often comparable for both groups. Unlike their hearing peers, however, students with hearing impairments face the formidable problems associated with being unable to communicate effectively.

Teaching Communication Skills. There are four common approaches to teaching communication skills to students with hearing impairments: auditory, oral, manual, and total communication. There is a long history of controversy regarding which approach is the most appropriate for students with hearing impairments (Moores, 1990). However, as Ling (1984b) indicated, no single method or collection of methods can meet the individual needs of all children with hearing impairments. It is not our purpose to enter into the controversy regarding these approaches but to present a brief description of each approach.

The auditory approach emphasizes the use of amplified sound and residual hearing to develop oral communication skills. The auditory channel is considered the primary avenue for language development, regardless of the severity or type of hearing loss. Students are strongly encouraged to learn normal speech production, and the use of manual communication (other than natural gestures) is discouraged. In addition to the common body-type and behind-the-ear hearing aids, the approach utilizes a variety of electroacoustic devices to enhance residual hearing. Although the traditional portable desk trainer may still be found

FOCUS 10

Identify four approaches to teaching communication skills to persons with hearing impairments.

INTERACTING IN NATURAL SETTINGS ·········· People with Hearing Impairments ············

EARLY CHILDHOOD YEARS

Tips for the Family

◆ Promote family learning about diversity in all people in the context of understanding the child with a hearing impairment.

◆ Keep informed about organizations and civic groups that can provide support to the young child with a hearing impairment and also the family.

◆ Get in touch with your local health, social services, and education agencies about infant, toddler, and preschool programs for children with hearing impairments. Become familiar with the individualized family service plan (IFSP) and how it can serve as a planning tool to support the inclusion of your child in early intervention programs.

◆ Focus on the development of communication for your child. Work with professionals to determine what mode of communication (oral, manual, and/or total communication) will be most effective in developing early language skills.

◆ Label stimuli (e.g., objects and people) both visually and verbally as often as possible to provide the child with multiple sources of input.

Tips for the Preschool Teacher

◆ Language deficits are a fundamental problem for young children with hearing impairments. Focus on developing some form of expressive and receptive communication in the classroom as early as possible. Help young children with hearing impairments to understand words that are abstract, have multiple meanings, and are part of idiomatic expressions (e.g. *run* down the street versus *run* for president).

◆ Help hearing classmates interact with the child with a hearing impairment. Help hearing children be both verbal and visual with the student who is hearing impaired. If the child with a hearing impairment doesn't respond to sound, have the hearing children learn to stand in the line of sight. Teach them to gain the attention of the child with a hearing impairment without physical prompting.

◆ Work closely with parents so that early communication and skill development for the young child with a hearing impairment is consistent across school and home environments.

◆ Become very familiar with acoustical devices (e.g., hearing aids) that may be used by the young child with a hearing impairment. Make sure that these devices are worn properly and work in the classroom environment.

Tips for Preschool Personnel

◆ Support the inclusion of young children with hearing impairments in your classrooms and programs.

◆ Support teachers, staff, and volunteers as they attempt to create successful experiences for the young child with a hearing impairment in the preschool setting.

◆ Work very closely with families to keep them informed and active members of the school community.

Tips for Neighbors and Friends

◆ Work with the family of a young child with a hearing impairment to seek opportunities for interactions with hearing children in neighborhood play settings.

◆ Focus on the capabilities of the young child with a hearing impairment rather than the disabilities. Understand how the child communicates: orally? manually? or both? If the child uses sign language, take the time to learn fundamental signs that will enhance your communication with him or her.

ELEMENTARY YEARS

Tips for the Family

◆ Learn about your rights as parents of a child with a hearing impairment. Actively participate in the development of your child's individualized education program (IEP). Through active participation, fight for the goals that you would like to see on the IEP that will focus on your child developing social interaction and communication skills in natural settings.

◆ Participate in as many school functions for parents as is reasonable (e.g., PTA, parent advisory groups, volunteering, etc.) to connect your family to the school.

◆ Seek information on in-school and extracurricular activities available that will enhance opportunities for your child to interact with hearing peers.

◆ Keep the school informed about the medical needs of your child. If he or she needs or uses acoustical devices to enhance hearing capability, help school personnel to understand how these devices work.

Tips for the Regular Classroom Teacher

◆ Outline school work (e.g., the schedule for the day) on paper or the blackboard so the student with a hearing impairment can see it.

◆ As much as possible, require classroom work to be answered in complete sentences to provide the necessary practice for students with hearing impairments.

◆ Remember that students with hearing impairments don't always know how words fit together to make understandable sentences. Help them develop skills by always writing in complete sentences.

- Have the student with a hearing impairment sit where he or she can see the rest of the class as easily as possible. Choose a buddy to sit by and keep him or her aware of what is going on in class.
- When lecturing, have the student with a hearing impairment sit as close to you as possible.
- Don't be surprised to see gaps in learning. Demonstrations of disgust or amazement will make the student feel he or she is at fault.
- Be sure to help the student with a hearing impairment know what is going on at all times (e.g., pass on announcements made over the intercom).
- Always give short, concise instructions and then make sure the student with a hearing impairment understood them by having him or her repeat the information before performing the task.
- Type scripts (or outlines of scripts) for movies and videotapes used in class. Let the student read the script for the movie.

Tips for School Personnel
- Integrate school resources as well as children. Wherever possible, help regular classroom teachers access the human and material resources necessary to meet the needs of students with hearing impairments. For example:
  — *The audiologist:* Keep in close contact with this professional and seek advice on the student's hearing and the acoustical devices being used.
  — *The special education teacher trained in hearing impairments:* This professional is necessary as both a teacher of students with hearing impairments and as a consultant to regular educators. Activities can range from working on the development of effective communications skills to dealing with behavioral difficulties. The regular education teacher may even decide to work with the special education teacher on learning sign language, if appropriate.
  — *Speech and language specialists:* Many students with hearing impairments will need help with speech acquisition and application in the school setting.
- Assist regular and special education teachers to develop peer-partner and support networks for students with hearing impairments. These peer partners may help by serving as tutors or just by reviewing for tests and class assignments.
- Work to help the student with a hearing impairment strive for independence. Assistance from peers is sometimes helpful, but it should never reach the point where other students are doing work for the student with a hearing impairment.

Tips for Neighbors and Friends
- Help families with a child who is hearing impaired to be an integral part of neighborhood and friendship networks. Seek ways to include the family and the child wherever possible in neighborhood activities (e.g., outings, barbecues, outdoor yard and street cleanups, crime watches, etc.).

SECONDARY/TRANSITION YEARS

Tips for the Family
- Become familiar with adult services systems (e.g., rehabilitation services, social security, health care) while your son or daughter is still in high school. Understand the type of vocational or employment training that he or she will need prior to graduation. Find out the school's view on what a high school should be doing to assist someone who is hearing impaired make the transition from school to adult life.
- Create opportunities out of school for your son or daughter to participate in activities with same-age hearing peers.

Tips for the Regular Classroom Teacher
- Collaborate with specialists in hearing impairments and other school personnel to help students adapt to subject matter in your classroom (e.g., science, math, physical education).
- Become aware of the needs of and resources available for students with hearing impairments in your classroom. Facilitate student learning by establishing peer-support systems (e.g., note-takers) to help students with hearing impairments be successful.
- Use diagrams, graphs, and visual representations whenever possible when presenting new concepts.
- Help the student with a hearing impairment become involved in the extracurricular high school activities. If you are the faculty sponsor of a club or organization, explore whether the student is interested and how he or she could get involved.

Tips for School Personnel
- Advocate for parents of high-school-age students with hearing impairments to participate in school activities (e.g., committees, PTA).
- Parents will be more active when school personnel have regular and positive contact with the family.

Tips for Neighbors, Friends, and Potential Employers
- Seek ways to become part of a community support network for individuals with hearing impairments. Be alert to ways that these individuals can become and remain actively involved in community employment, neighborhood recreational activities, and local church functions.
- As potential employers in the community, seek out information on employment of people with hearing impairments.

in schools, the general trend is more toward the "high-powered frequency modulated radio-frequency (FM-RF) body units" (Garwood, 1987, p. 440). These units use a one-way wireless system on radio-frequency bands. The receiver unit is worn by the student, and a microphone-transmitter-antennae unit is worn by the teacher. Although these body units have the advantage of presence (the child's ears are only inches away from the teacher's mouth), they are seldom preferred by students due to their conspicuousness (Garwood, 1987).

The oral approach to teaching communication skills also emphasizes the use of amplified sound and residual hearing to develop oral language. According to Ling (1984a), "The philosophy of oral education is that hearing-impaired children should be given the opportunity to speak and to understand speech, learn through spoken language in school, and later function as independent adults in a world in which people's primary mode of communication is speech" (p. 9). In addition to electroacoustical amplification, the teacher may employ speech reading, reading and writing, and **motokinesthetic** speech training (feeling an individual's face and reproducing breath and voice patterns). Speech reading (sometimes referred to as lipreading) is the process of understanding another person's speech by watching lip movement and facial and body gestures. This skill is difficult to master, especially for the person who has been deaf since an early age and thus never acquired speech. Problems with speech reading include that many sounds are not distinguishable on the lips and that the reader must attend carefully to every word spoken, a difficult task for preschool and primary-age children. Additionally, the speech reader must be able to see the speaker's mouth at all times.

The manual approach to teaching communication skills stresses the use of signs in teaching children who are deaf to communicate. The use of signs is based on the premise that many children who are deaf are unable to develop oral language and consequently must have some other means of communication. **Manual communication** systems are divided into two main categories: sign languages and sign systems.

Sign languages are a systematic and complex combination of hand movements that communicate whole words and complete thoughts rather than the individual letters of the alphabet. One of the most common sign languages is the **American Sign Language (ASL),** which has a vocabulary of about 6,000 signs. Examples of ASL signs are shown in

While American Sign Language has largely supplanted finger-spelling systems, some combination of the two is often used. (Leif Skoogfors/Woodfin Camp & Associates)

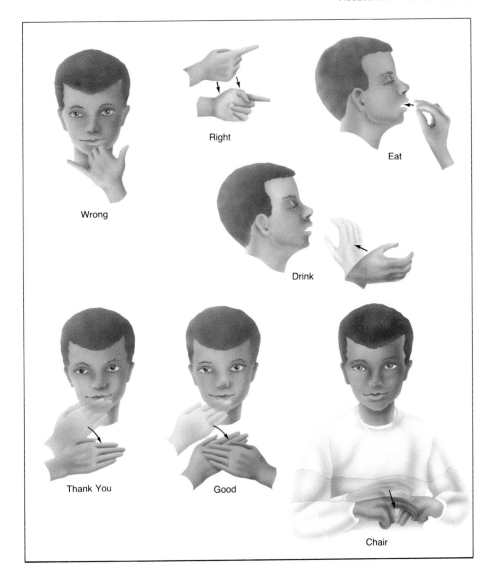

FIGURE 10–2

Examples of American Sign
Language Signs

Figure 10–2. ASL is currently the most widely used sign language among many adults who are deaf because it is easy to master, and has historically been the preferred mode of communication. It is a language, but it is not English. In fact, it is more similar to Chinese in that its signs represent concepts rather than single words.

Sign systems are different from sign languages in that they attempt to create visual equivalents of oral language through manual gestures. **Finger spelling** is a signing system that incorporates all 26 letters of the English alphabet. Each letter is signed independently on one hand to form words. Figure 10–3 illustrates the manual alphabet. In recent years, finger spelling, which is probably the oldest form of signing, has become more of a supplement to ASL. It is not uncommon to see a person who is deaf use finger spelling in a situation where there is no ASL sign for a word.

The four sign systems used in the United States are Seeing Exact English, Signing Exact English, Linguistics of Visual English, and Signed Exact English. Today, few educators

FIGURE 10-3

The American Manual Alphabet

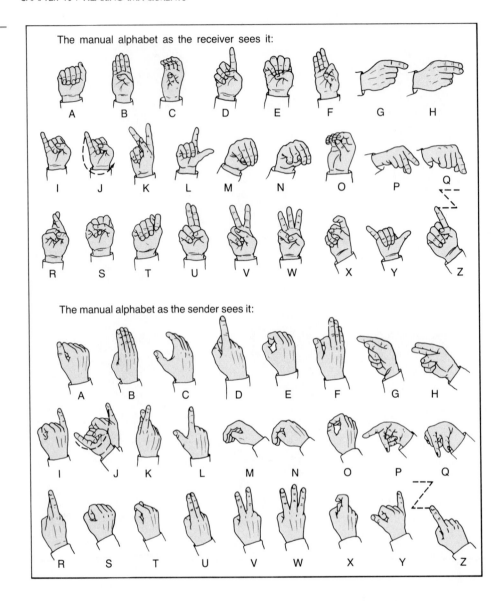

The manual alphabet as the receiver sees it:

A   B   C   D   E   F   G   H
I   J   K   L   M   N   O   P   Q
R   S   T   U   V   W   X   Y   Z

The manual alphabet as the sender sees it:

A   B   C   D   E   F   G   H
I   J   K   L   M   N   O   P   Q
R   S   T   U   V   W   X   Y   Z

rely solely on the manual system to teach communication skills. However, the system is in common use as a component of the fourth, combined approach to teaching communication skills known as total communication.

Total communication, often described as a new concept in the teaching of communication skills to people with hearing impairments, actually has roots that can be traced to the sixteenth century (Lowenbraun & Thompson, 1989). Over the past four centuries, many professionals advocated for an instructional system that employed every method possible to teach communication skills. This approach was known as the *combined system* or *simultaneous method*. The methodology of the early combined system was imprecise; essentially, any recognized approach to teaching communication was used as long as it included a manual component. The concept of total communication differs from the older combined system in that it is not used only when the oral method fails or when critical learning periods have long since passed. In fact, total communication is not a *system* at all but a *philosophy* (Lowenbraun & Thompson, 1989; Pahz & Pahz, 1978).

The philosophy of total communication is that the simultaneous presentation of signs and speech will enhance each person's opportunity to understand and use both systems more effectively (Ling, 1984b). Total communication programs use residual hearing, amplification, speech reading, speech training, reading, and writing in combination with manual systems. A method that may be used as an aid to total communication but is not a necessary component of the approach is **cued speech.** Cued speech is intended to facilitate the development of oral communication by combining hand signals with speech reading. Gestures provide additional information concerning sounds not identifiable by lipreading. The result is that an individual has access to all sounds in the English language through either the lips or the hands.

Technology.   Educational and leisure-time opportunities for people with hearing impairments have been greatly expanded through technological advances such as **closed-caption television** and computer-assisted instruction. The closed-captioning process translates the dialogue from a television program into captions—subtitles. These captions are then converted to electronic codes that can be inserted into the television picture on sets that are specially adapted with decoding devices. The process is called the *line-21 system,* because the caption is inserted into blank line 21 of the picture.

FOCUS 11

Describe the uses of closed-captioned television and computer-assisted instruction for people with hearing impairments.

TODAY'S TECHNOLOGY

From Alexander Graham Bell to the Modern Telephone

Alexander Graham Bell's initial efforts at transmitting speech over a wire were intended to decrease the social isolation of his wife (who was deaf) and others with hearing impairments. Now, a century later, the telephone has become a modern necessity for the hearing world but has not had the effect Bell intended for those who are hearing impaired. People with hearing impairments needed the *visible* cues for speech that are a part of daily conversation. The irony is that Bell's creation has played a major role in an ever-expanding technological society that has continuously isolated those who cannot hear.

People who are hearing impaired primarily communicate through speech that involves listening to the speaker while simultaneously looking for visual cues. This has not been possible through the auditory-only telephone. As we move into the 1990s, the advent of the videophone (live, two-way, audiovisual interaction) is on the horizon, perhaps less than a decade away. In fact, the technology exists today, as evidenced by the expanding use of live interactive television. The only issue that remains is when this technology will reach the homes and workplaces of people with hearing impairments. Until then, more and more attempts are being made to improve the technology of the telephone to meet the needs of people with hearing impairments. Here are some examples:

◆ Many pay phones are now equipped with auditory enhancers. The simple push of a button will increase the volume on the receiver.

◆ Although phones are routinely equipped with buttons that increase the loudness of the telephone bell, this is often not enough for people with profound hearing losses. A special acoustic device can be placed in the telephone as a substitute for the standard bell. This device has the same on-and-off repeating pattern as the conventional ring, but the acoustic signal operates at a low range of frequency that is considerably more audible to listeners who are hearing impaired. It is also possible to replace any "ringer" with a flashing light-signaling system that has a distinctive repeating pattern when a call is coming in.

◆ An amplifier with a strong acoustic signal can now be built into any standard telephone to make speech signals stronger. Portable, battery-powered amplifiers are also available for any standard telephone receiver.

◆ Most hearing aids are now equipped with components that, with a flick of a switch, enable the person to choose between sound that is airborne (microphone) or from a telephone (T) receiver. By switching the hearing aid to the T position, outside noise is reduced, and the individual generally finds it easier to understand speech over the phone.

Source: From *Telephone Communication and Hearing Impairment* by N. P. Erber, 1985, San Diego: College-Hill Press. Copyright 1985 by College-Hill Press. Adapted by permission.

REFLECT ON THIS

10–5 Signs across America: Different Strokes for Different Folks

You may have thought that the signs used in American Sign Language (ASL) were universal, that no matter where you went in the United States — from Tallahassee, Florida to Seattle, Washington — signs were interchangeable. Think again! Edgar and Susan Shroyer visited 25 states and found some surprising differences in the signs people used to describe the same word. Here is just one example:

FAINT: My mother fainted from the ammonia fumes

1 Alabama, Hawaii

2 Arkansas, Florida, Kentucky, Louisiana, Maine, North Carolina, South Carolina, Virginia

3 California, Illinois, Utah

4 Colorado, Texas (1 of 2)

5 Massachusetts

6 Michigan, Ohio

Captioning is not a new idea. In fact, it was first used on motion picture film in 1958. Most libraries in the United States distribute captioned films for individuals who are deaf. Closed captioning on television has experienced steady growth in a short period of time. The service has been available only since 1980. In its first year of operation, national closed-captioned programing was available about 30 hours per week. By 1987, more than 200 hours per week of national programing were captioned in a wide range of topics, from news and information to entertainment and commercials.

Computer-assisted instruction offers an exciting dimension to learning for persons with hearing impairments. The microcomputer places the individual in an interactive setting with the subject matter. It is a powerful motivator. Most people find microcomputers fun and interesting to work with on a variety of tasks. Additionally, computer-assisted instruction allows for individualized instruction so students are able to gain independence by working at their own pace and level.

Microcomputer programs are now available for instructional support in a variety of academic subject areas, from reading and writing to learning basic sign language. A recent

7 Missouri, New Mexico, Washington

8 New York

9 North Dakota

10 Pennsylvania

11 Texas (2 of 2)

12 Wisconsin

Source: Reprinted by permission of the publisher. From E. Shroyer and S. Shroyer, *Signs Across America* (1984): 78–80. Washington, DC: Gallaudet University Press. Copyright 1984 by Gallaudet University. Adapted by permission.

innovation is a software program that will display an individual's speech in visual form on the screen to assist in the development of articulation skills.

The interactive videodisc is another important innovation in computer-assisted instruction. The videodisc, a recordlike platter, is placed in a videodisc player that is connected to a microcomputer and television monitor. The laser-driven disc is interactive, allowing the individual to move through instruction at his or her own pace. Instant repetitions of subject matter are available to the learner at the touch of a button.

Another major advance is the development of telecommunication devices for individuals who are deaf (TDD). **TDD systems** send, receive, and print messages through thousands of stations across the United States. "The TDDs may also provide an excellent tool for the production and improvement of written language skills in deaf children. Coupling the graphic display with the written dialogue is extremely helpful in the development of language forms" (McAnally et al., 1987, p. 114).

The teletypewriter and printer (TTY) is also an effective use of technology for people who are deaf. It allows people who are deaf to communicate by phone with a typewriter that converts typed letters into electric signals through a modem. These signals are sent through the phone lines and then translated into typed messages and printed on a typewriter connected to a phone on the other end.

From captioning to TDD systems, a new world of technology is opening up for people with hearing impairments. This technology—along with advances in medical, social, and educational services—is helping people with hearing impairments join their peers in the hearing world. This is not to ignore the many problems that still face individuals with hearing impairments (e.g., underemployment, social isolation). But certainly, much has been accomplished.

Debate Forum · · · · · · · · · · · · · Living in a Deaf Community · · · · · · · · · · · · · ·

The inability to hear and understand speech may lead an individual to seek community ties and social relationships primarily with other individuals who are deaf. These individuals may choose to isolate themselves from hearing peers and live, learn, work, and play in a social subculture known as "a deaf community." An example of this strong sense of community occurred in 1988, when the appointment of a hearing person as President of Gallaudet University, a university for people who are deaf, resulted in widespread student protest and the eventual appointment of the university's first deaf president.

Point   The deaf community is a necessary and important component of life for many individuals who are deaf. The individual who is deaf has a great deal of difficulty adjusting to life in a hearing world. Through the deaf community, this person can find other individuals with similar problems, common interests, a common language (e.g., sign language), and a common culture. Membership in the deaf community is an achieved status that must be earned by the individual who is deaf. The individual must demonstrate a strong identification with the deaf world, understand and share experiences that come with being deaf, and be willing to actively participate in

the deaf community's activities. The deaf community gives the individual an identity that can't be found among their hearing peers.

Counterpoint   Participation in the deaf community only further isolates individuals who are deaf from those who hear. A separate subculture unnecessarily accents the differences between people who can and cannot hear. The life of the individual who is deaf need be no different from that of anyone else. Individuals who are deaf can live side by side with their hearing peers in local communities, sharing common bonds and interests. There is no reason why they can't participate together in the arts, enjoy sports, and share leisure-time and recreational interests. Membership in the deaf community may only further reinforce the idea that people who are disabled should grow up and live in a culture away from those who are not disabled. The fact is, the majority of people who are deaf do not seek membership in the deaf community. These individuals are concerned that the existence of such a community makes it all the more difficult for them to assimilate into society at large.

REVIEW ·

FOCUS 1   Describe how sound is transmitted through the human ear.

◆ A vibrator—such as a string, reed, or column of air—causes displacement of air particles.

◆ Vibrations are carried by air, metal, water, or other substances.

◆ Sound waves are displaced air particles that produce a pattern of circular waves that move away from the source to a receiver.

◆ The human ear collects, processes, and transmits sounds to the brain, where they are decoded into meaningful language.

FOCUS 2   Distinguish between the terms *deaf* and *hard of hearing*.

◆ A person who is deaf typically has profound or total loss of auditory sensitivity and very little if any auditory perception.

◆ For the person who is deaf, the primary means of information input is through vision; speech received through the ears is not understood.

◆ A person who is hard of hearing (partially hearing) generally has residual hearing through the use of a hearing aid, which is sufficient to process language through the ear successfully.

FOCUS 3   Why is it important to consider age of onset and anatomical site when defining a hearing impairment?

◆ Age of onset is critical in determining the type and extent of intervention necessary to minimize the effect of the hearing impairment.

◆ Three types of peripheral hearing loss are associated with anatomical site: conductive, sensorineural, and mixed.

◆ Central auditory hearing loss occurs when there is a dysfunction in the cerebral cortex (outer layer of gray matter in the brain).

FOCUS 4   What are the estimated prevalence and causes of hearing impairments?

- It has been extremely difficult to determine the prevalence of hearing impairments. Estimates of hearing loss in the United States go as high as 28 million people, or 11 percent of the total population.
- The most accurate estimates of prevalence are for school-age children. Approximately 1.4 percent of the 4 million students with disabilities have hearing impairments.
- There are more than sixty types of hereditary-related hearing impairments.
- A common hereditary disorder is otosclerosis (bone destruction in the middle ear).
- Nonhereditary hearing problems evident at birth may be associated with maternal health problems: infections (e.g., rubella), anemia, jaundice, central nervous system disorders, the use of drugs, venereal disease, chicken pox, anoxia, and birth trauma.
- Acquired hearing impairments are associated with postnatal infections, such as measles, mumps, influenza, typhoid fever, and scarlet fever.
- Environmental factors associated with hearing impairments include extreme changes in air pressure caused by explosions, head trauma, foreign objects in the ear, and loud noise.

FOCUS 5   Describe the basic intelligence, speech and language skills, educational achievement, and social development associated with people who are hearing impaired.

- The distribution of IQ scores of individuals with hearing impairments is similar to that of hearing children, although the mean score is slightly lower.
- On performance subtests of IQ batteries, the scores of children who are deaf fall in the average range for nonverbal intelligence.
- For people with mild and moderate losses, the effects on speech and language may be minimal. Although individuals with moderate losses cannot hear unvoiced sounds and distant speech, language delays can be prevented if the hearing loss is diagnosed and treated early.
- The majority of people with hearing impairments are able to use speech as the primary mode for language acquisition. People who are congenitally deaf are unable to receive information through the speech process unless they have learned to lipread (speech read). Sounds produced by the person who is deaf are extremely low in intelligibility.
- Reading is the academic area most adversely affected for students with hearing impairments.
- Arithmetic computation skills are deficient for students with hearing impairments in comparison to those of their hearing peers.
- Research has lent support to the notion that some individuals with hearing impairments may be more socially immature than their hearing peers. There is little agreement as to why this may be, but there is a relationship between the severity and type of hearing loss and social problems.

FOCUS 6   Why is the early detection of hearing loss so important?

- Early detection of hearing loss can prevent or minimize the impact of the impairment on the overall development of an individual.

FOCUS 7   Distinguish between an *otologist* and an *audiologist.*

- An otologist is a medical specialist who is concerned with the hearing organ and its diseases.
- An audiologist is concerned with the sociological and educational impact of hearing loss on an individual.
- Both the audiologist and otologist assist in the process of selecting and using a hearing aid.

FOCUS 8   Identify factors that may impede the social integration of people who are deaf into the hearing world.

- The inability to hear and understand speech has isolated some people who are deaf from their hearing peers.
- Societal views of deafness may reinforce isolation.

FOCUS 9   Why are educational services for students who are hearing impaired described as being in the process of change?

- The availability of educational services for students with hearing impairments, from preschool through adolescence, continues to increase.
- Educational programing is becoming more individualized in order to meet the needs of each student.

FOCUS 10   Identify four approaches to teaching communication skills to persons with hearing impairments.

- The auditory approach to communication emphasizes the use of amplified sound and residual hearing to develop oral communication skills.
- The oral approach to communication emphasizes the use of amplified sound and residual hearing but may also employ speech reading, reading and writing, and motokinesthetic speech training.
- The manual approach stresses the use of signs in teaching children who are deaf to communicate.
- Total communication employs the use of residual hearing, amplification, speech reading, speech training, reading, and writing in combination with manual systems to teach communication skills to children with hearing impairments.

FOCUS 11   Describe the uses of closed-captioned television and computer-assisted instruction for people with hearing impairments.

- Closed-captioned television translates the dialogue from a television program into captions (subtitles) that are broadcast on the television screen.
- Closed-captioned television provides the person with a hearing impairment greater access to information and entertainment than was previously thought possible.
- Microcomputers are powerful motivators that place people with hearing impairments in interactive settings with access to vast amounts of information.
- TDD systems provide efficient ways for people who are deaf to communicate over long distances.
- TTY devices allow people who are deaf to use a typewriter, modem, and printer to communicate over the phone.

Chapter Eleven
Visual Impairments

TO BEGIN WITH . . .

♦ "In Ann Arbor, Michigan, Phillip Jones, a 78-year-old widower [who is blind], delights in his Personal Reader's ability to inject excitement into its intonation when it sees an exclamation point. He also likes how it can read a page of German or Italian with a pronounced American accent. "It's easy for me to understand because the machine reads those languages the same way I would read them" (Ziegler, 1991, p. 119).

♦ "I'm appalled at the attitude of some . . . of the current generation of blind law students, who are constantly demanding more readers and other services provided without charge by the state. I believe that society should treat us normally while being sensitive to our physical limitations" (Judge William H. McCready, as cited in Attmore, 1990, p. 80).

♦ "A daily frustration of blindness: Not being able to scope out the shortest check-out line at the grocery store" (Susan, personal communication).

♦ "In 1970, the Library of Congress began producing Braille editions of magazines, including *Playboy*. In 1985, Congress cut funds that largely supported the production of Braille *Playboy*. Blind subscribers went to court and won. The judge reasoned that blind persons have a fundamental constitutional right to read *Playboy*. Printing of the Braille edition resumed (Kilpatrick, 1986).

JAMIE

JAMIE. By the time Jamie was 3 months old, it was evident that he was not responding to objects within his visual field. His parents became concerned and sought the help of a medical specialist. The ophthalmologist confirmed their suspicions: "Your child has a visual impairment caused by a congenital cataract."

As a young child, Jamie learned what it meant to move through his world with limited vision. He stumbled and fell frequently as he attempted to orient himself to people and objects around him. On entering school, it was clear that Jamie would need assistance from a vision specialist, but he could still remain with his age-mates in a regular classroom setting. The vision specialist worked with Jamie and his teacher on basic adaptive techniques in the classroom, such as the elimination of unnecessary glare on table and books, the removal of objects that might impede mobility and learning, and the introduction of special lighting to enhance his residual vision. Today, at the age of 28, Jamie's visual impairment has not prevented him from pursuing career and leisure-time interests. He is currently a successful sales representative for a local department store chain. His leisure time is spent hiking, enjoying good novels, and attending college sporting events.

*I*NTRODUCTION

Through the visual process, we observe the world around us and develop an appreciation for and a greater understanding of the physical environment. Vision is one of our most important sources for the acquisition and assimilation of knowledge, but we often take it for granted. From the moment we wake up in the morning, our dependence on sight is obvious. We rely on our eyes to guide us around our surroundings, inform us through the written word, and give us pleasure and relaxation.

What if this precious sight were lost or impaired? How would our perceptions of the world change? The fear of losing sight is often nurtured by the misconception that persons with visual impairments are helpless and unable to lead satisfying or productive lives (Bishop, 1987). It is not uncommon for people with sight to have little understanding of those who are visually impaired. People who are sighted may believe that most adults who are blind are likely to live a deprived socioeconomic and cultural existence. Children who have sight may believe that their peers who are blind are incapable of learning many basic skills, such as telling time or using a computer, or enjoying leisure-time and recreational activities such as swimming or television. Another attitudinal barrier is the religious belief that blindness is a punishment for sins (Bishop, 1987). However, as Window 11–1 about Jamie strongly suggests, these negative perceptions of people with visual impairments are often inaccurate. Jamie is an independent adult, with a successful career, who did not allow his visual impairment to keep him from the work and leisure activities that he values.

In order to more clearly understand the nature of visual impairments within the context of normal sight, we begin our discussion with an overview of the visual process. Since vision is basically defined as the act of seeing with the eye, we first review the physical components of the visual system.

THE VISUAL PROCESS

The physical components of the visual system include the eye, the visual center in the brain, and the **optic nerve,** which connects the eye to the visual center. The basic anatomy of the human eye is illustrated in Figure 11–1. The **cornea** is the external covering of the eye, and in the presence of light, it reflects visual stimuli. These reflected light rays pass through the

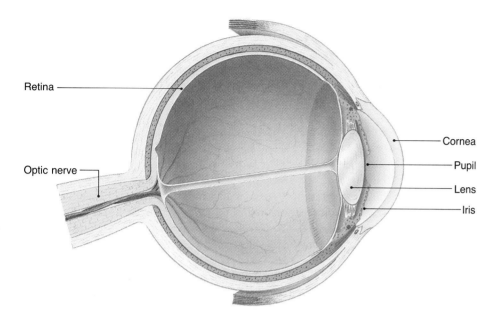

FIGURE 11–1

The Basic Anatomy
of the Human Eye

Retina

Optic nerve

Cornea

Pupil

Lens

Iris

pupil, which is an opening in the **iris.** The pupil expands or contracts to control the amount of light entering the eye. The iris is the colored portion of the eye and consists of membranous tissue and muscles whose function is to adjust the size of the pupil. The lens focuses the light rays by changing their direction so they strike the **retina** directly. As in a camera lens, the lens of the eye reverses the images. The retina consists of light-sensitive cells that transmit the image to the brain by means of the optic nerve. Images from the retina remain upside down until they are flipped over in the visual center of the brain.

The visual process is a much more complex phenomenon than suggested by a description of the physical components involved. The process is an important link to the physical world, helping us to gain information beyond the range of other senses, while also helping us to integrate the information acquired primarily through hearing, touch, smell, and taste. For example, our sense of touch can tell us that what we are feeling is furry, soft, and warm, but only our eyes can tell that it is a brown rabbit with a white tail and pink eyes. Our nose may perceive something with yeast and spices cooking, but our eyes can confirm that it is a large pepperoni pizza with bubbling mozzarella and green peppers. Our hearing can tell us that a friend sounds angry and upset, but only our vision can perceive the scowl, clenched jaw, and stiff posture. The way we perceive visual stimuli shapes our interactions with and reactions to the environment while providing a foundation for the development of a more complex learning structure.

DEFINITIONS AND CLASSIFICATION

Definitions

The term *visual impairment* describes people with a wide range of educational, social, and medical needs directly related to a partial or complete loss of sight. As suggested by Warren (1989), visual impairments encompass people who

> have never had any visual function, those who had normal vision for some years before becoming gradually or suddenly partially or totally blind, those with [disabilities] in addition to the visual loss, those with selective impairments of parts of the visual field, and those with a general degradation of acuity across the visual field. (p. 155)

FOCUS 1

Why is it important to understand the visual process as well as know the physical components of the eye?

FOCUS 2

Distinguish between the terms *blind* and *partially sighted*.

A variety of terms are used to describe levels of visual impairment, and this has created some confusion among professionals in various fields of study. The rationale for the development of various definitions is directly related to their intended use. For example, in order to be eligible for income-tax exemptions or special assistance from the American Printing House for the Blind, individuals with visual impairments must qualify under one of two general subcategories: **blind** or **partially sighted.**

Blindness.   Blindness has many diverse meanings. In fact, there are over 150 citations for *blind* in an unabridged dictionary. *Legal blindness,* as defined by the Social Security Administration, is visual acuity of 20/200 or worse in the best eye with best correction, as measured on the **Snellen test,** or a visual field of 20 percent or less (Kirchner, 1989). This definition of blindness employs two basic criteria: visual acuity and the field of vision.

Visual acuity is determined by the use of an index that refers to the distance from which an object can be recognized. The person with normal eyesight is defined as having 20/20 vision. However, if an individual is able to read at 20 feet what a person with normal vision can read at 200 feet, then his or her visual acuity would be described as 20/200. Most people consider those who are legally blind to have some light perception; only about 20 percent are totally without sight.

A person is also considered blind if his or her field of vision is limited at its widest angle to 20 degrees or less (see Figure 11–2). A restricted field is also referred to as **tunnel vision,** *pinhole vision,* or *tubular vision.* A restricted field of vision severely limits a person's ability to participate in athletics, read, or drive a car.

Blindness can also be characterized as an educational disability. Educational definitions of blindness focus primarily on students' ability to use vision as an avenue for learning.

FIGURE 11–2

The Field of Vision

Children who are unable to use their sight and rely on other senses, such as hearing and touch, are described as *educationally blind*. Educational blindness, in its simplest form, can be defined by whether the student must use braille when reading. Regardless of the definition used, the purpose of labeling a child educationally blind is to ensure that he or she receives an appropriate instructional program. This program must assist the student who is blind in utilizing other senses as a means to succeed in a classroom setting, and in the future as an independent and productive adult.

Partial Sight.   People who are partially sighted have a visual acuity greater than 20/200 but not greater than 20/70 in the best eye after correction. The field of education also distinguishes between blind and partially sighted in order to determine the level and extent of additional support services required by a student. The term *partially sighted* describes people who are able to use their vision as a primary source of learning. Jamie, the individual from Window 11–1, is partially sighted. While in school, a vision specialist worked with Jamie to make the best possible use of his remaining vision. This included the elimination of unnecessary glare in the work area, removal of obstacles that could impede mobility, use of large-print books, and special lighting to enhance visual opportunities.

Two very distinct positions have been formed regarding the individual who is partially sighted and the use of residual vision. The first suggests that the individual should make maximal use of his or her functional residual vision through the use of magnification, illumination, specialized teaching aids (e.g., large-print books and posters), as well as any exercises that will increase the efficiency of remaining vision. This position is contrary to the traditional philosophy of sight conservation or sight saving, which advocates restricted use of the eye. It was once believed that students with a visual impairment could keep what vision they had much longer if it was used sparingly. However, extended reliance on residual vision in conjunction with visual stimulation training now appears to actually improve a person's ability to use sight as an avenue for learning.

The distinction between the terms *blind* and *partially sighted* has not significantly minimized the confusion related to the terminology associated with visual problems. In an

These two photos show what a person without a visual impairment sees (right) compared to what a person with a limited visual field might see (left). (Craig Blouin/Offshoot Stock)

attempt to refine the terminology and to group various levels of visual problems by function, Barraga (1986) proposed the following descriptors:

1. *Profound visual disability.* Performance of the most basic visual task may be very difficult; vision is not used at all for detailed tasks.
2. *Severe visual disability.* More time and energy are needed to perform visual tasks; additionally, performance may be less accurate than that of sighted individuals, even though visual aids and modifications may be in use.
3. *Moderate visual disability.* Visual tasks may be performed with the use of special aids and lighting; performance may be comparable to that of students with normal vision.

Classification

Visual impairments may be classified according to the anatomical site of the problem. Anatomical disorders include impairment of the refractive structures of the eye, muscle anomalies in the visual system, and problems of the receptive structures of the eye.

FOCUS 3

Distinguish among refractive eye problems, muscle disorders, and receptive eye problems.

Refractive Eye Problems.   **Refractive problems** are the most common type of visual impairments and occur when the refractive structures of the eye (**cornea, aqueous humor, lens,** and **vitreous fluid**) fail to focus light rays properly on the retina. The four types of refractive problems are (1) **hyperopia,** or farsightedness; (2) **myopia,** or nearsightedness; (3) **astigmatism,** or blurred vision; and (4) **cataracts.**

Hyperopia occurs when the eyeball is excessively short (has a flat corneal structure), forcing light rays to focus behind the retina. The person with hyperopia is able to visualize objects at a distance clearly but unable to see them at close range. This individual may require reading glasses.

Myopia occurs when the eyeball is excessively long (has increased curvature of the corneal surface), forcing light rays to focus in front of the retina. The person with myopia is able to view objects at close range clearly but unable to see them from any distance (e.g., 100 feet). This individual requires eyeglasses to assist in focusing on distant objects. Figure 11–3 shows the myopic and hyperopic eyeballs and compares them to the normal human eye.

Astigmatism occurs when the surface of the cornea is uneven (the lens is structurally defective), preventing light rays from converging at one point. The rays of light are refracted in different directions, and the visual images are unclear and distorted. Astigmatism may occur independently of or in conjunction with myopia or hyperopia.

Cataracts occur when the lens becomes opaque, resulting in severely distorted vision or total blindness. Surgical treatment for cataracts has advanced rapidly in recent years, preventing many serious visual problems. Jamie was born with congenital cataracts; as a result of surgery, he has been able to retain some vision throughout his life (see Window 11–1).

Muscle Disorders.   Muscular defects of the visual system occur when the major muscles within the eye are inadequately developed or atrophic, resulting in a loss of control and an inability to maintain tension. People with muscle disorders are unable to maintain their focus on a given object for even short periods of time. The three types of muscle disorders include **nystagmus** (uncontrolled rapid eye movement), **strabismus** (crossed eyes), and **amblyopia** (loss of vision due to muscle imbalance).

Nystagmus is a continuous, involuntary, rapid movement of the eyeballs. The nystagmus pattern may be either circular or side to side.

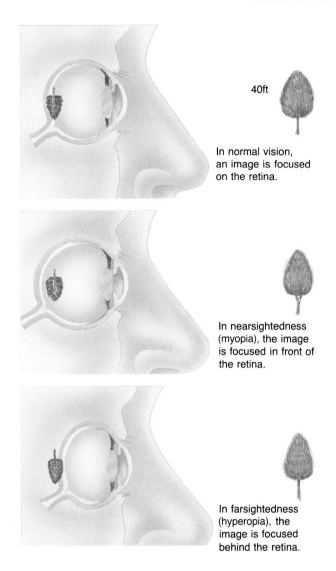

40ft

In normal vision, an image is focused on the retina.

In nearsightedness (myopia), the image is focused in front of the retina.

In farsightedness (hyperopia), the image is focused behind the retina.

FIGURE 11–3

The Normal, Myopic, and Hyperopic Eyeballs. (The image is focused on the retina upside down, but the brain immediately reverses it.)

Strabismus occurs when the muscles of the eyes are unable to pull equally, and the eyes therefore cannot focus together on the same object. Internal strabismus occurs when the eyes are pulled inward toward the nose. External strabismus occurs when the eyes are pulled out toward the ears. The eyes may also shift on a vertical plane (up or down), but this is rare. Strabismus can be corrected through surgical intervention. Persons with strabismus often experience a phenomenon known as *double vision*. In order to correct the double vision and reduce visual confusion, the brain attempts to suppress the image in one eye. As a result, the unused eye atrophies and loses its ability to see. This condition is known as *amblyopia*. Amblyopia can also be corrected by surgery or by forcing the affected eye into focus by covering the unaffected eye with a patch.

Receptive Eye Problems.   Disorders associated with the receptive structures of the eye occur when there is a degeneration of or damage to the retina and the optic nerve. These disorders include **optic atrophy, retinitis pigmentosa, retinal detachment, retrolental fibroplasia,** and **glaucoma.** Optic atrophy is a degenerative disease that results from the deterioration of nerve fibers connecting the retina to the brain. Retinitis pigmentosa is a

11–1   Flashback: Small Wonder of the World

It was May 1963, and the crowd at Chicago's Regal Theater was in a stone-whacked, hot-wired, ready-Freddy frenzy. This kid, this 12-year-old phenom, was going *wild* onstage. Finishing a bongo solo on a jazzy bossa nova number called "Fingertips," the kid suddenly started improvising—blowing fierce harmonica riffs, shouting, "Everybody say *yeah!*" and whipping the crowd and his grown-up band into a madhouse instrumental jam. Things got so chaotic that a confused bass player from Mary Wells' group, the next act on the Motown Revue bill, rushed in from the wings too early and found himself playing with strangers, yelling, "What key? What key?"

It was a turnaround night for Little Stevie Wonder. *Born prematurely, blinded when too much oxygen was pumped into his incubator,* Steveland Judkins Morris began his musical career by banging spoons on a table. By the time he turned 8, the Detroit prodigy had graduated to percussion, piano, and harmonica. Signed to Motown Records three years later by founder Berry Gordy, Jr., who gave him his stage name, Wonder was having trouble breaking through. His first three singles failed to chart; there was even an odd attempt to link Wonder with Ray Charles by having him sing an album of cover tunes called *A Tribute to Uncle Ray*. Realizing that Wonder drew the greatest response whenever he performed in front of an audience, Gordy then decided to record a stage show at the Regal Theater.

Capturing the raw energy of Wonder's performance, "Fingertips—Pt. 2" hit the charts on June 22, 1963. The song had clocked in at an incredible seven minutes—so long it had to be split in two as a single. Side one ("Fingertips—Pt. 1," which hardly anyone remembers) includes the brassy melody and extended bongo solo; the second boasts the rousing finale. "Fingertips—Pt. 2" became the first live recording ever to reach No. 1, and it marked the first time that a single and its album (*The 12-Year-Old Genius*) topped the charts at the same time.

Source: From "Flashback: Small Wonder of the World" by J. Ressner, 21 June 1991, *Entertainment Weekly*, p. 72. Copyright © 1991 by Entertainment Weekly Magazine. Reprinted with permission.

hereditary condition resulting from a break in the choroid, a vascular membrane containing pigment cells that lies between the retina and the sclera. The condition appears initially as night blindness but eventually results in total blindness.

Retinal detachment is a condition that occurs when the retina is separated from the choroid and the sclera. This detachment may result from such disorders as glaucoma, retinal degeneration, or extreme myopia. It can also be caused by trauma to the eye, such as a boxer's receiving a hard right hook to the face.

Until recently, retrolental fibroplasia (RLF) was one of the most devastating eye disorders in young children. It occurs when too much oxygen is administered to premature infants. Scar tissue forms behind the lens of the eye and prevents light rays from reaching the retina. Retrolental fibroplasia gained widespread attention in the early 1940s, with the advent of improved incubators for premature infants. These incubators substantially improved the concentration of oxygen available to the infant but resulted in a drastic increase in the number of children who were visually impaired. The disorder has also been associated with neurological, speech, and behavior problems in children and adolescents. Now that a relationship has been clearly established between increased oxygen levels and blindness, premature infants are protected by carefully controlling the amount of oxygen received in the early months of life.

FOCUS 4

What are the estimated prevalence and causes of visual impairments?

PREVALENCE

The prevalence of various visual impairments is often difficult to determine (Kirchner, 1988, 1989). For example, Reynolds and Birch (1982) indicated that at least 20 percent of the population have some visual problems, but most of these defects can be corrected to a level where they do not interfere with learning. LaPlante (1991) estimated that approximately 1,438,000 individuals of all ages have visual impairments that are significant enough to limit their activities. The figure of 0.1 percent is the most frequently cited prevalence figure for school-age children who meet the legal definitions of blindness and partial sight. Based on the U.S. Department of Education's *Thirteenth Annual Report to Congress* (1991), approximately 22,960 school-age children with visual impairments receive specialized services in U.S. public schools.

Thousands of children born blind during the maternal rubella epidemic in 1963 and 1964 constituted a significant percentage of the enrollment in special education and residential schools for the blind in the 1970s and 1980s. Maternal rubella is now essentially under control, since the introduction of a rubella vaccine. Retrolental fibroplasia (RLF), another major etiological factor in the 1960s, has also declined. However, a large percentage of the cases of blindness still have unknown causes (see following section).

Thus far, we have focused on prevalence figures as they relate to school-age children. Blindness also occurs as a function of increasing age. Approximately 75 percent of all people who are blind are over 45 years old.

CAUSATION

Genetically Determined Disorders

A number of genetic conditions may result in visual impairments, including **choroido-retinal degeneration** (a deterioration of the choroid and retina), **retinoblastoma** (a malignant tumor in the retina), **pseudoglioma** (a nonmalignant intraocular disturbance resulting from the detachment of the retina), optic atrophy (loss of function of optic nerve fibers), cataracts, myopia associated with retinal detachment, lesions of the cornea, abnormalities of the iris (coloboma or aniridia), **microphthalmus** (abnormally small eyeball), **anophthalmos** (absence of the eyeball), and **buphthalmos** or glaucoma (abnormal distention and enlargement of the eyeball) (Chapman & Stone, 1989). In addition, visual impairments may be the result of other malformations. For example, hydrocephalus (excess cerebrospinal fluid in the brain) may lead to optic atrophy.

Acquired Disorders

Acquired disorders can occur prior to, during, or after birth. Several factors present prior to birth, such as radiation or the introduction of drugs into the fetal system, may result in visual impairments. A major cause of blindness in the fetus is infection, which may be due to such diseases as rubella and syphilis. Ward (1986) estimated that about 14 percent of all cases of legal blindness are caused by infectious diseases. Other diseases that may result in blindness include influenza, mumps, and measles.

The leading cause of blindness in children during the 1940s and 1950s was retrolental fibroplasia, now known as **retinopathy of prematurity.** As previously noted, RLF results from the administration of oxygen over prolonged periods of time to low-birthweight infants. Lowenfeld (1980) indicated that, "in the peak years of this disease, some states reported that almost 80 percent of their preschool blind children had lost their sight as a result of RLF. It has been established that RLF caused blindness in more than 10,000 babies who have not reached adulthood" (p. 259).

Visual impairments occurring after birth may be due to several factors. Accidents, infections, inflammations, and tumors are all associated with loss of sight. Although the majority of visual impairments occur prior to adolescence or the adult years and approximately 60 percent occur before the age of 1, some visual problems are associated with factors occurring during adulthood, including injuries, disease, and degeneration.

FOCUS 5

Describe how a visual impairment can affect intelligence, speech and language skills, educational achievement, social development, orientation and mobility, and perceptual-motor development.

CHARACTERISTICS

A visual impairment present at birth will have a more significant effect on individual development than one that occurs later in life. Useful visual imagery may disappear if sight is lost prior to the age of 5 (Toth, 1983). If sight is lost after the age of 5, it is possible for the person to retain some visual frame of reference. This frame of reference may be maintained over a period of years, depending on the severity of the visual problem. Total blindness that occurs prior to age 5 has the greatest negative influence on overall functioning. However, many people who are blind from birth or early childhood are able to function at a level consistent with sighted persons of equal ability.

Intelligence

For a child with a visual impairment, his or her perceptions of the world may be based on input from senses other than vision. This is particularly true of the child who is blind, whose learning experiences are significantly restricted by the lack of vision. Consequently, everyday learning experiences that people with sight take for granted are substantially diminished.

Warren (1984, 1989) reviewed the literature on intellectual development and reported that children with visual impairments differ from their sighted peers in some areas of intelligence, ranging from understanding spatial concepts to a general knowledge of the world. Parsons and Sabornie (1987) confirmed that, on tests of intelligence, the performance of individuals with visual impairments may be negatively affected. However, it may not be appropriate to compare the performances of individuals with and without sight if those with sight have an advantage. The only valid way to compare the intellectual capabilities of children who are sighted versus blind is on tasks in which visual impairment does not interfere with performance.

Speech and Language Skills

For children with sight, speech and language development occurs primarily through the integration of visual experiences and the symbols of the spoken word. Depending on the degree of loss, children with visual impairments are at a distinct disadvantage in developing speech and language skills because they are unable to visually associate words with objects. Such children cannot learn speech by visual imitation and must rely on hearing or touch for input. Consequently, speech may develop at a slower rate for those who are congenitally blind. Once these children have learned speech, however, it is typically fluent.

There is some conflicting evidence regarding the differences in overall language development between children with visual impairments and their sighted peers (Chapman and Stone, 1989; Warren, 1989). Warren suggested that,

> while there are some differences in language usage and word meaning, most of these have clear explanations in the experiential base of visually [disabled] children. . . . Visually [disabled] children should be exposed to a full range of age-appropriate vocabulary, and should be provided with concrete physical experience as well as verbal explanations of referents for the development of meaning. (1989, p. 164)

However, Parsons and Sabornie (1987) reported that preschool-age children with limited vision performed significantly lower than their sighted peers on a language scale in the areas of auditory comprehension, verbal ability, and overall language. The preschool-age child with a visual impairment may develop a phenomenon known as **verbalism,** or the excessive use of speech (wordiness) in which individuals use words that have little meaning to them. Finally, Anderson, Dunlea, and Kekalis (1984) reported that the language development of six children who were blind, as studied over a three-year period, appeared to be comparable to that of their sighted peers. However, the investigators were concerned that, in terms of quality, children who were blind seemed to have more difficulty understanding words as symbolic vehicles and formed hypotheses about word meaning much more slowly than their sighted peers.

Educational Achievement

The educational achievement of students with visual impairments may be significantly delayed when compared to that of sighted peers (Lowenfeld, 1980). Some of the variables influencing educational achievement may include excessive school absences due to the need for eye surgery or treatment as well as years of failure in programs that did not meet each student's specialized needs.

On the average, children who are blind are two years behind sighted children in grade level. Thus, any direct comparisons of students with visual impairments to those with sight would indicate significantly delayed academic growth. However, this age phenomenon may have resulted from entering school at a later age, absence from school due to medical problems, and the lack of appropriate school facilities.

Social Development

The ability to adapt to the social environment depends on a number of factors, both hereditary and experiential. It is true that each of us experiences the world in his or her own way, but there are common bonds that provide a foundation on which to build perceptions of the world around us. One such bond is vision. Without vision, perceptions about ourselves and those around us would be drastically different.

For the person with a visual impairment, these differences in perception may result in some social-emotional difficulties. For example, people who are visually impaired are unable to imitate the physical mannerisms of others and therefore do not develop one very important component of a social communication system: body language. The subtleties of nonverbal communication may significantly alter the intended meaning of spoken words. A person's inability to develop a nonverbal communication system through the acquisition of visual cues (e.g., facial expressions, hand gestures) has profound consequences on interpersonal interactions, not only for the reception or interpretation of verbal language but also for what he or she expresses to others. Namely, the sighted person may misinterpret the meaning of what is said by the person who is visually impaired because the visual cues are not consistent with the spoken words.

Social problems may also result from the exclusion of persons with visual impairments from social activities that are integrally related to the use of vision (e.g., sports, movies). Individuals with visual impairments are often excluded from such activities without a second thought simply because they cannot see. This only serves to reinforce the mistaken notion that they do not want to participate and would not enjoy these activities (Tuttle, 1984). However, as we learned from Jamie (see Window 11–1), many people who have visual impairments seek activities in which vision may be viewed as necessary, such as hiking, golfing, and spectator sports. Excluding them from social experiences more often stems from negative public attitudes toward visual impairment than from these individuals' lack of social adjustment skills. In sum, as expressed by Warren, "Social development of visually [disabled] children is different in several ways from that of sighted children, and the factors that produce these differences, as well as the substantial variations among visually [disabled] children, are complex" (1989, p. 166).

Orientation and mobility are the most significant challenges faced by people with severe visual impairments. Mobility training and guidance equipment enable these individuals to achieve some level of independence. (Nurion Industries)

Orientation and Mobility

A visual impairment may have a direct effect on orientation and mobility in several ways. The individual may be unable to orient to other people or objects in the environment simply because he or she cannot see them. This lack of sight may prevent the person with a visual impairment from understanding his or her own relative position in space; consequently, he or she may be unable to move in the right direction. This may lead to fear of getting injured and an attempt to restrict movements to protect oneself. In addition, parents and professionals may contribute to such fears by protecting the person who is visually impaired from everyday risk. Any unnecessary retrictions will hinder the individual's acquisition of independent mobility skills and create an atmosphere for lifelong dependence.

A visual impairment may also have an affect on fine motor coordination and interfere with the ability to manipulate objects. Poor eye-hand coordination interferes with learning how to use tools necessary for everyday functioning and occupational efficiency (e.g., eating utensils, a toothbrush, a screwdriver). In order to prevent or remediate fine motor problems, many people with visual impairments require extensive training that must begin early and focus directly on experiences that will enhance opportunities for independent living (Chapman & Stone, 1989).

Perceptual-Motor Development

Perceptual-motor development is essential in the development of locomotion skills, but it is also important in the development of cognition, language, socialization, and personality. In a comprehensive review of the literature, Warren (1984) reported that perceptual discrimination abilities (e.g., discriminating texture, weight, and sound) of children who are blind are comparable to those of sighted peers. However, children who are blind do not perform as well on more complex tasks of perception, including form identification, spatial relations, and perceptual-motor integration. An early visual experience prior to the onset of

---

W I N D O W   11–2

ATTITUDES OF PEOPLE WITH VISION
TOWARD THOSE WITH IMPAIRMENTS

I Never Had the Chance to Know
Any Kids Who Are Blind

People who are blind have always evoked negative and fright-ening feelings in me. I guess part of my reaction stems from my fear of becoming blind. I really believe that such feelings come from my lack of experience with the blind. When I was in school, I never had the chance to get to know a person who was blind. There was a special class in my school for children who were blind, but they never seemed to be around. I remember that they came to school at a different time, had different lunch periods, and never participated in school activities. I don't know whether this

bothered them, but I know it never gave me the chance to know even one of these schoolmates.

Jeff, An Adult with Sight

Sure I Know Some Kids Who Are Blind

Sure, I know some kids who can't see. They go to my school, and some are in my class. Jenny is in my reading group. Her face almost touches the book when she reads. My teacher tries to give her books where the words are bigger on the page. Sometimes she works with another teacher who helps her because she can't see. When school started, I used to walk with her to the library or the bathroom, so she wouldn't get lost. She doesn't need help anymore. She knows where everything is in our class and goes all over the school with no help.

Malcolm, A Child with Sight

---

blindness or partial loss of sight may provide a child with some advantage in the acquisition of manipulatory and locomotor skills.

A popular misconception regarding the perceptual abilities of persons with visual im-pairments is that, because of their diminished sight, they develop greater capacity in other sensory areas. For example, people who are blind are supposedly able to hear or smell some things that people with normal vision cannot perceive. This notion has never been empir-ically validated.

ASSESSMENT AND INTERVENTIONS

Medical Interventions

Initial screenings for visual impairments are usually based on the individual's visual acuity. Visual acuity may be measured through the use of the Snellen test, developed in 1862 by Dutch ophthalmologist Herman Snellen. This visual screening test is used primarily to mea-sure central distance vision. The subject stands 20 feet from a letter or E-chart (standard eye-test chart) and reads each symbol, beginning with the top row. The different sizes of each row or symbol represent what a person with normal vision would see at the various distances indicated on the chart. As indicated earlier in this chapter, a person's visual acuity is then determined by the use of an index that refers to the distance at which an object can be recognized. The person with normal eyesight is defined as having 20/20 vision.

Since the Snellen test only measures visual acuity, it must be used primarily as an initial screening device that is supplemented by more in-depth assessments, such as a thorough ophthalmological examination. Parents, physicians, school nurses, and educators must also carefully observe the child's behavior, and a complete history of any presenting symptoms of a visual impairment should be documented. These observable symptoms fall into three categories: appearance, behavior, and complaints. Reflect on This 11–2 describes some warning signs of visual impairment. The existence of symptoms does not necessarily mean a person has a visual impairment, but it does indicate that an appropriate specialist should be consulted for further examination.

Prevention.   Prevention of visual impairments is one of the major goals within the field of medicine. Prevention measures can be grouped into three categories: (1) genetic

FOCUS 6
What steps can be taken to prevent and medically treat visual impair-ments?

11–2 Is There a Visual Problem? Keeping an Eye on the Warning Signs

Physical Symptoms
- Are the eyes crossed?
- Are the eyes functioning in unison?
- Are the eyelids swollen and crusted with red rims?
- Are the eyes overly sensitive to light?
- Are there frequent sties?
- Are the eyes frequently bloodshot?
- Are the pupils of different sizes?
- Are the eyes constantly in motion?

Observable Behavior
Does the individual:
- blink constantly?
- trip or stumble frequently?
- cover one eye when reading?
- hold reading material either very close or far away?
- distort the face or frown when concentrating on something in the distance?
- walk cautiously?
- fail to see objects that are to one side or the other?

Complaints
Does the individual complain of:
- frequent dizziness?
- frequent headaches?
- pain in the eyes?
- itching or burning of the eyes or eyelids?
- double vision?

screening and counseling; (2) appropriate prenatal care; and (3) early developmental assessment.

Since many causes of blindness are hereditary, it is important for the family to be aware of genetic services. One purpose of genetic screening is to identify those who are planning for a family and who may possess certain detrimental genotypes that can be passed on to their descendants. Screening may also be conducted after conception in order to determine whether the unborn fetus possesses any genetic abnormalities. Following the screening, a genetic counselor informs the parents of the results of the tests so that the family is able to make an informed decision about conceiving a child or carrying a fetus to term.

Adequate prenatal care is another means of preventing problems. Parents must be made aware of the potential hazards associated with poor nutritional habits, the use of drugs, and exposure to radiation (e.g., x-rays) during pregnancy. One example of preventive care during this period is the use of antibiotics to treat various infections (e.g., influenza, measles, syphilis), thus reducing the risk of infection to the unborn fetus.

Developmental screening is also a widely recognized means of prevention. It was through early developmental screening that a medical specialist confirmed that Jamie had a serious visual impairment and would require the assistance of a trained vision specialist (see Window 11–1). Early screening of developmental problems enables the family physician to analyze several treatment alternatives and, when necessary, to refer the child to an appropriate specialist. The specialist conducts a more thorough evaluation of the child's developmental delays.

Early visual screening—which also includes hearing, speech, motor, and psychological development—should be a component of this general development assessment. Early screening would include a medical examination at birth, with an emphasis not only on the physical condition of the newborn but also on a complete family history. The eyes should be carefully examined for any abnormalities, such as infection or trauma.

At 6 weeks of age, visual screening should be a component of another general developmental assessment. This examination should include input from the parents concerning how their child is responding (e.g., smiling and looking at objects or faces). The physician should check eye movement, as well as search for any infection, crusting on the eyes, or **epiphora** (an overflow of tears from obstruction of the lacrimal ducts).

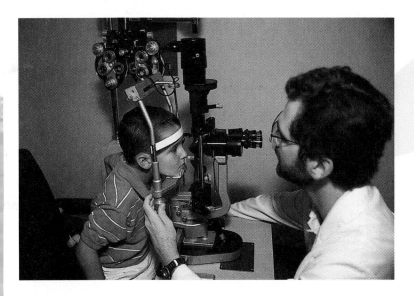

Regular eye examinations should begin early in every child's life and continue throughout adulthood. (Alese & Mort Pechter/The Stock Market)

The next examination should occur at about 6 months of age. A defensive blink should be present at this age, and eye movement should be full and coordinated. If there is any imbalance in eye movements, a more thorough examination should be conducted. Family history is extremely important, since in many cases, there is a familial pattern.

Between the ages of 1 and 5, visual evaluation should be conducted at regular intervals. A particularly important period is the time just prior to the child's entering school. Visual problems must not go undetected as these children attempt to cope with the new and complex demands of the educational environment.

Treatment. In addition to medicine's emphasis on prevention of visual impairments, significant strides have also been made in the treatment of these problems. The nature of medical interventions depends on the type and severity of the impairment. For individuals who are partially sighted, use of an optical aid can vastly improve access to the visual world. Most of these aids are in the form of corrective glasses or contact lenses, which are designed to magnify the image on the retina. Some aids are able to improve muscle control within the eye, while others clarify the retinal image. Appropriate use of optical aids, in conjunction with regular medical examinations, not only helps correct existing visual problems but may also prevent further deterioration of existing vision.

Surgery and drug therapy have also played important roles in treating visual impairments. Treatment in these areas may range from the extremely complex surgical procedures associated with corneal transplants to the process known as **atropinization.** Atropinization is the treatment for cataracts that involves washing out the eye with the alkaloid drug atropine, which permanently dilates the pupil.

Social Interventions

Some individuals with visual impairments may have social adjustment problems, which include poor self-concept and general feelings of inferiority. To minimalize these problems, it is important for mental health services to be available as early as possible in the person's life. These services may begin with infant stimulation programs and counseling for the family. As the child grows older, group counseling may assist in coping with feelings concerning blindness. In addition, the individual may need some guidance in the area of human

FOCUS 7

Why is the availability of appropriate mental health services important for people with visual impairments?

People with Visual Impairments Enjoying the Visual Arts

Irma Shore has been losing her eyesight to diabetes for several years. Her longtime passion for art, which has taken her to many museums, has not diminished, however. Frustrated with the limitations that impeded her enjoyment of art, Shore set out on a mission: to make art accessible to people with limited vision and other disabilities.

Her project, Access to Art, is permanently based at the Museum of American Folk Art in New York. The core of the exhibit is a large display of *tactile* art, in which every object is meant to be touched. Many three-dimensional folk art objects are particularly well suited to this exhibit, including a turn-of-the-century carved wooden carousel horse, colorful quilts from New England and the Midwest, a shaggy late-nineteenth-century "ravel knit" rug from Kentucky, a Shaker rocking chair, early-twentieth-century bird and fish decoys, and a contemporary grotesquely carved stoneware "face" jug from North Carolina.

Next to each item is a large, laminated photograph of it, which helps individuals with partial sight or color blindness see perspective and detail. Labels and catalogs are provided both in large-print and braille formats. The floor in the exhibit is designed so that those who use canes can guide themselves easily among the displays.

The Access to Art exhibit is not only geared to visitors with visual impairments. It is also designed to accommodate people with wheelchairs, and several sign language lectures are offered for those with hearing impairments. Visitors who wish to use them may also make use of audiotaped guided tours that not only explain the social and historical significance of the works but also describe them in vivid detail.

The museum has trained a number of volunteers to serve as *docents,* or personal guides for the exhibit. Part of their job training is completion of a disability awareness workshop, which teaches them to feel comfortable around individuals with disabilities and to unlearn certain ingrained behaviors. Above all else, docents are taught to relax. For example, individuals with visual impairments won't take offense if some-

The Museum of American Folk Art in New York offers a tactile exhibit, which makes art available to museum goers with visual impairments as well as other disabilities. (J. Chenet/Woodfin Camp & Associates, Inc.)

one uses the phrase "you see." And speaking in a loud voice does really not help people with visual problems.

The Access to Art exhibit has been immensely popular, dispelling the myth that, if you're blind, you aren't interested in art. Shore emphasizes, however, that "the exhibit is for everyone. It's not just for people with disabilities, and it's not *about* disabilities."

Perhaps the real key to the success of the exhibit is the freedom it offers all museum goers to experience art through more than just visual means. Most people respond with enthusiasm to being allowed to touch, particularly in an environment that usually warns against this. To be sure, there are no "Please don't touch" signs in the Access to Art exhibit.

Source: From "Please Touch the Artworks," *Newsweek,* November 6, 1989.

sexuality. Limited vision may distort perception of the physical body. Counseling eventually extends into matters focusing on marriage, family, and adult relationships. For the adult with a visual impairment, special guidance may also be necessary in preparation for employment and independent living.

Other services that facilitate participation of people with visual impairments in the community include specialized library and newspaper services, with books that have large print, are available on cassette, and are printed in braille. The *New York Times* publishes a weekly special edition with type three times the size of its regular type.

The mobility of the person with a visual impairment may be greatly enhanced in large cities by the use of auditory pedestrian signals at crosswalks. The "walk" and "don't walk" signals are indicated by auditory cues, such as different bird chirps for each signal. Restaurants can assist people with visual impairments through the availability of braille menus.

Educational Interventions

Educational Assessment. In the area of education, the assessment process is no different for students who are visually impaired than it is for students who are sighted. The educational team is interested in assessing the cognitive ability, academic achievement, language skills, motor performance, and social-emotional functioning of the student. Assessment must also focus specifically on how the student utilizes any remaining vision (visual efficiency) in conjunction with other senses.

The nature and severity of the visual problem determine the assessment instruments to be used. Some assessment instruments have been developed specifically for students with visual impairments. Others are intended for sighted students but have been adapted to students with visual impairments. There are also instruments that were developed for sighted students and are used in their original form with students who are visually impaired. Regardless of the instruments employed, educational assessment, in conjunction with medical and psychological data, must provide the diagnostic information that will ensure an appropriate educational experience for the student who is visually impaired.

Educational Placement. Historically, education for individuals with visual impairments—specifically, blindness—was provided through specialized residential facilities. These segregated centers have traditionally been referred to as *asylums, institutions,* or *schools.* One of the first such facilities in the United States was the New England Asylum for the Blind, later named the Perkins School. This facility opened its doors in 1832 and was one of several eastern schools that used treatment models borrowed from well-established European institutions. For the most part, the early U.S. institutions operated as closed schools, where a person who was blind would live and learn in an environment that was essentially separate from the outside world. The philosophy was to get the person who was blind "ready for the outside world," even though this approach provided little real exposure to it.

More recently, some residential schools have advocated an open system of intervention. These programs are based on the philosophy that children who are blind should have every opportunity to gain the same kinds of experiences that would be available if they were growing up in their own communities.

Both open and closed residential facilities exist today as alternative intervention modes, but they are no longer the primary social or educational systems available to people who are blind. As was true for Jamie in Window 11–1, the vast majority of individuals who are blind or partially sighted now live at home, attend local public schools, and interact within the community.

Educational programs for students with visual impairments are based on the principle of flexible placement. A wide variety of services are available for these students in the public schools, ranging from regular class placement, with little or no assistance from specialists, to segregated residential schools. Between these extremes, the public schools generally offer several alternative classroom structures, including the use of consulting teachers, resource rooms, part-time special classes, or full-time special classes. Placement of a student into one of these programs depends on the extent to which the visual impairment affects his or her overall educational achievement. Many students with visual impairments are able to function

FOCUS 8
What range of educational services are available to students with visual impairments?

successfully within regular education settings if the learning environment is adapted to meet their needs.

Whether the student is to be integrated into the regular classroom or taught in a special class, a *vision specialist* must be available, either to support the regular classroom teacher or to provide direct instruction to the student. A vision specialist has received concentrated training in the education of students with visual impairments. This specialist and the rest of the educational support team must be knowledgeable concerning appropriate educational assessment techniques, specialized curriculum materials and teaching approaches, and the use of various communication media. Specialized instruction for students who are visually impaired may include a major modification in curricula, including teaching concepts that children who are sighted learn incidentally (e.g., walking down the street, getting from one room to the next in the school building, getting meals in the cafeteria, and using public transportation) (Hatlen & Curry, 1987).

INTERACTING IN NATURAL SETTINGS .... People with Visual Impairments ....

EARLY CHILDHOOD YEARS

Tips for the Family

◆ Assist your child with a visual impairment in learning how to get around in the home environment. Then give him or her the freedom to move freely about.

◆ Help your child orient to the environment by removing all unnecessary obstacles around home (e.g., shoes left on the floor, partially opened doors, a vacuum cleaner left out). Keep him or her informed of any changes in room arrangements.

◆ Instruction in special mobility techniques should begin as early as possible with the young child who is visually impaired.

◆ Keep informed about organizations and civic groups that can provide support to the child and the family.

◆ Get in touch with your local health, social services, and education agencies about infant, toddler, and preschool programs for children with visual impairments. Become familiar with the individualized family service plan (IFSP) and how it can serve as a planning tool to include your child in early intervention programs.

Tips for the Preschool Teacher

◆ Mobility is a fundamental part of early intervention programs for children with visual impairments. Help them learn to explore the environment in the classroom, school, and local neighborhood.

◆ Work with the child on developing a sense of touch and using hearing to acquire information. The young child may also need assistance in learning to smile and make eye contact.

◆ Work closely with the family to develop orientation and mobility strategies that can be learned and applied in both home and school settings.

◆ Help other sighted children in the classroom to interact with the young child with a visual impairment by teaching them to

speak directly to him or her in a normal tone of voice so as not to raise the noise level.

◆ Become very familiar with both tactile (e.g., braille) and auditory aids (e.g., Kurzweil Personal Readers) that may be used by the young child to acquire information.

Tips for Preschool Personnel

◆ Support the inclusion of young children with visual impairments in your classrooms and programs.

◆ Support teachers, staff, and volunteers as they attempt to create successful experiences for the young child with visual impairments in the preschool setting.

◆ Work very closely with families to keep them informed and active members of the school community.

Tips for Neighbors and Friends

◆ Never assume that, because a young child has a visual problem, he or she cannot or should not participate in family and neighborhood activities that are associated with sight (e.g., board games, sports, hide-and-seek).

◆ Work with the young child's family to seek opportunities for interaction with sighted children in neighborhood play settings.

ELEMENTARY YEARS

Tips for the Family

◆ Learn about the programs and services available during the school years for your child with a visual impairment. Learn about your child's right to an appropriate education, and actively participate in the development of your child's individualized education program (IEP).

◆ Participate in as many school functions for parents as is reasonable to connect your family to the school (e.g., PTA, parent advisory groups, volunteering, etc.).

- Seek information on in-school and extracurricular activities that will enhance opportunities for your child to interact with sighted peers.
- Keep the school informed about the medical needs of your child.
- If your child needs or uses specialized mobility devices to enhance access to the environment, help school personnel to understand how these devices work.

Tips for the Regular Classroom Teacher

- Remove obstacles in the classroom that may interfere with the mobility of students with visual impairments, including small things like litter on the floor, to desks that are blocking aisles.
- Place the child's desk as close as necessary to you during group instruction. He or she should also sit as close as possible to visual objects associated with instruction (e.g., blackboard, video monitor, or classroom bulletin board).
- Be consistent in where you place classroom materials so that the child with a visual impairment can locate them independently.
- When providing instruction, always try to stand with your back to the windows. It is very difficult for a person with a visual impairment to look directly into a light source.
- Work closely with a vision specialist to determine any specialized mobility or lighting needs for the student with a visual impairment (e.g., special desk lamp, cassette recorder, large-print books, personal reader).
- Help the student gain confidence in you by letting him or her know where you are in the classroom. It is especially helpful to let the student know when you are planning to leave the classroom.

Tips for School Personnel

- Integrate school resources as well as children. Wherever possible, help regular classroom teachers access the human and material resources necessary to meet the needs of students with visual impairments. For example:
  - —A vision specialist: A professional trained in the education of students with visual impairments can serve as an effective consultant to you and the children in several areas (e.g., mobility training, use of special equipment, communication media, instructional strategies).
  - —An ophthalmologist: Students with visual impairments often have associated medical problems. It is helpful for the teacher to understand any related medical needs that can effect the child's educational experience.
  - —Peer-buddy and support systems: Peer support can be an effective tool for learning in a classroom setting. Peer-buddy systems can be established in the school to help the child with initial mobility needs and/or any tutoring that would help him or her succeed in the regular classroom.
- Support keeping the school as barrier free as possible; this includes providing adequate lighting in classrooms and hallways.

- It is critical that children with visual impairments have access to appropriate reading materials (e.g., braille books, large-print books, cassette recordings of books) in the school library and media center.

Tips for Neighbors and Friends

- Help the family of a child who is visually impaired be an integral part of the neighborhood and friendship networks. Seek ways to include the family and child wherever possible in neighborhood activities.

SECONDARY/TRANSITION YEARS

Tips for the Family

- Become familiar with the adult services system (e.g., rehabilitation services, social security, health care) while your child is still in high school. Understand the type of vocational or employment training that he or she will need prior to graduation.
- Find out the school's view on what it should do to assist students with visual impairments in making the transition from school to adult life.
- Create opportunities for your child to participate in out-of-school activities with same-age sighted peers.

Tips for the Regular Classroom Teacher

- Assist students with visual impairments to adapt to subject matter in your classroom while you adapt the classroom to meet their needs (e.g., in terms of seating, oral instruction, mobility, large-print or braille textbooks).
- Access to auditory devices (e.g., cassette recorders for lectures) can facilitate students' learning.
- Support the student with a visual impairment in becoming involved in extracurricular activities. If you are the faculty sponsor of a club or organization, explore whether the student is interested and how he or she could get involved.

Tips for School Personnel

- Assist parents of students with visual impairments to actively participate in school activities (e.g., parent/teacher groups and advisory committees).
- Maintain positive and ongoing contact with the family.

Tips for Neighbors, Friends, and Potential Employers

- Seek ways of becoming part of a community support network for the individuals with visual impairments. Be alert to ways that individuals can become and remain actively involved in community employment, neighborhood recreational activities, and local church functions.
- As potential employers in the local community, seek information on employment of people with visual impairments.

FOCUS 9
Identify two content areas that should be included in educational programs for students with visual impairments.

Mobility Training and Daily Living Skills.   The educational needs of students with visual impairments are comparable to those of their sighted counterparts. In addition, many of the instructional methods currently used with students who are sighted are applicable with students who are visually impaired. However, it is important for the educator to be aware of certain content areas that are essential to the success of students with visual impairments in the educational environment but are usually not a focal point for sighted students. These areas include mobility and orientation training as well as acquisition of daily living skills.

The ability to move safely and efficiently through the environment enhances the individual's opportunities to learn more about the world and thus be less dependent on others for survival. Lack of mobility restricts individuals with visual impairments in nearly every aspect of their educational life. Such students may be unable to orient to physical structures in the classroom (e.g., desks, chairs, and aisles), hallways, restrooms, library, or cafeteria. Whereas a person with sight is able automatically to establish a relative position in space, the individual with a visual impairment must be taught some means of compensating for a lack of visual input. This may be accomplished in a number of ways. It is important that students who are visually impaired not only learn the physical structure of their school but also develop specific techniques that can be employed to orient them to unfamiliar surroundings.

These orientation techniques involve using the other senses. For example, the senses of touch and hearing can be used to help identify cues that designate where the bathroom is in the school. Although it is not true that people who are blind have superior hearing abilities, they may learn to use their hearing more effectively by focusing on subtle auditory cues that often go unnoticed. The efficient use of hearing, in conjunction with the other senses (including any remaining vision), is the key to independent travel for people who are visually impaired.

Independent travel with a sighted companion but without the use of a cane, guide dog, or electronic device is the most common form of travel for young school-age children. As these children grow older, they may be instructed in the use of a long cane or **Mowat Sensor.** The Mowat Sensor, approximately the size of a flashlight, is a hand-held ultrasound travel aid that vibrates at different rates to warn of obstacles in front of the individual.

Guide dogs or electronic mobility devices may be appropriate for the adolescent or adult, since the need to travel independently significantly increases with age. A variety of

Despite advances in electronic mobility devices, the guide dog continues to be an important source of support for people who are blind.
(Brent Jones/Monkmeyer Press)

electronic mobility devices are currently being used; they do everything from enhancing hearing efficiency to detecting obstacles. The **Laser cane** converts infrared light into sound as light beams strike objects in the path of the person who is blind. The **Sonicguide,** which is worn on the head, emits ultrasound and is able to convert reflections from objects into audible noise. The individual is then able to learn about the structure of an object through the characteristics of the sound that is echoed back to the Sonicguide. For example, loudness indicates size: The louder the noise, the larger the object.

The acquisition of daily living skills is another curriculum area that is important to success in the classroom and independence in society. Most people take for granted many routine events of the day, such as eating, dressing, bathing, and toileting. An individual with sight learns very early in life the tasks associated with perceptual-motor development, including grasping, lifting, balancing, pouring, and manipulating objects. These daily living tasks become more complex during the school years as a child learns personal hygiene, grooming, and social etiquette. Eventually, individuals with sight acquire many complex daily living skills that later contribute to their independence as adults. Money management, grocery shopping, laundry, cooking, cleaning, repairing, sewing, mowing, and trimming are all a part of the daily tasks associated with adult life, which are learned from experiences that are not usually a part of an individual's formalized educational program.

For someone with a visual impairment, however, routine daily living skills are not learned through everyday experiences. In fact, children with visual impairments may be discouraged from developing self-help skills and protected from the challenges and risks of everyday life by their parents, siblings, or other family members and friends.

Traditional Curriculum Content Areas.   Mobility training and the acquisition of daily living skills are components of an educational program that must also concentrate on the traditional curriculum areas. Particular emphasis must be placed on developing receptive and expressive language skills. Students with visual impairments must learn to listen in order to understand the auditory world more clearly. Finely tuned receptive skills contribute to the development of expressive language, which allows these children to orally describe their perceptions of the world. Oral expression can then be expanded to include handwriting as a means of communication. The acquisition of social and instructional language skills opens the door to many areas, including mathematics and reading.

Abstract mathematical concepts may be difficult for students who are blind. These students will probably require additional practice in learning to master symbols, number facts, and higher-level calculations. As concepts become more complex, additional aids may be necessary to facilitate learning. Specially designed talking microcomputers, calculators, rulers, compasses, and the Crammer abacus have been developed to assist students in this area.

Reading is another activity that can greatly expand the knowledge base for individuals who are visually impaired. For people who are partially sighted, various optical aids are available: video systems that magnify print, hand-held magnifiers, magnifiers attached to eyeglasses, and other telescopic aids. Another means to facilitate reading for partially sighted students is the use of large-print books. They are generally available through the American Printing House for the Blind and come in several print sizes (see Figure 11–4). Other factors that must be considered in teaching reading to students who are partially sighted include adequate illumination and the reduction of glare.

Communication Media.   For students who are partially sighted, their limited vision remains a means of obtaining information. The use of optical aids in conjunction with auditory and tactile stimuli allows these individuals an integrated sensory approach to learning. However, this approach is not possible for students who are blind. They do not have access

FOCUS 10

How can communication media facilitate learning for people with visual impairments?

FIGURE 11–4   Illustrations of Large-Print Type

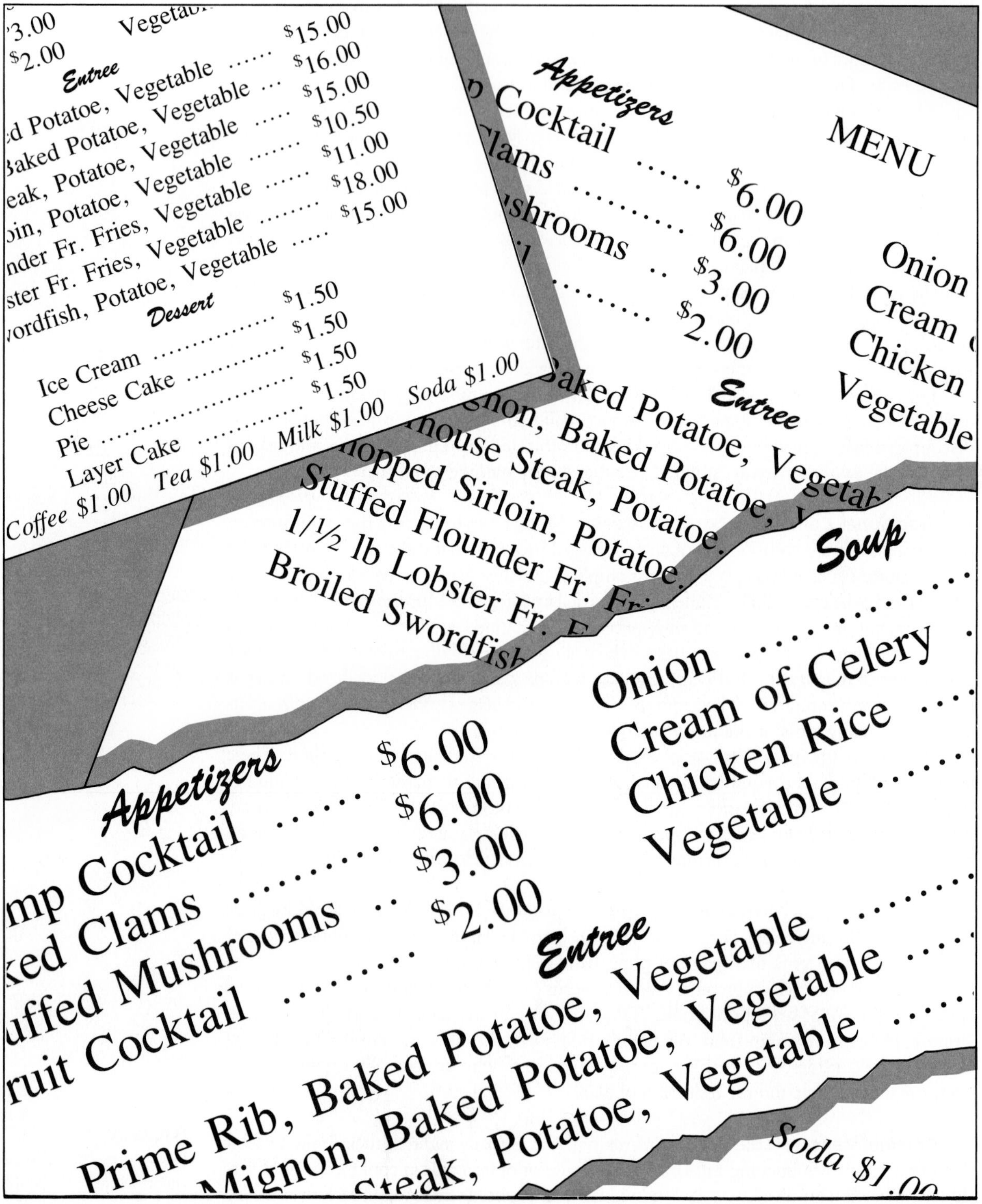

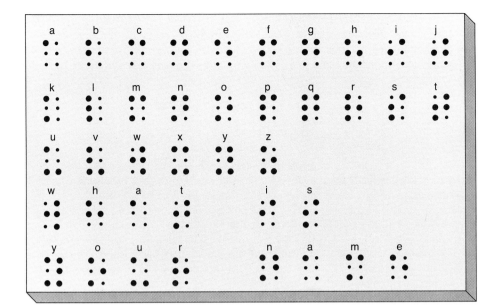

FIGURE 11–5

The Braille Alphabet

to visual stimuli and must compensate for this loss through the use of tactile and auditory media. Through these media, children who are blind develop an understanding of themselves and the world around them. One facet of this development process is the acquisition of language, and one facet of language acquisition is learning to read.

For the student who is blind, the tactile sense represents entry into the symbolic world of reading. Currently, the most widely used tactile medium for teaching reading is the raised-line **braille** system. This system, which originated with the work of Louis Braille in 1829, is a code that utilizes a six-dot cell to form 63 different alphabetical, numerical, and grammatical characters. In order to become a proficient braille reader, an individual must learn 263 different configurations, including alphabet letters, punctuation marks, short-form words, and contractions. As illustrated in Figure 11–5, braille is not a tactile reproduction of the standard English alphabet but a separate code for reading and writing.

Braille is still considered by a significant number of people who are blind to be an efficient means for teaching reading and writing. Critics of the system argue that most readers who use braille are much slower than those who read from print. Besides, braille materials are bulky and tedious. It can be argued, however, that, without braille, people who are blind would be much less independent. Individuals who are unable to read braille are more dependent on sight readers and recordings. Simple tasks—such as labeling cans, boxes, or cartons in a bathroom or kitchen—become nearly impossible to complete.

Braille writing is accomplished through the use of a slate and stylus. Using this procedure, a student writes a mirror image of the reading code, moving from right to left. The writing process may be facilitated by using a braille writer. This hand-operated machine has six keys that correspond to each dot in the braille cell.

An innovation for braille readers that reduces some of the problems associated with the medium is the **paperless brailler.** One such machine, the Rose Braille Display Reader, comes in a compact desktop unit where braille is recorded and retrieved on standard magnetic tape cassettes, thus significantly reducing the space necessary for storage. This machine is representative of the continuing research in the development of communication media for people who are blind. The Rose Braille Display Reader has been described by the National Federation for the Blind as "revolutionary as the development of the Braille system by Louis Braille more than a century and a half ago" (*Braille: An Overview*, 1982, p. 181). However, many newer systems do not incorporate braille as the medium for communication. Although it is the most widely known tactile medium, braille may not be functional for all individuals who are blind (e.g., those who do not have tactile sensitivity, including elderly people).

The Magic Machines of Ray Kurzweil

Lawyer Melea Rodgers has just arrived for work at the Decatur, Alabama, City Hall. The petite young woman with shoulder-length blond hair sits down at her desk and picks up her stack of morning mail. She opens the first letter and presses a switch on a briefcase-size machine on her desk.

"Hello, this is Perfect Paul," says a resonant male voice coming from the device. "I am ready." Rodgers picks up a palm-size scanner and slowly begins to slide it back and forth on the letter. In a moment, Perfect Paul continues. "Dear Miss Rodgers," he says, as he begins reading the entire letter.

Melea Rodgers went blind as a result of diabetes several years ago. Until she received this Kurzweil Personal Reader, she depended on office-mates and her mother to read not only her daily mail, but thousands of pages of regulations and court documents.

Now she can have any page read aloud to her in any of nine distinct voice-styles—from the resonant bass of Huge Harry to the breathy tones of Whispering Wendy. "Ever since I got my Kurzweil last year, I've been on my own. It's a wonderful feeling," says Rodgers.

The Kurzweil whose name adorns the machine is Raymond Kurzweil, one of the most remarkable inventors alive. A soft-spoken businessman-scientist in Waltham, Massachusetts, Kurzweil has repeatedly astonished colleagues and competitors with his "smart machines" that are transforming the lives of millions.

◆ Paul Scher, rehabilitation-services consultant for Sears in Chicago, can now enjoy his evenings instead of using them to keep up with office paper work. "I used to depend on a device that converts written material into a tactile pattern," says Scher. "It took forever. The Kurzweil is a fantastic breakthrough." . . .

◆ Judge Craig Alston of Bay City, Michigan, suffers from a degenerative eye disease. Now legally blind, Alston often addresses students and community groups on the dangers of drinking and driving. To add dramatic impact, he sometimes brings along his Personal Reader and has Perfect Paul read from medical, scientific and accident reports.

Few things give Ray Kurzweil more of a sense of fulfillment than hearing such stories. "I've received hundreds of letters from blind people who say they couldn't have gotten their college degree or couldn't hold their current job if it hadn't been for the Reader. It's a great feeling."

As a small boy growing up in Queens, New York, Kurzweil was an accomplished magician. Then in 1960, at age 12, he discovered the computer. Within three years he had written a program that saved so much time in doing statistical analyses that IBM later distributed it to customers throughout the country.

"I was already interested in how we recognize things—how we pick up patterns. That, to me, is the key to intelligence. And I began dreaming of making pattern recognition the area where I would concentrate," says Kurzweil. . . .

On a freezing January morning in 1976, the young inventor staged a demonstration for the press that caused a sensation. That evening the robot-like voice of his prototype reading machine delivered Walter Cronkite's sign-off on the "CBS Evening News."

The following day, singer Stevie Wonder heard Kurzweil demonstrating his reader on the "Today Show" and traveled to Cambridge to meet the inventor. "He wanted one right away," Kurzweil recalls. "The first machine weighed about 350 pounds and cost $50,000, but we loaded it right into his car." Wonder stayed up all that night reading. In the years since, the Kurzweil machine has been "a brother and a friend," he says. . . .

The Personal Reader is also used in schools to aid students with reading disabilities. Researchers have discovered that these students can sometimes overcome their [impairment] if they scan a page of a book, then follow along with Perfect Paul as he pronounces each word, like an infinitely patient teacher.

Ray Kurzweil is now devoting much of his time to new and different machines. The Kurzweil music synthesizer has become the standard for such stars as Stevie Wonder, Kenny Rogers and Neil Diamond. Kurzweil has also created a voice-recognition mechanism that permits a busy doctor to speak into a hand-held device after completing an examination and receive a typed report in minutes. . . .

Even though braille is used less frequently today than in the past, it remains an important reading and writing tool for people with visual impairments. (Craig Hammell/The Stock Market)

One of the most popular tactile devices that does not use the braille system is the **Optacon Scanner.** Printed material is exposed to a camera and then reproduced on a fingerpad using a series of vibrating pins that are tactile reproductions of the printed material. The Optacon was developed by J. C. Bliss and became available commercially in 1971. Currently, thousands are in use worldwide. Although the Optacon greatly expands access to the printed word, it has drawbacks, as well. It requires tactile sensitivity; as such, reading remains a slow, laborious process. Additionally, the Optacon requires considerable training for the individual to become a skilled user.

For some individuals who are blind, the tactile medium may not be the most functional or most efficient means of acquiring information. Some individuals must rely solely on the auditory sense, while others are able to integrate tactile and auditory input. Specialized auditory media for people who are blind are becoming increasingly available. One example is the **Kurzweil Personal Reader,** which converts printed matter into synthetic speech at a rate of more than 350 words per minute. Although the cost of today's Personal Reader

Kurzweil Personal Readers convert printed material into synthetic speech for readers with visual impairments. (Kurzweil/Xerox)

(about $8,000) is prohibitive, the American Foundation for the Blind and the Bank of Boston currently provide low-interest loans for people with visual impairments to purchase the device (Ziegler, 1991). There are projections for a book-size model in the near future that will cost around $1,000. Other auditory aids that assist people who are blind include talking calculators, talking-book machines, record players, and audiotape recorders.

Debate   Forum ·············· Regular Schools versus Special Schools— ··············· Where Should Children Who Are Blind Be Educated?

In 1900, the first class for students with blindness opened in the Chicago public schools. Prior to this, such children were educated in state residential schools, where they lived away from their families. Until 1950, the ratio of students attending schools for the blind to those in regular public schools was about 10 to 1. However, in that year, the incidence of children with retrolental fibroplasia increased, resulting in more children who were blind attending regular public schools. By 1960, more children with blindness were being educated with their nondisabled peers in regular public schools than in schools for the blind. Nonetheless, the issue of what is the most appropriate educational environment for children who are blind continues to be debated internationally.

Point   Children who are blind should be educated in regular schools and classrooms alongside their seeing peers. This allows children who are blind to remain at home with the family and live in a local neighborhood, which is just as important for these children as it is for their sighted friends. Schools for children who are blind have endeavored over the years to offer the best education possible, one that is intended to be equivalent to that offered to children who can see. However, these schools cannot duplicate the experiences of living at

home and being part of the local community. Although it can be argued that the special school is geared entirely to the needs of the child who is blind, there is much more to education than a segregated educational environment can provide. During the child's growing years, he or she must be directly involved in the seeing world in order to have the opportunity to adjust and become a part of society.

Counterpoint   The special school for children who are blind provides for these individuals a complete education that is oriented entirely to their unique needs. The teachers in these schools have years of experience in working exclusively with children who are blind and are well aware of what educational experiences are needed to help them reach their fullest potential. Additionally, special schools are equipped with a multitude of educational resources developed for children who are blind. Regular schools and classrooms cannot offer the intensive and individualized programs in such areas as music, physical education, arts and crafts, and the like that are available through schools for the blind. The strength of the special school is that it is entirely geared to the specialized needs of the child who is blind. Thus, it can more effectively teach him or her the skills necessary to adapt to life experiences.

REVIEW ···

FOCUS 1   Why is it important to understand the visual process as well as know the physical components of the eye?

- The visual process is an important link to the physical world, helping people to gain information beyond that provided by the other senses and also helping to integrate the information acquired primarily through sound, touch, smell, and taste.
- Our interactions with the environment are shaped by the way we perceive visual stimuli.

FOCUS 2   Distinguish between the terms *blind* and *partially sighted.*

- Legal blindness is visual acuity of 20/200 or worse in the best eye, or a field of vision of 20 percent or less.
- Educational definitions of blindness focus primarily on the individual's inability to use vision as an avenue for learning.

- A person who is partially sighted has a visual acuity greater than 20/200 but not greater than 20/70 in the best eye after correction.
- A person who is partially sighted can still use vision as a primary means of learning.

FOCUS 3   Distinguish among refractive eye problems, muscle disorders, and receptive eye problems.

- Refractive eye problems occur when the refractive structures of the eye (cornea, aqueous humor, lens, and vitreous fluid) fail to focus light rays properly on the retina. Refractive problems include hyperopia (farsightedness), myopia (nearsightedness), astigmatism (blurred vision), and cataracts.
- Muscle disorders occur when the major muscles within the eye are inadequately developed or atrophic, resulting in a loss of

control and an inability to maintain tension. Muscle disorders include nystagmus (uncontrolled rapid eye movement), strabismus (crossed eyes), and amblyopia (loss of vision due to muscle imbalance).

◆ Receptive eye problems occur when the receptive structures of the eye (retina and optic nerve) degenerate or become damaged. Receptive eye problems include optic atrophy, retinitis pigmentosa, retinal detachment, retrolental fibroplasia, and glaucoma.

FOCUS 4 What are the estimated prevalence and causes of visual impairments?

◆ At least 20 percent of the general population have some visual impairments.

◆ About 0.1 percent of all school-age children meet the legal definition of being blind or partially sighted. Nearly 23,000 students have visual impairments and receive specialized services in the U.S. public schools.

◆ Approximately 75 percent of all people who are blind are over 45 years of age.

FOCUS 5 Describe how a visual impairment can affect intelligence, speech and language skills, educational achievement, social development, orientation and mobility, and perceptual-motor development.

◆ Performance on tests of intelligence may be negatively affected by a visual impairment in areas ranging from spatial concepts to general world knowledge.

◆ Children with visual impairments are at a distinct disadvantage in developing speech and language skills because they are unable to visually associate words with objects.

◆ Children with visual impairments cannot learn speech by visual imitation but must rely on hearing or touch for input.

◆ Factors that may influence the educational achievement of a student with a visual impairment include (a) late entry to school; (b) failure in inappropriate school programs; (c) loss of time in school due to illness, treatment, or surgery; (d) lack of opportunity; and (e) slow rate of acquiring information.

◆ People with visual impairments are unable to imitate the physical mannerisms of sighted peers and thus do not develop body language, an important form of social communication.

◆ A person with sight may misinterpret what is said by a person with a visual impairment because his or her visual cues may not be consistent with the spoken word.

◆ People with visual impairments are often excluded from social activities that are integrally related to the use of vision, thus reinforcing the mistaken idea that they do not want to participate.

◆ The lack of sight may prevent a person with a visual impairment from understanding his or her own relative position in space.

◆ A visual impairment may affect fine motor coordination and interfere with the ability to manipulate objects.

◆ The perceptual discrimination abilities of people with visual impairments in the areas of texture, weight, and sound are comparable to those of sighted peers.

◆ People who are blind do not perform as well as people with sight on complex tasks of perception, including form identification, spatial relations, and perceptual-motor integration.

FOCUS 6 What steps can be taken to prevent and medically treat visual impairments?

◆ Visual impairments can be prevented through genetic screening and counseling, appropriate prenatal care, and early developmental assessment.

◆ The development of optical aids, including corrective glasses and contact lenses, has greatly improved access to the sighted world for people with visual impairments.

◆ Medical treatment may range from extremely complex surgical procedures associated with corneal transplants to drug therapy (e.g., atropinization).

FOCUS 7 Why is the availability of appropriate mental health services important for people with visual impairments?

◆ Mental health services are important in addressing individual problems with self-concept and feelings of inferiority that often stem from being visually impaired.

◆ Mental health services include infant stimulation programs, family counseling, and individual counseling relative to preparation for employment and independent living.

FOCUS 8 What range of educational services are available to students with visual impairments?

◆ Residential facilities try to provide children who are blind opportunities for the same kinds of experiences that would be available if they were growing up in their own communities.

◆ The vast majority of individuals with visual impairments live at home, attend public schools, and interact within their own communities.

◆ Services available within the public schools range from regular class placement, with little or no assistance, to special day schools.

FOCUS 9 Identify two content areas that should be included in educational programs for students with visual impairments.

◆ Mobility and orientation training
◆ The acquisition of daily living skills

FOCUS 10 How can communication media facilitate learning for people with visual impairments?

◆ Through communication media—such as optical aids in conjunction with auditory and tactile stimuli—individuals with visual impairments can better develop an understanding of themselves and the world around them.

◆ Tactile media—including the raised-line braille system and the Optacon Scanner—can greatly enhance the individual's access to information.

◆ Specialized auditory media—including the Kurzweil Personal Readers, talking calculators, talking-book machines, record players, and audiotape recorders—provide opportunities for people with visual impairments that were not thought possible only a few years ago.

Chapter Twelve
Physical and Health Disorders

TO BEGIN WITH . . .

◆ More than 80 percent of the children with AIDS got the infection from their mothers (Ordovensky, 1991).

◆ "My old wooden legs weighed about 15 pounds a piece and hurt my stumps—I'd clomp two blocks and have to sit and rest . . . My new legs weigh half as much and flex like real" (Canby, 1989, p. 746).

◆ One-fifth of all children in the United States are not covered by any health care insurance (Center for the Study of Social Policy, 1991).

◆ New York City will spend an estimated $795 million dollars during the next 10 years on special education for children affected by cocaine (Toufexis, Cronin, Ludtke, & Willwerth, 1991).

◆ The World Health Organization has estimated that 3 million women and children will die during the 1990s from AIDS-related complications worldwide (Chin, 1990).

DR. JOHNS, JR.

I WAS ALWAYS CHOSEN LAST.   I can still remember the half hour we had for recess twice a day in elementary school. On good weather days, the main sport was softball. I was in the third grade when I really grew interested in recess softball. I didn't own a softball mitt, and wouldn't have known how to use it if I had one. I lost most of my right arm in a clothes washer motor when I was 10 months old. The boys always brought their mitts to recess, and the best players were elected to be the captains who chose the teams. In the third grade, I was always chosen last.

When I told my dad what was happening, he immediately took me to buy a first baseman's mitt. I began to practice every night, throwing a tennis ball against the garage door and finding a way to get my mitt back on before the ball returned. I tried everything with that mitt: putting it on the ground after I had caught the ball, throwing it in the air and trying to get the ball to drop out of it, and other awkward systems.

I eventually found that, after catching the ball with my left hand, I could put my mitt under my right arm in one motion and pull the ball out in a second motion and throw it. I worked every night on this method with my dad and brothers and many hours of just throwing the ball against the door myself.

Between the third and fourth grades, I moved up from being chosen last at recess to being a captain who chose the teams. I eventually played in the Little League as a pitcher and first baseman, was an all-star in our Babe Ruth League, and captain of a Yankee baseball team in Northern England. I still use the technique I developed in third grade for playing on our over-the-hill church softball team.

Dick Johns, **M.D.**

*I*NTRODUCTION

Dr. Johns' physical disability never became a serious liability for him (see Window 12–1). His achievements to a great degree came from the support he received in his home environment, particularly that provided by his father and mother during his formative years. Their support and that of others in his neighborhood and community made it possible for Dr. Johns to become an active participant in just about every activity appropriate for his age. With encouragement and high expectations from parents, coaches, teachers, and others, he became a capable student; a skilled baseball pitcher, tennis player, and golfer; and eventually, a talented physician. In fact, Dr. Johns successfully hit two "hole in ones" during recent golf tournaments.

The degree to which children with physical and health disorders become integral participants in their neighborhoods and communities is directly related to the treatment they receive from caring professionals. Additionally, the full integration of people with physical and health disorders is a function of the ways in which we, as neighbors and community members, interact with them. Hopefully, the quality of our interactions will match that of the strides being made in the medical, pharmaceutical, and engineering fields.

PHYSICAL DISORDERS

Physical disorders are impairments that may interfere with an individual's mobility and coordination. They may also affect his or her capacity to communicate, learn, and adjust.

Advanced Materials

We had jogged a hundred feet, and already the man beside me was straining. But his face showed triumph—triumph over the impossible.

Sixteen years ago in Fremont, Nebraska, a seed truck crushed Roger Charter's legs. Both were amputated above the knee. For more than a decade the onetime star athlete fought for a normal life with traditional wooden legs. But the hopelessness of it ate away at his spirit.

Now, thanks to that resilient spirit and new limbs made possible by the miracles of advanced materials, Roger Charter is the first such amputee ever to run.

"My old wooden legs weighed 15 pounds apiece and hurt my stumps—I'd clomp two blocks and have to sit and rest," said Mr. Charter, today a dispatcher for the Union Pacific Railroad in Omaha. "My new legs weigh half as much and flex like real."

Those high-tech legs comprise a tidy little inventory of advanced materials: knees and ankles of light titanium alloys born of the space age, shins of a powerful composite of carbon fibers pressed into a matrix of resin, sockets of a flexible but strong new polyethylene to fit comfortably on the residual limbs.

And the feet? "The most difficult part," acknowledged John Sabolich, president of a prosthetics firm in Oklahoma City and a pioneering designer in advanced materials. "The human arch is like a complex leaf spring, almost impossible to duplicate. Fortunately a new plastic provided the springiness."

Source: From "Reshaping Our Lives" by T. Y. Canby, December 1989, *National Geographic*, p. 746.

The Individuals with Disabilities Education Act (IDEA) uses the term *orthopedically impaired* to describe children with physical disorders. These disorders or physical impairments are usually diagnosed by a physician early in a child's life. As the child with physical or health disorders grows older, his or her treatment program may involve professionals from many different disciplines, including medicine, psychology, education, and vocational rehabilitation.

Our discussion of physical disorders will be limited to a representative sample of physically disabling conditions. They include traumatic brain injury, cerebral palsy, spina bifida, spinal cord injuries, amputations, and muscular dystrophy.

Physical impairments cannot be used to justify excluding children from mainstream educational opportunities. (Bob Daemmrich/Stock, Boston)

WINDOW 12–2

CHRISTINA

According to her parents, Christina was a bright, verbal child who before she was 2 years old could talk in full sentences, recite the alphabet, sing several nursery songs, and loved to have stories read to her. She was a cuddly child who often asked for hugs but who was also physically active and had a mind of her own. By the time of her injury when she was almost two years of age, she and her parents had developed a very loving relationship.

When she was 23 months old, she was admitted to a local hospital emergency room comatose, with severe traumatic brain injuries after a fall backward off of a porch onto a cement side-walk. She had multiple fractures of the skull bones in the back of her head and massive bleeding in her brain. The pressure from the bleeding was pushing her brain over toward the left side. Because brain swelling was so severe, she underwent surgery; most of the right side of her brain needed to be removed. When she came to the rehabilitation hospital, Christina was not able to sit by herself, could not move the left side of her body, was fed by a tube in her nose, and made sounds if she was uncomfortable. She did not appear to recognize her parents, but she would look at objects and people around her.

Source: From *Psychological Management of Traumatic Brain Injuries in Children and Adolescents* (p. 54) by E. Lehr, 1990, Rockville, MD: Aspen Publishers. Copyright 1990 by Aspen Publishers. Reprinted by permission.

Traumatic Brain Injury

Definitions and Concepts.   **Traumatic brain injury (TBI)** is a new category that was designated by IDEA. In children, TBI consists "of rapid acceleration and deceleration of the brain, including shearing (tearing) of nerve fibers, contusion (bruising) of the brain tissue against the skull, brain stem injuries, and edema (swelling) (Lehr, 1990, p. 15). Injuries that do not involve penetration of the skull are referred to as *closed-head* or *generalized* head injuries. Children's head injuries are usually of this type. *Focal* or *open-head* injuries, such as a gunshot wound, are not common in children.

Two types of brain damage, primary and secondary, have been described by medical professionals. *Primary damage* is a direct outcome of the initial impact to the brain. For instance, a child who is hit accidentally with a baseball bat may develop a hematoma, an area

---

R E F L E C T   O N   T H I S

12–1 Common Characteristics of Students with Traumatic Brain Injury

◆ When a student suffers from a traumatic brain injury, it usually affects the cognitive, fine/gross motor, and social/behavioral functions. The educational plan should consider and be sensitive to the interrelationship of all three domains. The teacher should work with the abilities the students presently have, instead of trying to make the student the same as before the accident.

◆ Many students experience a lack of motivation, initiative, and organization. Help the student concentrate on success rather than failures.

◆ It will take longer for the student to process information. Shorter assignments and more time to complete tasks will be helpful.

◆ Most students will experience problems with concentration, memory, and learning new materials. Strategies need to be taught to compensate for poor memory and retrieval problems.

◆ Behavior tends to be rather erratic, impulsive, and verbally intrusive. One day they may behave very appropriately, and the next be totally out of control. A behavior management program should be part of the school re-integration program.

◆ Unlike most learning disabilities, students with traumatic brain injury have a condition that was acquired. The student remembers how things were before the accident and becomes frustrated because they are unable to perform the same or rely on strategies that were once effective.

◆ It is common to see the student become a dependent rather than independent thinker. The teacher usually needs to give more individual instruction and reinforce success.

Source: From "A Horse of a Different Color" by J. Copenhaver, 1991, *Special Educator, 12*(2), pp. 8–9. Copyright 1991 by *Special Educator*. Reprinted by permission.

of internal bleeding within the brain. This may be the primary damage. However, with the passage of time, the brain's response to the initial injury may be pervasive swelling, which will cause additional insult to the brain. This is referred to as *secondary damage*.

Causation and Prevalence.   The causes of TBI vary according to the age and developmental status of the affected individual. However, the greatest cause of injury in all age groups is automobile-related accidents.

Injuries during infancy, excluding those caused by birth-related events, result primarily from falls and child abuse. Very young children can sustain significant brain trauma from being severely shaken; there may not be clear external signs of abuse or injury (Duhaime et al., 1987). Second only to adolescents, preschoolers sustain a significant number of injuries. Again, the major causes of injury are falls and pedestrian-related accidents. School-age children are the least susceptible to head injuries when compared with other age groups. However, the greatest cause of injuries continues to be motor vehicle related. Sports-related injuries also become more prevalent during this period.

The prevalence of brain injuries takes a dramatic jump during the adolescent years (Gross, Wolf, Kunitz, & Jane, 1985). The number of injuries that occur between the ages of 15 and 19 years old usually equals the total number of injuries sustained during the entire previous 14 years. Again, a significant portion of these injuries are sustained in automobiles.

Each year in the United States, over 1 million children sustain traumatic brain injuries. This number represents about one-third of all head injuries (Lehr, 1990). In all but the youngest age groups, the number of head injuries in boys exceeds that of girls. As a rule, boys are two to four times more likely to sustain serious head injuries. This is particularly true during adolescence (Gross et al., 1985).

REFLECT ON THIS

12–2   Student Corner

Hi, my name is Lindsey Beecroft, I am 11 years old and in the 5th grade at Sparkman Elementary in Temecula, California. . . .

◆ I was on my summer vacation when my accident happened. I was at my friend's house playing when a gun in another room discharged and struck me.

◆ I was Life Flighted to the Primary Children's Medical Center where I stayed for three long weeks. My long blonde hair had to be cut and I looked very different. Things were very hard for me at first, but I had such great doctors and therapists that I soon got on the road to a good recovery.

◆ After 10 weeks, . . . I was able to go back to California. (My first airplane ride I was able to remember.)

I have a very special teacher. Her name is Mrs. Zavenstoski. She is so nice and helps a lot!! I am on the Student Council, my job is Pep Commissioner. I was afraid they would not let me do this because of my injury, but everyone is very supportive and they all help me a lot.

◆ School is different now. I try very hard to do my best at all times. I have very good friends. . . . They don't treat me any different because of my injury.

◆ Spelling and English are especially hard and homework takes more time to complete.

◆ I am happy I am doing well. I have made many friends in the hospital and in therapy. I'd like to tell them thanks for everything!! I hope someday I can become a doctor and help others like me.

Lindsey Beecroft

The past few months have been real trying and rewarding for us. We have watched our child struggle and then watched her smile as she finds success. She is a real hard worker and never gives up. She tries too hard to do everything and it is frustrating for her when she can't. We are so fortunate to have found such great doctors and therapists who really care. With everyone's help, our child is happy about herself once again.

Gayle Beecroft, Lindsey's Mother

Source: From "Student Corner" by L. Beecroft and G. Beecroft, 1991, *Brainwaves*, 2(2), p. 3. Reprinted by permission. (The newsletter, renamed *NeuroDevelopments*, is published by the Pediatric Brain Injury Resource Center, 230 South 500 East, Suite 100, Salt Lake City, UT 84102-2015.)

R
E
F
L
E
C
T

O
N

T
H
I
S

12–3   Questions and Answers

Q: My [child, who has a severe head injury,] refuses to give up his goals of becoming a physician. How should I handle this?

A: Perhaps one of the most difficult confrontations that parents experience subsequent to a child's severe head injury is disillusionment, the potential loss of hopes, dreams, and aspirations for the future. Parent reaction to this loss is extremely varied. Many parents choose to cope with it by ruling out all hope of any such accomplishment and making a pointed effort of helping their child to be "realistic" in their goal aspirations. Unfortunately, such a confrontation is often very destructive and results in considerable loss of the child's hope or optimism. There is the conscious and/or unconscious fear on the part of the parent that their child will be disappointed, struggle with that disappointment, and thus seek to avoid the pain. While such concern is understandable, it is a very strong and limiting message to the child.

My preference is to provide the child with a greater optimism for the future. I would not shoot down the long-term goal, but would rather let time and self-discovery make the adjustment. Even though pre-injury goals may be unreasonable or perhaps overly ambitious, his day-to-day struggles will be sufficient to shape his decision-making process over time, even with severe injury. Over time, he will learn his limitations more realistically and will adjust his expectations. For now, dreams and "unrealistic" aspirations will fuel his recovery. Like many young professionals, I used to have a strong need to be able to predict the future for children with neurologic compromise that followed. I finally quit predicting when I realized my "predictions" were below chance levels (i.e., 50 percent).

Source: From "Questions and Answers" by D. E. Nilsson, 1991, *Brainwaves*, *2*(2), p. 7. Reprinted by permission. (The newsletter, renamed *NeuroDevelopments*, is published by the Pediatric Brain Injury Resource Center, 230 South 500 East, Suite 100, Salt Lake City, UT 84102-2015.)

FOCUS 1

Identify the stages of treatment for children with traumatic brain injuries.

Interventions.   Treatment of TBI proceeds in stages. At the onset of the injury, medical personnel focus on maintaining the child's life, minimizing complications, and reducing the level of **coma.** This stage of the treatment is often characterized by strained interactions between physicians and parents. Many physicians are unable to respond satisfactorily to the overwhelming psychological needs of parents and family members because of the immense and complex medical demands presented by the injured child. Other trained personnel—such as social workers, psychologists, and ministers—should address the parents' and family's needs.

If the child remains in a coma, physical or occupational therapists may use specialized stimulation techniques to reduce the depth of the coma. If the young person is unduly agitated by stimuli, steps may be taken to control or reduce them. As the injured child comes out of the coma, personnel focus on orienting him or her. Many children who have had TBIs do not remember their accidents or the resulting medical activities or hospitalization.

The next stage of treatment focuses on relearning and performing preinjury skills and behaviors. This may take time and considerable effort. Gradually, children are prepared for return to their homes and appropriate school environments. Their families prepare as well, receiving ongoing support and counseling. Additionally, arrangements are made for appropriate **physical therapy** and **occupational therapy** and specialized teaching as necessary.

The last stages of intervention focus on (1) providing counseling and therapy to help the child cope with the injury and resultant effects, (2) assisting the child and family in maintaining the gains achieved, (3) terminating specific head injury services, and (4) referring the child and family to community agencies for additional services that may be needed.

Cerebral Palsy

Definitions and Concepts.   **Cerebral palsy** is a disability resulting from damage to the brain before or during birth. It is often evidenced by motor problems, general physical

■ **Table 12–1** Motor Classification Scheme for Cerebral Palsy

Classification	Brief Description
Spasticity	Characterized by great difficulty in using muscles for movement; involuntary contractions occur with attempts to stretch or use various muscle groups; spasticity prevents performance of controlled, voluntary motions.
Athetosis	Characterized by constant contorted twisting motions, particularly in the wrists and fingers; facial contortions are also common; continual movement and contraction of successive muscle groups prevents any well-controlled use of muscular motion.
Ataxia	Characterized by extreme difficulties in controlling both gross and fine motor movements; problems related to balance, position in space, and directionality make coordinated movement extremely difficult if not impossible.
Rigidity	Characterizes one of the most severe and rare types of cerebral palsy; involves continuous and diffuse tension as the limbs are extended; walking or movement of any type is extremely difficult.
Tremor	Characterized by motions that are constant, involuntary, and uncontrollable; are of a rhythmic, alternating, or pendular pattern and result from muscle contractions that occur continuously.
Atonia	Characterized by little if any muscle tone; muscles fail to respond to any stimulation; condition is extremely rare in its true form.
Mixed	Characterized by combinations of all the conditions described above.

weakness, lack of coordination, and speech disorders. The syndrome is not contagious, progressive, or remittent. Its seriousness and overall impact can range from very mild to very severe. A variety of classification schemes have been used to describe the different types of cerebral palsy, but the two major approaches focus on motor and topographical characteristics (see Tables 12–1 and 12–2). The motor scheme emphasizes the type and nature of physiological involvement or impairment. The topographical scheme focuses on the various body parts or limbs that are affected.

■ **Table 12–2** Topographical Classification of Cerebral Palsy and Paralytic Conditions

Classification	Affected Area
Monoplegia	One limb
Paraplegia	Lower body and both legs
Hemiplegia	One side of the body
Triplegia	Three appendages or limbs, usually both legs and one arm
Quadriplegia	All four extremities and usually the trunk
Diplegia	Legs are more involved than arms
Double hemiplegia	Both halves of the body, with one side more involved than the other

FOCUS 2

Why are many individuals with cerebral palsy considered to be multidisabled?

Cerebral palsy is a complicated and perplexing condition. The individual with cerebral palsy is likely to have mild to severe problems in nonmotor areas of functioning as well as motor areas. These difficulties may include hearing impairments, speech and language disorders, intellectual deficits, visual impairments, and general perceptual problems. Because of the multifaceted nature of this condition, many people with cerebral palsy are considered to be multidisabled. Thus, cerebral palsy cannot be characterized by a set of homogeneous symptoms. It is a condition in which a variety of problems may be present in differing degrees of severity.

Causation and Prevalence.   The causes of cerebral palsy are varied. Any condition that can adversely affect the brain may cause cerebral palsy. Chronic disease, maternal infection, birth trauma, fetal infection, and hemorrhage may all be sources of this neurological-motor disorder.

The prevalence of cerebral palsy ranges from 1.5 to 5 per 1,000 live births (Anderson, 1986; Whaley & Wong, 1985). These figures fluctuate as a function of several variables. For instance, many children born with cerebral palsy come from families who are unable to obtain medical care. Consequently, many of these children do not become known to physicians or agencies that collect prevalence information.

Interventions.   Treatment of cerebral palsy is best undertaken in a multidisciplinary fashion. Medical and motor aspects are handled by orthopedic personnel. Surgery may be necessary for treatment of muscle and tendon problems. Physical therapists provide training in muscle use, including how to utilize prosthetic and bracing devices effectively. Medical and physical therapies are aimed at achieving more controlled mobility and psychomotor behavior.

Speech and language clinicians provide therapies directed at developing the individual's communication skills. Speech synthesizers are beginning to play a major role in helping people with cerebral palsy communicate with their peers, teachers, and other individuals (Tarnowski & Drabman, 1986). Communication inaccuracies, error rates, and response times have been cut practically in half through the use of such devices.

Spina Bifida

Definitions and Concepts.   **Spina bifida** is a birth defect characterized by an abnormal opening in the spinal column. Until about the twelfth week of pregnancy, the backbone of a developing fetus remains open. Spina bifida occurs when the spinal column fails to close properly. This abnormal opening may allow the contents of the spinal canal to flow between the bone structures that did not fully close. Spina bifida frequently involves some paralysis of various portions of the body, depending on the location of the opening. It may or may not influence intellectual functioning. There are two types of spina bifida: spina bifida occulta and spina bifida cystica.

Spina bifida occulta is a very mild condition in which a small slit is present in one or more of the vertebral structures. Most people with spina bifida occulta are unaware of its presence unless they have had a spinal x-ray for diagnosis of some other condition. Spina bifida occulta has little if any impact on a developing infant.

Spina bifida cystica is a malformation of the spinal column in which a tumorlike sac grows on the infant's back (see Figure 12–1). It exists in one of two forms: **spina bifida meningocele** and **spina bifida myelomeningocele.** In the meningocele type, the sac contains spinal fluid but no nerve tissue. In contrast, in the myelomeningocele type, the sac does contain nerve tissue. The latter is the most serious variety of spina bifida in that it generally includes paralysis or partial paralysis of certain body areas, causing lack of bowel

FOCUS 3

What is spina bifida myelomeningocele?

FIGURE 12-1   Side Views of a Normal Spine, Spina Bifida Occulta, and Spina Bifida Cystica

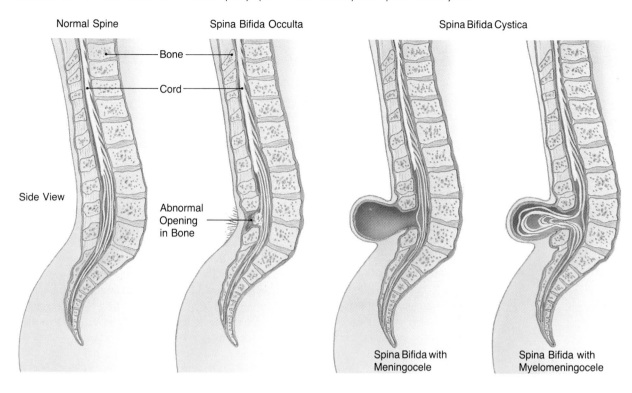

Normal Spine   Spina Bifida Occulta   Spina Bifida Cystica

Bone

Cord

Side View

Abnormal
Opening
in Bone

Spina Bifida with
Meningocele

Spina Bifida with
Myelomeningocele

and bladder control. There are two types of myelomeningocele: one in which the tumorlike sac is open, revealing the neural tissue, and one in which the sac is closed or covered with a combination of skin and membrane.

Children with spina bifida occulta exhibit the normal range of intelligence. Most children with myelomeningocele also have normal IQs (Hoekelmann, Blatman, Nelson, Friedman, & Seidel, 1987). For children whose learning capacity is normal or above average, no special educational programing is required.

Most children with spina bifida are of normal intelligence. (Alexander Tsiaras, Science Source/Photo Researchers, Inc.)

Causation and Prevalence.   The exact cause of spina bifida is unknown; however, there is a slight tendency for the condition to run in families. In fact, myelomeningocele appears to be transmitted genetically, probably as a function of certain prenatal factors interacting with genetic predispositions. It is also possible that certain harmful agents taken by the mother prior to or during the first few days of pregnancy or the absence of certain elements (vitamin A or folic acid) may be responsible for the defect. **Teratogens** that may induce malformations in the spine include radiation, maternal hyperthermia (high fever), vitamin A deficiency, excess glucose, and folic acid deficiency.

Prevalence figures for spina bifida, both myelomeningocele and meningocele, vary. In the United States, estimates range from 1.05 to 1.22 in 1,000 births (Tachdjian, 1990).

Interventions.   It is now possible to identify babies with myelomeningocele before they are born by means of certain sophisticated instruments and techniques. One means of doing so is ultrasonic scanning of the fetus late in pregnancy.

Immediate action is often called for when the child with myelomeningocele is born, depending on the nature of the lesion, its position on the spine, and the presence of other related conditions. Decisions regarding medical interventions are extremely difficult to make, for they often entail problems and issues that are not easily or quickly resolved. For example, in 80 percent of the children with spina bifida myelomeningocele, an area of the spinal cord is exposed. This places them at great risk for developing **meningitis,** which has a mortality rate of over 50 percent.

The decision to undertake surgery is often made quickly if the tissue sac is located very low on the infant's back and there is no presence of hydrocephalus. The purpose of the surgery is to close the spinal opening and lessen the potential for infection. In cases where the myelomeningocele is relatively high on the spine and other conditions are present (e.g., meningitis), surgery may not be performed.

Children with spina bifida myelomeningocele have little if any bowel or bladder control. This is directly attributable to the paralysis caused by malformation of the spinal cord. As these children mature, they can be trained to regulate their bowel movements through the use of suppositories.

Physical therapists play a critical role in helping children as they learn to cope with the paralysis caused by myelomeningocele. Paralysis obviously limits the children's exploratory activities, which are critical to later learning and perceptual motor performance. With this in mind, many such children are fitted with modified skateboards, which allows them to explore their surroundings. Utilizing the strength in their arms and hands, they may become quite adept at exploring their home environments. Gradually, they move to leg braces, crutches, a wheelchair, or a combination of the three.

Spinal Cord Injury

Definitions and Concepts.   **Spinal cord injury** occurs when the spinal cord is traumatized or severed. The cord can be traumatized through extreme extension or flexing from a fall, an automobile accident, or a sports injury. The cord may also be severed through the same types of accidents, although such occurrences are extremely rare. Usually in such cases, the cord is bruised or otherwise injured. Shortly thereafter, it swells, and within hours, bleeding often occurs. Gradually, a self-destructive process ensues in which the affected area slowly deteriorates and the damage becomes irreversible. The greatest number of spinal cord injuries occur between the ages of 16 and 30.

The overall impact of injury on an individual depends on the site and nature of the insult. If the injury occurs in the neck or upper back, the resulting paralysis and effects are

WINDOW 12-3

I'M NOT OPPOSED TO MIRACLES

My means of motion is one of two wheelchairs. One of these chairs is a typical wheelchair, not unlike many that you frequently see in hospitals for transporting patients. The other chair is a new, electronically driven model. It is powered by several batteries and is a real boon to me, since I can direct the motion and speed of the chair by myself. Also, I can use this chair without an assistant. When I use my old wheelchair, I must be propelled by an aide, another adult, or one of my children.

I like my new chair and the freedom it allows me, but there are still a lot of barriers that interfere with my getting around. Take my church, for example. I have no trouble getting into the church. It has a very suitable ramp, and I have access to many areas in the church. But I can't easily attend my Sunday school class without considerable effort on the part of others, and I get tired of having people help me. I like to do things on my own. I like to be as independent as I can. This is one of the reasons I enjoy my new electronic chair so much. With it, I can get around without major assistance from others. However, the electronic chair isn't yet equipped with "stair climbers."

Let me put it this way. My Sunday school class is a mere six steps up from a major hallway in the church. In order to get to my Sunday school class, I need someone to lift me and my chair up six steps to the second level of the building. You might say to yourself, What's the problem? Aren't the members of your church compassionate?

The problem is basically this: If I choose to be independent by using my new electronic wheelchair, I can enter the church almost unaided. I can also move from one room to another on the main floor of the church without being propelled by someone else. But the electronic chair weighs about 120 pounds. If you add my weight to that of the chair, you have the hefty sum of 250-plus pounds. Raising me the six steps vertically to attend my Sunday school class is nothing short of a modern-day miracle. I'm not opposed to miracles. I just like to be independent.

Mark, A Securities Firm Owner

Mitch Longley: A Face to Remember

When magazine readers turn to Ralph Lauren ads featuring black-and-white close-ups of Mitch Longley's striking profile, they tend to overlook the designer's gray, striped suit. Instead, they linger over Longley's perfectly sculpted face; his shoulder-length, jet-black hair; his sensuous dark eyes. What most people would not be able to overlook, were they to meet Longley in person, is the characteristic that differentiates him from many of his chin-jutting competitors: Longley uses a wheelchair.

One night in 1983, a few months before his high school graduation, Longley partied, having a few beers with friends. On the short drive to his Connecticut home, at 2:30 A.M., alone and not intoxicated, Longley fell asleep at the wheel and crashed into a stone wall. He awoke in a hospital bed, his back broken. He learned that he had paraplegia. His doctors told him that he would never walk again.

Instead of spending that spring working out with the school tennis team (he had hoped to turn pro one day), Longley spent it in agonizing physical therapy sessions. Three months later, with the aid of leg braces, he was able to walk down the aisle at his high school graduation. His optimism throughout the ordeal served him well. Indeed, according to high school buddy Peter Ahl, 26, one of the two friends who found Longley after the accident, "He's a little bit cocky and a little bit arrogant, and I think that helped him out a lot."

Aside from Longley's work as a model and an actor (including a recurring role on the soap opera *Another World*), his passion has been to create a foundation dedicated to changing people's attitudes toward those with disabilities. "I had watched a lot of TV (in the hospital), and I noticed that they never used disabled people in ads or as characters. That bothered me."

Longley has lectured widely on the subject of disabilities, both here and at the American University in Cairo, Egypt, where he became specifically interested in helping individuals with disabilities who lived in developing countries. According to Longley, the United States could learn a thing or two from the Third World about how to treat people with disabilities.

"We have the sophisticated laws. We have the accessible buildings. But [the United States] has major fears in dealing with disabled people. I think it is because our culture is so shallow, so young. It's such a white, male place. When I went to Egypt, no one stared at my wheelchair. They looked right at my face. Unfortunately, we haven't developed enough to treat people who are different as equal."

Source: From Karen Brailsford, "A Model Advocate," *Elle*, March, 1992, p. 198; David M. Hutchings, "A Face to Remember," *People Weekly*, October 21, 1991, pp. 72–74.

A variety of technologies, particularly computer-assisted devices, enable people who have limited use of their limbs to accomplish work. (James D. Wilson/Woodfin Camp & Associates, Inc.)

usually quite extensive. If the injury occurs in the lower back, paralysis is confined to the lower extremities.

The physical characteristics of spinal cord injuries are similar to those of spina bifida myelomeningocele. The terms used to describe the impact are identical: **paraplegia, quadriplegia,** and **hemiplegia.** It is worth noting, however, that these terms are global descriptions of functioning and not precise enough to accurately convey an individual's actual level of functioning.

Causation and Prevalence. While falls, accidents, and sports injuries can cause spinal cord injury, various diseases can have the same result. Motor vehicle accidents are responsible for approximately half of all spinal cord injuries. Twenty-five percent result from falls, while 10 percent are sports related. Some 5,000 to 10,000 new cases of spinal cord injuries appear each year, 75 percent of which involve males. Individuals in the age-range from 15 to 34 are most likely to incur such injuries. The overall prevalence rate for spinal cord injury is 3 of every 100,000 individuals (Yashon, 1986).

FOCUS 4

Identify specific treatments for individuals with spinal cord injuries.

Interventions. The immediate care rendered to a person with a spinal cord injury is critical. The impact of the injury can be magnified if proper procedures are not employed early after the accident or onset of the condition.

The first phase of treatment provided by a receiving hospital is the management of shock. Quickly thereafter, the individual is immobilized in order to prevent movement and possibly further damage. As a rule, surgical procedures are not undertaken immediately. The major goal of medical treatment at this point is to stabilize the spine and prevent further complications. Catheterization may be employed to control urine flow, and steps may be taken to reduce swelling and bleeding at the injury site. Traction may be used to stabilize certain portions of the spinal column and cord. Medical treatment of spinal cord injuries is lengthy and often tedious.

Once physicians have successfully stabilized the spine and treated any other medical conditions, the rehabilitation process promptly proceeds. The individual is taught to use new muscles and take advantage of any and all residual muscle strength. He or she is also taught to use orthopedic equipment, such as handsplints, braces, reachers, headsticks (for

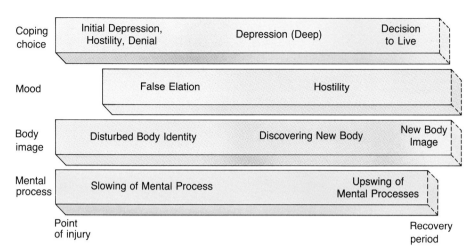

FIGURE 12–2

Psychological Changes after Spinal Cord Injury

Source: From "Coping with Spinal Cord Injury in Adolescents" by S. LeBaron, D. Currie, and L. Zeltzer, in *Chronic Illness and Disability in Childhood and Adolescence*, R. W. Blum (Ed.), 1984, Boston: Allyn and Bacon. Copyright © 1984 by Allyn and Bacon. Reprinted with permission.

typing), and plateguards. Together with an orthopedic specialist, occupational and physical therapists become responsible for the reeducation and training process.

Psychiatric and other support personnel are also engaged in rehabilitation activities. Psychological adjustment to a spinal cord injury and the impact it has on the individual's functioning can take a great deal of time (see Figure 12–2). The goal of all treatment is to help the injured individual become as independent as possible.

As the individual masters necessary self-care skills, other educational and career objectives can be pursued with the assistance of the rehabilitation team. The members of this team change constantly with the skills and needs of the individual. Education for individuals with spinal cord injuries is similar to that for any uninjured children or adults.

Environmental Control Systems

In the future, biomedical engineers, in conjunction with other health professionals, will have a profound effect on the lives of individuals with amputations. Presently, a variety of environmental control systems allow those with amputations and other physical disabilities to operate home appliances and other devices (Dickey & Shealey, 1987). These systems typically have several important components. They include a visual display, a central processing unit (CPU), and a transducer (control switch). In some cases, the transducer allows individuals to activate various devices in their home environments without using their hands. The transducer may be ac- tivated by a dual control, a "sip-puff" switch, an input controller from a powered wheelchair, a computer, an electronic communication aid, or a voice-recognition component. Using these switching devices, individuals with physical disorders may operate telephones, radios, stereos, televisions, video equipment, electronic beds, call signals for requesting assistance, intercoms, and even page turners. The visual display allows the individual to see if the outside doors are locked, if the lights are on in the kitchen, or if the alarm clock has been set. If the kitchen lights have been left on, the individual may turn them off with a voiced command.

Bionic Person: A Distant Reality?

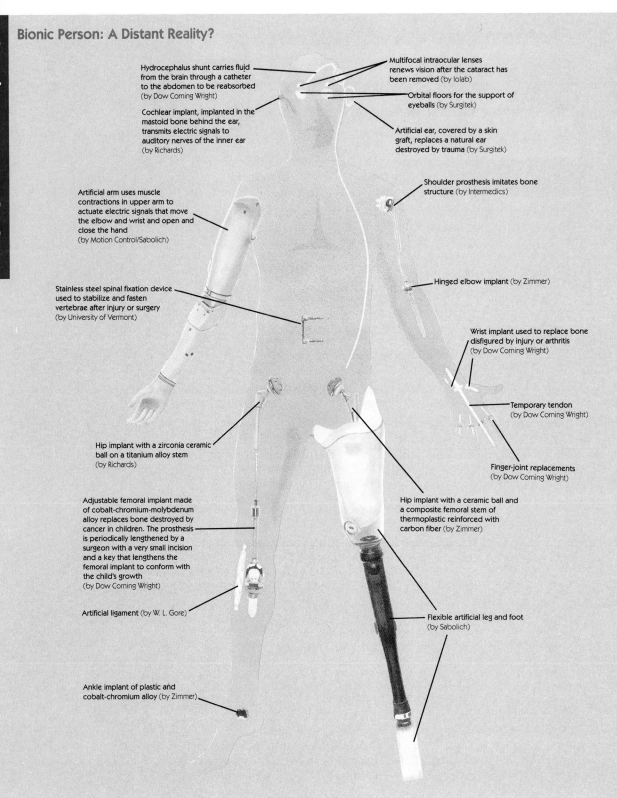

Hydrocephalus shunt carries fluid from the brain through a catheter to the abdomen to be reabsorbed (by Dow Corning Wright)

Cochlear implant, implanted in the mastoid bone behind the ear, transmits electric signals to auditory nerves of the inner ear (by Richards)

Multifocal intraocular lenses renews vision after the cataract has been removed (by Iolab)

Orbital floors for the support of eyeballs (by Surgitek)

Artificial ear, covered by a skin graft, replaces a natural ear destroyed by trauma (by Surgitek)

Artificial arm uses muscle contractions in upper arm to actuate electric signals that move the elbow and wrist and open and close the hand (by Motion Control/Sabolich)

Shoulder prosthesis imitates bone structure (by Intermedics)

Hinged elbow implant (by Zimmer)

Stainless steel spinal fixation device used to stabilize and fasten vertebrae after injury or surgery (by University of Vermont)

Wrist implant used to replace bone disfigured by injury or arthritis (by Dow Corning Wright)

Temporary tendon (by Dow Corning Wright)

Hip implant with a zirconia ceramic ball on a titanium alloy stem (by Richards)

Finger-joint replacements (by Dow Corning Wright)

Adjustable femoral implant made of cobalt-chromium-molybdenum alloy replaces bone destroyed by cancer in children. The prosthesis is periodically lengthened by a surgeon with a very small incision and a key that lengthens the femoral implant to conform with the child's growth (by Dow Corning Wright)

Hip implant with a ceramic ball and a composite femoral stem of thermoplastic reinforced with carbon fiber (by Zimmer)

Artificial ligament (by W. L. Gore)

Flexible artificial leg and foot (by Sabolich)

Ankle implant of plastic and cobalt-chromium alloy (by Zimmer)

Improvements in the design and manufacture of prosthetic equipment have made it easier to use and more functional in various applications. (Jim Argo/Picture Group)

Amputations

Definitions and Concepts.   There are two types of **amputation:** congenital and acquired. Congenital amputations, which are apparent at birth, occur for a variety of reasons that are not fully understood. Acquired amputations are generally the result of an injury or therapeutic surgical procedure. Relatively few children have acquired amputations; most result from accidents or injuries later in life.

Causation and Prevalence.   The causes of congenital amputation are not completely understood. Over the years, a variety of substances have been shown to adversely affect the development of the fetus. Thalidomide, quinine, aminoprotein, and Myleran have all been implicated in congenital amputations in children whose mothers used these drugs during pregnancy. All drugs taken during pregnancy must be considered potentially harmful. Certain genetic or inherited predispositions for congenital abnormalities in the limbs have also been identified. The reasons for the actual triggering of these predispositions remain unknown, but the presence of certain agents, such as those mentioned, heightens the chance for birth defects. The same is true of the rubella virus.

Accurate prevalence figures are difficult to obtain. The current prevalence rate is 1.7 to 8.6 amputees per 1,000 people (Sanders, 1986). Prevalence figures regarding children suggest that about 15 in every 100,000 children have amputations (Jones, 1988).

Interventions.   Children born with congenital amputations generally have an easier time adjusting to treatments and therapies than do individuals who undergo amputations later in life. Children with congenital amputations also adjust more readily to prosthetic equipment and are less reluctant to use it in public settings. Early encouragement of prosthesis use is based on the notion that exposure and practice early in life enhance the skill eventually achieved as well as acceptance of prostheses.

FOCUS 5
Identify treatment goals for individuals with congenital and acquired amputations.

Use of various prostheses occurs in a developmental fashion. Children born with incomplete legs may be provided with customized skateboards to assist them with crawling activities. Later, they may be fitted with artificial legs tailored to their physical dimensions. As children grow and develop, prosthetic devices must be redesigned and modified according to children's changing physical needs. Maintenance and replacement of these devices is very costly.

Individuals with acquired amputations—for instance, due to an accident during their teen or adult years—generally experience shock, consternation, and adjustment problems. The first step in treatment is typically medical. An orthopedic surgeon is responsible for preparing the remainder of the arm or leg for use with a prosthetic device. Following surgery, the second phase of treatment begins, in which the individual is helped to cope with the feelings and self-perceptions that emerge from the loss of a limb. Rehabilitation is the third phase of treatment. During this stage, the orthopedic specialist, prosthetist, occupational therapist, physical therapist, and rehabilitation personnel work together to help the individual with an amputation adjust to his or her condition and prosthetic device.

Muscular Dystrophy

FOCUS 6

Describe the physical limitations associated with muscular dystrophy.

Definitions and Concepts. "Muscular dystrophies are a group of chronic, inherited disorders characterized by progressive weakening and wasting of the voluntary skeletal muscles" (U.S. Department of Health and Human Services, 1980, p. 1). They affect the muscles of the hips, legs, shoulders, and arms. Individuals with **muscular dystrophy** progressively lose their ability to walk and also the effective use of their arms and hands. The loss of ability is attributable to fatty tissue that gradually replaces muscle tissue. Heart muscle may also be affected, in which case symptoms of heart failure may occur. The seriousness of the various dystrophies is influenced by heredity, age of onset, the physical location and nature of onset, and the rate at which the condition progresses.

Causation and Prevalence. The exact causes of the various forms of muscular dystrophy remain unknown. However, some progress has been made in identifying the genes responsible for at least one form of the disease. The etiology of this muscular dystrophy may be related to enzyme disturbances that subsequently affect muscle metabolism.

About 200,000 people are affected by muscular dystrophies and other related disorders. Some estimates indicate that 0.14 in 1,000 people develop muscular dystrophy (Whaley & Wong, 1985).

Interventions. There is no known cure for muscular dystrophy. The focus of treatment is maintaining or improving the individual's functioning and preserving his or her ambulatory independence for as long as possible (Schock, 1985). The first phases of maintenance and prevention are handled by a physical therapist, who works to prevent or correct contractures (a permanent shortening and thickening of muscle fibers). As the condition becomes more serious, treatment generally includes prescribing supportive devices, such as walkers, braces, nightsplints, surgical corsets, and hospital beds. Eventually, the person with muscular dystrophy may be confined to a wheelchair.

People with muscular dystrophy are frequently given some type of medication in hopes of increasing muscle strength and counteracting the disease's effect on the heart. If a child receives medication, parents and teachers play an important role in observing any peculiar reactions that occur. As the condition advances, respiratory muscles are often affected, and the individual may be unable to cough strongly enough to expel mucus and phlegm; this sometimes leads to recurrent pneumonia.

HEALTH DISORDERS

Health disorders affect children, youth, and adults in a variety of ways. For example, a child with juvenile diabetes who has engaged in some vigorous physical activities with classmates may need to drink a little fruit juice or soda pop just before or after the activity to regulate blood sugar levels. Likewise, a youth with a seizure disorder may need to take his or her medication consistently.

As described in IDEA, **health disorders** cause individuals to have "limited strength, vitality or alertness, due to chronic or acute health problems such as a heart condition, tuberculosis, rheumatic fever, nephritis, asthma, sickle cell anemia, hemophilia, epilepsy, lead poisoning, leukemia, or diabetes which adversely affect . . . educational performance" (23 Code of Federal Regulations, Section 300.5 [7]).

Not all of these health conditions will be discussed in this chapter. We will, however, review in some depth acquired immune deficiency syndrome (AIDS), seizure disorders (epilepsy), diabetes, cystic fibrosis, and sickle cell anemia. We will also discuss a number of medical conditions such as child abuse and neglect, adolescent pregnancy, suicide, and cocaine addiction that are not typically thought of as health disorders but nonetheless place children and youth at risk for failure in school, family, and community environments.

Acquired Immune Deficiency Syndrome (AIDS)

Definitions and Concepts.   AIDS in children is defined by the following characteristics: (1) presence of the **human immunodeficiency virus (HIV),** a virus that attacks specialized white cells within the body and/or the presence of antibodies to HIV in the blood or tissues as well as (2) recurrent bacterial diseases (Falloon, Eddy, Roper, & Pizzo, 1988). First reports regarding some of the features of AIDS were received by the Centers for Disease Control in the spring of 1981. These reports dealt exclusively with young men who had a

Ryan White's long battle with AIDS drew attention to the fact that *all* people are vulnerable to this disease. (Max Winter/Picture Group)

rare form of pneumonia. Reports were received simultaneously by the Centers for Disease Control regarding an increased incidence of a rare skin tumor, Kaposi's sarcoma. Individuals who had developed these conditions were homosexual men in their thirties and forties. Many died or were severely debilitated within 12 months of diagnosis.

Prior to the spring of 1981, primary-care physicians in New York, San Francisco, and other large cities had seen many cases of swollen lymph nodes in homosexual men. Many of these individuals exhibited this condition for months or even years after their initial diagnosis without suffering serious side effects. However, those who developed **opportunistic infections** often experienced severe side effects or even death. Eventually, these opportunistic infections were linked to a breakdown in the functioning of the **immune system.** People affected with these infections exhibit pronounced depletions of a particular subset of white blood cells, T lymphocytes. White blood cells fight infections; without sufficient numbers and kinds of them, the body is rendered defenseless. Individuals with this condition become subject to a wide range of opportunistic infections and tumors affecting the gastrointestinal system, central nervous system, and skin.

Causation and Prevalence.   Once the particular elements of AIDS had been identified, scientific and medical communities focused their attention on identifying its cause. Late in 1983, scientists in France and the United States were able to isolate two viruses with affinities for T lymphocytes. Several names were generated for these viruses, but eventually, the designation that prevailed was *human immunodeficiency virus (HIV)*. This virus is passed from one person to another through blood and unscreened blood products, semen, cervical and vaginal secretions, and perhaps breast milk.

Children may receive the HIV virus through a number of pathways. Some children and teenagers have been exposed through blood transfusions. In the past, individuals with hemophilia were particularly at risk for receiving blood that contained HIV. However, tests are now available to detect its presence in donated blood.

Another way in which children acquire the virus is through their mothers. Mothers who are pregnant and have received the virus through intravenous drug use or other means transmit it to their unborn children. Many of these children develop AIDS and die before their second birthday. In a very few cases, sexual abuse is the source of AIDS in children (Falloon et al., 1988).

Currently, more than 110,000 cases of AIDS have been reported in the United States (Osmond, 1990a). However, the number of individuals infected with the HIV virus range from 0.5 to 3 million individuals. Preliminary studies have suggested that 0.9 to 3.2 per 1,000 infants are born with HIV (Osmond, 1990b). The World Health Organization has estimated that 3 million women and children will die during the 1990s from AIDS-related complications worldwide (Chin, 1990). It has further been predicted that, between 1993 and 1996, a total of 10 million individuals worldwide will die of AIDS (Gotta, 1989).

At least two factors will influence the incidence figures as well as deaths related to AIDS in the United States and elsewhere during the 1990s: (1) the success or failure of various interventions and (2) the emergence of new, related viruses (Goedert & Blattner, 1988).

Information regarding the prevalence of AIDS among children and infants is far less accurate and complete than that for adults. In August 1987, there were 558 confirmed cases of AIDS in children under 13 years of age in the United States. It is anticipated that the number of AIDS cases in children in the United States will swell well beyond 3,000 within the next several years. Sixty percent of the children who test positive for HIV and eventually develop AIDS die. "Which children or what proportion of children will progress to symptoms, opportunistic infections, malignancy or death cannot be predicted" (Falloon et al., 1988, p. 346). Children who develop AIDS at a young age appear to have a shorter median survival rate than those who develop it when they are older.

Interventions.   To date, there is no known cure for AIDS. Although much work is being done with new drugs (e.g., interferon, interleukin II, ribavain, zidovudine, and azidothymidine), no effective treatment has been found (Polsky & Armstrong, 1988). However, progress is being made, and certain agents are now ready for testing or have been tested in human beings.

Interventions for infants and children with AIDS are in the beginning stages. The medication most frequently used with infants and children having AIDS is immunoglobin. It is used to control, to the degree possible, the infectious diseases that attack these children. Eventually, more use will be made of the antiviral therapies that are being developed for adults (Falloon et al., 1988).

Prevention of AIDS in children as well as others is a multifaceted and very complicated process (Christi, Siegel, & Moynihan, 1988). Motivating people to change their behaviors through public information campaigns and education programs has met with some success (Homans & Aggleton, 1988). There appear to be reductions in new cases of AIDS, particularly among homosexual males. Less progress has been made in reducing the incidence among intravenous drug users. Unfortunately, many innocent children become victims of AIDS because of the drug abuse of their mothers or their AIDS-infected partners.

At this point, prevention is the single most effective means of controlling the spread of AIDS. At the heart of prevention is informed choice and individual empowerment to make responsible decisions regarding one's own health, as well as that of others. Current health education programs emphasize health enhancement and an understanding of the personal, social, environmental, and economic factors that influence healthy behavior rather than mere information distribution about the causes and effects of AIDS (Homans & Aggleton, 1988). In many parts of the United States, counseling is now an integral part of prevention programs. When provided with information about safe sexual practices—including the cautious selection of sexual partners, abstinence, and the use of prophylactics—individuals in greater numbers are making choices that favor good health for them and their intimates (McKusick, Horstman, & Coates, 1985; Silverman, 1986).

Seizure Disorders (Epilepsy)

Definitions and Concepts.   The terms **seizure disorders** and **epilepsy** are used to describe a variety of disorders of brain function characterized by recurrent seizures. A **seizure** is a cluster of behaviors that occur in response to abnormal neurochemical activity in the brain. It typically has the effect of altering the individual's level of consciousness while simultaneously resulting in certain characteristic motor patterns. Several classification schemes have been employed to describe the various types of seizure disorders. We will briefly discuss two types of seizures: tonic/clonic and absence (Dreifuss, 1988).

Tonic/clonic seizures, formerly called *grand mal seizures,* are seizures in which the entire brain is affected. The **tonic** phase of these seizures is characterized by a stiffening of the body. The **clonic** phase is characterized by repeated muscle contractions and relaxations. Tonic/clonic seizures are often preceded by a warning signal known as an **aura,** in which the individual senses a unique sound, odor, or physical sensation just prior to the onset of the seizure. In some instances, the seizure is also signaled by a cry or other similar sound. The tonic phase of the seizure begins with a loss of consciousness, after which the individual falls to the ground. Initially, the trunk and head of the body become rigid during the tonic phase. The clonic phase follows and consists of involuntary muscle contractions (violent shaking) of the extremities. Irregular breathing, blueness in the lips and face, increased salivation, loss of bladder and bowel control, and perspiration may occur to some degree.

The nature, scope, frequency, and duration of tonic/clonic seizures vary greatly from person to person. Such seizures may last as long as 20 minutes or less than 1 minute. One

FOCUS 7
What steps should be taken to assist infants and children with AIDS?

FOCUS 8
Describe immediate treatment for a person who is experiencing a tonic/clonic seizure.

of the most dangerous aspects of tonic/clonic seizures is potential injury from falling and striking objects in the environment. In responding to this type of seizure, it is best to ease the person to the floor, if possible; remove any dangerous objects from the immediate vicinity; place a soft pad under his or her head, such as a coat or blanket; and allow him or her to rest after the seizure has terminated.

A period of sleepiness and confusion usually follows a tonic/clonic seizure. The individual may exhibit drowsiness, nausea, headache, or a combination of these symptoms. Such symptoms should be treated with appropriate rest, medication, or other therapeutic remedies. Seizure characteristics and aftereffects vary along a number of dimensions and should be treated with this in mind.

Absence seizures, formerly identified as *petit mal seizures,* are characterized by brief periods (moments or seconds) of inattention that may be accompanied by rapid eye blinking and head twitching. During these seizures, "the brain's normal activity shuts down" (Dreifuss, 1988, p. 3). The individual's consciousness is altered in an almost imperceptible manner. People with this type of seizure disorder may experience these miniseizures as often as 100 times a day.

Such inattentive behavior may be viewed as daydreaming by a teacher or work supervisor, but the episode is really due to a momentary burst of abnormal brain activity that the individual does not consciously control. The lapses in attention caused by this form of epilepsy can greatly hamper the individual's ability to respond properly to or profit from a teacher's presentation or a supervisor's instruction. Treatment and control of absence seizures is generally achieved through prescribed medication.

Causation and Prevalence.   Exact causation of the various types of epilepsy remains unclear. Similarly, precise reasons for the actual triggering of a seizure are also unknown. However, any condition that adversely affects the brain is a potential cause, such as head trauma, neural chemical irregularities, inflammation, and tumors.

Prevalence figures for seizure disorders vary, in part because of the social stigma associated with them. Studies have indicated that 0.6 to 0.9 percent of the population is directly affected by seizure disorders (Dreifuss, 1988). Seventy-five percent of all individuals who have seizures experience their first one prior to their eighteenth birthday (Dreifuss, 1988).

Interventions.   Treatment of epileptic conditions takes a variety of forms. The electroencephalograph is fundamental to the diagnostic process and assists physicians in assessing brain wave activity. This instrument is also helpful in identifying structural abnormalities within the brain. It should be noted that many seizure disorders are not detectable through electroencephalographic measures. A **CAT scan** of the brain is usually obtained to rule out the presence of structural abnormalities (e.g., brain tumors) or hemorrhaging.

Many types of seizures can be successfully treated with careful medical and drug management. Antiepileptic drugs must be chosen very carefully, however. The risk-benefit proportion of each medication must be balanced. Once an antiepileptic drug has been prescribed, families should be educated in its use to be aware of any side effects and the necessity for consistent administration. Maintaining a regular medication regimen can be very challenging for children and their parents. In some instances, medication may be discontinued after several years of seizure-free behavior (Dreifuss, 1988). This is particularly true for those young children who do not have some form of underlying brain pathology.

As with other neurological conditions, some individuals with seizure disorders also have serious accompanying problems, such as mental retardation, cerebral palsy, and emotional difficulties. Each individual with a seizure disorder must be treated with an array of medical, educational, social, and psychological strategies. Special education is not generally required for children with seizure disorders, unless the seizures are symptomatic of other more serious disabilities that adversely affect their academic and social functioning.

Individuals with seizure disorders need responses from others that are calm and supportive. Treatment efforts of various professionals and family members must be carefully orchestrated to provide these individuals with an optimal chance to use their abilities and talents.

Diabetes

Definitions and Concepts.   **Diabetes** is a developmental or hereditary disorder characterized by inadequate secretion or use of insulin produced by the pancreas to process carbohydrates. Glucose—a sugar, one of the end products of digesting carbohydrates—is used by the body for energy. Some glucose is used quickly, while some is stored in the liver and muscles for later use. However, muscle and liver cells cannot absorb and store the energy produced by glucose without **insulin,** a hormone produced by the pancreas that converts glucose into energy for use in body cells to perform their various functions. Without insulin, glucose accumulates in the blood, causing a condition known as *hyperglycemia*. Left untreated, this condition can cause serious, immediate problems for people with diabetes, leading to loss of consciousness or diabetic coma.

Typical symptoms associated with glucose buildup in the blood are extreme hunger, thirst, and frequent urination. Although progress has been made in regulating insulin levels, the prevention and treatment of the complications that accompany diabetes—including blindness, cardiovascular disease, and kidney disease—still pose tremendous challenges for health care specialists.

Juvenile diabetes is particularly troublesome. Compared to the adult form, the juvenile disease tends to be more severe and progresses more quickly. Generally, the symptoms are easily recognized. The child develops an unusual thirst for water and other liquids. His or

The regular intake of insulin is essential for youth with juvenile diabetes. (Jean-Claude Lejeune/Stock, Boston)

FOCUS 9
Identify three problems that individuals with diabetes may eventually experience.

her appetite also increases substantially, but listlessness and fatigue occur despite increased food and liquid intake.

Causation and Prevalence.   The causes of diabetes remain obscure, although considerable research has been conducted on the biochemical mechanisms responsible for it. An individual's environment and heredity interact in determining the severity and the long-term nature of the condition. Juvenile diabetes, more so than the adult form, appears to be more clearly linked to hereditary factors.

It is estimated that 5 percent of the U.S. population has diabetes. The prevalence rate for children with insulin-dependent (i.e., must administer insulin) diabetes is approximately 10 per 100,000 children. The peak incidence periods occur between 11 and 14 years of age (Greenberg, 1987). Recent studies indicate that, by age 18, approximately 1 in 300 to 400 Caucasian children in the United States have acquired insulin-dependent diabetes (Ross, Bernstein, & Rifkin, 1983).

Interventions.   Medical treatment centers around the regular administration of insulin, which is essential for children with juvenile diabetes. Several exciting advances have been made in recent years to monitor blood sugar levels and deliver insulin to people with diabetes. Also, recent success with pancreas transplants has virtually eliminated the disease for some individuals.

Maintaining normal levels of glucose is now achieved in many instances with an **insulin infusion pump,** which is worn by persons with diabetes and powered by small batteries. The infusion pump operates continuously and delivers the dose of insulin determined by the physician and the patient. This form of treatment is only effective if used in combination with carefully followed diet and exercise programs (Raskin, 1983).

Juvenile diabetes is a lifelong condition that can have a pronounced effect on the child in a number of areas. Complications for children with long-standing diabetes include blindness, heart attacks, and kidney problems. Many of these problems can be delayed or prevented by maintaining adequate blood sugar levels.

Cystic Fibrosis

Definitions and Concepts.   **Cystic fibrosis (CF)** is an inherited, systemic, generalized disease that begins at conception. Although the life span of persons with CF has been lengthened through new treatments, death within the early adult years is often inevitable. CF is a disorder of the secretion glands, which produce abnormal amounts of mucus, sweat, and saliva. Three major organ systems are affected: the lungs, pancreas, and sweat glands. The gluelike mucus in the lungs obstructs their functioning and increases the likelihood of infection. After repeated infection, the lungs are gradually destroyed. As lung deterioration occurs, the heart is burdened, and heart failure may result. The pancreas is affected in a similar fashion. Excessive amounts of mucus prevent critical digestive enzymes from reaching the small intestine. Without these enzymes, proteins and fats consumed by the individual with CF are lost in frequent, greasy, flatulent stools.

Causation and Prevalence.   The causes of cystic fibrosis are unclear, and many theories exist regarding its origin (Boat & Dearborn, 1984). It is known, however, that cystic fibrosis is an inherited disease (Cystic Fibrosis Foundation, 1988).

Cystic fibrosis is primarily a Caucasian phenomenon. Studies conducted in the United States have demonstrated a minimum prevalence range of from 1 in 2,000 Caucasian children to 1 in 17,000 African-American children (Doershuk & Boat, 1987).

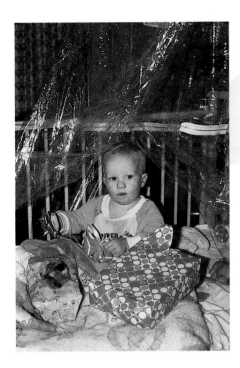

Management of respiratory conditions is critical to the well-being of individuals with cystic fibrosis. (Alan Carey/Photo Researchers, Inc.)

Interventions. The prognosis for an individual with cystic fibrosis depends on a number of factors. The two most critical are early diagnosis of the condition and the quality of care provided after diagnosis. If diagnosis occurs late, preliminary damage may have already occurred and be irreversible. With early diagnosis and appropriate medical care, most individuals with CF can achieve weight and growth gains similar to those of their normal peers. Early diagnosis and improved treatment strategies have lengthened the average life span of children with cystic fibrosis; more than half now live beyond their twentieth year (Walker, Durie, Hamilton, Walker-Smith, & Watkins, 1991).

Interventions for cystic fibrosis are varied and complex, with treatment continuing throughout the person's lifetime. Consistent and appropriate application of medical, social, educational, and psychological components of treatment allow these individuals to live longer and with less discomfort and fewer complications than in years past.

Treatment of cystic fibrosis is designed to accomplish a number of goals. The first is to diagnose the condition before any severe symptoms are exhibited. Other goals include control of chest infection, maintenance of adequate nutrition, education of the family regarding the condition, and provision of a suitable education for the child.

Management of respiratory disease caused by cystic fibrosis is critical. If respiratory insufficiency can be prevented or minimized, the individual's life will be greatly enhanced and prolonged. Diet management is also essential for the child with cystic fibrosis. Generally, the child with this condition requires more caloric intake than his or her normal peers. The diet should be high in protein and adjusted appropriately if the child fails to grow and/or make appropriate weight gains.

The major social and psychological problems of children with CF relate to chronic coughing, small stature, offensive stools, gas, delayed onset of puberty and secondary sex characteristics, and unsatisfying social relationships. Children with CF may also experience chronic physical complications that portend death. Counseling or psychiatric support and a sensitive teacher may be helpful to children who have these problems.

FOCUS 10
Identify interventions used in treating children with cystic fibrosis.

INTERACTING IN NATURAL SETTINGS · · · · · · · · · · · · People with Physical and Health Disorders · · · · · · · · · ·

EARLY CHILDHOOD YEARS

Tips for the Family

- Work closely with medical personnel to lessen the overall impact of the disorder over time.
- Provide the child with physical or health disorders opportunities to freely explore his or her environment to the maximum degree possible. This may require some adaptations or specialized equipment (e.g., custom-made wheelchairs, prosthetic devices, etc.).
- Involve the child with other children as time and energy permit. Only children can teach each other certain things.
- Join advocacy/support groups that provide the information and assistance that you need.

Tips for the Preschool Teacher

- Be sure that the physical environment in the classroom lends itself to the needs of children who may have physical or health disorders (e.g., aisles in the classroom are sufficiently large for free movement in a wheelchair).
- Become aware of specific needs of the child by consulting with parents. For example, the child may need to refrain from highly physical activities.

Tips for Preschool Personnel

- Be sure that other key personnel in the school who interact directly with the child are informed of his or her needs.
- Orient all the children in your classroom setting to the needs of the child with physical or health disorders.
- Be sure that arrangements have been made for emergency situations. Classmates should know how they may be helpful in directing and assisting the child during a fire drill or other emergency procedure.

Tips for Neighbors and Friends

- Involve the child with physical or health disorders and his or her family in holiday gatherings.
- Become aware of the things that you may need to do that may require a little additional effort. For example, you may need to know what you should do if the child has a seizure.
- Be inclusive rather than exclusive. Involve the child in all activities that you normally would, given his or her abilities and interests.

ELEMENTARY YEARS

Tips for the Family

- Maintain a healthy and ongoing relationship with the care providers that are a part of your child's life.
- Continue to be involved with advocacy/support groups.

- Stay informed by subscribing to newsletters that are produced and disseminated by advocacy organizations.
- Develop and maintain good relationships with the persons who teach and serve your child within the school setting.
- Remember that the goal over time is your child's development of independence or appropriate interdependence.

Tips for the Regular School Teacher

- Be informed and willing to learn about the unique needs of the child with physical or health disorders in your classroom. For example, schedule a conference with the child's parents before the year begins to talk about medications, prosthetic devices, levels of desired physical activities, and so on.
- Assume that "we are all in this together!" Think about what you would want for this child if you were his or her parent.
- Inform the other children in the class. Help them become aware of their critical role contributing to the well-being of the child with physical or health disorders.
- Use socially competent and mature peers to assist you (e.g., providing tutoring, physical assistance, social support in recess activities).
- Be sure that plans have been made and practiced for dealing with emergency situations (e.g., some children may need to be carried out of a building or room).
- If the child's condition is progressive and life threatening, begin to discuss the ramifications of death and loss. Many excellent books about this topic are available for children.

Tips for School Personnel

- Be sure that all key personnel in the school setting who interact with the child on a regular basis are informed. If they know what to do, they can perform with confidence.
- Meet periodically as professionals to deal with emergent problems, brainstorm for solutions, and identify suitable actions.
- Create an environment within the school that is inclusive and child centered. Children can be involved periodically in brainstorming activities that focus on involving the child with physical or health disorders to the maximum degree possible.
- Institute cross-age tutoring and support. When possible, have the child with a physical or health condition become a tutor.
- Be aware that the delivery of medical care and other related services may, from time to time, interfere with the child's performance.

Neighbors and Friends

- Involve the child with physical or health disorders in your family activities.
- Provide parents with some respite care. They will appreciate the time to themselves.
- Be informed! Be aware of the needs of the child by regularly talking to his or her parents. They will sincerely appreciate your concern.

Tips for the Family

- Remember that, for some individuals with physical or health disorders, the secondary or young adult years may be the most trying, particularly if the conditions are progressive in nature.
- Continue in your efforts to contribute to the individual's independence. Remember, this is the "letting go" phase.
- Begin planning early in the secondary school years for the youth's transition from the public school to the adult world.
- Be sure that you are well informed about the adult services offered in your community and state.

Tips for the Regular School Teacher

- Continue to be aware of the potential needs for accommodation and adjustment.
- Treat the individual as an adult.
- Realize that the youth's studies may be interrupted from time to time with medical treatments or other important health care services.

Tips for School Personnel

- Develop a school climate that is supportive of all students. Personnel should make a point to interact with students with phys-ical and health disorders in all appropriate settings (e.g., athletic events, dances, etc.).
- Provide opportunities for all students to receive recognition and be involved in school-related activities.
- Realize that peer assistance and tutoring may be particularly helpful to certain students. Social involvement outside the school setting should be encouraged (e.g., going to movies, attending concerts, etc.).
- Use members of teacher assistance teams to assist with unique problems that surface from time to time.
- Provide recognition to those school personnel who make significant contributions to students with disabilities (e.g., regular class teachers, counselors, custodians, etc.).

Tips for Neighbors, Friends, and Potential Employers

- Continue to be involved in the individual's life.
- Be aware of assistance that you might provide in the event of a youth's gradual deterioration or death.
- Involve the individual in age-appropriate activities (e.g., cookouts, video nights, or community events).
- Encourage your own teens to volunteer as peer tutors or volunteers.
- If you are an employer, provide opportunities for job sampling, on-the-job training, or actual employment.

Sickle Cell Anemia

Definitions and Concepts.   **Sickle cell anemia (SCA)** is a chronic disorder that has a profound impact on the function and structure of red blood cells. The hemoglobin molecule in the red blood cells of individuals with SCA is abnormal. More specifically, the hemoglobin molecule is vulnerable to structural collapse when the blood–oxygen level is significantly diminished. As the blood–oxygen level declines, these blood cells become distorted and form bizarre shapes. This distortion process is known as *sickling.* Cells that normally have donutlike shapes now appear as microscopic sickle blades.

People affected by sickle cell anemia experience unrelenting **anemia.** In some cases, it is tolerated well; in others, the condition is quite debilitating (Huntsman, 1987). Another aspect of SCA involves periodic vascular blockage, which occurs as a function of the sickled cells blocking microvascular channels. The blocking can often cause severe and chronic pain in the extremities, abdomen, or back. In addition, the disease may affect any organ system of the body (Serjeant, 1985). SCA also has a significant negative effect on the physical growth and development of infants and children (Bunn & Forget, 1986).

Causation and Prevalence.   Sickle cell anemia is caused by various combinations of genes that are inherited. A child who receives a mutant S-hemoglobin gene from each parent exhibits SCA to one degree or another.

SCA occurs in about 0.1 to 1.3 percent of the African-American population. The actual prevalence of SCA in African Americans is 141 per 100,000 (Wintrobe et al., 1981).

Interventions.   A number of treatments may be employed to deal with the problems and pain caused by sickle cell anemia. Individuals usually learn to adapt to their anemia and

FOCUS 11

Describe the impact of the sickling of cells on body tissues.

lead relatively normal lives. When their lives are interrupted by crises, a variety of treatment approaches may be used. Medication may help those with severe anemia. Other medical procedures may be aimed at raising the hemoglobin level in the blood.

Several factors predispose an individual to a SCA crisis: dehydration from fever, reduced liquid intake, and hypoxia (air that is poor in oxygen content). Stress, fatigue, and exposure to cold temperatures should be avoided by those who have a history of SCA crises.

Treatment of crises is generally directed at keeping the individual warm, increasing liquid intake, ensuring good blood oxygenation, and administering medication for infection. Assistance can also be provided during crisis periods by partial-exchange blood transfusions with fresh, normal red cells. Transfusions may also be necessary for individuals with SCA who are preparing for surgery or are pregnant.

Child Abuse and Neglect

Definitions and Concepts. **Child abuse** is defined as nonaccidental harm inflicted by family members or other individuals that negatively impacts a child's development and functioning. The abuse may be sexual, psychological, or physical in nature. We will review briefly each of these forms of abuse.

Child abuse can be regarded as a means of coping by the abuser, although an unfortunate and inappropriate one. All parents and caregivers are confronted with personal and family challenges that influence their responses to children. Some parents are able to cope with these challenges with adaptive behaviors that are not harmful to their children, while others respond with maladaptive behaviors that are harmful.

Child neglect results when parents choose to deal with pressures and strains by not caring for or abandoning their children. In short, children who are not adequately cared for are considered neglected. They are often malnourished, infrequently bathed or changed, left without suitable supervision, and rarely held or appropriately stimulated.

A seven-year-old boy who was sexually abused by his father drew this picture. He explains the purpose of the boat: "So I can take my father away." (Courtesy of Lears)

Another form of child mistreatment is **sexual abuse**—incest, assault, or sexual exploitation. Forty-four percent of sexual abusers are parents, members of the victim's immediate family, other relatives, neighbors, or close acquaintances of the family (Summit, 1985). Some refer to sexual abuse as a "psychological time bomb." This bomb may go off at any time, having profound psychological effects on children as youth or adults.

Other forms of abuse are much more elusive. The psychological and verbal abuse that some children experience is viewed by most professionals to be just as serious as physical abuse. Verbal abuse in the form of put-downs and sarcasm may have a profound impact on a child's self-esteem and overall personality development. The psychological and emotional injuries suffered by all abused and neglected children may never heal entirely.

Causation and Prevalence.   A number of variables may cause a parent or caregiver to be abusive. In fact, the phenomenon is the product of several constellations of interacting factors. Research has indicated that 30 to 35 percent of abusive parents were mistreated by their own mothers and fathers (Kaufman & Zigler, 1987); the intergenerational nature of child abuse is a strong causative factor. There are many other contributing factors, as well, including crises caused by unemployment, unwanted pregnancy, and economic difficulties (Meier, 1985).

Establishing accurate and precise prevalence estimates for child abuse is very difficult. In addition to the problem of underreporting, much of the difficulty is attributable to the lack of consistent criteria for child abuse and reporting procedures used in various states. Current prevalence estimates for physical abuse, neglect, and sexual exploitation of children 18 years old and younger are 1.25 to 1.5 percent. During 1989, 2.4 million cases of child abuse were reported (National Center on Child Abuse Prevention Research, 1990). Twenty-seven percent involved charges of physical abuse, 16 percent involved charges of sexual abuse, 8 percent were attributed to emotional maltreatment, and 55 percent involved charges of child neglect. Approximately 1,100 to 1,200 children in the United States die as a result of physical abuse each year (National Center on Child Abuse Prevention Research, 1990). The overall mortality rate due to child abuse is approximately 3 percent (Meier, 1985).

Child abuse and neglect occur among all ethnic groups and at all socioeconomic levels. Thus, all educators of children and youth must be aware of its existence and be willing to address it. Most state laws designate educators and other professionals who work with children (e.g., health care providers, police officers, social workers, clergy) as *mandated reporters,* which means they have a legal responsibility to report suspected abuse or neglect to their administrators and/or appropriate law enforcement or child protection agencies. Laws vary from state to state; thus, educators must become familiar with the definition of abuse used in their jurisdiction, as well as what their responsibilities are in reporting. Depending on the circumstances, most jurisdictions allow for immediate action to safeguard a child from imminent danger once a report has been made.

Clearly, reporting child abuse or neglect is a serious undertaking; however, the responsibility need not be intimidating. While the reporter should have ample reason to *suspect* that abuse or neglect has occurred, he or she is not responsible for *proving* that it has. Moreover, laws often protect individuals who report abuse and neglect by ensuring some level of confidentiality. The reporter's primary consideration should be the welfare of the child.

Interventions.   Treatment of child abuse and neglect is a multifaceted process (Kempe, 1987). The entire family must be involved. The first goal is to treat the abused child for any serious injuries and simultaneously prevent further harm or neglect. Hospitalization may be necessary to deal with immediate physical injuries or other complications. During hospitalization, the child protection and treatment team, in conjunction with the

FOCUS 12
Identify four factors that may contribute to child abuse and neglect.

family, develop a comprehensive treatment plan. Once the child's immediate medical needs have been met, a variety of treatment options may be employed: individual play therapy, therapeutic play school, regular preschool, foster care, residential care, hospitalization, and/or group treatment.

Treatment for parents and families of abused children is similar to that provided for the children. Treatment options include but are not limited to individual psychotherapy, marital and family therapy, group therapy, crisis hotlines, and crisis nurseries (Meier, 1985).

Adolescent Pregnancy

Definitions and Concepts.   Adolescent pregnancy is the outcome of conception in girls 19 years or younger. Three-quarters of the pregnancies that occur during the adolescent years are unwanted. The great majority of teen parents remain unmarried, leave school, experience severe financial problems, and frequently become reliant on welfare (Compton, Duncan, & Hruska, 1987).

Teens undergo a large number of developmental changes during adolescence: the construction of an identity; development of personal relationships and responsibilities; gradual preparation for vocational or professional work through education; emancipation from their parents; and various adjustments to a complex society. Many if not all of these developmental changes are significantly affected by pregnancy.

The risks associated with adolescent pregnancy are substantial if the mother is 15 years old or younger. Children born to these mothers experience higher rates of (1) infant mortality, (2) birth defects, (3) mental retardation, (4) central nervous system problems, and (5) intelligence deficits (Delano, 1986). Additionally, adolescent fathers are often fathers in absentia; few truly assume the role of a parent. It is the adolescent mother and her immediate family who shoulder most of the burden of caring for and supporting the child.

Teens who become pregnant, as well as their families, require support and counseling to address personal issues and make decisions about the welfare of their unborn children. (Ulrike Welsch)

Causation and Prevalence.   Adolescent girls become pregnant for a number of varied and complex reasons. Delano (1986) suggested several different types of contributing factors. General factors include a lack of knowledge about conception and sexuality, lack of access to contraceptives, misuse of contraceptives, a desire to escape family control, an attempt to be more adult, a desire to have someone to love, a means of gaining attention and care, and an inability to make sound decisions. Societal factors also play a role in the increased number of adolescents who become pregnant; contributing factors include greater permissiveness and freedom, social pressure from peers, and continual exposure to sexuality through the media.

FOCUS 13
Identify factors that may contribute to the increased prevalence of adolescent pregnancy.

The prevalence of adolescent pregnancy is staggering. In the United States, 8.2 percent of all births are to unwed, teenage mothers (Center of the Study of Social Policy, 1991). Twenty-five percent of all women become pregnant before age 18 and about 45 percent by age 21. For African-American women, the statistics are even more overwhelming: 40 percent become pregnant by age 18, and nearly 66 percent by age 21 (Hayes, 1987).

It is important to remember that not all pregnancies end in childbirth. In fact, about 40 percent of all teenagers choose abortion, and slightly more than 10 percent suffer miscarriages (Hayes, 1987).

Interventions.   The goals of treatment for the pregnant adolescent can be many and varied. The first goal for the prospective mother is to help her cope with the discovery of being pregnant. What emerges from this discovery is a crisis—for her, for the father, and for the families of both individuals. Adolescents may respond with denial, disbelief, bitterness, disillusionment, or a variety of other feelings. Parents often react to the announcement with anger, often followed by shame and guilt.

Treatment during this period is focused on reducing interpersonal and intrapersonal strain and tension. A wise counselor involves the family in crisis intervention, which is achieved through careful mediation and problem solving. For many adolescents, this period involves some very intense decision making: Should I keep the baby? Should I have the baby and then put it up for adoption? Should I have an abortion? If the adolescent chooses to have the baby, nutritional support for the developing infant, quality prenatal care, training for eventual child care, education, and employment skills become the focus of the intervention efforts (Delano, 1986).

Group processes have been used extensively in the rehabilitation and treatment of pregnant adolescents (Sadler, Corbett, & Meyer, 1987). Groups provide adolescents with an opportunity to develop friendships based on mutual needs. The communication that takes place in such group settings is often uniquely suited to the needs and perspectives of the adolescents involved. Members of the group likewise provide a form of psychological support for each other. As relationships and friendships grow, other types of support also emerge.

Unfortunately, many services rendered to pregnant adolescents fade after delivery of the child. This is most unfortunate, for the problem is one that requires ongoing attention and follow-up; problems do not cease with delivery. The development of functional life skills for independent living is a long-term educational and rehabilitation process. If adolescents are not assisted in developing these survival skills, they are likely to return to the decision-making processes and behaviors of the past.

Suicide in Youth

Definitions and Concepts.   **Suicide** in youth is generally a premeditated act that culminates in the taking of one's life (Hicks, 1990). It is a means of satisfying needs, alleviating

12–4　　What to Do If a Friend Is Thinking of Suicide

1. Do not be afraid to talk about suicide or to use the word. This will not put the idea in a friend's head or influence him or her to do it.
2. Try to get your friend to talk about what it is in life that makes him or her feel this way. The more talking, the better.
3. Try to convince your friend to speak to a trusted adult: parents, a teacher, a coach, or a counselor. Tell your friend that you want him or her to get more help than you alone can give. Go with your friend to speak with an adult, if necessary.
4. Unless you are absolutely certain that your friend has spoken to an adult about suicide, you should speak to an adult about your concern. It is better if you tell your friend you intend to do this.
5. Confidentiality. If your friend asks you not to tell anyone, should you keep the secret? NO. There is no rule of confidentiality when it comes to potential suicide. It does no good to keep the secret and lose the person.
6. Your friend may be angry and try to convince you that you will get him or her in trouble if you tell. If you still believe your friend is at risk, act now. All you can do is try to convey the idea that you are sincerely trying to help.

Source: From *Adolescent Suicidal Behavior* (pp. 187–188) by D. K. Curran, 1987, Washington, DC: Hemisphere Publishing Corporation.

---

pain, and coping with the challenges and stressors that are inherent to being a youth in today's society. Suicide is now the third most common form of death in young people 15 to 24 years of age in the United States (Pfeffer, 1986). Well over 5,000 adolescents and young adults commit suicide each year.

FOCUS 14

Identify the major causes of youth suicide.

Causation and Prevalence.　　The causes of suicide are multidimensional (Pfeffer, 1986). As Novick (1984) suggested, "Suicide is best viewed as the result of a complex interaction of many factors taking place over a long span of time" (p. 135). Suicide is rarely, if ever, an impulsive act. Generally, it is the culmination of serious, numerous, and long-standing problems (Curran, 1987). As a child moves into adolescence, these problems often become more serious.

Another key factor is repeated failure. Despite their best efforts in attempting to resolve problems, many youth are simply unsuccessful. Progressive failure leads to isolation from meaningful relationships. Often, just prior to a youth's suicide, there is a dissolution of any remaining important relationships.

Obviously, the sequence of events varies for each youth; however, the antecedents are generally the same. Often, it is not the presence of certain critical events in the lives of these young people but their perception of these events that is so decisive. Some of these events include abandonment, parents' divorce, death of a parent, remarriage of a parent, major moves, and school changes. Collectively, the events may be described as a series of losses and disruptions. Another important feature of these events is that they seem endless.

Other causative factors of suicide by youth have been identified by researchers. Some have suggested that suicide is a product of heredity triggered by overwhelming environmental stress (Ford, Rushforth, & Sudak, 1984; Kety, 1985). Suicide may also be an outgrowth of major depressive disorders. Studies have indicated that many depressed youth who exhibit these disorders have accompanying abnormalities in several hormonal systems of the body (Ambrosini, Rabinovich, & Puig-Antich, 1984).

Substance abuse of all forms also contributes to suicide (Curran, 1987). Due to the effects of drugs or alcohol, a young person's effectiveness in dealing with the primary problems of adolescence will be reduced, and numerous secondary problems may result, as well. Still another major contributor to the dramatic rise in suicide in youth may be the changes that have occurred in the structure and stability of the family (Fuchs, 1983).

The reported prevalence of suicide among young people is 8.7 per 100,000 (Curran, 1987). However, most professionals believe that this figure represents only a small portion of the actual number of youth suicides (Guetzloe, 1989). Far more young males than females commit suicide; the most conservative estimate suggests that the ratio of male to female suicides is 5 to 1 (Hicks, 1990).

Interventions. Treatment of suicidal youth is directed at protecting them from further harm, decreasing acute suicidal tendencies, and decreasing suicide risk factors. Interventions are also aimed at enhancing factors that protect against suicidal tendencies and decrease vulnerability to repeated suicidal behavior (Pfeffer, 1986).

Hospitalization may be the first step. Any physical injuries or complications that the youth may have suffered are addressed first. Then, a variety of professionals, together with parents, begin the planning process and implementation of treatment. Therapies directed at decreasing the problems manifested by suicide attempters include individual, peer-group, and family therapy.

Multiple levels and kinds of prevention may be implemented for youth who are suicidal. For example, crisis intervention is directed at moving youth away from imminent suicide and making referrals for appropriate treatment. In contrast, prevention programs are designed to provide early intervention, assist youth in developing coping skills, teach them how to manage stress, and provide counseling and other therapeutic services for children and adolescents throughout their school years (Curran, 1987; Hicks, 1990). Prevention is a community endeavor in many ways. The goal is to develop a network of social connections that give adolescents meaningful experiences with peers and other individuals. These connections may avert the problems that are often associated with loneliness and alienation.

Cocaine Addiction

Definition and Concepts. Expectant mothers who use cocaine intravenously, intranasally, or through smoking place themselves as well as their babies at risk for a variety of serious and sometimes life-threatening problems. Problems for these pregnant women include seizures, shortness of breath, lung damage, nasal membrane burns, respiratory paralysis with overdoses, cardiovascular problems (cardiac failure, high blood pressure, etc.), anorexia, and premature labor (Smith, 1988).

Although data regarding the impact of "crack" on babies is limited and somewhat ambiguous at this time, preliminary studies have suggested that the negative effects of cocaine on the emerging infant may be quite profound (Smith, 1991). Some of these effects include increased irritability, elevated respiratory rate and heartrates, diarrhea, poor tolerance for oral feeding, neurological damage, gastrointestinal problems, and disturbed sleep patterns (see Figure 12–3). Evidence has indicated that these babies are also at greater risk for sudden infant death syndrome (SIDS) and perinatal obstruction of arteries in the brain. Compared with infants born to mothers who have not used drugs, the babies of cocaine users are shorter in length, weigh less, and have smaller head circumferences.

Present information regarding the long-term impact of cocaine on these children is unclear. Some have argued that the impact is permanent and severe. Others have suggested that the problems derived from exposure to cocaine can be successfully treated without lasting damage to the affected children (Greer, 1990; Select Committee on Narcotics Abuse and Control, 1988).

Causation and Prevalence. Cocaine is inexpensive, readily available, easily ingested, and highly addictive. In fact, it is the drug of choice for many substance abusers. It

FOCUS 15

Identify the potential effects of cocaine on the developing fetus.

FIGURE 12–3 The Effects of Maternal Cocaine Use on Mothers and Fetuses/Babies

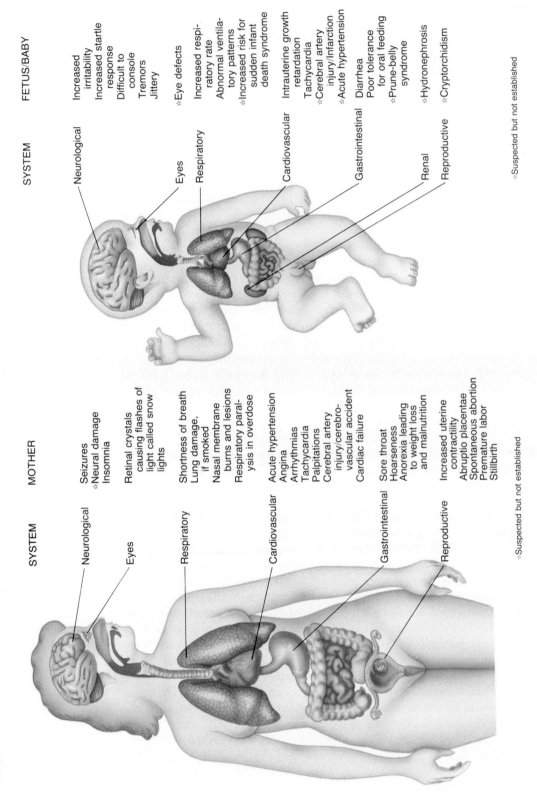

SYSTEM	MOTHER
Neurological	Seizures ☆Neural damage Insomnia
Eyes	Retinal crystals causing flashes of light called snow lights
Respiratory	Shortness of breath Lung damage, if smoked Nasal membrane burns and lesions Respiratory paral- ysis in overdose
Cardiovascular	Acute hypertension Angina Arrhythmias Tachycardia Palpitations Cerebral artery injury/cerebro- vascular accident Cardiac failure
Gastrointestinal	Sore throat Hoarseness Anorexia leading to weight loss and malnutrition
Reproductive	Increased uterine contractility Abruptio placentae Spontaneous abortion Premature labor Stillbirth

☆Suspected but not established

SYSTEM	FETUS/BABY
Neurological	Increased irritability Increased startle response Difficult to console Tremors Jittery
Eyes	☆Eye defects
Respiratory	Increased respi- ratory rate Abnormal ventila- tory patterns ☆Increased risk for sudden infant death syndrome
Cardiovascular	Intrauterine growth retardation Tachycardia ☆Cerebral artery injury/Infarction ☆Acute hypertension
Gastrointestinal	Diarrhea Poor tolerance for oral feeding ☆Prune-belly syndrome
Renal	☆Hydronephrosis
Reproductive	☆Cryptorchidism

☆Suspected but not established

Source: From "The Dangers of Prenatal Cocaine Use" by J. Smith, 1988, *American Journal of Maternal Child Nursing*, 13(3), p. 175. Copyright 1988 by *American Journal of Maternal Child Nursing*. Reprinted by permission.

is estimated that 1 million women in the United States use cocaine regularly. Unfortunately, far too many of these users are pregnant women. Because of the low molecular weight of cocaine, it readily crosses the placenta to the developing fetus or child. Once cocaine enters the baby, it easily passes through the blood-brain barrier, thereby altering the chemistry and functioning of the brain. Cocaine may also be passed from the mother to the child through her breast milk. The regular presence of cocaine in the developing fetus or child impacts its development and functioning in a variety of detrimental ways (see Figure 12–3).

The actual prevalence of babies directly affected by cocaine is difficult to determine. The National Association for Perinatal Addiction Research and Education has suggested that 1 in every 10 newborns is exposed in utero to one or more illicit drugs (Chasnoff, 1988). Many expectant mothers are reluctant to reveal their use of cocaine for fear that they will be prosecuted for child abuse. Additionally, cocaine is often difficult to detect in mothers or their babies because it is so rapidly metabolized.

In some urban areas, the percentage of babies testing positive for cocaine is as high as 20 percent of all normal deliveries (Select Committee on Narcotics Abuse and Control, 1988). The average prevalence rate nationwide is 8 to 10 percent (Little, Snell, Palmore & Gilstrap, 1988; Neerhof, MacGregor, Retzky & Sullivan, 1989).

Interventions. Planning and implementing interventions for mothers and their babies who have been exposed to cocaine is a challenging and complex process, particularly if the mother is addicted. Mothers with serious drug abuse histories may need as much treatment as their affected infants. In fact, in many instances, mothers may need more assistance. Think for a moment about being a neonatologist or pediatrician, faced with the decision of releasing an infant who is at risk and needs sophisticated care to a mother suspected of drug abuse. What action would you take? Some babies are initially placed with grandparents or other caregivers until their mothers are capable of caring for them.

The first line of treatment for cocaine babies should be directed at their mothers. Women with serious addiction problems should be helped before they become pregnant or early in their pregnancies. However, few drug treatment programs have been designed for drug-dependent women who are pregnant or already have children.

Preliminary treatments for preschoolers affected by cocaine center around (1) designing highly structured learning environments; (2) creating small classes (eight children per teacher); (3) providing learning environments that are free of loud sounds and other distracting stimulation; and (4) providing learning activities that are experiential rather than paper-and-pencil-type tasks. Programs for school-age children are beginning to emerge as we learn more about the impact of cocaine and other drugs on the development and performance of children.

Debate Forum ·················· AIDS and the Public Schools ·················

Guillermo is a first-grader. Unless you knew him well, you would assume that he was a very normal kid. He likes cold drinks and pizza and watches cartoons every Saturday morning.

In school, he performs reasonably well. He's not an academic superstar, but he is learning to read and write quite well. His teacher likes him and says that he is quite sociable for his age and size. Guillermo is a little on the small side, but he doesn't let that get in the way of his enjoying most things in life.

Since his foster parents have had him, he has been quite happy. The crying and whining that characterized his first weeks in their home have disappeared. He is now pretty much a part of the family.

His older foster brother, John, likes him a lot. John and Guillermo spend a good deal of time together. They are about 16 months apart in age. John is a second-grader and a mighty good one at that. He has always excelled in school, and he loves to help Guillermo when he can.

Guillermo, from day one of his placement, has been ill regularly. He has one infection after another. Of course, his foster parents knew that this would be the case, since Guillermo has AIDS. His biological mother could not care for him, as she was a drug addict and has AIDS herself.

Keeping a secret is sometimes very hard, and such was the case for John. From the very beginning of Guillermo's placement in his home, John knew that there was something special about him. His parents have talked to him about Guillermo and his condition. It was a family decision to have Guillermo live in their home.

John is often scared, not for himself but for Guillermo. He wonders how long he will be able to play with his young friend and constant companion. Also, it is often hard to keep the family secret about Guillermo.

Guillermo attends the neighborhood school. Those who are aware of his condition are his classmates, their parents, his teacher, the principal, the school board members, and of course, John. Just about everyone kept the secret at first, and Guillermo was well received by the overwhelming majority of his classmates. He played with them, enjoyed stories with them, and had a good wrestle now and then with some of the boys in his class.

However, over time, other parents and students learned about his condition. Then there was a big uproar about Guillermo being in school. The PTA was divided. The principal was in favor of Guillermo's continued attendance, but a few vocal parents began a petition to have Guillermo taught by a teacher for the homebound.

Point   Given our current knowledge about the ways in which AIDS is spread in adults and children, there is no reason to remove Guillermo from his neighborhood school. His behavior and physical condition do not place other children at risk for acquiring the HIV virus or developing AIDS.

Counterpoint   With the limited knowledge we have about AIDS and its transmission, we should not let children with AIDS or the HIV virus attend neighborhood schools. We should wait until we know a great deal more about the disease. The potential risks for other children are too great and far reaching.

REVIEW

FOCUS 1   Identify the stages of treatment for children with traumatic brain injuries.

◆ Maintaining the child's life, minimizing complications with appropriate treatment, and bringing the child out of the coma.

◆ Orienting the child after the coma has come to an end.

◆ Relearning and performing preinjury skills.

◆ Preparing the child for the return to the home, neighborhood, and school environments.

◆ Providing counseling and therapy as needed for the parents, family, and child.

FOCUS 2   Why are many individuals with cerebral palsy considered to be multidisabled?

◆ Often, individuals with cerebral palsy have several disabilities, including hearing impairments, speech and language disorders, intellectual deficits, visual impairments, and general perceptual problems.

FOCUS 3   What is spina bifida myelomeningocele?

◆ Spina bifida myelomeningocele is a defect in the spinal column. The meningocele type presents itself in the form of a tumorlike sac on the back of the infant, which contains spinal fluid and nerve tissue.

◆ Myelomeningocele is also the most serious variety of spina bifida in that it generally includes paralysis or partial paralysis of certain body areas, causing lack of bowel and bladder control.

FOCUS 4   Identify specific treatments for individuals with spinal cord injuries.

◆ Immediate stabilization of the spine is critical to the overall outcome of the injury.

◆ Once the spine has been stabilized, the rehabilitation process begins. Physical therapy helps the affected individual make full use of any and all residual muscle strength.

◆ The individual is also taught to use orthopedic devices, such as handsplints, braces, reachers, and headsticks.

◆ Psychological adjustment is aided by psychiatric and psychological personnel.

◆ Rehabilitation specialists aid the individual in becoming retrained or reeducated; they may also assist in securing new employment.

◆ Some individuals will need part-time or full-time attendant care for assistance with daily activities (e.g., bathing, dressing, and shopping).

FOCUS 5   Identify several treatment goals for individuals with congenital and acquired amputations.

◆ Children with congenital amputations are fitted with prosthetic devices as soon as they are able to use them.

◆ As children grow, their prosthetic devices are modified and customized.

◆ Individuals with acquired amputations are treated surgically. A surgeon treats the affected limb area and prepares it for eventual use in conjunction with a prosthetic device.

◆ Generally, people with acquired amputations experience greater difficulties in adjusting to the challenges inherent in their injuries than do children who have had the defect since birth.

◆ Occupational, physical, and other therapists play critical roles in helping people with congenital and acquired amputations realize their full potential in a variety of domains.

FOCUS 6 Describe the physical limitations associated with muscular dystrophy.

◆ Individuals with muscular dystrophy progressively lose their ability to walk and use their arms and hands effectively because fatty tissue begins to replace muscle tissue.

FOCUS 7 What steps should be taken to assist infants and children with AIDS?

◆ Infants and children should be provided with the most effective medical care available (e.g., medications, vaccinations, etc.).

◆ Children with AIDS should attend school unless they exhibit behaviors that are dangerous to others or are at risk for developing infectious diseases that would exacerbate their condition.

FOCUS 8 Describe immediate treatment for a person who is experiencing a tonic/clonic seizure.

◆ Ease the person to the floor.

◆ Remove any dangerous objects from the immediate vicinity.

◆ Place a soft pad under the person's head (e.g., a coat or blanket).

◆ Allow the person to rest after the seizure has terminated.

FOCUS 9 Identify three problems that individuals with diabetes may eventually experience.

◆ Structural abnormalities that occur over time may result in blindness, cardiovascular disease, and kidney disease.

FOCUS 10 Identify interventions used in treating children with cystic fibrosis.

◆ Drug therapy for prevention and treatment of chest infections

◆ Diet management

◆ Family education regarding the condition

◆ Chest physiotherapy and postural drainage

◆ Inhalation therapy

◆ Psychological and psychiatric counseling

FOCUS 11 Describe the impact of the sickling of cells on body tissues.

◆ Sickled cells are more rigid than normal cells; as such, they frequently block microvascular channels. The blockage of channels reduces or terminates circulation in these areas, and tissues in need of blood nutrients and oxygen die.

FOCUS 12 Identify four factors that may contribute to child abuse and neglect.

◆ Intergenerational patterns

◆ Parent's loss of employment

◆ Mother's unwanted pregnancy

◆ Inadequate preparation for parenting

◆ Challenging economic difficulties

FOCUS 13 Identify factors that may contribute to the increased prevalence of adolescent pregnancy.

◆ General factors include a lack of knowledge about conception and sexuality, a desire to escape family control, an attempt to be more adult, a desire to have someone to love, a means of gaining attention and love, and an inability to make sound decisions.

◆ Societal factors include greater sexual permissiveness and freedom, social pressure from peers, and continual exposure to sexuality through the media.

FOCUS 14 Identify the major causes of youth suicide.

◆ The causes of suicide are multidimensional. Suicide in adolescents is a culmination of serious, numerous, and long-standing problems.

◆ Other causative factors include a genetic predisposition triggered by overwhelming environmental stress and major depressive disorders accompanied by imbalances in several hormonal systems of the body.

FOCUS 15 Identify the potential effects of cocaine on the developing fetus.

◆ The effects include increased irritability, elevated respiratory rate and heartrate, diarrhea, poor tolerance for oral feeding, neurological damage, gastrointestinal problems, and disturbed sleep patterns.

◆ The child is also at risk for sudden infant death syndrome (SIDS) and perinatal obstruction of arteries in the brain.

Chapter Thirteen

Children and Youth Who Are Gifted, Creative, and Talented

TO BEGIN WITH . . .

◆ Interview questions composed by Samantha W., age 8, in a class for gifted and talented children:

"Dear Adam and Eve,

Did you guys feel yourself being created?
What did you eat beside the apple you weren't supposed to eat?
Tell me, how did you keep fit and trim?
Where is the garden now?"

◆ "One of my colleagues, a psychologist at an elementary school, recently told me that of the 20 or so children (mostly boys) referred over the previous months because of school failure in school and social inadaptation in class, more than half turned out to be decidedly above average in terms of intellectual giftedness (IQ scores over 130)" (Gagne, 1991, p. 66).

◆ "Researchers have consistently found parenting to be the most potent factor in the development of giftedness, creativity, and eminence" (Silverman, 1991, p. 308).

DWIGHT

DWIGHT. Dwight spends most of his time in a variety of creative business endeavors. He is currently president of Broadcast International, a company that specializes in using satellite technologies to deliver information to businesses and consumers throughout the United States.

Dwight is an exceptionally talented musician, composer, and arranger. He plays a number of instruments with great skill, including the bass viol, the fender bass, the guitar, the drums, and the piano. In addition, he has perfect pitch and sings well. During his early twenties, he was the musical director for a popular rock group that performed on television and in concerts around the world. In this capacity, he wrote musical scores, arranged songs and instrumentals, and developed an extensive library of recordings for radio stations.

As a youngster, Dwight's siblings and classmates referred to him as "the little professor" or "Doc." Throughout his school years, Dwight easily mastered the content in his classes, from science to math to creative writing. His interests were broad, and school was a sheer pleasure.

As a senior in high school, Dwight composed and arranged all types of musical scores. One example of his tremendous talent involved an audiotape that he created when he was 17. The tape included 15 contemporary songs, each systematically produced using the instruments he played himself. First, he recorded the piano on one tape track, then drums on another track, and so on. The result was a musical presentation that would have impressed many professional producers.

INTRODUCTION

Gifted, creative, and talented are terms associated with a special group of people who have extraordinary abilities in one or more areas of performance. In many cases, we admire such individuals and occasionally are a little envious of their talents. The ease with which they are able to master diverse and difficult concepts is impressive. Because of their unusual abilities and skills, we are often reluctant to provide them with the support they need to fully realize their potential.

For many years, behavioral scientists described children with exceptionally high intelligence as being *gifted*. Only recently have researchers and practitioners included in the adjectives *creative* and *talented* in their descriptions. These terms are typically employed to suggest domains of performance other than those measured by intelligence tests. Dwight is one of those individuals who is probably gifted, creative, and talented (see Window 13–1). Not only did he excel in intellectual (traditional academic) endeavors, but he also exhibited tremendous prowess with regard to producing and performing music. Certainly, the behaviors and traits associated with these terms interact with one another to produce the various constellations of giftedness. Some individuals soar to exceptional heights in the talent domain, others achieve in intellectual areas, and still others excel in creative endeavors. Furthermore, a select few exhibit remarkable levels of behavior and aptitude across several domains or areas.

HISTORICAL BACKGROUND

FOCUS 1
Briefly describe several historical developments that are directly related to the measurement of various types of giftedness.

Definitions describing the unusually able in terms of intelligence quotients and creativity measures are recent phenomena. Until the beginning of the twentieth century, there was no suitable method for quantifying or measuring the human attribute of intelligence. The breakthrough occurred in Europe when Alfred Binet, a French psychologist, constructed

WINDOW 13–2

EDUARDO

Eduardo and his family are recent immigrants to the United States. At age 10, he has become quite adept in speaking English. His primary language is Spanish. He is the oldest of seven children.

Eduardo's father is a supervisor on a large farm in southern California. With a lot of effort, he developed sufficient English skills to be of great value to farm owners who now employ him full time. They have hired him to work directly with migrant workers who regularly assist with the harvest of various kinds of produce and fruit. He is also skilled mechanically and, in the off-season, repairs equipment and farm machinery.

Eduardo's schooling has been quite irregular until the past two years. Prior to having a stable residence, he traveled with his family up and down the west coast of the United States, like many migrant farm families.

Eduardo's schoolmates really enjoy him. He has lots of friends and is invited frequently to birthday parties and social events. He

seems to have a real knack for creating friends and having adults like him.

Eduardo's parents view him as being especially alert and bright. He seems to be interested in many topics and is rarely bored. At the moment, he is intrigued with tractors. His mother indicates that he has always "questioned her to death." Moreover, he seems to be capable of easily entertaining himself. Recently, he spent an entire afternoon looking through a farm magazine and drawing farm equipment that caught his attention.

Since the beginning of this schoolyear, Eduardo has made phenomenal gains in reading, math, and English. In fact, he has become an avid reader of both Spanish and English books that are available at his school. Although it has been difficult to assess his innate ability, he appears to be a child of some promise, intellectually and socially. However, his parents are worried about providing him with the necessary resources to fully utilize his curiosity and ability. They are also concerned about his late start with consistent schooling.

the first developmental assessment scale for children in the early 1900s. This scale was created by observing children at various ages to identify specific tasks that ordinary children were able to perform at each age. These tasks were then sequenced according to age-appropriate levels. Children who could perform tasks well above that which was normal for their chronological age were identified as being developmentally advanced.

Gradually the notion of **mental age** emerged. The mental age of a child was derived by matching the tasks the child was able to perform to the age scale (typical performance of children at various ages) developed by Binet and Théodore Simon (1905, 1908). Although this scale was initially developed and used to identify mentally retarded children in the Parisian schools, it eventually became an important means for identifying those who had higher than average mental ages, as well.

Over the past decades, definitions of what constitutes giftedness have changed to consider more than IQ scores. (Kevin Horan/Picture Group)

REFLECT ON THIS

13–1   Eleven Years Old and . . .

John is just a few days away from being 11 years old. On the Washington Pre-College Test (WPC) he recently scored at the eightieth percentile on the verbal portion of the test and at the tenth percentile on the quantitative portion. For the past two years, he has been enrolled at the California State University, Los Angeles (CSULA), taking math and other college-level courses. During this time period, he has endeavored to improve his math performance. By the way, John's junior high has an excellent program for students who are highly gifted, and he has been enrolled in that program. But he finds his university classes to be more challenging and varied.

John's initial experiences with his university course work were fraught with problems. His elementary school training had not provided him with any skill in taking notes. His parents, however, were and are very supportive. When they discovered that he was having difficulty in taking notes, his mother obtained permission to attend some of his courses with him. They both took notes and then made comparisons each day after class. Within three weeks, John had mastered the skill and was well on his way to becoming a competent note-taker.

When he first began his university work, John viewed himself as being a "mathematical moron" because of his low entry scores on the WPC. The change in his self-perception as a mathematician came when he enrolled in a chemistry course at CSULA. It really captured his attention and interest. He soon discovered that an understanding of algebra was central to succeeding in the course. Motivated by this discovery, he soon became proficient in algebra. In his most recent test, he scored at the seventieth percentile on the quantitative portion of the WPC.

John's general feelings about himself and his capacity fluctuated a lot after his early entrance to college. Sometimes, he felt overconfident and other times discouraged. Now he has a realistic view of his strengths and weaknesses and is pursuing his university course work with a balanced perspective on himself.

This fall, John will enroll full time as a college student. He is now 14 and has a full year of college credit under his belt. By the time he is 15, he will be a junior. Today, he is probably thinking about the graduate school he would like to attend after finishing his bachelor's degree.

Lewis M. Terman, an American educator and psychologist, expanded the concepts and procedures developed by Binet. He was convinced that Binet and Simon had developed an approach for measuring intellectual abilities in all children. This belief prompted him to revise the Binet instrument, adding greater breadth to the scale. In 1916, Terman published the **Stanford-Binet Intelligence Scale** in conjunction with Stanford University. During this period, Terman developed the term **intelligence quotient, or IQ.** The IQ score was obtained by dividing a child's mental age by his or her chronological age and multiplying that figure by 100 (MA/CA × 100 = IQ). For example, a child with a mental age of 12, and a chronological age of 8 would have an IQ of 150 (12/8 × 100 = 150).

Gradually, other researchers became interested in studying the nature and assessment of intelligence. They tended to view intelligence as an underlying ability or capacity that expressed itself in a variety of ways. The unitary IQ scores that were derived from the Stanford-Binet tests were representative of and contributed to this notion.

Over time, however, other researchers came to believe that intellect was represented by a variety of distinct capacities and abilities (Cattell, 1971; Guilford, 1959). This line of thinking suggested that each distinct, intellectual capacity could be identified and assessed. Several mental abilities were investigated, including memory capacity, divergent thinking, vocabulary usage, and reasoning ability. Gradually, the multiple ability approach became more popular than the unitary intelligence notion. Its proponents were convinced that the universe of intellectual functions was extensive. Moreover, they believed that the intelligence assessment instruments utilized at that time measured a very small portion of an individual's true intellectual capacities.

One of the key contributors to the multidimensional theory regarding intelligence was J. P. Guilford (1950, 1959). Guilford's work led many researchers to consider intelligence more than a broad, unitary ability. He saw intelligence as a diverse range of intellectual and creative abilities. His theoretical contributions prompted many researchers to focus their scientific efforts on the emerging field of creativity and its various subcomponents, such as divergent thinking, problem solving, and decision making. Gradually, tests or measures of creativity were developed, using the constructs drawn from models created by Guilford and others.

In summary, conceptions of giftedness during the early 1920s were closely tied to the score that an individual obtained on an intelligence test. Thus, a single score, an IQ, was the index by which one was identified as being gifted. Commencing with the work of Guilford (1950, 1959) and Torrance (1961, 1965, 1968), notions regarding giftedness were greatly expanded. Giftedness began to refer not only to those with high IQs but also to those who demonstrated high aptitude on creativity measures. More recently, the term *talented* has been added to the descriptors associated with giftedness. As a result, individuals who demonstrate remarkable skills in the visual or performing arts or who excel in other areas of performance may be designated as gifted.

Currently, there is no federal mandate in the United States requiring educational services for students identified as gifted, as is the case with other exceptional conditions. The funding and provision of services are a state-by-state challenge, and as such, there is tremendous variability in the quality and types of programs offered to students. Unfortunately, due to the lack of a national policy, we are seriously neglecting the development of one of our most important natural resources: children who are gifted, talented, and creative.

DEFINITIONS AND CONCEPTS

Definitions of giftedness have been influenced by a variety of innovative and knowledgeable individuals. One definition characterizing the changes that have occurred over time is that provided by Purcell (1978):

> The term "gifted and talented" means children, and whenever applicable, youth who are identified at the preschool, elementary, or secondary level as possessing demonstrated or potential abilities that give evidence of high performance capability in areas such as intellectual, creative, specific academic or leadership ability, or in performing and visual arts and who by reason thereof require services or activities not ordinarily provided by the school. (Section 902)

Capturing the essence of any human condition in a definition can be very perplexing. This is certainly the case in defining the human attributes, abilities, and potentialities that constitute giftedness. However, definitions serve a number of important purposes. For example, definitions may have a profound influence on the following: (1) the number of students that are ultimately selected; (2) the types of instruments and selection procedures utilized; (3) the scores an individual must obtain in order to qualify for specialized instruction; (4) the types of education provided; (5) the amount of funding required to provide services; and (6) the types of training individuals need to teach the gifted and talented. Thus, definitions are important from both practical and theoretical perspectives (Kitano & Kirby, 1986).

Renzulli (1978) presented a "three-ring conception" of giftedness that has influenced the thinking and procedures employed by many practitioners. He pioneered the notion that giftedness was a combination of interacting clusters of behavior and that one could not be identified as being gifted based on only one cluster of behavior. Renzulli's definition stated:

> Giftedness consists of an interaction among three basic clusters of human traits—these clusters being above-average general abilities, high levels of task commitment, and high levels of creativity. Gifted and talented children are those possessing or

FOCUS 2

Identify six major components of definitions that have been developed to describe giftedness.

Creativity in children should always be encouraged. (Bob Daemmrich Photography)

capable of developing this composite set of traits and applying them to any potentially valuable area of human performance. Children who manifest or are capable of developing an interaction among the three clusters require a wide variety of educational opportunities and services that are not ordinarily provided through regular instructional programs. (1978, p. 261)

The clusters emphasized in this definition were drawn from research dealing with individuals who, as adults or youth, had distinguished themselves by their remarkable achievement or creative contributions. Renzulli (1978) claimed that his definition was an operational one because it met several important criteria. First, he developed the definition based on research on gifted individuals and their characteristics. Second, he asserted that it provided direction for selecting or developing instruments and procedures that could be used to devise defensible identification plans. In addition, he believed that such a definition directed practitioners to focus their programs on the essential characteristics of giftedness that really lead to future achievements and contributions.

New conceptualizations of giftedness and intelligence have recently emerged from theoretical and research literature (Colangelo & Davis, 1991). One of the new approaches to intelligence is Sternberg's triarchic theory of human intelligence (Sternberg, 1981), according to which intellectual performance is divided into three parts: (1) analytic, (2) synthetic, and (3) practical. *Analytic* intelligence is exhibited by people who perform well on aptitude and intelligence tests. Individuals with *synthetic* giftedness are unconventional thinkers who are creative, intuitive, and insightful. People with *practical* intelligence are extraordinarily adept in dealing with problems of everyday life and those presented in the work environment.

Another emerging view of giftedness has been developed by Ramos-Ford and Gardner (1991). They have defined *intelligence* or *giftedness* as "an ability or set of abilities that permit an individual to solve problems or fashion products that are of consequence in a particular cultural setting" (Ramos-Ford & Gardner, 1991, p. 56). This perspective of giftedness is referred to as the *theory of multiple intelligence*. Intelligence manifests itself in linguistic, logical-mathematical, spatial, musical, bodily-kinesthetic, interpersonal, and intrapersonal behaviors.

As you can see, we have come a long way from the unitary measure of IQ as the major measure of an individual's potential giftedness. However, despite the movement away from IQ scores and other changes in definitions of giftedness, critics argue that many if not most local, district, and state definitions are elitist in nature and favor the "white, middle class, and academically achieving" (Richert, 1991, p. 81).

There are diverse and competing definitions of giftedness. Each of the definitions presented reveals the complexity associated with defining the nature of giftedness, a difficulty that is common to definitions in the behavioral sciences. In a multicultural, pluralistic society, such as that of the United States, different abilities and capacities are encouraged and valued by different parents and teachers. Also, definitions of giftedness are often a function of educational, societal, and political priorities at a particular time. The problems of definition and description are not easily resolved, yet such efforts are vital to both research and practice.

PREVALENCE

Determining the number of children who are gifted is a challenging matter. The complexity of the task is directly related to problems inherent in determining who is gifted and what constitutes giftedness. As we know, giftedness has been defined in several ways. Some definitions are quite restrictive in terms of the number of children to which they apply; others are very inclusive and broad. Consequently, there is tremendous variability in prevalence estimates.

Prevalence figures prior to the 1950s were primarily limited to the intellectually gifted: those identified for the most part by intelligence tests. At that time, 2 to 3 percent of the general population was considered gifted. During the 1950s, a number of writers advocated an expanded view of giftedness (Conant, 1959; DeHann & Havighurst, 1957). Such work had a substantial effect on the prevalence figures suggested for program planning. Terms such as *academically talented* were used to refer to the upper 15 to 20 percent of the general school population.

Thus, prevalence estimates have fluctuated, depending on the views of researchers and professionals during various periods of the twentieth century. Currently, 3 to 15 percent of the students in the school population may be identified as gifted. However, regulations governing the number of students that can be identified and served vary from state to state.

CHARACTERISTICS

Accurately identifying the characteristics of gifted people is an enormous task. Many characteristics attributed to those who are gifted have been generated by different types of studies (MacKinnon, 1962; Terman, 1925). Frequently, these studies served as catalysts for the production of lists of distinctive characteristics. Gradually, what emerged from the studies was a stereotypical view of giftedness.

Unfortunately, much of the initial research relating to the characteristics of giftedness was conducted with restricted population samples. Generally, the studies did not include adequate samples of females or individuals from various ethnic and cultural groups; nor did early researchers carefully control for factors directly related to socioeconomic status. Therefore, characteristics generated by these studies may not be representative of the population of gifted individuals as a whole but rather a reflection of a select group from advantaged environments (Olszewski-Kubilius, Kulieke & Krasney, 1988).

Given the present multifaceted definitions of giftedness, we must conclude that gifted people are members of a heterogeneous population. Consequently, research findings of the past and present must be interpreted with great caution by practitioners assessing a particular child's behavior and attributes.

FOCUS 3

Identify four problems inherent in accurately describing the characteristics of individuals who are gifted.

■ **Table 13–1** Terman's Findings in the Study of People Who Are Gifted

Domains	Differentiating Characteristics
Physical characteristics	◆ Robust and in good health ◆ Above average in physical stature
Personality attributes and psychological adjustment	◆ Above average in willpower, popularity, perseverance, emotional maturity, aesthetic perceptivity, and moral reasoning ◆ Keen sense of humor and high levels of self-confidence. ◆ Equal to peers in marital adjustment ◆ Well adjusted as adults; few problems with substance abuse, suicide, and mental health
Educational attainment	◆ Generally read before school entrance ◆ Frequently promoted ◆ Excelled in reading and mathematical reasoning ◆ Consistently scored in the top 10 percent on achievement tests
Career achievement	◆ Mates primarily involved in professional and managerial positions ◆ Women primarily teachers or homemakers (probably due to cultural expectations at the time) ◆ By age 40 had completed 67 books, 1,400 scientific and professional papers, 700 short stories, and a variety of other creative and scholarly works ◆ Adult achievers came primarily from encouraging home environments

Shortly after the publication of the Stanford-Binet Intelligence Scale, Terman (1925) was funded to begin his intriguing *Genetic Studies of Genius*. His initial group of subjects included more than 1,500 students who had obtained IQ scores at or above 140 on the Stanford-Binet. The subjects were drawn from both elementary and secondary classroom settings. In conjunction with other associates, he investigated their physical characteristics, personality attributes, psychological and marital adjustment, educational attainment, and career achievement at the average ages of 20, 35, and so on (see Table 13–1). Terman's work provided the impetus for the systematic study of individuals who are gifted.

Since 1929, other researchers have sought to add to the knowledge base about the characteristics of populations of gifted people. Recent work completed by Adler, Mueller, and Ary (1987) has suggested that elementary students who are gifted are frequently sought out as helpmates. The "bookworm" or social-loner image that frequently comes to mind when we think of children who are gifted is simply not accurate. Students who are gifted are sought out more frequently by their less able peers and play an important role in the learning and growth of others.

Clark (1988) synthesized the work of past investigators and developed a comprehensive listing of differential characteristics of the gifted, their needs, and their possible problems. Table 13–2 presents a representative listing of some of the characteristics of children and

■ **Table 13–2** Representative Characteristics of People Who Are Gifted and Potential Concomitant Problems

Domains	Differentiating Characteristics	Problems
Cognitive (thinking)	Extraordinary quantity of information, unusual retentiveness	Boredom with regular curriculum; impatience with waiting for group
	High level of language development	Perceived as showoff by children of the same age
	Persistent, goal-directed behavior	Perceived as stubborn, willful, uncooperative
	Unusual capacity for processing information	Resent being interrupted; perceived as too serious; dislike for routine and drill
Affective (feeling)	Unusual sensitivity to the expectations and feelings of others	Unusually vulnerable to criticism of others; high level of need for success and recognition
	Keen sense of humor—may be gentle or hostile	Use of humor for critical attack on others, resulting in damage to interpersonal relationships
	Unusual emotional depth and intensity	Unusual vulnerability; problem focusing on realistic goals for life's work
	Advanced levels of moral judgement	Intolerance of and lack of understanding from peer group, leading to rejection and possible isolation
Physical (sensation)	Unusual discrepancy between physical and intellectual development	Result in adults who function with a mind/body dichotomy; children are comfortable expressing themselves only in mental activity, resulting in a limited development both physically and mentally
	Low tolerance for lag between standards and athletic skills	Refusal to take part in any activities where they do not excel, limiting experience with otherwise pleasurable, constructive physical activities
Intuitive	Early involvement and concern for intuitive knowing and metaphysical ideas and phenomena	Ridiculed by peers; not taken seriously by elders; considered weird or strange
	Creativity apparent in all areas of endeavor	Seen as deviant; become bored with mundane tasks; may be viewed as troublemaker
Societal	Strongly motivated by self-actualization needs	Frustration of not feeling challenged; loss of unrealized talents
	Leadership	Lack of opportunity to use social ability contructively may result in its disappearance from child's repertoire or its being turned into a negative characteristic (e.g., gang leadership)
	Solutions to social and environmental problems	Loss to society if these traits are not allowed to develop with guidance and opportunity for meaningful involvement

Source: Adapted with permission of Merrill an imprint of Macmillan Publishing Company from *Growing Up Gifted* 3rd edition by Barbara Clark. Copyright © 1988, 1983, 1979 by Macmillan Publishing Company.

youth who are gifted, according to Clark's five domains: cognitive, affective, physical, intuitive, and societal. Again, remember that individuals who are gifted vary greatly in the extent that they exhibit any or all of the characteristics identified by researchers. One of the interesting features of Clark's listing is the delineation of possible concomitant problems that may surface as a result of the individual's characteristics.

ORIGINS OF GIFTEDNESS

FOCUS 4

Identify four factors that appear to contribute significantly to the emergence of various forms of giftedness.

Scientists have long been interested in identifying the contributing sources of intelligence. Conclusions have varied greatly. For years, many scientists adhered to a hereditary explanation of intelligence: that people inherit their intellectual capacity at conception. Thus, intelligence was viewed as an innate capacity that remained relatively fixed during an individual's lifetime. The prevailing belief then was that little could be done to enhance intellectual ability.

During the 1920s and 1930s, scientists such as John Watson began to explore the new notion of *behavioral psychology,* or *behaviorism.* Like other behaviorists who followed him, Watson believed that the environment played an important role in the development of intelligence as well as personality traits. Initially, Watson largely discounted the role of heredity and its importance in intellectual development. Later, however, he moderated his views, moving somewhat toward a theoretical perspective in which both hereditary and environment contributed to an individual's intellectual ability.

During the 1930s, many investigators sought to determine the proportional influence of heredity and environment on intellectual development. Some genetic proponents asserted that as much as 70 to 80 percent of an individual's capacity is determined by heredity and the remainder by environmental influences. Environmentalists believed otherwise. The controversy regarding the respective contributions of heredity and environment to intelligence (known as the **nature versus nurture** controversy) is likely to continue for some time, in part because of the complexity and breadth of the issues involved.

Thus far, we have focused on the origins of intelligence rather than giftedness per se. Many of the theories regarding the emergence or essence of giftedness have been derived from the study of general intelligence. Few authors have focused directly on the origins of giftedness. Moreover, the ongoing changes in the definitions of giftedness have further complicated the precise investigation of its origins.

Research continues to provide a range of answers in terms of the inheritability of high intellectual capacity, creativity, and other exceptional talents. Davis and Rimm (1989) concluded that "heredity and environment, working together in some favorable combination, are obvious explanations for the origin of high talent" (p. 32).

The nature-nurture issue is also present in the literature pertaining to the origins of creativity. For example, Gowan, Khatena, and Torrance (1979) defined creativity as "an emergent characteristic of the escalation of developmental process when the requisite degrees of mental ability and environmental stimulation are present" (p. 276). The latter part of this definition illustrates the nature-nurture interactionist point of view, that is, that creativity cannot emerge without the requisite degrees of mental ability and environmental stimulation.

In this regard, Gowan et al. (1979) identified three major theories regarding the origins of creativity. The first is directly related to mental ability as conceptualized by Guilford (1959) in his structure of intellect model (see Figure 13–1). In particular, individuals endowed with unusually high levels of ability in the divergent production "slice" of Guilford's model have an excellent chance of becoming very creative. The second theory posits that creativity is an outcome of good mental health or progress toward self-actualization (full utilization of

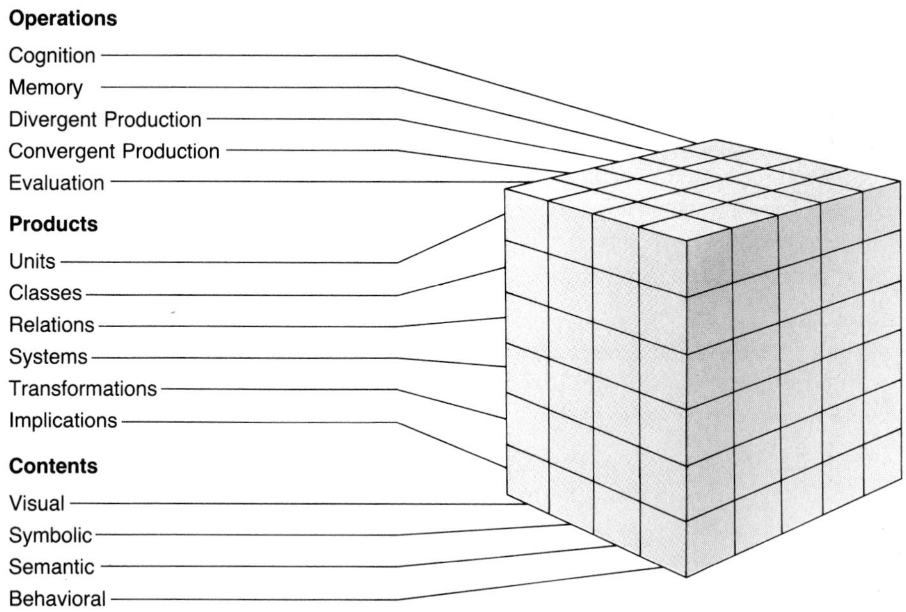

Operations

Cognition

Memory

Divergent Production

Convergent Production

Evaluation

Products

Units

Classes

Relations

Systems

Transformations

Implications

Contents

Visual

Symbolic

Semantic

Behavioral

Source: From *Way Beyond the IQ: Guide to Improving Intelligence and Creativity* [p. 151] by J. P. Guilford, 1977, Buffalo, NY: Creative Education Foundation. Copyright 1977 by Creative Education Foundation. Reprinted by permission.

FIGURE 13–1

Guilford's Structure of Intellect Model. Each little cube represents a unique combination of one kind of operation, one kind of content, and one kind of product, and hence a distinctly different intellectual ability or function.

one's potential). The third theory is directly related to environmental aspects of an individual's upbringing. Individuals who are reared in democratic family environments that foster risk taking, openness, and spontaneity are more likely to be creative as youth and adults.

Research pertaining to the origins of exceptional talent is limited. This is in part a function of the imprecise definitions to date regarding the nature of remarkable talents. Bloom (1985) studied the development of talent in young people in five fields: music, art, athletics, mathematics, and science. Each of the 120 talented individuals was selected because he or she was considered to be among the top 25 individuals within his or her talent area in the United States. Bloom's (1985) summary of his and others' research regarding these extremely talented individuals is as follows:*

> The majority of parents were strongly committed to the work ethic. . . . Typically the talented individuals that we studied tended to be good exemplars of the work ethic, and this was especially true in their talent field. (p. 539)

> Our present findings point to the conclusion that exceptional levels of talent development require certain types of environmental support, special experiences, excellent teaching, and appropriate motivational encouragement at each stage of development. No matter what the quality of initial gifts, each of the individuals we have studied went through many years of special development under the care of attentive parents and the tutelage and supervision of a remarkable series of teachers and coaches. (p. 543)

> Only rarely were the individuals in our study given their initial instruction in the talent field because parents or teachers saw in the child unusual gifts to be developed

* From *Developing Talent in Young People,* by Benjamin Bloom. Copyright © 1985 by Benjamin Bloom. Reprinted by permission of Ballantine Books, a division of Random House, Inc.

more fully. They were given the initial instruction and encouragement because their parents placed very high value on one of the areas—music and the arts, sports, or intellectual activities. The parents wanted all of their children to have a good opportunity to learn in the talent area that they preferred.

We speculated that if the talented individuals we studied had been reared in a very different home environment, it is probable that their initial instruction and encouragement to learn would have been very different. And it is not likely that they would have reached the level or type of talent for which they were included in this study. (pp. 542–544)

It was the child's small successes and interests that resulted in early learning in a talent field that teachers and parents noted. . . . These early minor achievements, rather than evidence of unusual gifts and qualities, were the basis for providing the child with further opportunities to develop in the talent field. (p. 544).

Thus, the precise origins of the various forms of giftedness are yet to be determined. Current thinking favors an interaction of natural endowment and appropriate environmental stimulation. All children who are capable of becoming gifted should have the opportunity to realize their creative and intellectual potential. Future research will enhance our abilities to provide this opportunity for all children, regardless of their ethnicity, social-class standing, or geographic location.

ASSESSMENT

The focus of assessment procedures for identifying potential giftedness is beginning to change (Richert, 1991). Elitist definitions are being replaced with defensible, inclusive definitions. Tests for identifying persons with potential for gifted performance are being more carefully selected; that is, tests are being used with the children or youth for which they were designed. In this regard, tests and procedures that are inappropriate for certain children are not being used in the identification process. Children and youth who were once excluded from programs for the gifted because of formal or standard cut-off scores that favored particular groups of students are now being included as candidates. Multiple sources of information are now collected and reviewed in determining who is potentially gifted rather than relying on limited sources of information (Richert, 1991). Additionally, the identification process is now directed at identifying needs and potentials rather than labeling individuals as gifted.

FOCUS 5

Describe the range of assessment devices used to identify the various types of giftedness.

Young gifted children are identified using several approaches. The first task of parents and other care providers is to be aware of the behaviors that may signal giftedness in their child or children (Anderson, 1987). Given the heterogeneous nature of giftedness, this can be a challenging task. Children identified as gifted develop in vastly different ways. Some may read, walk, and talk quite early, while others may be slow in these areas. Aspects of giftedness may emerge early in a child's development or later on as the child matures. Consequently, the identification process continues throughout a child's developmental years.

Elementary and secondary students who are gifted are identified in a variety of ways. The first step is generally screening. During this phase, teachers, psychologists, and other school personnel attempt to select all students who are potentially gifted. A number of procedures are employed in the screening process. Historically, information obtained from group intelligence tests and teacher nominations has been used to select the initial pool of students. However, many other measures and data-collection techniques have been instituted since the perspective of giftedness changed from a unidimensional to multidimensional

Giftedness may be recognized very early in a child's life or not until he or she is older, depending in part on what opportunities for learning have been available. (G. Moltini/The Image Bank)

approach (Irvine, 1987). They may include developmental inventories, achievement tests, creativity tests, newly developed information-processing tests, biographical inventories, motivation assessment, teacher nominations, and evaluation of student projects (Benbow & Minor, 1990; Sowell, Bergwall, Zeigler, & Cartwright, 1990). However, the most commonly used instrument for identifying learners who are gifted continues to be one of the Wechsler scales, even though other instruments and approaches have been developed (Klausmeier, Mishra, & Maker, 1987). We will highlight briefly some of the findings related to teacher nomination, intelligence testing, achievement testing, information-processing tests, and assessment of creativity.

Teacher Nomination

Teacher nomination has been an integral part of many screening approaches. This approach is, however, fraught with problems. Teachers often favor children who are well dressed, cooperative, and task oriented. Students who are bright underachievers as well as those who are bright and disruptive may be overlooked. Moreover, teachers are often given few if any specific criteria for nominating students thought to be gifted. Another problem is the restriction on the number of students teachers are allowed to nominate.

Fortunately, some of these problems have been addressed. There are now several scales and guidelines to aid teachers and others responsible for making nominations (Borland, 1978; Osborne & Byrnes, 1990; Renzulli, Reis, & Smith, 1981; Renzulli, Smith, White, Callahan, & Hartman, 1976; Schack & Starko, 1990; Steffens, 1989).

Intelligence and Achievement Tests

Intelligence testing has and continues to be a major approach to identifying intellectual gift-edness. Research related to intelligence assessment, however, reveals some interesting find-ings. Wallach (1976) analyzed a series of studies on the relationship between future profes-sional achievement and scores obtained earlier on academic aptitude tests or intelligence tests. He found that performance scores in the upper ranges, particularly those frequently used to screen and identify students who are gifted, served as poor criteria for predicting future creative and productive achievement.

Other criticisms have been aimed at intelligence tests and their uses, some of which we discussed earlier in this chapter. One of the major criticisms relates to the restrictiveness of such instruments (Tannenbaum, 1991). Many of the higher mental processes that charac-terize the functioning of individuals who are gifted are not measured adequately, and some are not assessed at all. Another criticism involves the limitations inherent in using the typical intelligence tests with individuals who are culturally different. Few of the instruments cur-rently available are suitably designed to assess the abilities of those who are substantially different from the core culture. The use of nonverbal intelligence tests as well as chrono-metric devices that monitor closely the speed with which students respond to various stimuli may prove useful in identifying children from minority groups who are gifted (Baldwin, 1987).

Similar problems are inherent in achievement tests. For example, achievement tests are not generally designed to measure the true achievement of children who are academically gifted. Such individuals are often prevented from demonstrating their unusual prowess be-cause of the restricted range of the test items. These **ceiling effects,** as they are known, prevent children who are gifted from demonstrating their achievement at higher levels.

Information-Processing Tests

Researchers have recently become interested in the ways in which normal students and students who are gifted process information and the relationship of these processing skills to intellectual giftedness (Davidson & Sternberg, 1984; Sternberg, 1981, 1987). Sternberg (1981) developed a means for analyzing human problem solving and identified five ele-mentary information processes or metacomponents: (1) planning and (2) decision-making procedures; (3) acquisition; (4) retention; and (5) transfer of problem-solving approaches to other types of problems. From this perspective, individuals who are gifted have superior skills in processing information for the purpose of problem solving. Kaufman and Kaufman (1983) developed an assessment battery for children that purportedly measures the mental-processing or problem-solving abilities of children. This battery and others that will be developed in the near future may provide an alternative and more accurate means of assessing giftedness in all children.

Creativity Tests

Because of the nature of creativity and the many forms in which it can be expressed, de-veloping tests to assess its presence and magnitude is a formidable task (Davis & Rimm, 1989). In spite of these challenges, a number of creativity tests have been formulated (Tor-rance, 1966; Williams, 1980). There are presently two main categories of creativity tests: (1) tests designed to assess divergent thinking and (2) inventories that provide information about students' personalities and biographical traits. Callahan (1991) has suggested that mul-tiple measures of creativity be used in order to substantiate prowess in this area of perfor-

FIGURE 13–2

Selected Items from the Biographical Inventory, Form U (Institute for Behavioral Research in Creativity, Salt Lake City, Utah, 1979)

13. Do you make your own decisions when you can?
  A. Almost always
  B. Usually
  C. Sometimes
  D. Not very often
  E. Almost never

18. Compared to other students in your class, how often do you ask the teacher questions about the class subject?
  A. Much more often than the other students
  B. A little more than the other students
  C. About as often as the other students
  D. A little less often than others
  E. Much less often than others

34. How often do you, on your own, work math problems which have not been assigned to you in courses?
  A. Not very often
  B. About once or twice a month
  C. About once a week
  D. A few times a week

136. What is your ability to do assignments in new and different ways?
  A. Outstanding
  B. Excellent
  C. Somewhat above average
  D. About average
  E. Somewhat below average
  F. Once a day or more

mance. A typical question on a divergent thinking test may read as follows: What would happen if your eyes could be adjusted to see things as small as germs?

Taylor and Ellison (1983) reported on their successful use of various **biographical inventories** in identifying children and adults who were gifted. These inventories encompass a wide range of questions about childhood activities, sources of satisfaction, descriptions of parents, self-descriptions, self-evaluations, and academic experiences (see Figure 13–2).

REFLECT ON THIS

| 13–2 | The Prodigy: Norbert Wiener

At one period I was an infant prodigy in the full sense of the word, for I entered college before the age of twelve, obtained my bachelor's degree before fifteen, and my doctorate before nineteen. Yet any man who has reached the age of fifty-seven is certainly no longer an infant prodigy; and if he has accomplished anything in life, whatever temporary conspicuousness he may have had as a prodigy has lost all importance in view of the much greater issues of success or failure in his later life. (p. 3)

Mother used to read to me in the garden. I know now that the yard was a mere three or four feet of grass outside the front steps, but then it seemed to me enormous. The book from which she most enjoyed reading was Kipling's *Jungle Book,* and her favorite story was "Rikki-Tikki-Tavi." I myself was beginning to read at the time, but I was only three and a half years old, and there were many words that caused me difficulty. My books were not particularly adapted to my years. (p. 34)

Source: From *Ex-Prodigy: My Childhood and Youth.* Copyright © 1953 by Norbert Wiener. Copyright Renewed: 1981 by Margaret Wiener. Reprinted by permission of SIMON & SCHUSTER.

■ **Table 13–3** Characteristics of Student Who Are Gifted That Tend to Screen Them Out of Programs

Behaviors	Associated with:
Bored with routine tasks, refuses to do rote homework No interest in details; hands in messy work Makes jokes or puns at inappropriate times	**CREATIVITY** • High tolerance of ambiguity • Independent, divergent thinking • Risk taking • Imaginative, sensitive
Refuses to accept authority; nonconforming, stubborn Difficult to get her to move onto another topic	
Emotionally sensitive–may overreact, get angry easily, or be ready to cry if things go wrong	**MOTIVATION** • Persistence in interest areas • Intensity of feelings and values • Independence
Tends to dominate others Often disagrees vocally with others or with the teachers about ideas or values	**CRITICAL THINKING** • Sees discrepancies between real/ideal truth/expression • Sets high standards • Capable of analysis and evaluation
Is self-critical, impatient with failures Is critical of others, of the teachers	

Source: From E. S. Richert, "Rampant Problems and Promising Practices in Identification." In HANDBOOK OF GIFTED EDUCATION, by N. Colangelo and G. A. Davis (Eds.), Copyright 1991 by Allyn and Bacon. Reprinted with permission.

The questions were derived from biographical research dealing with highly creative research scientists, effective leaders, and other very creative individuals. Thus, children or youth whose inventory results compare favorably to the criteria established by adults who are gifted may, as both students and later in life, make significant contributions to their selected fields of endeavor.

Once the screening steps have been completed, the actual identification and selection of students is begun. During this phase, each of the previously screened students is carefully evaluated again, using more individualized procedures and assessment tools. Ideally, these techniques should be closely related to the definition of giftedness used by the district or school system and the nature of the program envisioned for students (Callahan, 1991).

Historically, a single index or IQ score was used as the basis for placing or serving young people in programs for the gifted. Now a variety of different types of measures and scores can be utilized to determine whether a student ought to be served. Richert (1991) has also identified behaviors that may cause selection committee members to screen out certain individuals who are potentially gifted (see Table 13–3).

INTERVENTIONS

Early Childhood

Parents can promote the early learning and development of their children in a number of ways (Koopmans-Dayton & Feldhusen, 1987; Lewis & Louis, 1991). During the first 18 months of life, 90 percent of all social interactions with children take place during such activities as feeding, bathing, changing diapers, and dressing (Clark, 1988). Parents who are interested in advancing their child's mental and social development use these occasions for talking to him or her; providing varied sensory experiences such as bare-skin cuddling, tickling, and smiling; and conveying a sense of trust.

As children gradually progress through infancy, toddler, and preschool periods, the experiences provided become more varied and uniquely suited to the child's emerging interests. Language and cognitive development are encouraged by means of stories that are read and told. Children are also urged to make up their own stories. Brief periods are also reserved for discussions or spontaneous conversations that arise from events that have momentarily captured their attention. Requests for help in saying or printing a word are promptly fulfilled. Thus, many children who are gifted learn to read before they enter kindergarten or first grade.

During the school years, parents continue to advance their children's development by providing opportunities that correspond to their children's strengths and interests (Shaughnessy & Neely, 1987). The simple identification games played during the preschool period now become more complex. Discussions frequently take place with peers and other interesting adults in addition to parents. The nature of the discussions and the types of questions asked become more sophisticated. Parents assist their children in moving to higher levels of learning by asking questions that involve analysis (comparing and contrasting ideas), synthesis (integrating and combining ideas into new and novel forms), and evaluation (judging and disputing books, newspaper articles, etc.). Other ways parents can help include (1) furnishing books and reading materials on a broad range of topics; (2) providing appropriate equipment as various interests surface (e.g., microscopes, telescopes, chemistry sets, etc.); (3) encouraging regular trips to the public library and other learning-resource centers;

Parents play a critical role in encouraging their children's curiosity and building self-esteem.
(Myrleen Ferguson/PhotoEdit)

Putting on the Pressure

The regular education system in the United States has come under increasing fire for not pressuring students to meet minimum education requirements, much less achieve scholastic excellence. But what about the opposite end of the spectrum? When it comes to students who are gifted and talented, has too much pressure been put on them to succeed?

Educators at the privately funded Johns Hopkins Center for Talented Youth and many similar programs would say no. In fact, part of their educational philosophy is that learning to deal with pressure is as important as learning facts, figures, and logic. Programs such as the one at Johns Hopkins involve students from 11 to 17 years old whose combined SAT scores are at least 930 out of 1,600. (The national average for college-bound seniors is 896.) These students attend accelerated classes during the summer and after school to supplement the supposedly "lightweight fare" available to them in the regular education system.

In addition to the differences in content offered, some regular education programs take a different psychological approach to teaching, as well. Namely, promoting students' self-esteem has become the primary issue in many programs. Students of various interests and abilities receive praise and support from teachers and peers. Competition and its inherent tendency to bruise fragile egos is often downplayed.

William Durden, director of the program at Johns Hopkins, takes issue with this approach, saying, "*Stress* is not a dirty word." Facing competition and pressure are certainly part of achieving success in the real world. But how much stress is appropriate?

Consider the following scenario of a writing session involving students who are gifted: A 14-year-old girl sits in the middle of a circle formed by her teacher and eight classmates. She looks ready to cry. Everyone in the circle has read her essay and takes a turn offering criticism, some of it quite blunt. The teacher has the last word, saying, "Your observations are insightful, but your writing sounds stupid." The girl bites her lip and looks down, but she does not cry.

Is this approach too harsh? The teacher involved in the writing session explains that students who are gifted but have attended regular schools are so used to getting good grades and receiving praise for everything they do that they no longer feel challenged. Thus, their interest and drive are restored when they face criticism and competition in special programs with peers of similar ability. "They generally thank me for the constructive criticism they never had," says the teacher.

Not everyone is convinced. Some educators and parents feel that programs for students who are gifted and talented are sometimes elitist and unnecessarily stressful. Moreover, it is difficult to say what lasting mark such pressure may leave on children and youth. As one individual stated, "While gifted programs are great, they're not worth making our kids crazy about."

Source: David Machan, "Spare the prod, spoil the child," *Forbes*, October 14, 1991. Excerpts reprinted with permission by Forbes Inc., copyright 1991.

(4) providing opportunities for participation in cultural events, lectures, and exhibits of various kinds; (5) encouraging participation in extracurricular and community activities outside the home; and (6) fostering relationships with potential mentors (Hendricks & Scott, 1987) and other resource people in the community.

Preschool Programs.　A variety of preschool programs have been developed for young children who are gifted (Gross & Kirsten, 1987). Some children are involved in traditional programs, which are characterized by activities and curricula devoted primarily to the development of academic skills. Many of the traditional programs emphasize affective and social developments, as well. The entry criteria for these programs is varied, but the primary considerations are usually the child's IQ and social maturity. Moreover, the child must be skilled in following directions, attending to tasks of some duration, and controlling impulsive behavior.

Creativity programs are designed to help children develop their natural endowments in a number of artistic and creative domains. Another purpose of such programs is to help the children discover their own areas of promise. Children in these programs are also prepared for eventual involvement in the traditional academic areas of schooling.

13–3 The Prodigy: Norbert Wiener— Self-Analysis

There is one point which I would append to the discussion of my early reminiscences. It is probably of considerable interest to the reader to know how the very early intellectual development of the prodigy differs from that of other children. It is, however, impossible for the child, whether he be prodigy or not, to compare the earlier stages of his intellectual development with those of other children until he has reached a level of social consciousness which does not begin until late childhood.

I was well along in childhood, probably seven or eight, before I knew enough about the intellectual development of other children to comment in my own mind on their relative speed of learning and my own. By this time the earlier stages of the process of learning how to read and even the simpler aspects of learning my arithmetic had receded into the past almost as thoroughly as the average child's consciousness of learning how to speak. For this reason what I shall have to say about these matters will scarcely be distinguishable from the history of any other child, except on the basis of the precise year and month in my life at which I passed various stages of development. (p. 44)

Source: From *Ex-Prodigy: My Childhood and Youth.* Copyright © 1953 by Norbert Wiener. Copyright Renewed: 1981 by Margaret Wiener. Reprinted by permission of SIMON & SCHUSTER.

Preschool Programs for Children with Disabilities. Preschoolers with disabilities who are gifted are now served in several programs in the United States (Karnes & Johnson, 1991). Each program pursues the education and development process in varied ways. Some programs use Bloom's (1969) taxonomy of educational objectives, while others employ Guilford's (1956) structure of intellect model as the basis for advancing children's thinking processes. Individualization is a key component in the process.

Programs also vary according to the amount of structure provided in the preschool environment. The RAPYHT Program (Retrieval and Acceleration of Promising Young Handicapped and Talented) provides children with open-classroom as well as structured-classroom experiences. The open-classroom experience provides children with opportunities to initiate their own learning activities. The children also select the pace at which they will accomplish goals. Teachers in this classroom environment serve as facilitators. In contrast, the structured classroom is teacher directed. Learning activities are selected by the teacher, and the sequence of learning experiences is tightly structured (Karnes & Johnson, 1991).

Childhood and Adolescence

Giftedness in elementary and secondary students may be nurtured in a variety of ways (VanTassel-Baska, 1988). A number of service delivery systems and approaches are used in responding to the needs of students who are gifted. Frequently, the nurturing process has been referred to as **differentiated education,** that is, an education uniquely and predominately suited to the capacities and interests of individuals who are gifted.

Intervention Approaches. Selection of intervention approaches and organizational structures occurs as a function of a variety of factors (VanTassel-Baska, 1988; Williams, 1988). First, a school system must determine what types of giftedness it is capable of serving. It must also establish identification criteria and measures that allow it to select qualified students fairly. For example, if the system is primarily interested in advancing creativity, measures and indices of creativity should be utilized. If the focus of the program is accelerating math achievement and understanding, instruments measuring mathematical aptitude and achievement should be employed. With regard to identifying giftedness in students who are culturally different, progress in instrumentation and measurement development has been made (Baldwin, 1991; Khatena, 1982; Kirschenbaum, 1988). A variety of formal and informal approaches have been developed that allow practitioners to measure potential giftedness in culturally divergent students (Calahan, 1991; Richert, 1991; Robinson, Bradley, & Stanley, 1990). Second, the school system must select the organizational structures through which children who are gifted are to receive their differentiated educations. Third, school personnel must select the intervention approaches that are to be utilized within each program setting. Fourth, school personnel must select continuous evaluation procedures and techniques that help them assess the overall effectiveness of the program. Data generated from program evaluation efforts can serve as a catalyst for making appropriate changes.

Service Delivery Systems.   Once the types of giftedness to be emphasized have been selected and appropriate identification procedures have been established, planning must be directed at selecting suitable service delivery systems. Organizational structures for students who are gifted are similar to those found in other areas of special education. Clark (1983) described a continuum model that has been used to develop services for students who are gifted (see Figure 13–3). Each of the learning environments in the model has inherent advantages and disadvantages (Kramer, 1987a, 1987b). For example, students who are enrolled in regular classrooms and given opportunities to spend time in seminars, resource rooms, special classes, and other novel learning circumstances profit from the experiences because they are allowed to work at their own levels of ability (Parke, 1989). Furthermore, such pull-out activities provide a means for students to interact with each other and to pursue areas of interest that may not be part of the usual school curriculum (Renzulli & VanTassel-Baska, 1987). However, the disadvantages of such a program are many. The major part of

FIGURE 13–3

Clark's Continuum Model for Ability Grouping

(Adapted with permission of Merrill, an imprint of Macmillan Publishing Company, from *Growing Up Gifted* 3rd edition by Barbara Clark. Copyright © 1988, 1983, 1979 by Macmillan Publishing Company.)

Regular Classroom

Regular Class with Cluster

Regular Class with Pullout

Regular Class with Cluster and Pullout

Individualized Classroom

Individualized Classroom with Cluster

Individualized Classroom with Pullout

Individualized Classroom with Cluster and Pullout

Special Class with Some Integrated Classes

Special Class

Special School

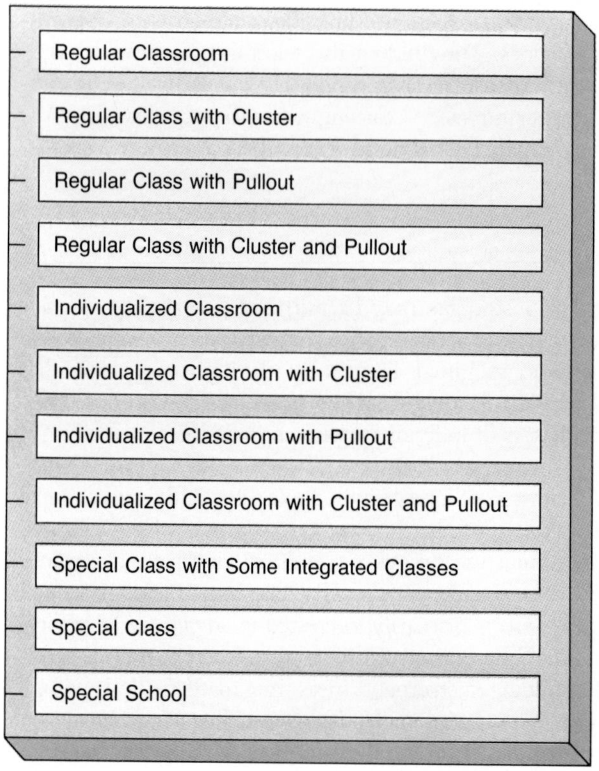

the instructional week is spent doing things that may not be appropriate for students who are gifted, given their abilities and interests. Additionally, when they return to regular school classes, they are frequently required to make up missed assignments.

Another example of Clark's continuum is the special class with opportunities for course work integrated with regular classes. This approach has many advantages. Students have the best of both worlds, academically and socially. Directed independent studies, seminars, mentorships, and cooperative studies are types of involvement that are made possible through this arrangement. Students who are gifted are able to interact in an intensive fashion with other able students as well as normal students in their integrated classes. This program also has disadvantages, however. A special class requires a well-trained teacher, and many school systems simply do not have sufficient funds to secure the services of a specially trained teacher. Without a skilled teacher, the special class instruction or other specialized learning activities may just be more of the regular curriculum. Unfortunately, many of the special classes that have been developed for students who are gifted emphasize quantity of assignments rather than quality.

The selection of service delivery systems is a function of available financing and human resources (e.g., trained personnel, specialists in gifted education, mentors, etc.) as well as local community values and conditions. Optimally, delivery systems should facilitate achievement of program goals. Furthermore, the selection of delivery systems should correspond with the types of giftedness being nurtured.

Acceleration.   Traditionally, programs for students who are gifted have emphasized the practices of acceleration and enrichment. **Acceleration** allows students to achieve at rates consonant with their capacities. Acceleration approaches provide for one or many of the following options: grade skipping, telescoped programs, rapid progress through subject matter, and early entry to college or advanced placement (Schiever & Maker, 1991). Grade skipping used to be a common administrative practice in providing for the needs of learners of high abilities, but it takes place much less frequently now. The decline in this practice is attributed to the conviction of some individuals that grade skipping may heighten a student's likelihood of becoming socially maladjusted. Others believe that accelerated students will experience significant gaps in learning because of grade skipping. Acceleration is generally limited to two years in the typical elementary school program.

Another practice related to grade skipping is telescoped or condensed schooling, which makes it possible for students to progress through the content of several grades in a significantly reduced timespan. An allied practice is that of allowing students to progress rapidly through a particular course or content offering. Acceleration of this nature provides students with the sequential, basic learning at a pace commensurate with their abilities. School programs that are ungraded are particularly suitable for telescoping. Because of their very nature, students, regardless of their chronological ages, may progress through a learning or curriculum sequence that is not constricted by artificial grade boundaries.

Other forms of condensed programing that occur at the high school level include earning credit by examination, enrolling in extra courses for early graduation, reducing or eliminating certain course work, enrolling in intensive summer programs, and completing university requirements while taking approved high school courses. Many of these options make it possible for students to enter college early or begin bachelor's programs with other advanced students. Dwight, the talented musician and broadcasting entrepreneur described in Window 13–1, was able to profit from honors courses in high school by earning college credit before his actual enrollment in a university. Many students who are gifted are ready for college-level course work at age 14, 15, or 16. Some students of unusually high abilities are prepared for college-level experiences prior to age 14.

Research on acceleration and its impact suggests that carefully selected students profit greatly from such experiences (Brody & Benbow, 1987; Kulik & Kulik, 1984; Thomas, 1987). The major benefits of acceleration, as established by research and effective practice, include improved motivation and confidence and early completion of advanced or professional training. In addition, acceleration prevents the "habits of mental laziness" (VanTassel-Baska, 1989a, p. 189).

Enrichment.   **Enrichment** refers to experiences that extend or broaden a person's knowledge in a vertical or horizontal fashion (Aylward, 1987; Klausmeier, 1986; Schiever & Maker, 1991). *Horizontal* enrichment refers to courses of study such as music appreciation, foreign languages, and mythology that are added to a student's curriculum. These courses are usually not any more difficult than other classes in which the student is involved. By contrast, *vertical* enrichment involves experiences in which the student develops sophisticated thinking skills (i.e., synthesis, analysis, interpretation, and evaluation) or opportunities to develop and master advanced concepts in a particular subject area (McAuliff & Stoskin, 1987). Some forms of enrichment are actually types of acceleration. A student whose enrichment involves having an opportunity to fully pursue mathematical concepts that are well beyond his or her present grade level is experiencing a form of acceleration. Obviously, the two approaches are interrelated.

The enrichment approach is the most common administrative provision utilized in serving students who are gifted. It is also the most abused approach in that it is often applied in name only and in a sporadic fashion, without well-delineated objectives or rationale. There are also other problems with the enrichment approach. It is the least expensive service delivery option; consequently, it is often utilized by school systems in a superficial fashion, as a token response to the demands of parents of children who are gifted. Enrichment activities are viewed by some professionals as periods devoted to educational trivia or instruction heavy in student assignments but light in content. Quality enrichment programs are characterized by carefully selected activities, modules, or units; challenging but not overwhelming assignments; and evaluations that are rigorous yet fair. Additionally, good enrichment programs are characterized by "a systematic plan for extended student learning" (Schiever & Maker, 1991, p. 99).

Students who are gifted do not appear to suffer socially from involvement in enrichment programs that take place outside the regular classroom. (Kevin Horan/Picture Group)

13–4   The Prodigy: Norbert Wiener— High School Years

I entered the Ayer high school in the fall of 1903 at the age of nine as a special student. We left the problem of my eventual classification for the future to decide. It soon became clear that the greater part of my work belonged to the third year of high school, so when the year was over I was transferred to the senior class to be graduated in June, 1906.

I had not attended school since I had gone to the Peabody School in Cambridge at the age of eight, and I had never attended school regularly. Now at the Ayer high school the seats were much too big for me and my adolescent fellow students seemed to me already full adults. I know that

Miss Leavitt tried to relieve me from the alarm of being in this unfamiliar place among unfamiliar figures, and on one occasion during my first few months at school, she took me on her lap during a recitation of the class. This kind act did not lead to any outburst of laughter or ridicule by the class, who seemed to consider me as the equivalent of their kid brothers. It was quite natural for a friendly teacher to take such a child on her lap when he visited the high school. (p. 93)

There, in my last year of high school and at the age of eleven, I fell in love with a girl who played the piano at our school concerts. She was about fifteen, the freckled daughter of a railroad man. Futile as it was, it was real love, and not the almost sexless affection of undeveloped children. She was

developed beyond her years. I was only eleven, but I was not even physically the typical eleven-year-old. My make-up was a mosaic of elements as young as eight and at least as old as fourteen. This calf love was quite as ridiculous to me as it must have seemed to others, and I was ashamed of it. I tried to show off in what was actually the least effective way open to me, and to compose a piece of music for her—I, the least musical of all boys. Like so many of these primitive attempts at composition, it sounded like nothing so much as the black keys of the piano struck in succession. (p. 99)

Source: From *Ex-Prodigy: My Childhood and Youth.* Copyright © 1953 by Norbert Wiener. Copyright Renewed: 1981 by Margaret Wiener. Reprinted by permission of SIMON & SCHUSTER.

There is a paucity of systematic experimental research regarding enrichment programs. Despite many of the limitations of current and past research, evidence supports the effectiveness of enrichment approaches (Callahan, 1981). However, little long-term experimental research addressing the effectiveness of enrichment programs has been conducted (Klausmeier, 1986). Nonexperimental evaluations of enrichment programs have indicated that students, teachers, and parents are generally satisfied with their nature and content. Enrichment activities do not appear to detract from the success students experience on regularly administered achievement tests. Sociometric data regarding students who are pulled out of regular classrooms for enrichment activities are also positive. Students do not appear to suffer socially from involvement in enrichment programs that take place outside normal classrooms.

Special Programs and Schools.   Programs designed to advance the talents of individuals in nonacademic areas, such as the visual and performing arts, have grown rapidly in recent years. Students involved in these programs frequently spend half their school day working in academic subjects and the other half in arts studies. Often the arts instruction is provided by an independent institution, but some school systems maintain their own separate schools. Most programs provide training in the visual and performing arts, but a few emphasize instruction in creative writing, motion picture and television production, and photography.

So-called *governor's schools* (distinctive summer programs generally held at university sites) and specialized residential or high schools in various states also provide valuable opportunities for students who are talented and academically gifted (Carpenter, 1987; Gold, Koch, Jordan, & Pendavis, 1987; Taffel, 1987). Competitively selected students are provided with curricular experiences that are closely tailored to their individual aptitudes and interests. Faculties for these schools are meticulously selected for competence in various areas and for

REFLECT ON THIS

13–5 The Prodigy: Norbert Wiener—College Years

I was admitted to Tufts on the basis of my high school record and a few easy examinations, which in my case were mostly oral. We bought a nearly finished house on the Hillside from the contractor builder, who lived next door to us, and had him complete it in accordance with our requirements. (p. 102)

My life was sharply divided between the sphere of the student and that of the child. I was not so much a mixture of child and man as wholly a child for purposes of companionship and nearly completely a man for purposes of study. Both my playmates and the college students were aware of this. My playmates accepted me as a child with them, although I might have been a slightly incomprehensible child, while my fellow students were willing to allow me to participate in their bull sessions if I wasn't too loud and too insistent. I was homesick for the earlier days when I had had a wealth of playmates in Cambridge. (p. 106–107)

In spite of this interest in biology, it was in mathematics that I was graduated. I had studied mathematics every year in college, largely under Dean Wren whose point of view was more nearly that of the engineer than that of Professor Ransom, who had taught me in my freshman year. I found the courses on calculus and differential equations quite easy, and I used to discuss them with my father who was thoroughly oriented in the ordinary college mathematics. For my routine of double recitation has not changed so far as my mathematical and cultural courses were concerned. In these my father remained my complete master, and there was not the slightest slackening in his stream of invectives. (p. 112)

Source: From *Ex-Prodigy: My Childhood and Youth.* Copyright © 1953 by Norbert Wiener. Copyright Renewed: 1981 by Margaret Wiener. Reprinted by permission of SIMON & SCHUSTER.

their ability to stimulate and motivate students. In Pennsylvania, the governor's school focuses solely on the visual and performing arts. Also, a number of universities offer exciting summer and year-round programs for high school students who are gifted (Clark & Zimmerman, 1987; Feldhusen, 1991; Hollingsworth, 1987; Leroux & DeFazio, 1987; Olszewski-Kubilius, 1989).

Career Education. Career education and career guidance are essential components of a comprehensive program for students who are gifted (VanTassel-Baska, 1989b). Ultimately, career education activities and experiences are designed to help students make educational and occupational decisions. Differentiated learning experiences provide elementary and middle school students with opportunities to investigate and explore. Many of these investigations and explorations are career related and designed to help students understand what it might be like to be a zoologist, neurosurgeon, or filmmaker. Students also become familiar with the training and effort necessary for work in these fields. In group meetings, they may discuss the factors that influenced a scientist to pursue a given problem or experiments that led to his or her eminence.

As students who are gifted grow and mature, both cognitively and physically, the nature and scope of their career education activities become more sophisticated and varied. New programs for individuals who are gifted emphasize leadership development and prepare them for active involvement in all kinds of organizations (Addison, Oliver, & Cooper, 1987).

Mentoring. Some students are provided opportunities to work directly with research scientists or other professionals who are conducting studies and investigations. Students may spend as many as two days a week, three or four working hours a day, in laboratory facilities. These students are mentored by the scientists and professionals with whom they work. Other students rely on intensive workshops or summer programs in which they are exposed to specialized careers through internships and individually tailored instruction.

Career Choices and Challenges. As you might surmise, there is a broad array of career choices and problems that students who are gifted must contend with in selecting a career. By virtue of their multifaceted abilities and interests, these individuals are often perplexed about what direction they should take in pursuing their studies. The following statements exemplify the dilemmas they face:

I have found that if I apply myself I can do almost anything. I don't seem to have a serious lack of aptitude in any field. I find an English assignment equally as difficult as a physics problem. I find them also to be equally as challenging and equally as interesting. The same goes for math, social studies, music, speech, or any other subject area. . . . Nothing is so simple for me that I can do a perfect job without effort, but nothing is so hard that I cannot do it. That is why it is so difficult to decide my place in the future. Many people wouldn't consider this much of a problem; but to me, this lack of one area to stand out in is a very grave problem indeed.★

When I look for a career in my future, the clouds really thicken. There are so many things I'd like to do and be, and I'd like to try them all; where to start is the problem. Sometimes there is so much happiness and loneliness and passion and joy and despair in me that I practically take off over the trees, and when I get like that I love to write poetry. Sometimes I go for months without writing any, and then it kind of bursts out of me like spontaneous combustion. I'll probably always be like this, but I would also like to be able to discipline myself enough to write more short stories or novels. I'd like to be a physical therapist, a foreign correspondent, a psychiatrist, an anthropologist, a linguist, a folk singer, an espionage agent, and a social worker.★★

Career guidance and other forms of counseling play an important role in helping people who are gifted utilize their remarkable abilities and talents. These students may have a difficult time making educational and career choices *because of* their multiple talents; may feel an inordinate amount of pressure to select a certain career or achieve in a certain manner because of the expectations of others; experience social isolation as a result of their unique abilities and preferences; and have problems selecting career options because of traditional cultural values and expectations. These problems can be addressed and perhaps solved if appropriate assistance is provided by skilled counselors and parents (Silverman, 1989).

The techniques used by counselors vary according to the nature of the problems and the student's characteristics. In some instances, students need help in resolving personal or social problems before they are able to address issues regarding career development and preparation. If the problem is social isolation, the counselor may help the student by involving him or her in a social skills group or group counseling program that emphasizes self-understanding and positive peer feedback. Problems caused by excessive or inappropriate parental expectations may need to be addressed in a family context, wherein the counselor helps parents develop realistic expectations that fit their child's abilities and true interests.

Problems and Challenges of Giftedness. Students who are gifted must cope with a number of problems (Buescher, 1991; VanTassel-Baska, 1989b). One problem is the expectations they have of themselves and those that have been explicitly and implicitly imposed

★ Reprinted, by permission, from Bruce G. Milne, "Career Education," in *The Gifted and the Talented: Their Education and Development, Seventy-Eighth Yearbook of the National Society for the Study of Education, Part 2,* A. Harry Passow (Ed.) (Chicago: University of Chicago Press, 1979), pp. 253–254.
★★M. P. Sanborn. (1979). Career development: Problems of gifted and talented students. In N. Colangelo and R. T. Zaffran (Eds.), *New Voices in Counseling the Gifted.* Dubuque, Iowa: Kendall Hunt Publishing Co. Copyright © 1979. Reprinted by permission of Kendall/Hunt Publishing Company.

REFLECT ON THIS

13–6 The Prodigy: Norbert Wiener— Outlook on the Future

I had not realized until my graduation how much the three years at Tufts had taken out of me. I was exhausted, but I could not stop the wheels from going around, and I could not rest. I did not prosper physically that summer. . . . My emotional state corresponded with my physical condition. The feeling of growing up out of the protection of childhood into that of responsibility had not been welcome to me. With my undergraduate days over, and an unknown future confronting me, I felt at loose ends.

I had had my due share of the brief gratification of commencement; but behind this happy moment were running the great questions: what should I do in the future and what hopes might I have of success?

The first question had been partly answered by my decision to do graduate work at Harvard. But the question of my success had an added poignancy. Though I had graduated *cum laude,* I had not been elected to Phi Beta Kappa. My record could be interpreted in two ways, and both my appointment and my nonappointment were defensible. But I was given to understand that the chief reason I did not receive the appointment was the doubt as to whether the future of an infant prodigy would justify the honor. This was the first time that I became fully aware of the fact that I was considered a freak of nature, and

I began to suspect that some of those about me might be awaiting my failure.

Fifteen years later when I received the honor denied me at my graduation, I had begun to make my mark on the scientific world. To appoint me then was to bet on a horse after the race was over. The appointment at the time of my graduation would have meant a trust in myself and in my future which would have been a source of strength. For a good measure of conceit mingled in me with a greater measure of unsureness. (p. 115–116)

———

Source: From *Ex-Prodigy: My Childhood and Youth.* Copyright © 1953 by Norbert Wiener. Copyright Renewed: 1981 by Margaret Wiener. Reprinted by permission of SIMON & SCHUSTER.

by parents, teachers, and others. Students who are gifted frequently feel an inordinate amount of pressure to achieve high grades or to select particular professions. They often feel obligated or duty bound to achieve and contribute with excellence in every area. Such pressure often fosters a kind of conformity, preventing students from selecting avenues of endeavor that truly fit them and their personal interests. A "survival guide" was developed by Delisle and Galbraith (1987) to help students 11 to 18 years of age deal with the challenges and problems of being gifted.

The importance of adult role models, or mentors, to children who are gifted and talented cannot be overemphasized. (Laima Druskis/Photo Researchers, Inc.)

INTERACTING IN NATURAL SETTINGS ·········· Children and Youth Who Are Gifted ··········

EARLY CHILDHOOD YEARS

Tips for the Family

◆ Realize that giftedness is evidenced in many ways (e.g., concentration, memory, pleasure in learning, sense of humor, social knowledge, task orientation, ability to follow and lead, capacity and desire to compete, information capacity, etc.).

◆ Provide toys for children who are gifted that may be used for a variety of activities.

◆ Take trips to museums, exhibits, fairs, and other places of interest.

◆ Provide an environment that is appropriately challenging.

◆ Supply proper visual, auditory, verbal, and kinesthetic stimulation.

◆ Talk to the child in ways that foster a give-and-take conversation.

◆ Begin to expose the child to picture books and ask him or her to find certain objects or animals or respond to age-appropriate questions.

◆ Avoid unnecessary restrictions.

◆ Provide play materials that are developmentally appropriate and maybe a little challenging.

Tips for the Preschool Teacher

◆ Look for ways in which various talents and skills may be expressed (e.g., cognitive, artistic, leadership, socialization, motor ability, memory, special knowledge, imagination, etc.).

◆ Provide opportunities for the child who is gifted to express these talents.

◆ Capitalize on the child's curiosity. Develop learning activities that relate to his or her passions.

◆ Allow the child to experiment with all the elements of language as he or she is ready—even written language.

Tips for Preschool Personnel

◆ Remember that conversation is critical to the child's development. Do not be reluctant to spend a great deal of time asking the child various questions as he or she engages in various activities.

◆ Become a specialist in looking for gifts and talents across a variety of domains (e.g., artistic, social, cognitive, etc.).

◆ Allow for rapid mastery of concepts and then allow the child to move on to other more challenging activities rather than holding him or her back.

Tips for Neighbors and Friends

◆ Recognize that people have a variety of gifts and talents that can be encouraged.

◆ Provide preschool opportunities for all children who are potentially gifted to have the necessary environmental ingredients to fully use their talents or gifts.

◆ Enjoy and sometimes endure the neighborhood child who has chosen your home as his or her lab for various experiments in cooking, painting, and building.

ELEMENTARY YEARS

Tips for the Family

◆ Maintain the search for individual gifts and talents; some qualities may not be evident until the child is older.

◆ Provide out-of-school experiences that foster talent or skill development (e.g., artistic, physical, academic, leadership, etc.).

◆ Enroll the child who is gifted in summer programs that are offered by universities or colleges.

◆ Monitor the child's school environment to be sure that adequate steps are being taken to respond to his or her unique skills.

◆ Join an advocacy group for parents in your community or state.

◆ Subscribe to child publications that are related to your child's current interests.

◆ Encourage you child's friendships and associations with other people who have like interests and aptitudes.

Tips for the Regular School Teacher

◆ Provide opportunities for enrichment as well as acceleration.

◆ Allow students who are gifted to pursue individual projects that require sophisticated forms of thinking or production.

◆ Become involved in professional organizations that provide assistance to teachers of students who are gifted.

◆ Take a course that specifically addresses the instructional strategies that might be used with children who are gifted.

◆ Encourage children to become active participants in various events that emphasize particular skill or knowledge areas (e.g., science fairs, music competitions).

Tips for School Personnel

◆ Develop clubs and programs that allow children who are gifted to pursue their talents.

◆ Create award programs that encourage talent development across a variety of domains.

◆ Involve community members in offering enrichment and acceleration activities (e.g., artists, engineers, writers).

◆ Foster the use of inclusive procedures for identifying students who are potentially gifted from minority and disadvantaged groups.

Tips for Neighbors and Friends

◆ Contribute to organizations that foster talent development.
◆ Volunteer to serve as judges for competitive events.
◆ Be willing to share your talents with young, emergent scholars, musicians, athletes, and artists.
◆ Become a mentor for someone in your community.

SECONDARY/TRANSITION YEARS

Tips for the Family

◆ Continue to provide sources of support for talent development outside of the home.
◆ Regularly counsel your child about courses that he or she will take.
◆ Provide access to tools (e.g., computers, video cameras) and resources (e.g., specialists, coaches, mentors) that contribute to the child's performance.
◆ Expect variations in performance from time to time.
◆ Provide opportunities for rest and relaxation from demanding schedules.
◆ Continue to encourage involvement with peers who have like interests and aptitudes.

Tips for the Regular School Teacher

◆ Provide a range of activities for students with varying abilities.
◆ Provide opportunities for students who are gifted to deal with real problems or develop actual products.
◆ Give opportunities for genuine enrichment activities, not just more work.
◆ Remember that giftedness manifests itself in many ways. How can various types of giftedness be expressed in your content domain?

◆ Help eliminate conflicting and confusing signals about career choices and fields of study often given to young women who are gifted.

Tips for School Personnel

◆ Provide, to the degree possible, a variety of curriculum options, activities, clubs, and the like.
◆ Acknowledge excellence in a variety of performance areas (e.g., leadership, visual and performing arts, academics).
◆ Continue to use inclusive procedures in identifying individuals who are potentially gifted and talented.
◆ Encourage participation in competitive activities in which students are able to use their gifts and talents (e.g., science fairs, debate tournaments, music competitions).

Tips for Neighbors, Friends, and Potential Employers

◆ Provide opportunities for students to "shadow" talented professionals.
◆ Volunteer as a professional to work directly with students who are gifted in pursuing a real problem or producing an actual product.
◆ Become a mentor for a student who is interested in what you do professionally.
◆ Support the funding of programs for students who are gifted and talented and who come from disadvantaged environments.
◆ Provide summer internships for students who have a particular interest in your profession.
◆ Serve as an advisor for a high school club or other organization that gives students additional opportunities to pursue talent areas.

VanTassel-Baska (1986b) identified a number of social-emotional needs of students who are gifted that differentiate them from their same-age peers. Such special needs include:

◆ Understanding how they are different from and similar to their peers
◆ Appreciating and valuing their own uniqueness as well as that of others
◆ Understanding and developing relationship skills
◆ Developing and valuing their high-level sensitivity
◆ Gaining a realistic understanding of their own abilities and talents
◆ Identifying ways of nurturing and developing their own abilities and talents
◆ Adequately distinguishing between pursuits of excellence and pursuits of perfection
◆ Developing the behaviors associated with negotiation and compromise

Students who are gifted often have access to adult role models who have interests and abilities that parallel theirs; the importance of these role models cannot be underestimated (Haeger & Feldhusen, 1987; Seeley, 1985). Role models are particularly important for able students who grow up and receive their schooling in rural and remote areas. Such students often complete their public schooling without the benefit of having a mentor or professional person with whom they can talk or discuss various educational and career-related issues.

WINDOW 13–3

SARAH

Sarah is now 20. She works as a motel clerk in a very small community in West Virginia. She is incredibly adept at her job, but it provides her with few if any challenges. She does most of the bookkeeping for the motel and manages its newly installed computer system.

Sarah enjoyed her schooling in her rural community and often helped other students when they struggled with their studies. Everything seemed to come easily to her. Her teachers were always impressed with her prowess in reading, broad interests, and solid performance on achievement tests. However, she was not directly encouraged to further her schooling.

No one in Sarah's family has ever gone to a university or community college. Her dad and his family have always been involved in mining. Her mother is a homemaker. Two nights a week, Sarah worked in a local cafe as a waitress. Earnings and tips from this job were used to take care of the family during the lean times when Dad was out of work. When Sarah finished high school, she knew she could work full time at the motel.

Sarah had no idea she was gifted. Nor did she know that she had the "smarts" necessary for college or university training. Going to school after high school was not something that had been encouraged in her family. Sarah had no role models or mentors.

HISTORICALLY NEGLECTED GROUPS

Females

Silverman (1986, p. 43) posed the question, "What happens to the gifted girl?" The number of girls identified as gifted appears to decline with age. This phenomenon is peculiar when we realize that girls tend to walk and talk earlier than their male counterparts; that girls, as a group, read earlier; that girls score higher than boys on IQ tests during the preschool years; and that the grade-point averages of girls during the elementary years are higher than those of boys (Silverman, 1986). Just exactly what happens to girls? Is the decline related to their socialization over time? Does some innate physiological or biological mechanism account for this decline? The answers to these and other important questions are gradually emerging.

REFLECT ON THIS

13–7   Encouraging Giftedness in Daughters

- Hold high expectations for daughters.
- Do not purchase gender-role-stereotyped toys.
- Avoid overprotectiveness.
- Encourage high levels of activity.
- Allow girls to get dirty.
- Instill beliefs in their capabilities.
- Support their interests.
- Get them identified as gifted during their preschool years.
- Find for them playmates who are gifted to identify with and emulate.

- Foster interests in mathematics outside of school.
- Consider early entrance and other opportunities to accelerate.
- Encourage daughters to take every mathematics course possible.
- Introduce them to professional women in many occupations.
- Encourage their mothers to acknowledge their own giftedness.
- Encourage their mothers to work at least part time outside the home.
- Encourage fathers to spend time alone with daughters in so-called masculine activities.
- Share household duties equally between the parents.
- Assign chores to siblings on a nonsexist basis.

- Discourage the use of sexist language or teasing in the home.
- Monitor television programs for sexist stereotypes, and discuss these with children of both genders.
- Encourage siblings to treat each other equitably, rather than according to the traditional gender-role stereotypes they see outside the home.

Source: From Silverman, L. K. (1986). What happens to the gifted girl? In C. J. Maker (Ed.), *Critical issues in gifted education, Vol. 1: Defensible programs for the gifted* (pp. 43–89). Austin, TX: Pro-Ed. (Copyright owned by author.) Adapted by permission.

REFLECT ON THIS

| 13–8 | Suggestions for Teachers and Counselors in Fostering Giftedness in Girls |

♦ Believe in girls' logicomathematical abilities, and provide many opportunities for them to practice mathematical reasoning within other subject areas.

♦ Accelerate girls through the science and mathematics curriculum whenever possible.

♦ Have special clubs in mathematics for girls who are high achieving.

♦ Design coeducational career development classes in which both girls and boys learn about career potentialities for women.

♦ Expose boys and girls to role models of women in various careers.

♦ Discuss nontraditional careers for women, including salaries for men and women and schooling requirements.

♦ Help girls set long-term goals.

♦ Discuss underachievement among females who are gifted and ask how they can combat it in themselves and others.

♦ Have girls read biographies of famous women.

♦ Arrange opportunities for girls to "shadow" a female professional for a few days to see what her work entails.

♦ Discourage sexist remarks and attitudes in the classroom.

♦ Boycott sexist classroom materials, and write to the publishers for their immediate correction.

♦ Discuss sexist messages in the media.

♦ Advocate special classes and after-school enrichment opportunities for students who are gifted.

♦ Form support groups for girls with similar interests.

Source: From Silverman, L. K. (1986). What happens to the gifted girl? In C. J. Maker (Ed.), *Critical issues in gifted education, Vol. 1: Defensible programs for the gifted* (pp. 43–89). Austin, TX: Pro-Ed. (Copyright owned by author.) Adapted by permission.

FOCUS 7

Identify six problems that complicate the selection of careers or professional pursuits for youth who are gifted.

FOCUS 8

Identify some of the problems that girls who are gifted experience in careers and other pursuits.

One of the explanations given for this decline is the gender-role socialization that girls receive. Behaviors associated with competitiveness, risk taking, and independence are not generally encouraged in girls. Behaviors that are generally fostered in girls include dependence, cooperation, and nurturing. The elimination of independent behaviors in girls is viewed by Silverman (1986) as being the most damaging aspect of their socialization. Without independence, the development of high levels of creativity, achievement, and leadership are severely limited. Research indicates that females who achieve a high degree of excellence as adults combine the beliefs, values, expectations, and behaviors that are a composite of both genders (Silverman, 1986).

Females, who are gifted and talented experience unique problems, in addition to those identified above (Feldhusen, VanTassel-Baska, & Seeley, 1989; Kerr, 1991; Silverman, 1986). These problems include fear of success, competition between marital and career aspirations, stress induced by traditional cultural and societal expectations, and self-imposed and/or culturally imposed restrictions related to educational and occupational choices (Buescher, Olszewski, & Higham, 1987; Kerr, 1985). Although many of these problems are far from being resolved at this point, some progress is being made (Fox & Tobin, 1988; Goldsmith, 1987; Hollinger & Fleming, 1988). Women in greater numbers are choosing to enter professions traditionally pursued primarily by men.

Fortunately, multiple role assignments are emerging in many family units, wherein the usual tasks of mothers are shared by all members of the family or are completed by someone outside the family. Cultural expectations are changing, and as a result, options for women who are gifted are rapidly expanding.

Persons with Disabilities

For some time, intellectual giftedness has been largely associated with high IQs and high scores on aptitude tests. These tests, by their very nature and structure, measure a limited range of mental abilities. Because of their limitations, they have not been particularly helpful

Daniel Day-Lewis won an Oscar for his portrayal of the character Christy Brown in the film *My Left Foot,* the true story of a gifted writer who has cerebral palsy. (Miramax/Shooting Star)

in identifying persons with disabilities who are intellectually gifted. However, researchers and clinicians have discovered that persons with disabilities such as cerebral palsy, learning disabilities, and other disabling conditions can in fact be gifted (Karnes & Johnson, 1991; Whitmore & Maker, 1985). Helen Keller was a prime example of an individual who was disabled and also gifted.

In this context, the person who is gifted is defined as "one who has exhibited exceptional potential for (a) learning, (b) achieving academic excellence in one or more subject areas,

13–9 Specific Characteristics of Mexican-American Students Who May Be Gifted

- Rapidly acquires English language skills once exposed to the language and given an opportunity to use it expressively
- Exhibits leadership ability, be it open or unobtrusive, with heavy emphasis on interpersonal skills
- Has older playmates and easily engages adults in lively conversation
- Enjoys intelligent (or effective) risk-taking behavior, often accompanied by a sense of drama
- Is able to keep busy and entertained, especially by imaginative games and ingenious applications, such as getting the most out of a few simple toys and objects
- Accepts responsibilities at home normally reserved for older children, such as supervising younger siblings or helping others do their homework
- Is "street-wise" and recognized by others as someone who has the ability to "make it" in the Anglo-dominated society

Sources: Bernal, 1974; VanTassel-Baska, 1989c.

and (c) manifesting superior abilities through language, problem solving and creative production" (Whitmore & Maker, 1985, p. 10). Although many challenges are still associated with identifying individuals who are disabled and gifted, much progress has been made. Factors critical to successful identification of giftedness include environments that elicit signs of mental giftedness and information about the individual's performance gathered from many sources. With regard to these eliciting environments, it is important that the child or youth be given opportunities to perform tasks that are not impeded by his or her disabling condition. Also, if and when tests of mental ability are used, they must be appropriately adapted, both in administration and scoring (Whitmore & Maker, 1985).

Differential education for children and youth who are disabled and gifted is still in its infancy. A great deal of progress has been made, particularly in the adaptive uses of computers and related technologies, but much development work remains to be done. Additionally, a great deal is still unknown about the service delivery systems and materials that are best suited for these individuals.

Children and Youth Who Are Disadvantaged

Typical identification procedures often fail to identify children and youth as being gifted when they come from minority groups or disadvantaged environments. However, recent research conducted by VanTassel-Baska and Chepko-Sade (1986) has suggested that as many as 15.5 percent of the gifted population may be children who are disadvantaged. In fact, the actual number of students who are disadvantaged and also gifted may be even greater, given the identification criteria used in this study. By definition, children and youth who are gifted and come from economically deprived or culturally different environments do not have the resources to "make it on their own" (VanTassel-Baska, 1989c, p. 54).

Several procedures have been developed to more accurately identify children who are disadvantaged and also gifted: employing nontraditional measures; using multiple criteria; considering broader ranges of scores for inclusion in special programs; peer nomination; parent nomination; assessments by persons other than educational personnel; and information provided by adaptive behavior assessments (Robinson, Bradley & Stanley, 1990). For example, if 60 percent of the students in a given school population come from a certain cultural minority group and only 2 percent are identified as gifted using traditional measures, the screening committee may reexamine its identification procedures or adjust the cutoff scores for students who represent the minority group.

Intervention programs for children and youth who are disadvantaged and gifted have several key components. There is a general consensus that the programs should begin early. The programs should also be tailored to the needs of individual children. Often the emphasis in the early years is on reading instruction, language development, and foundation skills. Other key components include parental involvement in the educational program model, experiential education that provides children with many opportunities for hands-on learning, activities that foster self-expression, plentiful use of mentors and role models who represent the child's cultural or ethnic group, involvement of the community, and counseling throughout the schoolyears that gives serious consideration to the cultural values of the family and the child who is gifted (VanTassel-Baska, 1989c).

Debate   Forum   · What Would You Do with Jane? · · · · · · · · · · · · · · · · · · ·

Many children who are gifted are prevented from accelerating their growth and learning for fear that they will be hurt emotionally and socially. Parents' comments such as these are common: "She's so young." "Won't she miss a great deal if she doesn't go through the fourth- and fifth-grade experiences?" "What about her friends?" "Who will her friends be if she goes to college at such a young age?" "Will she have the social skills to interact with kids that are much older?" "If she skips these two grades, won't there be gaps in her learning and social development?"

On the other hand, the nature of the questions or comments by parents about acceleration may also be positive: "She is young in years only! She will adjust extremely well." "Maybe she is emotionally mature enough to handle this type of acceleration." "The increased opportunities provided through university training will give her greater chances to develop her talents and capacities." "Perhaps the older students with whom she will interact are better suited to her intellectual and social needs."

Let us consider Jane. She is a child who is gifted. In third grade, she thrived in school, and just about everything associated with her schooling at that time was positive. Her teacher was responsive and allowed her and others to explore well beyond the usual "read-the-text-then-respond-to-the-ditto-sheet" routine. A lot of self-pacing was possible. Materials galore were presented for both independent studies and queries.

In the fourth and fifth grades, however, things began to change radically. Jane's teachers were simply unable to provide enough interesting and challenging work for her. It was during the latter part of the fourth grade that she began to view herself as being different. Not only did she know, but her classmates knew that learning came exceptionally easily to her. At this same time, Jane was beginning to change dramatically in her cognitive capacity. Unfortunately, her teachers persisted in unnecessary drills and other mundane assignments. Jane gradually became bored and lapsed into a type of passive learning. Rather than attacking assignments with vigor, she performed them carelessly, often making many stupid errors. Gradually, what ensued was a child who was very unhappy in school. Where she most wanted to be before she entered fourth grade became a source of pain and boredom.

Jane's parents decided that they needed to know more about her capacities and talents. Although it was expensive and quite time consuming, they visited a nearby university center for psychological services. Jane was tested, and the results were very revealing. For the first time, Jane's parents had some objective information about her capacities. She was in fact an unusually bright and talented young lady. Jane's parents then began to consider the educational alternatives available to her.

The counselor who provided the interpretation of the results at the university center strongly recommended that Jane be advanced to the seventh grade in a school that provided services to students who were talented and gifted. This meant that Jane would skip one year of elementary school and have an opportunity to move very rapidly through her junior and senior high school studies. Furthermore, she would potentially be able to enter the university well in advance of her peers.

Jane's parents know that her performance has diminished significantly in the last year. Moreover, her attitude and disposition about school seem to be worsening. What would you do as her parents? What factors would you consider important in making the decision? Or is the decision Jane's and hers alone?

Point   Jane should be allowed to accelerate her educational pace. Moving to the seventh grade will benefit her greatly, intellectually and socially. Most girls develop more rapidly physically and socially than boys do. Skipping one grade will not hinder her social development at all. In fact, she will benefit from the interactions that she will have with other able students, some of whom will also have skipped a grade or two. Additionally, the research regarding the impact of accelerating students is positive, particularly if the students are carefully selected. Jane has been carefully evaluated and deserves to have the opportunity to be excited about learning and achieving again.

Counterpoint   There are some inherent risks in having Jane skip her sixth-grade experience and move on to the seventh grade. Jane is neither socially nor emotionally prepared to deal with the junior high environment. She may be very able intellectually and her achievement may be superior, but this is not the time to move her into junior high. Socially, she is still quite awkward for her age. This awkwardness would be intensified in the junior high setting. Acceleration for Jane should be considered later on, when she has matured more socially.

She should be able to receive the acceleration that she needs in her present elementary school. Certainly, there are other able students in her school who would benefit from joining together for various activities and learning experiences. The acceleration should take place in her own school, with other students who are gifted and of her own age. Maybe all Jane needs is some release time to attend a class or two elsewhere. Using this approach, she could benefit from involvement with her same-age peers and still receive the stimulation that she so desperately needs. Allowing her to skip a grade now would hurt her emotionally and socially in the long run.

REVIEW ••

FOCUS 1   Briefly describe several historical developments directly related to the measurement of various types of giftedness.

◆ Alfred Binet developed the first developmental scale for children during the early 1900s.

◆ Gradually, the notion of mental age emerged, that is, a representation of what the child was capable of doing compared to age-specific developmental tasks.

◆ Lewis M. Terman translated the Binet scale and made modifications suitable for children in the United States.

◆ Gradually, the intelligence quotient, or

$$IQ \text{ (mental age/chronological age} \times 100 = IQ),$$

became the gauge for determining giftedness.

◆ Intelligence, for a long time, was viewed as being a unitary structure or underlying ability. But gradually, the view of the nature of intelligence changed, and researchers began to believe that intelligence was represented in a variety of distinct capacities and abilities. J. P. Guilford and other social scientists began to develop a multidimensional theory of intelligence, which prompted researchers to develop models and assessment devices for examining creativity.

◆ Programs were gradually developed to foster and develop creativity in young people.

FOCUS 2   Identify six major components of definitions that have been developed to describe giftedness.

◆ Gifted individuals should be identified by qualified assessment personnel.

◆ Gifted individuals may demonstrate their extraordinary abilities in a variety of domains—general intellectual abilities, specific academic aptitude, creative or productive thinking, leadership abilities, achievements in visual or performing arts, and psychomotor ability.

◆ Children who are gifted may be identified during the preschool, elementary, or secondary school periods.

◆ Children who are gifted exhibit high levels of task commitment and creativity.

◆ Such children combine their high levels of intelligence, task commitment, and creativity to eventually make lasting contributions in their fields of endeavor.

◆ Children who are gifted need special educational opportunities in order to realize their full intellectual and creative potential.

FOCUS 3   Identify four problems inherent in accurately describing the characteristics of individuals who are gifted.

◆ Individuals who are gifted vary significantly on a variety of characteristics; they are not a homogeneous group.

◆ Research regarding the characteristics of people who are gifted has been conducted with different population groups; therefore, the characteristics that have surfaced represent the population studied rather than the population as a whole.

◆ Many early studies of individuals who are gifted led to a stereotypical view of giftedness.

◆ Historically, studies regarding the characteristics of individuals who are gifted have not included adequate samples of females, minority or ethnic groups, or socioeconomic groups.

FOCUS 4   Identify four factors that appear to contribute significantly to the emergence of various forms of giftedness.

◆ Genetic endowment certainly contributes to manifestations of giftedness in all of its varieties.

◆ Environmental stimulation provided by parents, teachers, coaches, tutors, and others contributes significantly to the emergence of giftedness.

◆ The interaction of innate abilities with environmental influences and encouragement fosters the development and expression of giftedness.

◆ The development of high levels of task commitment in individuals who are gifted determines the level and nature of contributions that they eventually make to themselves and their extended communities.

FOCUS 5   Describe the range of assessment devices used to identify the various types of giftedness.

◆ Developmental checklists and scales
◆ Parent and teacher inventories
◆ Intelligence and achievement tests
◆ Problem-solving and information-processing tests
◆ Creativity tests
◆ Biographical inventories
◆ Other observational measures

FOCUS 6   Identify eight interventions that are utilized to foster the development of children and youth who are gifted.

◆ Environmental stimulation provided by parents from infancy through adolescence

◆ Differentiated education and specialized service delivery systems that provide enrichment activities and/or possibilities for acceleration: grade skipping; early entrance to college; honors programs at the high school and college levels; specialized schools in the performing and visual arts; mentor programs with university professors and other talented individuals; and specialized counseling facilities.

FOCUS 7   Identify six problems that complicate the selection of careers or professional pursuits for youth who are gifted.

◆ Because individuals who are gifted are often talented, capable, and interested in a broad spectrum of areas, they find it difficult to make an appropriate choice relative to a career or profession.

◆ Women who are gifted may lack adequate models or mentors with whom to identify in pursuing various career and professional options.

◆ They may also be influenced by traditional cultural and societal expectations that are restrictive.

◆ Youth who are gifted may be unduly influenced by their parents' expectations, their own expectations, and their preconceived notions as to what people who are gifted ought to do professionally or academically.

◆ Some youth who are gifted are socially isolated in the sense that they do not have access to peers who are gifted and with whom they can discuss their aspirations, interests, and problems.

◆ Youth who are gifted and live in rural or remote areas may have few if any role models with whom they can relate or identify.

FOCUS 8   Identify some of the problems that girls who are gifted experience in careers and other pursuits.

◆ Fear of success

◆ Competition between marital and career aspirations

◆ Stress induced by traditional cultural and societal expectations

◆ Self-imposed or culturally imposed restrictions related to educational and occupational choices

Chapter Fourteen

Impact of Exceptionality on the Family

TO BEGIN WITH . . .

- No one plans to have a child with disabilities.

- "The birth of a child with a disability is an unanticipated event. No family—regardless of race, ethnicity, or socioeconomic status—is immune to childhood disability; yet almost all are poorly prepared to cope with its occurrence" (Seligman & Darling, 1989, p. vii).

- "[I was most worried about] how he would develop. It was the uncertainty of not knowing whether he'd be able to go to school and get a job or whether he'd always be dependent on us. It was just not knowing what was likely to happen and what the future held for him and for us" (Baxter, 1986, p. 85).

- For every 100 babies born, 3 will have major defects. This statistic has remained stable since 1960, when researchers first began to collect these data (Adler, 1987).

- It can cost a family over $100,000 to raise a child with a disability to the age of 18. There is some feeling that costs of equipment, in particular, may be inflated. For example, in 1982 a motorized wheelchair cost $3,450. In comparison, a two-seated motorized golf cart cost $1,900, while a farm tractor cost $3,000 (Hutchinson, 1982).

- Since 1970, over 80 percent of the litigation for rights and services has been decided in favor of children with disabilities and their families. However, subsequent improvement in opportunities and programs has not matched the extent of the legal victories (Blatt, 1988).

CHARLES

WHAT DO I DO NOW? I learned of my son's condition when my wife telephoned me to come to the hospital soon after the birth of our fourth child. This was the third day of life for my son, and it was then that I learned he was mongoloid—a term I soon replaced with the description Down syndrome.

My first reaction was: What do I do now? How do I take care of this person? It was a feeling of helplessness and despair. One of my wife's first comments was, "I don't even want to hold him!" This impulse to reject the new baby lasted only one or two days but was replaced by a numbness. After that, a feeling of self-pity and wondering why this had happened to us came along. We then got tired of not doing anything, so we began looking for help from people and organizations. My wife and I decided to treat our son in the same manner as we did our other children as much as possible. Our expectations have been great, and in most cases, our son has fulfilled them.

I wouldn't wish this traumatic experience on any family, but after 16 years, my son has brought a whole new dimension of understanding, patience, and happiness to me and other members of our family.

Charles, A Father

*I*NTRODUCTION

Nowhere is the impact of an individual who is exceptional felt so strongly as in the family. The birth of an infant with disabilities may alter the family as a social unit in a variety of ways. Parents and siblings may react with shock, disappointment, anger, depression, guilt, and confusion. Relationships between family members often change, in either a positive or a negative manner. The impact of such an event is great, and it is unlikely that the family unit will ever be the same.

A child with physical, intellectual, or behavioral problems presents unique and diverse challenges to the family unit. In one instance, the child may hurl the family into crisis, resulting in major conflicts among its members. Family relationships may be weakened by the added and unexpected physical, emotional, and financial stress imposed on them (Shelton, Jeppson, & Johnson, 1987). In another instance, family members may see this child as a source of unity that bonds them and actually strengthens relationships. Many factors influence the reactions of family members: the emotional stability of each individual, religious values and beliefs, socioeconomic status, the severity of the child's disability, and the type of disability, to identify only a few.

In this chapter, we discuss how rearing children with disabilities affects parents. We examine a broad array of family and parental issues directly related to rearing children with various types and degrees of exceptional conditions. We review the family as a social system defined by a set of purposes, roles, and expectations. Each family member fulfills various roles that are consistent with expectations established by discussion, tradition, or other means. Each member functions in an interdependent manner with other members to pursue family goals. Using a social system framework, we can see how changes in one family member can have an effect on every other member and consequently the entire family system. If we accept the notions and concepts associated with this sociological view of a family, we can see how the birth and continued presence of a child with a disorder can significantly affect the family unit over time.

FOCUS 1

Identify five factors that influence the ways in which families respond to infants with birth defects or disabilities.

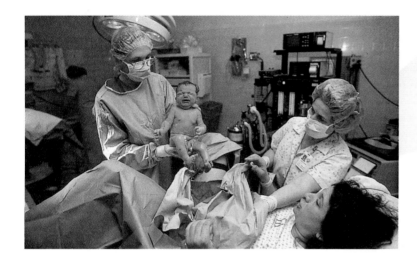

The initial diagnosis that their child has a disability has a heavy and complex impact on parents. (M Richards/PhotoEdit)

FAMILY CRISIS: THE INITIAL IMPACT

The birth of an infant with significant disabilities has a profound impact on the family. The expected or fantasized child whom the parents and other family members have anticipated does not arrive. The birth of an infant with a conspicuous **congenital** defect or abnormality throws parents into a kind of emotional shock (Seligman & Darling, 1989).

Some conditions, such as spina bifida or **Down syndrome,** are readily apparent at birth (Volpe & Koenigsberger, 1981), while others, such as hearing disorders and learning disabilities, are not detectable until later. Even if attending physicians suspect the presence of a disabling condition, they may be unable to give a confirmed diagnosis without the passage of some time and further testing. When the parents also suspect that something may be wrong, waiting for a diagnosis can be agonizing.

The most immediate and predictable reaction to the birth of a child with a disorder is depression, often exhibited in the form of grief or mourning. Some parents describe the mourning as being very much like that suffered after the death of a loved one. Mothers whose abnormal babies survive frequently suffer more acute feelings of grief than mothers whose abnormal infants die. Mothers also tend to mourn for a longer period before they recover in this instance (D'Arcy, 1968). Recurrent sorrow and frequent feelings of inadequacy are persistent emotions that many parents experience as they gradually adjust to having an infant who is atypical (Peterson, 1987).

Other reactions on the part of family members include shock, uncertainty, disappointment, anger, frustration, guilt, denial, fear, withdrawal, and rejection (Blacher, 1984; Bristor, 1984; Gargiulo, 1985; Rose, 1987). The level of impact varies, but for most parents, such an event creates a family crisis of considerable magnitude.

Gargiulo (1985) suggested that parental responses may be separated into three stages: (1) the primary phase, which is characterized by shock, denial, and finally grief, often accompanied by depression; (2) the secondary phase, marked by ambivalence, followed by guilt and then anger, shame, and embarrassment; and (3) the tertiary phase, which begins with bargaining, then adaptation and reorganization, and lastly, acceptance and adjustment. However, research completed by Blacher (1984) suggested that the stage approach used by many professionals to understand, predict, and help parents deal with their newborn children with disabilities needs further refinement and validation.

What we can assume is that parents of children with disabilities experience common feelings and reactions that may occur during certain periods of time. However, the nature

FOCUS 2

What three statements can be made about the stages that parents may experience in responding to infants or young children with disabilities?

of the feelings, their intensity, their relationship to specific stages, and the eventual adjustments that are made personally and collectively by family members vary from one person to another. Stages associated with various kinds of emotions may overlap with one another. Emotions of one period may resurface again during another period. Some parents may go through distinct periods of adjustment, whereas others may adjust without passing through any sequence of stages.

Further research will help us understand the very complex, multifaceted relationships that exist among these factors and the responses that parents and other family members make during the lifetime of a child with a disability. We can, however, say that the process of adjustment for parents is continuous and distinctively individual.

> When our son was born my husband and I were told that the parents of a [disabled] child move through certain stages of reaction: shock, guilt, reaction, and anger, all terminating in the final, blissful stage of adjustment. I do not believe in this pattern. I now know too many parents of [disabled] children to be a believer in any set pattern.
>
> I feel we do move through these emotions, and just because we have come to adjustment (which I prefer to call "acceptance" because we spend our whole lives adjusting, although we may at one point accept the situation), that does not mean we never return to other emotions. We may continue to feel any of these emotions at any time, in any order. (West, 1981, p. S10)

In sum, mothers and fathers of children with disabilities are affected in diverse ways. The range and sequence of emotions can be highly variable. Some parents move through distinct stages and phases, while others seem not to follow any emotional pattern. At this juncture, we analyze some of the phases that parents may experience in responding to their child, illustrating the vast array of feelings parents may face.

Shock

The initial response to the birth of an infant who is disabled is generally shock. This phase may be distinguished by feelings of anxiety, guilt, numbness, confusion, helplessness, anger, disbelief, denial, and despair. Sometimes, there are feelings of detachment, bewilderment, or bereavement. At this time, when many parents are most in need of assistance, the least amount of help may be available. The length of time it takes parents to deal with these feelings or move through this period depends on their psychological makeup, the types of assistance rendered, and the seriousness of the disabling condition.

During the initial shock period, parents may be unable to process or comprehend information provided by medical and other health-related personnel. For this reason, information given to parents may need to be repeated on several occasions until they have fully grasped the concepts presented. Also during this time, parents may experience the greatest assaults on their self-worth and value systems. They may blame themselves for the disabilities present in their child. They may seriously question their positive perceptions of themselves. Likewise, they may be forced to reassess the meaning of life and the reasons for their present challenges. Blacher (1984) has referred to this stage as *the period of emotional disorganization*.

Realization

The stage of realization is characterized by several types of parental behavior. Parents may be anxious or fearful about their ability to cope with the demands of caring for a child with unique needs. They may be easily irritated or upset. Considerable time may be spent in self-accusation, self-pity, or self-hate. Information provided by health care professionals during this period may still be rejected or denied. However, during this stage, parents come to understand the actual demands and constraints that will come with raising a child who is exceptional. This realization frequently overwhelms couples, and as a result, they may remove themselves from family and social activities for a period of time.

Defensive Retreat

The stage of defensive retreat is one in which parents attempt to avoid dealing with the anxiety-producing realities of their child's condition. They may try to solve their dilemma by seeking placement for the child in a clinic, institution, or residential setting. Some parents respond by disappearing for a while or by retreating to a safer and less demanding environment. One mother, on returning home from the hospital with her infant with Down syndrome, quickly packed her suitcase and left with the infant in the family car, not knowing exactly what her destination would be. She simply did not want to face her immediate family or relatives. After driving around for several hours, she decided to return home. Within several months, she adapted very well to her daughter's needs and began to provide the stimulation necessary for gradual, persistent growth. Her daughter is now married and works full time in a day-care center for young children.

Acknowledgement

Acknowledgement is the stage in which parents are able to mobilize their strengths to confront the conditions created by having a child who is exceptional. At this stage, parents become capable of involving themselves in the intervention and treatment process. They

Once parents acknowledge their child's disability, they become a very important part of the intervention process. Zabala/Monkmeyer Press)

are also better able to comprehend information or directions provided by a specialist concerning their child's condition and treatment. At this time, some parents become interested in joining an advocacy organization that is suited to their child's condition and the needs of the family. During this stage, parents begin to accept the child with the disability as well as others and even themselves. It is during this stage that parents become capable of directing their energies to tasks and problems outside of themselves.

FOCUS 3

Identify four major concerns of parents of children who are exceptional.

We must remember, however, that patterns of parental response are highly variable. Parents and families respond to the birth and ongoing development of children and siblings with disabilities in common yet divergent ways. Furthermore, the time required for parents and others to make the various adjustments is extremely variable. The stage approach provides us with one frame of reference for understanding the ongoing reactions and adjustments parents make in rearing children with congenital or acquired disabilities. Further research will help us to understand the range, duration, and nature of these parental responses.

Parents of children who are exceptional have many other concerns. They especially want to know what their child's future educational and social needs will be. They want to know what their child will be capable of doing as he or she grows older and becomes an adult. They want to know how the presence of the child will affect other family members. Most importantly, they want to know how to maintain normal family functioning and manage the stress associated with having a child who is exceptional.

CHANGES IN FAMILY ROLES AND PATTERNS

FOCUS 4

Identify three ways in which a newborn child with disabilities influences the manner in which family members respond to each other.

The birth and continued presence of a child with disabilities strongly influence the manner in which family members respond to one another, particularly if the child is severely disabled or has multiple disabilities. In many families, it is often the mother who experiences the greatest amount of trauma and strain in responding to conditions created by the presence of a child who is exceptional. In caring for the child, she may no longer be able to handle the other tasks she once performed, such as preparing meals, doing laundry, doing the weekly grocery shopping, and assisting with homework assignments. Her time with the family may also be greatly reduced because of time spent taking care of the child's unique needs.

When the mother is drawn away from the tasks she used to perform, other family members must often assume more responsibility. It may be difficult for family members to adjust to the new roles and routines that result from having a child who is exceptional in the family. Each family member may need to alter his or her personal routine in order to assist the mother. Initially, the demands and needs of the child may be numerous and time consuming. For families that are already experiencing serious emotional, financial, or other problems, the addition of a child who is exceptional may serve as the catalyst for dissolution.

As the child grows older, the mother is frequently faced with a unique dilemma: how to strike a balance between the nurturing activities she associates with her role as caregiver and the activities associated with fostering independence. It can be difficult for mothers to see their children struggle with new tasks and suffer some of the natural consequences of trying new behaviors. For many mothers, overprotectiveness is extremely difficult to conquer, but it can be accomplished with help provided by others who have already experienced and mastered this problem. If the mother or other care providers continue to be overprotective, the results can be disastrous, particularly when the child reaches late adolescence and is unprepared for entry into adulthood or semi-independent living.

Each family exhibits a characteristic pattern of conveying information to family members. The pattern and type of communication vary according to the size of the family, its cultural background, and its members' ages. Generally, information conveyed to the family regarding the nature of a child's disorder is provided by the father, particularly if the exceptionality is diagnosed at birth. Once initial information regarding the child's condition has been conveyed to siblings, older children frequently become responsible for providing additional clarification to younger ones.

At first, a new closeness may occur in families who discover that one of the children has a disorder. During this period, the mother frequently senses this closeness, and it serves to support her. Over time, however, this support may wane, and family members may gradually move away from the family unit to associate more closely with peers or friends. Questions that children may want to ask parents regarding family issues may be posed to older siblings, or they may not be asked at all. Such behavior is probably a function of the strain that the children sense in their parents. It is a natural outcome and one that is to be expected in families in which parents must direct a great deal of their attention to a child with a disability.

Mothers often develop strong **dyadic relationships** with their children who are exceptional. Other dyadic relationships may also develop between various other members of the family. Certain siblings may turn to each other for support and nurturing. Older siblings may take on the role of parent substitutes as a result of their new caregiving responsibilities. Younger children, who come to depend on older siblings for care, then tend to develop strong relationships with them.

R E F L E C T O N T H I S

14–1 Innovative Approaches to Family Support

Chicago Pilot Program for Home Care

In a northern suburb of Chicago, Illinois, one family with a child with a developmental disability has successfully fought for the resources to care for that family member at home. By receiving state and federal reimbursement equal to what it would cost to care for their daughter in a group home, Ellen and Ed M. have been able to hire respite caregivers for Laura, who is fourteen, and to keep her at home.

Laura had been placed in a group home at the age of ten. Non-ambulatory and non-verbal, Laura required extensive assistance. . . . But the M.'s were not happy with placing Laura away from home. Ellen M. said: "It just didn't make sense that a child would leave the family at 10 years. There was this emptiness that something wasn't the way it should be."

With the help of Community Alternatives Unlimited, a case management services provider, the M.'s and their friends formed Community Living Inc. (CLI), a nonprofit group dedicated to aiding the families of children with disabilities in Chicago's northern suburbs. CLI asked the state to authorize a pilot project for Laura; the proposal was approved. In March 1989, Laura returned home.

The state agreed to provide the same level of funding that it was providing for Laura in the group home, which is about half of what it would have cost to move her to a state-run institution, and to assist the M.'s in home adaptations, including installation of outdoor and indoor chairlifts. Two other resources were the Social Security Administration's SSI program and the state's respite care program. The state funds actually go to CLI, which, with no administrative expenses, use all of the available resources to pay for the caregivers. Laura is home now because the M.'s have caregivers for 47 hours in a typical week—from 3 P.M. to 8 P.M. during the week

and eleven hours a day on Saturdays and Sundays. During the week, Laura attends Wilmette Junior High School for half the day where she has a busy schedule assisted by three other seventh grade girls who have volunteered their services, and an aide. She helps catalogue materials in the library as part of her schedule, and also takes a computer class with the help of assistive technology.

Ellen M. is hopeful that Laura's community integration will continue to grow as everyone involved recognizes its value to both her and to her community. Although the M.'s acknowledge that a home-care program may not be the best alternative for every family with a child with a disability, they believe that, in Laura's case, "As long as she's a child, this is where she belongs, under our roof."

Source: From "Innovative Approaches to Family Support: Chicago Pilot Program for Home Care," Fall 1990, *Family Support Bulletin*, p. 9. Reprinted by permission from *Family Support Bulletin*. Published by United Cerebral Palsy Associations, Inc.

WINDOW 14–2

VIEW FROM A HUSBAND

We were just beginning to get our feet on the ground when it happened. We had been in our new home for about two years. My job had been demanding yet fulfilling. Our daughter, Maria, was doing well in the fifth grade, and everything about our family life and marriage was almost ideal. Angela was pregnant, and we were excited about having our last child. I was hoping for a boy, and I think Angela was, too.

Our boy, Juan, did arrive, but during the birth process, he suffered extensive brain damage. From that point on, the tone of

our marriage and family life went from optimism to pessimism and continual doubt. My wife spent so much time reading books about brain damage, keeping medical appointments, and caring for Juan that Maria and I have been forced to pursue other activities. We often avoid contact with my wife, since she has become demanding and domineering. I find it difficult to communicate with her. Somehow, we have lost the affection and affinity we once had for each other.

Carlos

FOCUS 5

What kind of relationship may develop between the mother and her child with a disability?

Every family has a unique power structure. In some families, most of the power or control is held by the father. In other families, the governance of the family lies with the mother or the family at large. Power, in the context of this discussion, is defined as the amount of control or influence a family member or group of family members exerts in managing family decisions, assigning family tasks, and implementing family activities. Families vary greatly in their membership and their organization. Some families have both parents living at home, while others have only one. In a similar fashion, the power structure within each family varies according to the characteristics of each family member. The family power structure is often altered substantially by the arrival of an infant with disabilities. It is not uncommon for older siblings to assume greater power than before, as they also assume more responsibility.

Husband-Wife Relationships

The excerpt in Window 14–2 illustrates some of the interactions and outcomes that a couple experiences in dealing with a child with a disability. According to Featherstone (1980), "A child's [disability] attacks the fabric of a marriage in four ways. It excites powerful emotions in both parents. It acts as a dispiriting symbol of shared failure. It reshapes the organization of the family. It creates fertile ground for conflict" (p. 91). An infant with disabilities may require more immediate and prolonged attention from the mother for feeding, treatment, and general care. Her attention may become riveted on the life of the child. The balance that once existed between being a mother and a wife will now be absent. The wife may become so involved with caring for the child that other relationships may lose their quality and intensity.

FOCUS 6

Identify three factors in raising a child who is exceptional that contribute to marital stress.

Comments representative of some of these feelings are exemplified in the following statements (see Window 14–2): "Angela spends so much time with Juan that she has little energy left for me. It is as if she has become consumed with his care." "You ask me to pay attention to Juan, but you rarely spend any time with me. When am I going to be a part of your life again?" "I am developing a resentment toward you and Juan. Who wants to come home when all your time is spent waiting on him?" One can sense from these comments the types of feelings a husband might have regarding a wife's involvement with the child. Husbands may also become excessively involved with their children's lives, promoting the same kinds of feelings in their wives.

Marital partners also have other types of feelings. Fear, anger, guilt, resentment, and other related feelings often interfere with a couple's capacity to communicate and seek realistic solutions. Fatigue also has a profound effect on the ways in which couples function

R
E
F
L
E
C
T

O
N

T
H
I
S

14-2 Respite Care for Parents

Lisa—That Special Someone for the Browns

Lisa is a very special member of the Brown family. She was not born into our family but entered it as a Respite Worker because of our son, Aaron, 9 years old.

I remember the first day Lisa came into our house with her eyes huge as she looked at Aaron and saw the extent of his medical and physical needs. I could see she had serious doubts about her abilities. . . .

Lisa supported our family's vision of integration and inclusion for Aaron in all aspects of community life. . . . She was Aaron's resource person at Y-camp, she took him all around the city on walks on field trips, and honed her sign language so that she could give him additional input about the world around him. Lisa always put on Aaron's hearing aids and glasses when they were reading a story, watching TV or going for a walk so that Aaron could experience his world more completely. Sometimes she'd suggest a different way she did something that worked well and I was grateful for her thoughtful insights and helpful hints. She even sometimes ran a load of wash, folded laundry or did a sink of dishes. . . . I didn't expect it but it always made me say "Thanks."

Also because of Lisa's superior abilities, my husband and I were able to go out of town on two occasions for an overnight. These were the first times we had gone away together since having children.

Our son Aaron blossomed whenever Lisa and he did things together. People watching them felt comfortable about joining in the fun and getting to know both of them. She believes in kids and they recognize this and rise to do the best they can, . . . kids with special needs and typical ones, too. I came in from work one day and, lying on our kitchen table, were Lisa's keys to our van and our house. We had entrusted them to her for two years. And when I saw those keys, I cried. What a gap there is when someone leaves who has filled your life so wonderfully! Boy, do we miss her! Lisa and her husband moved to St. Paul, MN where she is to do an internship in occupational therapy. It's been exciting to have been so involved in HER life, too, her growing and learning during the time she worked for our family. It wasn't all a one-way street. It took patience, flexibility and give-and-take on all our parts.

Source: From "People in the News, Lisa—That Special Someone for the Browns" by L. Brown, Fall 1990, pp. 13–14. Reprinted by Permission from *Family Support Bulletin.* Published by United Cerebral Palsy Associations, Inc.

and communicate. All these feelings and conditions are exacerbated by the presence of a child who is exceptional in the home. Some parents join together to create respite care programs (Cobb, 1987), which give them a chance to be away from the demands of child rearing. Moreover, respite care gives parents the opportunity to relax and renew their relationship.

A number of other factors may also contribute to marital stress: unusually heavy financial burdens incurred by the family to provide medical treatment or therapy; frequent visits to treatment facilities; a reduction of time spent together in couple-related activities; decreased time for sleep, particularly in the early years of the child's life; and social isolation from relatives and friends (Beckman-Bell, 1981; Blackard & Barsh, 1982; Fredericks, 1985; Gallagher, Beckman-Bell, & Cross, 1983).

Research related to marital stress and instability is limited and contradictory (Seligman & Darling, 1989). Some families appear to experience extreme marital turmoil (Gabel, McDowell, & Cerreto, 1983; Schell, 1981). However, other families "report no more frequent problems than comparison families" (Seligman & Darling, 1989, p. 93). Still other families report an improvement in the marital relationship following diagnosis of a child with a disability.

Cleveland (1980) studied the adaptations made by 17 families after a child in each family had experienced traumatic spinal cord injury. She examined the family's adaptation shortly after the accident and also one year later. Changes in family functioning and specific intra-familial relationships were the focus of the study. With regard to marital functioning, Cleveland identified several sources of spousal irritation and distress. As a rule, mothers in each

14–3 When I Think about Having Another Child, I . . .

When I think about having another child, I panic. In fact, I have consumed hours of psychological time thinking about my little boy and our response to him. Actually, my husband and I really haven't dealt successfully with the feelings that seem to be ever present in our thinking.

The problem is simply this: Two years ago, I gave birth to a little boy who was severely disabled. At the time, I was about 26 years old and my husband was 27. We married later than most, and having this little boy was something that was neither planned nor unplanned. We did know that we wanted to have children, and so we let nature take its course.

We didn't know much about children, let alone children with disabilities, nor did we ever think that we would have a child who would be seriously disabled. When the pediatrician suggested institutionalization for the child, we just nodded our heads. Believe it or not, I had not even touched our son. I had merely looked at him through the observation windows once or twice.

After the baby's birth, I didn't return to work. In fact, within several days after the delivery and placement of the child, my husband and I decided to take a vacation to sort things out. Well, the "sorting" didn't really take place. Gradually since that time, I have become less and less interested in things. I sleep a lot more, and to be honest with you, I don't really look

forward to getting up each day. My old friends have stopped coming by, and my husband chooses to do less and less with me. He spends his free time with old friends because I have little energy for any activity outside our home.

Recently, my husband gave me an ultimatum: "Either you decide to have some children, or I'm going to find someone who will." (There are, of course, other things that are bothering him.) But since the birth of this child, I have been absolutely terrified of becoming pregnant again. As a result, my responses to my husband's needs for physical affection have been practically absent—or should I say, nonexistent. I'm driving not only myself crazy but also my husband. I guess you could say I really need some help.

of the families assumed the major role of caring for the injured children. Husbands reported feeling angry toward their wives because of their involvement with the injured children. Conversely, wives expressed hostility toward their husbands for a lack of empathy and understanding about the care they provided. In addition, overprotectiveness by the mothers was identified as a major source of tension for couples. Most husbands felt that their spouses were overly solicitous and shielding in their caregiving activities. Generally, couples reported that their marriages had been made neither better nor worse as a function of the injury to their child. They were, however, concerned about the prolonged period of parenthood that they would have to provide. They also felt they would have to alter some of the plans they had made for the postparenthood phase of their lives.

Parent counseling and training can be extremely helpful in avoiding many of the problems encountered in coping with having a child with disabilities in the family. Counseling may help parents work through such feelings as anger, resentment, and discouragement. Parent training may help parents develop appropriate expectations for their child's current and future achievement. In addition, parents may acquire specific skills to help them respond more effectively and therapeutically to their child's difficulties.

Single Parenthood

Information and research specifically related to single parents of children with disabilities is extremely scant (Seligman & Darling, 1989). We can, however, assume that the number of children with disabilities who grow up in households with one parent is on the rise. Available research indicates that many of these single parents experience serious financial and family problems, have significant needs for basic respite care, and desire increased social and personal support in caring for their children (Beckman, 1983; Wikler, 1981). As you might guess, many of these parents are women who are likely to be unemployed and dependent on social services funding for maintaining their households (Wikler, 1981). The only kind of external support that is consistently available to many of these mothers is that provided by their own parents (Seligman & Darling, 1989). In these instances, grandparents play a crucial role in both the child's and mother's well-being.

Parent-Child Relationships

The relationships between parents and children are a function of many factors. Some of the most critical factors include the child's age, the child's gender, the family's socioeconomic status, the family's coping strength, the nature and seriousness of the disability, and the family's composition (one-parent family, two-parent family, or reconstituted family).

Families go through a developmental cycle in responding to the needs and nuances of caring for children with disabilities. The cycle includes the following phases: (1) the time at which parents learn about or suspect a disability in their child; (2) the period in which the parents determine what action to take regarding the child's education; (3) the point at which the individual who is disabled has completed his or her education; and (4) the time when the parents become older and may be unable to care for their adult offspring. We do not review all of these periods here, but we highlight some of the most common relationship patterns that appear over time in the life of an individual with disabilities. Of course, the nature and severity of the disability and the willingness of the parents to make adjustments and to educate themselves regarding their role in helping the child have an appreciable influence on the parent-child relationship that eventually emerges.

The Mother-Child Relationship.   If a child's impairment is congenital and readily apparent at birth, it is often the mother who becomes primarily responsible for relating to the child and his or her needs. If the infant is born prematurely or needs extensive, early medical assistance, the relationship that emerges may be slow in coming, for many reasons. The mother may be prevented from engaging in typical feeding and caregiving activities that most mothers would perform with a new infant. The child may need to spend many weeks in an isolette supported by sophisticated medical equipment. Some mothers come to question whether they really had a baby because of the remoteness they experience in not being able to interact immediately with their infant in a personally satisfying manner. Many mothers report that they are not given adequate direction as to how to become involved with their disabled infants.

FOCUS 7
Identify four general phases of the developmental cycle that parents go through in rearing a child with a disability.

FOCUS 8
Identify four factors that influence the relationship that develops between infants with disabilities and their mothers.

===== **W I N D O W   14–3** =====

VIEW FROM A MOTHER

My initial response to Tyrone's birth was very negative. I didn't quite know what to do. My pediatrician came into my room right after the delivery and said something to the effect, "I think we have a problem." What he was trying to say was, "Your child has Down syndrome." The emotional surge of feelings I had then cannot be accurately described.

I can distinctively remember the first thoughts that I had as I spoke to my husband after I had my brief visit with the pediatrician. I wanted to throw my new son out the window . . . not literally, but somehow I didn't want to deal with this immensely new and complex problem. At least, that's how I viewed the situation at the time.

In retrospect, as I think about those earlier feelings regarding Tyrone, I am sorry I felt that way. But I think my thoughts at that time were really very typical. I didn't know a lot about Down syndrome and I wasn't sure what to expect, so I expected the worst.

Without minimal levels of involvement and appropriate support from other adults or professionals, many mothers become estranged from their infants and find it difficult to begin the caring process. Physicians, nurses, and other health-related personnel responsible for providing parents with appropriate explanations, instruction, and expectations set the stage for the development of healthy and realistic parent-infant relationships. The mother's expectations are particularly important, for they shape the types of responses she will later make in caring and seeking assistance for her infant (Lavelle & Keogh, 1980).

In other cases, the mother may be virtually forced into a close physical and emotional relationship with her child who is injured or disabled. The bond that develops between mother and child is one that is strong and often impenetrable (Leigh, 1987). The mother becomes, according to Cleveland (1980), the "guardian of affective needs." She assumes primary responsibility for fostering the child's emotional adjustment. She also becomes the child's personal representative or interpreter. In this role, the mother has the responsibility of communicating the child's needs and desires to other family members.

Because of the sheer weight of these responsibilities, other relationships often wane or even disappear. The mother who assumes this role and develops a very close relationship with her offspring who is exceptional often walks a variety of tightropes. In her desire to protect her child, she often overprotects him or her, thus preventing the child from having optimal opportunities to practice the skills and participate in the activities that ultimately lead to independence. The mother may also underestimate her child's capacities. She may be reluctant to allow her child to engage in challenging or risky ventures. In this regard, the mother might be described as being overprotective. On the other hand, some mothers may neglect their children with disabilities and not provide the stimulation so critical to their optimal development. This constitutes child neglect and should receive the prompt attention of appropriate child-care workers.

Hackney (1981) identified several ways in which children who are gifted impact family functioning. He found that children who are gifted can alter family roles. For example, their adultlike capacities may lead them to occasionally serve as the "third parent" in the family. Disciplining children who are verbally and intellectually skilled also poses some challenges for parents. The usual pat answers provided by parents for choosing a particular discipline remedy may be logically and quickly challenged and repudiated. Furthermore, parents may feel greater pressure to provide additional learning experiences or talent-enhancement activities for these children. Last, children who are gifted and also socially skillful are often viewed by their parents as being highly manipulative. The tenacity and skill with which such children pursue their goals and desires can be a perplexing problem for mothers and fathers.

The Father-Child Relationship.   Not much has been written about fathers and their relationships with children with disabilities. The information available is primarily anecdotal in nature or appears in the form of case studies.

As indicated earlier, the father is often responsible for conveying the news that the mother has given birth to a child who is exceptional, and for a time, the father may well be responsible for keeping the family aware of the mother's status and the child's condition. The father's reactions to the birth of a child who is injured or disabled are generally more reserved than those of other family members (Lamb, 1983). Fathers are more likely to internalize their feelings than to express them openly. They may respond with such coping mechanisms as withdrawal, sublimation, and intellectualization. Fathers of children with mental retardation are typically more concerned than mothers about their children's capacity to develop socially adequate behavior, particularly their sons'. Fathers are also more concerned about their children's eventual social and educational status. Likewise, they are more affected by the visibility of their children's retardation than are mothers (Lamb, 1983).

FOCUS 9

Identify three ways in which fathers may respond to their children with disabilities.

R	14–4	What about Fathers?
E		
F		
L		
E		
C		
T		
O		
N		
T		
H		
I		
S		

14–4 What about Fathers?

The following questions are those of a concerned father of a child with disabilities. Think about the extent to which professionals address these questions as they work with families and particularly fathers of children with disabilities.

◆ Do we encourage fathers to come to appointments if at all possible?

◆ Are we flexible in our scheduling, setting meetings and appointments early in the morning or late in the afternoon so that men (like mothers who work out of the home) can also attend?

◆ When we call home and Dad answers the phone, do we speak to him or automatically ask for his wife?

◆ Do we inquire about fathers when the mothers come for weekly appointments?

◆ If a couple is divorced, do we send information to both parents?

◆ Have we provided effective support networks for men to gain information, to deal with their grief, and to learn appropriate ways to interact with their children?★

Source: ★ From "Commentary: What about Fathers?" by J. May, Fall 1990, p. 19. Reprinted by Permission from *Family Support Bulletin*. Published by United Cerebral Palsy Associations, Inc.

The relationships that emerge between fathers and children who are exceptional are a function of the same factors reviewed concerning mother–child relationships. One important factor may be the gender of the child. If the child is male and the father had idealized the role he would eventually assume in interacting with a son, the adjustment for the father can be very difficult. The father may have had hopes of playing football with the child, having him eventually become a business partner, or participating with his son in a variety of activities. Many of these hopes may never be realized with a child who is disabled.

Recent research has indicated that fathers, in comparison to mothers, of preschool children with developmental disabilities experience fewer symptoms of distress, exhibit higher levels of self-esteem, and demonstrate more internal locus of control in responding to their children with disabilities (Goldberg, Marcovitch, MacGregor, & Lojkasek, 1986). In cases in which fathers do withdraw or are uninvolved with the child, other family members, particularly mothers, must shoulder more of the child-care responsibilities. This withdrawal often creates significant stress for mothers and other family members.

Several advocacy organizations have created support and discussion groups that have been carefully tailored to the needs of fathers (Vadasy, Fewell, Greenberg, & Meyer, 1986). These groups are often led by a professional and a father of a child with a disability. The groups often provide a safe environment in which fathers may express strong feelings and concerns about their child and other family challenges. Participation in these groups is quite positive for fathers as well as other family members (Vadasy, Fewell, Greenberg, Desmond, & Meyer, 1986). Positive outcomes include lower levels of stress and depression, higher satisfaction regarding social support, increased family cohesion, and decreased family rigidity in dealing with the challenges of rearing a child who is exceptional.

Sibling Relationships

Siblings respond to family members who are exceptional in a variety of ways. The titles of several recent articles in a popular publication for parents of children who are exceptional illustrate this point: "I'm Not Going to Be John's Baby Sitter Forever: Siblings, Planning, and the Disabled Child" (1987) and "When I Grow Up, I'm Never Coming Back! The Adolescent and the Family" (1988).

The responses siblings make to their sister or brother with a disability are subject to a number of variables. Farber (1962) identified several factors that may be predictive of family

W I N D O W   14–4

VIEW FROM A SIBLING

I found that I was purely fascinated by my brother. Why didn't he speak? How did he think if he didn't know words? As a sibling, I could be intrigued without the pains of reality and natural motherly awareness of a son's abnormalities. I could take him out shopping in supermarkets, which he loved, and not be bothered or embarrassed if he accidentally knocked down a huge display. My sister would have become nervous and distraught, while my mother would have been close to tears. Taking a walk around the beach with him was an education in people. I learned from their fearful expressions, their sympathy, their ignorance. Yet, some did not notice anything unusual, as he was so physically beautiful, except when he would flap his hands or do his little foot shuffle. Then they often noticed. . . .

I consider myself to have had a very special upbringing. I learned so much from my brother, indirectly. I enjoy being around people like him, although, of course, there is no one as special as my brother Ben. (Lettick, 1979, p. 294)

---

and sibling adjustment to a brother or sister who is retarded. These include the quality of the interpersonal relationship between the child's parents, the retarded child's gender, the social class of the family, and the interaction patterns of the family. Grossman (1972a, 1972b) found that families in upper income brackets are capable of relieving their normal children of some burdens associated with caring for a sibling who is retarded. By contrast, lower-income families often place much of the burden for the child's care on older, female siblings.

FOCUS 10

Identify four ways in which siblings respond to their brothers or sisters who are exceptional.

Siblings who learn that they have a brother or sister with a disability are frequently encumbered with many different kinds of concerns. A number of questions are commonly asked: "Why did this happen?" "Is my brother contagious? Can I catch what he has?" "What am I going to say to my friends?" "Am I going to have to take care of him all of my life?"

Like their parents, siblings want to know and understand as much as they can about the condition of their sibling (Wasserman, 1983). They want to know how they should respond and how their lives might be different as a result of this event. If these concerns can

Sibling relationships involving children with disabilities have unique dynamics. This boy with mental retardation can benefit from taking some responsibility for his baby sister. (Brent Petersen/The Stock Market)

be adequately addressed, the prognosis for positive sibling involvement with the brother or sister who is disabled is much better than otherwise. Lamb (1980) reviewed a number of books that may be used therapeutically to help children accept their exceptional siblings. Through these stories, children may become vicariously involved with the problems of having a sister or brother who is exceptional.

We would be remiss in our discussion of this topic if we were to leave the impression that all sibling problems can be handled through appropriate orientation, education, and counseling. Even with excellent counseling support and assistance, having a child who is disabled in the family can be challenging and painful for both parents and siblings. In spite of assistance, many siblings may continue to resent and be embarrassed by their brother or sister.

The attitudes and behaviors of the parents have a significant impact on the attitudes of children toward siblings who are exceptional (McHale, Sloan, & Simeonsson, 1986), since children tend to mirror the attitudes and values of their parents. If parents are optimistic and realistic in their views toward the children who are exceptional, then siblings are likely to share these attitudes. If siblings are kindly disposed toward assisting the exceptional child, they can be a real source of support (McHale, Sloan, & Simeonsson, 1986). Many siblings play a critical role in fostering the intellectual, social, and affective development of a brother or sister who is exceptional.

Anger is one of the many feelings that siblings may express or feel. Loneliness, anxiety, guilt, and envy are also common. Feelings of loneliness may surface in children who wanted a brother or sister with whom they could play. Anxiety may be present in a youth who wonders who will care for the sibling who is disabled when the parents are no longer capable or alive. Guilt may come from many sources. Siblings may feel that they are obligated to care for the sibling who is disabled. In their minds, failure to provide such care would make them bad or immoral. Similarly, they may feel guilty about the real thoughts and feelings they have about their sibling. These feelings may include frustration, resentment, and even hate. Realizing that many parents would not respond positively to the expression of such feelings, some siblings carry them inside for a long time, only to express them later.

Many siblings resent the time and attention parents devote to their sister or brother. This resentment may also take the form of jealousy (Forbes, 1987; McHale, Sloan & Simeonsson, 1986; Simeonsson & Bailey, 1986). Some siblings feel as if they are emotionally neglected, that their parents are not responsive to their needs for attention and emotional support. For some siblings, the predominant feeling is one of bitter resentment or even rage. For others, the predominant attitude toward the family experience of growing up with a brother or sister who is disabled is a feeling of deprivation. They feel as if their social, educational, and recreational pursuits have been seriously limited because of the presence of the sibling.

The following statements are examples of such feelings: "We never went on a family vacation because of my brother, Steven." "How could I invite a friend over? I never knew how my autistic brother would behave." "How do you explain to a date that you have a sister who is retarded?" "Many of my friends stopped coming to my house because they didn't know how to handle my brother, Mike, who is deaf. They simply could not understand him." "I was always shackled with the responsibilities of tending my little sister. I didn't have time to have fun with my friends." "I want a real brother, not a retarded one."

As mentioned earlier, Grossman (1972a) found that older, female siblings from low-income families frequently have to assume responsibility for caring for the disabled family member. In these cases, many siblings resent having to assume the role of caregiver and feel deprived of some of the important opportunities most young people want to have in growing up.

REFLECT ON THIS

14–5   Letter from Aviva Rich

My Family and I

My name is Aviva Rich. I turned 11 years old in February. I have a sister named Tammy. She is 14. I have a brother named Richard. He is 12. Both my sister and brother are adopted. My sister is blind. My brother can't use his right hand. But they still act normal.

My sister came to my family when I was 4 and she was 9. For a while we didn't talk that much. She was going to a school for the blind for a while then changed to a public school called Rushmore. My sister has a lot of friends. Sometimes we play together. I like Tammy a lot.

My brother came to my family when I was eight. Lots of people used to make fun of his right hand. My brother has learning disabilities. He goes to a public school. He can't have sugar. But once in a while he is allowed to have it. He likes sports, food, games and music. But he hates going to bed and hates going to school. I like my brother.

I have always been with my family. I play the flute and the piano. I started school early, but I had to take a test. I am the youngest person in fifth grade.

I like gymnastics, drawing, writing, playing the flute, chocolate, pizza and reading.

I share a room with my sister. I have over fifty dolls from around the world. I am half Jewish and half Christian. I go to temple. My favorite holidays are Purim, Chanuka, Christmas and my birthday.

I like my whole family, not just one part of it, my whole family.

Source: From "My Family and I" by A. Rich, 1984, *Exceptional Parent, 14*(5), p. C2. Reprinted with permission of *Exceptional Parent*, 1170 Commonwealth Avenue, Boston, MA 02134.

Siblings of children who are exceptional may also feel as if they must compensate for their parents' disappointment about having a child who is disabled. They may feel an undue amount of pressure to excel or to be successful in a particular academic or artistic pursuit. Such pressure can have a profound effect on siblings' physical and mental health. Likewise, the expressed expectations of parents can serve as a source of pressure and emotional pain to siblings: "Why do I always feel as if I have to be the perfect child or the one who always does things right? I'm getting tired of constantly having to win my parents' admiration. Why can't I just be average for once?"

Sibling support groups for families with children who are exceptional are emerging and can be particularly helpful to adolescents. In these groups, children and youth can be introduced to the important aspects of having such a sibling in the family (Atkins, 1987).

REFLECT ON THIS

14–6   Help for Siblings

Children who have brothers or sisters who are disabled may experience a number of problems in dealing with their parents, their friends, and other situations both inside and outside the home. A new and innovative organization has been established for the siblings of disabled individuals.

This organization is the Sibling Information Network. Its members enjoy the following resources: a quarterly newsletter with quality resource materials; a bibliography of children's literature related to disabling conditions; a list of media on siblings; a list of all its members and persons who have organized sibling groups; a bibliography of journal articles on siblings; and a collection of articles from the newsletter on various programs and workshops. The headquarters for this new network is located at the University of Connecticut, Department of Educational Psychology, Storrs, Connecticut.

Involvement with this network may be very helpful to children who are experiencing difficulties in relating to a new sibling who is disabled.

Appropriate expectations can be established, and questions that children may be hesitant to ask in a family context may be freely discussed. These groups may also provide a therapeutic means by which these individuals can analyze family problems and identify practical solutions.

Extended Family Relationships

The term **extended family** is frequently used to describe a household in which an immediate (nuclear) family lives accompanied by a number of close relatives. For the purposes of this section, the term *extended family* is used to identify those individuals who are close relatives of the immediate family and have regular and frequent contacts with it even though they do not necessarily live in the same household. These individuals may include grandparents, uncles, aunts, or cousins.

When a child is born and becomes part of a family, he or she also becomes part of an extended family. Usually, the grandparents make the first official family visit or call to the hospital. This visit can be extraordinarily taxing and difficult if it entails providing congratulations and support to a daughter who has given birth to a child with a disability. In a very real fashion, grandparents perceive grandchildren as extensions of themselves. They look forward to babying, bragging about, and showing snapshots of their grandchildren, without worrying about the burdens of responsibility that parents must assume.

When a grandchild is born with an impairment, the joy of the occasion may dissipate. Like parents, grandparents are hurled into a crisis that necessitates reevaluation and reorientation (Seligman & Darling, 1989). They must decide not only how they will respond to their child, who is now a parent, but also how they will relate to the new grandchild. Many grandparents grew up in a time when deviancy of almost any variety was barely tolerated, much less understood. Therefore, they enter the crisis process without much understanding. In their day, such a birth may have signified the presence of "bad blood" within a family.

W I N D O W   14–5

VIEW FROM A MOTHER ABOUT HER IN-LAWS

I can distinctly remember the tears of my father-in-law and my mother-in-law's reluctance to visit me in the hospital when they discovered that I had given birth to a child with an open spine (spina bifida). During my mother-in-law's first visit, all she could talk about was the dinner party she had held the night before and her upcoming vacation. All I could think about was my baby and whether he was going to make it through the night. At the time, I was extremely angry and upset by her lack of sympathy and understanding. I could not figure out why she was so insensitive to my feelings and my son's condition.

Because of the seriousness of our son's defect, the consulting physicians recommended that Eric immediately undergo an operation. Shortly thereafter, my mother-in-law asked me who had given permission for this operation, implying that it might have been better to have allowed Eric not to survive or die on his own. Attempting to be stoic in spite of my heightened feelings of hos-

tility, I remained silent. The silence was broken with another hurtful comment: "My son will be burdened for life." These and other similar comments were common during the first 24 months of Eric's life. It was as though I had burdened *her*.

As I reflect on this time period, I can see that I was simply too overwhelmed by my own feelings to give careful consideration to the comments made by my in-laws, neighbors, and friends. With the passage of time, however, I have come to understand my husband's parents and their responses to our exceptional son. They, in turn, have also developed an appreciation and understanding of our son and us. It took quite a bit of time, and we all had to adapt and change a great deal.

Eric is now 10. He loves both of his grandparents and looks forward to spending time with them on special weekend visits. It is during these weekends that my husband and I take time to renew our relationship and restore ourselves with recreational activities.

Parents and siblings often feel overextended by the extra care required by a child with disabilities. Grandparents and other family members can contribute much to supporting the primary family unit. (Will & Deni McIntyre/Photo Researchers, Inc.)

As a result of this attitude and other similar perceptions, the mother or father of the newborn child may be selected as the scapegoat. But blaming only provides a temporary form of relief. It does little to promote the optimal family functioning that becomes so necessary in the weeks and months to come.

Grandparents and other family members may contribute much to the primary family unit (Sonnek, 1986; Wilcoxon, 1987). If they live near the family, they may become an integral part of the resource network. They may also be able to provide support before the energies of their children are so severely depleted that they need additional, costly help. In order to be of assistance, grandparents must be prepared and informed, which can be achieved in a variety of ways. They must have an opportunity to voice their questions, feelings, and concerns about the disorder and its complications. They must have means by which they can become informed. Parents can aid in this process by sharing with their own parents and siblings pamphlets, materials, and books suggested by health and educational personnel. They may also encourage their families to become involved in parent and grandparent discussion groups. In such informal meetings, they learn about the struggles and feelings of their own children. These meetings are also catalysts for frank and open conversation. Extended family members need positive feedback regarding their efforts and support. When these conditions are met, they can be an important part of the total treatment process. Norma McPhee, grandmother of a child with cerebral palsy, shares some of her feelings in Window 14–6.

Often, the initial response of grandparents to the newly born child with a disability may be to provide evidence that they are "pure and not responsible for the present suffering" (McPhee, 1982, p. 14). This is, of course, very counterproductive to the well-being of the mother and father of the newborn child. Research has indicated that grandparents, particularly during the diagnosis phase, play an influential role in how their children, the new parents, respond to the child with a disability. If the grandparents are understanding and

WINDOW 14–6

VIEW FROM A GRANDMOTHER

I was determined to find ways to stimulate him and motivate him. I tried to verbalize for him his frustrations and to help him find outlets for expression. I became aware of things that I did that didn't require speaking, using my hands or my feet.

Story records went his way and he loved them. I scoured stores for cookie cutters to help him with holiday preparations. He could hold them and wait until they were needed.

We carried on one-way, long-distance telephone conversations. I cried the first time I heard his sounds in response on the other end of the line. We shared canoe rides and picnics on a camping trip. We visited an orchard and picked apples.

One day I stopped by his picture, saw the lopsided smile and realized what a very special magic there is between grandparents and grandchildren. I realize just how much I loved him—just as he was. (McPhee, 1982, p. 16)

---

emotionally supportive and provide good role models of effective coping, they may have a positive impact on their own children, the mother and father. If the grandparents are critical or unaccepting, they may add to the present burden and complicate it even further (Seligman & Darling, 1989).

As time passes, other responses may emerge. Generally, these center around three conceptual themes: avoidance, trivialization, and fantasizing (Meyer & Vadasy, 1986). Each of these themes is evident in the respective statements that follow: (1) "I don't think those doctors really know what they are talking about. Our grandchild certainly isn't disabled." (2) "We are not going to worry about this anymore. We're sure he will come out of this." (3) "There has to be a cure! We'll find a physician who really knows how to handle this condition."

Actually, many grandparents experience many of the same stages and have many of the same needs as the child's parents. And, like parents, grandparents need to receive information when they will best understand it. Additionally, they need to be informed about the disability and the available therapies or treatment approaches. Lastly, they need to know about the child's potential over time (Vadasy, Fewell, & Meyer, 1986).

REFLECT ON THIS

14–7 We Decided to Educate Ourselves

When I discovered that our grandson, Richard, was retarded, I wasn't sure how I should respond. You must remember that, in my day, children who were retarded weren't talked about a lot. They were actually hidden or sent away to a state hospital or something like that. My husband was particularly perplexed by the birth of our new grandson. He really didn't know what to say or how to respond. Of course, I wasn't much better. We decided that we needed to educate ourselves. Our daughter was kind enough to give us a few pamphlets that helped us learn about our new grandson's condition. We also talked to some other friends of ours who have a granddaughter with Down syndrome. They didn't know a whole lot more than we did, but the talking did us both some good.

Since that time, we've tried to be supportive of our daughter and her situation. We try to volunteer whatever assistance we can when she seems to be pressed or to need a reprieve for a couple of hours. We're glad that we live somewhat close to her.

I remember our first contacts with Richard. We weren't sure how different he would be. Actually, it took very little time for us to realize that Richard wasn't all that different. We found that he does things a little bit more slowly, but other than that, he's pretty much normal.

We think our daughter and her husband, John, have handled this situation extremely well. In fact, we're very proud of them. And we realize that this could happen to anyone.

We enjoy Richard a lot. Yes, we worry a little about his future and what he'll do when he's older, but we've learned from John and Marilyn that sometimes, it's better to take things one day at a time.

Betty, A Grandmother

REFLECT ON THIS

14–8   My Dreams Are No Different . . .

My dreams for Christopher are no different from the dreams any grandmother has for her grandson. I want him to have self-esteem and a sense that he is a competent person. I want him to live a life of integrity that is rich, that has friendships and laughter and sharing and love. I want him to give himself the freedom to fail, to take risks, to make independent decisions and to live with the consequences. I want him to know that to do his best is enough. I want him to have an appreciation for good music, good food, and good ideas. I want him to know the satisfaction of leaving the world a better place. I want him to have confidence in his abilities, whatever they may be, and to value the unique and wonderful qualities he has been given. Most of all, I want him to understand that the challenge of life for all of us is to make the most of what we have even when what we have is less than what we want to have and maybe less than what others have.

Our family tries to look at life as a boxing match. You can lose the first fourteen rounds and still win. All you have to do is knock out your opponent in the last ten seconds of the 15th round and you are the World Heavyweight Champion. Our plan is to keep getting up from the mat every time we fail, hoping for that one lucky punch.

Source: From "Evolving Attitudes about Family Support" by N. Johnson, Fall 1990, p. 13. Reprinted by Permission from *Family Support Bulletin*. Published by United Cerebral Palsy Associations, Inc.

FOCUS 11

Identify three types of assistance that grandparents may render to families with children who are exceptional.

Grandparents may be helpful in several ways (Seligman & Darling, 1989), providing much needed **respite care.** They may be able to give parents a weekend reprieve from the pressures of maintaining the household, as did Norma McPhee. They may also assist with transportation or baby-sitting. Grandparents may often serve as third-party evaluators, providing solutions to seemingly unresolvable problems. The child with an impairment profits from the unique attention that only grandparents can provide. This attention can be a natural part of such special occasions as birthdays, vacations, fishing trips, or other traditional family activities.

We have highlighted the positive ways in which extended family members may assist the primary family unit, but the types of assistance and support described may be difficult to arrange. For instance, few family members freely volunteer to tend a child with an attention-deficit disorder. Baby-sitting exchanges and other similar arrangements are also

Sharing experiences with other parents of children with disabilities can provide useful information and emotional support. (S. Pick/Stock, Boston)

R E F L E C T   O N   T H I S

14–9

Baby-Sitters! We Need Just One!

Marcia's a pretty mature girl for her age, but she becomes almost terrified when she thinks that she might have to hold our new son, Jeremy. He has multiple disabilities.

I don't dare leave him with our other two children, Amy and Mary Ann. They're much too young to handle Jeremy. But I need to get away from the demands that seem to be ever present in caring for Jeremy. If I could just find one person who could help us, even just once a month, things would be a lot better for me and my family.

A dilemma faced by many parents of children who are severely disabled or chronically ill is finding a baby-sitter. The challenge is far greater than one might imagine: Frequently the parents of such children never find someone who can provide them and their other children with the reprieve they so much need.

As you might guess, the more severe the child's disability, the more difficult it is to find a person who can provide the needed care. Unfortunately, many parents discover all too late how much a good baby-sitter could have helped them. What are the reasons for endeavoring to find a baby-sitter?

We have learned that the presence of a child who is disabled or seriously ill in the family can produce a lot of strain, not only for the parents but also for other members of the family. Having an opportunity to be away from the child who is disabled provides the immediate caregivers and siblings with a chance to have some of their own needs met. It also gives parents an opportunity to become recharged or revitalized for the demanding regimen they often have to follow in taking care of such a child. Moreover, respites in which the siblings of the child who is disabled are able to have the exclusive attention of their parents reaffirm their importance in the family and their value as individuals.

In some areas of the country, enterprising teenagers have developed baby-sitting businesses that specialize in tending children who are disabled or otherwise require special care. Frequently, local disability associations can also be helpful in providing qualified assistance in the important area of baby-sitting.

---

much more difficult to set up when the situation involves a difficult child. Such is the case with many family activities. The child with disabilities is not as likely as others to be invited to participate in recreational activities such as sleeping overnight at a friend's or cousin's house, eating dinner with neighbors, or going with another family on a weekend camping trip.

In addition, relatives and neighbors may be critical of management procedures that parents have been encouraged to employ with their child. Procedures such as social isolation and various forms of punishment may be viewed as abusive parental behavior by close friends and relatives. Other types of treatment may also be viewed with a jaundiced eye if they include the use of stimulant drugs, very controlled diets, or point systems. Parents who must administer these home-based interventions often feel that they are completely alone. On the other hand, the support provided by extended family members, if properly applied, can have a positive effect on the physical and social-emotional well-being of the primary family.

THE FAMILY DILEMMA: LEARNING TO WORK WITH PROFESSIONALS

The interaction between professionals and parents is often marked by confusion, dissatisfaction, disappointment, and anger. Several writers have documented these and other negative feelings in parents (Dembo, 1984; Muir-Hutchinson, 1987; Seligman & Darling, 1989). What are the sources of these feelings? Are they to be expected? A certain amount of dissatisfaction is present in even the best relationships. However, the research information available has led many observers to believe that the relationship between parents and professionals could be significantly improved (Kotze, 1986; Kroth, 1987).

Many professionals are inadequately prepared to deal with the challenges of informing parents of their child's exceptionality. In a similar vein, many professionals do not have the

REFLECT ON THIS

14–10   Our First IEP Meeting

I also remember the first IEP [individualized education program] Meeting we attended. Christopher had been in the program for several weeks and we were feeling pretty proud of his progress. The meeting was attended by his teacher, his three therapists, his mother and me. Each staff member reviewed their most recent evaluations of Christopher's developmental status and one after the other informed us of just how far behind Christopher was. I sat there listening, feeling sick inside, as I heard that he was four months delayed in this skill and five months delayed in that skill with skills emerging to only a 3 month delay in another area. One or two staff members made a positive comment, but the emphasis was certainly on his deficit. I went home that night and cried to my husband, "Nobody said anything positive about what a wonderful child he is. Nobody mentioned how much he smiles, how well he relates to people. Nobody mentioned how hard he tries to do new things in therapy!" It was truly one of my saddest days!

Source: From "Evolving Attitudes about Family Support" by N. Johnson, p. 13. Reprinted by Permission from *Family Support Bulletin*. Published by United Cerebral Palsy Associations, Inc.

FOCUS 12

Identify three types of professional understanding that are essential to establishing positive relationships with parents and families of children who are exceptional.

counseling skills necessary for the development of satisfactory relationships with patients and their families. In examining these problems, Seligman and Seligman (1980) identified three types of professional understanding essential to establishing positive working relationships with families. First, professionals need to understand the impact they have on parents. Second, they need to understand the impact the individual who is exceptional has on the family over time. Third, they need to understand the impact the child and family have on them, the professionals.

Medical and other health-related personnel have a profound impact on the ways parents respond to the birth or injury of a child. They cannot prevent the shock felt by parents as they learn of the child's impairment, but they can lessen its impact. They can also provide parents with perspective and direction as they attempt to adjust their lives and make room for the child (Seligman & Darling, 1989).

Physicians set the stage and prepare the family for the first few days, weeks, and months. Unfortunately, some are not adequately prepared to counsel parents regarding the

The home environment can be the most important source of learning and emotional support available to a child with disabilities. (Gabe Palmer/The Stock Market)

steps to take. In fact, many medical personnel are unaware of the resources and services available for infants and children who have disabilities. They are also unprepared to deal with the parents' present situation and feelings. Therefore, parents frequently leave the hospital or clinic confused and disoriented, not knowing exactly what their options are or how they should proceed.

Professional Burnout

Little has been written about the impact the child who is exceptional and his or her family have on the lives of educational and health personnel. The information available is primarily anecdotal in nature. Like parents, professionals are subject to emotional exhaustion, which may exhibit itself in numerous ways. Professionals may become apathetic, pessimistic, or cynical about their work and involvement with patients, students, and clients. They may focus on the negative aspects of their work and feel that their perceptions have become constricted. Depression is also a common characteristic of emotional exhaustion. Personnel affected this way may feel they have no power to enact meaningful changes in their work environments (Pagel & Price, 1980).

Emotional and physical exhaustion cannot be attributed entirely to the actions of families and children, but they do play an important role. As physicians, educators, and therapists interact with children who are disabled and their families, problems frequently arise. Caring for an individual who is disabled in a medical or educational setting can be very challenging. Progress may be exceedingly slow. Interventions may be unsuccessful. The individual may not make the progress anticipated. Parents may be disappointed with the quality of services and may complain or even threaten to sue. Prescribed medication may be ineffective. These conditions can have an immense impact on the physical and mental well-being of professionals who feel responsible for the individuals and their families. The recurring frustration, tedium, pressure, and dissatisfaction that characterize the work of helping professionals can at times be overwhelming and debilitating.

FOCUS 13

Identify three ways in which children with disabilities and their families impact teachers and health care workers.

REFLECT ON THIS

14–11 Parents Comment

"What is the most helpful thing a professional ever said to you?"

- It's not your fault. You are not powerful enough to have caused the kinds of problems your child has.
- What do you need for yourself?
- I think your son could be a success story for our agency.
- I value your input.
- Under the circumstances, you are doing the best you can do. Frankly, I don't know what I would do or how I would be able to carry on.

- If you were a perfect parent, your son would still be in this condition.
- I agree with you.
- Your child has made progress and I know he can do more, so we will continue to work with him.
- Why are you taking all of the blame? It takes two to make or break a relationship.
- I don't know. I can't tell you what's wrong with your child or what caused the problem.
- Your child knows right from wrong. She knows most of society's values and that's because you taught them to her.
- There is a lot of love in your family.
- You know, it's okay to take care of yourself too.

- I don't know. I have to give that serious thought.
- I believe in your instincts. You're the expert on your child.
- You're being too hard on yourself.
- Our agency will take your case.
- Thanks so much for your participation in the group [parent support group]. Your intelligence and your calm reasonableness are important influences in the group.

Source: From "What Is the Most Helpful Thing a Professional Ever Said to You?" Spring 1991, p. 20. Reprinted by Permission from *Family Support Bulletin*. Published by United Cerebral Palsy Associations, Inc.

14–12   My Students Are
Incredibly Challenging

Actually, I really enjoy teaching and working with my students. Yes, they are at times incredibly challenging. For example, a third grader in my self-contained class recently climbed up on his desk and engaged in a little urine-sprinkling activity. At first, I couldn't believe what I was seeing, but nothing surprises me anymore.

The kids are the least of my problems, however. It's the paperwork, the legal requirements, regular teachers who are strongly opposed to main-streaming, uncooperative parents who won't even sign a simple end-of-the-day-report, and administrative personnel who provide little, if any, support that really bother me. Also, the teaching resources and materials I have are very meager. How can anyone expect me to do a good job of teaching when I don't even have the essential tools and materials?

By the way, when I do need some help dealing with serious student problems, I generally get it quite quickly. The assistance usually is provided by John, our school psychologist, or by Jane, the social worker. Each of them has really made a difference. John has helped me deal with some superaggressive students. Jane has been helpful with some of my children's parents. I wish I had something good to say about my principal, but he's practically worthless when it comes to supporting special education. He has no idea what needs to be done.

Sarah, A Teacher of Young Children
with Behavior Disorders

Because of the stress inherent in working with persons who are exceptional, many professionals experience a phenomenon known as **burnout.** Child care workers in a variety of settings leave their professional pursuits because of the excessive demands they confront. Smith and Cline (1980) evaluated the sources of stress for special education personnel. In order of importance, the following tasks were identified as causing stress in teachers: (1) completing individual educational programs and due-process paperwork; (2) coping with parents; (3) taking care of school-related work after the usual hours; (4) dealing with excessive student loads; (5) diagnosing and assessing; and (6) working with other teachers. It is interesting to note that the second most stressful item was dealing with parents. In a related study, Pagel and Price (1980) reported similar findings. They found that teachers were frequently bothered by "disruptive and unmotivated students" as well as "uncooperative parents" (p. 46).

Communication and understanding must prevail if parents and professionals are to share in the task of helping individuals who are exceptional achieve their fullest potential. Much work remains to be done. Both parents and professionals need to become more sensitive to one another and their respective needs. Schools that prepare people for the helping professions must provide better training for those who will be responsible for helping and counseling parents.

Training for Professionals and Parents

Fortunately, professional and parent training programs are being developed to help teachers and parents communicate and work more effectively with each other (Chandler, Fowler, & Lubeck, 1985; Guralnick, Bennett, Heiser & Richardson, 1987; Tynan & Fritsch, 1987). Many teachers and parents are truly unprepared to consult and work with one another (McKinney & Hocutt, 1982). Teachers have been prepared primarily to work with children, not with parents and families. Parents may have little understanding of the educational processes involved in evaluating, placing, and instructing children with disabilities. Therefore, parents may have difficulty responding knowledgeably and productively in the usual planning, placement, and annual evaluation meetings.

However, as training programs for parents and teachers emerge, the problems should be lessened, particularly if parent training is individualized, a need stressed by Turnbull and Turnbull (1986). The outcomes of effective parental involvement are very positive (Bristol

& Gallagher, 1982; Cartwright, 1981). The engagement and cooperation of parents can add greatly to the overall rate and quality of success that children and teachers experience in achieving academic, social, and vocational skills.

Debate / Forum

Health Care Industry Forces Family Impoverishment

On September 19, 1990, . . . Donald P. of South Bend, Indiana, testified before the House Energy and Commerce Subcommittee on Commerce, Consumer Protection and Competitiveness. . . . At a hearing entitled "Access to Health Insurance: Who Is Medically Insurable?" . . . Mr. P. testified about his eight-year-old son Michael who has multiple disabilities.

"My name is Donald P. and I live in South Bend, Indiana with my wife, Vickie, and our three children, ages 11, 8 and 4. . . . My wife and I were high school sweethearts and have been married for 15 years. We were both born and raised in the State of Indiana; that is where we have our roots and our extended family.

We have three children; Jeffrey, age 11, Michael, age 8, and Steven, age 4. Michael was born on June 3, 1982. He is a child with multiple disabilities—his diagnosis is colpocephaly (a brain malformation), hypotonia, seizure disorder, scoliosis, with a communication disorder, mental retardation, and multiple developmental delays—or in short, cerebral palsy, meaning he cannot walk, talk, dress, toilet, feed or fend for himself. Michael is physically dependent upon us for his every need, and probably will be dependent upon us and others for physical assistance and support throughout his lifetime.

As a head of a household with a child with multiple disabilities, I have learned a great deal more than I ever wanted to know about the health insurance industry and its impact on my family and thousands of families like mine.

While my wife was pregnant with Michael, my employer . . . was taken over in a merger by another company and I was let go. . . . I didn't opt for the [insurance] conversion policy when the company policy ended . . . because there seemed to be better coverage by purchasing a private "family" policy for myself, my wife and my son Jeffrey from Blue Cross–Blue Shield of Indiana, at a premium of $93.60 per month. . . ."

Between June 1982 and April 1986 the following sequence of events forced the P.'s to impoverish themselves to qualify for Medicaid coverage for their son.

◆ Blue Cross–Blue Shield insurance premiums increased 175 percent in a twelve-month period;

◆ After being rehired by a prior employer and restored to a prior plan, uncertainty about the future led Mr. P. to retain the Blue Cross–Blue Shield policy as a personal expense;

◆ Attempts to add Michael to the family plan were ignored by Blue Cross; instead, he was enrolled as an individual policyholder on a separate policy with $1,000 deductible, with a "1.XVXV benefits code";

◆ Blue Cross continued the family, minus Michael, in a policy with a $250 deductible with an "XRR benefits code";

◆ After collecting monthly premiums of $50.43 for Michael and $112.31 for the rest of the family for a period of time, Blue Cross canceled both policies, stating in a form letter to all policyholders in Indiana that they could no longer afford to administer the plan;

◆ The re-hire by the previous employer and acceptance into the Company's self-insured health benefits followed by a termination created a sense of panic and led to a choice not to purchase a conversion plan for fear the premium would be too high;

◆ All health insurance coverage lapsed until Mr. P. was employed by a small firm where he was informed that the company health insurance plan would not cover Michael "because of his health conditions." He therefore withheld Michael's name from the application for insurance, in effect denying his son's existence so that the rest of the family could have health insurance coverage;

◆ Unable to buy insurance for Michael because no one in Indiana was selling it, Mr. P. stated, "The health insurance industry forced me to turn to Medicaid." To qualify, all family assets, savings, individual retirement accounts, and life insurance policies were "spent down" leaving the family impoverished, unprotected and vulnerable to financial disaster.

◆ A current employer provides a group plan that covers all of the family, except Michael. Medicaid has paid for Michael's wheelchair and a custom seat insert, a total of $5,400 (or $350 per month since Medicaid covered him). Medicaid denied payment for the lift necessary to get Michael's wheelchair into the family van saying it was not "medically necessary." Private charities, other family members and friends contributed $3,430 for a used wheelchair lift. The family sacrificed Medicaid's respite care allowance for one year so that the $600 allowed could be used instead for the lift.

Mr. P. says they have been stigmatized and excluded, they have "suffered" and will continue to suffer until the health industry is compelled to modify or eliminate current underwriting principles. Because of their commitment to raise their son with disabilities at home, they "are not very free to pursue economic growth and the American Dream." Instead they are compelled to:

◆ set financial restrictions on their standard of living;

♦ deny themselves additional education and career advancement;

♦ forego saving for their children's college educations and their own retirement;

♦ foresake any inheritance from other family members.★

Point   Families with children with disabilities should have access to health insurance that covers reasonable health care for all family members. Insurance companies currently base their coverage on "experience ratings" rather than "community ratings." Using experience ratings, they identify groups of individuals with whom they can make significant profits given their past health care requirements. They should use community ratings which consider the health needs of all individuals in a given area or location. Additionally, their pricing and potential profit structures should be based on these community ratings. As a society, we should be willing to share the expense of providing basic medical care to all families and their members. Present insurance policies are patently discriminatory.

Counterpoint   Insurance companies are private entities and for-profit businesses. As such, they must operate in ways that allow them to make profits as well as fund the expenses that they incur in paying for health care delivered to families and individuals. If insurance companies were to alter their current underwriting standards, their expenses would exceed their incomes, and they would not be able to provide health insurance for anyone.

Source: ★ From "Public Testimony, Health Care Industry Forces Family Impoverishment: UCPA Witness Testifies on Access to Health Insurance" by A. I. Bergman and J. Simpson, Fall 1990, *Family Support Bulletin*, pp. 19–20. Reprinted by permission from *Family Support Bulletin*. Published by the United Cerebral Palsy Associations, Inc.

REVIEW

FOCUS 1   Identify five factors that influence the ways in which families respond to infants with birth defects or disabilities.

♦ The emotional stability of each family member,

♦ Religious values and beliefs,

♦ Socioeconomic status,

♦ The severity of the disability,

♦ The type of disability

FOCUS 2   What three statements can be made about the stages that parents may experience in responding to infants or young children with disabilities?

♦ The stage approach needs further refinement and validation before it can be used accurately to understand, predict, or help parents deal with young infants and children with disabilities.

♦ Parental responses are highly variable.

♦ The adjustment process, for most parents, is continuous and distinctively individual.

FOCUS 3   Identify four major concerns of parents of children who are exceptional.

♦ What are our child's future educational and social needs?

♦ What will our child be capable of doing as an adult?

♦ How will our child influence our other children and our family as a whole?

♦ How can we maintain our normal family functioning with the presence of this child?

FOCUS 4   Identify three ways in which a newborn child with disabilities influences the manner in which family members respond to each other.

♦ The mother may have less time to relate to the other children in the family.

♦ The other members of the family may have to assume some of the roles and responsibilities that were once the mother's.

♦ The mother's need for support and assistance may bring the family closer together as a unit.

FOCUS 5   What kind of relationship may develop between the mother and her child with a disability?

♦ A strong dyadic relationship

FOCUS 6   Identify three factors in raising a child who is exceptional that contribute to marital stress.

♦ A decrease in the amount of time available for the couple's activities

♦ Sometimes heavy financial burdens

♦ Fatigue

FOCUS 7   Identify four general phases of the developmental cycle that parents go through in rearing a child with a disability.

♦ The diagnostic period: Does the child truly have a disability?

♦ The school period (elementary and secondary) with its inherent challenges: dealing with teasing and other peer-related behaviors; learning academic, social, and vocational skills. Included in this period are the challenges of adolescence.

♦ The postschool period: The child makes the transition from school to other educational or vocational activities.

♦ The period when the parents are no longer able to provide direct care and guidance for their son or daughter.

FOCUS 8 Identify four factors that influence the relationship that develops between infants with disabilities and their mothers.

◆ The mother may be unable to engage in typical feeding and caregiving activities because of the intensive medical care being provided.

◆ Some mothers may have difficulty bonding to children with whom they have little physical and social interaction.

◆ Some mothers are given little direction as to how they might become involved with their children. Without minimal involvement, some mothers become estranged from their children and find it difficult to begin the caring process.

◆ The expectations that mothers have about their children and their functions in nurturing them play a significant role in the relationship that develops.

FOCUS 9 Identify three ways in which fathers may respond to their children with disabilities.

◆ Fathers are more likely to internalize their feelings than are mothers.

◆ Fathers often respond to sons with disabilities differently from how they respond to daughters.

◆ Fathers may resent the time their wives spend in caring for their children with disabilities.

FOCUS 10 Identify four ways in which siblings respond to their brothers or sisters who are exceptional.

◆ Siblings tend to mirror the attitudes and behaviors of their parents toward a child with disabilities.

◆ Siblings may play a critical role in fostering the intellectual, social, and affective development of the child who is exceptional.

◆ Some siblings respond by eventually becoming members of helping professions that serve populations that are exceptional.

◆ Some siblings respond with feelings of resentment or deprivation.

FOCUS 11 Identify three types of assistance that grandparents may render to families with children who are exceptional.

◆ They may provide their own children with weekend reprieves from the pressures of the home environment.

◆ They may assist occasionally with baby-sitting or transportation.

◆ They may help their children in times of crisis by listening and helping them deal with seemingly unresolvable problems.

FOCUS 12 Identify three types of professional understanding that are essential to establishing positive relationships with parents and families of children who are exceptional.

◆ Professionals need to understand the impact that they have on the family over time.

◆ Professionals need to understand the impact that the child with disabilities has on the family over time.

◆ Professionals need to understand the impact that the child with disabilities and his or her family have on them.

FOCUS 13 Identify three ways in which children with disabilities and their families impact teachers and health care workers.

◆ Professionals may become emotionally exhausted from the pressures involved in educating or helping children who are exceptional.

◆ Professionals may become apathetic, pessimistic, or cynical about their work with patients, clients, and students.

◆ Professionals may feel powerless to enact meaningful changes in their work environments.

Appendix A

The 1992 Definition of Mental Retardation as Adopted by the American Association on Mental Retardation

In 1992, the American Association on Mental Retardation (AAMR) undertook the organization's fourth revision of the definition of mental retardation in the past 30 years. The definition is published in the AAMR manual entitled *Mental Retardation: Definitions, Classification, and Systems of Support* (9th ed.) and is to be field tested over the next several years. For the most part, this new definition has maintained the basic elements of the 1983 definition (see pages 96–97 of this book) but has a much stronger emphasis on adaptive and functional skills.

1992 AAMR DEFINITION OF MENTAL RETARDATION

Mental retardation refers to substantial limitations in present functioning. It is characterized by significantly subaverage intellectual functioning, existing concurrently with related limitations in two or more of the following applicable adaptive skill areas: communication, self-care, home living, social skills, community use, self-direction, health and safety, functional academics, leisure and work. Mental retardation manifests before age 18.

APPLICATION OF THE DEFINITION

AAMR has developed four assumptions that are viewed as essential as professionals and consumers begin to use the definition in practice:

1. Valid assessment considers cultural and linguistic diversity and differences in communication and behavioral factors.

2. The existence of limitations in adaptive skills occurs within the context of community environments typical of the individual's age peers and is indexed to the person's individualized needs support.

3. Specific adaptive limitations often coexist with strengths in other adaptive skills or other personal capabilities.

4. With appropriate supports over a sustained period, the life functioning of the person with mental retardation will generally improve.

STEPS FOR DIAGNOSIS, CLASSIFICATION, AND IDENTIFICATION OF SUPPORTS

1. *Diagnosis of Mental Retardation*—This step determines eligibility for support services:
   a. The person's intellectual functioning level is below IQ 70–75.
   b. The age of onset is 18 years or younger.
   c. There are significant disabilities in two or more adaptive skill areas.

2. *Classification and Description*—This step identifies needed supports:
   a. Describe the person's strengths and weaknesses in reference to psychological/emotional considerations.
   b. Describe the person's overall physical health and indicate the condition's etiology (cause).
   c. Describe the person's current environmental placement and the optimal environment that would facilitate the person's continued growth and development.

3. *Identification of the Pattern and Intensity of Supports Needed*—This step results in a profile of support needs:
   a. Intermittent
   b. Limited
   c. Extensive
   d. Pervasive

Source: Material in this section is from *Mental Retardation: Definitions, Classification, and Systems of Supports* (9th ed) by R. Luckasson, D. Coulter, E. Polloway, S. Reiss, R. Schalock, M. Snell, D. Spitalnik, and J. Stark, 1992, Washington, DC: American Association on Mental Retardation.

Levels of Supports

Intermittent.   Supports are provided on an "as-needed basis"; characterized as episodic (i.e., person does not always need supports) or short-term during life-span transitions (e.g., job loss or acute medical crisis). Intermittent supports may be of high or low intensity when provided.

Limited.   Supports are characterized by consistency; time required may be limited but not intermittent. Fewer staff may be required and costs may be lower than for more intensive levels of support (e.g., time-limited employment training or transitional supports during school-to-adult provider period).

Extensive.   Supports are characterized by regular involvement (e.g., daily) in at least some environments, such as work or home; supports are not time limited (e.g., long-term job and home-living support).

Pervasive.   Supports are characterized by constancy and high intensity and provided across environments; they have a potential life-sustaining nature. Pervasive supports typically involve more staff and are more intrusive than extensive or time-limited supports.

Appendix B

Americans with Disabilities Act of 1990: PL 101-336

SECTION 1. SHORT TITLE; TABLE OF CONTENTS.

(a) SHORT TITLE.—This Act may be cited as the "Americans with Disabilities Act of 1990."

(b) TABLE OF CONTENTS.—The table of contents is as follows:

Source: Material in this section is from Report 101–596 issued by the House of Representatives, July 12, 1990, 101st Congress, 2d session.

SECTION 2. FINDINGS AND PURPOSES.

(a)   FINDINGS.—The Congress finds that—

(1)   some 43,000,000 Americans have one or more physical or mental disabilities, and this number is increasing as the population as a whole is growing older;

(2)   historically, society has tended to isolate and segregate individuals with disabilities, and, despite some improvements, such forms of discrimination against individuals with disabilities continue to be a serious and pervasive social problem;

(3)   discrimination against individuals with disabilities persists in such critical areas as employment, housing, public accommodations, education, transportation, communication, recreation, institutionalization, health services, voting, and access to public services;

(4)   unlike individuals who have experienced discrimination on the basis of race, color, sex, national origin, religion, or age, individuals who have experienced discrimination on the basis of disability have often had no legal recourse to redress such discrimination;

(5)   individuals with disabilities continually encounter various forms of discrimination, including outright intentional exclusion, the discriminatory effects of architectural, transportation, and communication barriers, overprotective rules and policies, failure to make modifications to existing facilities and practices, exclusionary qualification standards and criteria, segregation, and relegation to lesser services, programs, activities, benefits, jobs, or other opportunities;

(6)   census data, national polls, and other studies have documented that people with disabilities, as a group, occupy an inferior status in our society, and are severely disadvantaged socially, vocationally, economically, and educationally;

(7)   individuals with disabilities are a discrete and insular minority who have been faced with restrictions and limitations, subjected to a history of purposeful unequal treatment, and relegated to a position of political powerlessness in our society, based on characteristics that are beyond the control of such individuals and resulting from stereotypic assumptions not truly indicative of the individual ability of such individuals to participate in, and contribute to, society;

(8)   the Nation's proper goals regarding individuals with disabilities are to assure equality of opportunity, full participation, independent living, and economic self-sufficiency for such individuals; and

(9)   the continuing existence of unfair and unnecessary discrimination and prejudice denies people with disabilities the opportunity to compete on an equal basis and to pursue those opportunities for which our free society is justifiably famous, and costs the United States billions of dollars in unnecessary expenses resulting from dependency and nonproductivity.

(b)   PURPOSE—It is the purpose of this Act—

(1)   to provide a clear and comprehensive national mandate for the elimination of discrimination against individuals with disabilities;

(2) to provide clear, strong, consistent, enforceable standards addressing discrimination against individuals with disabilities;

(3) to ensure that the Federal Government plays a central role in enforcing the standards established in this Act on behalf of individuals with disabilities; and

(4) to invoke the sweep of congressional authority, including the power to enforce the fourteenth amendment and to regulate commerce, in order to address the major areas of discrimination faced day-to-day by people with disabilities.

SECTION 3. DEFINITIONS.

As used in this Act:

(1) AUXILIARY AIDS AND SERVICES.—The term "auxiliary aids and services" includes—

(A) qualified interpreters or other effective methods of making aurally delivered materials available to individuals with hearing impairments;

(B) qualified readers, taped texts, or other effective methods of making visually delivered materials available to individuals with visual impairments;

(C) acquisition or modification of equipment or devices; and

(D) other similar services and actions.

(2) DISABILITY.—The term "disability" means, with respect to an individual—

(A) a physical or mental impairment that substantially limits one or more of the major life activities of such individual;

(B) a record of such an impairment; or

(C) being regarded as having such an impairment.

(3) STATE.—The term "State" means each of the several States, the District of Columbia, the Commonwealth of Puerto Rico, Guam, American Samoa, the Virgin Islands, the Trust Territory of the Pacific Islands, and the Commonwealth of the Northern Mariana Islands.

TITLE I—EMPLOYMENT

Section 101. Definitions.

As used in this title:

(1) COMMISSION.—The term "Commission" means the Equal Employment Opportunity Com-

mission established by section 705 of the Civil Rights Act of 1964 (42 U.S.C. 2000e–4).

(2) COVERED ENTITY.—The term "covered entity" means an employer, employment agency, labor organization, or joint labor-management committee.

(3) DIRECT THREAT.—The term "direct threat" means a significant risk to the health or safety of others that cannot be eliminated by reasonable accommodation.

(4) EMPLOYEE—The term "employee" means an individual employed by an employer.

(5) EMPLOYER.—

(A) IN GENERAL.—The term "employer" means a person engaged in an industry affecting commerce who has 15 or more employees for each working day in each of 20 or more calendar weeks in the current or preceding calendar year, and any agent of such person, except that, for two years following the effective date of this title, an employer means a person engaged in an industry affecting commerce who has 25 or more employees for each working day in each of 20 or more calendar weeks in the current or preceding year, and any agent of such person.

(B) EXCEPTIONS.—The term "employer" does not include—

(i) the United States, a corporation wholly owned by the government of the United States, or an Indian tribe; or

(ii) a bona fide private membership club (other than a labor organization) that is exempt from taxation under section 501(c) of the Internal Revenue Code of 1986.

(6) ILLEGAL USE OF DRUGS.—

(A) IN GENERAL.—The term "illegal use of drugs" means the use of drugs, the possession or distribution of which is unlawful under the Controlled Substances Act (21 U.S.C. 812). Such term does not include the use of a drug taken under supervision by a licensed health care professional, or other uses authorized by the Controlled Substances Act or other provisions of Federal law.

(B) DRUGS.—The term "drug" means a controlled substance, as defined in schedules I through V of section 202 of the Controlled Substances Act.

(7) PERSON, ETC.—The terms "person", "labor organization", "employment agency", "commerce", and "industry affecting commerce", shall have the same meaning given such terms in section 701 of the Civil Rights Act of 1964 (42 U.S.C. 2000e).

(8) QUALIFIED INDIVIDUAL WITH A DISABILITY.—The term "qualified individual with a disability" means an individual with a disability who, with or without reasonable accommodation, can perform the essential functions of the employment position that such individual holds or desires. For the purposes of this title, consideration shall be given to the employer's judgment as to what functions of a job are essential, and if an employer has prepared a written description before advertising or interviewing applicants for the job, this description shall be considered evidence of the essential functions of the job.

(9) REASONABLE ACCOMMODATION.— The term "reasonable accommodation" may include—

(A) making existing facilities used by employees readily accessible to and usable by individuals with disabilities; and

(B) job restructuring, part-time or modified work schedules, reassignment to a vacant position, acquisition or modification of equipment or devices, appropriate adjustment or modifications of examinations, training materials or policies, the provision of qualified readers or interpreters, and other similar accommodations for individuals with disabilities.

(10) UNDUE HARDSHIP.—

(A) IN GENERAL.—The term "undue hardship" means an action requiring significant difficulty or expense, when considered in light of the factors set forth in subparagraph (B).

(B) FACTORS TO BE CONSIDERED.—In determining whether an accommodation would impose an undue hardship on a covered entity, factors to be considered include—

(i) the nature and cost of the accommodation needed under this Act;

(ii) the overall financial resources of the facility or facilities involved in the provision of the reasonable accommodation; the number of persons employed at such facility; the effect on expenses and resources, or the impact otherwise of such accommodation upon the operation of the facility;

(iii) the overall financial resources of the covered entity; the overall size of the business of a covered entity with respect to the number of its employees; the number, type, and location of its facilities; and

(iv) the type of operation or operations of the covered entity, including the composition, structure, and functions of the workforce of such entity; the geographic separateness, administrative, or fiscal relationship of the facility or facilities in question to the covered entity.

Section 102. Discrimination.

(a) GENERAL RULE.—No covered entity shall discriminate against a qualified individual with a disability because of the disability of such individual in regard to job application procedures, the hiring, advancement, or discharge of employees, employee compensation, job training, and other terms, conditions, and privileges of employment.

(b) CONSTRUCTION.—As used in subsection (a), the term "discriminate" includes—

(1) limiting, segregating, or classifying a job applicant or employee in a way that adversely affects the opportunities or status of such applicant or employee because of the disability of such applicant or employee;

(2) participating in a contractual or other arrangement or relationship that has the effect of subjecting a covered entity's qualified applicant or employee with a disability to the discrimination prohibited by this title (such relationship includes a relationship with an employment or referral agency, labor union, an organization providing fringe benefits to an employee of the covered entity, or an organization providing training and apprenticeship programs);

(3) utilizing standards, criteria, or methods of administration—

    (A) that have the effect of discrimination on the basis of disability; or

    (B) that perpetuate the discrimination of others who are subject to common administrative control;

(4) excluding or otherwise denying equal jobs or benefits to a qualified individual because of the known disability of an individual with whom the qualified individual is known to have a relationship or association;

(5) (A) not making reasonable accommodations to the known physical or mental limitations of an otherwise qualified individual with a disability who is an applicant or employee, unless such covered entity can demonstrate that the accommodation would impose an undue hardship on the operation of the business of such covered entity; or

    (B) denying employment opportunities to a job applicant or employee who is an otherwise qualified individual with a disability, if such denial is based on the need of such covered entity to make reasonable accommodation to the physical or mental impairments of the employee or applicant;

(6) using qualification standards, employment tests or other selection criteria that screen out or tend to screen out an individual with a disability or a class of individuals with disabilities unless the standard, test or other selection criteria, as used by the covered entity, is shown to be job-related for the position in question and is consistent with business necessity; and

(7) failing to select and administer tests concerning employment in the most effective manner to ensure that, when such test is administered to a job applicant or employee who has a disability that impairs sensory, manual, or speaking skills, such test results accurately reflect the skills, aptitude, or whatever other factor of such applicant or employee that such test purports to measure, rather than reflecting the impaired sensory, manual, or speaking skills of such employee or applicant (except where such skills are the factors that the test purports to measure).

(c) MEDICAL EXAMINATIONS AND INQUIRIES.—

ination as referred to in subsection (a) shall include medical examinations and inquiries.

(2) PREEMPLOYMENT.—

    (A) PROHIBITED EXAMINATION OR INQUIRY.—Except as provided in paragraph (3), a covered entity shall not conduct a medical examination or make inquiries of a job applicant as to whether such applicant is an individual with a disability or as to the nature or severity of such disability.

    (B) ACCEPTABLE INQUIRY.—A covered entity may make preemployment inquiries into the ability of an applicant to perform job-related functions.

(3) EMPLOYMENT ENTRANCE EXAMINATION.—A covered entity may require a medical examination after an offer of employment has been made to a job applicant and prior to the commencement of the employment duties of such applicant, and may condition an offer of employment on the results of such examination, if—

    (A) all entering employees are subjected to such an examination regardless of disability;

    (B) information obtained regarding the medical condition or history of the applicant is collected and maintained on separate forms and in separate medical files and is treated as a confidential medical record, except that—

        (i) supervisors and managers may be informed regarding necessary restrictions on the work or duties of the employee and necessary accommodations;

        (ii) first aid and safety personnel may be informed, when appropriate, if the disability might require emergency treatment; and

        (iii) government officials investigating compliance with this Act shall be provided relevant information on request; and

    (C) the results of such examination are used only in accordance with this title.

(4) EXAMINATION AND INQUIRY.—

    (A) PROHIBITED EXAMINATIONS AND INQUIRIES.—A covered entity shall not require a medical examination and shall not make inquiries of an employee as to whether such employee is an individual with a disability or as to the nature or severity of the disability, unless such examination or inquiry is shown to be job-related and consistent with business necessity.

(B)   ACCEPTABLE EXAMINATIONS AND INQUIRIES.—A covered entity may conduct voluntary medical examinations, including voluntary medical histories, which are part of an employee health program available to employees at that work site. A covered entity may make inquiries into the ability of an employee to perform job-related functions.

(C)   REQUIREMENT.—Information obtained under subparagraph (B) regarding the medical condition or history of any employee are subject to the requirements of subparagraphs (B) and (C) of paragraph (3).

Section 103. Defenses.

(a)   IN GENERAL.—It may be a defense to a charge of discrimination under this Act that an alleged application of qualification standards, tests, or selection criteria that screen out or tend to screen out or otherwise deny a job or benefit to an individual with a disability has been shown to be job-related and consistent with business necessity, and such performance cannot be accomplished by reasonable accommodation, as required under this title.

(b)   QUALIFICATION STANDARDS.—The term "qualification standards" may include a requirement that an individual shall not pose a direct threat to the health or safety of other individuals in the workplace.

(c)   RELIGIOUS ENTITIES.—

(1)   IN GENERAL.—This title shall not prohibit a religious corporation, association, educational institution, or society from giving preference in employment to individuals of a particular religion to perform work connected with the carrying on by such corporation, association, educational institution, or society of its activities.

(2)   RELIGIOUS TENETS REQUIREMENT.— Under this title, a religious organization may require that all applicants and employees conform to the religious tenets of such organization.

(d)   LIST OF INFECTIOUS AND COMMUNICABLE DISEASES.—

(1)   IN GENERAL.—The Secretary of Health and Human Services, not later than 6 months after the date of enactment of this Act, shall—

(A)   review all infectious and communicable diseases which may be transmitted through handling the food supply;

(B)   publish a list of infectious and communicable diseases which are transmitted through handling the food supply;

(C)   publish the methods by which such diseases are transmitted; and

(D)   widely disseminate such information regarding the list of diseases and their modes of transmissability to the general public.

Such list shall be updated annually.

(2)   APPLICATIONS.—In any case in which an individual has an infectious or communicable disease that is transmitted to others through the handling of food, that is included on the list developed by the Secretary of Health and Human Services under paragraph (1), and which cannot be eliminated by reasonable accommodation, a covered entity may refuse to assign or continue to assign such individual to a job involving food handling.

(3)   CONSTRUCTION.—Nothing in this Act shall be construed to preempt, modify, or amend any State, county, or local law, ordinance, or regulation applicable to food handling which is designed to protect the public health from individuals who pose a significant risk to the health or safety of others, which cannot be eliminated by reasonable accommodation, pursuant to the list of infectious or communicable diseases and the modes of transmissability published by the Secretary of Health and Human Services.

Section 104. Illegal Use of Drugs and Alcohol.

(a)   QUALIFIED INDIVIDUAL WITH A DISABILITY.—For purposes of this title, the term "qualified individual with a disability" shall not include any employee or applicant who is currently engaging in the illegal use of drugs, when the covered entity acts on the basis of such use.

(b)   RULES OF CONSTRUCTION.—Nothing in subsection (a) shall be construed to exclude as a qualified individual with a disability an individual who—

(1)   has successfully completed a supervised drug rehabilitation program and is no longer engaging in the illegal use of drugs, or has otherwise been rehabili-

tated successfully and is no longer engaging in such use;

(2) is participating in a supervised rehabilitation program and is no longer engaging in such use; or

(3) is erroneously regarded as engaging in such use, but is not engaging in such use;

except that it shall not be a violation of this Act for a covered entity to adopt or administer reasonable policies or procedures, including but not limited to drug testing, designed to ensure that an individual described in paragraph (1) or (2) is no longer engaging in the illegal use of drugs.

(c) AUTHORITY OF COVERED ENTITY.—A covered entity—

(1) may prohibit the illegal use of drugs and the use of alcohol at the workplace by all employees;

(2) may require that employees shall not be under the influence of alcohol or be engaging in the illegal use of drugs at the workplace;

(3) may require that employees behave in conformance with the requirements established under the Drug-Free Workplace Act of 1988 (41 U.S.C. 701 et seq.);

(4) may hold an employee who engages in the illegal use of drugs or who is an alcoholic to the same qualification standards for employment or job performance and behavior that such entity holds other employees, even if any unsatisfactory performance or behavior is related to the drug use or alcoholism of such employee; and

(5) may, with respect to Federal regulations regarding alcohol and the illegal use of drugs, require that—

(A) employees comply with the standards established in such regulations of the Department of Defense, if the employees of the covered entity are employed in an industry subject to such regulations, including complying with regulations (if any) that apply to employment in sensitive positions in such an industry, in the case of employees of the covered entity who are employed in such positions (as defined in the regulations of the Department of Defense);

(B) employees comply with the standards established in such regulations of the Nuclear Regulatory Commission, if the employees of the covered entity are employed in an industry subject to such regulations, including complying with regulations (if any) that apply to employment in sensitive positions in such an industry, in the case of employees of the covered

entity who are employed in such positions (as defined in the regulations of the Nuclear Regulatory Commission); and

(C) employees comply with the standards established in such regulations of the Department of Transportation, if the employees of the covered entity are employed in a transportation industry subject to such regulations, including complying with such regulations (if any) that apply to employment in sensitive positions in such an industry, in the case of employees of the covered entity who are employed in such positions (as defined in the regulations of the Department of Transportation).

(d) DRUG TESTING.—

(1) IN GENERAL.—For purposes of this title, a test to determine the illegal use of drugs shall not be considered a medical examination.

(2) CONSTRUCTION.—Nothing in this title shall be construed to encourage, prohibit, or authorize the conducting of drug testing for the illegal use of drugs by job applicants or employees or making employment decisions based on such test results.

(e) TRANSPORTATION EMPLOYEES.—Nothing in this title shall be construed to encourage, prohibit, restrict, or authorize the otherwise lawful exercise by entities subject to the jurisdiction of the Department of Transportation of authority to—

(1) test employees of such entities in, and applicants for, positions involving safety-sensitive duties for the illegal use of drugs and for on-duty impairment by alcohol; and

(2) remove such persons who test positive for illegal use of drugs and on-duty impairment by alcohol pursuant to paragraph (1) from safety-sensitive duties in implementing subsection (c).

Section 105. Posting Notices.

Every employer, employment agency, labor organization, or joint labor-management committee covered under this title shall post notices in an accessible format to applicants, employees, and members describing the applicable provisions of this Act, in the manner prescribed by section 711 of the Civil Rights Act of 1964 (42 U.S.C. 2000e-10).

Section 106. Regulations.

Not later than 1 year after the date of enactment of this Act, the Commission shall issue regulations in an accessible format to carry out this title in accordance with subchapter II of chapter 5 of title 5, United States Code.

Section 107. Enforcement.

(a) POWERS, REMEDIES, AND PROCEDURES.— The powers, remedies, and procedures set forth in sections 705, 706, 707, 709, and 710 of the Civil Rights Act of 1964 (42 U.S.C. 2000e-4, 2000e-5, 2000e-6, 2000e-8, and 2000e-9) shall be the powers, remedies, and procedures this title provides to the Commission, to the Attorney General, or to any person alleging discrimination on the basis of disability in violation of any provision of this Act, or regulations promulgated under section 106, concerning employment.

(b) COORDINATION.—The agencies with enforcement authority for actions which allege employment discrimination under this title and under the Rehabilitation Act of 1973 shall develop procedures to ensure that administrative complaints filed under this title and under the Rehabilitation Act of 1973 are dealt with in a manner that avoids duplication of effort and prevents imposition of inconsistent or conflicting standards for the same requirements under this title and the Rehabilitation Act of 1973. The Commission, the Attorney General, and the Office of Federal Contract Compliance Programs shall establish such coordinating mechanisms (similar to provisions contained in the joint regulations promulgated by the Commission and the Attorney General at part 42 of title 28 and part 1691 of title 29, Code of Federal Regulations, and the Memorandum of Understanding between the Commission and the Office of Federal Contract Compliance Programs dated January 16, 1981 (46 Fed. Reg. 7435, January 23, 1981)) in regulations implementing this title and the Rehabilitation Act of 1973 not later than 18 months after the date of enactment of this Act.

Section 108. Effective Date.

This title shall become effective 24 months after the date of enactment.

TITLE II—PUBLIC SERVICES

SUBTITLE A—Prohibition Against Discrimination and Other Generally Applicable Provisions

Section 201. Definition.

As used in this title:

(1) PUBLIC ENTITY.—The term "public entity" means—

    (A) any State or local government;

    (B) any department, agency, special purpose district, or other instrumentality of a State or States or local government; and

    (C) the National Railroad Passenger Corporation, and any commuter authority (as defined in section 103(8) of the Rail Passenger Service Act).

(2) QUALIFIED INDIVIDUAL WITH A DISABILITY.—The term "qualified individual with a disability" means an individual with a disability who, with or without reasonable modifications to rules, policies, or practices, the removal of architectural, communication, or transportation barriers, or the provision of auxiliary aids and services, meets the essential eligibility requirements for the receipt of services or the participation in programs or activities provided by a public entity.

Section 202. Discrimination.

Subject to the provisions of this title, no qualified individual with a disability shall, by reason of such disability, be excluded from participation in or be denied the benefits of the services, programs, or activities of a public entity, or be subjected to discrimination by any such entity.

Section 203. Enforcement.

The remedies, procedures, and rights set forth in section 505 of the Rehabilitation Act of 1973 (29 U.S.C. 794a) shall be the remedies, procedures and rights this title provides to any person alleging discrimination on the basis of disability in violation of section 202.

Section 204. Regulations.

(a) IN GENERAL.—Not later than 1 year after the date of enactment of this Act, the Attorney General shall promulgate regulations in an accessible format that implement this subtitle. Such regulations shall not include any matter within the scope of the authority of the Secretary of Transportation under section 223, 229, or 244.

(b) RELATIONSHIP TO OTHER REGULATIONS.— Except for "program accessibility, existing facilities", and "communications", regulations under subsection (a) shall be consistent with this Act and with the coordination regulations under part 41 of title 28, Code of Federal Regulations (as promulgated by the Department of Health, Education, and Welfare on January 13, 1978), applicable to recipients of Federal financial assistance under section 504 of the Rehabilitation Act of 1973 (29 U.S.C. 794). With respect to "program accessibility, existing facilities", and "communications", such regulations shall be consistent with regulations and analysis as in part 39 of title 28 of the Code of Federal Regulations, applicable to federally conducted activities under such section 504.

(c) STANDARDS.—Regulations under subsection (a) shall include standards applicable to facilities and vehicles covered by this subtitle, other than facilities, stations, rail passenger cars, and vehicles covered by subtitle B. Such standards shall be consistent with the minimum guidelines and requirements issued by the Architectural and Transportation Barriers Compliance Board in accordance with section 504(a) of this Act.

Section 205. Effective Date.

(a) GENERAL RULE.—Except as provided in subsection (b), this subtitle shall become effective 18 months after the date of enactment of this Act.

(b) EXCEPTION.—Section 204 shall become effective on the date of enactment of this Act.

SUBTITLE B—Actions Applicable to Public Transportation Provided by Public Entities Considered Discriminatory

PART I—Public Transportation Other Than by Aircraft or Certain Rail Operations

Section 221. Definitions.

As used in this part:

(1) DEMAND RESPONSIVE SYSTEM.—The term "demand responsive system" means any sys-tem of providing designated public transportation which is not a fixed route system.

(2) DESIGNATED PUBLIC TRANSPORTA-TION.—The term "designated public transportation" means transportation (other than public school transportation) by bus, rail, or any other conveyance (other than transportation by aircraft or intercity or commuter rail transportation (as defined in section 241)) that provides the general public with general or special service (including charter service) on a regular and continuing basis.

(3) FIXED ROUTE SYSTEM.—The term "fixed route system" means a system of providing designated public transportation on which a vehicle is operated along a prescribed route according to a fixed schedule.

(4) OPERATES.—The term "operates", as used with respect to a fixed route system or demand responsive system, includes operation of such system by a person under a contractual or other arrangement or relationship with a public entity.

(5) PUBLIC SCHOOL TRANSPORTATION.— The term "public school transportation" means transportation by schoolbus vehicles of schoolchildren, personnel, and equipment to and from a public elementary or secondary school and school-related activities.

(6) SECRETARY.—The term "Secretary" means the Secretary of Transportation.

Section 222. Public Entities Operating Fixed Route Systems.

(a) PURCHASE AND LEASE OF NEW VEHICLES.— It shall be considered discrimination for purposes of section 202 of this Act and section 504 of the Rehabilitation Act of 1973 (29 U.S.C. 794) for a public entity which operates a fixed route system to purchase or lease a new bus, a new rapid rail vehicle, a new light rail vehicle, or any other new vehicle to be used on such system, if the solicitation for such purchase or lease is made after the 30th day following the effective date of this subsection and if such bus, rail vehicle, or other vehicle is not readily accessible to and usable by individuals with disabilities, including individuals who use wheelchairs.

(b) PURCHASE AND LEASE OF USED VEHICLES.—

Subject to subsection (c)(1), it shall be considered discrimination for purposes of section 202 of this Act and section 504 of the Rehabilitation Act of 1973 (29 U.S.C. 794) for a public entity which operates a fixed route system to purchase or lease, after the 30th day following the effective date of this subsection, a used vehicle for use on such system unless such entity makes demonstrated good faith efforts to purchase or lease a used vehicle for use on such system that is readily accessible to and usable by individuals with disabilities, including individuals who use wheelchairs.

(c) REMANUFACTURED VEHICLES.—

(1) GENERAL RULE.—Except as provided in paragraph (2), it shall be considered discrimination for purposes of section 202 of this Act and section 504 of the Rehabilitation Act of 1973 (29 U.S.C. 794) for a public entity which operates a fixed route system—

(A) to remanufacture a vehicle for use on such system so as to extend its usable life for 5 years or more, which remanufacture begins (or for which the solicitation is made) after the 30th day following the effective date of this subsection; or

(B) to purchase or lease for use on such system a remanufactured vehicle which has been remanufactured so as to extend its usable life for 5 years or more, which purchase or lease occurs after such 30th day and during the period in which the usable life is extended;

unless, after remanufacture, the vehicle is, to the maximum extent feasible, readily accessible to and usable by individuals with disabilities, including individuals who use wheelchairs.

(2) EXCEPTION FOR HISTORIC VEHICLES.—

(A) GENERAL RULE.—If a public entity operates a fixed route system any segment of which is included on the National Register of Historic Places and if making a vehicle of historic character to be used solely on such segment readily accessible to and usable by individuals with disabilities would significantly alter the historic character of such vehicle, the public entity only has to make (or to purchase or lease a remanufactured vehicle with) those modifications which are necessary to meet the requirements of paragraph (1) and which do not significantly alter the historic character of such vehicle.

(B) VEHICLES OF HISTORIC CHARACTER DEFINED BY REGULATIONS.—For purposes of this paragraph and section 228(b), a vehicle of historic character shall be defined by the regulations issued by the Secretary to carry out this subsection.

Section 223. Paratransit as a Complement to Fixed Route Service.

(a) GENERAL RULE.—It shall be considered discrimination for purposes of section 202 of this Act and section 504 of the Rehabilitation Act of 1973 (29 U.S.C. 794) for a public entity which operates a fixed route system (other than a system which provides solely commuter bus service) to fail to provide with respect to the operations of its fixed route system, in accordance with this section, paratransit and other special transportation services to individuals with disabilities, including individuals who use wheelchairs, that are sufficient to provide to such individuals a level of service (1) which is comparable to the level of designated public transportation services provided to individuals without disabilities using such system; or (2) in the case of response time, which is comparable, to the extent practicable, to the level of designated public transportation services provided to individuals without disabilities using such system.

(b) ISSUANCE OF REGULATIONS.—Not later than 1 year after the effective date of this subsection, the Secretary shall issue final regulations to carry out this section.

(c) REQUIRED CONTENTS OF REGULATIONS.—

(1) ELIGIBLE RECIPIENTS OF SERVICE.—The regulations issued under this section shall require each public entity which operates a fixed route system to provide the paratransit and other special transportation services required under this section—

(A) (i) to any individual with a disability who is unable, as a result of a physical or mental impairment (including a vision impairment) and without the assistance of another individual (except an operator of a wheelchair lift or other boarding assistance device), to board, ride, or disembark from any vehicle on the system which is readily accessible to and usable by individuals with disabilities;

(ii) to any individual with a disability who needs the assistance of a wheelchair lift or other boarding assistance device (and is able with such assistance) to board, ride, and disembark from any vehicle which is readily accessible to and usable by individuals with disabilities if the individual wants to travel on a route on the system during the hours of operation of the system at a time (or within a reasonable period of such time) when such a vehicle is not being used to provide designated public transportation on the route; and

(iii) to any individual with a disability who has a specific impairment-related condition which prevents such individual from traveling to a boarding location or from a disembarking location on such system;

(B) to 1 other individual accompanying the individual with the disability; and

(C) to other individuals, in addition to the one individual described in subparagraph (B), accompanying the individual with a disability provided that space for these additional individuals is available on the paratransit vehicle carrying the individual with a disability and that the transportation of such additional individuals will not result in a denial of service to individuals with disabilities.

For purposes of clauses (i) and (ii) of subparagraph (A), boarding or disembarking from a vehicle does not include travel to the boarding location or from the disembarking location.

(2) SERVICE AREA.—The regulations issued under this section shall require the provision of paratransit and special transportation services required under this section in the service area of each public entity which operates a fixed route system, other than any portion of the service area in which the public entity solely provides commuter bus service.

(3) SERVICE CRITERIA.—Subject to paragraphs (1) and (2), the regulations issued under this section shall establish minimum service criteria for determining the level of services to be required under this section.

(4) UNDUE FINANCIAL BURDEN LIMITATION.—The regulations issued under this section shall provide that, if the public entity is able to demonstrate to the satisfaction of the Secretary that the provision of paratransit and other special transportation services otherwise required under this section would impose an undue financial burden on the public entity, notwithstanding any other provision of this section (other than paragraph (5)), shall only be required to provide such services to the extent that providing such services would not impose such a burden.

(5) ADDITIONAL SERVICES.—The regulations issued under this section shall establish circumstances under which the Secretary may require a public entity to provide, notwithstanding paragraph (4), paratransit and other special transportation services under this section beyond the level of paratransit and other special transportation services which would otherwise be required under paragraph (4).

(6) PUBLIC PARTICIPATION.—The regulations issued under this section shall require that each public entity which operates a fixed route system hold a public hearing, provide an opportunity for public comment, and consult with individuals with disabilities in preparing its plan under paragraph (7).

(7) PLANS.—The regulations issued under this section shall require that each public entity which operates a fixed route system—

(A) within 18 months after the effective date of this subsection, submit to the Secretary, and commence implementation of, a plan for providing paratransit and other special transportation services which meets the requirements of this section; and

(B) on an annual basis thereafter, submit to the Secretary, and commence implementation of, a plan for providing such services.

(8) PROVISION OF SERVICES BY OTHERS.—The regulations issued under this section shall—

(A) require that a public entity submitting a plan to the Secretary under this section identify in the plan any person or other public entity which is providing a paratransit or other special transportation service for individuals with disabilities in the service area to which the plan applies; and

(B) provide that the public entity submitting the plan does not have to provide under the plan such service for individuals with disabilities.

(9) OTHER PROVISIONS.—The regulations issued under this section shall include such other provisions

and requirements as the Secretary determines are necessary to carry out the objectives of this section.

(d) REVIEW OF PLAN.—

(1) GENERAL RULE.—The Secretary shall review a plan submitted under this section for the purpose of determining whether or not such plan meets the requirements of this section, including the regulations issued under this section.

(2) DISAPPROVAL.—If the Secretary determines that a plan reviewed under this subsection fails to meet the requirements of this section, the Secretary shall disapprove the plan and notify the public entity which submitted the plan of such disapproval and the reasons therefor.

(3) MODIFICATION OF DISAPPROVED PLAN.—Not later than 90 days after the date of disapproval of a plan under this subsection, the public entity which submitted the plan shall modify the plan to meet the requirements of this section and shall submit to the Secretary, and commence implementation of, such modified plan.

(e) DISCRIMINATION DEFINED.—As used in subsection (a), the term "discrimination" includes—

(1) a failure of a public entity to which the regulations issued under this section apply to submit, or commence implementation of, a plan in accordance with subsections (c)(6) and (c)(7);

(2) a failure of such entity to submit, or commence implementation of, a modified plan in accordance with subsection (d)(3);

(3) submission to the Secretary of a modified plan under subsection (d)(3) which does not meet the requirements of this section; or

(4) a failure of such entity to provide paratransit or other special transportation services in accordance with the plan or modified plan the public entity submitted to the Secretary under this section.

(f) STATUTORY CONSTRUCTION.—Nothing in this section shall be construed as preventing a public entity—

(1) from providing paratransit or other special transportation services at a level which is greater than the level of such services which are required by this section,

(2) from providing paratransit or other special transportation services in addition to those paratransit and special transportation services required by this section, or

(3) from providing such services to individuals in addition to those individuals to whom such services are required to be provided by this section.

Section 224. Public Entity Operating a Demand Responsive System.

If a public entity operates a demand responsive system, it shall be considered discrimination, for purposes of section 202 of this Act and section 504 of the Rehabilitation Act of 1973 (29 U.S.C. 794), for such entity to purchase or lease a new vehicle for use on such system, for which a solicitation is made after the 30th day following the effective date of this section, that is not readily accessible to and usable by individuals with disabilities, including individuals who use wheelchairs, unless such system, when viewed in its entirety, provides a level of service to such individuals equivalent to the level of service such system provides to individuals without disabilities.

Section 225. Temporary Relief Where Lifts Are Unavailable.

(a) GRANTING.—With respect to the purchase of new buses, a public entity may apply for, and the Secretary may temporarily relieve such public entity from the obligation under section 222(a) or 224 to purchase new buses that are readily accessible to and usable by individuals with disabilities if such public entity demonstrates to the satisfaction of the Secretary—

(1) that the initial solicitation for new buses made by the public entity specified that all new buses were to be lift-equipped and were to be otherwise accessible to and usable by individuals with disabilities;

(2) the unavailability from any qualified manufacturer of hydraulic, electromechanical, or other lifts for such new buses;

(3) that the public entity seeking temporary relief has made good faith efforts to locate a qualified manufacturer to supply the lifts to the manufacturer of such buses in sufficient time to comply with such solicitation; and

(4) that any further delay in purchasing new buses necessary to obtain such lifts would significantly impair transportation services in the community served by the public entity.

(b) DURATION AND NOTICE TO CONGRESS.— Any relief granted under subsection (a) shall be limited in duration by a specified date, and the appropriate committees of Congress shall be notified of any such relief granted.

(c) FRAUDULENT APPLICATION.—If, at any time, the Secretary has reasonable cause to believe that any relief granted under subsection (a) was fraudulently applied for, the Secretary shall—

(1) cancel such relief if such relief is still in effect; and

(2) take such other action as the Secretary considers appropriate.

Section 226. New Facilities.

For purposes of section 202 of this Act and section 504 of the Rehabilitation Act of 1973 (29 U.S.C. 794), it shall be considered discrimination for a public entity to construct a new facility to be used in the provision of designated public transportation services unless such facility is readily accessible to and usable by individuals with disabilities, including individuals who use wheelchairs.

Section 227. Alterations of Existing Facilities.

(a) GENERAL RULE.—With respect to alterations of an existing facility or part thereof used in the provision of designated public transportation services that affect or could affect the usability of the facility or part thereof, it shall be considered discrimination, for purposes of section 202 of this Act and section 504 of the Rehabilitation Act of 1973 (29 U.S.C. 794), for a public entity to fail to make such alterations (or to ensure that the alterations are made) in such a manner that, to the maximum extent feasible, the altered portions of the facility are readily accessible to and usable by individuals with disabilities, including individuals who use wheelchairs, upon the completion of such alterations. Where the public entity is undertaking an alteration that affects or could affect usability of or access to an area of the facility containing a primary function, the entity shall also make the alterations in such a manner that, to the maximum extent feasible, the path of travel to the altered area and the bathrooms, telephones, and drinking fountains serving the altered area, are readily accessible to and usable by individuals with disabilities, including individuals who use wheelchairs, upon completion of such alterations, where such alterations to the path of travel or the bathrooms, telephones, and drinking fountains serving the altered area are not disproportionate to the overall alterations in terms of cost and scope (as determined under criteria established by the Attorney General).

(b) SPECIAL RULE FOR STATIONS.—

(1) GENERAL RULE.—For purposes of section 202 of this Act and section 504 of the Rehabilitation Act of 1973 (29 U.S.C. 794), it shall be considered discrimination for a public entity that provides designated public transportation to fail, in accordance with the provisions of this subsection, to make key stations (as determined under criteria established by the Secretary by regulation) in rapid rail and light rail systems readily accessible to and usable by individuals with disabilities, including individuals who use wheelchairs.

(2) RAPID RAIL AND LIGHT RAIL KEY STATIONS.—

(A) ACCESSIBILITY.—Except as otherwise provided in this paragraph, all key stations (as determined under criteria established by the Secretary by regulation) in rapid rail and light rail systems shall be made readily accessible to and usable by individuals with disabilities, including individuals who use wheelchairs, as soon as practicable but in no event later than the last day of the 3-year period beginning on the effective date of this paragraph.

(B) EXTENSION FOR EXTRAORDINARILY EXPENSIVE STRUCTURAL CHANGES.—The Secretary may extend the 3-year period under subparagraph (A) up to a 30-year period for key stations in a rapid rail or light rail system which stations need extraordinarily expensive structural changes to, or replacement of, existing facilities; except that by the last day of the 20th year following the date of the enactment of this Act at least ⅔ of such key stations must be readily accessible to and usable by individuals with disabilities.

(3) PLANS AND MILESTONES.—The Secretary shall require the appropriate public entity to develop and submit to the Secretary a plan for compliance with this subsection—

(A) that reflects consultation with individuals with disabilities affected by such plan and the results of a public hearing and public comments on such plan, and

(B) that establishes milestones for achievement of the requirements of this subsection.

Section 228. Public Transportation Programs and Activities in Existing Facilities and One Car per Train Rule.

(a) PUBLIC TRANSPORTATION PROGRAMS AND ACTIVITIES IN EXISTING FACILITIES.—

    (1) IN GENERAL.—With respect to existing facilities used in the provision of designated public transportation services, it shall be considered discrimination, for purposes of section 202 of this Act and section 504 of the Rehabilitation Act of 1973 (29 U.S.C. 794), for a public entity to fail to operate a designated public transportation program or activity conducted in such facilities so that, when viewed in the entirety, the program or activity is readily accessible to and usable by individuals with disabilities.

    (2) EXCEPTION.—Paragraph (1) shall not require a public entity to make structural changes to existing facilities in order to make such facilities accessible to individuals who use wheelchairs, unless and to the extent required by section 227(a) (relating to alterations) or section 227(b) (relating to key stations).

    (3) UTILIZATION.—Paragraph (1) shall not require a public entity to which paragraph (2) applies, to provide to individuals who use wheelchairs services made available to the general public at such facilities when such individuals could not utilize or benefit from such services provided at such facilities.

(b) ONE CAR PER TRAIN RULE.—

    (1) GENERAL RULE.—Subject to paragraph (2), with respect to 2 or more vehicles operated as a train by a light or rapid rail system, for purposes of section 202 of this Act and section 504 of the Rehabilitation Act of 1973 (29 U.S.C. 794), it shall be considered discrimination for a public entity to fail to have at least 1 vehicle per train that is accessible to individuals with disabilities, including individuals who use wheelchairs, as soon as practicable but in no event later than the last day of the 5-year period beginning on the effective date of this section.

    (2) HISTORIC TRAINS.—In order to comply with paragraph (1) with respect to the remanufacture of a vehicle of historic character which is to be used on a segment of a light or rapid rail system which is included on the National Register of Historic Places, if making such vehicle readily accessible to and usable by individuals with disabilities would significantly alter the historic character of such vehicle, the public entity which operates such system only has to make (or to purchase or lease a remanufactured vehicle with) those modifications which are necessary to meet the requirements of section 222(c)(1) and which do not significantly alter the historic character of such vehicle.

Section 229. Regulations.

(a) IN GENERAL.—Not later than 1 year after the date of enactment of this Act, the Secretary of Transportation shall issue regulations, in an accessible format, necessary for carrying out this part (other than section 223).

(b) STANDARDS.—The regulations issued under this section and section 223 shall include standards applicable to facilities and vehicles covered by this subtitle. The standards shall be consistent with the minimum guidelines and requirements issued by the Architectural and Transportation Barriers Compliance Board in accordance with section 504 of this Act.

Section 230. Interim Accessibility Requirements.

If final regulations have not been issued pursuant to section 229, for new construction or alterations for which a valid and appropriate State or local building permit is obtained prior to the issuance of final regulations under such section, and for which the construction or alteration authorized by such permit begins within one year of the receipt of such permit and is completed under the terms of such permit, compliance with the Uniform Federal Accessibility Standards in effect at the time the building permit is issued shall suffice to satisfy the requirement that facilities be readily accessible to and usable by persons with disabilities as required under sections 226 and 227, except that, if such final regulations have not been issued one year after the Architectural and Transportation Barriers Compliance Board has issued the supplemental minimum guidelines required under section 504(a) of this Act, compliance with such supplemental minimum guidelines shall be necessary to satisfy the requirement that facilities be readily accessible to and usable by persons with disabilities prior to issuance of the final regulations.

Section 231. Effective Date.

(a) GENERAL RULE.—Except as provided in subsection (b), this part shall become effective 18 months after the date of enactment of this Act.

(b)   EXCEPTION.—Sections 222, 223 (other than subsection (a)), 224, 225, 227(b), 228(b), and 229 shall become effective on the date of enactment of this Act.

PART II—Public Transportation by Intercity and Commuter Rail

Section 241. Definitions.

As used in this part:

(1)   COMMUTER   AUTHORITY.—The   term "commuter authority" has the meaning given such term in section 103(8) of the Rail Passenger Service Act (45 U.S.C. 502(8)).

(2)   COMMUTER RAIL TRANSPORTATION.— The term "commuter rail transportation" has the meaning given the term "commuter service" in section 103(9) of the Rail Passenger Service Act (45 U.S.C. 502(9)).

(3)   INTERCITY   RAIL   TRANSPORTATION.— The term "intercity rail transportation" means transportation provided by the National Railroad Passenger Corporation.

(4)   RAIL PASSENGER CAR.—The term "rail passenger car" means, with respect to intercity rail transportation, single-level and bi-level coach cars, single-level and bi-level dining cars, single-level and bi-level sleeping cars, single-level and bi-level lounge cars, and food service cars.

(5)   RESPONSIBLE PERSON.—The term "responsible person" means—

(A)   in the case of a station more than 50 percent of which is owned by a public entity, such public entity;

(B)   in the case of a station more than 50 percent of which is owned by a private party, the persons providing intercity or commuter rail transportation to such station, as allocated on an equitable basis by regulation by the Secretary of Transportation; and

(C)   in a case where no party owns more than 50 percent of a station, the persons providing intercity or commuter rail transportation to such station and the owners of the station, other than private party owners, as allocated on an equitable basis by regulation by the Secretary of Transportation.

(6)   STATION.—The term "station" means the portion of a property located appurtenant to a right-of-way on which intercity or commuter rail transportation is operated, where such portion is used by the general public and is related to the provision of such transportation, including passenger platforms, designated waiting areas, ticketing areas, restrooms, and, where a public entity providing rail transportation owns the property, concession areas, to the extent that such public entity exercises control over the selection, design, construction, or alteration of the property, but such term does not include flag stops.

Section 242. Intercity and Commuter Rail Actions Considered Discriminatory.

(a)   INTERCITY RAIL TRANSPORTATION.—

(1)   ONE CAR PER TRAIN RULE.—It shall be considered discrimination for purposes of section 202 of this Act and section 504 of the Rehabilitation Act of 1973 (29 U.S.C. 794) for a person who provides intercity rail transportation to fail to have at least one passenger car per train that is readily accessible to and usable by individuals with disabilities, including individuals who use wheelchairs, in accordance with regulations issued under section 244, as soon as practicable, but in no event later than 5 years after the date of enactment of this Act.

(2)   NEW INTERCITY CARS.—

(A)   GENERAL RULE.—Except as otherwise provided in this subsection with respect to individuals who use wheelchairs, it shall be considered discrimination for purposes of section 202 of this Act and section 504 of the Rehabilitation Act of 1973 (29 U.S.C. 794) for a person to purchase or lease any new rail passenger cars for use in intercity rail transportation, and for which a solicitation is made later than 30 days after the effective date of this section, unless all such rail cars are readily accessible to and usable by individuals with disabilities, including individuals who use wheelchairs, as prescribed by the Secretary of Transportation in regulations issued under section 244.

(B)   SPECIAL RULE FOR SINGLE-LEVEL

PASSENGER COACHES FOR INDIVID-
UALS WHO USE WHEELCHAIRS.—
Single-level passenger coaches shall be re-
quired to—

   (i)   be able to be entered by an individual
who uses a wheelchair;

   (ii)   have space to park and secure a
wheelchair;

   (iii)   have a seat to which a passenger in a
wheelchair can transfer, and a space to
fold and store such passenger's wheelchair; and

   (iv)   have a restroom usable by an individual
who uses a wheelchair,

only to the extent provided in paragraph (3).

(C) SPECIAL RULE FOR SINGLE-LEVEL
DINING CARS FOR INDIVIDUALS
WHO USE WHEELCHAIRS.—Single-
level dining cars shall not be required to—

   (i)   be able to be entered from the station
platform by an individual who uses a
wheelchair; or

   (ii)   have a restroom usable by an individual
who uses a wheelchair if no restroom is
provided in such car for any passenger.

(D) SPECIAL RULE FOR BI-LEVEL DINING
CARS FOR INDIVIDUALS WHO USE
WHEELCHAIRS.—Bi-level dining cars
shall not be required to—

   (i)   be able to be entered by an individual
who uses a wheelchair;

   (ii)   have space to park and secure a
wheelchair;

   (iii)   have a seat to which a passenger in a
wheelchair can transfer, or a space to
fold and store such passenger's wheelchair; or

   (iv)   have a restroom usable by an individual
who uses a wheelchair.

(3) ACCESSIBILITY OF SINGLE-LEVEL
COACHES.—

  (A) GENERAL RULE.—It shall be considered
discrimination for purposes of section 202 of
this Act and section 504 of the Rehabilitation
Act of 1973 (29 U.S.C. 794) for a person who
provides intercity rail transportation to fail to
have on each train which includes one or more
single-level rail passenger coaches—

   (i)   a number of spaces—

     (I)   to park and secure wheelchairs (to
accommodate individuals who
wish to remain in their wheelchairs) equal to not less than one-
half of the number of single-level
rail passenger coaches in such train;
and

     (II)   to fold and store wheelchairs (to ac-
commodate individuals who wish
to transfer to coach seats) equal to
not less than one-half of the number of single-level rail passenger
coaches in such train,

as soon as practicable, but in no event
later than 5 years after the date of enactment of this Act; and

   (ii)   a number of spaces—

     (I)   to park and secure wheelchairs (to
accommodate individuals who
wish to remain in their wheelchairs) equal to not less than the total number of single-level rail passenger coaches in such train; and

     (II)   to fold and store wheelchairs (to ac-
commodate individuals who wish
to transfer to coach seats) equal to
not less than the total number of
single-level rail passenger coaches
in such train,

as soon as practicable, but in no event
later than 10 years after the date of enactment of this Act.

(B) LOCATION.—Spaces required by subparagraph (A) shall be located in single-level rail
passenger coaches or food service cars.

(C) LIMITATION.—Of the number of spaces
required on a train by subparagraph (A), not
more than two spaces to park and secure
wheelchairs nor more than two spaces to fold
and store wheelchairs shall be located in any
one coach or food service car.

(D) OTHER ACCESSIBILITY FEATURES.—
Single-level rail passenger coaches and food
service cars on which the spaces required by
subparagraph (A) are located shall have a restroom usable by an individual who uses a
wheelchair and shall be able to be entered from
the station platform by an individual who uses
a wheelchair.

(4) FOOD SERVICE.—
   (A) SINGLE-LEVEL DINING CARS.—On any train in which a single-level dining car is used to provide food service—
      (i) if such single-level dining car was purchased after the date of enactment of this Act, table service in such car shall be provided to a passenger who uses a wheelchair if—
         (I) the car adjacent to the end of the dining car through which a wheelchair may enter is itself accessible to a wheelchair;
         (II) such passenger can exit to the platform from the car such passenger occupies, move down the platform, and enter the adjacent accessible car described in subclause (I) without the necessity of the train being moved within the station; and
         (III) space to park and secure a wheelchair is available in the dining car at the time such passenger wishes to eat (if such passenger wishes to remain in a wheelchair), or space to store and fold a wheelchair is available in the dining car at the time such passenger wishes to eat (if such passenger wishes to transfer to a dining car seat); and
      (ii) appropriate auxiliary aids and services, including a hard surface on which to eat, shall be provided to ensure that other equivalent food service is available to individuals with disabilities, including individuals who use wheelchairs, and to passengers traveling with such individuals.
   Unless not practicable, a person providing intercity rail transportation shall place an accessible car adjacent to the end of a dining car described in clause (i) through which an individual who uses a wheelchair may enter.
   (B) BI-LEVEL DINING CARS.—On any train in which a bi-level dining car is used to provide food service—
      (i) if such train includes a bi-level lounge car purchased after the date of enactment of this Act, table service in such lounge car shall be provided to individuals who use wheelchairs and to other passengers; and
      (ii) appropriate auxiliary aids and services, including a hard surface on which to eat, shall be provided to ensure that other equivalent food service is available to individuals with disabilities, including individuals who use wheelchairs, and to passengers traveling with such individuals.

(b) COMMUTER RAIL TRANSPORTATION.—
   (1) ONE CAR PER TRAIN RULE.—It shall be considered discrimination for purposes of section 202 of this Act and section 504 of the Rehabilitation Act of 1973 (29 U.S.C. 794) for a person who provides commuter rail transportation to fail to have at least one passenger car per train that is readily accessible to and usable by individuals with disabilities, including individuals who use wheelchairs, in accordance with regulations issued under section 244, as soon as practicable, but in no event later than 5 years after the date of enactment of this Act.
   (2) NEW COMMUTER RAIL CARS.—
      (A) GENERAL RULE.—It shall be considered discrimination for purposes of section 202 of this Act and section 504 of the Rehabilitation Act of 1973 (29 U.S.C. 794) for a person to purchase or lease any new rail passenger cars for use in commuter rail transportation, and for which a solicitation is made later than 30 days after the effective date of this section, unless all such rail cars are readily accessible to and usable by individuals with disabilities, including individuals who use wheelchairs, as prescribed by the Secretary of Transportation in regulations issued under section 244.
      (B) ACCESSIBILITY.—For purposes of section 202 of this Act and section 504 of the Rehabilitation Act of 1973 (29 U.S.C. 794), a requirement that a rail passenger car used in commuter rail transportation be accessible to or readily accessible to and usable by individuals with disabilities, including individuals who use wheelchairs, shall not be construed to require—
         (i) a restroom usable by an individual who uses a wheelchair if no restroom is provided in such car for any passenger;

(ii) space to fold and store a wheelchair; or

(iii) a seat to which a passenger who uses a wheelchair can transfer.

(c) USED RAIL CARS.—It shall be considered discrimination for purposes of section 202 of this Act and section 504 of the Rehabilitation Act of 1973 (29 U.S.C. 794) for a person to purchase or lease a used rail passenger car for use in intercity or commuter rail transportation, unless such person makes demonstrated good faith efforts to purchase or lease a used rail car that is readily accessible to and usable by individuals with disabilities, including individuals who use wheelchairs, as prescribed by the Secretary of Transportation in regulations issued under section 244.

(d) REMANUFACTURED RAIL CARS.—

(1) REMANUFACTURING.—It shall be considered discrimination for purposes of section 202 of this Act and section 504 of the Rehabilitation Act of 1973 (29 U.S.C. 794) for a person to remanufacture a rail passenger car for use in intercity or commuter rail transportation so as to extend its usable life for 10 years or more, unless the rail car, to the maximum extent feasible, is made readily accessible to and usable by individuals with disabilities, including individuals who use wheelchairs, as prescribed by the Secretary of Transportation in regulations issued under section 244.

(2) PURCHASE OR LEASE.—It shall be considered discrimination for purposes of section 202 of this Act and section 504 of the Rehabilitation Act of 1973 (29 U.S.C. 794) for a person to purchase or lease a remanufactured rail passenger car for use in intercity or commuter rail transportation unless such car was remanufactured in accordance with paragraph (1).

(e) STATIONS.—

(1) NEW STATIONS.—It shall be considered discrimination for purposes of section 202 of this Act and section 504 of the Rehabilitation Act of 1973 (29 U.S.C. 794) for a person to build a new station for use in intercity or commuter rail transportation that is not readily accessible to and usable by individuals with disabilities, including individuals who use wheelchairs, as prescribed by the Secretary of Transportation in regulations issued under section 244.

(2) EXISTING STATIONS.—

(A) FAILURE TO MAKE READILY ACCESSIBLE.—

(i) GENERAL RULE.—It shall be considered discrimination for purposes of section 202 of this Act and section 504 of the Rehabilitation Act of 1973 (29 U.S.C. 794) for a responsible person to fail to make existing stations in the intercity rail transportation system, and existing key stations in commuter rail transportation systems, readily accessible to and usable by individuals with disabilities, including individuals who use wheelchairs, as prescribed by the Secretary of Transportation in regulations issued under section 244.

(ii) PERIOD FOR COMPLIANCE.—

(I) INTERCITY RAIL.—All stations in the intercity rail transportation system shall be made readily accessible to and usable by individuals with disabilities, including individuals who use wheelchairs, as soon as practicable, but in no event later than 20 years after the date of enactment of this Act.

(II) COMMUTER RAIL.—Key stations in commuter rail transportation systems shall be made readily accessible to and usable by individuals with disabilities, including individuals who use wheelchairs, as soon as practicable but in no event later than 3 years after the date of enactment of this Act, except that the time limit may be extended by the Secretary of Transportation up to 20 years after the date of enactment of this Act in a case where the raising of the entire passenger platform is the only means available of attaining accessibility or where other extraordinarily expensive structural changes are necessary to attain accessibility.

(iii) DESIGNATION OF KEY STATIONS.—Each commuter authority shall designate the key stations in its commuter rail transportation system, in consultation with individuals with disabilities and organizations representing such individuals, taking into consideration such factors as high ridership and whether such station serves as a transfer or feeder station. Before the final designation of key stations under this clause, a commuter authority shall hold a public hearing.

(iv) PLANS AND MILESTONES.—The Secretary of Transportation shall require the appropriate person to develop a plan for carrying out this subparagraph that reflects consultation with individuals with disabilities affected by such plan and that establishes milestones for achievement of the requirements of this subparagraph.

(B) REQUIREMENT WHEN MAKING ALTERATIONS.—

(i) GENERAL RULE.—It shall be considered discrimination, for purposes of section 202 of this Act and section 504 of the Rehabilitation Act of 1973 (29 U.S.C. 794), with respect to alterations of an existing station or part thereof in the intercity or commuter rail transportation systems that affect or could affect the usability of the station or part thereof, for the responsible person, owner, or person in control of the station to fail to make the alterations in such a manner that, to the maximum extent feasible, the altered portions of the station are readily accessible to and usable by individuals with disabilities, including individuals who use wheelchairs, upon completion of such alterations.

(ii) ALTERATIONS TO A PRIMARY FUNCTION AREA.—It shall be considered discrimination, for purposes of section 202 of this Act and section 504 of the Rehabilitation Act of 1973 (29 U.S.C. 794), with respect to alterations that affect or could affect the usability of or access to an area of the station containing a primary function, for the responsible person, owner, or person in control of the station to fail to make the

alterations in such a manner that, to the maximum extent feasible, the path of travel to the altered area, and the bathrooms, telephones, and drinking fountains serving the altered area, are readily accessible to and usable by individuals with disabilities, including individuals who use wheelchairs, upon completion of such alterations, where such alterations to the path of travel or the bathrooms, telephones, and drinking fountains serving the altered area are not disproportionate to the overall alterations in terms of cost and scope (as determined under criteria established by the Attorney General).

(C) REQUIRED COOPERATION.—It shall be considered discrimination for purposes of section 202 of this Act and section 504 of the Rehabilitation Act of 1973 (29 U.S.C. 794) for an owner, or person in control, of a station governed by subparagraph (A) or (B) to fail to provide reasonable cooperation to a responsible person with respect to such station in that responsible person's efforts to comply with such subparagraph. An owner, or person in control, of a station shall be liable to a responsible person for any failure to provide reasonable cooperation as required by this subparagraph. Failure to receive reasonable cooperation required by this subparagraph shall not be a defense to a claim of discrimination under this Act.

Section 243. Conformance of Accessibility Standards.

Accessibility standards included in regulations issued under this part shall be consistent with the minimum guidelines issued by the Architectural and Transportation Barriers Compliance Board under section 504(a) of this Act.

Section 244. Regulations.

Not later than 1 year after the date of enactment of this Act, the Secretary of Transportation shall issue regulations, in an accessible format, necessary for carrying out this part.

Section 245. Interim Accessibility Requirements.

(a) STATIONS.—If final regulations have not been issued pursuant to section 244, for new construction or alterations for which a valid and appropriate State or local building permit is obtained prior to the issuance of final regulations under such section, and for which the construction or alteration authorized by such permit begins within one year of the receipt of such permit and is completed under the terms of such permit, compliance with the Uniform Federal Accessibility Standards in effect at the time the building permit is issued shall suffice to satisfy the requirement that stations be readily accessible to and usable by persons with disabilities as required under section 242(e), except that, if such final regulations have not been issued one year after the Architectural and Transportation Barriers Compliance Board has issued the supplemental minimum guidelines required under section 504(a) of this Act, compliance with such supplemental minimum guidelines shall be necessary to satisfy the requirement that stations be readily accessible to and usable by persons with disabilities prior to issuance of the final regulations.

(b) RAIL PASSENGER CARS.—If final regulations have not been issued pursuant to section 244, a person shall be considered to have complied with the requirements of section 242(a) through (d) that a rail passenger car be readily accessible to and usable by individuals with disabilities, if the design for such car complies with the laws and regulations (including the Minimum Guidelines and Requirements for Accessible Design and such supplemental minimum guidelines as are issued under section 504(a) of this Act) governing accessibility of such cars, to the extent that such laws and regulations are not inconsistent with this part and are in effect at the time such design is substantially completed.

Section 246. Effective Date.

(a) GENERAL RULE.—Except as provided in subsection (b), this part shall become effective 18 months after the date of enactment of this Act.

(b) EXCEPTION.—Sections 242 and 244 shall become effective on the date of enactment of this Act.

TITLE III—PUBLIC ACCOMMODATIONS AND SERVICES OPERATED BY PRIVATE ENTITIES

Section 301. Definitions.

As used in this title:

(1) COMMERCE.—The term "commerce" means travel, trade, traffic, commerce, transportation, or communication—
  (A) among the several States;
  (B) between any foreign country or any territory or possession and any State; or
  (C) between points in the same State but through another State or foreign country.

(2) COMMERCIAL FACILITIES.—The term "commercial facilities" means facilities—
  (A) that are intended for nonresidential use; and
  (B) whose operations will affect commerce.
  Such term shall not include railroad locomotives, railroad freight cars, railroad cabooses, railroad cars described in section 242 or covered under this title, railroad rights-of-way, or facilities that are covered or expressly exempted from coverage under the Fair Housing Act of 1968 (42 U.S.C. 3601 et seq.).

(3) DEMAND RESPONSIVE SYSTEM.—The term "demand responsive system" means any system of providing transportation of individuals by a vehicle, other than a system which is a fixed route system.

(4) FIXED ROUTE SYSTEM.—The term "fixed route system" means a system of providing transportation of individuals (other than by aircraft) on which a vehicle is operated along a prescribed route according to a fixed schedule.

(5) OVER-THE-ROAD BUS.—The term "over-the-road bus" means a bus characterized by an elevated passenger deck located over a baggage compartment.

(6) PRIVATE ENTITY.—The term "private entity" means any entity other than a public entity (as defined in section 201(1)).

(7) PUBLIC ACCOMMODATION.—The following private entities are considered public accommodations for purposes of this title, if the operations of such entities affect commerce—
  (A) an inn, hotel, motel, or other place of lodging, except for an establishment located within a

building that contains not more than five rooms for rent or hire and that is actually occupied by the proprietor of such establishment as the residence of such proprietor;

(B) a restaurant, bar, or other establishment serving food or drink;

(C) a motion picture house, theater, concert hall, stadium, or other place of exhibition or entertainment;

(D) an auditorium, convention center, lecture hall, or other place of public gathering;

(E) a bakery, grocery store, clothing store, hardware store, shopping center, or other sales or rental establishment;

(F) a laundromat, dry-cleaner, bank, barber shop, beauty shop, travel service, shoe repair service, funeral parlor, gas station, office of an accountant or lawyer, pharmacy, insurance office, professional office of a health care provider, hospital, or other service establishment;

(G) a terminal, depot, or other station used for specified public transportation;

(H) a museum, library, gallery, or other place of public display or collection;

(I) a park, zoo, amusement park, or other place of recreation;

(J) a nursery, elementary, secondary, undergraduate, or postgraduate private school, or other place of education;

(K) a day care center, senior citizen center, homeless shelter, food bank, adoption agency, or other social service center establishment; and

(L) a gymnasium, health spa, bowling alley, golf course, or other place of exercise or recreation.

(8) RAIL AND RAILROAD.—The terms "rail" and "railroad" have the meaning given the term "railroad" in section 202(e) of the Federal Railroad Safety Act of 1970 (45 U.S.C. 431(e)).

(9) READILY ACHIEVABLE.—The term "readily achievable" means easily accomplishable and able to be carried out without much difficulty or expense. In determining whether an action is readily achievable, factors to be considered include—

(A) the nature and cost of the action needed under this Act;

(B) the overall financial resources of the facility or facilities involved in the action; the number of

persons employed at such facility; the effect on expenses and resources, or the impact otherwise of such action upon the operation of the facility;

(C) the overall financial resources of the covered entity; the overall size of the business of a covered entity with respect to the number of its employees; the number, type, and location of its facilities; and

(D) the type of operation or operations of the covered entity, including the composition, structure, and functions of the workforce of such entity; the geographic separateness, administrative or fiscal relationship of the facility or facilities in question to the covered entity.

(10) SPECIFIED PUBLIC TRANSPORTATION.—The term "specified public transportation" means transportation by bus, rail, or any other conveyance (other than by aircraft) that provides the general public with general or special service (including charter service) on a regular and continuing basis.

(11) VEHICLE.—The term "vehicle" does not include a rail passenger car, railroad locomotive, railroad freight car, railroad caboose, or a railroad car described in section 242 or covered under this title.

Section 302. Prohibition of Discrimination by Public Accommodations.

(a) GENERAL RULE.—No individual shall be discriminated against on the basis of disability in the full and equal enjoyment of the goods, services, facilities, privileges, advantages, or accommodations of any place of public accommodation by any person who owns, leases (or leases to), or operates a place of public accommodation.

(b) CONSTRUCTION.—

(1) GENERAL PROHIBITION.—

(A) ACTIVITIES.—

(i) DENIAL OF PARTICIPATION.—It shall be discriminatory to subject an individual or class of individuals on the basis of a disability or disabilities of such individual or class, directly, or through contractual, licensing, or other arrangements, to a denial of the opportunity of the individual or class to participate in or benefit from the goods, services, facilities, privileges, advantages, or accommodations of an entity.

(ii) PARTICIPATION IN UNEQUAL BENEFIT.—It shall be discriminatory to afford an individual or class of individuals, on the basis of a disability or disabilities of such individual or class, directly, or through contractual, licensing, or other arrangements with the opportunity to participate in or benefit from a good, service, facility, privilege, advantage, or accommodation that is not equal to that afforded to other individuals.

(iii) SEPARATE BENEFIT.—It shall be discriminatory to provide an individual or class of individuals, on the basis of a disability or disabilities of such individual or class, directly, or through contractual, licensing, or other arrangements with a good, service, facility, privilege, advantage, or accommodation that is different or separate from that provided to other individuals, unless such action is necessary to provide the individual or class of individuals with a good, service, facility, privilege, advantage, or accommodation, or other opportunity that is as effective as that provided to others.

(iv) INDIVIDUAL OR CLASS OF INDIVIDUALS.—For purposes of clauses (i) through (iii) of this subparagraph, the term "individual or class of individuals" refers to the clients or customers of the covered public accommodation that enters into the contractual, licensing or other arrangement.

(B) INTEGRATED SETTINGS.—Goods, services, facilities, privileges, advantages, and accommodations shall be afforded to an individual with a disability in the most integrated setting appropriate to the needs of the individual.

(C) OPPORTUNITY TO PARTICIPATE.—Notwithstanding the existence of separate or different programs or activities provided in ac-

cordance with this section, an individual with a disability shall not be denied the opportunity to participate in such programs or activities that are not separate or different.

(D) ADMINISTRATIVE METHODS.—An individual or entity shall not, directly or through contractual or other arrangements, utilize standards or criteria or methods of administration—

(i) that have the effect of discriminating on the basis of disability; or

(ii) that perpetuate the discrimination of others who are subject to common administrative control.

(E) ASSOCIATION.—It shall be discriminatory to exclude or otherwise deny equal goods, services, facilities, privileges, advantages, accommodations, or other opportunities to an individual or entity because of the known disability of an individual with whom the individual or entity is known to have a relationship or association.

(2) SPECIFIC PROHIBITIONS.—

(A) DISCRIMINATION.—For purposes of subsection (a), discrimination includes—

(i) the imposition or application of eligibility criteria that screen out or tend to screen out an individual with a disability or any class of individuals with disabilities from fully and equally enjoying any goods, services, facilities, privileges, advantages, or accommodations, unless such criteria can be shown to be necessary for the provision of the goods, services, facilities, privileges, advantages, or accommodations being offered;

(ii) a failure to make reasonable modifications in policies, practices, or procedures, when such modifications are necessary to afford such goods, services, facilities, privileges, advantages, or accommodations to individuals with disabilities, unless the entity can demonstrate that making such modifications would fundamentally alter the nature of such goods, services, facilities, privileges, advantages, or accommodations;

(iii) a failure to take such steps as may be necessary to ensure that no individual with a disability is excluded, denied services, segregated or otherwise treated differently than other individuals because of the absence of auxiliary aids and services, unless the entity can demonstrate that taking such steps would fundamentally alter the nature of the good, service, facility, privilege, advantage, or accommodation being offered or would result in an undue burden;

(iv) a failure to remove architectural barriers, and communication barriers that are structural in nature, in existing facilities, and transportation barriers in existing vehicles and rail passenger cars used by an establishment for transporting individuals (not including barriers that can only be removed through the retrofitting of vehicles or rail passenger cars by the installation of a hydraulic or other lift), where such removal is readily achievable; and

(v) where an entity can demonstrate that the removal of a barrier under clause (iv) is not readily achievable, a failure to make such goods, services, facilities, privileges, advantages, or accommodations available through alternative methods if such methods are readily achievable.

(B) FIXED ROUTE SYSTEM.—

(i) ACCESSIBILITY.—It shall be considered discrimination for a private entity which operates a fixed route system and which is not subject to section 304 to purchase or lease a vehicle with a seating capacity in excess of 16 passengers (including the driver) for use on such system, for which a solicitation is made after the 30th day following the effective date of this subparagraph, that is not readily accessible to and usable by individuals with disabilities, including individuals who use wheelchairs.

(ii) EQUIVALENT SERVICE.—If a private entity which operates a fixed route system and which is not subject to section 304 purchases or leases a vehicle with a seating capacity of 16 passengers or less (including the driver) for use on such system after the effective date of this subparagraph that is not readily accessible to or usable by individuals with disabilities, it shall be considered discrimination for such entity to fail to operate such system so that, when viewed in its entirety, such system ensures a level of service to individuals with disabilities, including individuals who use wheelchairs, equivalent to the level of service provided to individuals without disabilities.

(C) DEMAND RESPONSIVE SYSTEM.—For purposes of subsection (a), discrimination includes—

(i) a failure of a private entity which operates a demand responsive system and which is not subject to section 304 to operate such system so that, when viewed in its entirety, such system ensures a level of service to individuals with disabilities, including individuals who use wheelchairs, equivalent to the level of service provided to individuals without disabilities; and

(ii) the purchase or lease by such entity for use on such system of a vehicle with a seating capacity in excess of 16 passengers (including the driver), for which solicitations are made after the 30th day following the effective date of this subparagraph, that is not readily accessible to and usable by individuals with disabilities (including individuals who use wheelchairs) unless such entity can demonstrate that such system, when viewed in its entirety, provides a level of service to individuals with disabilities equivalent to that provided to individuals without disabilities.

(D) OVER-THE-ROAD BUSES.—

(i) LIMITATION ON APPLICABILITY.—Subparagraphs (B) and (C) do not apply to over-the-road buses.

(ii) ACCESSIBILITY REQUIREMENTS.—For purposes of subsection

(a), discrimination includes (I) the purchase or lease of an over-the-road bus which does not comply with the regulations issued under section 306(a)(2) by a private entity which provides transportation of individuals and which is not primarily engaged in the business of transporting people, and (II) any other failure of such entity to comply with such regulations.

(3) SPECIFIC CONSTRUCTION.—Nothing in this title shall require an entity to permit an individual to participate in or benefit from the goods, services, facilities, privileges, advantages and accommodations of such entity where such individual poses a direct threat to the health or safety of others. The term "direct threat" means a significant risk to the health or safety of others that cannot be eliminated by a modification of policies, practices, or procedures or by the provision of auxiliary aids or services.

Section 303. New Construction and Alterations in Public Accommodations and Commercial Facilities.

(a) APPLICATION OF TERM.—Except as provided in subsection (b), as applied to public accommodations and commercial facilities, discrimination for purposes of section 302(a) includes—

(1) a failure to design and construct facilities for first occupancy later than 30 months after the date of enactment of this Act that are readily accessible to and usable by individuals with disabilities, except where an entity can demonstrate that it is structurally impracticable to meet the requirements of such subsection in accordance with standards set forth or incorporated by reference in regulations issued under this title; and

(2) with respect to a facility or part thereof that is altered by, on behalf of, or for the use of an establishment in a manner that affects or could affect the usability of the facility or part thereof, a failure to make alterations in such a manner that, to the maximum extent feasible, the altered portions of the facility are readily accessible to and usable by individuals with disabilities, including individuals who use wheelchairs. Where the entity is undertaking an alteration that affects or could affect usability of or access to an area of the facility containing a primary function, the entity shall also make the alterations in such a manner that, to the maximum extent feasible, the path of travel to the altered area and the bathrooms, telephones, and drinking fountains serving the altered area, are readily accessible to and usable by individuals with disabilities where such alterations to the path of travel or the bathrooms, telephones, and drinking fountains serving the altered area are not disproportionate to the overall alterations in terms of cost and scope (as determined under criteria established by the Attorney General).

(b) ELEVATOR.—Subsection (a) shall not be construed to require the installation of an elevator for facilities that are less than three stories or have less than 3,000 square feet per story unless the building is a shopping center, a shopping mall, or the professional office of a health care provider or unless the Attorney General determines that a particular category of such facilities requires the installation of elevators based on the usage of such facilities.

Section 304. Prohibition of Discrimination in Specified Public Transportation Services Provided by Private Entities.

(a) GENERAL RULE.—No individual shall be discriminated against on the basis of disability in the full and equal enjoyment of specified public transportation services provided by a private entity that is primarily engaged in the business of transporting people and whose operations affect commerce.

(b) CONSTRUCTION.—For purposes of subsection (a), discrimination includes—

(1) the imposition or application by an entity described in subsection (a) of eligibility criteria that screen out or tend to screen out an individual with a disability or any class of individuals with disabilities from fully enjoying the specified public transportation services provided by the entity, unless such criteria can be shown to be necessary for the provision of the services being offered;

(2) the failure of such entity to—

(A) make reasonable modifications consistent with those required under section 302(b)(2)(A)(ii);

(B) provide auxiliary aids and services consistent with the requirements of section 302(b)(2)(A)(iii); and

(C) remove barriers consistent with the requirements of section 302(b)(2)(A) and with the requirements of section 303(a)(2);

(3) the purchase or lease by such entity of a new vehicle (other than an automobile, a van with a seating capacity of less than 8 passengers, including the driver, or an over-the-road bus) which is to be used to provide specified public transportation and for which a solicitation is made after the 30th day following the effective date of this section, that is not readily accessible to and usable by individuals with disabilities, including individuals who use wheelchairs; except that the new vehicle need not be readily accessible to and usable by such individuals if the new vehicle is to be used solely in a demand responsive system and if the entity can demonstrate that such system, when viewed in its entirety, provides a level of service to such individuals equivalent to the level of service provided to the general public;

(4) (A) the purchase or lease by such entity of an over-the-road bus which does not comply with the regulations issued under section 306(a)(2); and

(B) any other failure of such entity to comply with such regulations; and

(5) the purchase or lease by such entity of a new van with a seating capacity of less than 8 passengers, including the driver, which is to be used to provide specified public transportation and for which a solicitation is made after the 30th day following the effective date of this section that is not readily accessible to or usable by individuals with disabilities, including individuals who use wheelchairs; except that the new van need not be readily accessible to and usable by such individuals if the entity can demonstrate that the system for which the van is being purchased or leased, when viewed in its entirety, provides a level of service to such individuals equivalent to the level of service provided to the general public;

(6) the purchase or lease by such entity of a new rail passenger car that is to be used to provide specified public transportation, and for which a solicitation is made later than 30 days after the effective date of this paragraph, that is not readily accessible to and usable by individuals with disabilities, including individuals who use wheelchairs; and

(7) the remanufacture by such entity of a rail passenger car that is to be used to provide specified public transportation so as to extend its usable life for 10 years or more, or the purchase or lease by such entity of such a rail car, unless the rail car, to the maximum extent feasible, is made readily accessible to and usable by individuals with disabilities, including individuals who use wheelchairs.

(c) HISTORICAL OR ANTIQUATED CARS.—

(1) EXCEPTION.—To the extent that compliance with subsection (b)(2)(C) or (b)(7) would significantly alter the historic or antiquated character of a historical or antiquated rail passenger car, or a rail station served exclusively by such cars, or would result in violation of any rule, regulation, standard, or order issued by the Secretary of Transportation under the Federal Railroad Safety Act of 1970, such compliance shall not be required.

(2) DEFINITION.—As used in this subsection, the term "historical or antiquated rail passenger car" means a rail passenger car—

(A) which is not less than 30 years old at the time of its use for transporting individuals;

(B) the manufacturer of which is no longer in the business of manufacturing rail passenger cars; and

(C) which—

(i) has a consequential association with events or persons significant to the past; or

(ii) embodies, or is being restored to embody, the distinctive characteristics of a type of rail passenger car used in the past, or to represent a time period which has passed.

Section 305. Study.

(a) PURPOSES.—The Office of Technology Assessment shall undertake a study to determine—

(1) the access needs of individuals with disabilities to over-the-road buses and over-the-road bus service; and

(2) the most cost-effective methods for providing access to over-the-road buses and over-the-road bus service to individuals with disabilities, particularly individuals who use wheelchairs, through all forms of boarding options.

(b) CONTENTS.—The study shall include, at a minimum, an analysis of the following:

(1) The anticipated demand by individuals with disabilities for accessible over-the-road buses and over-the-road bus service.

(2) The degree to which such buses and service, including any service required under sections 304(b)(4) and 306(a)(2), are readily accessible to and usable by individuals with disabilities.

(3) The effectiveness of various methods of providing accessibility to such buses and service to individuals with disabilities.

(4) The cost of providing accessible over-the-road buses and bus service to individuals with disabilities, including consideration of recent technological and cost saving developments in equipment and devices.

(5) Possible design changes in over-the-road buses that could enhance accessibility, including the installation of accessible restrooms which do not result in a loss of seating capacity.

(6) The impact of accessibility requirements on the continuation of over-the-road bus service, with particular consideration of the impact of such requirements on such service to rural communities.

(c) ADVISORY COMMITTEE.—In conducting the study required by subsection (a), the Office of Technology Assessment shall establish an advisory committee, which shall consist of—

(1) members selected from among private operators and manufacturers of over-the-road buses;

(2) members selected from among individuals with disabilities, particularly individuals who use wheelchairs, who are potential riders of such buses; and

(3) members selected for their technical expertise on issues included in the study, including manufacturers of boarding assistance equipment and devices.

The number of members selected under each of paragraphs (1) and (2) shall be equal, and the total number of members selected under paragraphs (1) and (2) shall exceed the number of members selected under paragraph (3).

(d) DEADLINE.—The study required by subsection (a), along with recommendations by the Office of Technology Assessment, including any policy options for legislative action, shall be submitted to the President and Congress within 36 months after the date of the enactment of this Act. If the President determines that compliance with the regulations issued pursuant to section 306(a)(2)(B) on or before the applicable deadlines specified in section 306(a)(2)(B) will result in a significant reduction in intercity over-the-road bus service, the President shall extend each such deadline by 1 year.

(e) REVIEW.—In developing the study required by subsection (a), the Office of Technology Assessment shall provide a preliminary draft of such study to the Architectural and Transportation Barriers Compliance Board established under section 502 of the Rehabilitation Act of 1973 (29 U.S.C. 792). The Board shall have an opportunity to comment on such draft study, and any such comments by the Board made in writing within 120 days after the Board's receipt of the draft study shall be incorporated as part of the final study required to be submitted under subsection (d).

Section 306. Regulations.

(a) TRANSPORTATION PROVISIONS.—

(1) GENERAL RULE.—Not later than 1 year after the date of the enactment of this Act, the Secretary of Transportation shall issue regulations in an accessible format to carry out sections 302(b)(2)(B) and (C) and to carry out section 304 (other than subsection (b)(4)).

(2) SPECIAL RULES FOR PROVIDING ACCESS TO OVER-THE-ROAD BUSES.—

(A) INTERIM REQUIREMENTS—

(i) ISSUANCE.—Not later than 1 year after the date of the enactment of this Act, the Secretary of Transportation shall issue regulations in an accessible format to carry out sections 304(b)(4) and 302(b)(2)(D)(ii) that require each private entity which uses an over-the-road bus to provide transportation of individuals to provide accessibility to such bus; except that such regulations shall not require any structural changes in over-the-road buses in order to provide access to individuals who use wheelchairs during the effective period of such regulations and shall not require the purchase of boarding assistance devices to provide access to such individuals.

(ii) EFFECTIVE PERIOD.—The regulations issued pursuant to this subparagraph shall be effective until the effective date of the regulations issued under subparagraph (B).

(B) FINAL REQUIREMENT.—

    (i) REVIEW OF STUDY AND INTERIM REQUIREMENTS.—The Secretary shall review the study submitted under section 305 and the regulations issued pursuant to subparagraph (A).

    (ii) ISSUANCE.—Not later than 1 year after the date of the submission of the study under section 305, the Secretary shall issue in an accessible format new regulations to carry out sections 304(b)(4) and 302(b)(2)(D)(ii) that require, taking into account the purposes of the study under section 305 and any recommendations resulting from such study, each private entity which uses an over-the-road bus to provide transportation to individuals to provide accessibility to such bus to individuals with disabilities, including individuals who use wheelchairs.

    (iii) EFFECTIVE PERIOD.—Subject to section 305(d), the regulations issued pursuant to this subparagraph shall take effect—

        (I) with respect to small providers of transportation (as defined by the Secretary), 7 years after the date of the enactment of this Act; and

        (II) with respect to other providers of transportation, 6 years after such date of enactment.

(C) LIMITATION ON REQUIRING INSTALLATION OF ACCESSIBLE RESTROOMS.—The regulations issued pursuant to this paragraph shall not require the installation of accessible restrooms in over-the-road buses if such installation would result in a loss of seating capacity.

(3) STANDARDS.—The regulations issued pursuant to this subsection shall include standards applicable to facilities and vehicles covered by sections 302(b)(2) and 304.

(b) OTHER PROVISIONS.—Not later than 1 year after the date of the enactment of this Act, the Attorney General shall issue regulations in an accessible format to carry out the provisions of this title not referred to in subsection (a) that include standards applicable to facilities and vehicles covered under section 302.

(c) CONSISTENCY WITH ATBCB GUIDELINES.—Standards included in regulations issued under subsections (a) and (b) shall be consistent with the minimum guidelines and requirements issued by the Architectural and Transportation Barriers Compliance Board in accordance with section 504 of this Act.

(d) INTERIM ACCESSIBILITY STANDARDS.—

(1) FACILITIES.—If final regulations have not been issued pursuant to this section, for new construction or alterations for which a valid and appropriate State or local building permit is obtained prior to the issuance of final regulations under this section, and for which the construction or alteration authorized by such permit begins within one year of the receipt of such permit and is completed under the terms of such permit, compliance with the Uniform Federal Accessibility Standards in effect at the time the building permit is issued shall suffice to satisfy the requirement that facilities be readily accessible to and usable by persons with disabilities as required under section 303, except that, if such final regulations have not been issued one year after the Architectural and Transportation Barriers Compliance Board has issued the supplemental minimum guidelines required under section 504(a) of this Act, compliance with such supplemental minimum guidelines shall be necessary to satisfy the requirement that facilities be readily accessible to and usable by persons with disabilities prior to issuance of the final regulations.

(2) VEHICLES AND RAIL PASSENGER CARS.—If final regulations have not been issued pursuant to this section, a private entity shall be considered to have complied with the requirements of this title, if any, that a vehicle or rail passenger car be readily accessible to and usable by individuals with disabilities, if the design for such vehicle or car complies with the laws and regulations (including the Minimum Guidelines and Requirements for Accessible Design and such supplemental minimum guidelines as are issued under section 504(a) of this Act) governing accessibility of such vehicles or cars, to the extent that such laws and regulations are not incon-

sistent with this title and are in effect at the time such design is substantially completed.

Section 307. Exemptions for Private Clubs and Religious Organizations.

The provisions of this title shall not apply to private clubs or establishments exempted from coverage under title II of the Civil Rights Act of 1964 (42 U.S.C. 2000-a(e)) or to religious organizations or entities controlled by religious organizations, including places of worship.

Section 308. Enforcement.

(a) IN GENERAL.—
    (1) AVAILABILITY OF REMEDIES AND PROCEDURES.—The remedies and procedures set forth in section 204(a) of the Civil Rights Act of 1964 (42 U.S.C. 2000a-3(a)) are the remedies and procedures this title provides to any person who is being subjected to discrimination on the basis of disability in violation of this title or who has reasonable grounds for believing that such person is about to be subjected to discrimination in violation of section 303. Nothing in this section shall require a person with a disability to engage in a futile gesture if such person has actual notice that a person or organization covered by this title does not intend to comply with its provisions.

    (2) INJUNCTIVE RELIEF.—In the case of violations of section 302(b)(2)(A)(iv) and section 303(a), injunctive relief shall include an order to alter facilities to make such facilities readily accessible to and usable by individuals with disabilities to the extent required by this title. Where appropriate, injunctive relief shall also include requiring the provision of an auxiliary aid or service, modification of a policy, or provision of alternative methods, to the extent required by this title.

(b) ENFORCEMENT BY THE ATTORNEY GENERAL.—
    (1) DENIAL OF RIGHTS.—
      (A) DUTY TO INVESTIGATE.—
        (i) IN GENERAL.—The Attorney General shall investigate alleged violations of this title, and shall undertake periodic reviews of compliance of covered entities under this title.

        (ii) ATTORNEY GENERAL CERTIFICATION.—On the application of a State or local government, the Attorney General may, in consultation with the Architectural and Transportation Barriers Compliance Board, and after prior notice and a public hearing at which persons, including individuals with disabilities, are provided an opportunity to testify against such certification, certify that a State law or local building code or similar ordinance that establishes accessibility requirements meets or exceeds the minimum requirements of this Act for the accessibility and usability of covered facilities under this title. At any enforcement proceeding under this section, such certification by the Attorney General shall be rebuttable evidence that such State law or local ordinance does meet or exceed the minimum requirements of this Act.

      (B) POTENTIAL VIOLATION.—If the Attorney General has reasonable cause to believe that—
        (i) any person or group of persons is engaged in a pattern or practice of discrimination under this title; or
        (ii) any person or group of persons has been discriminated against under this title and such discrimination raises an issue of general public importance,
the Attorney General may commence a civil action in any appropriate United States district court.

    (2) AUTHORITY OF COURT.—In a civil action under paragraph (1)(B), the court—
    (A) may grant any equitable relief that such court considers to be appropriate, including, to the extent required by this title—
      (i) granting temporary, preliminary, or permanent relief;
      (ii) providing an auxiliary aid or service, modification of policy, practice, or procedure, or alternative method; and

(iii) making facilities readily accessible to and usable by individuals with disabilities;

(B) may award such other relief as the court considers to be appropriate, including monetary damages to persons aggrieved when requested by the Attorney General; and

(C) may, to vindicate the public interest, assess a civil penalty against the entity in an amount—

(i) not exceeding $50,000 for a first violation; and

(ii) not exceeding $100,000 for any subsequent violation.

(3) SINGLE VIOLATION.—For purposes of paragraph (2)(C), in determining whether a first or subsequent violation has occurred, a determination in a single action, by judgment or settlement, that the covered entity has engaged in more than one discriminatory act shall be counted as a single violation.

(4) PUNITIVE DAMAGES.—For purposes of subsection (b)(2)(B), the term "monetary damages" and "such other relief" does not include punitive damages.

(5) JUDICIAL CONSIDERATION.—In a civil action under paragraph (1)(B), the court, when considering what amount of civil penalty, if any, is appropriate, shall give consideration to any good faith effort or attempt to comply with this Act by the entity. In evaluating good faith, the court shall consider, among other factors it deems relevant, whether the entity could have reasonably anticipated the need for an appropriate type of auxiliary aid needed to accommodate the unique needs of a particular individual with a disability.

Section 309. Examinations and Courses.

Any person that offers examinations or courses related to applications, licensing, certification, or credentialing for secondary or postsecondary education, professional, or trade purposes shall offer such examinations or courses in a place and manner accessible to persons with disabilities or offer alternative accessible arrangements for such individuals.

Section 310. Effective Date.

(a) GENERAL RULE.—Except as provided in subsections (b) and (c), this title shall become effective 18 months after the date of the enactment of this Act.

(b) CIVIL ACTIONS.—Except for any civil action brought for a violation of section 303, no civil action shall be brought for any act or omission described in section 302 which occurs—

(1) during the first 6 months after the effective date, against businesses that employ 25 or fewer employees and have gross receipts of $1,000,000 or less; and

(2) during the first year after the effective date, against businesses that employ 10 or fewer employees and have gross receipts of $500,000 or less.

(c) EXCEPTION.—Sections 302(a) for purposes of section 302(b)(2)(B) and (C) only, 304(a) for purposes of section 304(b)(3) only, 304(b)(3), 305, and 306 shall take effect on the date of the enactment of this Act.

TITLE IV—TELECOMMUNICATIONS

Section 401. Telecommunications Relay Services for Hearing-Impaired and Speech-Impaired Individuals.

(a) TELECOMMUNICATIONS.—Title II of the Communications Act of 1934 (47 U.S.C. 201 et seq.) is amended by adding at the end thereof the following new section:

"Section 225. Telecommunications Services for Hearing-Impaired and Speech-Impaired Individuals.

"(a) DEFINITIONS.—As used in this section—

"(1) COMMON CARRIER OR CARRIER.—The term 'common carrier' or 'carrier' includes any common carrier engaged in interstate communication by wire or radio as defined in section 3(h) and any common carrier engaged in intrastate communication by wire or radio, notwithstanding sections 2(b) and 221(b).

"(2) TDD.—The term 'TDD' means a Telecommunications Device for the Deaf, which is a machine that employs graphic communication in the transmission of coded signals through a wire or radio communication system.

"(3) TELECOMMUNICATIONS RELAY SERVICES.—The term 'telecommunications relay services' means telephone transmission services that provide the ability for an individual who has a hearing impairment or speech impairment to engage in communication by wire or radio with a hearing individual in a manner that is functionally equivalent to the ability of an individual who does not have a hearing impairment or speech impairment to communicate using voice communication services by wire or radio. Such term includes services that enable two-way communication between an individual who uses a TDD or other nonvoice terminal device and an individual who does not use such a device.

"(b) AVAILABILITY OF TELECOMMUNICATIONS RELAY SERVICES.—

"(1) IN GENERAL.—In order to carry out the purposes established under section 1, to make available to all individuals in the United States a rapid, efficient nationwide communication service, and to increase the utility of the telephone system of the Nation, the Commission shall ensure that interstate and intrastate telecommunications relay services are available, to the extent possible and in the most efficient manner, to hearing-impaired and speech-impaired individuals in the United States.

"(2) USE OF GENERAL AUTHORITY AND REMEDIES.—For the purposes of administering and enforcing the provisions of this section and the regulations prescribed thereunder, the Commission shall have the same authority, power, and functions with respect to common carriers engaged in intrastate communication as the Commission has in administering and enforcing the provisions of this title with respect to any common carrier engaged in interstate communication. Any violation of this section by any common carrier engaged in intrastate communication shall be subject to the same remedies, penalties, and procedures as are applicable to a violation of this Act by a common carrier engaged in interstate communication.

"(c) PROVISION OF SERVICES.—Each common carrier providing telephone voice transmission services shall, not later than 3 years after the date of enactment of this section, provide in compliance with the regulations prescribed under this section, throughout the area in which it offers service, telecommunications relay services, individually, through designees, through a competitively selected vendor, or in concert with other carriers. A common carrier shall be considered to be in compliance with such regulations—

"(1) with respect to intrastate telecommunications relay services in any State that does not have a certified program under subsection (f) and with respect to interstate telecommunications relay services, if such common carrier (or other entity through which the carrier is providing such relay services) is in compliance with the Commission's regulations under subsection (d); or

"(2) with respect to intrastate telecommunications relay services in any State that has a certified program under subsection (f) for such State, if such common carrier (or other entity through which the carrier is providing such relay services) is in compliance with the program certified under subsection (f) for such State.

"(d) REGULATIONS.—

"(1) IN GENERAL.—The Commission shall, not later than 1 year after the date of enactment of this section, prescribe regulations to implement this section, including regulations that—

"(A) establish functional requirements, guidelines, and operations procedures for telecommunications relay services;

"(B) establish minimum standards that shall be met in carrying out subsection (c);

"(C) require that telecommunications relay services operate every day for 24 hours per day;

"(D) require that users of telecommunications relay services pay rates no greater than the rates paid for functionally equivalent voice communication services with respect to such factors as the duration of the call, the time of day, and the distance from point of origination to point of termination;

"(E) prohibit relay operators from failing to fulfill the obligations of common carriers by refusing calls or limiting the length of calls that use telecommunications relay services;

"(F) prohibit relay operators from disclosing the content of any relayed conversation and from keeping records of the content of any such conversation beyond the duration of the call; and

"(G) prohibit relay operators from intentionally altering a relayed conversation.

"(2) TECHNOLOGY.—The Commission shall ensure that regulations prescribed to implement this section encourage, consistent with section 7(a) of this Act, the use of existing technology and do not discourage or impair the development of improved technology.

"(3) JURISDICTIONAL SEPARATION OF COSTS.—

"(A) IN GENERAL.—Consistent with the provisions of section 410 of this Act, the Commission shall prescribe regulations governing the jurisdictional separation of costs for the services provided pursuant to this section.

"(B) RECOVERING COSTS.—Such regulations shall generally provide that costs caused by interstate telecommunications relay services shall be recovered from all subscribers for every interstate service and costs caused by intrastate telecommunications relay services shall be recovered from the intrastate jurisdiction. In a State that has a certified program under subsection (f), a State commission shall permit a common carrier to recover the costs incurred in providing intrastate telecommunications relay services by a method consistent with the requirements of this section.

"(e) ENFORCEMENT.—

"(1) IN GENERAL.—Subject to subsections (f) and (g), the Commission shall enforce this section.

"(2) COMPLAINT.—The Commission shall resolve, by final order, a complaint alleging a violation of this section within 180 days after the date such complaint is filed.

"(f) CERTIFICATION.—

"(1) STATE DOCUMENTATION.—Any State desiring to establish a State program under this section shall submit documentation to the Commission that describes the program of such State for implementing intrastate telecommunications relay services and the procedures and remedies available for enforcing any requirements imposed by the State program.

"(2) REQUIREMENTS FOR CERTIFICATION.—After review of such documentation, the Commission shall certify the State program if the Commission determines that—

"(A) the program makes available to hearing-impaired and speech-impaired individuals, either directly, through designees,

through a competitively selected vendor, or through regulation of intrastate common carriers, intrastate telecommunications relay services in such State in a manner that meets or exceeds the requirements of regulations prescribed by the Commission under subsection (d); and

"(B) the program makes available adequate procedures and remedies for enforcing the requirements of the State program.

"(3) METHOD OF FUNDING.—Except as provided in subsection (d), the Commission shall not refuse to certify a State program based solely on the method such State will implement for funding intrastate telecommunication relay services.

"(4) SUSPENSION OR REVOCATION OF CERTIFICATION.—The Commission may suspend or revoke such certification if, after notice and opportunity for hearing, the Commission determines that such certification is no longer warranted. In a State whose program has been suspended or revoked, the Commission shall take such steps as may be necessary, consistent with this section, to ensure continuity of telecommunications relay services.

"(g) COMPLAINT.—

"(1) REFERRAL OF COMPLAINT.—If a complaint to the Commission alleges a violation of this section with respect to intrastate telecommunications relay services within a State and certification of the program of such State under subsection (f) is in effect, the Commission shall refer such complaint to such State.

"(2) JURISDICTION OF COMMISSION.—After referring a complaint to a State under paragraph (1), the Commission shall exercise jurisdiction over such complaint only if--

"(A) final action under such State program has not been taken on such complaint by such State—

"(i) within 180 days after the complaint is filed with such State; or

"(ii) within a shorter period as prescribed by the regulations of such State; or

"(B) the Commission determines that such State program is no longer qualified for certification under subsection (f)."

(b) CONFORMING AMENDMENTS.—The Communications Act of 1934 (47 U.S.C. 151 et seq.) is amended—

(1)   in section 2(b) (47 U.S.C. 152(b)), by striking "section 224" and inserting "sections 224 and 225"; and

(2)   in section 221(b) (47 U.S.C. 221(b)), by striking "section 301" and inserting "sections 225 and 301".

Section 402. Closed-Captioning of Public Service Announcements.

Section 711 of the Communications Act of 1934 is amended to read as follows:

"Section 711. Closed-Captioning of Public Service Announcements.

"Any television public service announcement that is produced or funded in whole or in part by any agency or instrumentality of Federal government shall include closed captioning of the verbal content of such announcement. A television broadcast station licensee—

"(1)   shall not be required to supply closed captioning for any such announcement that fails to include it; and

"(2)   shall not be liable for broadcasting any such announcement without transmitting a closed caption unless the licensee intentionally fails to transmit the closed caption that was included with the announcement."

TITLE V—MISCELLANEOUS PROVISIONS

Section 501. Construction.

(a)   IN GENERAL.—Except as otherwise provided in this Act, nothing in this Act shall be construed to apply a lesser standard than the standards applied under title V of the Rehabilitation Act of 1973 (29 U.S.C. 790 et seq.) or the regulations issued by Federal agencies pursuant to such title.

(b)   RELATIONSHIP TO OTHER LAWS.—Nothing in this Act shall be construed to invalidate or limit the remedies, rights, and procedures of any Federal law or law of any State or political subdivision of any State or jurisdiction that provides greater or equal protection for the rights of individuals with disabilities than are afforded by this Act. Nothing in this Act shall be construed to preclude the prohibition of, or the imposition of restrictions on, smoking in places of employment covered by title I, in transportation covered by title II or III, or in places of public accommodation covered by title III.

(c)   INSURANCE.—Titles I through IV of this Act shall not be construed to prohibit or restrict—

(1)   an insurer, hospital or medical service company, health maintenance organization, or any agent, or entity that administers benefit plans, or similar organizations from underwriting risks, classifying risks, or administering such risks that are based on or not inconsistent with State law; or

(2)   a person or organization covered by this Act from establishing, sponsoring, observing or administering the terms of a bona fide benefit plan that are based on underwriting risks, classifying risks, or administering such risks that are based on or not inconsistent with State law; or

(3)   a person or organization covered by this Act from establishing, sponsoring, observing or administering the terms of a bona fide benefit plan that is not subject to State laws that regulate insurance.

Paragraphs (1), (2), and (3) shall not be used as a subterfuge to evade the purposes of title I and III.

(d)   ACCOMMODATIONS AND SERVICES.—Nothing in this Act shall be construed to require an individual with a disability to accept an accommodation, aid, service, opportunity, or benefit which such individual chooses not to accept.

Section 502. State Immunity.

A State shall not be immune under the eleventh amendment to the Constitution of the United States from an action in Federal or State court of competent jurisdiction for a violation of this Act. In any action against a State for a violation of the requirements of this Act, remedies (including remedies both at law and in equity) are available for such a violation to the same extent as such remedies are available for such a violation in an action against any public or private entity other than a State.

Section 503. Prohibition Against Retaliation and Coercion.

(a)   RETALIATION.—No person shall discriminate against any individual because such individual has opposed any act or practice made unlawful by this Act or because such individual made a charge, testified, assisted, or participated in any manner in an investigation, proceeding, or hearing under this Act.

(b) INTERFERENCE, COERCION, OR INTIMIDATION.—It shall be unlawful to coerce, intimidate, threaten, or interfere with any individual in the exercise or enjoyment of, or on account of his or her having exercised or enjoyed, or on account of his or her having aided or encouraged any other individual in the exercise or enjoyment of, any right granted or protected by this Act.

(c) REMEDIES AND PROCEDURES.—The remedies and procedures available under sections 107, 203, and 308 of this Act shall be available to aggrieved persons for violations of subsections (a) and (b), with respect to title I, title II and title III, respectively.

Section 504. Regulations by the Architectural and Transportation Barriers Compliance Board.

(a) ISSUANCE OF GUIDELINES.—Not later than 9 months after the date of enactment of this Act, the Architectural and Transportation Barriers Compliance Board shall issue minimum guidelines that shall supplement the existing Minimum Guidelines and Requirements for Accessible Design for purposes of titles II and III of this Act.

(b) CONTENTS OF GUIDELINES.—The supplemental guidelines issued under subsection (a) shall establish additional requirements, consistent with this Act, to ensure that buildings, facilities, rail passenger cars, and vehicles are accessible, in terms of architecture and design, transportation, and communication, to individuals with disabilities.

(c) QUALIFIED HISTORIC PROPERTIES.—
(1) IN GENERAL.—The supplemental guidelines issued under subsection (a) shall include procedures and requirements for alterations that will threaten or destroy the historic significance of qualified historic buildings and facilities as defined in 4.1.7 (1)(a) of the Uniform Federal Accessibility Standards.
(2) SITES ELIGIBLE FOR LISTING IN NATIONAL REGISTER.—With respect to alterations of buildings or facilities that are eligible for listing in the National Register of Historic Places under the National Historic Preservation Act (16 U.S.C.

470 et seq.), the guidelines described in paragraph (1) shall, at a minimum, maintain the procedures and requirements established in 4.1.7 (1) and (2) of the Uniform Federal Accessibility Standards.
(3) OTHER SITES.—With respect to alterations of buildings or facilities designated as historic under State or local law, the guidelines described in paragraph (1) shall establish procedures equivalent to those established by 4.1.7(1) (b) and (c) of the Uniform Federal Accessibility Standards, and shall require, at a minimum, compliance with the requirements established in 4.1.7(2) of such standards.

Section 505. Attorney's Fees.

In any action or administrative proceeding commenced pursuant to this Act, the court or agency, in its discretion, may allow the prevailing party, other than the United States, a reasonable attorney's fee, including litigation expenses, and costs, and the United States shall be liable for the foregoing the same as a private individual.

Section 506. Technical Assistance.

(a) PLAN FOR ASSISTANCE.—
(1) IN GENERAL.—Not later than 180 days after the date of enactment of this Act, the Attorney General, in consultation with the Chair of the Equal Employment Opportunity Commission, the Secretary of Transportation, the Chair of the Architectural and Transportation Barriers Compliance Board, and the Chairman of the Federal Communications Commission, shall develop a plan to assist entities covered under this Act, and other Federal agencies, in understanding the responsibility of such entities and agencies under this Act.
(2) PUBLICATION OF PLAN.—The Attorney General shall publish the plan referred to in paragraph (1) for public comment in accordance with subchapter II of chapter 5 of title 5, United States Code (commonly known as the Administrative Procedure Act).

(b) AGENCY AND PUBLIC ASSISTANCE.—The Attorney General may obtain the assistance of other Federal agencies in carrying out subsection (a), including the National Council on Disability, the President's Committee on Employment of People with Disabilities, the Small Business Administration, and the Department of Commerce.

(c) IMPLEMENTATION.—
(1) RENDERING ASSISTANCE.—Each Federal agency that has responsibility under paragraph (2) for implementing this Act may render technical assistance to individuals and institutions that have rights or duties under the respective title or titles for which such agency has responsibility.

(2) IMPLEMENTATION OF TITLES.—
(A) TITLE I.—The Equal Employment Opportunity Commission and the Attorney General shall implement the plan for assistance developed under subsection (a), for title I.

(B) TITLE II.—
(i) SUBTITLE A.—The Attorney General shall implement such plan for assistance for subtitle A of title II.
(ii) SUBTITLE B.—The Secretary of Transportation shall implement such plan for assistance for subtitle B of title II.

(C) TITLE III.—The Attorney General, in coordination with the Secretary of Transportation and the Chair of the Architectural Transportation Barriers Compliance Board, shall implement such plan for assistance for title III, except for section 304, the plan for assistance for which shall be implemented by the Secretary of Transportation.

(D) TITLE IV.—The Chairman of the Federal Communications Commission, in coordination with the Attorney General, shall implement such plan for assistance for title IV.

(3) TECHNICAL ASSISTANCE MANUALS.— Each Federal agency that has responsibility under paragraph (2) for implementing this Act shall, as part of its implementation responsibilities, ensure the availability and provision of appropriate technical assistance manuals to individuals or entities with rights or duties under this Act no later than six months after applicable final regulations are published under titles I, II, III, and IV.

(d) GRANTS AND CONTRACTS.—
(1) IN GENERAL.—Each Federal agency that has responsibility under subsection (c)(2) for implementing this Act may make grants or award contracts to effectuate the purposes of this section, subject to the availability of appropriations. Such grants and contracts may be awarded to individuals, institutions not organized for profit and no part of the net earnings of which inures to the benefit of any private shareholder or individual (including educational institutions), and associations representing individuals who have rights or duties under this Act. Contracts may be awarded to entities organized for profit, but such entities may not be the recipients of grants described in this paragraph.

(2) DISSEMINATION OF INFORMATION.— Such grants and contracts, among other uses, may be designed to ensure wide dissemination of information about the rights and duties established by this Act and to provide information and technical assistance about techniques for effective compliance with this Act.

(e) FAILURE TO RECEIVE ASSISTANCE.—An employer, public accommodation, or other entity covered under this Act shall not be excused from compliance with the requirements of this Act because of any failure to receive technical assistance under this section, including any failure in the development or dissemination of any technical assistance manual authorized by this section.

Section 507. Federal Wilderness Areas.

(a) STUDY.—The National Council on Disability shall conduct a study and report on the effect that wilderness designations and wilderness land management practices have on the ability of individuals with disabilities to use and enjoy the National Wilderness Preservation System as established under the Wilderness Act (16 U.S.C. 1131 et seq.).

(b) SUBMISSION OF REPORT.—Not later than 1 year after the enactment of this Act, the National Council on Disability shall submit the report required under subsection (a) to Congress.

(c) SPECIFIC WILDERNESS ACCESS.—
(1) IN GENERAL.—Congress reaffirms that nothing in the Wilderness Act is to be construed as prohibiting the use of a wheelchair in a wilderness area by an individual whose disability requires use of a wheelchair, and consistent with the Wilderness Act no agency is required to provide any form of special treatment or accommodation, or to construct any

facilities or modify any conditions of lands within a wilderness area in order to facilitate such use.

(2) DEFINITION.—For purposes of paragraph (1), the term "wheelchair" means a device designed solely for use by a mobility-impaired person for locomotion, that is suitable for use in an indoor pedestrian area.

Section 508. Transvestites.

For the purposes of this Act, the term "disabled" or "disability" shall not apply to an individual solely because that individual is a transvestite.

Section 509. Coverage of Congress and the Agencies of the Legislative Branch.

(a) COVERAGE OF THE SENATE.—
(1) COMMITMENT TO RULE XLII.—The Senate reaffirms its commitment to Rule XLII of the Standing Rules of the Senate which provides as follows:
   "No member, officer, or employee of the Senate shall, with respect to employment by the Senate or any office thereof—
   "(a) fail or refuse to hire an individual;
   "(b) discharge an individual; or
   "(c) otherwise discriminate against an individual with respect to promotion, compensation, or terms, conditions, or privileges of employment
   on the basis of such individual's race, color, religion, sex, national origin, age, or state of physical handicap.".
(2) APPLICATION TO SENATE EMPLOYMENT.—The rights and protections provided pursuant to this Act, the Civil Rights Act of 1990 (S. 2104, 101st Congress), the Civil Rights Act of 1964, the Age Discrimination in Employment Act of 1967, and the Rehabilitation Act of 1973 shall apply with respect to employment by the United States Senate.
(3) INVESTIGATION AND ADJUDICATION OF CLAIMS.—All claims raised by any individual with respect to Senate employment, pursuant to the Acts referred to in paragraph (2), shall be investi-gated and adjudicated by the Select Committee on Ethics, pursuant to S. Res. 338, 88th Congress, as amended, or such other entity as the Senate may designate.

(4) RIGHTS OF EMPLOYEES.—The Committee on Rules and Administration shall ensure that Senate employees are informed of their rights under the Acts referred to in paragraph (2).
(5) APPLICABLE REMEDIES.—When assigning remedies to individuals found to have a valid claim under the Acts referred to in paragraph (2), the Select Committee on Ethics, or such other entity as the Senate may designate, should to the extent practicable apply the same remedies applicable to all other employees covered by the Acts referred to in paragraph (2). Such remedies shall apply exclusively.
(6) MATTERS OTHER THAN EMPLOYMENT.—
   (A) IN GENERAL.—The rights and protections under this Act shall, subject to subparagraph (B), apply with respect to the conduct of the Senate regarding matters other than employment.
   (B) REMEDIES.—The Architect of the Capitol shall establish remedies and procedures to be utilized with respect to the rights and protections provided pursuant to subparagraph (A). Such remedies and procedures shall apply exclusively, after approval in accordance with subparagraph (C).
   (C) PROPOSED REMEDIES AND PROCEDURES.—For purposes of subparagraph (B), the Architect of the Capitol shall submit proposed remedies and procedures to the Senate Committee on Rules and Administration. The remedies and procedures shall be effective upon the approval of the Committee on Rules and Administration.
(7) EXERCISE OF RULEMAKING POWER.—Notwithstanding any other provision of law, enforcement and adjudication of the rights and protections referred to in paragraphs (2) and (6)(A) shall be within the exclusive jurisdiction of the United States Senate. The provisions of paragraphs (1), (3), (4), (5), (6)(B), and (6)(C) are enacted by the Senate as an exercise of the rulemaking power of the Senate, with full recognition of the right of the Senate to change its rules, in the same manner, and to the same extent, as in the case of any other rule of the Senate.

(b) COVERAGE OF THE HOUSE OF REPRESEN-TATIVES.—

(1) IN GENERAL.—Notwithstanding any other provision of this Act or of law, the purposes of this Act shall, subject to paragraphs (2) and (3), apply in their entirety to the House of Representatives.

(2) EMPLOYMENT IN THE HOUSE.—

(A) APPLICATION.—The rights and protections under this Act shall, subject to subparagraph (B), apply with respect to any employee in an employment position in the House of Representatives and any employing authority of the House of Representatives.

(B) ADMINISTRATION.—

(i) IN GENERAL.—In the administration of this paragraph, the remedies and procedures made applicable pursuant to the resolution described in clause (ii) shall apply exclusively.

(ii) RESOLUTION.—The resolution referred to in clause (i) is House Resolution 15 of the One Hundredth First Congress, as agreed to January 3, 1989, or any other provision that continues in effect the provisions of, or is a successor to, the Fair Employment Practices Resolution (House Resolution 558 of the One Hundredth Congress, as agreed to October 4, 1988).

(C) EXERCISE OF RULEMAKING POWER.—The provisions of subparagraph (B) are enacted by the House of Representatives as an exercise of the rulemaking power of the House of Representatives, with full recognition of the right of the House to change its rules, in the same manner, and to the same extent as in the case of any other rule of the House.

(3) MATTERS OTHER THAN EMPLOYMENT.—

(A) IN GENERAL.—The rights and protections under this Act shall, subject to subparagraph (B), apply with respect to the conduct of the House of Representatives regarding matters other than employment.

(B) REMEDIES.—The Architect of the Capitol shall establish remedies and procedures to be utilized with respect to the rights and protections provided pursuant to subparagraph (A). Such remedies and procedures shall apply exclusively, after approval in accordance with subparagraph (C).

(C) APPROVAL.—For purposes of subparagraph (B), the Architect of the Capitol shall submit proposed remedies and procedures to the Speaker of the House of Representatives. The remedies and procedures shall be effective upon the approval of the Speaker, after consultation with the House Office Building Commission.

(c) INSTRUMENTALITIES OF CONGRESS.—

(1) IN GENERAL.—The rights and protections under this Act shall, subject to paragraph (2), apply with respect to the conduct of each instrumentality of the Congress.

(2) ESTABLISHMENT OF REMEDIES AND PROCEDURES BY INSTRUMENTALITIES.—The chief official of each instrumentality of the Congress shall establish remedies and procedures to be utilized with respect to the rights and protections provided pursuant to paragraph (1). Such remedies and procedures shall apply exclusively.

(3) REPORT TO CONGRESS.—The chief official of each instrumentality of the Congress shall, after establishing remedies and procedures for purposes of paragraph (2), submit to the Congress a report describing the remedies and procedures.

(4) DEFINITION OF INSTRUMENTALITIES.—For purposes of this section, instrumentalities of the Congress include the following: the Architect of the Capitol, the Congressional Budget Office, the General Accounting Office, the Government Printing Office, the Library of Congress, the Office of Technology Assessment, and the United States Botanic Garden.

(5) CONSTRUCTION.—Nothing in this section shall alter the enforcement procedures for individuals with disabilities provided in the General Accounting Office Personnel Act of 1980 and regulations promulgated pursuant to that Act.

Section 510. Illegal Use of Drugs.

(a) IN GENERAL.—For purposes of this Act, the term "individual with a disability" does not include an individual who is currently engaging in the illegal use of drugs, when the covered entity acts on the basis of such use.

(b) RULES OF CONSTRUCTION.—Nothing in subsection (a) shall be construed to exclude as an individual with a disability an individual who—

(1) has successfully completed a supervised drug rehabilitation program and is no longer engaging in the illegal use of drugs, or has otherwise been rehabilitated successfully and is no longer engaging in such use;

(2) is participating in a supervised rehabilitation program and is no longer engaging in such use; or

(3) is erroneously regarded as engaging in such use, but is not engaging in such use;

except that it shall not be a violation of this Act for a covered entity to adopt or administer reasonable policies or procedures, including but not limited to drug testing, designed to ensure that an individual described in paragraph (1) or (2) is no longer engaging in the illegal use of drugs; however, nothing in this section shall be construed to encourage, prohibit, restrict, or authorize the conducting of testing for the illegal use of drugs.

(c) HEALTH AND OTHER SERVICES.—Notwithstanding subsection (a) and section 511(b)(3), an individual shall not be denied health services, or services provided in connection with drug rehabilitation, on the basis of the current illegal use of drugs if the individual is otherwise entitled to such services.

(d) DEFINITION OF ILLEGAL USE OF DRUGS.—

(1) IN GENERAL.—The term "illegal use of drugs" means the use of drugs, the possession or distribution of which is unlawful under the Controlled Substances Act (21 U.S.C. 812). Such term does not include the use of a drug taken under supervision by a licensed health care professional, or other uses authorized by the Controlled Substances Act or other provisions of Federal law.

(2) DRUGS.—The term "drug" means a controlled substance, as defined in schedules I through V of section 202 of the Controlled Substances Act.

Section 511. Definitions.

(a) HOMOSEXUALITY AND BISEXUALITY.—For purposes of the definition of "disability" in section 3(2),

homosexuality and bisexuality are not impairments and as such are not disabilities under this Act.

(b) CERTAIN CONDITIONS.—Under this Act, the term "disability" shall not include—

(1) transvestism, transsexualism, pedophilia, exhibitionism, voyeurism, gender identity disorders not resulting from physical impairments, or other sexual behavior disorders;

(2) compulsive gambling, kleptomania, or pyromania; or

(3) psychoactive substance use disorders resulting from current illegal use of drugs.

Section 512. Amendments to the Rehabilitation Act.

(a) DEFINITION OF HANDICAPPED INDIVIDUAL.—Section 7(8) of the Rehabilitation Act of 1973 (29 U.S.C. 706(8)) is amended by redesignating subparagraph (C) as subparagraph (D), and by inserting after subparagraph (B) the following subparagraph:

"(C) (i) For purposes of title V, the term 'individual with handicaps' does not include an individual who is currently engaging in the illegal use of drugs, when a covered entity acts on the basis of such use.

"(ii) Nothing in clause (i) shall be construed to exclude as an individual with handicaps an individual who—

"(I) has successfully completed a supervised drug rehabilitation program and is no longer engaging in the illegal use of drugs, or has otherwise been rehabilitated successfully and is no longer engaging in such use;

"(II) is participating in a supervised rehabilitation program and is no longer engaging in such use; or

"(III) is erroneously regarded as engaging in such use, but is not engaging in such use;

except that it shall not be a violation of this Act for a covered entity to adopt or administer reasonable policies or procedures, including but not limited to drug testing, designed to ensure that an individual described in subclause (I) or (II) is no longer engaging in the illegal use of drugs.

"(iii)   Notwithstanding clause (i), for purposes of programs and activities providing health services and services provided under titles I, II, and III, an individual shall not be excluded from the benefits of such programs or activities on the basis of his or her current illegal use of drugs if he or she is otherwise entitled to such services.

"(iv)   For purposes of programs and activities providing educational services, local educational agencies may take disciplinary action pertaining to the use or possession of illegal drugs or alcohol against any handicapped student who currently is engaging in the illegal use of drugs or in the use of alcohol to the same extent that such disciplinary action is taken against non-handicapped students. Furthermore, the due process procedures at 34 CFR 104.36 shall not apply to such disciplinary actions.

"(v)   For purposes of sections 503 and 504 as such sections relate to employment, the term 'individual with handicaps' does not include any individual who is an alcoholic whose current use of alcohol prevents such individual from performing the duties of the job in question or whose employment, by reason of such current alcohol abuse, would constitute a direct threat to property or the safety of others."

(b)   DEFINITION OF ILLEGAL DRUGS.—Section 7 of the Rehabilitation Act of 1973 (29 U.S.C. 706) is amended by adding at the end the following new paragraph:

"(22)   (A)   The term 'drug' means a controlled substance, as defined in schedules I through V of section 202 of the Controlled Substances Act (21 U.S.C. 812).

"(B)   The term 'illegal use of drugs' means the use of drugs, the possession or distribution of which is unlawful under the Controlled Substances Act. Such term does not include the use of a drug taken under supervision by a licensed health care professional, or other uses authorized by the Controlled Substances Act or other provisions of Federal law."

(c)   CONFORMING AMENDMENTS.—Section 7(8)(B) of the Rehabilitation Act of 1973 (29 U.S.C. 706(8)(B)) is amended—

(1)   in the first sentence, by striking "Subject to the second sentence of this subparagraph," and inserting "Subject to subparagraphs (C) and (D),"; and

(2)   by striking the second sentence.

Section 513. Alternative Means of Dispute Resolution.

Where appropriate and to the extent authorized by law, the use of alternative means of dispute resolution, including settlement negotiations, conciliation, facilitation, mediation, factfinding, minitrials, and arbitration, is encouraged to resolve disputes arising under this act.

Section 514. Severability.

Should any provision in this Act be found to be unconstitutional by a court of law, such provision shall be severed from the remainder of the Act, and such action shall not affect the enforceability of the remaining provisions of the Act.

And the House agree to the same.

CONGRESSIONAL VOTES ON THE FINAL PASSAGE OF THE AMERICANS WITH DISABILITIES ACT

In the House of Representatives

July 12, 1990 the House agreed to the conference report on S. 933, to establish a clear and comprehensive prohibition of discrimination on the basis of disability. This cleared the measure for Senate action.

For—377   **Against—28**   **Not Voting—27**

In the Senate

July 13, 1990 the U.S. Senate agreed to the conference report on S. 933, to establish a clear and comprehensive prohibition of discrimination on the basis of disability.

For—91   **Against—6**   **Not Voting—3**

The Americans with Disabilities Act became law when it was signed by President George Bush at 10:26 AM on July 26, 1990.

Glossary

A

Abnormal behavior. General classification of behavior that is unusual to the degree that it exceeds what society views as normal.

Absence seizures. Seizures characterized by brief lapses of attention, usually not more than 10 seconds; may be accompanied by eye blinking and head twitching; formerly called *petit mal seizures.*

Academic achievement. Level of proficiency attained in academic subjects (e.g., math, reading).

Acceleration. Instructional approach in which students who are gifted are allowed to achieve at rates consonant with their capacities.

Activity group therapy. Group-oriented approach used for treatment of children with behavior disorders.

Adaptive behavior. Classification of behavior that reflects the individual's ability to be socially appropriate and personally responsible.

Adaptive fit. Degree of compatibility between the demands of a task or setting and the individual's needs and abilities.

Adaptive instruction. Instructional approach in which the learning environment is modified to accommodate unique learner characteristics.

Adult service agencies. Agencies whose major focus is on providing necessary services to assist individuals with disabilities in becoming more independent as adults (e.g., rehabilitation services, social services, mental health services, etc.).

Alternative communication. See **Augmentative communication**

Amblyopia. Condition characterized by loss of vision due to imbalance of the eye muscles.

American Association on Mental Retardation (AAMR). Organization of professionals from many disciplines involved in the study and treatment of mental retardation.

American Sign Language (ASL). Type of sign language in which signs represent whole words and complete thoughts rather than single letters; commonly used by people with hearing impairments. See also **Sign systems**

Americans with Disabilities Act (ADA) (1990, PL 101-336). U.S. Civil rights legislation that prohibited discrimination against people with disabilities in private-sector employment, public services, and public accommodations, transportation, and telecommunications.

Amniocentesis. Prenatal assessment of the fetus involving analysis of amniotic fluid to screen for possible abnormalities.

Amputation. Absence of a limb due to a birth defect (congenital) or accident or surgery (acquired).

Anemia. Condition characterized by a deficient level of red blood cells.

Anencephaly. Condition characterized by partial or complete absence of cerebral tissue.

Anophthalmos. Condition characterized by absence of the eyeball.

Anoxia. Condition characterized by a lack of oxygen; may result in permanent brain damage.

Anticonvulsant. Medication used to control convulsions.

Antiretroviral agent. Agent that inhibits activity of a retrovirus (i.e., a virus characterized by reversal of the transfer of genetic code information from one type to another).

Anti-Rh gamma globulin (RhoGAM). Medication used to combat incompatibility in blood type between the mother and fetus. See also **Rh incompatibility**

Anxiety disorders. Conditions characterized by difficulty in anxiety-provoking situations (e.g., child's fear of separation from parents, unrealistic worries about the future or achievement, constant need for reassurance).

Apgar scoring. Evaluation of a newborn that assesses heartrate, respiratory condition, muscle tone, reflexes, and color.

Aphasia. Condition characterized by complete or partial impairment of language comprehension, formulation, and use; caused by brain damage.

Aqueous humor. Fluid between the lens and cornea of the eye.

ARC (The). Familiar title of A National Organization on Mental Retardation; acronym derived from Association for Retarded Citizens.

Articulation disorders. Speech problems such as omissions, substitutions, additions, and distortions.

Asphyxia. Condition characterized by impaired or absent exchange of oxygen and carbon dioxide; usually caused by interruption in breathing.

Assistive communication. Communication forms that supplement or replace verbal speech. See also **Augmentative communication**

Asthma. Condition characterized by continuously labored breathing and wheezing, a sense of constriction in the chest, and attacks of coughing and gasping; commonly of allergic origin.

Astigmatism. Condition characterized by a refractive visual disorder that occurs when the surface of the cornea is uneven or structurally defective, preventing light rays from converging at one point; blurred vision.

At-risk students. See **Students at risk**

Ataxia. Condition characterized by extreme difficulty in controlling fine and gross motor movements.

Athetosis. Condition characterized by constant, contorted twisting motions in the wrists and fingers.

Atonia. Condition characterized by lack of muscle tone.

Atresia. Absence of a normal opening.

Atropinization. Treatment for cataracts that involves washing the eye with atropine, permanently dilating the pupil.

Attention-deficit disorder (ADD). See **Attention-deficit hyperactivity disorder (ADHD)**

Attention-deficit hyperactivity disorder (ADHD). Condition in children characterized by difficulty maintaining attention because of limited ability to concentrate; also exhibit impulsive actions and hyperactive behavior. See also **Undifferentiated attention-deficit disorder**

Audiogram. Record produced by an audiometer that graphs an individual's threshold of hearing at various sound frequencies. See also **Audiometer**

Audiologist. Medical specialist in assessment of hearing ability.

Audiometer. Electronic device used to detect an individual's response to sound stimuli.

Audition. Act or sense of hearing.

Auditory association. Ability to associate verbally presented ideas or information.

Auditory blending. Ability to blend the parts of words into integrated wholes when speaking.

Auditory discrimination. Ability to distinguish between the sounds of different words or syllables or environmental sounds.

Auditory memory. Ability to recall verbally presented information.

Augmentative communication. Communication forms that employ nonspeech alternatives.

Aura. Sensation that occurs just before a seizure; characterized by unique sound, odor, or feeling.

Autism. Condition characterized by extreme withdrawal, self-stimulation, intellectual deficits, and language disorders; age of onset usually prior to 36 months.

B

Bacterial meningitis. Condition characterized by inflammation of the membranes in the brain or spinal cord; caused by bacterial infection.

Barrier-free facility. Building or other structure designed and constructed so that people with mobility disabilities (e.g., those in wheelchairs) can access all areas without encountering architectural obstructions.

Basic-skills approach. Instructional approach in which the groundwork is laid for further development and higher levels of functioning.

Behavior disorders. Conditions in which the emotional or behavioral responses of individuals in various environments are significantly different from their peer, ethnic, and cultural groups. These responses seriously affect their social relationships, personal adjustment, schooling, and employment.

Behavioral contract. Agreement, written or oral, between people stating that, if one behaves in a certain manner (e.g., student completes homework), the other (i.e., teacher, parent) will give him or her a specific reward.

Binet-Simon Scale. Individual test of intelligence developed in France in 1905 by Alfred Binet and Théodore Simon; later translated into English (1908) and revised and standardized by Lewis Terman (1916). See **Stanford-Binet Individual Intelligence Scale**

Biographical inventories. Information about a wide range of activities, interests, and achievements of the individual being studied.

Blind. Describes an individual whose central visual acuity does not exceed 20/200 in the best eye with correcting lenses or whose visual acuity, if better than 20/200, is limited in the central field of vision. See also **Visual acuity**

Braille. Writing system used by many people who are blind; involves combinations of six raised dots punched into paper that are read with the fingertips.

Buphthalmos. Condition characterized by abnormal distention and enlargement of the eyeball.

Burnout. Condition characterized by fatigue, demoralization, and depression; afflicts the individual when physical and emotional demands of work or life exceed his or her tolerance; common in helping professions.

C

Case management. Process that includes planning, implementing, and monitoring an individual's program(s) from assessment through intervention.

CAT scan. Precise x-ray taken of the brain or other area of the body to determine the presence of structural abnormalities (e.g., tumors); abbreviation for computerized axial tomography (CAT).

Cataract. Condition characterized by the eye lens becoming opaque and cloudy; results in distorted vision or total blindness.

Categorical descriptors. Descriptors that classify learning and behavior disabilities according to traditional categories (e.g., mental retardation, behavior disorders, and learning disabilities). See also **Cross-categorical definitions**

Ceiling effects. Effects produced when students who are academically gifted are unable to demonstrate their true capacities of achievement due to use of a restricted range of test questions or problems.

Cerebral palsy. Condition characterized by motor problems, general physical weakness, lack of coordination, and speech disorders; neurological in origin; results from brain damage before or during birth.

Chest physiotherapy. Physical therapy applied to the chest.

Child abuse. Situation in which a child is the victim of inflicted, nonaccidental, sexual, physical, and/or psychological trauma and/or injury. See also **Child neglect; Sexual abuse**

Child find. System within a state or local area that attempts to identify all children who are disabled or at risk and makes referrals for appropriate support services.

Child neglect. Situation in which a child is not adequately cared for by parents or caregivers; involves neglect of physical and/or emotional needs. See also **Child abuse**

Choroido-retinal degeneration. Condition characterized by deterioration of the choroid and retina.

Chromosomal abnormalities. Defects in chromosomes, thread-like materials that carry genes and therefore play central role in heredity.

Civil Rights Act (1964). U.S. legislation that prohibited discrimination against individuals on the basis of race, gender, religion, or national origin.

Cleft palate. Condition characterized by a gap in the soft palate and roof of the mouth, sometimes extending through the upper lip.

Clonic. Describes the phase of a seizure in which the muscles repeatedly contract and relax.

Closed-captioned TV. System by which people with hearing impairments are provided translated dialogue from television programs in the form of subtitles; also called the *line-21 system* since the caption is inserted into blank line 21 of the picture.

Cluttering. Condition characterized by excessively rapid, disorganized speech, often including random or unnecessary words.

Cochlea. Structure in the inner ear that converts sound coming from the middle ear into electrical signals that are transmitted to the brain.

Cochlear implant. Surgical procedure in which an electronic prosthetic component is implanted in the ear to stimulate the auditory nerve and restore hearing. See also **Transducer**

Cognition. Act of thinking, knowing, or processing information.

Cognitive functioning. Ability to think and process information and knowledge.

Cognitive-behavioral training. Instructional approach in which the individual is taught to use internalized speech strategies to respond to problematic situations.

Collaboration. People working together to attain a common goal; sometimes referred to as *professional partnerships*.

Coma. Condition characterized by abnormally deep stupor; caused by injury, disease, or poison.

Communication. Interchange of information between senders and receivers.

Community-based instruction. Instructional approach that focuses on individuals' learning and applying skills in community settings.

Computer-assisted instruction. Instructional approach in which computers are used to provide instruction, rehearsal, and testing.

Conditioning. Process in which new objects or situations elicit responses that were previously elicited by other stimuli.

Conductive. Describes hearing loss due to poor conduction of sound along passages leading to the inner ear.

Congenital. Describes a condition existing at birth.

Congenital rubella. Condition commonly called *German measles;* when contracted by a woman during pregnancy, causes a variety of problems in offspring (e.g., mental retardation, deafness, blindness, and other neurological problems).

Consulting teacher. Educator who provides support to regular classroom teachers and students through specialized training and assistance (e.g., modifying curricula and environment to accommodate students with diverse needs).

Consultive services. Assistance provided to teachers and students by specialists in general education settings to improve the quality of education or other interventions for students with disabilities.

Continuum of placements. Range of educational placements required by IDEA to meet the least restrictive environment mandate for students with disabilities; extends from regular classrooms with support services to homebound and hospital programs.

Cooperative learning. Instructional approach in which students work together to achieve group goals or rewards.

Cornea. External covering of the eye; reflects visual stimuli in the presence of light.

Corti's organ. Structure within the cochlea of highly specialized cells that translate vibrations into nerve impulses that are sent to the brain. See also **Cochlea**

Criterion-referenced assessment. Assessment in which an individual's performance is compared to an established standard or goal (i.e., a criterion); individual performance is not compared with that of others; sometimes associated with intraindividual differences. See **Intraindividual**

Cross-categorical definitions. Classification approach in which individuals with learning and behavior disabilities are grouped on the basis of the severity of the problem (mild, moderate, severe) rather than placed in traditional categories. See also **Categorical descriptors**

Cued speech. Communication method that combines hand signals with speech reading; gestures provide additional information regarding sounds not identifiable by lipreading; used by people with hearing impairments. See also **Speech reading**

Cultural approach. Labeling approach in which *normal* is defined according to standards established by a given culture.

Cultural pluralism. Instructional approach that advocates multiple cultural subgroups living together in a manner that maintains subsocietal differences, thereby continuing each group's cultural or ethnic traditions.

Cultural-familial retardation. Condition in which retardation may be attributable to both sociocultural and genetic factors.

Curriculum specialist. Educator who provides consultive support services to classroom teachers in developing curriculum design and implementation strategies.

Curriculum-based assessment. Assessment that uses the objectives of an individual's curriculum as the criteria against which progress is evaluated.

Cystic fibrosis (CF). Condition characterized by a disorder of the secretion glands; affects the lungs, pancreas, and sweat glands; begins at conception and is usually diagnosed in childhood.

Cytomegalic inclusion. Condition in newborns due to infection by cytomegalovirus (CMV); characterized by jaundice, mental retardation, and hearing impairment.

D

Deaf. Describes the individual who has a hearing loss greater than 75 to 80 db and cannot understand speech through the ear; vision is his or her primary means of input.

Deaf-blind. Describes the condition of or individual having simultaneous vision and hearing deficiencies.

Delayed speech. Condition characterized by delay in the acquisition of speech skills; individual performs like someone much younger.

Denasality. Condition characterized by too little voice resonance from the nasal passages (i.e., sounds like the individual has a cold).

Developmental approach. Labeling approach based on deviations from what is considered normal growth.

Developmental disorders. Conditions characterized by severe delays in the acquisition of cognitive, language, motor, and social skills.

Developmental period. Period of time between birth and age 18 (as provided in AAMR definition of mental retardation).

Deviant. Describes the behavior of individuals who are unable to adapt to social roles or establish appropriate interpersonal relationships.

Diabetes. Condition characterized by inadequate utilization of insulin; results in disordered metabolism of carbohydrates, fats, and proteins; developmental or hereditary.

Differentiated education. Instructional approach in which learning activities are uniquely and predominantly suited to capacities and interests of students who are gifted.

Disability. Condition characterized by a loss of physical functioning or difficulty in learning and social adjustment that significantly interferes with normal growth and development; as defined by the Americans with Disabilities Act, "A person with a disability has a physical or mental impairment that substantially limits the person in some major life activity. The person has a history that this physical or mental impairment results in discrimination."

Disorder. Condition characterized by general malfunctioning of mental, physical, or psychological processes.

Disruptive behavior disorders. Conditions characterized by attention or conduct disorders (e.g., problems in attending, following directions, interacting with others, listening, taking turns, relating aggressive behaviors to negative outcomes).

Down syndrome. Condition characterized by unique physical characteristics and varying degrees of mental retardation; results from chromosomal abnormality; historically described as *mongolism,* a term no longer acceptable.

Drug therapy. Medical approach in which physician attempts to aid the individual by prescribing medication specifically designed for his or her identified problem(s) (e.g., antidepressants, antipsychotics, anticonvulsants).

Dyadic relationship. A significant affiliation between two individuals.

Dyslexia. Condition characterized by severe impairment of the ability to read.

E

Early intervention. Intervention approach in which comprehensive services are provided for infants and toddlers who are disabled or at risk of eventually becoming disabled and their families; services may include education, health care, and/or social-psychological assistance.

Eating disorders. Conditions characterized by gross disturbances in eating behaviors (e.g., anorexia nervosa, bulimia).

Echolalia. Condition characterized by meaningless repetition or imitation of speech.

Ecological approach. Psychological approach that attributes abnormal behavior primarily to the interaction of an individual with the environment rather than disease.

Educationally disadvantaged. See **Students at risk**

Electroacoustic aids. Electronic devices that assist an individual in hearing; types include body and behind-the-ear aids.

Elimination disorders. Conditions characterized by soiling and wetting behaviors in older children that are not attributable to inherent physical problems.

Emotional disturbance. Condition characterized by difficulty expressing or dealing with emotions produced from normal family-, school-, or work-related experiences; behavior problems that are frequently internal in nature. See **Behavior disorders**

Emotionally disturbed. Describes the condition of or individual having emotional disturbances. See **Emotional disturbances**

Emphysema. Condition characterized by distention of tissues (i.e., expanded space between) and damage to walls in lungs; effects include shortness of breath.

Encephalitis. Condition characterized by inflammation of the brain tissue; may cause permanent damage to the central nervous system.

Enrichment. Instructional approach in which experiences are provided for students who are gifted to enhance thinking skills and extend knowledge.

Epilepsy. Condition characterized by cerebral dysfunction; effects include different types of recurrent seizures. See also **Seizures**

Epileptic. Describes the condition of or individual having epilepsy.

Epiphora. Condition characterized by overflow of tears from obstruction of lacrimal ducts.

Eustachian tube. Structure that extends from the throat to the middle-ear cavity; equalizes air pressure on the eardrum with that of outside by controlling airflow into the cavity.

Exceptional. Describes the condition of or individual having physical, mental, or behavioral performance that deviates substantially from the average (higher or lower).

Expressive language disorders. Conditions characterized by difficulty in language production or formulating and using spoken language.

Extended family. Family unit that includes the immediate family and close relatives who have regular and frequent contacts with it even though they don't necessarily live together.

F

Facilitative communication. Communication forms that facilitate or augment general communication ability (e.g., prompting). See also **Augmentative communication**

Feebleminded. Describes the condition of or individual having mental incompetence; roughly means "of weak mind"; term is outdated.

Fenestration.   Surgical technique in which a new opening is created in the labyrinth of the ear to restore hearing.

Fetal alcohol syndrome.   Condition characterized by damage to fetus due to the mother's consumption of alcohol during pregnancy; effects include facial deformities and various degrees of mental retardation.

Fetoscopy.   Procedure for examining the fetus using a needlelike camera that is inserted into the womb; used to detect visible abnormalities.

Figure-ground discrimination.   Ability to distinguish an object from its background.

Finger spelling.   Sign system of communication that incorporates all letters of the English alphabet; each letter is signed independently on one hand to form words. See also **Sign systems**

Fluency disorder.   Condition characterized by repeated interruptions, hesitations, or repetitions that interrupt the flow and rhythm of speech.

Fragile X syndrome.   Condition characterized by damage to the chromosome structure; appears as breaking or splitting at the end of an X chromosome; found in some males with autism.

Fraternal twins.   Twins that develop from two fertilized eggs and develop in two placentas; many times do not resemble one another closely.

Full inclusion.   Instructional approach in which students who are disabled or at risk receive all instruction in a regular classroom setting; support services come to the students.

Functional articulation disorders.   Conditions characterized by articulation problems that are not due to structural defects or neurological problems but likely result from environmental or psychological influences.

Functional life/compensatory approach.   Instructional approach in which only those practical skills are taught that will facilitate a student's accommodation to the natural setting, whether the classroom, home, or neighborhood (e.g., self-care, personal social skills, and occupational/vocational skills).

G

Galactosemia.   Condition characterized by a metabolic problem in which the infant has difficulty processing lactose; may cause mental retardation and other problems.

Gender-identity disorders.   Conditions characterized by incongruence between an individual's perception of his or her biologically assigned sex and gender identity.

Genetic counselor.   Professional who counsels people considering having a child regarding the chances of disability occurring based on their genetic history.

Geneticist.   Professional who specializes in the study of heredity.

Gifted, creative, and talented.   Describes the condition of or individual having extraordinary abilities in one or more areas.

Gifts and talents.   Extraordinary abilities in one or more areas.

Glaucoma.   Condition characterized by high pressure inside the eyeball.

H

Handicap.   Limitation imposed on an individual by the environment and his or her capacity to cope with that limitation.

Haptic.   Describes the sensation of touch and the information transmitted through body movements and/or positions.

Hard-of-hearing.   Describes the condition of or individual having deficient but somewhat functional hearing.

Health disorders.   Conditions characterized by limited strength, vitality, and alertness; may interfere with an individual's functioning but do not necessarily or initially impact the ability to move about independently in various settings.

Hemiplegia.   Condition characterized by paralysis of one side of the body.

Hertz (Hz).   Unit used to measure sound frequency in terms of number of cycles that vibrating molecules complete per second.

Human immunodeficiency virus (HIV).   Condition characterized by weakening of the immune system; causes AIDS.

Hydrocephalus.   Condition characterized by accumulation of cerebrospinal fluid in the skull; often results in head enlargement with pressure on the brain; may cause mental retardation.

Hyperactivity.   Condition characterized by hyperkinetic behavior. See **Hyperkinetic behavior**

Hyperkinetic behavior.   Behavior that is excessive in inappropriate circumstances.

Hypernasality.   Condition characterized by excessive voice resonance (i.e., too many sounds) from the nasal passages (i.e., causes a twang in speech).

Hyperopia.   Condition characterized by refractive problem in which the eyeball is excessively short and light rays are focused behind the retina; farsightedness.

Hyponasality.   Condition characterized by too little voice resonance from the nasal passages (i.e., sounds like the individual has a cold).

Hypotonia.   Condition characterized by poor muscle tone.

I

Identical twins.   Twins that develop from a single fertilized egg in a single placental sack; will be of the same sex and usually resemble one another closely.

Idiot.   Individual characterized by extreme mental deficiency; outdated term.

Immune system.   Physiological system that protects the body from disease when functioning normally.

In utero.   Describes fetal development before birth; means "in the uterus"; may be used to describe abnormalities or accidents that occur during this time (e.g., in utero infection).

Incidence.   Number of new cases of a condition identified within a specific period of time (e.g., one year). See also **Prevalence**

Individual approach.   Labeling approach in which labels are self-imposed and thus reflect how an individual perceives himself or herself.

Individualized education program (IEP). Instructional program based on multidisciplinary assessment and designed to meet the individual needs of a student with disabilities; as required by IDEA, the program developed and implemented must account for the student's present level of performance and provide for annual goals, short-term instructional objectives, related services, percentage of time in regular education, timeline for special education services, and annual evaluation.

Individualized family service plan (IFSP). Intervention plan for preschool-age children similar in content to an IEP; includes statements regarding the child's present development level, family's strengths and needs, major outcomes expected, delineation of specific interventions and delivery systems needed, dates of initiation and duration of services, and plan for transition into public schools. See also **Individualized education program (IEP)**

Individuals with Disabilities Education Act (IDEA) (1990, PL 101–476). New name for PL 94–142 (Part B of the Education for the Handicapped Act); added two new categories of disability: autism and traumatic brain injury. See also **Public Law 94–142**

Infant stimulation. Approach emphasizing early intervention in which the infant is provided with an array of visual, auditory, and physical stimuli to promote development.

Information processing. Model used to study the way individuals acquire, remember, and manipulate information.

Insane. Describes the condition of or individual having serious mental illness; outdated term.

Institution. Establishment or facility governed by a collection of fundamental rules.

Insulin. Hormone produced by the pancreas that converts glucose to energy, allowing it to enter the body's cells. See also **Diabetes**

Insulin infusion pump. Battery-operated devices that dispense insulin on a continuous basis to diabetic patients.

Intelligence quotient (IQ). Score obtained from an intelligence test that provides a measure of mental ability in relation to age.

Intensive-care specialists. Medical professionals that provide care to newborns who are seriously ill, disabled, or at risk of serious medical problems (e.g., physicians, nurses); also referred to as *neonatal specialists*.

Interdisciplinary. Describes team approach to intervention; during assessment, team members conduct independent assessments; program planning involves collaboration across disciplines; beyond planning, collaboration often ceases.

Interindividual. Describes analysis of an individual's performance in comparison with that of age-mates.

Intoxication. Condition characterized by an excessive level of some toxic agent in the mother-fetus system; may cause brain damage.

Intraindividual. Describes analysis of an individual's different areas of performance, emphasizing his or her own strengths and weaknesses.

IQ. See **Intelligence quotient**

Iris. Colored portion of the eye; adjusts to the size of the pupil.

Itinerant teacher. Educator who moves from place to place (e.g., school to school, school to hospital, home to home) to provide instruction and support to students with special needs.

K

Ketoacidosis. Condition associated with diabetes; characterized by dehydration, vomiting, drowsiness, labored breathing, and frequent urination.

Kinesthetic. Describes the sensation of body position, presence, or movement resulting chiefly from stimulation of sensory nerve endings in the muscles, tendons, and joints.

Kurzweil Personal Readers. Reading devices for individuals who are blind; convert printed material into synthetic speech.

L

Language. Systematic means of communicating ideas through the use of common symbols; a component of communication. See also **Communication**

Language delay. Condition characterized by interruption in the normal rate of language development; developmental sequence remains intact.

Language disorders. Conditions characterized by serious disruption of the language-development process.

Laryngeal. Describing that which pertains to the larynx.

Larynx. Portion of the throat that contains the vocal mechanism.

Laser cane. Mobility device for individuals who are blind; converts infrared light into sound as light beams strike objects.

Latchkey kids. Children who do not have any after-school support (e.g., because both parents work, etc.).

Learning disabilities. Conditions characterized by deficiency in one or more of the basic psychological processes used in understanding or using language.

Learning disabled. Describes the condition of or individual having a learning disability. See **Learning disability**

Learning disorders. Conditions characterized by significantly below-average learning performance.

Least restrictive environment (LRE). Environment as similar as possible to that of the regular classroom setting (i.e., with fewest restrictions) in which an individual with a disability can be educated; IDEA required that students with disabilities be educated with their nondisabled peers to the maximum extent appropriate.

Lens. Clear structure in the eye that focuses light rays on the retina.

Low birthweight. Describes newborns that weigh 5.5 pounds (2,500 grams) or less.

M

Mainstreaming. Instructional approach in which students with disabilities are integrated into general education classes with their nondisabled peers; refers to both instructional and social integration.

Malocclusion. Condition characterized by an abnormal fit of the upper and lower dental structures.

Manual communication. Communication form that involves sign language.

Marital and family therapy. Therapeutic approach in which family members are given opportunities to learn and practice more effective ways of relating to each other.

Master teacher. Highly trained and skilled educator who serves on a supervisory and consultive basis, assisting other teachers in meeting the diverse needs of students in classroom settings. See also **Consultive services**

Maternal infection. Condition characterized by infection in the mother during pregnancy; may injure the fetus.

Measurement bias. Error introduced during testing when results are unfair or inaccurate due to factors such as cultural background, sex, or race. See also **Test bias.**

Medical model. Model in which human development is described as having two dimensions: normal (i.e., absence of biological problems) and pathological (i.e., alterations caused by disease).

Melting pot. Concept that many cultures blend together into one, losing their distinctive and diverse elements; often associated with the United States.

Meningitis. Condition characterized by inflammation of the membranes covering the brain and spinal cord.

Mental age. Concept used in psychological assessment that relates to the general mental ability possessed by an individual of a given chronological age.

Mental retardation. Condition characterized by significantly subaverage general intellectual functioning existing concurrently with deficits in adaptive behavior; manifested during the developmental period (birth to age 18).

Mentally retarded. Describes the condition of or individual having mental retardation. See **Mental retardation**

Metabolic. Describes the body's ability to process (metabolize) substances.

Metacognitive processes. Processes employed by an individual in problem solving, monitoring, and evaluation.

Microphthalmos. Condition characterized by an abnormally small eyeball.

Mild learning and behavior disabilities. Conditions characterized by academic and/or social-interpersonal performance deficits that range from one to two standard deviations below the interindividual and/or intraindividual mean on the measures being recorded; a cross-categorical classification of disabilities; generally become evident in school-related settings and necessitate support services beyond those typically offered.

Mirror writing. Writing backward from right to left; letters appear as ordinary writing seen in a mirror.

Mixed. Describes hearing loss due to a combination of conductive and sensorineural problems. See also **Conductive; Sensorineural**

Modeling. Instruction approach in which the instructor demonstrates the appropriate behavior or skill to be learned.

Moderate learning and behavior disabilities. Conditions characterized by intellectual, academic and/or social-interpersonal performance deficits that range from two to three standard deviations below the interindividual and/or intraindividual mean on the measures being recorded; a cross-categorical classification of disabilities; cause may be identified in some cases but typically cannot;

performance deficits are not limited to any given setting; individuals require substantially altered patterns of service and treatment and perhaps environmental accommodations.

Morphology. Form and internal structure of words; transformations of words in such areas as tense and number.

Motokinesthetic. Describes a type of speech training in which an individual who is hearing impaired feels another individual's face and then imitates breath and voice patterns.

Mowat Sensor. Hand-held travel aid (approximately size of a flashlight) used by people who are blind; vibrates at different rates to warn the individual of obstacles in front of him or her.

Multicultural education. Instructional approach that promotes cultural pluralism (i.e., learning about multiple cultures and their values). See also **Cultural pluralism**

Multidisciplinary team. Group of professionals from several disciplines (e.g., educators, psychologists, and social workers) who work together for a common goal; required by IDEA for developing an individualized education program (involving parents, as well). See also **Individualized education program (IEP)**

Multiple handicaps. Conditions characterized by the presence of multiple disabling conditions that impair an individual's physical and mental development.

Muscular dystrophy. Condition characterized by deterioration and weakening of the voluntary skeletal muscles; includes a group of inherited, chronic disorders.

Myopia. Condition in which the eyeball is excessively long and focuses light in front of the retina; nearsightedness.

Myringoplasty. Surgical reconstruction of a perforated eardrum.

N

Nature versus nurture. Describes concept of whether an individual's ability is related primarily to sociocultural influences (nurture) or genetic factors (nature).

Negativism. Condition characterized by an individual withdrawing and refusing to speak in response to demands that exceed his or her performance level (e.g., child in response to parents' expectations).

Neurofibromatosis. Condition characterized by tumors of the skin and other tissue (e.g., the brain); causes mental retardation in 10 percent of cases; hereditary.

Neurological. Describes that pertaining to the nervous system.

Neuroses. Conditions characterized by partial disorganization and involving combinations of anxieties, compulsions, obsessions, and phobias.

Neurotic disorders. See **Neuroses**

Nondiscriminatory and multidisciplinary assessment. Assessment done in an individual's native or primary language; as required by IDEA, testing procedures must be selected and administered to prevent cultural or racial discrimination, assessment tools must be validated for the purpose they are being used, and multidisciplinary teams must use several pieces of information to formulate placement decisions.

Norm-based averages. See **Norm-referenced assessment**

Norm-referenced assessment.   Assessment in which a person's performance is compared with that of others, such as age-mates (i.e., a norm).

Normalization.   Concept of making available to individuals with disabilities the patterns and conditions that are as close as possible to those of everyday life in mainstream society.

Nystagmus.   Condition characterized by uncontrolled rapid eye movements.

O

Occlusion.   Closure and fitting together of dental structures.

Occupational therapist.   Professional who performs occupational therapy. See **Occupational therapy**

Occupational therapy.   Treatment approach that involves the design and delivery of instruction related to potential work-related activities.

Opportunistic infection.   Condition caused by germs that are not usually capable of causing infection in normal people (i.e., with normal immunity); associated with AIDS. See also **Human immunodeficiency virus (HIV)**

Optacon Scanner.   Tactile scanner that reads printed material and reproduces it on a fingerpad through a series of vibrating pins; used by people who are blind and do not use braille.

Optic atrophy.   Condition characterized by deterioration of the nerve fibers connecting the retina to the brain.

Optic nerve.   Nerve that connects the eye to the visual center of the brain.

Orthopedic impairments.   See **Physical disorders**

Ossicular chain.   Group of three small bones (malleus/incus/stapes or hammer/anvil/stirrup) that transmit vibrations from the external ear through the middle-ear cavity to the inner ear.

Otitis media.   Condition characterized by inflammation of the middle ear.

Otologist.   Professional who studies the ear and its diseases.

Otoxic drugs.   Drugs that can have harmful effects on the organs that control hearing and balance.

P

Paperless brailler.   Device for writing in braille in which the information is recorded and retrieved in some manner not using paper (e.g., standard magnetic tape cassette).

Paraplegia.   Condition characterized by paralysis of the lower body and both legs.

Partially sighted.   Describes the condition of or persons having visual acuity greater than 20/200 but not greater than 20/70 in the best eye after correction.

Pathological.   Describes alterations in an organism caused by disease.

Peer and cross-age tutoring.   Instructional approach that uses a cooperative learning situation in which one or more peers provide instruction to other students to achieve instructional goals; includes students of different ages tutoring each other.

Peer-mediated instruction.   Instructional approach that uses structured interactions between two or more students that are designed by school personnel to achieve instructional goals.

Perceptual disorders.   Conditions characterized by an ability to use one or more of the senses.

Perceptual-motor.   Describes the interaction between various channels of perception and motor activity.

Performance feedback.   Information regarding performance given to students by teachers or therapists.

Pervasive developmental disorder.   Condition characterized by qualitative impairment in the development of social interaction abilities and communication skills; term used by the American Psychiatric Association in DSM-III-R referring to a general class of psychological disorders.

Phenylketonuria (PKU).   Condition characterized by an infant's inability to process phenylalanine; may cause mental retardation if left untreated; genetic in origin.

Phonology.   System of speech sounds and the rules that govern their use.

Physical disorders.   Conditions characterized by bodily impairments that interfere with an individual's mobility, coordination, communication, learning, and/or personal adjustment.

Physical therapist.   Professional who performs physical therapy. See **Physical therapy**

Physical therapy.   Treatment approach of a physical deficiency through means such as stretching, exercise, or massage.

Postlingual disorders.   Conditions characterized by hearing impairment that occurs at any age following speech development.

Postural drainage.   Drainage of fluids through changing the posture of an individual; done with individuals with cystic fibrosis.

Pragmatics.   Language components concerned with the use of language in social contexts (e.g., rules that govern language functions, forms of messages).

Precipitous birth.   Delivery wherein the time between the onset of labor and birth is unusually short (e.g., less than two hours).

Precision teaching.   Instructional approach in which the skills to be taught are specifically designated, the initial performance level of those skills is measured, goals and objectives for improvements are stated, and evaluation is done on a daily basis in order to alter the program design if progress is not sufficient.

Prelingual disorders.   Conditions characterized by hearing impairment that occurs prior to the time of speech development (i.e., age 2).

Prematurity.   Situation in which the newborn is delivered early (i.e., before full term, which is 37 weeks from the first day of the mother's last menstrual period).

Prevalence.   Number of persons in a given population who exhibit a particular condition, problem, or status at a specific point in time. See also **Incidence**

Project Head Start.   Federally funded program for disadvantaged preschool students; attempts to identify and instruct children who are at risk prior to entering public school.

Prosthetic.   Describes a device that replaces or supports a missing or malfunctioning part of the body (e.g., an arm, joint, teeth).

Pseudoglioma.   Condition characterized by a nonmalignant intraocular disturbance resulting from detachment of the retina.

Psychodynamic. Describes an approach to psychological disorders that attributes causation to unconscious conflicts and anxieties (e.g., family interaction).

Psychosis. Condition characterized by serious behavior disorders resulting in loss of contact with reality; effects include delusions, hallucinations, and illusions.

Psychotic disorders. See **Psychosis**

Public Law 94-142 (1975). Part B of the Education of the Handicapped Act (EHA), mandating that all eligible students, regardless of the extent or type of disability, are to receive at public expense the special education services necessary to meet their individual needs. See also **Individuals with Disabilities Education Act**

Public Law 99-457 (1986). U.S. legislation that extended the rights and protections of IDEA (formerly PL 94-142) to preschool-age children (ages 3 through 5); also established a program for infants and toddlers with disabilities. See also **Individuals with Disabilities Education Act; Public Law 94-142**

Pull-out program. Instructional approach in which students with disabilities are removed from the regular classroom and placed in separate classes for at least part of the school day.

Pupil. Opening in the iris; expands or contracts to control the amount of light entering the eye.

Q

Quadriplegia. Condition characterized by paralysis of all four extremities and usually the trunk.

R

Receptive language disorders. Conditions characterized by difficulties in comprehending speech.

Refractive problems. Visual disorders that occur when the refractive structures of the eye fail to properly focus light rays on the retina.

Regular education initiative. See **Full inclusion**

Reinforcement. Process in which rewards are given to build, strengthen, or maintain specific adaptive behaviors.

Related services. Services necessary to ensure that students with disabilities benefit from their educational experience; include special transportation and other support services (e.g., speech pathology, psychological services, physical and occupational therapy, recreation, rehabilitation counseling, social work, and medical services).

Remedial readers. Students who need particular assistance in reading instruction; term was used in early literature to classify students who might now be described as learning disabled.

Remediation approach. Instructional approach that focuses on and attempts to remedy deficiencies in a student's repertoire of skills.

Research design. Procedural plan for undertaking research.

Resource room. Educational placement option for students with disabilities involving specialized instruction in a separate location for a specific period, depending on students' needs (most of the day is spent in the regular classroom, however); specialized assistance reinforces and supplements regular class instruction.

Resource-room teacher. Educator who provides instruction in a resource room. See also **Resource room**

Respite care. Assistance provided by individuals outside the immediate family that allows parents and siblings time away from the child with a disability (e.g., for a recreational event, vacation, etc.).

Retina. Light-sensitive cells in the interior of the eye that transmit images to the brain via the optic nerve.

Retinal detachment. Condition characterized by separation of the retina from the choroid and sclera.

Retinitis pigmentosa. Condition resulting from a break in the choroid; hereditary.

Retinoblastoma. Condition characterized by a malignant tumor in the retina.

Retinopathy of prematurity. Term now used for *retrolental fibroplasia*. See **Retrolental fibroplasia (RLF)**

Retrolental fibroplasia (RLF). Condition characterized by formation of scar tissue behind the lens, preventing light rays from reaching the retina; result of administering excessive oxygen to premature infants.

Rh incompatibility. Condition characterized by incompatibility between the mother's and fetus' blood types (i.e., mother has Rh-negative blood, fetus has Rh-positive blood); may result in birth defects.

Rigidity. Condition characterized by continuous and diffuse tension as the limbs are extended.

Role-playing. Instructional approach in which individuals practice behaviors they are to learn; often used to teach social behaviors.

Rubella. See **Congenital rubella**

S

Savant. Individual with highly proficient knowledge or ability, often in highly specific topics or skills.

Schoolwide assistance teams (SWATs). Groups of professionals, students, and parents working together toward the common goal of providing instructional support; employ strategies to assist school personnel in making referrals for students at risk of failure.

Scientific method. Systematic method of investigation that involves formulating a problem, collecting data, and establishing a theory.

Section 501 Vocational Rehabilitation Act (PL 93-12). Federal civil rights provision that states handicapped individuals cannot be excluded from participation in, denied benefits of, or be subjected to discrimination under any program or activity receiving federal financial assistance.

Seizure. Condition characterized by abnormal neurochemical activity in the brain; cluster of effects include altered consciousness and characteristic motor patterns.

Seizure disorders. Conditions characterized by recurrent seizures; effects include sudden altering of the individual's consciousness, accompanied by uncontrolled jerking and motor activity; includes a number of disorders, including epilepsy. See also **Seizure**

Selective attention.   Attending that often does not focus on centrally important tasks or information.

Self-fulfilling prophecy.   Theory that an individual will become what he or she is described (labeled) as being.

Semantics.   Components of language concerned with meaning.

Sensorineural.   Describes hearing loss due to an abnormal sense organ (inner ear) and damaged auditory nerve.

Sensory disorders.   Conditions characterized by differences in vision and hearing that affect individual performance.

Severe and profound/multiple disabilities.   Conditions characterized by physical, sensory, intellectual, and/or social-interpersonal performance deficits that range beyond three standard deviations below the interindividual and/or intraindividual mean on the measures being recorded; a cross-categorical classification; deficits are not limited to any given setting but are evident in all environmental settings and often involve several areas of performance; causation is more identifiable at this level of functioning but not exact in many cases; individuals with functional disabilities at this level require significantly altered environments with regard to care, treatment, and accommodations.

Sexual abuse.   Situation in which a child is sexually mistreated, involving incest, assault, or sexual exploitation. See also **Child abuse**

Sheltered workshop.   Segregated vocational training and employment setting for people with disabilities.

Short attention span.   Condition characterized by an inability to focus attention on a task for a sustained period (i.e., more than a few seconds or minutes).

Sickle cell anemia (SCA).   Condition characterized by distortion in the structures of red blood cells; causes unrelenting anemia. See also **Anemia**

Sign systems.   Communication forms that attempt to produce visual equivalents of oral language through manual gestures; different from sign language. See **American Sign Language**

"Six-hour retardate."   Term that evolved from observations that certain students appeared retarded only during the six hours that they were in school.

Snellen test.   Test of visual acuity.

Social maladjustment.   Condition characterized by an individual's inability or unwillingness to conform to social values or expectations; often used to describe individuals, particularly youth who break the law.

Socialized aggression.   Condition characterized by aggressive attitudes and behaviors toward society; often used to describe youth who belong to gangs and participate in delinquent subcultures.

Sonicguide.   Electronic mobility device worn on the head by people who are blind; emits ultrasound and converts reflections for objects into audible noise.

Spasticity.   Condition characterized by involuntary contractions of various muscle groups.

Special day schools.   See **Special schools**

Special education.   Specially designed instruction provided to students with disabilities in all settings (e.g., the classroom, physical education, at home, in the hospital) (as defined in IDEA).

Special education classroom.   Educational placement option for students with disabilities in which they are removed to separate classroom settings and taught under the supervision of qualified special educators for most of the day; integration is provided as appropriate for the student; individual needs are addressed through specialized instruction.

Special schools.   Educational placement option for students with disabilities in which they attend separate schools (i.e., away from nondisabled peers) that have been designed specifically to address individual students' needs.

Speech.   Audible production of language; a component of communication. See also **Communication; Language**

Speech and language disorders.   Conditions characterized by difficulty in communicating effectively. See also **Speech disorders**

Speech disorders.   Conditions characterized by speech behavior that is sufficiently deviant from normal or accepted speaking patterns; adversely affect communication for the speaker and/or listener.

Spina bifida.   Condition characterized by a developmental defect of the spinal column; congenital.

Spina bifida cystica.   Condition characterized by a malformation of the spinal column in which a tumorlike sac grows on the infant's back.

Spina bifida meningocele.   Condition characterized by cystic swelling or growth of a tumorlike sac that contains spinal fluid but no nerve tissue.

Spina bifida myelomeningocele.   Condition characterized by cystic swelling or growth of a tumorlike sac that contains both spinal fluid and nerve tissue.

Spina bifida occulta.   Condition characterized by an oblique slit present in one or several of the vertebral structures; a very mild condition of spina bifida.

Spinal cord injury.   Condition characterized by traumatization or severance of the spinal cord.

Spinal meningitis.   Condition characterized by inflammation of the membranes of the spinal cord.

Standard deviation.   Statistical measure of the amount an individual score deviates from average.

Stanford-Binet Intelligence Scale.   Standardized individual intelligence test; originally the Binet-Simon Scales, which were revised and standardized by Lewis Terman at Stanford University (1916).

Stapedectomy.   Surgical procedure in which a defective stapes is replaced with a prosthetic device to restore hearing.

Sterilization.   Process of making an individual unable to reproduce; usually accomplished surgically.

Strabismus.   Condition characterized by eyes that look inward (internal, "crossed eyes") or outward (external).

Students at risk.   Students who have not been identified as disabled but are described as vulnerable to failure and need specialized instruction and/or support (e.g., those who drop out of school, live in poverty or are homeless, have no medical care, are abused and/or neglected, etc.); some definitions include students with disabilities.

Stuttering. Condition characterized by abnormal repetitions, blockages, or prolongations during speech.

Suicide. Act of taking one's own life.

Supported employment. Intervention approach based on paid work in integrated community settings for individuals with severe disabilities who are expected to need continuous support services and for whom competitive employment has traditionally not been possible.

Syntax. Rules governing sentence structure; the order in which word sequences are combined into phrases and sentences.

T

T lymphocytes. Type of white blood cell that attacks infections and aids in production of antibodies.

TDD systems. Telecommunication devices for people who are deaf (thus, the acronym TDD) that send, receive, and print messages between stations at distant locations.

Teacher assistance teams (TATs). See **Schoolwide assistance teams (SWATs)**

Teratogens. Substances or conditions that cause malformations to occur.

Test bias. Error introduced during testing when a procedure or test instrument gives one group a particular advantage or disadvantage; usually involves factors unrelated to ability, such as culture, gender, and race. See also **Measurement bias**

Therapeutic abortion. Termination of pregnancy after a defect is found in the fetus during prenatal evaluation.

Tic disorders. Conditions characterized by stereotypical movements or vocalizations that are involuntary, rapid, and recurrent.

Tinnitus. Condition characterized by high-pitched throbbing or ringing sounds; associated with disease of the inner ear.

Token reinforcement systems. Instructional approach in which students may earn tokens (i.e., tangible items, such as chips, marbles, checkmarks) and exchange them for rewards (e.g., activities, food items, prizes, special privileges) for positive behavior changes.

Tonic/clonic seizures. Conditions characterized by stiffening of the body followed by repeated rapid muscle contractions and relaxations (extreme shaking); the entire brain is affected; formerly called *grand mal seizures*.

Tonic. Describes the phase of a seizure in which the entire body becomes very rigid and stiff.

Total communication. Communication approach that employs various combinations of elements from manual, oral, and other techniques; used by people with hearing impairments to facilitate understanding.

Toxoplasmosis. Condition characterized by infection caused by protozoa carried in raw meat and fecal material.

Transdisciplinary. Describes the team approach using a primary therapist or teacher; team members cooperate during assessment and program planning; implementation of instruction is usually carried out by one team member with collaboration and support from others.

Transducer. Device that receives energy from one system and retransmits it to another, often in a different form; used in cochlear implants to alter sound into electric nerve-stimulating signals. See also **Cochlear implant**

Transfer of training. Process of generalizing behaviors or skills learned in one setting to others.

Transition from school to adult life. Adjustment period for individuals with disabilities between leaving school and entering adult life. See **Transition plan; Transition services**

Transition plan. Individualized plan for a student with a disability that includes a statement of the services needed to facilitate his or her leaving school and entering adult life.

Transition services. Coordinated services for students with disabilities that facilitate the transition from school to adult life; factors considered include employment, further education, vocational training, independent living, and community participation; required by IDEA.

Traumatic brain injury (TBI). Condition characterized by direct injuries to the brain, either generalized (closed head) or focal (open head) (e.g., tearing of nerve fibers, bruising of brain tissue against the skull, brain stem trauma, swelling).

Triplegia. Condition characterized by paralysis of three appendages, usually both legs and one arm.

Trisomy 21. Type of Down syndrome in which the chromosomal pairs do not separate properly during the formation of sperm or egg cells, resulting in an extra chromosome on the twenty-first pair; all called *nondisjunction*.

Tuberous sclerosis. Condition characterized by tumors on many organs and related to mental retardation in about 66 percent of all cases.

Tunnel vision. Condition characterized by a restricted field of vision that is 20 degrees or less at its widest angle.

Type I diabetes. Condition characterized by nonexistent or insufficient production of insulin by the pancreas; a type of diabetes. See also **Diabetes mellitus**

Type II diabetes. Condition characterized by insufficient or ineffective production of insulin by the pancreas; a type of diabetes.

U

Ultrasound. Prenatal evaluation procedure in which high-frequency sound waves are bounced through the mother's abdomen to record tissue densities; may be used in prenatal assessment to locate fetal abnormalities.

Undifferentiated attention–deficit disorder (UADD). Condition characterized by a child's difficulty in maintaining attention because of limited ability to concentrate; exhibit impulsive actions but not hyperactive behavior. See also **Attention–deficit hyperactivity disorder**

V

Verbalism. Condition characterized by the excessive use of speech (wordiness) in which individuals use words that have little meaning to them.

Vermis. Cerebellum portion of the brain that appears to be underdeveloped in individuals with autism.

Vestibular mechanism. Structure in the inner ear containing three semicircular canals filled with fluid; sensitive to movement and assists the body in maintaining equilibrium.

Visual acuity. Sharpness or clearness of vision.

Visual discrimination. Ability to distinguish one visual stimulus from another.

Visual impairment. Condition characterized by loss of sight; includes conditions in which individuals are partially sighted and also blind.

Visually handicapped. See **Visual impairment**

Vitreous fluid. Jellylike substance that fills most of the interior of the eye.

Voice disorders. Conditions characterized by unusual or abnormal acoustical qualities of speech.

Voice problems. See **Voice disorders**

References

Chapter One

Aloia, G. F., & MacMillan, D. L. (1983). Influence of the EMR label on initial expectations of regular-classroom teachers. *American Journal of Mental Deficiency, 88*(3), 255–262.

Baird, J. L., & Workman, D. S. (1986). *Towards Solomon's mountain*. Philadelphia, PA: Temple University Press.

Bak, J. J., Cooper, E. M., Dobroth, K. M., & Siperstein, G. N. (1987). Special class placements as labels: Effects on children's attitudes toward learning handicapped peers. *Exceptional Children, 54*(2), 151–155.

Baron, R. A., & Byrne, D. (1991). *Social psychology: Understanding human interaction* (6th ed.). Boston: Allyn and Bacon.

Binet, A., & Simon, T. (1905). Methodes nouvelles pour le diagnostic du niveau ellectual des anormaux. *L'Annee Psychologique, 11*, 191–244.

Bogdan, R. (1986). The sociology of special education. In R. J. Morris & B. Blatt (Eds.), *Special education: Research and trends* (pp. 344–359). Elmsford, NY: Pergamon Press.

Brown v. Topeka, Kansas, Board of Education. (1954). 347 U.S. 483.

Carlson, N. R. (1990). *Psychology: The science of behavior*. Boston: Allyn and Bacon.

Cassidy, V. M., & Stanton, J. E. (1959). *An investigation of factors involved in the educational placement of mentally retarded children: A study of differences between children in special and regular classes in Ohio*. (U.S. Office of Education Cooperative Research Program, Project No. 043). Columbus: Ohio State University.

Cowen, E. (1973). Social and community interventions. In P. H. Mussen & M. R. Rosenzweig (Eds.), *Annual review of psychology* (Vol. 24) (pp. 423–472). Palo Alto, CA: Annual Reviews.

Danielsen, L. C., & Bellamy, G. T. (1989). State variation in placement of children with handicaps in segregated environments. *Exceptional Children, 55*(5), 448–455.

Davis, W. E., & McCaul, E. J. (1991). *The emerging crisis: Current and projected status of children in the United States* (Monograph). Orono, ME: Institute for the Study of At-Risk Students.

Dotter, D. L., & Roebuck, J. B. (1988). The labeling approach re-examined: Interactionism and the components of deviance. *Deviant Behavior, 9*(1), 19–32.

Drew, C. J., Logan, D. R., & Hardman, M. L. (1992). *Mental retardation: Life cycle approach* (4th ed.). St. Louis: Mosby.

Fiedler, C. R., & Simpson, R. L. (1987). Modifying the attitudes of nonhandicapped high school students toward handicapped peers. *Exceptional Children, 53*(4), 342–349.

Fink, D. (1988). *School-age children with special needs: What do they do when school is out?* Boston: Exceptional Parent Press.

Foster, G. G., Ysseldyke, J. E., & Reese, J. H. (1975). I wouldn't have seen it if I hadn't believed it. *Exceptional Children, 41*(7), 469–473.

Goddard, J. J. (1912). *The Kallikak family: A study in the heredity of feeblemindedness*. New York: Macmillan.

Graham, S., & Dwyer, A. (1987). Effects of the learning disability label, quality of writing performance, and examiner's level of expertise on the evaluation of written products. *Journal of Learning Disabilities, 20*(5), 317–318.

Harkin, T. (1990). Responses to issues raised about the Americans with Disabilities Act of 1990. Washington, D.C.: United States Senate.

Harris, L., & Associates. (1987). *International Center for the Disabled survey II: Employing disabled Americans*. New York: Author.

Harris, L., & Associates. (1989). *International Center for the Disabled survey III: A report card on special education*. New York: Author.

Homeward Bound v. Hissom Memorial Center (1988). 85-C-437-E. U.S. District Court, North District, Oklahoma.

James, W. (1890). *Principles of psychology*. New York: Henry Holt.

Johnson, G. O. (1961). *A comparative study of the personal and social adjustment of mentally handicapped children placed in special classes with mentally handicapped children who remain in regular classes*. Syracuse, NY: Syracuse University Research Institute, Office of Research in Special Education and Rehabilitation.

Johnson, G. O. (1962). Special education for the mentally handicapped— A paradox. *Exceptional Children, 29*, 62–69.

Jordan, A. M. (1959). Personal-social traits of mentally handicapped children. In T. G. Thurstone (Ed.), *An evaluation of educating mentally handicapped children in special classes and regular classes*. Chapel Hill: School of Education, University of North Carolina.

Kammeyer, K. C. W., Ritzer, G., & Yetman, N. T. (1990). *Sociology: Experiencing changing societies*. Boston: Allyn and Bacon.

Lakin, K. C., & Bruininks, R. J. (1985). Contemporary services for handicapped children and youth. In R. H. Bruininks and K. C. Lakin (Eds.), *Living and learning in the least restrictive environment* (pp. 3–22). Baltimore: Paul H. Brookes.

Leitch, D., & Sodhi, S. S. (1986). "Specialness" of special education. *British Columbia Journal of Special Education, 10*(4), 349–358.

Levin, H. M. (1988). *Accelerated schools for at-risk students* (CPRE Research Report Series, RR-010). New Brunswick, NJ: Center for Policy Research Education.

McCleary, I. D., Hardman, M. L., & Thomas, D. (1990). International special education. In T. Husen & T. N. Postlewaire (Eds.), *International encyclopedia of education: Research and studies* (pp. 608–615). New York: Pergamon Press.

Mills v. District of Columbia Board of Education. (1972). 348 F. Supp. 866 (D.D.C.).

National Commission on Excellence in Education. (1983). *A nation at risk: The imperative for educational reform*. Washington, DC: Author.

National Council on Disability. (1986). *Toward independence*. Washington, DC: Author.

National School Boards Association. (1989). *An equal chance: Educating at-risk children to succeed*. Alexandria, VA: Author.

Natriello, G., McDill, E. L., & Pallas, A. M. (1990). *Schooling disadvantaged children: Racing against catastrophe*. New York: Teachers College Press, Columbia University.

New *Individuals with Disabilities Education Act*. (1991, February 27). *Education of the Handicapped*. Alexandria, VA: Capitol Publications.

Organization for Economic Cooperation and Development (OECD). (1986). *Young people with handicaps: The road to adulthood*. Paris, France: Author.

Pennhurst State School and Hospital v. Halderman. (1981). 451 U.S. 1.

Pennsylvania Association for Retarded Citizens v. Commonwealth of Pennsylvania. (1971). 334 F. Supp. 1257 (E.D.Pa. 1971).

Peterson, B. (1988, December 10). Special student can't get after-school care. *Gastonia Gazette*.

Polloway, E. A. (1984). The integration of mildly retarded students in the schools: A historical review. *Remedial and Special Education, 5*(4), 18–28.

Resnick, L. B. (1987). Learning in school and out. *Educational Researcher, 16*(9), 13–20.

Reynolds, M. C., Wang, M. C., & Walberg, H. J. (1987). The necessary restructuring of special and regular education. *Exceptional Children, 53*(5), 391–398.

Robinson, B. E., Rowland, B. H., & Coleman, M. (1986). *Latchkey kids: Unlocking doors for children and their families*. Lexington, MA: Lexington Books.

Robinson, B. E., Rowland, B. H., & Coleman, M. (1989). *Home-alone kids: The working parent's complete guide to providing the best care for your child*. Lexington, MA: Lexington Books.

Rosenhan, D. L. (1973). On being sane in insane places. *Science, 179,* 250–258.

Rosenthal, R. (1987). Pygmalion effects: Existence, magnitude, and social importance. *Educational Researcher, 16*(9), 37–41.

Rosenthal, R., & Jacobsen, L. (1968). *Pygmalion in the classroom*. New York: Holt, Rinehart & Winston.

Rowland, B. H., & Robins, B. E. (1991, Spring). Latchkey kids with special needs. *Teaching Exceptional Children, 23*(3), 34–35.

Serving handicapped children: A special report. (1988). Princeton: NJ: The Robert Wood Johnson Foundation.

Smith, R. W., Osborne, L. T., Crim, D., & Rhu, A. H. (1986). Labeling theory as applied to learning disabilities. *Journal of Learning Disabilities, 19*(4), 195–202.

Thurstone, T. G. (1959). *An evaluation of educating mentally handicapped children in special classes and regular classes* (U.S. Office of Education, Cooperative Research Project No. OE-SAE 6452). Chapel Hill: University of North Carolina.

U.S. Department of Education. (1991). To assure the free appropriate public education of all handicapped children. *Thirteenth annual report to Congress on the implementation of the Education for All Handicapped Children Act*. Washington, DC: U.S. Government Printing Office.

U.S. Department of Labor. (1982). *Employers and child care: Establishing services through the workplace* (Pamphlet No. 23). Washington, DC: U.S. Government Printing Office.

Van Bourgondien, M. E. (1987). Children's responses to retarded peers as a function of social behaviors, labeling and age. *Exceptional Children, 53*(5), 432–439.

Watson, J. B., & Rayner, R. (1920). Conditioned emotional reactions. *Journal of Experimental Psychology, 3,* 1–14.

West, J. (1991). Implementing the act: Where do we begin? In J. West (Ed.), *The Americans with Disabilities Act: From policy to practice* (pp. xi–xxxi). New York: Millbank Memorial Fund.

Westling, D. L. (1986). *Introduction to mental retardation*. Englewood Cliffs, NJ: Prentice Hall.

Wineburg, S. S. (1987). The self-fulfillment of the self-fulfilling prophecy. *Educational Researcher, 16*(9), 28–37.

Wyatt v. Stickney. (1972). 344 F. Supp. 387, 344 F. Supp.4 373 (M.D.Ala. 1972).

Youngberg v. Romeo. (1982). No. 80-1429 U.S.

Ysseldyke, J. E., & Foster, G. G. (1978). Bias in teachers' observations of emotionally disturbed and learning disabled children. *Exceptional Children, 44*(8), 613–615.

Chapter Two

Baca, L. M., & Cervantes, H. T. (1989). *The bilingual special education interface* (2nd ed.). St. Louis, MO: Mosby.

Barresi, J. G. (1982). Educating handicapped migrants: Issues and options. *Exceptional Children, 48,* 473–488.

Bedell, F. D. (1989, June 7–8). Testimony delivered at hearings conducted by the National Council on the Handicapped, Washington DC.

Brooks-Gunn, J., & Furstenberg, F. F. (1986). The children of adolescent mothers: Physical, academic and psychological outcomes. *Developmental Review, 6,* 224–251.

Burt, C. (1921). *Mental and scholastic tests*. London: King.

Cattell, R. B. (1940). A culture-free intelligence test, I. *Journal of Educational Psychology, 31,* 161–180.

Cattell, R. B., Feingold, S. N., & Sarason, S. B. (1941). A culture-free intelligence test, II. Evaluation of cultural influences on test performance. *Journal of Educational Psychology, 32,* 81–100.

Children's Defense Fund. (1990a). *Children 1990: A report card, briefing book, and action primer*. Washington, DC: Author.

Children's Defense Fund. (1990b). *S.O.S. America: A children's defense budget*. Washington, DC: Author.

Collier, C., & Hoover, J. J. (1987). Sociocultural considerations when referring minority children for learning disabilities. *Learning Disabilities Focus, 3,* 39–45.

Correa, V. I. (1987). Working with Hispanic parents of visually impaired children: Cultural implications. *Journal of Visual Impairment and Blindness, 81,* 260–264.

Davis, W. E., & McCaul, E. J. (1991). *The emerging crisis: Current and projected status of children in the United States*. Orono, ME: Institute for the Study of At-Risk Students, University of Maine.

Diana v. State Board of Education. (1970, 1973). C-70, 37 RFP (N.D. Cal., 1970, 1973).

Drew, C. J. (1973). Criterion-referenced and norm-referenced assessment of minority group children. *Journal of School Psychology, 11,* 323–329.

Drew, C. J., Logan, D. R., & Hardman, M. L. (1992). *Mental retardation: A life-cycle approach* (5th ed.). Columbus, OH: Merrill.

Duran, R. P. (1989). Assessment and instruction of at-risk Hispanic students. *Exceptional Children, 56,* 154–158.

Elbert, J. C. (1984). Training in child diagnostic assessment: A survey of clinical psychology graduate programs. *Journal of Clinical Child Psychology, 13,* 122–133.

Field, T. (1980). Interactions of preterm and term infants with their lower and middle class teenage and adult mothers. In T. Field, S. Goldberg, D. Stern, & A. Sostek (Eds.), *High-risk infants and children: Adult and peer interactions.* New York: Academic Press.

Figueroa, R. A. (1989). Psychological testing of linguistic-minority students: Knowledge gaps and regulations. *Exceptional Children, 56,* 145–152.

Fishgrund, J. E., Cohen, O. P., & Clarkson, R. L. (1987). Hearing-impaired children in Black and Hispanic families. *Volta Review, 89*(5), 59–67.

Fradd, S. H., & Correa, V. I. (1989). Hispanic students at risk: Do we abdicate or advocate? *Exceptional Children, 56,* 105–110.

Fradd, S. H., Figueroa, R. A., & Correa, V. I. (1989). Meeting the multicultural needs of Hispanic students in special education. *Exceptional Children, 56,* 102–103.

Garcia, R. L. (1978). *Fostering a pluralistic society through multiethnic education.* Bloomington, IN: Phi Delta Kappa Educational Foundation.

Gelfand, D. M., Jenson, W. R., & Drew, C. J. (1988). *Understanding child behavior disorders* (2nd ed.). New York: Holt, Rinehart & Winston.

Gollnick, D. M., & Chinn, P. C. (1990). *Multicultural education in a pluralistic society.* (3rd ed.). Columbus, OH: Merrill.

Harry, B. (1992). *Cultural diversity, families, and the special education system: Communication and empowerment.* New York: Teachers College Press.

Heath, F., & Heath, B. *Language in the U.S.A.* Cited by C. J. Ovando (1989), Language diversity and education, in J. A. Banks & C. A. Banks (Eds.), *Multicultural education: Issues and perspectives.* Boston: Allyn and Bacon.

Hernandez, H. (1989). *Multicultural education: A teacher's guide to content and process.* Columbus, OH: Merrill.

Heward, W. L., & Orlansky, M. D. (1988). *Exceptional children* (3rd ed.). Columbus, OH: Merrill.

Hilliard, A. (1980). Cultural diversity and special education. *Exceptional Children, 46,* 584–588.

Hunter, B. (1982). Policy issues in special education for migrant students. *Exceptional Children, 48,* 469–472.

Kaufman, A. S. (1979) *Intelligence testing with the WISC-R.* New York: Wiley/Interscience.

Langdon, H. W. (1989). Language disorder or difference? Assessing the language skills of Hispanic students. *Exceptional Children, 56,* 160–167.

Larry P. v. Riles. (1972). C-71-2270 US.C, 343 F. Supp. 1306 (N.D. Cal. 1972).

Larry P. v. Riles. (1979). 343 F. Supp. 1306, 502 F.2d 963 (N.D. Cal. 1979).

Leung, B. (1987, February 20–22). *Cultural considerations in working with Asian parents.* Paper presented at the conference of the National Center for Clinical Infant Programs, Los Angeles.

Lopez, S. (1988). The empirical basis of ethnocultural and linguistic bias in mental health evaluations of Hispanics. *American Psychologist, 43,* 1095–1096.

Luftig, R. L. (1989). *Assessment of learners with special needs.* Boston: Allyn and Bacon.

Magrab, P. R., Sostek, A.M., & Powell, B. A. (1984). Prevention in the prenatal period. In M. C. Roberts & L. Peterson (Eds.), *Prevention of problems in childhood: Psychological research and applications.* New York: Wiley/Interscience.

Malgady, R. G., Rogler, L. H., & Constantino, G. (1987). Ethnocultural and linguistic bias in mental health evaluation of Hispanics. *American Psychologist, 42,* 228–234.

Manion, M. L., & Bersani, H. A. (1987). Mental retardation as a Western sociological construct: A crosscultural analysis. *Disability, Handicap, and Society, 2,* 231–245.

Mattes, L. J., & Omark, D. R. (1984). *Speech and language assessment for the bilingual handicapped.* San Diego: College-Hill Press.

McDavis, R. J. (1980). The black client. In N. A. Vacc & J. P. Wittmer (Eds.), *Let me be me: Special populations and the helping profession* (pp. 151–174). Muncie, IN: Accelerated Development.

Merton, R. K. (1948). The self-fulfilling prophecy. *Antioch Review, 8,* 193–210.

Merton, R. K. (1987). Three fragments from a sociologist's notebooks: Establishing the phenomenon, specified ignorance, and strategic research materials. *Annual Review of Sociology, 13,* 1–28.

Miller-Jones, D. (1989). Culture and testing. *American Psychologist, 44,* 360–366.

Morrow, R. D. (1987). Cultural differences—Be aware! *Academic Therapy, 23,* 143–149.

National Foundation for the Improvement of Education. (1982). *Bilingual education fact sheets, Public education strategies: Bilingual education.* Washington, DC: Author.

Natriello, G., McDill, E. L., & Pallas, A. M. (1990). *Schooling disadvantaged children: Racing against catastrophe.* New York: Teachers College Press.

Pai, Y. (1990). *Cultural foundations of education.* Columbus, OH: Merrill.

Patton, J. R., Payne, J. S., Kauffman, J. M., Brown, G. B., & Payne, R. A. (1987). *Exceptional children in focus.* Columbus, OH: Merrill.

Pepper, F. C. (1976). Teaching the American Indian child in mainstream settings. In R. L. Jones (Ed.), *Mainstreaming and the minority child* (pp. 133–158). Reston, VA: Council for Exceptional Children.

Prasse, D. P., & Reschly, D. J. (1986). Larry P.: A case of segregation, testing, or program efficacy? *Exceptional Children, 52,* 333–346.

Raven, J. C. (1938). *Guide to using the progressive matrices.* London: H. H. Lewis.

Reynolds, C. R. (1987). Race bias in testing. In R. J. Corsini (Ed.), *Concise encyclopedia of psychology* (pp. 953–954). New York: Wiley.

Reynolds, C. R., & Brown, R. T. (1984). *Perspectives on bias in mental testing.* New York: Plenum.

Roberts, E., & DeBlassie, R. R. (1983). Test bias and the culturally different early adolescent. *Adolescence, 18,* 837–843.

Rodriguez, F. (1982). Mainstreaming a multicultural concept into special education: Guidelines for teacher trainers. *Exceptional Children, 49,* 220–227.

Rosenthal, R. (1987). Pygmalion effects: Existence, magnitude and social importance. *Educational Researcher, 16*(9), 37–41.

Rosenthal, R., & Jacobson, L. (1968a). *Pygmalion in the classroom: Teacher expectation and pupils' intellectual development.* New York: Holt, Rinehart & Winston.

Rosenthal, R., & Jacobson, L. (1968b). Self-fulfilling prophecies in the classroom: Teachers' expectations as unintended determinants of pupils' intellectual competence. In M. Deutsch, I. Katz, & A. R. Jensen (Eds.), *Social class, race, and psychological development* (pp. 219–253). New York: Holt, Rinehart & Winston.

Rosenthal, R., & Jacobson, L. (1968c). Teacher expectations for the disadvantaged. *Scientific American, 218,* 19–23.

Salend, S. J., Michael, R. J., & Taylor, M. (1984). Competencies necessary for instructing migrant handicapped students. *Exceptional Children, 51,* 50–55.

Skowronski, J. J., & Carlston, D. E. (1989). Negativity and extremity biases in impression formation: A review of explanations. *Psychological Bulletin, 105,* 131–142.

Slate, N. M. (1983). Nonbiases assessment of adaptive behavior: Comparison of three instruments. *Exceptional Children, 50,* 67–70.

Smith, R. D. (1987, February 20–22). *Multicultural considerations: Working with families of developmentally disabled and high-risk children: The Hispanic perspective.* Paper presented at the conference of the National Center for Clinical Infant Programs, Los Angeles.

Turner, A. (1987, February 20–22). *Multicultural considerations: Working with families of developmentally disabled and high-risk children: The Black perspective.* Paper presented at the conference of the National Center for Clinical Infant Programs, Los Angeles.

U.S. Bureau of the Census (1990). *Statistical abstract of the United States: 1990.* Washington, DC: U.S. Government Printing Office.

U.S. Commission on Civil Rights. (1980). *Characters in textbooks.* (Clearinghouse Publication 62). Washington, DC: U.S. Government Printing Office.

Wagner, M. (1989). *The transition experience of youths with disabilities: A report from the national longitudinal transition study.* Menlo Park, CA: SRI International.

Wineburg, S. S. (1987). The self-fulfillment of the self-fulfilling prophecy. *Educational Researcher, 16*(9), 28–37.

Wood, F. H., Johnson, J. L., & Jenkins, J. R. (1986). The *Lora* case: Nonbiased referral, assessment, and placement procedures. *Exceptional Children, 52,* 323–331.

Yacobacci-Tam, P. (1987). Interacting with the culturally different family. *Volta Review, 89*(5), 46–58.

Chapter Three

Allington, R., & McGill-Franzen, A. (1989). Different programs, indifferent instruction. In D. K. Lipksky & A. Gartner (Eds.), *Beyond separate education: Quality education for all.* Baltimore: Paul H. Brookes.

Association for Persons with Severe Handicaps (TASH). (1990, November). Testimony on future directions for research presented to the U.S. Department of Education, National Institute on Disability and Rehabilitation Research. Washington, DC: Author.

Baker, G. (1990). Peer tutoring: A growth experience for both sides. *Special Educator, 2*(2), 3.

Bennett, T., Lingerfelt, B. V., & Nelson, D. E. (1990). *Developing individualized family support plans.* Cambridge, MA: Brookline.

Blalock, G. (1988). Transitions across the lifespan. In B. L. Ludlow, A. P. Turnbull, & R. Luckasson (Eds.), *Transitions to adult life for people with mental retardation—Principles and practices* (pp. 3–20). Baltimore: Paul H. Brookes.

Bloom, B. S. (1964). *Stability and change in human characteristics.* New York: Wiley & Sons.

Braaten, S., Kauffman, J., Braaten, B., Polsgrove, L., & Nelson, C. M. (1988). The regular education initiative: Patent medicine for behavioral disorders. *Exceptional Children, 55*(1), 21–27.

Brimer, R. W. (1990). *Students with severe disabilities: Current perspectives and practices.* Mountain View, CA: Mayfield.

Brinker, R. P. (1985). Interactions between severely mentally retarded students and other students in integrated and segregated public school settings. *American Journal of Mental Deficiency, 89*(6), 587–594.

Brolin, D. E. (1982). *Vocational preparation of persons with handicaps* (2nd ed.). Columbus, OH: Merrill.

Casto, G., & Mastropieri, M. A. (1985). *The efficacy of early intervention programs for handicapped children: A meta-analysis.* Logan, UT: Early Intervention Research Institute.

Casto, G., & White, K. R. (1984). The efficacy of early intervention programs with environmentally at-risk infants. *Journal of Children in Contemporary Society, 17,* 37–48.

Edgar, E. (1987). Secondary programs in special education: Are many of them justifiable? *Exceptional Children, 53,* 555–561.

Florian, L., & West, J. (1991). Beyond access: Special education in America. *European Journal of Special Needs Education, 6*(2), 124–132.

Fuchs, D., & Fuchs, L. (1991). Framing the REI debate: Abolitionists versus conservationists. In J. W. Lloyd, N. N. Singh, & A. C. Repp (Eds.), *Regular education initiative: Alternative perspectives on concepts, issues, and models* (pp. 241–255). Sycamore, IL: Sycamore.

Garber, H. L., Hodge, J. D., Rynders, J., Dever, R., & Velu, R. (1991). The Milwaukee Project: Setting the record straight. *American Journal on Mental Retardation, 95*(5), 493–525.

Gartner, A., & Lipsky, D. K. (1987). Beyond special education: Toward a quality system for all students. *Harvard Educational Review, 57*(4), 367–395.

Gartner, A., & Lipsky, D. K. (1989). New conceptualization for special education. *European Journal of Special Needs Education, 4*(1), 16–21.

Giangreco, M. F., & Putnam, J. W. (1991). Supporting the education of students with severe disabilities in regular education environments. In L. H. Meyer, C. A. Peck, & L. Brown (Eds.), *Critical issues in the lives of people with severe disabilities* (pp. 245–270). Baltimore: Paul H. Brookes.

Gillet, P. K. (1987). Transition: A special education perspective. In R. N. Iacacone & R. A. Stodden (Eds.), *Transition issues and directions* (pp. 113–119). Reston, VA: Council for Exceptional Children.

Hansen, C. L., & Eaton, M. D. (1978). Reading. In N. G. Haring, T. C. Lovitt, M. D. Eaton, & C. L. Hansen (Eds.), *The fourth R: Research in the classroom.* Columbus, OH: Merrill.

Hanson, M. J., & Lynch, E. W. (1989). *Early intervention.* Austin, TX: Pro-Ed.

Harris, L., & Associates. (1987). *International Center for the Disabled survey of disabled Americans: Bringing disabled Americans into the mainstream.* New York: Author.

Hart, V. (1977). The use of many disciplines with the severely and profoundly handicapped. In E. Sontag, J. Smith, & N. Certo (Eds.), *Educational programming for the severely and profoundly handicapped* (pp. 391–396). Reston, VA: Council for Exceptional Children.

Hasazi, S. B., Gordon, L. R., & Roe, C. A. (1985). Factors associated with the employment status of handicapped youth exiting high school from 1975 to 1983. *Exceptional Children, 51,* 455–469.

Hasazi, S. B., Johnson, R. E., Hasazi, J., Gordon, L. R., & Hull, M. (1989). A statewide follow-up survey of high school exiters: A comparison of former students with and without handicaps. *Journal of Special Education, 23,* 243–255.

Hunt, J. M. (1961). *Intelligence and experience.* New York: Ronald Press.

Hutinger, P. L. (1988). Linking screening, identification, and assessment with curriculum. In J. Jordan, J. Gallagher, P. Hutinger, & M. Karnes (Eds.), *Early childhood special education: Birth to three* (pp. 29–66). Reston, VA: Council for Exceptional Children.

Individuals with Disabilities Education Act of 1990, PL 101–476, §602[a][19].

Jenkins, J. R., Pious, C. G., Jewell, M. (1990). Special education and the regular education initiative: Basic assumptions. *Exceptional Children, 56*(6), 479–491.

Kauffman, J. M. (1991). Restructuring in sociopolitical context: Reservations about the effects of current reform proposals on students with disabilities. In J. W. Lloyd, N. N. Singh, & A. C. Repp (Eds.), *The regular education initiative: Alternative perspectives on concepts, issues, and models* (pp. 57–66). Sycamore, IL: Sycamore.

Lipsky, D. K., & Gartner, A. (1991). Restructuring for quality. In J. W. Lloyd, N. N. Singh, & A. C. Repp (Eds.), *The regular education initiative: Alternative perspectives on concepts, issues, and models* (pp. 43–56). Sycamore, IL: Sycamore.

McDonnell, A. P., & Hardman, M. L. (1988). A synthesis of best practice guidelines for early childhood services. *Journal of the Division for Early Childhood, 12*(4), 328–341.

McDonnell, A. P., & Hardman, M. L. (1989). The desegregation of America's special schools: Strategies for change. *Journal of the Association for Persons with Severe Handicaps, 14*(1), 68–74.

McDonnell, J., & Hardman, M. L. (1985). Planning the transition of severely handicapped youth from school to adult services: A framework for high school programs. *Education and Training of the Mentally Retarded, 20*(4), 275–286.

McDonnell, J., Wilcox, B., & Boles, S. M. (1985). *Do we know enough to plan transition? A national survey of state agencies responsible for service to persons with severe handicaps.* Unpublished manuscript, University of Oregon, Eugene.

McDonnell, J., Wilcox, B., & Hardman, M. L. (1991). *Secondary programs for students with developmental disabilities.* Boston: Allyn and Bacon.

Meisels, S. J. (1985). The efficacy of early intervention: Why are we still asking this question? *Topics in Early Childhood Special Education, 5*(2), 1–11.

Miller, J. A., & Peterson, D. W. (1987). Peer influenced academic interventions. In C. A. Maher & J. E. Zins (Eds.), *Psychoeducational interventions in the schools: Methods and procedures for enhancing student competence.* Elmsford, NY: Pergamon Press.

Mithaug, D. E., Horiuchi, C. N., & Fanning, P. N. (1985). A report of the Colorado statewide follow-up of special education students. *Exceptional Children, 51,* 397–404.

Morsink, C. V., Thomas, C. C., & Correa, V. I. (1991). *Interactive teaming: Consultation and collaboration in special programs.* New York: Macmillan.

National Association of State Directors of Special Education. (1991). [Reference notes for understanding the forces at work which are driving social policy.] Washington, DC: Author.

National Council on Disability. (1989). *The education of students with disabilities: Where do we stand?* Washington, DC: Author.

Peterson, N. L. (1987). *Early intervention for handicapped and at-risk children.* Denver: Love.

Piaget, J. (1970). Piaget's theory. In P. H. Mussen (Ed.), *Carmichael's manual of child psychology* (3rd ed., Vol. 1). New York: Wiley.

Ramey, C. T., & Baker-Ward, L. (1982). Psychosocial retardation and the early experience paradigm. In D. D. Bricker (Ed.), *Intervention with at-risk and handicapped infants: From research to application.* Baltimore: University Park Press.

Ramey, C. T., & MacPhee, D. (1985). Development of retardation among the poor: A system theory perspective on risk and prevention. In D. C. Farran & J. D. McKinney (Eds.), *Risk in intellectual and psychological development.* New York: Academic Press.

Reaves, J., & Burns, J. (1982). *An analysis of the impact of the handicapped children's early education program* (Final Report No. 2 for Special Education Programs, U.S. Department of Education, Contract No. 300-81-0661). Washington, DC: Roy Littlejohn Associates.

Reynolds, M. C., & Birch, J. W. (1987). Noncategorical special education: Models for research and practice. In M. C. Wang, M. C. Reynolds, and H. J. Walberg (Eds.), *Handbook of special education research and practice: Vol. 1. Learner characteristics and adaptive education* (pp. 331–356). Oxford, England: Pergamon Press.

Reynolds, M. C., & Birch, J. W. (1988). *Adaptive mainstreaming* (3rd ed.). New York: Longman.

Sailor, W., Anderson, J. L., Halvorsen, A. T., Doering, K., Filler, J., & Goetz, L. (1989). *The comprehensive local school: Regular education for all students with disabilities.* Baltimore: Paul H. Brookes.

Sailor, W., Gerry, M., & Wilson, W. C. (1990). Disability and school integration. In T. Husen & T. N. Postlewaite (Eds.), *International encyclopedia of education: Research and Studies (2nd suppl.)* (pp. 158–163). New York: Pergamon Press.

Schutz, J. B., Carpenter, C. D., & Turnbull, A. P. (1991). *Mainstreaming exceptional students: A guide for classroom teachers.* Boston: Allyn and Bacon.

Seigel, J. S. (1980). On the demography of aging. *Demography, 17,* 345–364.

Snell, M. E. (1991). Schools are for all kids: The importance of integration for students with severe disabilities and their peers. In J. W. Lloyd, N. N. Singh, & A. C. Repp (Eds.), *The regular education initiative: Alternative perspectives on concepts, issues, and models* (pp. 133–148). Sycamore, IL: Sycamore.

Stainback, W., & Stainback, S. (1989). Practical organizational strategies. In S. Stainback, W. Stainback, & M. Forest (Eds.), *Educating all students in the mainstream of education* (pp. 71–87). Baltimore: Paul H. Brookes.

Stainback, W., & Stainback, S. (1991). Rationale for integration and restructuring: A synopsis. In J. W. Lloyd, N. N. Singh, & A. C. Repp (Eds.), *The regular education initiative: Alternative perspectives on concepts, issues, and models* (pp. 225–240). Sycamore, IL: Sycamore.

Stainback, S., Stainback, W., & Forest, M. (Eds.). (1989). *Educating all students in the mainstream of regular education.* Baltimore: Paul H. Brookes.

Strain, P. (1984). Efficacy research with young handicapped children: A critique of the status quo. *Journal of the Division for Early Childhood, 9,* 4–10.

U.S. Department of Education (1991). To assure the free appropriate public education of all handicapped children. *Thirteenth annual report to Congress on the implementation of the Education of the Handicapped Act.* Washington, DC: U.S. Government Printing Office.

Wagner, M. (1989). *The transition experiences of youth with disabilities: A report from the National Longitudinal Transition Study.* Menlo Park, CA: SRI International.

Walberg, H. J., & Wang, M. C. (1987). Effective educational practices and provisions for individual differences. In M. C. Wang, M. C. Reynolds, & H. J. Walberg (Eds.), *Handbook of special education: Research and practice:*

Vol. 1. Learner characteristics and adaptive education (pp. 113–128). Oxford, England: Pergamon Press.

Wang, M. C. (1989). Accommodating student diversity through adaptive instruction. In S. Stainback, W. Stainback, & M. Forest (Eds.), *Educating all students in the mainstream of education* (pp. 183–197). Baltimore: Paul H. Brookes.

Wehman, P., Kregal, J., & Barcus, J. M. (1985). From school to work: A vocational transition model for handicapped students. *Exceptional Children, 52*(1), 25–37.

Westlake, C. R., & Kaiser, A. P. (1991). Early childhood services for children with severe disabilities. In L. H. Meyer, C. A. Peck, & L. Brown (Eds.), *Critical issues in the lives of people with severe disabilities* (pp. 429–458). Baltimore: Paul H. Brookes.

White, B. L. (1975). *The first three years of life.* Englewood Cliffs, NJ: Prentice Hall.

White, K. R., Mastropieri, M. A., & Casto, G. (1984). An analysis of special education early-childhood education projects approved by the joint dissemination review panel. *Journal of the Division for Early Childhood Education, 9,* 11–26.

Will, M. (1986). Educating children with learning problems: A shared responsibility. *Exceptional Children, 52,* 411–415.

Will, M. (1984). *OSERS programming for the transition of youth with disabilities: Bridges from school to work life.* Washington, DC: Office of Special Education and Rehabilitative Services.

Zins, J. E., Curtis, M. J., Graden, J. L., & Ponti, C. R. (1988). *Helping students succeed in the regular classroom.* San Francisco: Jossey-Bass.

Chapter Four

Abroms, K. L., & Bennett, J. W. (1983). Current findings in Down's syndrome. *Exceptional Children, 49* 449–450.

Agran, M., Salzberg, C. L., & Stowitchek, J. (1987). An analysis of the effects of a social-skills training program using self-instructions on the acquisition and generalization of two social behaviors in a work setting. *Journal of the Association for Persons with Severe Handicaps, 12*(2), 131–139.

American Psychiatric Association. (1987). *Diagnostic and statistical manual of mental disorders* (3rd ed., rev.). Washington, DC: Author.

Bailey, D. B., & Wolery, M. (1989). *Assessing infants and preschoolers with handicaps.* Columbus, OH: Merrill.

Batshaw, M. L., & Perret, Y. M. (1986). *Children with handicaps: A medical primer* (2nd ed.). Baltimore: H. Brookes.

Bensberg, G., & Siegelman, C. (1976). Definitions and prevalence. In L. Lloyd (Ed.), *Communication, assessment, and intervention strategies.* Baltimore: University Park Press.

Best, J. W., & Kahn, J. V. (1989). *Research in education.* Englewood Cliffs, NJ: Prentice Hall.

Borkowski, J. G., & Cavanaugh, J. C. (1979). Maintenance and generalization of skills and strategies by the retarded. In N. R. Ellis (Ed.), *Handbook of mental deficiency: Psychological theory and research* (2nd ed.). Hillsdale, NJ: Erlbaum.

Borkowski, J. G., & Day, J. (1987). *Cognition in special children: Comparative approaches to retardation, learning disabilities, and giftedness.* Norwood, NJ: Ablex.

Borkowski, J. G., Peck, V. A., & Damberg, P. R. (1983). Attention, memory, and cognition. In J. L. Matson & J. A. Mulich (Eds.), *Handbook of mental retardation* (pp. 479–497). New York: Pergamon Press.

Brickey, M. P., Campbell, K. M., & Browning, L. J. (1985). A five-year follow-up of sheltered workshop employees placed in competitive jobs. *Mental Retardation, 20*(2), 52–57.

Brimer, R. W. (1990). *Students with severe disabilities: Current perspectives and practices.* Mountain View, CA: Mayfield.

Brooks, P. H., & McCauley, C. (1984). Cognitive research in mental retardation. *American Journal of Mental Deficiency, 88,* 479–486.

Browder, D. M., & Snell, M. E. (1987). Functional academics. In M. E. Snell (Ed.), *Systematic instruction of persons with severe handicaps* (pp. 436–468). Columbus, OH: Merrill.

Bruininks, R. H., & McGrew, K. (1987). *Exploring the structure of adaptive behavior.* Minneapolis: University Affiliated Program on Developmental Disabilities, University of Minnesota.

Curtis, J., & Riding, M. (1989). Special school programs as the least restrictive environment. *Special Educator, 9*(5), 6.

Drew, C. J., Logan, D. R., & Hardman, M. L. (1992). *Mental retardation: Life cycle approach* (5th ed.). Columbus, OH: Merrill.

Ellison, J. (1988). Court plan and order of deinstitutionalization. *Homeward Bound v. Hissom Memorial Center.* Case No. 85-C-437-E.

Fink, W. (1981). *The distribution of clients and their characteristics in programs for the mentally retarded and other developmentally disabled throughout Oregon.* Unpublished manuscript, Oregon Mental Health Division, Eugene.

Gentry, D., & Olson, J. (1985). Severely mentally retarded young children. In D. Bricker & J. Filler (Eds.), *Severe mental retardation: From theory to practice* (pp. 50–75). Lancaster, PA: Division on Mental Retardation of the Council for Exceptional Children.

Glidden, I. M. (1985). Semantic processing, semantic memory, and recall. In N. R. Ellis (Ed.), *International review of research in mental retardation* (Vol. 13, pp. 247–278). New York: Academic Press.

Grossman, H. J. (Ed.) (1983). *Manual on terminology and classification in mental retardation.* Washington, DC: American Association on Mental Deficiency.

Hallahan, D. P., & Reeve, R. E. (1980). Selective attention and distractibility. In B. K. Keogh (Ed.), *Advances in special education: Vol. 1. Basic constructs and theoretical orientations.* Greenwich, CT: JAI Press.

Halvorsen, A. T., & Sailor, W. (1990). Integration of students with severe and profound disabilities: A review of research. In R. Gaylord-Ross (Ed.), *Issues and research in special education* (pp. 110–172). New York: Teachers College Press.

Hardman, M. L. (1988). Educational services for students with severe disabilities: The movement toward social integration. *Special Educator, 9*(1), 9–10.

Hasazi, S., Johnson, R. E., Hasazi, J., Gordon, L. R., & Hull, M. (1989). Employment of youth with and without handicaps following school: Outcomes and correlates. *Journal of Special Education, 23,* 243–245.

Hetherington, E. M., & Parke, R. D. (1986). *Child psychology: A contemporary viewpoint* (3rd ed.). New York: McGraw-Hill.

Homeward Bound v. Hissom Memorial Center, 85-C-437-E, U. S. District Court, North District, Oklahoma. (1988).

Kaiser, A. P., Alpert, C. L., & Warren, S. (1987). Teaching functional language: Strategies for language intervention. In M. E. Snell (Ed.), *Systematic instruction of persons with severe handicaps* (pp. 247–272). Columbus, OH: Merrill.

Joseph P. Kennedy, Jr., Foundation. (1991). *Facts about mental retardation.* Washington, D. C.: Author.

Kirk, S. A. (1940). *Teaching reading to slow-learning children.* Boston: Houghton Mifflin.

Luckasson, R., Coulter, D., Polloway, E., Reiss, S., Schalock, R., Snoll, M., Spitalnik, D., & Stark, J. (1992). *Classification in mental retardation* (9th ed.). Washington, DC: American Association on Mental Retardation.

MacMillan, D. L. (1982). *Mental retardation in school and society* (2nd ed.). Boston: Little, Brown.

March of Dimes Birth Defects Foundation. (1991). *Public health education information sheet: Genetic series.* White Plains, NY: Author.

McDonald, A. C., Carson, K. L., Palmer, D. J., & Slay, T. (1982). Physician's diagnostic information to parents of handicapped neonates. *Mental Retardation, 20*(1), 12–14.

McDonnell, A., & Hardman, M. L. (1988). A synthesis of "best practice" guidelines for early childhood services. *Journal of the Division for Early Childhood, 12*(4), 328–341.

McDonnell, A., & Hardman, M. L. (1989). The desegregation of America's special schools: Strategies for change. *Journal of the Association for Persons with Severe Handicaps, 14*(1), 68–74.

McDonnell, J., Wilcox, B., & Hardman, M. L. (1991). *Secondary programs for students with developmental disabilities.* Boston: Allyn and Bacon.

Meyer, L. H., Peck, C. A., & Brown, L. (Eds.) (1991). *Critical issues in the lives of people with severe disabilities.* Baltimore: Paul H. Brookes.

Meyers, L. (n.d.). *Computer-enhanced language interventions.* Unpublished manuscript, PEAL Software, Calabasas, CA.

Miller, J. F. (1981). Early psycholinguistic acquisition. In R. L. Schiefelbusch & D. D. Bricker (Eds.), *Early language: Acquisition and intervention* (pp. 331–337). Baltimore: University Park Press.

Minton, L. (1990, October 14). Fresh voices: Have you changed in the last year? *Parade Magazine,* p. 24.

Moon, M. S., & Bunker, L. (1987). Recreation and motor skills programming. In M. E. Snell (Ed.), *Systematic instruction of persons with severe handicaps* (3rd ed.) (pp. 214–244). Columbus, OH: Merrill.

Mori, A. A., & Masters, L. F. (1980). *Teaching with severely mentally retarded.* Rockville, MD: Aspen.

National Academy of Sciences. (1975). *Genetic screening: Programs, principles, and research.* Washington, DC: Author.

National Association of State Directors of Special Education. (1991). Reference notes for understanding the forces at work which are driving social policy. Washington, DC: Author.

Nirje, B. (1970). The normalization principle and its human management implications. *Journal of Mental Subnormality, 16,* 62–70.

Patton, J. R., Beirne-Smith, J., & Payne, J. S. (1990). *Mental retardation* (3rd ed.). Columbus, OH: Merrill.

Payne, J. S., Polloway, E. A., Smith, J. E., & Payne, R. A. (1981). *Strategies for teaching the mentally retarded* (2nd ed.). Columbus, OH: Merrill.

Perske, R., & Perske, M. (1988). *Circles of friends.* Nashville: Abingdon Press.

Peterson, N. L. (1987). *Early intervention for handicapped and at-risk children: An introduction to early childhood-special education.* Denver: Love.

President's Commission for the Study of Ethical Problems in Medicine and Biomedical and Behavioral Research. (1983). *Securing access to health care.* Washington, DC: U.S. Government Printing Office.

Rantakallio, P., & von Wendt, L. (1986). Mental retardation and subnormality in a birth cohort of 12,000 children in Northern Finland. *American Journal of Mental Deficiency, 90,* 380–387.

Robinson, N. M., & Robinson, H. B. (1976). *The mentally retarded child: A psychological approach.* (2nd ed.). New York: McGraw-Hill.

Smith, J. D. (1988, September). A position statement on the right of children with mental retardation to life sustaining medical care and treatment. *CEC-MReport.*

Stainback, W., & Stainback, S. (1990). *Support networks for inclusive schooling.* Baltimore: Paul H. Brookes.

Sternberg, R. J., & Spear, I. C. (1985). A triarchic theory of mental retardation. In N. R. Ellis (Ed.), *International review of research in mental retardation* (Vol. 13, pp. 301–326). New York: Academic Press.

U.S. Department of Education (1991). To assure the free appropriate public education of all handicapped children. *Thirteenth annual report to Congress on the implementation of the Education of the Handicapped Act.* Washington, DC: U.S. Government Printing Office.

Van Riper, C. (1972). *Speech corrections: Principles and methods* (5th ed.). Englewood Cliffs, NJ: Prentice Hall.

Wehman, P., & Hill, J. W. (1985). *Competitive employment for persons with mental retardation: From research to practice* (Vol. 1). Richmond: Rehabilitation Research and Training Center, Virginia Commonwealth University.

Wehman, P., Moon, M. S., Everson, J. M., Wood, W., & Barcus, J. M. (1988). *Transition from school to work: New challenges for youth with severe disabilities.* Baltimore: Paul H. Brookes.

Westling, D. (1986). *Introduction to mental retardation.* Englewood Cliffs, NJ: Prentice Hall.

Zigler, E., & Balla, D. (1981). Issues in personality and motivation of mentally retarded persons. In M. J. Begab, H. C. Haywood, & H. L. Garber (Eds.), *Psychosocial influences in retarded performance: Vol. 1. Issues and theories in development.* Baltimore: University Park Press.

Chapter Five

Achenbach, T. M. (1966). The classification of children's psychiatric symptoms: A factor analytic study. *Psychological Monographs: General and Applied, 615,* 1–37.

Achenbach, T. M. (1988). Child behavior checklist for ages 4–16 (11-88 ed.). Burlington: University of Vermont.

Achenbach, T. M., & Edelbrock, C. S. (1981). Child behavior checklist for ages 4–16. Burlington: University of Vermont.

Ager, C. L., & Cole, C. L. (1991). A review of cognitive-behavioral interventions for children and adolescents with behavior disorders. *Behavior Disorders, 16*(4), 276–287.

American Psychiatric Association. (1980). *Diagnostic and statistical manual of mental disorders* (3rd ed.). Washington, DC: Author.

American Psychiatric Association. (1987). *Diagnostic and statistical manual of mental disorders* (3rd ed., rev.). Washington, DC: Author.

Amish, P. L., Gesten, E. L., Smith, J. K., Clark, H. B., & Stark, C. (1988). Social problem-solving training for severely emotionally disturbed and behaviorally disordered children. *Behavior Disorders, 13*(3), 175–186.

Associated Press News Service. (1989, June 11). Children and mental illness.

Bauer, A. M., & Shea, T. M. (1988). Structuring classrooms through level systems. *Focus on Exceptional Children, 21*(3), 1–12.

Benson, D., Edwards, L., Roseel, J., & White, M. (1986). Inclusion of socially maladjusted children and youth in legal definition of the behaviorally disordered population: A debate. *Behavior Disorders, 11*(3), 213–222.

Bower, E. M. (1959). The emotionally handicapped child and the school. *Exceptional Children, 26,* 6–11.

Bower, E. M. (1981). *Early identification of emotionally handicapped children in the school* (3rd ed.). Springfield, IL: Charles C Thomas.

Bower, E. M. (1982). Defining emotional disturbance: Public policy and research. *Psychology in the Schools, 19,* 55–60.

Brandenburg, N. A., Friedman, R. M., & Silver, S. E. (1990). The epidemiology of childhood psychiatric disorders: Prevalence findings from recent studies. *Journal of the American Academy of Child and Adolescent Psychiatry, 29,* 76–83.

Browne, A., & Finkelhor, D. (1986). Impact of child sexual abuse: A review of research. *Psychological Bulletin, 99,* 66–77.

Burchard, J. D., & Clark, R. T. (1990). The role of individualized care in a service delivery system for children and adolescents with severely maladjusted behavior. *Journal of Mental Health Administration, 17*(1), 48–60.

Burchard, J. D., Clark, R. T., & Hamilton, R. I. (1988, May). *Project Wraparound: A state-university partnership in training clinical psychologists to serve severely emotionally disturbed children.* National Conference on Clinical Psychology: Improving Psychological Services for Children and Adolescents with Severe Mental Disorders, Washington, DC.

Center, D. B. (1986). Educational programming for children and youth with behavior disorders. *Behavior Disorders, 11*(3), 208–211.

Center, D. B. (1989a). *Social maladjustment: An interpretation.* Paper presented at the 67th Annual International Conference of the Council for Exceptional Children, San Francisco.

Center, D. B. (1989b). Social maladjustment: Definition, identification and programming. *Focus on Exceptional Children, 22*(1), 1–12.

Center for Social Policy. (1990). *Kids count data book.* Washington, DC: Author.

Children's Defense Fund. (1989). *A vision for America's future: An agenda for the 1990s.* Washington, DC: Author.

Clarizio, H. (1987). Differentiating emotionally impaired from socially maladjusted students. *Psychology in the Schools, 24,* 237–243.

Cline, D. H. (1990). A legal analysis of policy initiatives to exclude handicapped/disruptive students from special education. *Behavioral Disorders, 15,* 159–173.

Coleman, M. C. (1986). *Behavior disorders: Theory and practice.* Englewood Cliffs, NJ: Prentice Hall.

Council for Children with Behavior Disorders. (1987). Position paper on definition and identification of students with behavior disorders. *Behavior Disorders, 13*(1), 9–19.

Council for Children with Behavior Disorders. (1989). *A new proposed definition and terminology to replace "serious emotional disturbance" in Education of the Handicapped Act.* Reston, VA: Author.

Council for Children with Behavior Disorders. (1990). *Position paper on the exclusion of children with conduct disorders and behavior disorders.* Reston, VA: Author.

Council for Exceptional Children. (1991). *Report of the CEC advocacy and governmental relations committee regarding the new proposed U.S. federal definition of serious emotional disturbance.* Reston, VA: Author.

Coutinho, M. (1986). Reading achievement of students identified as behaviorally disordered at the secondary level. *Behavior Disorders, 11*(3), 200–207.

Cullinan, D., & Epstein, M. H. (1986). Behavior disorders. In N. Haring (Ed.), *Exceptional children and youth* (4th ed.). Columbus, OH: Merrill.

Dowrick, P. (1988). Alaska youth initiative. In P. Greenbaum, R. Friedman, A. Duchnowski, K. Kutash, & S. Silver (Eds.), *Children's mental health services and policy: Building a research base.* Tampa: Florida Mental Health Institute.

Emery, R. E., Hetherington, E. M., & DiLalla, L. F. (1984). Divorce, children and social policy. In H. W. Stevenson & A. E. Siegel (Eds.), *Child development research and social policy* (Vol. 1). Chicago: University of Chicago Press.

Epstein, M. H., & Olinger, E. (1987). Use of medication in school programs for behaviorally disordered pupils. *Behavior Disorders, 12*(2), 138–145.

Etscheidt, S. E. (1991). Reducing aggressive behavior and improving self-control: A cognitive-behavioral treatment program for behaviorally disordered adolescents. *Behavior Disorders, 16*(2), 107–115.

Fiedler, J. F., & Knight, R. P. (1986). Congruence between assessed needs and IEP goals of identified behaviorally disabled students. *Behavior Disorders, 12*(1), 22–27.

Forest, M., & Pearpoint, J. (1990). Supports for addressing severe maladaptive behavior. In W. Stainback & S. Stainback (Eds.), *Support networks for inclusive schooling: Interdependent integrated education.* Baltimore: Paul H. Brookes.

Forness, S. R. (1988). Planning for the needs of children with serious emotional disturbance: The national special education and mental health coalition. *Behavior Disorders, 13*(2), 127–133.

Forness, S. R., & Kavale, K. A. (1988). Psychopharmacologic treatment: A note on classroom effects. *Journal of Learning Disabilities, 21*(3), 144–147.

Forness, S. R., & Knitzer, J. K. (1990). *A new proposed definition and terminology to replace "serious emotional disturbance" in the Education of the Handicapped Act.* Alexandria, VA: National Mental Health Association.

Freeman, B. M., & Ritvo, E. R. (1984). The syndrome of autism: Establishing the diagnosis and principles of management. *Pediatric Annals, 13,* 284–296.

Gadow, K. D. (1986). *Children on medication: Vol. I. Hyperactivity, learning disabilities, and mental retardation.* Reston, VA: Council for Exceptional Children.

Gelfand, D. M., Jenson, W. R., & Drew, C. J. (1988). *Understanding child behavior disorders* (2nd ed.). New York: Holt, Rinehart & Winston.

Goldstein, A. P., & Glick, B. (1987). *Aggression replacement training: A comprehensive intervention for aggressive youth.* Champaign, IL: Research Press.

Graubard, P. S. (1964). The extent of academic retardation in a residential treatment center. *Journal of Education Research, 58,* 78–80.

Guidubaldi, J., Perry, J. D., & Cleminshaw, H. K. (1984). The legacy of parental divorce: A nationwide study of family status and selected mediating variables on children's academic and social competencies. In B. B. Lahey & A. E. Kazdin (Eds.), *Advances in clinical child psychology* (Vol. 7). New York: Plenum.

Harris, K. R., & Pressley, M. (1991). The nature of cognitive strategy instruction: Interactive strategy construction. *Exceptional Children, 57*(5), 392–404.

Hobbs, N. (1965). How the Re-ED plan developed. In N. J. Long, W. C. Morse, & R. G. Newman (Eds.), *Conflict in the classroom.* Belmont, CA: Wadsworth.

Hofmeister, A. M., & Ferrara, J. M. (1986). *Artificial intelligence application in special education: How feasible?* (Final Report). Logan: Utah State University.

Jay, D. E., & Padilla, C. L. (1987). *Special education dropouts.* Menlo Park, CA: SRI International.

Juul, K. D. (1986). Epidemiological studies of behavior disorders in children: An international survey. *International Journal of Special Education, 1*(1), 1–20.

Kauffman, J. M. (1985). *Characteristics of children's behavior disorders* (3rd ed.). Columbus, OH: Merrill.

Kauffman, J. M. (1987). Strategies for the nonrecognition of social deviance. *Journal of Special Education, 11*(3), 201–214.

Kauffman, J. M. (1989). *Characteristics of behavior disorders of children and youth* (4th ed.). Columbus, OH: Merrill.

Kavale, K. A., Forness, S. R., & Alper, A. E. (1986). Research in behavioral disorders/emotional disturbance: A survey of subject identification criteria. *Behavior Disorders, 11*(3), 159–167.

Kazdin, A. E. (1985). *Treatment of antisocial behavior in children and adolescents.* Homewood, IL: Dorsey Press.

Kelly, E. J. (1988). *The differential problem sorter manual: Rationale and procedures distinguishing between conduct problems and emotionally disturbed students and populations.* Las Vegas: University of Nevada–Las Vegas.

Knapczyk, D. R. (1988). Reducing aggressive behaviors in special and regular class settings by training alternative social responses. *Behavior Disorders, 14*(1), 27–39.

Knitzer, J. (1982). *Unclaimed children: The failure of public responsibility to children and adolescents in need of mental health services.* Washington, DC: Children's Defense Fund.

Knitzer, J., Steinberg, Z., & Fleish, B. (1990). *At the schoolhouse door: An examination of programs and policies for children with behavioral and emotional problems.* New York: Bank Street College of Education.

MacFarlane, K. (1978). Sexual abuse of children. In J. Chapman and M. Gates (Eds.), *The victimization of women.* Beverly Hills: Sage.

McGinnis, E., Goldstein, A. P., Sprafkin, R. P., & Gershaw, N. J. (1984). *Skillstreaming the elementary school child: A guide for teaching prosocial skills.* Champaign, IL: Research Press.

Meichenbaum, D. H. (1977). *Cognitive-behavior modification: An integrative approach.* New York: Plenum.

Morgan, D. P., & Jenson, W. R. (1988). *Teaching behaviorally disordered students.* Columbus, OH: Merrill.

Morse, W. C., Cutler, R. L., & Fink, A. H. (1964). *Public school classes for emotionally handicapped: A research analysis.* Washington, DC: Council for Exceptional Children.

Neel, R. S., Meadows, N., Levine, R., & Edgar, E. B. (1988). What happens after special education: A statewide follow-up study of secondary students who have behavioral disorders. *Behavior Disorders, 13*, 209–216.

Nelson, C. M., Rutherford, R. B., Center, D. B., & Walker, H. M. (1991). Do public schools have an obligation to serve troubled children and youth? *Exceptional Children, 57*(5), 406–415.

Newcomer, P. L. (1980). *Understanding and teaching emotionally disturbed children.* Boston: Allyn and Bacon.

O'Donnell, L. (1980). Intraindividual discrepancy in diagnosing specific learning disabilities. *Learning Disability Quarterly, 3*(1), 10–18.

Olson, J., Algozzine, B., & Schmid, R. E. (1980). Mild, moderate, and severe: An empty distinction. *Behavior Disorders, 5*(2), 96–101.

Patterson, G. R., & Bank, L. (1986). Bootstrapping your way in the normological thicket. *Behavioral Assessment, 8*, 49–73.

Peacock Hill Working Group. (1990). *Problems and promises in special education and related services for children and youth with emotional and behavioral disorders.* Charlottesville, VA: Author.

Peterson, N. L. (1987). *Early intervention for handicapped and at-risk children: An introduction to early childhood-special education.* Denver: Love.

Quay, H. C. (1975). Classification in the treatment of delinquency and antisocial behavior. In N. Hobbs (Ed.), *Issues in the classification of children* (Vol. 1). San Francisco: Jossey-Bass.

Quay, H. C. (1979). Classification. In H. C. Quay & J. S. Werry (Eds.), *Psychopathological disorders of childhood* (2nd ed.). New York: Wiley.

Radl, S. (1976). Why you are shy and how to cope with it. *Glamour*, 64–84.

Ramsey, E., & Walker, H. M. (1988). Family management correlates of antisocial behavior among middle school boys. *Behavior Disorders, 13*(3), 187–201.

Rogeness, G. A., Amrung, S., Macedo, C. A., Harris, W. R., & Fisher, C. (1986). Psychopathology in abused or neglected children. *Journal of the American Academy of Child Psychiatry, 24*(5), 659–665.

Rubin, R. A., & Balow, B. (1978). Prevalence of teacher identified behavior problems: A longitudinal study. *Exceptional Children, 45*, 102–111.

Rutherford, R. B., Nelson, C. M., & Wolford, B. I. (1985). Special education in the most restrictive environment: Correctional/special education. *Journal of Special Education, 19*(1), 59–71.

Sandler, A. G., Arnold, L. B., Gable, R. A., & Strain, P. S. (1987). Effects of peer pressure on disruptive behavior of behaviorally disordered classmates. *Behavior Disorders, 12*(2), 104–110.

Sasso, G. M., Melloy, K. J., & Kavale, K. A. (1990). Generalization, maintenance, and behavioral covariation associated with social skills training through structured learning. *Behavioral Disorders, 16*(1), 9–22.

Schloss, P. J., Schloss, C. N., Wood, C. E., & Kiehl, W. S. (1986). A critical review of social skills with behaviorally disordered students. *Behavior Disorders, 12*(1), 1–14.

Scruggs, T. E., & Mastropieri, M. A. (1986). Academic characteristics of behaviorally disordered and learning disabled students. *Behavior Disorders, 11*(3), 184–190.

Scruggs, T. E., Mastropieri, M. A., Cook, S. B., & Escobar, C. (1986). Early intervention for children with conduct disorders: A qualitative synthesis of single-subject research. *Behavior Disorders, 11*(4), 260–271.

Simpson, R. L. (1987). Social interaction of behaviorally disordered children and youth: Where are we and where do we need to go? *Behavior Disorders, 12*(4), 292–298.

Slate, J. R., & Saudargas, R. A. (1986). Differences in the classroom behaviors of behaviorally disordered and regular class children. *Behavior Disorders, 12*(1), 45–53.

Slenkovitch, J. E. (1983). *P.L. 94-142 as applied to DSM III diagnoses: An analysis of DSM III diagnoses vis-a-vis special education law.* Cupertino, CA: Kinghorn.

Smith, C. R. (1985). Identification of handicapped children and youth: A state agency perspective on behavior disorders. *Remedial and Special Education, 6*(4), 34–41.

Stainback, S., & Stainback, W. (1980). *Educating children with severe maladaptive behaviors.* New York: Grune & Stratton.

Stainback, W., & Stainback, S. (1990). *Supportive networks for inclusive schooling.* Baltimore: Paul H. Brookes.

Stone, F., & Rowley, V. N. (1964). Educational disability in emotionally disturbed children. *Exceptional Children, 30,* 423–426.

Swartz, S. L., Mosley, W. J., Koenig-Jerz, G. (1987, April). *Diagnosing behavior disorders: An analysis of eligibility criteria and recommended procedures.* Paper presented at the Annual Convention of the Council for Exceptional Children, Chicago, IL.

Tamkin, A. S. (1960). A survey of educational disability in emotionally disturbed children. *Journal of Educational Research, 53,* 313–315.

U.S. Department of Education. (1991). To assure the free appropriate public education of all handicapped children. *Thirteenth annual report to Congress on the implementation of the Education of the Handicapped Act.* Washington, DC: Division of Educational Services, Special Education Programs.

U.S. Department of Health, Education, and Welfare. (1977, August 23). Education of Handicapped Children (Implementation of Part B of the Education of the Handicapped Act). *Federal Register, 42*(173), 42478.

VanDenBurg, J. (1989). The Alaska Youth Initiative: An experiment in individualized treatment and education. In A. Algarin, R. M. Friedman, A. J. Duchnowski, K. Kutash, S. E. Silver, & M. K. Johnson (Eds.), *Children's mental health services and policy: Building a research base.* Tampa: Research and Training Center for Children's Mental Health, Florida Mental Health Institute, University of South Florida.

Von Isser, A., Quay, H. C., & Love, C. T. (1980). Interrelationships among three measures of deviant behavior. *Exceptional Children, 46,* 272–276.

Vorrath, H. H., & Brendtro, L. K. (1985). *Positive peer culture* (2nd ed.). New York: Aldine.

Weinstein, L. (1969). Project, Re-ED schools for emotionally disturbed children: Effectiveness as viewed by referring agencies, parents, and teachers. *Exceptional Children, 35,* 703–711.

Wicks-Nelson, R., & Israel, A. C. (1984). *Behavior disorders of childhood.* Englewood Cliffs, NJ: Prentice Hall.

Wolf, M. M., Braukmann, C. J., & Ramp, K. A. (1987). Serious delinquent behavior as part of a significantly handicapping condition: Cures and supportive environments. *Journal of Applied Behavior Analysis, 20*(4), 347–359.

Chapter Six

Achenbach, T. M. (1986). How is a parent rating scale used in the diagnosis of attention deficit disorder? *Journal of Children in Contemporary Society, 19,* 19–31.

Ackerman, P. T., Anhalt, B. S., & Dykman, R. A. (1986). Arithmetic automation failure in children with attention and reading disorder. *Journal of Learning Disabilities, 19,* 222–232.

Agrawal, R., & Kaushal, K. (1987). Attention and short-term memory in normal children, aggressive children, and nonaggressive children with attention deficit disorder. *Journal of General Psychology, 114,* 335–344.

Aleman, S. R. (1990, July 2). *Attention deficit disorder—Issue for the reauthorization of the discretionary grant programs of the Education of the Handicapped Act (EHA).* Memorandum prepared by the Education and Public Welfare Division of the Congressional Research Service, Library of Congress, Washington, DC.

Aman, M. G., & Turbott, S. H. (1986). Incidental learning, distraction, and sustained attention in hyperactive and control subjects. *Journal of Abnormal Child Psychology, 14,* 441–455.

American Psychiatric Association. (1987). *Diagnostic and statistical manual of mental disorders* (3rd ed., rev.). Washington, DC: Author.

Anderson, R. C., Hiebert, E. H., Scott, J. A., & Wilkinson, I. A. G. (1985). *Becoming a nation of readers.* Washington, DC: National Institute of Education.

Associated Press News Service (1989, June 3). 750,000 children take stimulants researchers say.

August, G. J. (1987). Production deficiencies in free recall: A comparison of hyperactive, learning-disabled, and normal children. *Journal of Abnormal Child Psychology, 15,* 429–440.

Bailet, L. L. (1990). Spelling rule usage among students with learning disabilities and normally achieving students. *Journal of Learning Disabilities, 23,* 121–128.

Baxley, G. G., & LeBlanc, J. M. (1976). The hyperactive child: Characteristics, treatment, and evaluation of research design. In H. Reese (Ed.), *Advances in child development and behavior* (Vol. 11). New York: Academic Press.

Bennett, D. E., & Clarizio, H. F. (1988). A comparison of methods for calculating a severe discrepancy. *Journal of School Psychology, 26,* 359–369.

Benton, A. L., & Pearl, D. (Eds.). (1978). *Dyslexia: An appraisal of current knowledge.* New York: Oxford University Press.

Blankenship, C. S. (1988). Structuring the classroom for success. *Australian Journal of Special Education, 12*(2), 25–30.

Bonnet, K. A. (1989). Learning disabilities: A neurobiological perspective in humans. *Journal of Remedial and Special Education, 10,* 8–19.

Bos, C. S., & Filip, D. (1984). Comprehension monitoring in learning-disabled and average students. *Journal of Learning Disabilities, 17,* 229–233.

Brown, L. (1986). Assessing socioemotional development. In D. D. Hammill (Ed.), *Assessing the abilities and instructional needs of students* (pp. 502–609). Austin, TX: Pro-Ed.

Choate, J. S., & Rakes, T. A. (1989). *Reading: Detection and correcting special needs.* Boston: Allyn & Bacon.

Connolly, A. J. (1985). *KeyMath teach and practice.* Circle Pines, MN: American Guidance Service.

Coons, H. W., Klorman, R., & Borgstedt, A. D. (1987). Effects of methylphenidate on adolescents with a childhood history of attention deficit disorder. *Journal of the American Academy of Child and Adolescent Psychiatry, 26,* 368–374.

Cotungo, A. J. (1987). Cognitive control functioning in hyperactive and nonhyperactive learning-disabled children. *Journal of Learning Disabilities, 20,* 563–567.

deHaas, P. A. (1986). Attention styles and peer relationships of hyperactive and normal boys and girls. *Journal of Abnormal Child Psychology, 14,* 457–467.

Deloach, T. F., Earl, J. M., Brown, B. S., Poplin, M. S., & Warner, M. M. (1981). LD teachers' perceptions of severely learning-disabled students. *Learning Disability Quarterly, 4*(4), 343–358.

Deshler, D. D., & Schumaker, J. B. (1983). Social skills of learning-disabled adolescents: Characteristics and interventions. *Topics in Learning and Learning Disabilities, 3*(2), 15–23.

Deshler, D. D., Schumaker, J. B., & Lenz, B. K. (1984). Academic and cognitive intervention for LD adolescents: Part I. *Journal of Learning Disabilities, 17,* 108–117.

Deshler, D. D., Schumaker, J. B., Lenz, B. K., & Ellis, E. (1984). Academic and cognitive interventions for LD adolescents: Part II. *Journal of Learning Disabilities, 17,* 170–179.

Draeger, S., Prior, M., & Sanson, A. (1986). Visual and auditory attention performance in hyperactive children: Competence or compliance. *Journal of Abnormal Child Psychology, 14,* 411–424.

Drew, C. J., Logan, D. R., & Hardman, M. L. (1992). *Mental retardation: A life cycle approach* (5th ed.). Columbus, OH: Merrill.

Dudley-Marling, C., & Edmiaston, R. (1985). Social status of learning-disabled children and adolescents: A review. *Learning Disability Quarterly, 8,* 189–204.

Dudley-Marling, C., & Searle, D. (1988). Enriching language learning environments for students with learning disabilities. *Journal of Learning Disabilities, 21,* 140–143.

Ellis, E. S., & Lenz, B. K. (1987). A component analysis of effective learning strategies for LD students. *Learning Disabilities Focus, 2,* 94–107.

Engelmann, S., & Carnine, D. (1972). *DISTAR arithmetic.* Chicago: SRA.

Englemann, S., & Carnine, D. (1982). *Corrective mathematics program.* Chicago: SRA.

Englert, C. A., & Palincsar, A. S. (1988). The reading process. In D. K. Reid (Ed.). *Teaching the learning disabled: A cognitive developmental approach* (pp. 162–189). Boston: Allyn and Bacon.

Englert, C. S., & Thomas, C. C. (1987). Sensitivity to text structure in reading and writing: A comparison of learning-disabled and nondisabled students. *Learning Disabilities Quarterly, 10,* 93–105.

Enright, B. E. (1989). *Basic mathematics: Detecting and correcting special needs.* Boston: Allyn and Bacon.

Fair, G. W. (1988). Mathematics instruction in junior and senior high school. In D. K. Reid (Ed.), *Teaching the learning disabled: A cognitive developmental approach* (pp. 378–415). Boston: Allyn and Bacon.

Finch, A. J., Jr., & Spirito, A. (1980). Use of cognitive training to change cognitive processes. *Exceptional Education Quarterly, 1,* 31–39.

Fleener, F. T. (1987). Learning disabilities and other attributes as factors in delinquent activities among adolescents in a nonurban area. *Psychological Reports, 60,* 327–334.

Fuchs, D., & Fuchs, L. S. (1986). Test procedure bias: A meta-analysis of examiner familiarity effects. *Review of Educational Research, 56,* 243–262.

Fuchs, L. S., & Fuchs, D. (1988). Curriculum-based measurement: A methodology for evaluating and improving student programs. *Diagnostique, 14,* 3–13.

Gaddes, W. H. (1985). *Learning disabilities and brain function: A neuropsychological approach* (2nd ed.). New York: Springer-Verlag.

Gartner, A., & Lipsky, D. K. (1989, June 7–8). Equity and excellence for all students. *The education of students with disabilities: Where do we stand?* Briefing paper for testimony given at hearings conducted by the National Council on the Handicapped, Washington, DC.

Gelfand, D. M., Jenson, W. R., & Drew, C. J. (1988). *Understanding child behavior disorders* (2nd ed.). New York: Holt, Rinehart & Winston.

Gerber, M. M. (1985). Spelling as concept-drive problem solving. In B. Hutson (Ed.), *Advances in reading/language research* (Vol. 3, pp. 39–75). Greenwich, CT: JAI Press.

Gerber, M. M. (1986). Generalization of spelling strategies by LD students as a result of contingent imitation/modeling and mastery criteria. *Journal of Learning Disabilities. 19,* 530–537.

Gordon, M. (1986). How is a computerized attention test used in the diagnosis of attention deficit disorder? *Journal of Children in Contemporary Society, 19,* 53–64.

Gottfredson, L. S., Finucci, J. M., & Childs, B. (1984). Explaining the adult careers of dyslexic boys. *Journal of Vocational Behavior, 24,* 355–373.

Griffith, P. L., Ripich, D. N., & Dastoli, S. L. (1986). Story structure, cohesion, and propositions in s ory recall by learning-disabled and non-disabled children. *Journal of Psycholinguistic Research, 15,* 539–555.

Grinnell, P. C. (1988). Teaching handwriting and spelling. In D. K. Reid (Ed.), *Teaching the learning disabled: A cognitive developmental approach* (pp. 245–278). Boston: Allyn and Bacon.

Gronlund, N. E., & Linn, R. L. (1990). *Measurement and evaluation in teaching.* New York: Macmillan.

Hall, R. J. (1980). Cognitive behavior modification and information processing skills of exceptional children. *Exceptional Education Quarterly, 1,* 9–15.

Hallahan, D. P., Kauffman, J. M., & Lloyd, J. W. (1985). *Introduction to learning disabilities* (2nd ed.). Englewood Cliffs, NJ: Prentice Hall.

Hamlett, K. W., Pellegrini, D. S., & Conners, C. K. (1987). An investigation of executive processes in the problem solving of attention deficit disorder-hyperactive children. *Journal of Pediatric Psychology, 12,* 227–240.

Hammill, D. D. (1990). On defining learning disabilities: An emerging consensus. *Journal of Learning Disabilities, 23,* 74–84.

Healy, J. M., & Aram, D. M. (1986). Hyperlexia and dyslexia: A family study. *Annals of Dyslexia, 36,* 237–252.

Hermann, K. (1959). *Reading disability: A medical study of word-blindness and related handicaps.* Springfield, IL: Charles C Thomas.

Hooper, S. R., & Willis, W. G. (1989). *Learning disability subtyping: Neuropsychological foundations, conceptual models, and issues in clinical differentiation.* New York: Springer-Verlag.

Houck, C. K. (1984). *Learning disabilities: Understanding concepts, characteristics, and issues.* Englewood Cliffs, NJ: Prentice Hall.

Idol, L. (Ed.). (1988). *Grace Fernald's remedial techniques in basic school subjects.* Austin, TX: Pro-Ed.

Johnston, R. B. (1987). *Learning disabilities, medicine, and myth: A guide to understanding the child and the physician.* Boston: Little, Brown.

Kaluger, G., & Kolson, C. J. (1978). *Reading and learning disabilities* (2nd ed.). Columbus, OH: Merrill.

Kavale, K., & Nye, C. (1981). Identification criteria for learning disabilities: A survey of the research literature. *Learning Disability Quarterly, 4*(4), 383–388.

Kirk, S. A. (1963). Behavioral diagnosis and remediation of learning disabilities. *Proceedings: Conference on exploration into the problems of the perceptually handicapped* (Vol. 1). First Annual Meeting, Chicago.

Kirk, S. A., & Chalfant, J. C. (1984). *Academic and developmental learning disabilities.* Denver: Love.

Kramer, J. R. (1986). Where are hyperactive children as young adults? *Journal of Children in Contemporary Society, 19,* 89–98.

la Greca, A. M. (1987). Children with learning disabilities: Interpersonal skills and social competence. *Journal of Reading, Writing, and Learning Disabilities International, 3,* 167–185.

Lahey, B. B., Schaughency, E. A., Hynd, G. W., Carlson, C. L., & Nieves, N. (1987). Attention deficit disorder with and without hyperactivity: Comparison of behavioral characteristics of clinic-referred children. *Journal of the American Academy of Child and Adolescent Psychiatry, 26,* 718–723.

Larsen, S. (1978). Learning disabilities and the professional educator. *Learning Disability Quarterly, 1*(1), 5–12.

Lerner, J. (1985). *Children with learning disabilities: Theories, diagnosis, and teaching strategies* (4th ed.). Boston: Houghton Mifflin.

Levy, F. (1989). CNS stimulant controversies. *Australian and New Zealand Journal of Psychiatry, 23*, 497–502.

Lindsey, J. D. (1987). *Computers and exceptional individuals.* Columbus, OH: Merrill.

Lynn, R., Gluckin, N. D., & Kripke, B. (1979). *Learning disabilities: An overview of theories, approaches, and politics.* New York: Free Press.

Margalit, M. (1989). Academic competence and social adjustment of boys with learning disabilities and boys with behavior disorders. *Journal of Learning Disabilities, 22*, 41–45.

McCue, P. M., Shelly, C., & Goldstein, G. (1986). Intellectual, academic, and neuropsychological performance levels in learning-disabled adults. *Journal of Learning Disabilities, 19*, 233–236.

McGee, R., Williams, S., & Silva, P. A. (1987). A comparison of girls and boys with teacher-identified problems of attention. *Journal of American Academy of Child and Adolescent Psychiatry, 26*, 711–717.

McKinney, J. D., & Haskins, R. (1980). Cognitive training and the development of problem-solving strategies. *Exceptional Education Quarterly, 1*, 41–51.

McLoughlin, J. A., Clark, F., Mauck, A. R., & Petrosko, J. (1987). A comparison of parent-child perceptions of student learning disabilities. *Journal of Special Education Technology, 4*, 50–58.

Meyen, E. (1989). Let's not confuse test scores with the substance of the discrepancy model. *Journal of Learning Disabilities, 22*, 482–483.

Miller, J. L. (1990). Apocalypse or Renaissance or something in between? Toward a realistic appraisal of *The Learning Mystique. Journal of Learning Disabilities, 23*, 86–91.

Morris, R. J. (1985). *Behavior modification with exceptional children: Principles and practices.* Glenview, IL: Scott, Foresman.

National Advisory Committee on Handicapped Children. (1968). *Special education for handicapped children: First annual report.* Washington, DC: Department of Health, Education, and Welfare.

National Association of State Directors of Special Education. (1991). *Reference notes for speechmaking or for understanding the forces at work which are driving social policy.* Washington, DC: author.

National Joint Committee on Learning Disabilities. (1988) [Letter to NJCLD member organizations].

Nelson, H. E. (1980). Analysis of spelling errors in normal and dyslexic children. In U. Frith (Ed.), *Cognitive processes in spelling* (pp. 475–493). London: Academic Press.

Nix, G. W., & Shapiro, J. (1986). Auditory perceptual processing in learning-assistance children: A preliminary report. *Journal of Research in Reading, 9*(2), 92–102.

Osman, B. R. (1987). Promoting social acceptance of children with learning disabilities: An educational responsibility. *Journal of Reading, Writing, and Learning Disabilities International, 3*, 111–118.

Parker, H. C. (1990). *C.H.A.D.D.: Children with attention deficit disorders: Parents supporting parents.* Education position paper, Plantation, FL.

Parrill, M. (1987). Developmental issues surrounding severe discrepancy. *Learning Disabilities Research, 3*, 32–42.

Patberg, J., Dewitz, P., & Samuels, S. J. (1981). The effect of context on the size of the perceptual unit used in word recognition. *Journal of Reading Behavior, 13*, 33–48.

Pelham, W. E. (1983). The effects of psychostimulants on academic achievement in hyperactive and learning-disabled children. *Thalmus,*

3(1), 2–48 (newsletter of the International Academy of Research in Learning Disabilities).

Pelham, W. E. (1986). What do we know about the use and effects of CNS stimulants in the treatment of ADD? *Journal of Children in Contemporary Society, 19*, 99–110.

Perkins, C. B. (1989). Curriculum based assessment: A new approach. *Principal, 69*(2), 44–45.

Perlmutter, B. F. (1987). Delinquency and learning disabilities: Evidence for compensatory behaviors and adaptation. *Journal of Youth and Adolescence, 16*, 89–95.

Polloway, E. A., & Smith, J. E. (1982). *Teaching language skills to exceptional learners.* Denver: Love.

Rakes, T. A., & Choate, J. S. (1989). *Language arts: Detecting and correcting special needs.* Boston: Allyn and Bacon.

Reid, D. K. (1988). Learning disabilities and the cognitive developmental approach. In D. K. Reid (Ed.), *Teaching the learning disabled: A cognitive developmental approach* (pp. 29–46). Boston: Allyn and Bacon.

Richards, G. P., Samuels, S. J., Turnure, J. E., & Ysseldyke, J. E. (1990). Sustained and selective attention in children with learning disabilities. *Journal of Learning Disabilities, 23*, 129–136.

Rosenberg, M. S. (1987). Psychopharmacological interventions with young hyperactive children. *Topics in Early Childhood Special Education, 6*(4), 62–74.

Rosenthal, R. H., & Allen, T. W. (1978). An examination of attention, arousal, and learning dysfunctions of hyperkinetic children. *Psychological Bulletin, 85*, 689–715.

Rourke, B. P. (1987). Syndrome of nonverbal learning disabilities: The final common pathway of white-matter disease/function. *Clinical Neuropsychologist, 1*(3), 209–234.

Samuels, S. J., & Kamil, M. L. (1984). Models of the reading process. In P. D. Pearson (Ed.), *Handbook of reading research* (pp. 185–229). New York: Longman.

Seidenberg, P. L. (1989). Relating text-processing research to reading and writing instruction for learning disabled students. *Learning Disabilities Focus, 5*, 4–12.

Siegel, L. S. (1989). IQ is irrelevant to the definition of learning disabilities. *Journal of Learning Disabilities, 22*, 469–478, 486.

Skinner, B. F. (1953). *Science and human behavior.* New York: Free Press.

Skinner, B. F. (1957). *Verbal behavior.* New York: Appleton-Century-Crofts.

Skinner, B. F. (1971). *Beyond freedom and dignity.* New York: Knopf.

Smith, D. D., & Lovitt, T. C. (1982). *The computational arithmetic program.* Austin, TX: Pro-Ed.

Smith, S. M. (1989). Congenital syndromes and mildly handicapped students: Implications for special educators. *Journal of Remedial and Special Education, 10*, 20–30.

Sorrel, A. L. (1990). Three reading comprehension strategies: TELLS, story mapping, and QARs. *Academic Therapy, 25*, 359–368.

Stanford Research Institute. (1989, June 7–8). National longitudinal transition study of special education students. *The education of students with disabilities: Where do we stand?* Briefing paper for testimony given at hearings conducted by the National Council on the Handicapped, Washington, DC.

Swanson, H. L. (1979). Developmental recall lag in learning-disabled children: Perceptual deficit or verbal mediation deficiency? *Journal of Abnormal Child Psychology, 7*, 199–210.

Swanson, H. L. (1988). Toward a metatheory of learning disabilities. *Journal of Learning Disabilities, 21,* 196–209.

Swanson, H. L., Cochran, K. F., & Ewers, C. A. (1990). Can learning disabilities be determined from working memory performance? *Journal of Learning Disabilities, 23,* 59–67.

Tansley, P., & Panckhurst, J. (1981). *Children with specific learning difficulties.* Windsor, England: NFER-Nelson Publishing.

Torgesen, J. K. (1989). Why IQ *is* relevant to the definition of learning disabilities. *Journal of Learning Disabilities, 22,* 484–486.

U.S. Department of Education. (1991). *Thirteenth annual report to Congress on the implementation of the Education of the Handicapped Act.* Washington, DC: Division of Educational Services, Special Education Programs.

U.S. Department of Health, Education, and Welfare. (1977, August 23). Education of Handicapped Children (Implementation of Part B of the Education of the Handicapped Act). *Federal Register, 42* (173), 42478.

Vogel, S. A. (1982). On developing LD college programs. *Journal of Learning Disabilities, 15,* 518–528.

Wallace, G., & McLoughlin, J. A. (1988). *Learning disabilities: Concepts and characteristics* (3rd ed.). Columbus, OH: Merrill.

Wallander, J. L. (1988). The relationship between attention problems in childhood and antisocial behavior eight years later. *Journal of Child Psychology and Psychiatry and Allied Disciplines, 29,* 53–61.

Warner, M. M., Schumaker, J. B., Alley, G. R., & Deshler, D. D. (1980). Learning-disabled adolescents in the public schools: Are they different from other low achievers? *Exceptional Education Quarterly, 1,* 27–36.

Weiss, G., & Hechtman, L. T. (1986). *Hyperactive children grown up: Empirical findings and theoretical considerations.* New York: Guilford Press.

Welch, M. W., & Jensen, J. (1991). Write, P.L.E.A.S.E.: A video-assisted strategic intervention to improve written expression of inefficient learners. *Journal of Remedial and Special Education, 12,* 37–47.

Weller, C., & Strawser, S. (1987). Adaptive behavior of subtypes of learning-disabled individuals. *Journal of Special Education, 21,* 101–115.

Weller, C., Strawser, S., & Buchanan, M. (1985). Adaptive behavior: Designator of a continuum of severity of learning-disabled individuals. *Journal of Learning Disabilities, 18*(4), 201–204.

Whalen, C. K. (1987, March). *High risk, but also high potential: The plight and the promise of children with attention deficit disorders.* Paper presented at the National Conference on Learning Disabilities, Washington, DC.

Whalen, C. K., & Henker, B. (1986). Cognitive behavior therapy for hyperactive children: What do we know? *Journal of Children in Contemporary Society, 19,* 123–241.

White, W. J., Deshler, D. D., Schumaker, J. B., Warner, M. M., Alley, G. R., & Clark, F. L. (1983). The effects of learning disabilities on post-school adjustment. *Journal of Rehabilitation, 49,* 46–50.

Wilson, L. R. (1985). Large-scale learning-disability identification: The reprieve of a concept. *Exceptional Children, 52,* 44–51.

Wiederholt, J. L. (1989). Restructuring special education services: The past, the present, the future. *Learning Disability Quarterly, 12,* 181–191.

Wong, B. Y. L. (1980). Activating the inactive learner: Use of question/prompts to enhance comprehension and retention of implied information in disabled children. *Learning Disability Quarterly, 3,* 29–37.

Wong, B. Y. L. (1989). Is IQ necessary in the definition of learning disabilities? Introduction to the special series. *Journal of Learning Disabilities, 22,* 468.

Wong, B. Y. L., & Sawatsky, D. (1984). Sentence elaboration and retention

of good, average, and poor readers. *Learning Disability Quarterly, 7,* 229–236.

Youngstrom, N. (1991). Most child clinicians support prescribing. *APA Monitor, 22*(3), 21.

Zentall, S. S., & Kruczek, T. (1988). The attraction of color for active attention-problems children. *Exceptional Children, 54,* 357–362.

Chapter Seven

Adelman, H. S. (1992). The classification problem. In W. Stainback & S. Stainback (Eds.), *Controversial issues confronting special education: Divergent perspectives* (pp. 97–108). Boston: Allyn and Bacon.

Braaten, S., Kauffman, J. M., Braaten, B., Polsgrove, L., & Nelson, C. M. (1988). The regular education initiative: Patent medicine for behavioral disorders. *Exceptional Children, 55*(1), 21–27.

Bryan, T., Bay, M., Lopez-Reyna, T., & Donahue, M. (1991). Characteristics of students with learning disabilities: The extant database and its implications for educational programs. In J. Lloyd, N. N. Singh, & A. C. Repp (Eds.), *The regular education initiative: Alternative perspectives on concepts, issues, and models* (pp. 113–132). Sycamore, IL: Sycamore.

Davis, W. E., & McCaul, E. J. (1991). *The emerging crisis: Current and projected status of children in the United States* (Monograph). Orono, ME: Institute for the Study of At-Risk Students.

Drew, C. J., Logan, D. R., & Hardman, M. L. (1992). *Mental retardation: Life cycle approach* (5th ed.). Columbus, OH: Merrill.

Gartner, A., & Lipsky, D. (1987). Beyond special education: Toward a quality system for all students. *Harvard Educational Review, 57*(4), 367–395.

Gartner, A., & Lipsky, D. (1989, June). Equity and excellence for all students. Testimony before the National Council on Disability, Washington, DC.

Goldman, J., & Gardner, H. (1989). Multiple paths to educational effectiveness. In D. K. Lipsky & A. Gartner (Eds.), *Beyond separate education: Quality education for all* (pp. 121–140). Baltimore: Paul H. Brookes.

Gottlieb, J., Alter, M., Gottlieb, B. W. (1991). Mainstreaming academically handicapped children in urban schools. In J. W. Lloyd, N. N. Singh, & A. C. Repp (Eds.), *The regular education initiative: Alternative perspectives on concepts, issues, and models* (pp. 95–112). Sycamore, IL: Sycamore.

Jenkins, J. R., Pious, C. G., & Peterson, D. L. (1988). Categorical programs for remedial and handicapped students: Issues of validity. *Exceptional Children, 55*(2), 147–158.

Kauffman, J. M., & Pullen, P. L. (1989). An historical perspective: A personal perspective on our history of service to mildly handicapped and at-risk students. *Remedial and Special Education, 10*(6), 12–14.

Larrivee, B. (1986). Effective teaching of mainstreamed students in effective teaching of all students. *Teacher Education and Special Education, 9*(4), 173–179.

Laycock, V. P. (1980). Environmental alternatives for mildly and moderately handicapped. In J. W. Schifani, R. M. Anderson, & S. J. Odle (Eds.), *Implementing learning in the least restrictive environment.* Baltimore: Paul H. Brookes.

Lilly, M. S. (1987). Lack of focus on special education in literature on educational reform. *Exceptional Children, 53*(4), 325–326.

Lilly, M. S. (1992). Labeling: A tired, overworked, yet unresolved issue in special education. In W. Stainback & S. Stainback (Eds.), *Controversial issues confronting special education: Divergent perspectives* (pp. 85–95). Boston: Allyn and Bacon.

Lipsky, D. K., & Gartner, A. (1991). Restructuring for quality. In J. Lloyd, N. N. Singh, & A. C. Repp (Eds.), *The regular education initiative: Alternative perspectives on concepts, issues, and models* (pp. 43–56). Sycamore, IL: Sycamore.

Marston, D. (1987). Does categorical teacher certification benefit the mildly handicapped child? *Exceptional Children, 53*(5), 423–431.

Meyer, L. H., Peck, C. A., & Brown, L. (1991). Definition of the people TASH serves. In L. H. Meyer, C. A. Peck, & L. Brown (Eds.), *Critical issues in the lives of people with disabilities* (p. 19). Baltimore: Paul H. Brookes.

Meyer, L. H., Peck, C. A., & Brown, L. (1991). Definitions and diagnosis. In L. H. Meyer, C. A. Peck, & L. Brown (Eds.), *Critical issues in the lives of people with disabilities* (p. 17). Baltimore: Paul H. Brookes.

Reynolds, M. C. (1991). Classification and labeling. In J. W. Lloyd, N. N. Singh, & A. C. Repp (Eds.), *The regular education initiative: Alternative perspectives on concepts, issues, and models* (pp. 29–41). Sycamore, IL: Sycamore.

Reynolds, M. C., & Birch, J. W. (1988). *Adaptive mainstreaming.* New York: Longman.

Reynolds, M. C., Wang, M. C., & Walberg, H. J. (1987). The necessary restructuring of special and regular education. *Exceptional Children, 53*(5), 391–398.

Snell, M. E. (1987). What does an "appropriate" education mean? In M. E. Snell (Ed.), *Systematic instruction of persons with severe handicaps* (pp. 1–6). Columbus, OH: Merrill.

Snell, M. E. (1991). Schools are for all kids: The importance of integration for students with severe disabilities and their peers. In J. Lloyd, N. N. Singh, & A. C. Repp (Eds.), *The regular education initiative: Alternative perspectives on concepts, issues, and models* (pp. 133–148). Sycamore, IL: Sycamore.

U.S. Department of Education. (1991). *Thirteenth annual report to Congress.* Washington, DC: Author.

Wang, M. C. (1989). Education of students with disabilities: Where do we stand? Testimony before the National Council on Disability, Washington, DC.

Wang, M. C., & Walberg, H. J. (1987). Four fallacies of segregation. *Exceptional Children, 55*(2), 128–137.

Ysseldyke, J. E. (1987). Classification of handicapped students. In M. C. Wang, M. C. Reynolds, & H. J. Walberg (Eds.), *Handbook of special education: Research and practice: Vol. 1. Learner characteristics and adaptive education.* New York: Pergamon Press.

Ysseldyke, J. E., Algozzine, B., Shinn, M., & McGue, M. (1982). Similarities and differences between low achievers and students classified as handicapped. *Journal of Special Education, 16,* 73–85.

Chapter Eight

Allen, D. V., & Bliss, L. S. (1987). Concurrent validity of two language screening tests. *Journal of Communication Disorders, 20,* 305–317.

Ausubel, D. P., Sullivan, E. V., & Ives, S. W. (1980). *Theory and problems of child development* (3rd ed.). New York: Grune & Stratton.

Bernstein, D. K. (1985). The nature of language and its disorders. In D. K. Bernstein and E. Tiegerman (Eds.), *Language and communication disorders in children* (pp. 1–19). Columbus, OH: Merrill.

Bialystok, E. (1986). Children's concept of word. *Journal of Psycholinguistic Research, 15,* 13–32.

Bishop, D. V. M., & Edmundson, A. (1987). Specific language impairment as a maturational lag: Evidence from longitudinal data on language and motor development. *Developmental Medicine and Child Neurology, 29,* 442–459.

Cassar, M. C. (1988). Stuttering and hypnosis: Processes of cortical control. *Australian Journal of Clinical Hypnotherapy and Hypnosis, 9*(2), 49–65.

Chapman, K. L., & Terrell, B. Y. (1988). "Verb-alizing": Facilitating action word usage in young language-impaired children. *Topics in Language Disorders, 8*(2), 1–13.

Cole, K. N., & Dale, P. S. (1986). Direct language instruction and interactive language instruction with language-delayed preschool children: A comparison study. *Journal of Speech and Hearing Research, 29,* 206–217.

Cole, M. L., & Cole, J. T. (1989). *Effective intervention with the language impaired child* (2nd ed.). Rockville, MD: Aspen.

Cooper, J. A., & Flowers, C. R. (1987). Children with a history of acquired aphasia: Residual language and academic impairments. *Journal of Speech and Hearing Disorders, 52,* 251–262.

Crestwood Company. (1987–1988). *Communication aids for children and adults* (Catalog). Milwaukee, WI: Author.

Cromer, R. F. (1981). Reconceptualizing language acquisition and cognitive development. In R. L. Schiefelbusch & D. D. Bricker (Eds.), *Early language acquisition and intervention.* Baltimore: University Park Press.

Cruz, M. delC., & Ayala, M. (1987). *Developmental variables and speech-language in a special education intervention model.* Paper presented at the 68th National American Educational Research Association Convention, Washington, DC.

Edwards, M., Cape, J., & Brown, D. (1989). Patterns of referral for children with speech disorders. *Child Care, Health and Development, 15,* 417–424.

Elias, A., Raven, R., Butcher, P., & Littlejohns, D. W. (1989). Speech therapy for psychogenic voice disorders: A survey of current practice and training. *British Journal of Disorders of Communication, 24,* 61–76.

Emerick, L. L., & Haynes, W. O. (1986). *Diagnosis and evaluation in speech pathology* (3rd ed.). Englewood Cliffs, NJ: Prentice Hall.

Ewing-Cobbs, L. (1987). Language functions following closed-head injury in children and adolescents. *Journal of Clinical and Experimental Neuropsychology, 9,* 575–592.

Fitzgerald, M. T., & Karnes, D. E. (1987). A parent-implemented language model for at-risk and developmentally delayed preschool children. *Topics in Language Disorders, 7*(3), 31–46.

Gardner, H. (1989). An investigation of maternal interaction with phonologically disordered children as compared to two groups of normally developing children. *British Journal of Disorders of Communication, 24,* 41–59.

Gelfand, D. M., Jenson, W. R., & Drew, C. J. (1988). *Understanding children's behavior disorders* (2nd ed.). New York: Holt, Rinehart & Winston.

Groshong, C. C. (1987). Assessing oral language comprehension: Are picture-vocabulary tests enough? *Learning Disabilities Focus, 2,* 108–115.

Harlan, N. T., & Tschiderer, P. A. (1987). *A primary prevention program: Teaching models I and II.* Paper presented at the Annual Convention of the American Speech-Language-Hearing Association, Detroit, MI.

Hasbrouck, J. M., Doherty, J., Mehlmann, M. A., Nelson, R., Randle, B., & Whitaker, R. (1987). Intensive stuttering therapy in a public school setting. *Language, Speech, and Hearing Services in Schools, 18,* 330–343.

Healey, E. C., & Howe, S. W. (1987). Speech shadowing characteristics of stutterers under diotic and dichotic conditions. *Journal of Communication Disorders, 20,* 493–506.

Henderson, V. W. (1990). Alalia, aphemia, and aphasia. *Archives of Neurology, 47,* 85–88.

Hornby, G., & Jensen-Proctor, G. (1984). Parental speech to language-delayed children: A home intervention study. *British Journal of Disorders of Communication, 19,* 97–103.

Kahane, J. C., & Mayo, R. (1989). The need for aggressive pursuit of healthy childhood voices. *Language, Speech, and Hearing Services in Schools, 20,* 102–107.

Kerbeshian, J., Gascon, G., & Burd, L. (1988). A role for biogenic amines in developmental language disorders. *Neuroscience and Biobehavioral Reviews, 12,* 289–293.

Klinger, H. (1987). Effects of pseudostuttering on normal speakers' self-ratings of beauty. *Journal of Communication Disorders, 20,* 353–358.

Koegel, R. L., Koegel, L. K., VanVoy, K., & Ingham, J. C. (1988). Within-clinic versus outside-of-clinic self-monitoring of articulation to promote generalization. *Journal of Speech and Hearing Disorders, 53,* 392–399.

Kraaimaat, F., Janssen, P., & Brutten, G. J. (1988). The relationship between stutterers' cognitive and autonomic anxiety and therapy outcome. *Journal of Fluency Disorders, 13,* 107–113.

Lucas, E. V. (1980). *Semantic and pragmatic language disorders: Assessment and remediation.* Rockville, MD: Aspen.

Mecham, M. J., & Willbrand, M. L. (1985). *Treatment approaches to language disorders in children: Psycholinguistic and neurolinguistic approaches.* Springfield, IL: Charles C Thomas.

Mowrer, D. E., & Conley, D. (1987). Effects of peer-administered consequences upon articulation responses of speech-defective children. *Journal of Communication Disorders, 20,* 319–326.

Murdoch, B. E., Killin, H., & McCaul, A. (1989). A kinematic analysis of respiratory function in a group of stutterers pre- and posttreatment. *Journal of Fluency Disorders, 14,* 323–350.

Peters, H., & Hulstijn, W. (Eds.). (1987). *Speech motor dynamics in stuttering.* New York: Springer-Verlag.

Pindzola, R. H. (1987). Durational characteristics of the fluent speech of stutterers and nonstutterers. *Folia Phonetica, 39,* 90–97.

Powell, M., Filter, M. D., & Williams, B. (1989). A longitudinal study of the prevalence of voice disorders in children from a rural school division. *Journal of Communication Disorders, 22,* 375–382.

Prosek, R. A. et al. (1987). Formant frequencies of stuttered and fluent vowels. *Journal of Speech and Hearing Research, 30,* 301–305.

Rastatter, M. P., & Dell, C. (1987). Vocal reaction times of stuttering subjects to tachistoscopically presented concrete and abstract words: A closer look at cerebral dominance and language processing. *Journal of Speech and Hearing Research, 30,* 306–310.

Rastatter, M. P., & Loren, C. A. (1988). Visual coding dominance in stuttering: Some evidence from central tachistoscopic stimulation (tachistoscopic viewing and stuttering). *Journal of Fluency Disorders, 13,* 89–95.

Raver, S. A. (1987). Practical procedures for increasing spontaneous language in language-delayed preschoolers. *Journal of the Division for Early Childhood, 11,* 226–232.

Reuter News Agency. (1991, March 25). Babbling with hands by deaf babies casts doubt on speech-language tie. *Salt Lake Tribune,* p. A1.

Richard, N. B. (1986). Interaction between mothers and infants with Down syndrome: Infant characteristics. *Topics in Early Childhood Special Education, 6*(3), 54–71.

Roberts, J. E., Rabinowitch, S., & Bryant, D. M. (1989). Language skills of children with different preschool experiences. *Journal of Speech and Hearing Research, 32,* 773–786.

Smith, C. R. (1991). *Learning disabilities: The interaction of learner, task, and setting* (2nd ed.). Boston: Allyn and Bacon.

Tiegerman, E. (1985). The social bases of language acquisition. In D. K. Bernstein and E. Tiegerman (Eds.), *Language and communication disorders in children* (pp. 20–30). Columbus, OH: Merrill.

U.S. Department of Education. (1991). To assure the free appropriate public education of all children with disabilities. *Thirteenth annual report to Congress on the implementation of the Individuals with Disabilities Act.* Washington, DC: Author.

Van Riper, C., & Emerick, L. (1990). *Speech correction: An introduction to speech pathology and audiology* (8th ed.). Englewood Cliffs, NJ: Prentice Hall.

Waldo, A. L. (1984). *Sacajawea* (rev. exp. ed.). New York: Avon Books.

Weaver-Spurlock, S., & Brasseur, J. (1988). The effects of simultaneous sound-position training on the generalization of (s). *Language, Speech, and Hearing Services in Schools, 19,* 259–271.

Webster, W. G. (1988). Neural mechanisms underlying stuttering: Evidence from bimanual handwriting performance. *Brain and Language, 33,* 226–244.

Wiig, E. H., & Semel, E. M. (1984). *Language assessment and intervention for the learning disabled* (2nd ed.). Columbus, OH: Merrill.

Wnuk, L. (1987). A review of the Bzoch-League Receptive-Expressive Emergent Language Scale and the Test for Auditory Comprehension Language. *Canadian Journal for Exceptional Children, 3,* 95–98.

Wood, K. S. (1971). Terminology and nomenclature. In L. E. Travis (Ed.), *Handbook of speech pathology and audiology.* New York: Appleton-Century-Crofts.

Ylvisaker, M. (1986). Language and communication disorders following pediatric head injury. *Journal of Head Trauma Rehabilitation, 1*(4), 48–56.

Chapter Nine

Accardo, P. (1988). Autism and plumbism. A possible association. *Clinical Pediatrics, 27,* 41–44.

Akyurek, A., & Kalverboer, A. F. (1986). Aspects of the behavioral repertoire of an autistic/epileptic child. *Perceptual and Motor Skills, 62,* 843–858.

American Psychiatric Association. (1987). *Diagnostic and statistical manual of mental disorders* (3rd ed., rev.). Washington, DC: Author.

Beavers, D. J. (1982). *Autism: Nightmare without end.* Port Washington, NY: Ashley Books.

Bebko, J. M. (1987). Parent and professional evaluations of family stress associated with characteristics of autism. *Journal of Autism and Developmental Disorders, 17,* 565–576.

Bemporad, J. R. (1979). Adult recollections of a formerly autistic child. *Journal of Autism and Developmental Disorders, 9,* 179–197.

Biklen, D. (1990). Communication unbound: Autism and praxis. *Harvard Educational Review, 60,* 291–314.

Bryson, S. E., Clark, B. S., & Smith, I. M. (1988). First report of a Canadian epidemiological study of autistic syndromes. *Journal of Child Psychology and Psychiatry and Allied Disciplines, 29,* 433–445.

Ciadella, P., & Mamelle, N. (1989). An epidemiological study of infantile autism in a French department (Rhone): A research note. *Journal of Child Psychology and Psychiatry and Allied Disciplines, 30,* 165–175.

Coleman, M., & Gillberg, C. (1985). *The biology of autistic syndromes.* New York: Praeger.

Courchesne, I., Yeung-Courchesne, R., Press, G. A., Hesselink, J. R., & Jernigan, T. L. (1988). Hypoplasia of cerebellar vermal lobules VI and VII in autism. *New England Journal of Medicine, 318,* 1349–1354.

Crossley, R., & McDonald, A. (1980). *Annie's coming out.* New York: Penguin.

Dalrymple, N. (1989). *Developing a functional and longitudinal individual plan. Functional programming for people with autism: A series.* Bloomington: Indiana Resource Center for Autism, Institute for the Study of Developmental Disabilities, Indiana University.

Dalrymple, N., Gray, S., & Ruble, L. (1991). *Sex education: Issues for the person with autism. Functional programming for people with autism: A series.* Bloomington: Indiana Resource Center for Autism, Institute for the Study of Developmental Disabilities, Indiana University.

Dawson, G., Finley, C., Phillips, S., & Lewy, A. (1989). A comparison of hemispheric asymmetries in speech-related brain potentials of autistic and dysphasic children. *Brain and Language, 37,* 26–41.

Department of Education. (1991, August 19). Notice of proposed rule-making. *Federal Register, 56*(160), 41271.

Donnellan, A. M., & Mirenda, P. L. (1984). Issues related to professional involvement with families of individuals with autism and other severe handicaps. *Journal of the Association for Persons with Severe Handicaps, 9,* 16–25.

Du Verglas, G., Banks, S. R., & Guyer, K. E. (1988). Clinical effects of fenfluramine on children with autism: A review of the research. *Journal of Autism and Developmental Disorders, 18,* 297–308.

Dunlap, G., Koegel, R. L., & O'Neill, R. (1985). Pervasive developmental disorders. In P. H. Bornstein & A. E. Kazdin (Eds.), *Handbook of clinical behavior therapy with children* (pp. 499–540). Homewood, IL: Dorsey Press.

Durand, V. M., & Carr, E. G. (1987). Social influences on "self-stimulatory" behavior: Analysis and treatment application. *Journal of Applied Behavior Analysis, 20,* 119–132.

Ekman, G., Miranda-Linne, F., Gillberg, C., Garle, M., & Wetterberg, L. (1989). Fenfluramine treatment of twenty children with autism. *Journal of Autism and Developmental Disorders, 19,* 511–532.

Fisch, G. S. (1989). Fragile X and autism. *Journal of the American Academy of Child and Adolescent Psychiatry, 28,* 965–966.

Folstein, S., & Rutter, M. (1988). Autism: Familial aggregation and genetic implications. *Journal of Autism and Developmental Disorders, 18,* 297–321.

Gelfand, D. M., Jenson, W. R., & Drew, C. J. (1988). *Understanding child behavior disorders* (2nd ed.). New York: Holt, Rinehart & Winston.

Gillberg, C. (1986). Brief report: Onset at age 14 of a typical autistic syndrome. A case report of a girl with herpes simplex encephalitis. *Journal of Autism and Developmental Disorders, 16,* 369–375.

Gillberg, C. (1990a). Autism and pervasive developmental disorders. *Journal of Child Psychology and Psychiatry and Allied Disciplines, 31,* 99–119.

Gillberg, C. (1990b). Infantile autism: Diagnosis and treatment. *Acta Psychiatrica Scandinavica, 81,* 209–215.

Groden, J., & Cautela, J. (1988). Procedures to increase social interaction among adolescents with autism: A multiple baseline analysis. *Journal of Behavior Therapy and Experimental Psychiatry, 19*(2), 87–93.

Harris, S. L. (1986). Families of children with autism: Issues for the behavior therapist. *Behavior Therapist, 9,* 175–177.

Ho, H. H., & Kalousek, D. K. (1989). Fragile X syndrome in autistic boys. *Journal of Autism and Developmental Disorders, 19,* 343–347.

Kanner, L. (1943). Autistic disturbances of affective contact. *Nervous Child, 3,* 217–250.

Koegel, R. L., & Koegel, L. K. (1990). Extended reductions in stereotypic behavior of students with autism through a self-management treatment package. *Journal of Applied Behavior Analysis, 23,* 119–127.

Konstantareas, M. M., & Homatidis, S. (1989). Assessing child symptom severity and stress in parents of autistic children. *Journal of Child Psychology and Psychiatry and Allied Disciplines, 30,* 459–470.

Lienemann, J., & Walker, F. D. (1989). Naltrexone for treatment of self-injury. *American Journal of Psychiatry, 146,* 1639–1640.

Lord, C. (1988). Enhancing communication in adolescents with autism. *Topics in Language Disorders, 9,* 72–81.

Lovaas, O. I. (1987). Behavioral treatment and normal educational and intellectual functioning in young autistic children. *Journal of Consulting and Clinical Psychology, 55,* 3–9.

Loveland, K. A., McEvoy, R. E., & Tunali, B. (1990). Narrative story telling in autism and Down's syndrome. *British Journal of Developmental Psychology, 8,* 9–23.

Marcus, L. M., & Mesibov, G. B. (1987). Comprehensive services for adolescents with autism. *International Journal of Adolescent Medicine and Health, 3,* 145–154.

McHale, S. M., Sloan, J., & Simeonsson, R. J. (1986). Sibling relationships of children with autistic, mentally retarded and nonhandicapped brothers and sisters. *Journal of Autism and Developmental Disorders, 16,* 399–413.

Mesibov, G. B., & Stephens, J. (1990). Perceptions of popularity among a group of high-functioning adults with autism. *Journal of Autism and Developmental Disorders, 20,* 33–43.

Moreno, S. J., & Donellan, A. M. (1991). *High-functioning individuals with autism: Advice and information for parents and others who care.* Crown Point, IN: Maap Services.

Oades, R. D., Stern, L. M., Walker, M. K., & Clark, C. R. (1990). Event-related potentials and monoamines in autistic children on a clinical trial of fenfluramine. *International Journal of Psychophysiology, 8,* 197–212.

Oshima-Takane, Y., & Benaroya, S. (1989). An alternative view of pronominal errors in autistic children. *Journal of Autism and Developmental Disorders, 19,* 73–85.

Park, C. C. (1982). *The siege: The first ten years of an autistic child, with an epilogue, fifteen years later* (2nd ed.). Boston: Little, Brown.

Paul, R., Fischer, M. L., & Cohen, D. J. (1988). Brief report: Sentence comprehension strategies in children with autism and specific language disorders. *Journal of Autism and Developmental Disorders, 18,* 669–679.

Pingree, C. B. (1983, August). So near and yet so far. *The Ensign.*

Pingree, C. B. (1984). Parents versus autism: Our pediatrician, the coach. *Pediatric Annals, 13,* 330–338.

Porco, B. (1989a). *Growing towards independence by learning functional skills and behaviors. Functional programming for people with autism: A series.*

Bloomington: Indiana Resource Center for Autism, Institute for the Study of Developmental Disabilities, Indiana University.

Porco, B. (1989b). *Reading. Functional programming for people with autism: A series*. Bloomington: Indiana Resource Center for Autism, Institute for the Study of Developmental Disabilities, Indiana University.

Prior, M. (1989). Biological factors in childhood autism. *NIMHANS Journal, 7,* 91–101.

Prizant, B. M., & Wetherby, A. M. (1988). Providing services to children with autism (ages 0 to 2 years) and their families. *Topics in Language Disorders, 9,* 1–23.

Ramm, S. (1990). The use of the duvet (quilt) for treatment of autistic, violent behaviors (an experiential account). *Journal of Autism and Developmental Disorders, 20,* 279–280.

Ricks, D. (1989). Child autism: II. Differential diagnosis. *NIMHANS Journal, 7,* 71–75.

Rincover, A., & Ducharme, J. M. (1987). Variables influencing stimulus overselectivity and "tunnel vision" in developmentally delayed children. *American Journal of Mental Deficiency, 91,* 422–430.

Ritvo, E. R., Freeman, B. J., Pingree, C., Mason-Brothers, A., Jorde, L., Jenson, W. R., McMahon, W. M., Petersen, P. B., Mo, A., & Ritvo, A. (1989). The UCLA–University of Utah epidemiologic survey of autism: Palence. *American Journal of Psychiatry, 146,* 194–199.

Rothenberger, A. (1990). The brain development and behavior of autistic children: Notes on the research situation. *European Journal of Child and Adolescent Psychiatry, 53,* 191–194.

Schopler, E., & Mesibov, G. (Eds.). (1984). *The effects of autism on the family.* New York: Plenum.

Schreibman, L. (1988). Diagnostic features of autism. *Journal of Child Neurology, 3*(Suppl.), 57–64.

Sherman, J., Factor, D. C., Swinson, R., & Darjes, R. W. (1989). The effects of fenfluramine (hydrochloride) on the behaviors of fifteen autistic children. *Journal of Autism and Developmental Disorders, 19,* 533–543.

Stewart, J. R., Myers, W. C., Burket, R. C., & Lyles, W. B. (1990). A review of the pharmacotherapy of aggression in children and adolescents. *Journal of the American Academy of Child and Adolescent Psychiatry, 29,* 269–277.

Sue, D., Sue, D., & Sue, S. (1990). *Understanding abnormal behavior* (3rd ed.). Boston, MA: Houghton Mifflin.

Szatmari, P., Bartolucci, G., & Bremner, R. (1989). Asperger's syndrome and autism: Comparison of early history and outcome. *Developmental Medicine and Child Neurology, 31,* 709–720.

Volkmar, F. R., Cicchetti, D. V., Dykens, E., Sparrow, S. S., Leckman, J. F., & Cohen, D. J. (1988). An evaluation of the Autism Behavior checklist. *Journal of Autism and Developmental Disorders, 18,* 81–97.

Volkmar, F. R., Sparrow, S. S., Goudreau, D., Cicchetti, D. V., Paul, R., & Cohen, D. J. (1987). Social deficits in autism: An operational approach using the Vineland Adaptive Behavior Scale. *Journal of the American Academy of Child and Adolescent Psychiatry, 26,* 156–161.

Walters, A. S., Barrett, R. P., Feinstein, C., & Mercurio, A. (1990). A case report of naltrexone treatment of self-injury and social withdrawal in autism. *Journal of Autism and Developmental Disorders, 20,* 169–176.

Wheeler, M., Rimstidt, S., Gray, S., & DePaula, V. (1991). *Facts about autism.* Bloomington: Indiana Resource Center for Autism, Institute for the Study of Developmental Disabilities, Indiana University.

Chapter Ten

Abroms, I. F. (1977). Nongenetic hearing loss. In B. F. Jaffe (Ed.), *Hearing loss in children.* Baltimore: University Park Press.

Allen, T. (1986). A study of the achievement pattern of hearing-impaired students: 1974–1983. In A. Schildroth & M. Karchmer (Eds.), *Deaf children in America* (pp. 161–206). San Diego: College-Hill Press.

American Speech-Language-Hearing Association. (1982). Joint Committee on Infant Hearing: Position statement. *Asha, 24,* 1017–1018.

Brill, R. G., MacNeil, B., & Newman, I. R. (1986). Framework for appropriate programs for deaf children. *American Annals of the Deaf, 131*(2), 65–77.

Carney, E., & Verlinde, R. (1987). Caption decoders: Expanding options for hearing impaired children and adults. *American Annals of the Deaf, 132*(2), 73–77.

Cole, P. R. (1987). Recognizing language disorders. In F. N. Martin (Ed.), *Hearing disorders in children* (pp. 113–150). Austin, TX: Pro-Ed.

Conrad, R. (1979). *The deaf schoolchild: Language and cognitive function.* London: Harper & Row.

Dipietro, L. J., Knight, C. H., & Sams, J. S. (1981, April). Health care delivery for deaf patients: The provider's role. *American Annals of the Deaf,* pp. 106–112.

Erber, N. P. (1985). *Telephone communication and hearing impairment.* San Diego: College-Hill Press.

Garwood, V. P. (1987). Public school audiology. In F. N. Martin (Ed.), *Hearing disorders in children* (pp. 427–467). Austin, TX: Pro-Ed.

Gentile, A., & McCarthy, B. (1973). *Additional handicapping conditions among hearing-impaired students, United States: 1971–72* (Series D, no. 14). Washington, DC: Office of Demographic Studies, Gallaudet College.

Greenberg, M. T., & Kusche, C. A. (1989). Cognitive, personal, and social development of deaf children and adolescents. In M. C. Wang, M. C. Reynolds, & H. J. Walberg (Eds.), *Handbook of special education: Research and practice: Vol. 3. Low incidence conditions* (pp. 95–129). Oxford, England: Pergamon Press.

Hanson, V. L., Shankweiler, D., & Fischer, F. W. (1983). Determinants of spelling ability in deaf and hearing adults: Access to linguistic structure. *Cognition, 14,* 323–344.

Hicks, D. E. (1970). Comparison profiles of rubella and nonrubella children. *American Annals of the Deaf, 115,* 86–92.

Higgins, P. C. (1990). *The challenges of educating together deaf and hearing youth: Making mainstreaming work.* Springfield, IL: Charles C Thomas.

Hodgson, W. R. (1987). Test of hearing–The infant. In F. N. Martin (Ed.), *Hearing disorders in children* (pp. 185–216). Austin, TX: Pro-Ed.

Hoemann, H. W., & Briga, J. S. (1981). Hearing impairments. In J. M. Kauffman & D. P. Hallahan (Eds.), *Handbook of special education.* Englewood Cliffs, NJ: Prentice Hall.

Individuals with Disabilities Education Act, PL 101-476, Amendments to the Education of the Handicapped Act (1990).

Jaffe, B. F. (1977). History and physical examination for evaluating hearing loss in children. In B. F. Jaffe (Ed.), *Hearing loss in children.* Baltimore: University Park Press.

Karchmer, M. A. (1985). Demographics and deaf adolescence. In G. B. Anderson & D. Watson (Eds.), *The habilitation and rehabilitation of deaf adolescents* (pp. 28–47). Washington, DC: Gallaudet College Press.

Lang, H. G. (1989). Academic development and preparation for work. In

M. C. Wang, M. C. Reynolds, & H. J. Walberg (Eds.), *Handbook of special education: Research and practice: Vol. 3. Low incidence conditions* (pp. 71–93). Oxford, England: Pergamon Press.

LaPlante, M. P. (1991). The demographics of disability. In J. West (Ed.), *The Americans with Disabilities Act: From policy to practice* (pp. 55–80). New York: Milbank Memorial Fund.

LaSasso, C. (1985, June). *National survey of materials and procedures used to teach reading to hearing-impaired students: Preliminary results.* Paper presented at the Conference on Reading Instruction for the Hearing Impaired, South Carolina State Department of Education, Office of Programs for the Handicapped, Columbia, SC.

Levitt, H. (1989). Speech and hearing in communication. In M. C. Wang, M. C. Reynolds, & H. J. Walberg (Eds.), *Handbook of special education: Research and practice: Vol. 3. Low incidence conditions* (pp. 23–45). Oxford, England: Pergamon Press.

Ling, D. (1984a). Early oral intervention: An introduction. In D. Ling (Ed.), *Early intervention for hearing-impaired children: Oral options.* San Diego: College-Hill Press.

Ling, D. (1984b). Early total communication intervention: An introduction. In D. Ling (Ed.), *Early intervention for hearing-impaired children: Total communication options.* San Diego: College-Hill Press.

Ling, D., & Milne, M. (1981). The development of speech in hearing-impaired children. In F. H. Bess, B. A. Freeman, & J. S. Sinclair (Eds.), *Amplification in education.* Washington, DC: Alexander Graham Bell Association for the Deaf.

Lovrinic, J. H. (1980). Pure tone and speech audiometry. In R. W. Keith (Ed.), *Audiology for the physician.* Baltimore: Williams & Wilkins.

Lowenbraun, S., & Thompson, M. (1989). Environments and strategies for learning and teaching. In M. C. Wang, M. C. Reynolds, & H. J. Walberg (Eds.), *Handbook of special education: Research and practice: Vol. 3. Low incidence conditions* (pp. 47–69). Oxford, England: Pergamon Press.

Mandell, C. J., & Fiscus, E. (1981). *Understanding exceptional people.* St. Paul, MN: West.

Martin, F. N. (1986). *Introduction to audiology* (3rd ed.) Englewood Cliffs, NJ: Prentice Hall.

Maxon, A. B. (1987). Pediatric amplification. In F. N. Martin (Ed.), *Hearing disorders in children* (pp. 361–393). Austin, TX: Pro-Ed.

McAnally, P. L., Rose, S., & Quigley, S. P. (1987). *Language learning practices with deaf children.* San Deigo: College-Hill Press.

Meadow, K. P. (1980). *Deafness and child development.* Berkeley: University of California Press.

Mental health needs of deaf Americans: Task panel reports submitted to the President's Commission on Mental Health (Vol. 3). (1978). Washington, DC: U.S. Government Printing Office.

Mertens, D. M. (1990). A conceptual model for academic achievement: Deaf student outcomes. In D. F. Moores & K. P. Meadow-Orlands (Eds.), *Educational and developmental aspects of deafness* (pp. 25–72). Washington, DC: Gallaudet University Press.

Moores, D. F. (1987). *Educating the deaf: Psychology, principles, and practices* (3rd ed.). Boston: Houghton Mifflin.

Moores, D. F. (1990). Research in educational aspects of deafness. In D. F. Moores & K. P. Meadow-Orlands (Eds.), *Educational and developmental aspects of deafness* (pp. 11–24), Washington, DC: Gallaudet University Press.

Morgan, A. B. (1987). Causes and treatment. In F. N. Martin (Ed.), *Hearing disorders in children* (pp. 5–48). Austin, TX: Pro-Ed.

National Captioning Institute. (n.d.) *Reading TV in the classroom: Suggestions for using captioned TV in the teaching of reading.* Falls Church, VA: Author.

Newton, L. (1987). The educational management of hearing-impaired children. In F. N. Martin (Ed.), *Hearing disorders in children* (pp. 321–360). Austin, TX: Pro-Ed.

Olmstead, R. W., Alvarez, M. D., Moroney, J. D., & Eversden, M. (1964). The pattern of hearing following acute Otitis Media. *Journal of Pediatrics, 65,* 252–255.

Pahz, J. A., & Pahz, C. S. (1978). *Total communication.* Springfield, IL: Charles C Thomas.

Patrick, P. E. (1987). Identification audiometry. In F. N. Martin (Ed.), *Hearing disorders in children* (pp. 402–425). Austin, TX: Pro-Ed.

Perkins, W. H., & Kent, R. D. (1986). *Functional anatomy of speech, language, and hearing.* San Diego: College-Hill Press.

Quigley, S. P., & King, C. (Eds.). (1984). *Reading milestones.* Beaverton, OR: Dormac.

Quigley, S. P., & Kretschmer, R. E. (1982). *The education of deaf children: Issues, theory and practice.* Baltimore: University Park Press.

Quigley, S. P., & Paul, P. V. (1989). English language development. In M. C. Wang, M. C. Reynolds, & H. J. Walberg (Eds.), *Handbook of special education: Research and practice: Vol. 3. Low incidence conditions* (pp. 3–22). Oxford, England: Pergamon Press.

Ross, M. (1977). Definitions and descriptions. In J. David (Ed.), *Our forgotten children: Hard-of-hearing pupils in the schools.* Minneapolis: Audiovisual Library Service, University of Minnesota.

Ross, M., & Calvert, D. R. (1984). Semantics of deafness revisited: Total communication and the use and misuse of residual hearing. *Audiology, 9*(9), 127–145.

Sanders, D. A. (1980). Psychological implications of hearing impairment. In W. M. Cruickshank (Ed.), *Psychology of exceptional children* (4th ed.). Englewood Cliffs, NJ: Prentice Hall.

Schlesinger, H. S., & Meadow, K. P. (1976). Emotional support for parents. In D. L. Lillie, P. L. Trohanis, & K. W. Goin (Eds.), *Teaching parents to teach.* New York: Walker & Col.

Schreiber, F. C. (1979). *National Association of the Deaf.* In L. J. Bradford & W. G. Hardy (Eds.), *Hearing and hearing impairment.* New York: Grune & Stratton.

Shroyer, E. H., & Shroyer, S. P. (1984). *Signs across America.* Washington, DC: Gallaudet University Press.

Stoel-Gammon, C., & Otomo, K. (1986). Babbling development of hearing-impaired and normally hearing subjects. *Journal of Speech and Hearing Disorders, 51,* 33–41.

Toufexis, A. (1991, August 5). Now hear this—If you can. *Time,* pp. 50–51.

Trybus, R. J. (1985). *Today's hearing-impaired children and youth: A demographic profile.* Washington, DC: Gallaudet Research Institute.

U.S. Department of Education. (1991). *Thirteenth annual report to Congress on the implementation of the Education of the Handicapped Act.* Washington, DC: United States Department of Education.

Van Cleve, J. V., & Crouch, B. A. (1989). *A place of their own.* Washington, DC: Gallaudet University Press.

Vernon, M. (1969). Sociological and psychological factors associated with hearing loss. *Journal of Speech and Hearing Research, 12,* 541–563.

Vernon, M., & Brown, B. (1964). A guide to psychological tests and testing procedures in the evaluation of deaf and hard-of-hearing children. *Journal of Speech and Hearing Disorders, 29,* 414–423.

A very special Santa. (1985, December). *Good Housekeeping*, p. 136.

Wixtrom, C. (1988, Summer). Alone in the crowd. *Deaf American, 38*(12), 14–15.

Woodward, J. (1982). *How you gonna get to heaven if you can't talk to Jesus?* Silver Spring, MD: T. J. Publishers.

You and your deafness. (1982). Washington, DC: Gallaudet College Press.

Chapter Eleven

Anderson, E., Dunlea, A., & Kekalis, L. (1984). Blind children's language: Resolving some differences. *Journal of Child Language, 11*(3), 645–664.

Attmore, M. (1990). *Career perspectives. Interviews with blind and visually impaired professionals.* New York: American Foundation for the Blind.

Barraga, N. C. (1986). Sensory perceptual development. In G. Scholl (Ed.), *Foundations of education for blind and visually handicapped children and youth.* New York: American Foundation for the Blind.

Bishop, V. E. (1987). Religion and blindness: From inheritance to opportunity. *Journal of Visual Impairment and Blindness, 1*(6), 256–259.

Braille: An overview—History, problems, technology, and future prospects. (1982). Baltimore: National Federation of the Blind.

Chapman, E. K., & Stone, J. M. (1989). *The visually handicapped child in your classroom.* London: Cassell.

Hatlen, P., & Curry, S. (1987). In support of specialized programs for blind and visually impaired children: The impact of vision loss on learning. *Journal of Visual Impairment and Blindness, 81*, 7–13.

Kilpatrick, J. J. (1986, September 8). "Right" of the blind to read *Playboy*. *Indianapolis Star*, p. 32.

Kirchner, C. (1988). *Data on blindness and visual impairment in the U.S.* New York: American Foundation for the Blind.

Kirchner, C. (1989). National estimates of children with visual impairments. In M. C. Wang, M. C. Reynolds, & H. J. Walberg (Eds.), *Handbook of special education: Research and practice: Vol. 3. Low incidence conditions* (pp. 155–172). Oxford, England: Pergamon Press.

LaPlante, M. P. (1991). The demographics of disability. In J. West (Ed.), *The Americans with Disabilities Act: From policy to practice* (pp. 55–80). New York: Milbank Memorial Fund.

Lowenfeld, B. (1980). Psychological problems of children with severely impaired vision. In W. M. Cruickshank (Ed.), *Psychology of exceptional children and youth* (4th ed.). Englewood Cliffs, NJ: Prentice Hall.

Parsons, A. S., & Sabornie, E. J. (1987). Language skills of young low-vision children: Performance on the preschool language scale. *Journal of the Division for Early Childhood, 11*(3) 217–225.

Ressner, J. (1991, June 21). Flashback: Small "Wonder" of the world. *Entertainment Weekly*, p. 72.

Reynolds, M. C., & Birch, J. W. (1982). *Teaching exceptional children in all America's schools.* Reston, VA: Council for Exceptional Children.

Toth, Z. (1983). *Die vorstellunswelt der blinden.* Leipzig: Johann Ambrosius Barth.

Tuttle, D. (1984). *Self-esteem and adjusting to blindness.* Springfield, IL: Charles C Thomas.

U.S. Department of Education. (1991). *Thirteenth annual report to Congress on the implementation of the Education of the Handicapped Act.* Washington, DC: Author.

Ward, M. (1986). The visual system. In G. Scholl (Ed.), *Foundations of education for blind and visually handicapped children and youth.* New York: American Foundation for the Blind.

Warren, D. H. (1984). *Blindness and early childhood development.* New York: American Foundation for the Blind.

Warren, D. H. (1989). Implications of visual impairments for child development. In M. C. Wang, M. C. Reynolds, & H. J. Walberg (Eds.), *Handbook of special education: Research and practice. Vol. 3. Low incidence conditions* (pp. 155–172) Oxford, England: Pergamon Press.

Ziegler, E. (1991, February). The magic machines of Ray Kurzweil. *Reader's Digest*, pp. 119–122.

Chapter Twelve

Ambrosini, P. J., Rabinovich, H., & Puig-Antich, J. (1984). Biological factors and the pharmacologic treatment in major depressive disorder in children and adolescents. In H. S. Sudak, A. B. Ford, & N. B. Rushforth (Eds.), *Suicide in the young.* Boston: John Wright PSG.

Anderson, K. M. (1986). The nervous system. In G. M. Scipien, M. U. Barnard, M. A. Chard, J. Howe, & P. J. Phillips (Eds.), *Comprehensive pediatric nursing.* New York: McGraw-Hill.

Beecroft, L., & Beecroft, G. (1991). Student corner. *Brainwaves, 2*(2), 3.

Boat, T. F., & Dearborn, D. G. (1984). Etiology and pathogenesis. In L. N. Taussig (Ed.), *Cystic fibrosis.* New York: Thieme-Stratton.

Bunn, H. F., & Forget, B. G. (1986). *Hemoglobin: Molecular, genetic and clinical aspects.* Philadelphia: Saunders.

Canby, T. Y. (1989, December). Reshaping our lives: Advanced materials. *National Geographic*, pp. 746–781.

Center for the Study of Social Policy. (1991). *Kids count data book.* Washington, DC: Author/Annie E. Casey Foundation.

Chasnoff, I. J. (1988, October). A first: National hospital incidence survey. *NAPARE Update*, p. 2.

Chin, J. (1990). Current and future dimensions of HIV/AIDS pandemic in women and children. *Lancet, 336* (8709), 221–224.

Christi, G. H., Siegel, K., & Moynihan, R. T. (1988). Psychosocial issues: Prevention and treatment. In V. T. Devita, Jr., S. Hellman, & S. A. Rosenberg (Eds.), *AIDS: Diagnosis, treatment and prevention.* Philadelphia: Lippincott.

Compton, N., Duncan, M., & Hruska, J. (1987). *How schools can help combat student pregnancy.* Washington, DC: National Education Association.

Copenhaver, J. (1991). A horse of a different color: Traumatic brain injury. *Special Educator, 12*(2), 8–9.

Curran, D. K. (1987). *Adolescent suicidal behavior.* Washington, DC: Hemisphere.

Cystic Fibrosis Foundation. (1988). *Living with cystic fibrosis.* Bethesda, MD: Consumer Focus Committee/Professional Education Committee.

Delano, C. (1986). Potential risks and hazards of adolescent pregnancies and implication for nursing practice. In J. Ouimette (Ed.), *Perinatal nursing: Care of the high-risk mother and infant.* Boston: Jones and Bartlett.

Dickey, R., & Shealey, S. H. (1987). Using technology to control the environment. *American Journal of Occupational Therapy, 41*(11), 717–721.

Doershuk, C. F., & Boat, T. F. (1987). In R. E. Behrman & V. C. Vaughan III (Eds.), *Nelson textbook of pediatrics* (13th ed.). Philadelphia: Saunders.

Dreifuss, F. E. (1988). What is epilepsy? In H. Reisner (Ed.), *Children with epilepsy.* Kensington, MD: Woodbine House.

Duhaime, A., Gennarelli, T. A., Thibault, L. E., Bruce, D. A., Margulies, S. S., & Wiser, R. (1987). The shaken baby syndrome: A clinical, pathological and biomedical study. *Journal of Neurosurgery, 66*, 409–415.

Falloon, J., Eddy, J., Roper, M., & Pizzo, P. (1988). AIDS in the pediatric population. In V. T. Devita, Jr., S. Hellman, & S. A. Rosenberg (Eds.), *AIDS: Diagnosis, treatment and prevention.* Philadelphia: Lippincott.

Ford, A. B., Rushforth, N. B., & Sudak, H. S. (1984). The causes of suicide. In H. S. Sudak, A. B. Ford, and N. B. Rushforth (Eds.), *Suicide in the young.* Boston: John Wright/PSG.

Fuchs, V. R. (1983). *How we live.* Cambridge, MA: Harvard University Press.

Goedert, J. J., & Blattner, W. A. (1988). The epidemiology and natural history of human immunodeficiency. In V. T. Devita, Jr., S. Hellman, & S. A. Rosenberg (Eds.), *AIDS: Diagnosis, treatment and prevention.* Philadelphia: Lippincott.

Gotta, A. W. (1989). The anesthesiologist and AIDS. In *1989 review of course lectures, International Anesthesia Research Society.* Cleveland, OH: International Anesthesia Research Society.

Greenberg, R. E. (1987). Diabetes mellitus. In R. A. Hoekelman, S. Blatman, N. M. Nelson, & H. M. Seidel (Eds.), *Primary pediatric care.* St. Louis: Mosby.

Greer, J. V. (1990). The drug babies. *Exceptional Children, 56,* 382–384.

Gross, C. R., Wolf, C., Kunitz, S. C., & Jane, J. A. (1985). Pilot traumatic coma data bank: A profile of head injuries in children. In R. G. Dacey, R. Winn, & R. Rimel (Eds.), *Trauma of the central nervous system.* New York: Raven Press.

Guetzloe, E. C. (1989). *Youth suicide: What should the educator know?* Reston, VA: ERIC Clearinghouse on Handicapped and Gifted Children.

Hayes, E. (Ed.). (1987). *Risking the future: adolescent sexuality, pregnancy, and childbearing* (Vol. 1). Washington, DC: National Academy Press.

Hicks, B. B. (1990). *Youth suicide: A comprehensive manual for prevention and intervention.* Bloomington, IN: National Educational Service.

Hoekelmann, R. A., Blatman, S., Nelson, N. M., Friedman, S. B., & Seidel, H. M. (1987). *Primary pediatric care.* St. Louis: Mosby.

Homans, H., & Aggleton, P. (1988). Health education, HIV infection and AIDS. In P. Aggleton & H. Homans (Eds.), *Social aspects of AIDS.* London: Falmer Press.

Huntsman, R. G. (1987). *Sickle-cell anemia and thalassemia: A primer for health care professionals.* Ontario, Canada: Canadian Sickle Cell Society.

Jones, L. E. (1988). The free limb scheme and the limb-deficient child in Australia. *Australian Paediatric Journal, 24*(5), 290–294.

Kamenetz, H. L. (1986). Wheelchairs and other indoor vehicles for the disabled. In J. B. Reford (Ed.), *Orthotics etcetera.* Baltimore: Williams & Wilkins.

Kaufman, J., & Zigler, E. (1987). Do abused children become abusive parents? *American Journal of Orthopsychiatry, 57*(2), 186–192.

Kempe, R. S. (1987). A developmental approach to treatment of the abused child. In R. E. Helfer & R. S. Kempe (Eds.), *The battered child* (4th ed.). Chicago: University of Chicago Press.

Kety, S. S. (1985). Genetic factors in suicide. In A. Roy (Ed.), *Suicide.* Baltimore: Williams & Wilkins.

LeBaron, S., Currie, D., & Zeltzer, L. (1984). In R. W. Blum (Ed.), *Chronic illness and disabilities in childhood and adolescence.* Orlando: Grune & Stratton.

Lehr, E. (1990). *Psychological management of traumatic brain injuries in children and adolescents.* Rockville, MD: Aspen.

Little, B. B., Snell, L. M., Palmore, M. K., & Gilstrap, L. C. (1988). "Cocaine Use in Pregnant Women in a Large Public Hospital," *American Journal of Perinatology, 5*(3), 202–207.

McKusick, L., Horstman, W., & Coates, T. J. (1985). AIDS and sexual behavior reported by gay men in San Francisco. *American Journal of Public Health, 75*(5), 493–496.

Meier, J. H. (1985). *Assault against children.* San Diego: College-Hill Press.

National Center on Child Abuse Prevention Research. (1990). *Current trends in child abuse: The results of the 1989 annual fifty state survey.* Chicago: National Committee for the Prevention of Child Abuse.

Neerhof, M. G., MacGregor, S. N., Retzky, S. S., & Sullivan, T. P. (1989). Cocaine abuse during pregnancy: Peripartum prevalence and perinatal outcome. *American Journal of Obstetrics and Gynecology, 16*(3), 633–638.

Nilsson, D. E. (1991). Questions and answers. *Brainwaves, 2*(2), 7.

Novick, J. (1984). Attempted suicide in adolescence: The suicide sequence. In H. S. Sudak, A. B. Ford, & N. B. Rushforth (Eds.), *Suicide in the young.* Boston: John Wright/PSG.

Ordovensky, P. (1991, 26 June). PTA backs tests to protect kids. *USA Today,* p. D1.

Osmond, D. (1990a). Number and demographic characteristics of U.S. cases. In P. T. Cohen, M. A. Sande, & P. A. Volberding (Eds.), *The AIDS knowledge base.* Waltham, MA: Medical Publishing Group.

Osmond, D. (1990b). Prevalence of infection and projections for the future. In P. T. Cohen, M. A. Sande, & P. A. Volberding (Eds.), *The AIDS knowledge base.* Waltham, MA: Medical Publishing Group.

Pfeffer, C. R. (1986). *The suicidal child.* New York: Guilford Press.

Polsky, B., & Armstong, D. (1988). Other agents in the treatment of AIDS. In V. T. Devita, Jr., S. Hellman, & S. A. Rosenberg (Eds.), *AIDS: Diagnosis, treatment and prevention.* Philadelphia: Lippincott.

Raskin, P. (1983). Open and closed insulin infusion systems: Newer methods of insulin delivery. In M. Ellenberg & H. Rifkin (Eds.), *Diabetes mellitus: Theory and practice* (3rd ed.). New Hyde Park, NY: Medical Examination Publishing.

Ross, H., Bernstein, G. & Rifkin, H. (1983). Relationship of metabolic control of diabetes mellitus to long-term complications. In M. Ellenberg & H. Rifkin (Eds.), *Diabetes mellitus: Theory and practice.* (3rd ed.). New Hyde Park, NY: Medical Examination Publishing.

Sadler, L. S., Corbett, M.-A., Meyer, J. H. (1987). Setting up an adolescent health care program. In M.-A. Corbett & J. H. Meyer (Eds.), *The adolescent and pregnancy.* Boston: Blackwell.

Sanders, G. (1986). *Lower limb amputations: A guide to rehabilitation.* Philadelphia: F. A. Davis.

Schock, N. (1985). *The child with muscular dystrophy in school* (rev. ed.). Lexington, MA: Appalachian Satellite Program Resource Center.

Select Committee on Narcotics Abuse and Control (1988). *Cocaine babies.* Washington, DC: U.S. Government Printing Office.

Serjeant, G. R. (1985). *Sickle cell disease.* Oxford, England: Oxford University Press.

Silverman, M. (1986). What have we learned? In L. McKusick (Ed.), *What to DO about AIDS.* Los Angeles: University of California Press.

Smith, J. (1988). The dangers of prenatal cocaine use. *American Journal of Maternal Child Nursing, 13*(3), 174–179.

Stroud, M., & Sutton, E. (1988). *Expanding options for older adults with developmental disabilities.* Baltimore: Paul H. Brookes.

Summit, R. (1985). Causes, consequences, treatment and prevention of sexual assault against children. In J. H. Meier (Ed.), *Assault against children.* San Diego: College-Hill Press.

Tachdjian, M. O. (1990). *Pediatric orthopedics* (2nd ed.). Philadelphia: Saunders.

Tarnowski, K. J., & Drabman, R. S. (1986). Increasing the communicator usage skills of a cerebral palsied adolescent. *Journal of Pediatric Psychology, 11*(4), 573–581.

Toufexis, A., Cronin, M., Ludtke, M., & Willwerth, J. (1991, May 13). Innocent victims. *Time*, pp. 56–60.

Twenty-Three Code of Federal Regulations (C.F.R.) 300.5 (7) (1984).

U.S. Department of Health and Human Services. (1980). *Muscular dystrophy and other neuromuscular disorders* (NIH Publication No. 80-1615). Bethesda, MD: Office of Scientific and Health Reports, National Institute of Neurological and Communicative Disorders and Stroke, National Institute of Health.

Walker, W. A., Durie, P. R., Hamilton, J. R., Walker-Smith, J. A., & Watkins, J. B. (1991). *Pediatric gastrointestinal disease: Pathophysiology, diagnosis, and management*. Philadelphia: B. C. Decker.

Whaley, F. F., & Wong, D. L. (1985). *Essentials of pediatric nursing*. St. Louis: Mosby.

Williams, S. E., & Matesi, D. V. (1988). Therapeutic intervention with an adapted toy. *American Journal of Occupational Therapy, 42*(10), 673–676.

Williamson, R., Wainwright, B., Cooper, C., Scambler, P., Farrall, M., Estivill, X., & Pedersen, P. (1987). The cystic fibrosis locus. *Enzyme, 38*(1–4), 8–13.

Wintrobe, M. M., Lee, G. R., Boggs, D. R., Bithell, T. C., Foerster, J., Athens, J. W., & Lukens, J. N. (1981). *Clinical hematology* (8th ed.). Philadelphia: Lea & Febiger.

Yashon, D. (1986). *Spinal injury* (2nd ed.). Norwalk, CT: Appleton-Century-Crofts.

Chapter Thirteen

Addison, L., Oliver, A. I., & Cooper, C. R. (1987). *Developing leadership potential in gifted children and youth (ERIC exceptional child education report)*. Reston, VA: ERIC Clearinghouse on Handicapped and Gifted Children.

Adler, J. C., Mueller, R. J., & Ary, D. (1987, April). *Nongifted elementary and middle-school children's sociometric choices of gifted vs. nongifted helpers*. Paper presented at the annual meeting of the American Education Research Association, Washington, DC.

Anderson, M. A. (1987). Facilitating parental understanding of the "gifted" label. *Techniques, 3*(3), 326–344.

Aylward, M. (1987). Enriched-students' program: Nova Scotia, Canada. *Gifted Child Today, 10*(4), 46–47.

Baldwin, A. Y. (1987). Undiscovered diamonds: The minority gifted child. *Journal for the Education of the Gifted, 10*(4), 271–285.

Baldwin, A. Y. (1991). Ethnic and cultural issues. In N. Colangelo & G. A. Davis (Eds.), *Handbook of gifted education* (pp. 416–427). Boston: Allyn and Bacon.

Benbow, C. P., & Minor, L. L. (1990). Cognitive profiles of verbally and mathematically precocious students: Implications for identifications of the gifted. *Gifted Child Quarterly, 34*(1), 21–26.

Bernal, E. M. (1974). Gifted Mexican-American children: An ethnoscientific perspective. *California Journal of Education Research, 25*(5), 261–273.

Binet, A., & Simon. T. (1905). Méthodes nouvelles pour le diagnostique du nivea intellectuel des anomaux. *L'Année Psychologique, 11*, 196–198.

Binet, A., & Simon, T. (1908). Le dévelopment de l'intelligence chez les enfants. *L'Année Psychologique, 14*, 1–94.

Bloom, B. (1969). *Taxonomy of educational objectives*. New York: David McKay.

Bloom, B. (1985). *Developing talent in young people*. New York: Ballantine Books.

Borland, J. (1978). Teacher identification of the gifted. *Journal for the Education of the Gifted, 2*, 22–31.

Brody, L. E., & Benbow, C. P. (1987). Accelerative strategies: How effective are they for the gifted? *Gifted Child Quarterly, 31*(3), 105–110.

Buescher, T. M. (1991). Gifted adolescents. In N. Colangelo & G. A. Davis (Eds.), *Handbook of gifted education* (pp. 382–401). Boston: Allyn and Bacon.

Buescher, T. M., Olszewski, P., & Higham, S. J. (1987, April). *Influences on strategies adolescents use to cope with their own recognized talents*. Paper presented at the biennial meeting of the Society for Research in Child Development, Baltimore, MD.

Callahan, C. M. (1981). Superior abilities. In J. M. Kauffman & D. P. Hallahan (Eds.), *Handbook of special education*. Englewood Cliffs, NJ: Prentice Hall.

Callahan, C. M. (1991). The assessment of creativity. In N. Colangelo & G. A. Davis (Eds.), *Handbook of gifted education* (pp. 219–235). Boston: Allyn and Bacon.

Carpenter, M. (1987). North Carolina school of the arts: ". . . infinitely the best school in America." *Gifted Child Today, 10*(5), 30–35.

Cattell, R. B. (1971). *Abilities: Their structure, growth, and action*. Boston: Houghton Mifflin.

Clark, B. (1983). *Growing up gifted* (2nd ed.). Columbus, OH: Merrill.

Clark, B. (1988). *Growing up gifted* (3rd ed.). Columbus, OH: Merrill.

Clark, G., & Zimmerman, E. (1987). More than meets the eye: Indiana University Summer Arts Institute. *Gifted Child Today, 10*(5), 42–44.

Colangelo, N., & Davis, G. A. (1991). *Handbook of gifted education*. Boston: Allyn and Bacon.

Conant, J. B. (1959). *The American high school today*. New York: McGraw-Hill.

Davidson, J. E., & Sternberg, R. J. (1984). The role of insight in intellectual giftedness. *Gifted Child Quarterly, 28*, 58–64.

Davis, G. A., & Rimm, S. B. (1989). *Education of the gifted and talented*. Englewood Cliffs, NJ: Prentice Hall.

DeHann, R., & Havighurst, R. J. (1957). *Educating gifted children*. Chicago: University of Chicago Press.

Delisle, J. R., & Galbraith, J. (1987). *The gifted kids survival guide II: A sequel to the original*. Minneapolis, MN: Free Spirit.

Feldhusen, J. F. (1991). Saturday and summer programs. In N. Colangelo & G. A. Davis (Eds.), *Handbook of gifted education* (pp. 197–208). Boston: Allyn and Bacon.

Feldhusen, J. F., VanTassel-Baska, J., & Seeley, K. (1989). *Excellence in educating the gifted*. Denver: Love.

Fox, L., & Tobin, D. (1988). Broadening career horizons for gifted girls. *Gifted Child Today, 11*(1), 9–13.

Gagne, F. (1991). Toward a differentiated model of giftedness and talent. In N. Colangelo & G. A. Davis (Eds.), *Handbook of gifted education* (pp. 65–80). Boston: Allyn and Bacon.

Gardner, H. (1983). *Frames of mind: The theory of multiple intelligences*. New York: Basic Books.

Gold, M., Koch, S., Jordan, W., & Pendavis, J. (1987). Twenty by twenty: A two-decade history of 20 members of the 1965 Georgia governor's honors program. *Gifted Child Today, 10*(5), 2–16.

Goldsmith, L. T. (1987). Girl prodigies: Some evidence and some speculations. *Roeper Review, 10*(2), 74–82.

Gowan, J. C., Khatena, J., & Torrance, E. P. (1979). *Educating the ablest.* Itasca, IL: F. E. Peacock.

Gross, M., & Kirsten, S. (1987). Linking education and community: Marvern, Australia. *Gifted Child Today, 10*(4), 44–45.

Guilford, J. P. ('950). Creativity. *American Psychologist, 5,* 444–454.

Guilford, J. P. (1956). Structure of intellect. *Psychological Bulletin, 53,* 267–293.

Guilford, J. P. (1959). Three faces of intellect. *American Psychologist, 14,* 469–479.

Haeger, W., & Feldhusen, J. (1987). *Developing a mentor program.* East Aurora, NY: DOK.

Hendricks, J., & Scott, M. (1987). Mentor companions in curiosity: A program for accepting and encouraging curiosity in young gifted children. *Creative Child and Adult Quarterly, 12*(2), 119–123.

Hollinger, C. L., & Fleming, E. S. (1988). Gifted and talented women: Antecedents and correlates of life satisfaction. *Gifted Child Quarterly, 32*(2), 254–259.

Hollingsworth, P. L. (1987). *The University of Tulsa School for Gifted Children.* Tulsa, OK: The University of Tulsa School for Gifted Children.

Irvine, D. J. (1987, August). *A three-dimensional model for individualizing instruction for gifted students.* Paper presented at the Seventh World Conference on Gifted and Talented Children, Salt Lake City, UT.

Karnes, B. K., & Johnson, L. J. (1991). Gifted handicapped. In N. Colangelo & G. A. Davis (Eds.), *Handbook of gifted education* (pp. 428–437). Boston: Allyn and Bacon.

Kaufman, A., & Kaufman, N. (1983). *Kaufman assessment battery for children: Sampler manual.* Circle Pines, MN: American Guidance Service.

Kerr, B. A. (1985). *Smart girls, gifted women.* Columbus: Ohio Psychology.

Kerr, B. A. (1991). Educating gifted girls. In N. Colangelo & G. A. Davis (Eds.), *Handbook of gifted education* (pp. 402–415). Boston: Allyn and Bacon.

Khatena, J. (1982). Myth: Creativity is too difficult to measure. *Gifted Child Quarterly, 26*(1), 21–23.

Kirschenbaum, R. (1988). Methods for identifying the gifted and talented. *Journal for the Education of the Gifted, 11,* 53–63.

Kitano, M. K., & Kirby, D. F. (1986). *Gifted education: A comprehensive view.* Boston: Little, Brown.

Klausmeier, K. (1986). Enrichment: An educational imperative for meeting the needs of gifted students. In C. J. Maker (Ed.), *Critical issues in gifted education: Defensible programs for the gifted.* Rockville, MD: Aspen.

Klausmeier, K., Mishra, S. P., & Maker, C. J. (1987). Identification of gifted learners: A national survey of assessment practices and training needs of school psychologists. *Gifted Child Quarterly, 31*(3), 135–137.

Koopsman-Dayton, J. D., & Feldhusen, J. F. (1987). A resource guide for parents of gifted preschoolers. *The Gifted Child Today, 10*(6), 2–7.

Kramer, L. R. (1987a, April). *Differences in learning and achieving in self-contained and resource-room programs for the gifted.* Paper presented at the annual conference of the American Education Research Association, Washington, DC.

Kramer, L. R. (1987b, April). *Self-contained and resource-room programs for the gifted: Factors influencing effectiveness.* Paper presented at the annual meeting of the American Education Research Association, Washington, DC.

Kulik, J. A., & Kulik, C. C. (1984). Effects of acceleration instruction on students. *Review of Educational Research, 54,* 409–425.

Leroux, J. A., & DeFazio, P. (1987, April). *University programs for high-ability adolescents.* Paper presented at the annual meeting of the American Education Research Association. Washington, DC.

Lewis, M., & Louis, B. (1991). Young gifted children. In N. Colangelo & G. A. Davis (Eds.), *Handbook of gifted education* (pp. 365–382). Boston: Allyn and Bacon.

MacKinnon, D. W. (1962). The nature and nurture of creative talent. *American Psychologist, 17*(7), 484–495.

McAuliff, J. H., & Stoskin, L. (1987). Synectic: The creative connection; Maryland, United States. *Gifted Child Today, 10*(4), 18–20.

Milne, B. G. (1979). Career education. In A. Harry Passow (Ed.), *The gifted and the talented: Their education and development, Seventy-eighth yearbook of the National Society for the Study of Education, Part 2.* Chicago: University of Chicago Press.

Olszewski-Kubilius, P. M. (1989). Development of academic talent: The role of summer programs. In J. L. VanTassel-Baska & P. Olszewski-Kubilius (Eds.), *Patterns of influence on gifted learners.* New York: Teachers College Press.

Olszewski-Kubilius, P. M., Kulieke, M. J., & Krasney, N. (1988). Personality dimensions of gifted adolescents: A review of the empirical literature. *Gifted Child Quarterly, 32*(4), 347–352.

Osborne, J. K., & Byrnes, D. A. (1990). Identifying gifted and talented students in an alternative learning center. *Gifted Child Quarterly, 34*(4), 143–146.

Parke, B. N. (1989). *Gifted students in the regular classroom.* Boston: Allyn and Bacon.

Perkins, D., & Simmons, R. (1988). The cognitive roots of scientific and mathematical ability. In J. Dreyden, G. Stanley, S. Gallagher, & R. Sawyer (Eds.), *The proceedings of the talent and identification programs/National Science Foundation conference on academic talent.* Durham, NC: Duke University Talent Identification Program.

Purcell, C. (1978). *Gifted and Talented Children's Education Act of 1978.* Washington, DC: U.S. Government Printing Office.

Ramos-Ford, V., & Gardner, H. (1991). Giftedness from a multiple intelligences perspective. In N. Colangelo & G. A. Davis (Eds.), *Handbook of gifted education* (pp. 55–64). Boston: Allyn and Bacon.

Renzulli, J. S. (1978). What makes giftedness? Reexamining a definition. *Phi Delta Kappan, 60*(3), 180–184, 261.

Renzulli, J. S., Reis, S. M., & Smith, L. M. (1981). *The revolving door identification model.* Wethersfield, CT: Creative Learning Press.

Renzulli, J. S., Smith, L. H., White, A. J., Callahan, C. M., & Hartman, R. K. (1976). *Scales for rating the behavioral characteristics of superior students.* Wethersfield, CT: Creative Learning Press.

Renzulli, J. S., & VanTassel-Baska, J. (1987). Point-counterpoint: The positive side of pull-out programs and the ineffectiveness of the pull-out program model in gifted education: A minority perspective. *Journal for the Education of the Gifted, 10*(4), 245–269.

Richert, E. S. (1991). Rampant problems and promising practices in identification. In N. Colangelo & G. A. Davis (Eds.), *Handbook of gifted education* (pp. 81–96). Boston: Allyn and Bacon.

Robinson, A., Bradley, R. H., & Stanley, T. D. (1990). Opportunity to achieve: Identifying mathematically gifted Black students. *Contemporary Educational Psychology, 15*(1), 1–2.

Sanborn, M. P. Career development: Problems of gifted and talented students. In N. Colangelo & R. T. Zaffran (Eds.), *New voices in counseling the gifted.* Dubuque, IA: Kendall/Hunt.

Schack, G. D., & Starko, A. J. (1990). Identification of gifted students: An analysis of criteria preferred by preservice teachers, classroom teachers, and teachers of the gifted. *Journal for the Education of the Gifted, 13*(4), 346–363.

Schiever, S. W., & Maker, C. J. (1991). Enrichment and acceleration: An overview and new directions. In N. Colangelo & G. A. Davis (Eds.), *Handbook of gifted education* (pp. 99–110). Boston: Allyn and Bacon.

Seeley, K. (1985). Facilitators for gifted learners. In J. Feldhusen (Ed.), *Toward excellence in gifted education.* Denver: Love.

Shaughnessy, M., & Neely, R. (1987). Parenting the prodigies: What if your child is highly verbal or mathematically precocious? *Creative Child and Adult Quarterly, 12*(1), 7–20.

Silverman, L. K. (1986). What happens to the gifted girls? In C. J. Maker (Ed.), *Critical issues in gifted education: Defensible programs for the gifted.* Rockville, MD: Aspen.

Silverman, L. K. (1989). Career counseling for the gifted. In J. L. VanTassel-Baska & P. M. Olszewski-Kubilius (Eds.), *Patterns of influence on gifted learners.* New York: Teachers College Press.

Silverman, L. K. (1991). Family counseling. In N. Colangelo & G. A. Davis (Eds.), *Handbook of gifted education.* Boston: Allyn and Bacon.

Sowell, E. J., Bergwall, L. K., Zeigler, A. J., & Cartwright, R. M. (1990). Identification and description of mathematically gifted students: A review of empirical research. *Gifted Child Quarterly, 34*(4), 147–154.

Steffens, K. (1989). Differentiating highly gifted students on a typological basis: An analysis of teachers' judgements. *Psychologie in Erziehung und Unterricht, 36*(2), 114–119.

Sternberg, R. J. (1981). A componential theory of intellectual giftedness. *Gifted Child Quarterly, 25,* 86–93.

Sternberg, R. J. (1987). *Beyond I.Q.* New York: Cambridge University Press.

Taffel, A. (1987). Fifty years of developing the gifted in science and mathematics. *Roeper Review, 10*(1), 21–24.

Tannenbaum, A. J. (1991). The social psychology of giftedness. In N. Colangelo & G. A. Davis (Eds.), *Handbook of gifted education* (pp. 27–44). Boston: Allyn and Bacon.

Taylor, C. W., & Ellison, R. L. (1983). Searching for talent resources. *Gifted Child Quarterly, 27*(3), 99–106.

Terman, L. M. (1925). *Genetic studies of genius: Vol. 1. Mental and physical traits of a thousand gifted children.* Stanford: Stanford University Press.

Thomas, T. A. (1987, April). *CSUS academic talent search follow-up report: After the first four years.* Paper presented at the annual meeting of the American Education Research Association, Washington, DC.

Torrance, E. P. (1961). Problems of highly creative children. *Gifted Child Quarterly, 5,* 31–34.

Torrance, E. P. (1965). *Gifted children in the classroom.* New York: Macmillan.

Torrance, E. P. (1966). *Torrance tests of creative thinking.* Bensenville, IL: Scholastic Testing Service.

Torrance, E. P. (1968). Finding hidden talent among disadvantaged children. *Gifted and Talented Quarterly, 12,* 131–137.

VanTassel-Baska, J. (1988). *Comprehensive curriculum for gifted learners.* Boston: Allyn and Bacon.

VanTassel-Baska, J. (1989a). Acceleration. In C. J. Maker (Ed.), *Critical issues in gifted education: Defensible programs for the gifted.* Rockville, MD: Aspen.

VanTassel-Baska, J. (1989b). Counseling the gifted. In J. Feldhusen, J. VanTassel-Baska, & K. Seeley (Eds.), *Excellence in educating the gifted.* Denver: Love.

VanTassel-Baska, J. (1989c). The disadvantaged gifted. In J. Feldhusen, J. VanTassel-Baska, & K. Seeley (Eds.), *Excellence in educating the gifted.* Denver: Love.

VanTassel-Baska, J., & Chepko-Sade, D. (1986). *An incidence study of disadvantaged gifted students in the Midwest.* Evanston, IL: Center for Talent Development, Northwestern University.

Wallach, M. A. (1976). Tests tell us little about talent. *American Scientist, 64,* 57.

Wiener, N. (1953). *Ex-prodigy: My childhood and youth.* New York: Simon and Schuster.

Whitmore, J. R., & Maker, C. J. (1985). *Intellectual giftedness in disabled persons.* Rockville, MD: Aspen.

Williams, F. E. (1980). Creativity assessment packet. East Aurora, NY: DOK.

Williams, F. E. (1988). A magic circle. *Gifted Child Today, 11*(1), 2–5.

Chapter Fourteen

Adler, J. (1987, March 17). Cause for concern—And optimism. *Newsweek,* pp. 63–66.

Atkins, D. V. (1987). Siblings of the hearing-impaired: Perspectives for parents. *Volta Review, 89*(5), 32–45.

Barsh, R. H. (1968). *The parent of the handicapped child: The study of child-rearing practices.* Springfield, IL: Charles C Thomas.

Baxter, C. (1986). *Intellectual disability: Parental perceptions and stigma as stress.* Unpublished doctoral dissertation, Monash University, Victoria, Australia.

Beckman, P. J. (1983). Influence of selected child characteristics on stress in families of handicapped infants. *American Journal of Mental Deficiency, 88,* 150–156.

Beckman-Bell, P. (1981). Child-related stress in families of handicapped children. *Topics in Early Childhood Special Education, 1*(3), 45–54.

Bergman, A. I., & Simpson, J. (1990, Fall). Public testimony, Health care industry forces family impoverishment: UCPA witness testifies on access to health insurance. *Family Support Bulletin,* pp. 19–20.

Berns, J. H. (1980). Grandparents of handicapped children. *Social Work, 15*(3), 238–239.

Blacher, J. (1984). Sequential stages of parental adjustment to the birth of a child with handicaps: Fact or artifact? *Mental Retardation, 22*(2) 55–68.

Blackard, M. K., & Barsh, E. T. (1982). Parents' and professionals' perceptions of the handicapped child's impact on the family. *Journal of the Association for the Severely Handicapped, 7,* 62–70.

Blatt, B. (1988). *Conquest of mental retardation.* Austin, TX: Pro-Ed.

Bristol, M. M., & Gallagher, J. J. (1982). A family focus for intervention. In E. T. Ramey & P. L. Trohanis (Eds.), *Finding and educating high-risk and handicapped infants.* Baltimore: University Park Press.

Bristor, M. W. (1984). The birth of a handicapped child—A holistic model for grieving. *Family Relations, 33*, 25–32.

Brown, L. (1990, Fall). People in the news, Lisa—that special someone for the Browns. *Family Support Bulletin*, pp. 13–14.

Busk, H. H. (1985). Setting the platitudes straight. *Exceptional Parents, 15*(7), 23–28.

Cartwright, C. A. (1981). Effective programs for parents of young handicapped children. *Topics in Early Childhood Special Education, 3*, 1–9.

Chandler, L. K., Fowler, S. A., & Lubeck, R. C. (1985). *Assessing family needs: The first step in providing family-focused intervention*. Washington, DC: Special Education Programs (ED/OSERS).

Cleveland, M. (1980). Family adaptation to traumatic spinal-cord injury: Response to crisis. *Family Therapy, 29*(4), 558–565.

Cobb, P. S. (1987). Creating respite-care programs. *Exceptional Parent, 15*(5), 31–33.

Crutcher, D. M. (1991). Family support in the home: Home visiting and public law 99-457, A parent's perspective. *American Psychologist, 46*(2), 138–140.

D'Arcy, E. (1968). Congenital defects: Mothers' reactions to first information. *British Medical Journal, 3*, 796–798.

Davis, R. D. (1967). Family processes in mental retardation. *American Journal of Psychiatry, 124*(3), 340–350.

Dembo, T. (1984). Sensitivity of one person to another. *Rehabilitation Literature, 45*, 90–95.

Farber, B. (1962). Effects of a severely retarded child on the family. In E. P. Trapp & P. Himelskin (Eds.), *Readings on the exceptional child*. New York: Appleton-Century-Crofts.

Featherstone, H. (1980). *A difference in the family: Living with a disabled child*. New York: Penguin.

Forbes, E. (1987). My brother, Warren. *Exceptional Parent, 17*(5), 50–52.

Fredericks, B. (1985). Parents/families of persons with severe mental retardation. In D. Bricker & J. Filler (Eds.), *Severe mental retardation: From theory to practice*. Reston, VA: Council for Exceptional Children.

Gabel, H., McDowell, J., & Cerreto, M. C. (1983). Family adaptation to the handicapped infant. In S. G. Garwood & R. R. Fewell (Eds.), *Educating handicapped infants* (pp. 455–493). Rockville, MD: Aspen.

Gallagher, J. R., Beckman-Bell, P., & Cross, A. H. (1983). Families of handicapped children: Sources of stress and its amelioration. *Exceptional Children, 50*, 10–19.

Gardner, J. F., & Markowitz, R. K. (1986). *Maryland family support services consortium, final report*. Baltimore: Maryland State Planning Council on Developmental Disabilities.

Gargiulo, R. M. (1985). *Working with professionals of exceptional children: A guide for professionals*. Boston: Houghton Mifflin.

Goldberg, S., Marcovitch, S., MacGregor, D., & Lojkasek, M. (1986). Family responses to developmentally delayed preschoolers: Etiology and the father's role. *American Journal of Mental Deficiency, 90*(6), 610–617.

Guralnick, M. J., Bennett, F. C., Heiser, K. E., & Richardson, H. B., Jr. (1987). Training future primary care pediatricians to serve handicapped children and their families. *Topics in Early Childhood Special Education, 6* 1–11.

Hackney, H. (1981). The child, the family, and the school. *Gifted Child Quarterly, 25*, 51–54.

Hutchinson, E. F. (1982). Wheelchairs. *Exceptional Parent, 12*(1), 7, 60.

I'm not going to be John's baby sitter forever: Sibling, planning, and the disabled (1987). *Exceptional Parent, 17*(8), 60–64.

Innovative approaches to family support: Chicago pilot program for home care. (1990, Fall). *Family Support Bulletin*. p. 9.

Johnson, N. (1990, Fall). Evolving attitudes about family support. *Family Support Bulletin*, pp. 12–13.

Kotze, J. M. A. (1986, July). *Educational aid to parents of young handicapped children*. Paper presented at the World Conference of O.M.E.P. World Organization for Preschool Education, Jerusalem, Israel.

Kraft, S. P., & Snell, M. A. (1980). Parent-teacher conflict: Coping with parental stress. *Pointer, 24*(2), 29–37.

Kroth, R. L. (1987). Mixed or missed messages between parents and professionals. *Volta Review, 89*(5), 1–10.

Lamb, C. B. (1980). Fostering acceptance of a disabled sibling through books. *Exceptional Parent, 10*(1), 12–13.

Lamb, M. E. (1983). Fathers of exceptional children. In M. Seligman (Ed.), *The family with a handicapped child: Understanding and treatment*. New York: Grune & Stratton.

Lavelle, N., & Keogh, B. K. (1980). Expectations and attributions of parents of handicapped children. In J. J. Gallagher (Ed.), *New directions for exceptional children, parents, and families of handicapped children*. San Francisco: Jossey-Bass.

Leigh, J. (1987). Parenting and the hearing-impaired. *Volta Review, 89*(5), 11–21.

Lettick, S. (1979). *Ben*. In Sullivan, R. (Ed.), "Siblings of Autistic Children." *The Journal of Autism and Developmental Disorders, 9*(3), 287–298.

Lipsky, D. K. (1987). *Family support for families with a disabled member* (Monograph No. 39). New York: World Rehabilitation Fund.

Luterman, D. (1987). *Deafness in the family*. Boston: Little, Brown.

May, J. (1991, Spring). Commentary: What about fathers? *Family Support Bulletin*, p. 19.

McHale, S. M., Sloan, J., & Simeonsson, R. J. (1986). Sibling relationships and adjustment of children with disabled brothers and sisters. *Journal of Children in Contemporary Society, 16*, 131–158.

McKinney, J. D., & Hocutt, A. M. (1982). Public school involvement of parents and learning-disabled children and average learners. *Exceptional Education Quarterly, 3*(2), 64–73.

McPhee, N. (1982). A very special magic: A grandparent's delight. *Exceptional Parent, 12*(3), 13–16.

Meyer, D. J., & Vadasy, P. F. (1986). *Grandparent workshops: How to organize workshops for grandparents of children with handicaps*. Seattle: University of Washington Press.

Muir-Hutchinson, L. (1987). Working with professionals. *Exceptional Parent, 17*(5), 8–10.

Pagel, S., & Price, J. (1980). Strategies to alleviate teacher stress. *Pointer, 24*(2), 45–53.

Peterson, N. L. (1987). *Early intervention for handicapped and at-risk children: An introduction to early-childhood special education*. Denver: Love.

Rich, A. (1984). My family and I. *Exceptional Parent, 14*(5), C2.

Rose, H. W. (1987). *Something's wrong with my child*. Springfield, IL: Charles C Thomas.

Salkever, M. (1981). Tammy: A part of our family. *Exceptional Parent, 11*(5), 11–16.

Schell, G. C. (1981). The young handicapped child: A family perspective. *Topics in Early Childhood Special Education, 1*(3), 21–28.

Seligman, M., & Darling, R. B. (1989). *Ordinary families, special children*. New York: Guilford Press.

Seligman, M., & Seligman, D. A. (1980). The professional's dilemma: Learning to work with parents. *Exceptional Parent, 10*(5), 511–513.

Shelton, T. L., Jeppson, E. S., & Johnson, B. H. (1987). *Family-centered care for children with special health-care needs*. Washington, DC: Association for the Care of Children's Health.

Simeonsson, R. J., & Bailey, D. B. (1986). Siblings of the handicapped child. In J. J. Gallagher & W. Vietze (Eds.), *Families of handicapped persons* (pp. 67–77). Baltimore: Paul H. Brooke.

Smith, J., & Cline, D. (1980). Quality programs. *Pointer, 24*(2), 80–87.

Somers, M. N. (1987). Parenting in the 1980s: Programming perspectives and issues. *Volta Review, 89*(5), 68–77.

Sonnek, I. M. (1986). Grandparents and the extended family of handicapped children. In R. R. Fewell & P. F. Vadasy (Eds.), *Families of handicapped children* (pp. 99–120). Austin, TX: Pro-Ed.

Turnbull, A. P., & Turnbull, H. R., III. (1986). *Families and professionals: Creating an exceptional partnership*. Columbus, OH: Merrill.

Tynan, D. D., & Fritsch, R. E. (1987). *Stress associated with handicapped children: Guidelines for family management* (ERIC Document Reproduction Service, No. Ed-285-314). Washington, DC: ERIC.

Vadasy, P. F., Fewell, R. R., Greenberg, M. T., Desmond, M. L., & Meyer, D. J. (1986). Follow-up evaluation of the effects of involvement in the fathers program. *Topics in Early Childhood Education, 6*, 16–31.

Vadasy, P. F., Fewell, R. R., & Meyer, D. J. (1986). Grandparents of children with special needs: insight into their experiences and concerns. *Journal of the Division for Early Childhood, 10*(1), 36–44.

Volpe, J. J., & Koenigsberger, R. (1981). Neurologic disorders. In G. B. Avery (Ed.), *Neonatology, pathophysiology, and management of the newborn* (2nd ed.). Philadelphia: Lippincott.

Wasserman, R. (1983). Identifying the counseling needs of the siblings of mentally retarded children. *Personnel and Guidance Journal, 61*, 622–627.

West, E. (1981). My child is blind—Thoughts on family life. *Exceptional Parent, 1*(1), S9–S12.

When I grow up, I'm never coming back! The adolescent and the family (1988, March). *Exceptional Parent*, 62–67.

Wikler, L. (1981). Chronic stresses of families of mentally retarded children. *Family Relations. 30*, 281–288.

Wilcoxon, A. S. (1987). Grandparents and grandchildren: an often neglected relationship between significant others. *Journal of Counseling and Development, 65*, 289–290.

Author Index

Subject Index

Sexual abuse, 150. *See also* Child abuse and neglect

Siblings, 273, 417, 423–427. *See also* Family issues

Sickle cell anemia, 363–364

Sight. *See* Visual impairments

Sign languages/systems, 302–304, 306–307. *See also* American Sign Language (ASL)

Simon, Théodore, 20

"Six-hour retardate," 214

Snellen Test, 314, 323

Social deviance, 12–13, 134

Social interventions
   and acquired immune deficiency syndrome (AIDS), 357
   and behavior disorders, 155–156, 164–166
   and gifted, creative, and talented, 397–398
   and hearing impairments, 295–298
   and mental retardation, 124–145
   and pregnancy, adolescent, 367
   and seizure disorders, 358–359
   and spinal cord injury, 351
   and traumatic brain injury (TBI), 344
   and visual impairments, 325–326
   and youth suicide, 369

Social isolation, 13–15. *See also* Institutions; Special education, special schools

Social services. *See* Social interventions

Socioeconomic factors, 31, 52–53, 131, 149, 406

Sociology, 12–13

Sociometric devices, 152

Sonicguide, 331

Special classes. *See* Special education, special classes

Special education
   costs, 26
   definition of, 22
   full-inclusion programs, 78–80, 89, 123
   history, 20–30
   and multicultural issues, 43–44
   placement options, 26–28
   pull-out programs, 78–80, 89
   special classes, 13, 20–21, 28, 78
   special schools, 28, 78, 123, 127–128, 298–299, 307–308, 327

Special Olympics, 98

Special schools. *See* Special education, special schools

Speech disorders, 139, 141, 234–249
   articulation, 242–247
   cluttering, 234
   defined, 234
   delayed speech, 237–242
   early childhood years, 240
   elementary years, 240–241
   family issues, 240–241
   fluency, 234–237
   individual interactions, 240–241
   prevalence, 249
   secondary/transition years, 241
   stuttering, 234–237
   technology, 255
   voice, 247–249

Spelling. *See* Academic achievement, spelling

Spina bifida, 346–348

Spinal cord injury, 348–349

Spinal meningitis, 278

Standard deviation, 211, 212, 218, 222

Stanford-Binet Intelligence Scale (1916), 20, 115, 378. *See also* Binet-Simon Intelligence Test; Binet-Simon Scales

Sterilization, 13

Stimulant drugs, 167

Strabismus, 316–317

Structural family therapy, 157

Students at-risk. *See* At-risk, students

Stuttering, 234–237

Substance abuse. *See* Alcohol use; Drug use

Suicide, youth, 131, 367–369

Supported
   employment, 84, 122
   living, 124–125

Syntax, 231, 232

T

Talented. *See* Gifted, creative, and talented

TASH. *See* Association for Persons with Severe Handicaps (TASH)

TDD systems. *See* Telecommunication devices

Teacher-assistance teams (TATs), 74, 75

Technology
   artificial intelligence, 144
   and autism, 272
   and behavior disorders, 144

closed-captioned television, 277, 305–306

computer-assisted instruction, 144, 255

and hearing impairments, 281, 294–295, 305–308

and language disorders, 255

and learning disabilities, 198–199, 200

and mental retardation, 116

and physical disorders, 351

and speech disorders, 255

telephones, 305

and visual impairments, 331–336

Telecommunication devices, 307–308

Telescoped programs, 395

Teratogens, 348

Terman, Lewis, 20

Test bias. *See* Assessment bias

Testing. *See* Assessment

Therapeutic interventions, 153–159
   activity group therapy, 155
   behavior therapy, 153, 156–157
   drug therapy, 153–154, 159, 195–197
   group psychotherapy, 153, 155–156
   insight-oriented therapy, 153, 154
   marital/family therapy, 153, 157
   play therapy, 153, 155
   structural family therapy, 157

Tic disorders, 139, 141

Total communication approach, 299, 304–305

Transdisciplinary approach (to instruction), 74–75

Transition from school to adult life, 82–88
   adult service agencies, 87–88
   definition of, 84–85
   and hearing impairments, 301
   and IDEA, 84–85, 87
   and learning disabilities, 194, 197, 201–204
   and mental retardation, 121–124
   parent involvement, 88
   plans, 86–87
   research on, 83–84, 88,
   schools, 85–86
   transition, definition of, 84–85
   and visual impairments, 329

Transition planning. *See* Transition from school to adult life, plans

Transition services. *See* Transition from school to adult life

Traumatic brain injury (TBI), 342–344

Triplegia, 345

Tunnel vision, 314

NOTES